CAT

FOREWORD

Hannah Shaw aka Kitten Lady

There may be no creature on the earth that has captured the human imagination more deeply than the house cat. Ever since the dawn of the human-feline relationship, when Neolithic people in the Fertile Crescent formed a mutualistic partnership with the African wildcat (*Felis silvestris lybica*) close to ten thousand years ago, these unlikely allies have embedded themselves into society in nearly every corner of the globe—and masterfully positioned themselves at the center. More than one quarter of households in the United States alone are now home to a cat, and there are 600 million cats and counting around the world. Across centuries and continents, art and popular culture, the cat has always been, and continues to be, a compelling main character.

If you want to understand how a society views cats, look no further than how it represents them in visual culture. Are they hidden in the landscape, or commanding the frame? Are they portrayed with regal poise, or memeified and downright derpy? Cats have been cast in diverse and even contradictory roles throughout history in art, fashion, television, and movies: the posh lap cat and the scrappy alley wanderer, the exalted goddess and the shadowy familiar, the tireless political mascot and the lazy lasagna lover. Perhaps the enduring appeal of the cat is that they seem to contain, quite effortlessly, all of these qualities at the same time.

I became fascinated by the historical representation of cats in art while working on *Cats of the World*, my best-selling book about global cat welfare and culture that was published in 2024. For that project, which was photographed by my husband, Andrew Marttila (a professional cat photographer whose work is also included in this volume; see p.217), we traveled to thirty countries to capture an intimate portrait of cat welfare around the world. This labor of love stemmed from my own life's work here in the United States: rescuing neonatal kittens, teaching kitten care courses for animal shelters and the public, and founding Orphan Kitten Club, a national nonprofit organization with a mission to save the lives of the tiniest and most vulnerable kittens. As someone constantly reflecting on the intersection between culture and feline welfare in the United States, I took *Cats of the World* as an opportunity to discover the relationship between society and its cats everywhere, from the mountains of Nepal to the islands of Kenya.

During a visit to a Parisian gallery of ancient artifacts curated by a French art historian, I was deeply drawn to a collection of carvings and paintings depicting black cats as fiendish sorcerers. My own beloved companion was a black cat, and these works offered a haunting lens into the fear and superstition that pervaded medieval French society's perception of beings like her. But we were not only there to reflect on the artistic legacy of felines. We were also there to meet Ponpon, a gloriously rotund, silky black cat adopted by the curator who now gallivants among the artifacts like a modern-day masterpiece. Ponpon's distinguished portrait permanently lives in the pages of our own curated collection, offering a quiet rebuttal to the centuries of suspicion that have preceded him.

I believe artistic representation has the power not only to reflect our perceptions but also to shape them. Because the human-feline bond tends to blossom in private spaces—behind closed doors or in the stillness of night—cats have historically been shrouded in more mystery than dogs, whose relationships with humans often unfold in public view. It makes sense that earlier artistic renderings often cast cats as enigmatic or otherworldly, while today's ubiquitous digital atmosphere brings a realism that reframes them as companions and community members. Intimate glimpses of feline life now circulate through our feeds as a steady stream of house cats pose like muses for the masses. Even community cats (sometimes referred to as "feral" cats), long misunderstood, meet the gaze of the camera and are suddenly seen. The lifesaving implications of this visibility are evident in the public's deepening affection for cats and the modern surge in volunteering, fostering, and adoption. When representation inspires compassion, art becomes advocacy.

The collection you hold in your hands, *Cat*, is a beautiful celebration of our ever-evolving, always enduring connection with felines. In so many of these images, I am struck by the echoes of cats I have loved: the tender weight of a darling black lap cat reflected in a modernist painting by Henri Matisse (see p.90), the quiet connection between a woman and her cat in a woodcut print by Fumi Yanagimoto (see p.215), the familiar face of a wily tabby carved into the curve of a wooden chair by Gérard Rigot (see p.62). As a lifelong devotee to cats and their welfare, I am moved by the depth and breadth of what is captured in these pages and am honored to have been a part of its curation. I invite you to savor it slowly—perhaps with a warm cup of tea and a beloved cat curled beside you.

A BRIEF HISTORY OF CATS IN VISUAL CULTURE

Leïla Jarbouai

The domestic cat (*Felis catus*) is one of the world's most beloved pets, overtaking its traditional rival, the dog, as the animal companion of choice in many countries and cultures, with more than 600 million existing today. Ambiguous by nature, these "wild domestic" animals have been a part of the human landscape and visual culture for millennia. Over the centuries, our complex relationship with our feline friends has shifted between fascination and repulsion. Humans' current passion for cats is the result of a lengthy process of social and cultural evolution, a process that we can see evolve in the images that we have made of them since ancient times.

Cats belong to the Felidae family and share the carnivorous nature and hunting instinct of big cats, as well as their extraordinary flexibility, speed, and precision of movement. Their subfamily, Felinae, includes specific carnivores, such as leopards and lynxes, that are distinguished from other felines by their ability to purr but not roar. Regardless, members of the species *Felis catus*, unlike their bigger cousins, are both predators—hunting small rodents, birds, snakes, and lizards—and prey—hunted by foxes, dogs, badgers, martens, and birds of prey—and they encompass contradictory characteristics of each.

A cat is a harmonious and surprising combination of opposites, alternately gentle and ferocious, tender and violent, domestic and wild, attached to its humans (that is, those who feed it, house it, pet it, if, indeed, it has any) and implacably independent, nonchalant and bouncing, lazy and tireless, stay-at-home and adventurous, cautious and curious. Whether they come from the city or the country, live out on the streets—where they may even appear spray-painted on buildings (see p.10)—or indoors, beyond their countless differences in character and their individualities, cats all have in common an elusive quality and an irrepressible freedom of spirit. With silky fur and elegant lines, or a coarse coat and wild features, cats always land on their feet. They openly display their sensuality and love of life and have a knack for finding the pleasantest of spots. To say the least, cats appreciate the pleasures of life, exuding traits guaranteed to inspire artists and enrich the never-ending iconographic history that has been prompted by the enduring connections between us and this ordinary yet extraordinary diminutive feline.

Our shared history goes back almost ten thousand years. The domestic cat (*F. catus*) is descended from *F. silvestris lybica*, a wildcat native to the Middle East and North Africa, itself coming from the larger *F. sylvestris* species, and has evolved little morphologically over its partnerships with humans that have survived thousands of years. Although much remains mysterious about how and when exactly cats became domesticated, farmers probably first tamed their feline neighbors during the Neolithic period as crop cultivation developed in the Fertile Crescent, with humans valuing their ability to catch the rodents that were otherwise destroying stocks of grain. Early depictions of the cat, from ancient Egyptian tomb paintings to Roman mosaics (see pp.36 and 155), depict its hunter's nature.

The cat is a rare exception in the history of interspecies relationships: humans have never been able to teach it new tricks, so to speak, or to use the animal in any capacity other than the one that comes naturally to it: as a catcher of rodents, which it hunts entirely at its own discretion. Unlike cattle, horses, and dogs, it has never been put to work. The cat is fundamentally a free animal, totally resistant to being confined or deprived of the independence that is essential to it wherever it is, even within the four walls of a tiny city apartment. Apart from its great usefulness as a hunter—which not only protected crops and helped limit the spread of disease, but also proved useful for monks and scholars in need of saving books and documents from the errant nibbler—now the cat has succeeded in convincing humans that its chief value comes from . . . not having one. Its importance lies simply in its unique presence, which makes it an object of delight to all humans, especially the artists who encounter it.

This fascination with felines can be traced most readily through how the cat has been depicted in visual culture, from paintings, sculpture, and prints to books, fashion, and popular culture, as far back as ancient Minoan seals (see p.57) all the way to the present in viral animated GIFs (see p.41). First and foremost, the cat has always had a sacred dimension, be it divine or diabolical. The fact that the animals are fecund creatures, producing several litters a year, has led cultures to associate them with fertility goddesses and good fortune. Perhaps most famously, in ancient Egypt, cats were strongly connected to the divine. Beloved pets, they were protected by law, mummified, and buried when they died as the object of strict mourning rituals on the part of their humans (see p.175). Many of the sitting cat sculptures (see p.29) that survive are actually not goddesses themselves but offerings to Bastet, the daughter of the sun god Ra. She sometimes took the form of a woman with the head of a female cat or the warrior-like form of the merciless lioness Sekhmet, and was the caring goddess of the home and protector of pregnant women and children. Astonishingly, we know only a single cat's name from ancient Egypt, that of Nedjem, recorded in a hieroglyph during the reign of Hatshepsut (c. 1473–1458 BCE).

From ancient Egypt, cats probably spread across the different continents by ship. Sailors, scholars, pilgrims, and all kinds of travelers took them aboard to protect their supplies of provisions or their precious cargo from vermin. It is thought that the Phoenicians brought them to Europe in the fifth century BCE, and, hundreds of years later, European colonists traveled with them to the Americas in the sixteenth century. About 1,400 years ago, cats caught a ride from the western Mediterranean through Central Asia to China along the Silk Road with merchants and diplomats as presents for members of the elite. In Japan, they were probably imported in the sixth century on Chinese ships carrying Buddhist scrolls, which the hunters were taken onboard to protect.

Since then, cats, or *neko*, have always occupied a special place in Japanese culture, acting as an inexhaustible source of inspiration. Ranging from cute to frightening, they are foundational characters in folklore, from the *maneki-neko* "lucky cat" to the *nekomata* cat monster (see pp.78 and 185). The realistic cats depicted in *ukiyo-e* prints by Utagawa Kuniyoshi and Utagawa Hiroshige in the nineteenth century (see pp.89 and 102) spread beyond Japan to become icons, helping popularize the cute exports of contemporary *kawaii*, such as the tiny Sonny Angel figurines by Dreams Inc. (see p.179), Hello Kitty, and the cat characters of Studio Ghibli films.

In the Islamic world, cats were similarly prized, but without reaching the level of deification. Legend has it that the prophet Muhammad once cut off his sleeve instead of waking a tomcat that had fallen asleep on it. Cats are allowed to go into mosques, and artists, such as Zeinab Saleh, have depicted them lounging serenely on prayer mats (see p.197). In cities throughout the Middle East and Mediterranean, street cats are a delight to both the inhabitants and photographers.

In some cultures in Western Europe, the cat did not enjoy as warm of a welcome. Although some depictions exist in art and ephemera, such as an ancient Greek krater from 420–400 BCE (see p.81), the cat is less present in the visual culture of premodern Europe. After the Christianization of the continent, the animal's sensuality and elusiveness, perceived greediness and shamelessness, and phosphorescent eyes that let it see in the dark made it a suspect creature. It was long associated with the devil, especially when it was unfortunate enough to be the color of darkness and have a black coat.

This modest little predator might have been a useful asset in daily life, but it was too much of a charmer to be innocent. Cats might appear as humorous doodles in the margins of illuminated medieval manuscripts (see p.106), but in Renaissance paintings, they were instead shown preying on birds that were associated with Christ or running from angels (see p.70). Between about 1450 and 1650, when witch hunts were at their height, cats were considered to be bringers of bad luck, accused not just as witches' familiars but as one of the forms witches could take.

During the Industrial Revolution and the urbanization of Europe throughout the nineteenth century, a radical shift occurred in Europeans' relationship to cats. No longer were they only considered pest controllers, but they began to assume the role that they had enjoyed in African, Middle Eastern, and Asian cultures for centuries, that of revered and independent companion. Much of this was thanks to revolutions in visual and popular culture—including the hilarious and relatable anthropomorphic illustrations of British artist Louis Wain (see p.220). Pedigree breeding also developed in Victorian England, which celebrated the glamour of groomed felines for a new bourgeois audience (see p.208).

Cats' newfound domesticity is reflected and refracted in art. They became household companions, members of the family who brought a tenderness to interior spaces, made all the more valuable because they were just as capable of doing the opposite and being ferocious. From the nineteenth century, artists, such as Henriëtte Ronner-Knip and John Henry Dolph, began to produce saccharine scenes of mother cats watching over their kittens or cats with puppies, which appealed to a burgeoning bourgeois clientele of cat owners (see pp.176 and 200). These tender images set an example of caretaking to children, and to young girls, in particular, who were often portrayed with their pets, such as in Pierre-Auguste Renoir's portrait of Julie Manet (see p.108), which manages to suggest the

animal purring through the paint. The special bond between children and felines continues today: one charming example from photographer Jamel Shabazz shows a little boy holding a kitten on the streets of 1980s New York (see p.43).

There have also been countless representations of the so-called special connection between women and their feline companions throughout art history, from Henri Matisse's colorful depiction of his daughter Marguerite with a black cat to Gordon Parks's tender 1952 photograph of Eartha Kitt with two kittens (see pp.90 and 214). Since the late twentieth century, artists' paintings that are specifically of men with cats have reflected new versions of masculinity that are less stridently virile and sometimes with a queer slant. In portraits by Alice Neel (see p.112) and Kerry James Marshall (see p.125), we see men who are not afraid to display their affection or their sensuality. With one of these little hunters at their feet or in their arms, they show themselves as unguarded and caring, the opposite of a male predator.

But if cats are depicted so widely and often, it is perhaps primarily for a simple reason: their incredible beauty. A few distinctive forms make them immediately recognizable—pointed ears, almond-shaped eyes, and paws with toe pads. The variety of their fur—the precise shade of color, positioning of patches, sizes of stripe, and length of hair—gives creatives a limitless palette with which to play. Their sinuous shape borders on the calligraphic, evident in the dynamic sculptures of Korean artist Lee Sangsoo (see p.73). Cats adopt the most improbable of positions, curling themselves into a ball one minute and stretching themselves into an endless long line the next, as captured by Serbian painter Endre Penovác (see p.165). The regal way they hold themselves and the quiet way they seem to glide noiselessly—like ballerinas forever walking on the tips of their toes—make them the most elegant creatures. They have an imperturbable look about them, with large lustrous eyes that they close now and again to show us they understand us.

Creatives have represented cats again and again as their equals, from Gwen John's quiet painting of her beloved tortoiseshell Edgar Quinet in 1904 (see p.126) to Tracey Emin's transcendent connection to her gray feline Docket in the new millennium (see p.66). Some artists' cats have gone down in history as famous lifelong companions with a name and character of their own, portrayed by their humans as a way of capturing their spark of life. Similarly, cats have become the classic companions of writers, a natural evolution, perhaps, from their medieval adoption by monks to protect their parchments from rodents (see p.54).

As seen in the photographs of contemporary Kenyan photographer Bill Muganda (see p.103) or on the canvases of American painter Hilary Pecis (see p.11), cats have remained library animals: they love peace and quiet, sleeping calmly for a long time in a studious atmosphere. Cats have also inspired writers to write, acting as muses to the likes of Dr. Seuss, Beatrix Potter, and T.S. Eliot (see pp.12, 42, and 69). Although their caterwauling was often linked to the witches' sabbath in earlier times, they have had a positive impact on pop music—Carole King's tabby Telemachus famously graced the cover of her 1971 album *Tapestry* and Freddie

Mercury was such a cat lover that he owned multiple feline-shaped plates (see pp.53 and 109).

This proliferation of the cat in visual culture matches the passion for cats in the real world, with more than one-quarter of households in the United States alone acting as home to these "wild domestic" companions. The adoration has not always been so widespread, and the black cat offers an interesting microcosm. After centuries of being perceived as a bad-luck charm, the black cat became emblematic of modernity in France during the nineteenth century, when it took a symbolic part in the revolutionary beginnings of modern art. Édouard Manet inserted a cat at the prostitute Olympia's feet in place of the dog traditionally associated with loyalty and marriage, and it gave its name to the bohemian cabaret in Montmartre, for which it was emblazoned on a poster by Théophile Alexandre Steinlen as a symbol of fin-de-siècle Paris (see pp.147 and 23). The once satanic cat, the familiar of witches, was now the cat of free spirits and artists.

Examples of the cool black cat still abound: painter Linda Stark celebrated hers in a surreal portrait, featuring its head as the heart of a fantastical flower, while fashion designer Thom Browne has created a handbag for fashionistas of all genders in the shape of one, complete with a swiveling head (see pp.20 and 171). Even so, black cats in some cultures have held on to their negative, witchy connotations, and are the least likely to be adopted from rescue centers due to the color of their coats, a reminder that our feline friends still rely on us for love and homes, regardless of how often they appear on canvases or in cute memes. The instrumentalization of all cats on social media in viral visuals raises ethical concerns, which this book of animal iconography tries to emphasize—that art can play a powerful role in improving our relationship with animals. The star of the 2024 Academy Award–winning film *Flow* (see p.152), for example, a heroic shorthair, has actually inspired an uptick in adoptions of black cats.

Regardless of how much passion they inspire, we need to remember that these creatures are living beings who should be respected in all their integrity and individuality. The collection of images presented in *Cat* is an insightful survey that illustrates the symbiotic relationship between humans and this beloved feline companion in art and popular culture. *Cat* is a celebration of our connection to these animals, a small attempt at thanking them for the well-being they bring us—when they want to. This volume proves that cats have infinitely inspired artists, authors, animal rescuers, musicians, photographers, fashion designers, filmmakers, and seemingly anyone who has ever had the pleasure of savoring the present moment alongside this animal. The pages that follow demonstrate how human beings have taken our lead from cats' own innate philosophy: be ourselves, whatever happens; remain true to our own being; and stay free without servility.

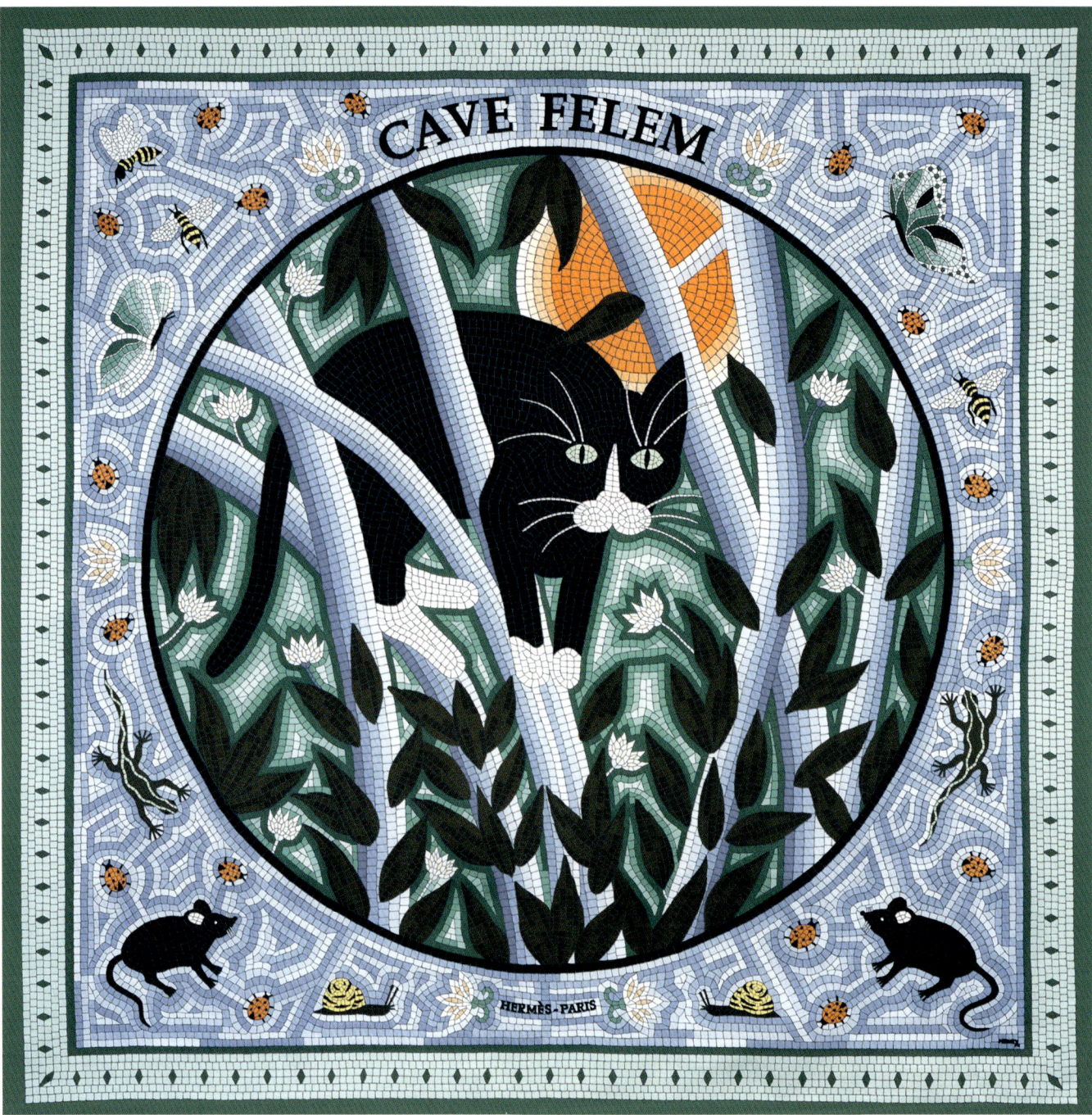

CHRISTINE HENRY FOR HERMÈS

Cave Felem, 1995
Silk, 35½ × 35½ in. / 90 × 90 cm
Hermès Collection, Paris

Although it may appear as such upon first glance, this colorful square is not an ancient mosaic but an ingeniously designed silk scarf. The first scarf project by French designer Christine Henry for Hermès, *Cave Felem* is inspired by the real-life Roman mosaic that covers the vestibule floor of a first-century villa in Pompeii, known as the House of the Tragic Poet. The original mosaic features a leashed but apparently vicious guard dog and the words *Cave Canem* (Latin for "beware of dog"), both symbol and text acting as a deterrent to potential burglars. Henry has put a feline twist on the motif, choosing instead to warn delightfully depicted critters—snails, bees, ladybugs, lizards, and mice—to "beware of cat," here a stealthy black-and-white hunter, unseen in lush foliage. Over her more than thirty-year collaboration with Hermès, Henry's designs have often been based on themes she sees as vital, such as mythology and history, environmental preservation, and the intricate beauty of nature. Hermès has an extensive record of collaboration with many illustrators for its prized silk scarf designs, beginning in 1937 when the first screenprinted scarf, *Jeu des omnibus et des dames blanches*, was launched. Now an iconic fashion accessory, the Hermès *carré* (French for "square") has been the canvas for almost three thousand bold designs, illustrating a rich variety of ideas, including beloved animal companions. With its beautiful scarves, Hermès Design Studio has continued to uphold a long-standing partnership between the atelier and the creative world.

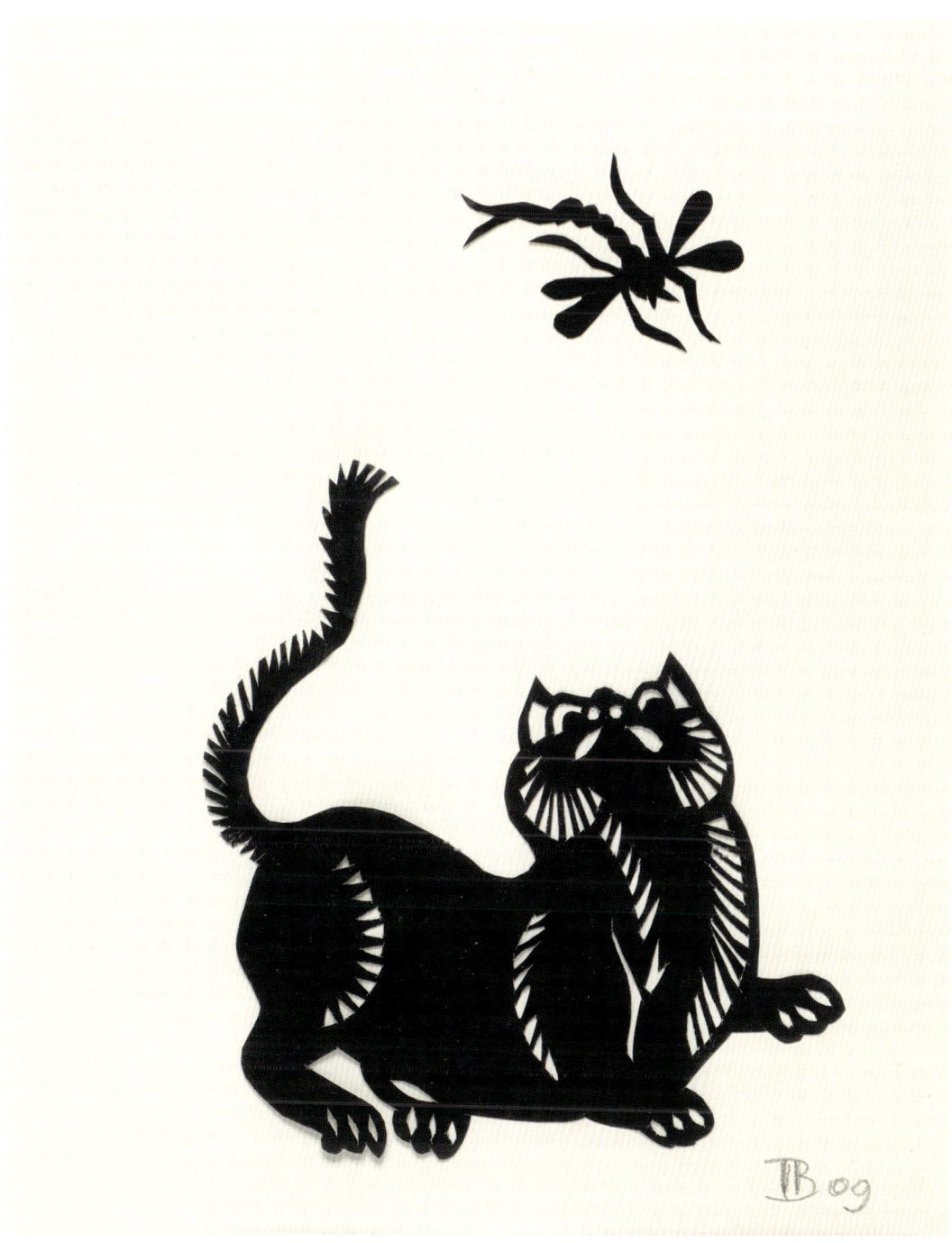

IRA BLOUNT

Cat and Dragonfly Silhouette, 2009
Paper and graphite, 14⅛ × 11⅛ in. / 36 × 20.3 cm
Anacostia Community Museum, Smithsonian,
Washington, DC

A black cat, with its head cocked back and its paw slightly raised ready to strike, looks intently at a dragonfly, which hovers teasingly above the feline's head. This charming image is a cut-paper silhouette made by American artist Ira Blount (1918–2020). Having meticulously clipped both cat and insect out of black paper, Blount brings the figures to life with deft shaping that gives a sense of texture to the animal's fur and the detail of the claws on each paw, as well as the intricate anatomy of the dragonfly. The cat's jagged tail is upright as it gets ready to pounce, but the viewer will never know if its hunt is successful, allowing one to engage fully with the sense of playfulness in the image. Blount, who became an outreach worker in his adopted city of Washington, DC, after serving in the army during World War II, was a polymath who worked in a variety of media, including calligraphy, quilting, woodworking, basketry, and origami, all of which require skills of intense precision, as evident here in the intricate cuts he has made in the paper. His love of craftwork and learning helped guide his path: he acknowledged them as "a strong force in turning my back on some of the bad habits I had." Over the course of a full life and career, Blount constantly shared his love of artisanal crafts with the many students he taught and inspired, donating more than two hundred works to the Smithsonian's Anacostia Community Museum when he died at the age of 101.

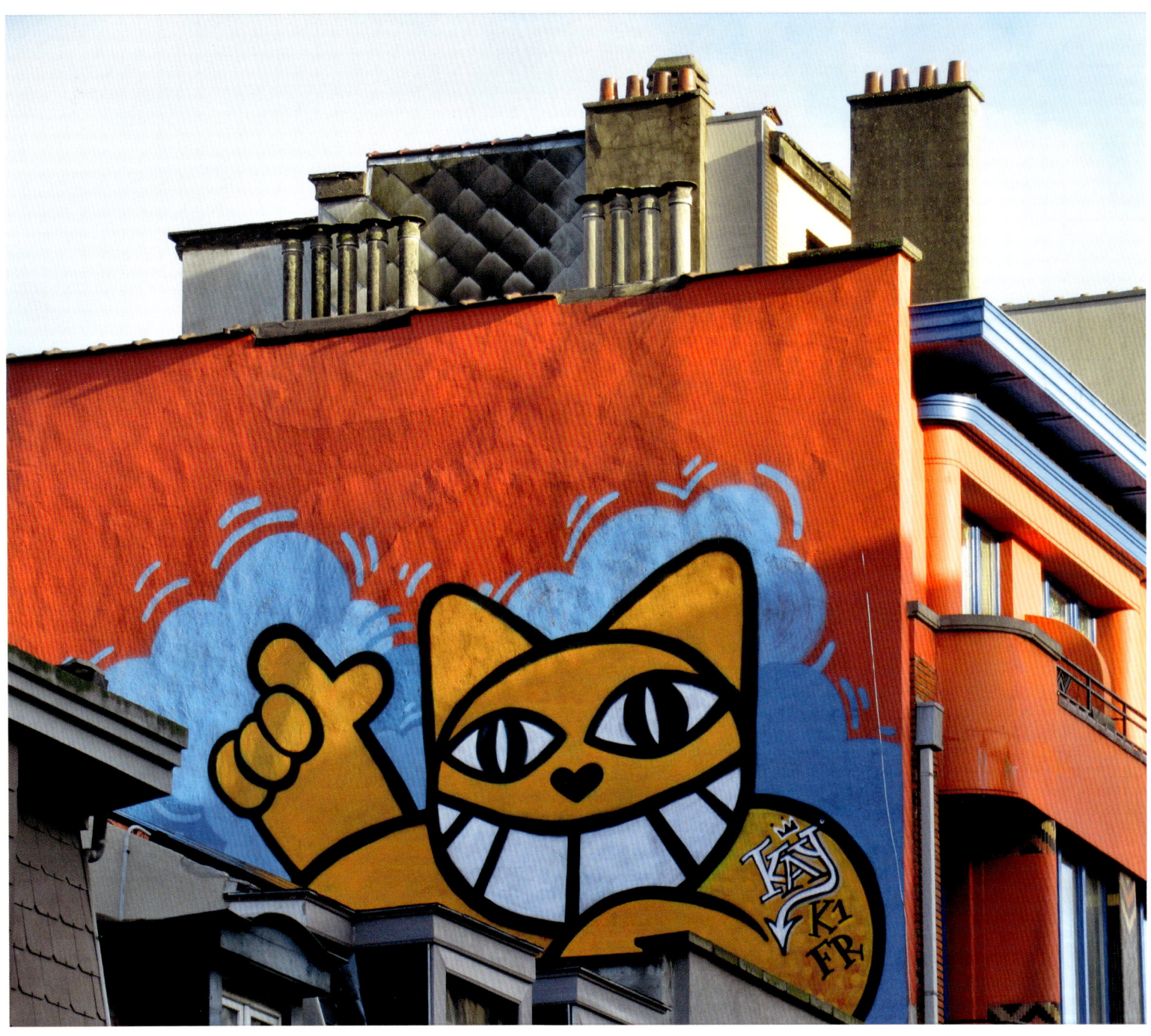

M.CHAT

M.Chat, Brussels, 2022
Graffiti, dimensions variable
Photograph by Ferdinand Feys

Encouraging passersby to look upward, this bright yellow cat grins effusively from a Brussels rooftop. The jaunty character, known as M.Chat (also Mr. Chat or Monsieur Chat), is the creation of Franco-Swiss street artist Thoma Vuille (b. 1977), who also goes by the same moniker as his creation, and is regularly seen in urban centers worldwide, from New York City and Hong Kong to São Paulo and Dakar. Characterized by a huge Cheshire Cat grin (see p.21), the benevolent feline brings joy and optimism to the drab, city environments in which he appears. Although M.Chat is often portrayed mid-leap, he sometimes flies with angel wings, emerges from a hole, or, as here, points to the sky. But whatever his pose, he is always grinning. Vuille began painting graffiti in 1992, although it wasn't until 1997,

when he was a student at the Orléans School of Art and Design in France, that M.Chat was born, first appearing on the city's rooftop chimneys and later on walls elsewhere in France, Europe, and the world. The iconic character has since become something of a cultural icon in France and was even the subject of a 2004 Chris Marker documentary, *The Case of the Grinning Cat*. Painting in secret, Vuille managed to protect his anonymity for more than a decade, but in 2007 he was apprehended by the police while working on a mural. The ensuing trial, which resulted in a suspended sentence, saw the prices of Vuille's gallery works soar, along with the popularity of his most famous creation.

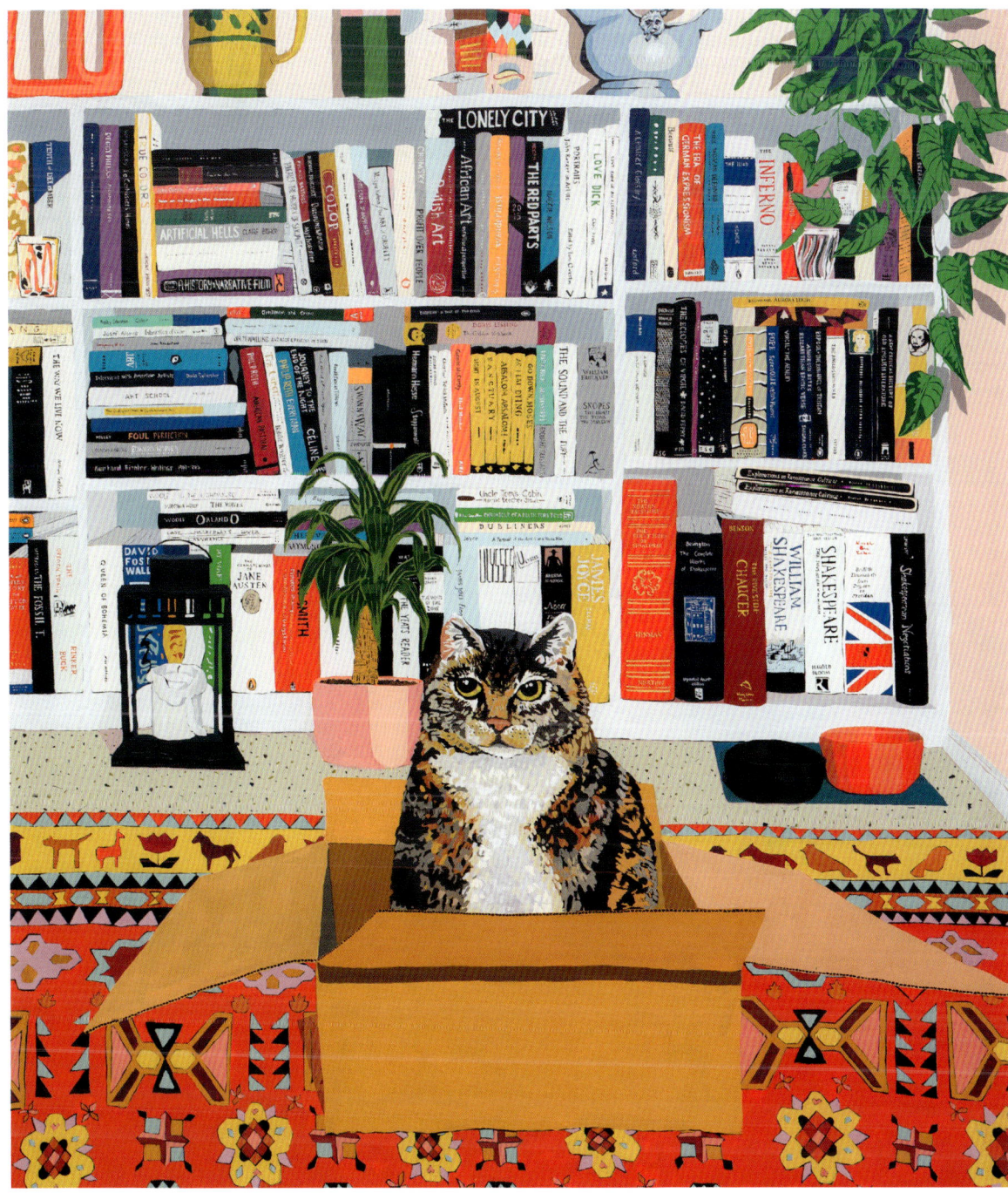

HILARY PECIS

Clementine's Bookshelf, 2021
Acrylic on linen
74 × 64 in. / 188 × 162.6 cm
Private collection

Cats have been a mainstay of libraries for centuries as effective deterrents against mice and rats that would otherwise cause damage to paper and books. Empress Elizabeth of Russia famously issued a royal decree in 1745 that the biggest, fiercest cats be dispatched to the Royal Palace's library (now the Hermitage Museum), and cats have been occupants there ever since. Indeed, the library or bookstore cat is a popular trope, the focus of scores of websites, memes, social media accounts, and books. American painter Hilary Pecis (b. 1979) depicted one such library lurker in *Clementine's Bookshelf*. A tabby sits directly in the center of the composition, tucked into a cardboard box (another classic cat motif) and on guard in front of the room's towering bookshelf, as if a sentry. Pecis, who paints from photographs,

has a particular fondness for capturing the written word, and many of her works contain books or other signage. The bright, color-splashed composition, rendered in flat, acrylic paint, exemplifies the Los Angeles–based artist's style, directly echoing the cheerful hues of her native Southern California. Her work hearkens to the vibrant palette and compressed perspective of the Fauvists, such as Henri Matisse (see p.90), although she rarely portrays figures in her work, instead favoring intimate interiors, full of objects and, yes, cats, that act as extensions of the people who live in those spaces, a modern update of the fusty rooms and feline portraits of painters past.

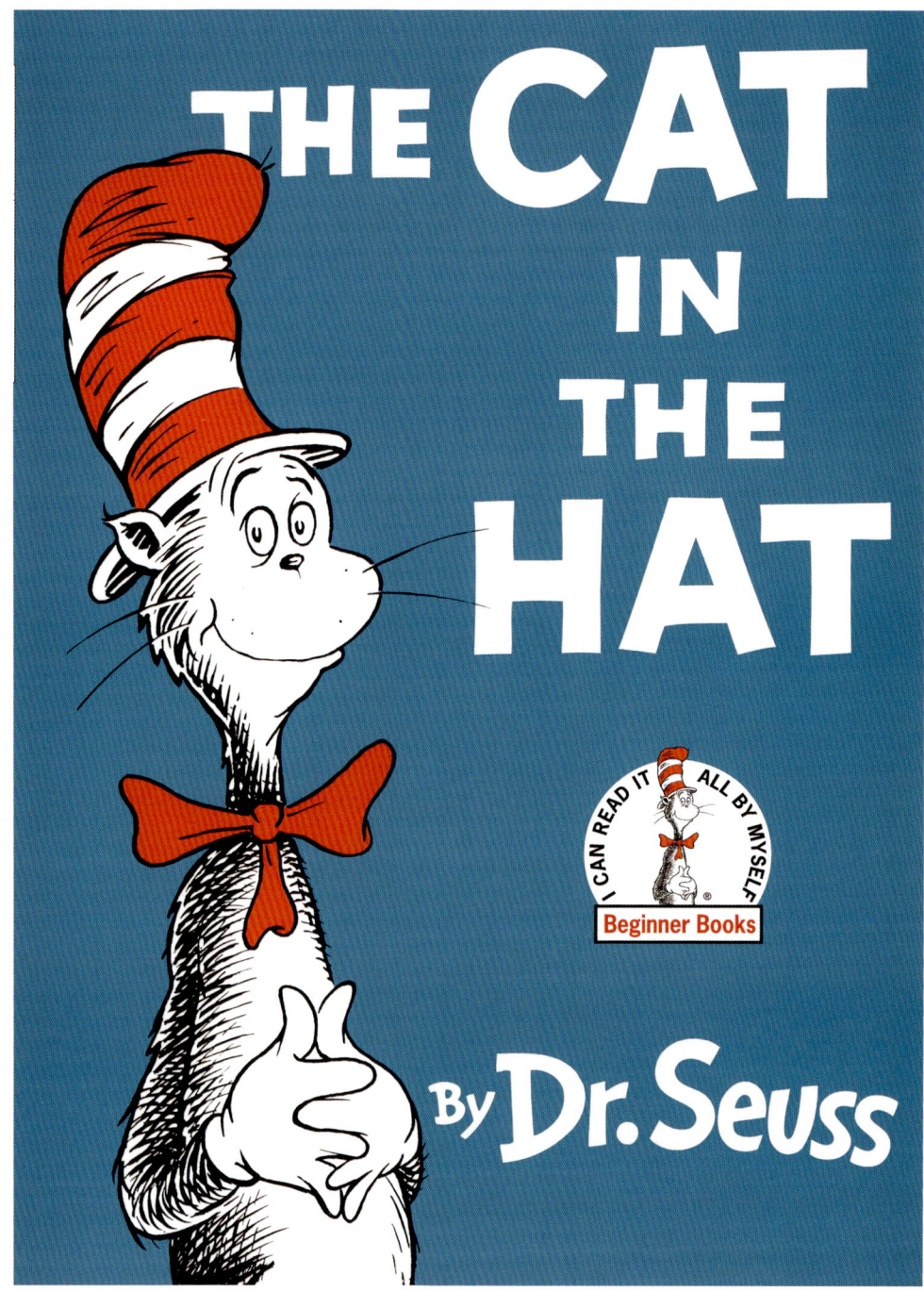

DR. SEUSS

The Cat in the Hat, 1957
Printed book, 11¼ × 8¼ in. / 28.6 × 21 cm

The mischievous Cat in the Hat is perhaps the most famous feline in literature, who teaches Sally and her brother some new games while they are home alone on a rainy day. Created by Theodor Seuss Geisel (1904–1991)—better known as Dr. Seuss—this iconic anthropomorphic black Cat in a striped top hat and red scarf became an unlikely symbol of children's literacy. Although Seuss had published a bestseller nearly every year since 1937, he had never written a primer, or any educational book that helps teach very young children how to read, until an editor asked him to "write me a story that first graders can't put down!" According to legend, Seuss was given a strict list of words to use that were friendly to new readers but frustrating to a freewheeling creative, so he based his story off the first rhyme he found—"cat" and "hat." Drawn in Seuss's colorful, imaginative style, the sly Cat and his twin blue-haired imps, Thing One and Thing Two, wreak havoc in the children's home, ignoring the complaints of their concerned pet fish. Just before their mother arrives home, the Cat cleans everything up with his fantastical machine, finishing a wild story that all the while emphasizes reading skills. *The Cat in the Hat* has never gone out of print, selling more than 15 million copies globally to teach children across the world both the joys of reading and the fun of a feline's tricks.

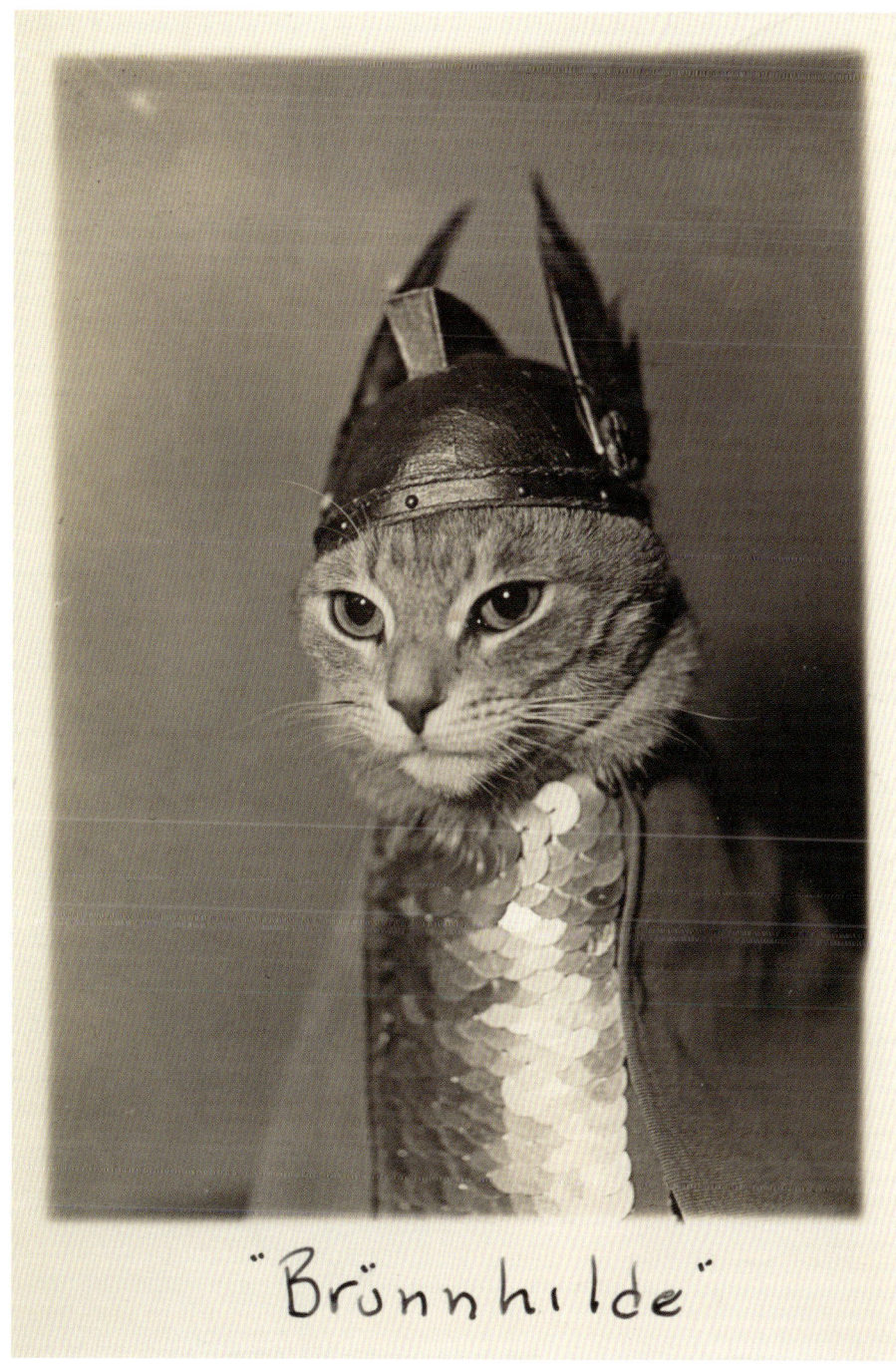

"Brünnhilde"

ADOLPH E. WEIDHAAS

Brünnhilde, 1936
Gelatin silver print, 4¾ × 3½ in. / 12 × 9 cm
Library of Congress, Washington, DC

In Norse mythology, the princess Brünnhilde was the most famous of all the Valkyries, the "shield maidens" of the god Odin who carried the souls of dead warriors to Valhalla. Her reputation continued all the way into the nineteenth century through her role in German composer Richard Wagner's opera cycle *Der Ring des Nibelungen* (1857). With her horned helmet and breastplate armor, the warrior maiden's image has been seared into the collective consciousness far beyond the opera house, as this photograph can attest. Taken by Adolph E. Weidhaas (1891–1971), a pioneer in the field of American advertising photography, this tabby Valkyrie was used to advertise a performance of Wagner's opera in 1936. The photograph was originally displayed with images of other cats in operatic costume, prominently placed in the window of the Snapshot Store on West 40th Street in New York, where it drew large crowds. A passerby described the throngs of people: "Elbowing closer we found the window filled with photographs of a cat dressed in costume for such operatic roles as Brunhild, Musetta, or the Bad Man in *Girl of the Golden West*." Along with Bugs Bunny's own unforgettable Brünnhilde costume, this handsome cat dressed in a winged helmet and breastplate is an indelible image of the shield maiden that appeals to new generations. Indeed, the feline *Brünnhilde* emerged as one of the most-loved images from a 2022 Library of Congress exhibition that mined its historic archives, *Not an Ostrich: & Other Images from America's Library*.

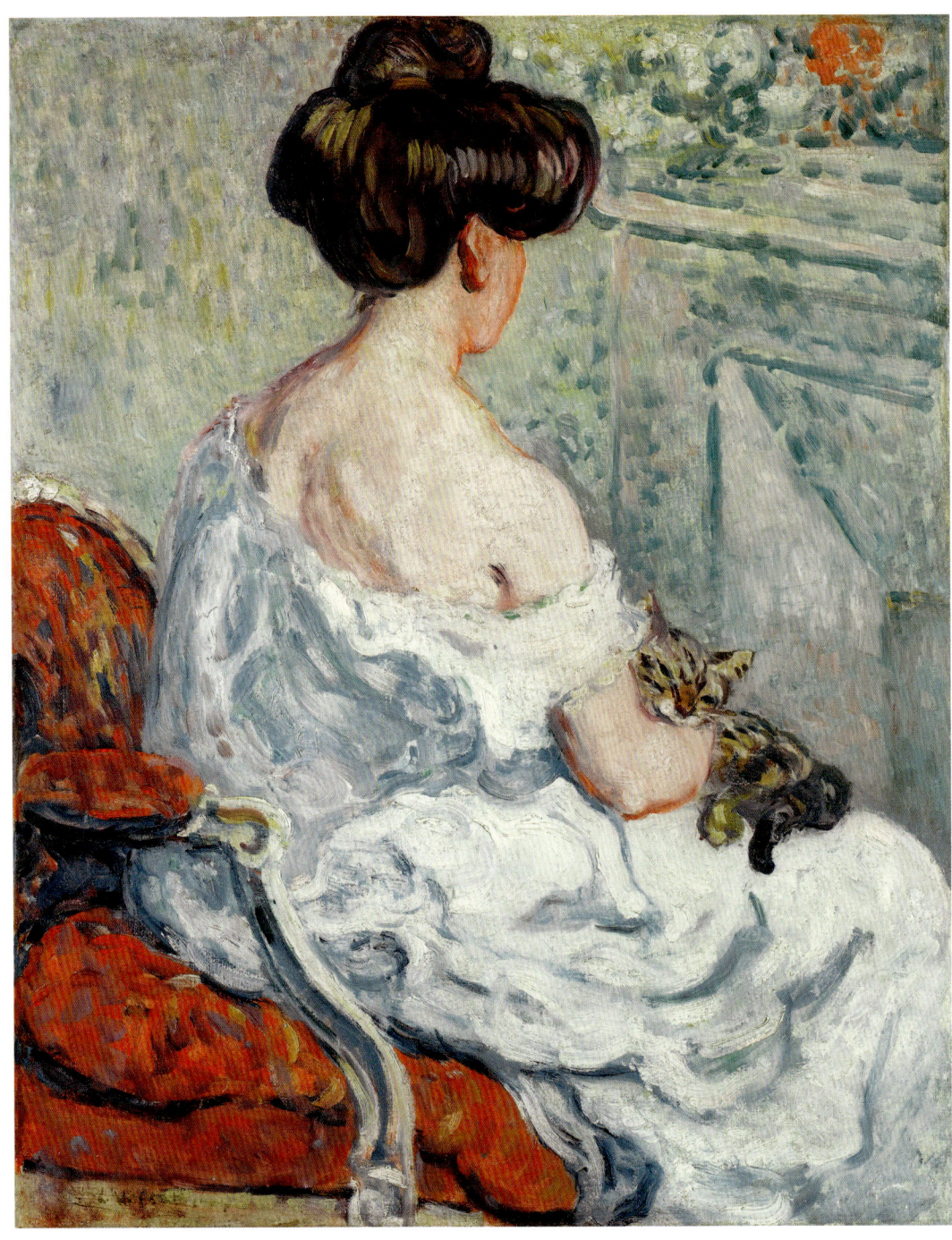

LOUIS VALTAT

Woman with a Cat, 1903
Oil on canvas, 37 × 28¾ in. / 94 × 73.1 cm
Metropolitan Museum of Art, New York

This painting catches a scantily clad (for 1903) woman in a moment of intimacy with a beloved pet, her dressing gown falling off her shoulders as she lovingly strokes a brown tabby in her lap. Created by French artist Louis Valtat (1869–1952), the aggressive brushstrokes and provocative subject matter are all hallmarks of the Fauves, an avant-garde group of late nineteenth- and early twentieth-century painters who broke both with Realist representation and the larger Impressionist movement. Although Valtat is most closely associated with the Fauves, as the bright hues of this painting attest, he never utilized the high-keyed, unnaturalistic colors for which they were known, as evident in the works of Henri Matisse (see p.90). Women and cats were a favorite subject of the Impressionists,

Post-Impressionists, and the Fauves, not only because these artists sought to represent real scenes from everyday and interior lives, but because most of them were simply crazy about cats. It has been claimed, for example, that Pierre-Auguste Renoir (see p.108) was cat obsessed, and authenticators have been able to use the cat hair stuck in the paint of his canvases to verify his works. Renoir showed Valtat's work to influential art dealer Ambroise Vollard, who took on the young painter as a client and organized his first solo exhibition in 1903, the same year this painting was produced. Indeed, one can see the echoes of Renoir in this sweetly romantic work, with its soft brushstrokes and muted palette.

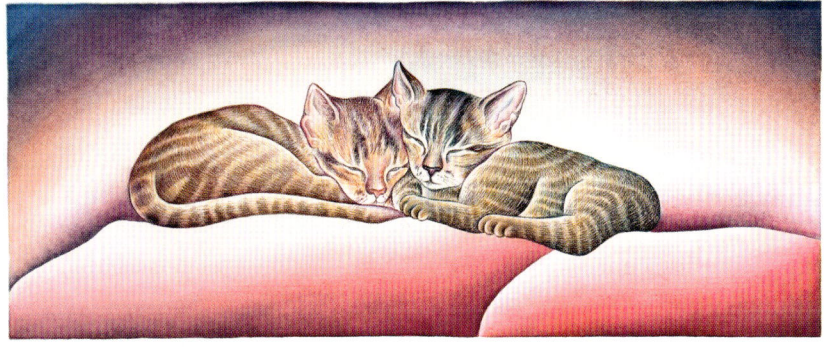

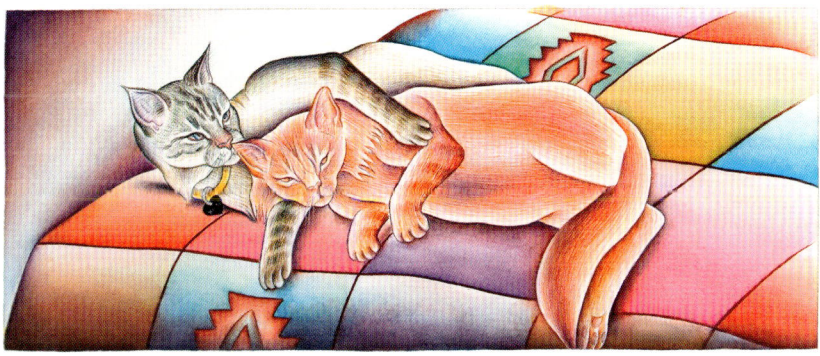

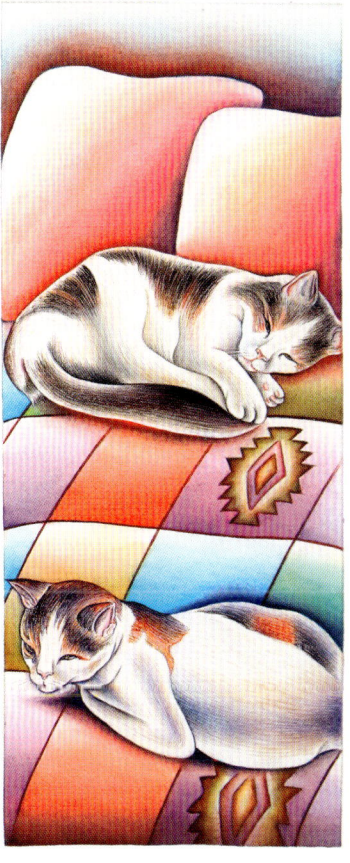

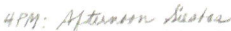

Judy Chicago 2001

JUDY CHICAGO

4 PM / Afternoon Siesta, from Kitty City, 1999–2004
Watercolor on Arches drawing paper
22 × 30 in. / 55.9 × 76.2 cm
Private collection

This three-part painting by American feminist artist Judy Chicago (b. 1939) evokes the famous title of a poem by English poet Eleanor Farjeon: "Cats Sleep Anywhere." A triple pair of felines snooze in different formations in the middle and on the edge of a colorful quilt-covered bed. While their fur coats are painted in true-to-life patterns, the overall palette and shading technique provide a vibrancy that contrasts with the sleepy creatures, although one has pricked ears, a reminder that even a dormant cat is highly alert to potential threats. The artist—a cat lover since her early twenties, when she took in a black kitten that showed up on her doorstep—made the work as part of a wider series representing cats at different times of day. This structure echoes a book of hours, an illustrated devotional book with

roots in medieval Europe that aided the daily prayer cycle. Chicago is most well-known for *The Dinner Party* (1974–79), an installation celebrating overlooked women from history in a ceramic dinner service with yonic imagery. This symbol of femininity is echoed as a pattern on the patchwork bedspread in two of the paintings here, indicating an intentional connection to women's sexuality, even in a subject as innocent as sleeping cats. This link was further amplified in a 2017 solo exhibition at Jessica Silverman Gallery in San Francisco, entitled *Judy Chicago's Pussies*, when Chicago reflected, "It wouldn't have been feasible to call an exhibition 'Pussies' before a generation of young women reclaimed the power and humor of the word."

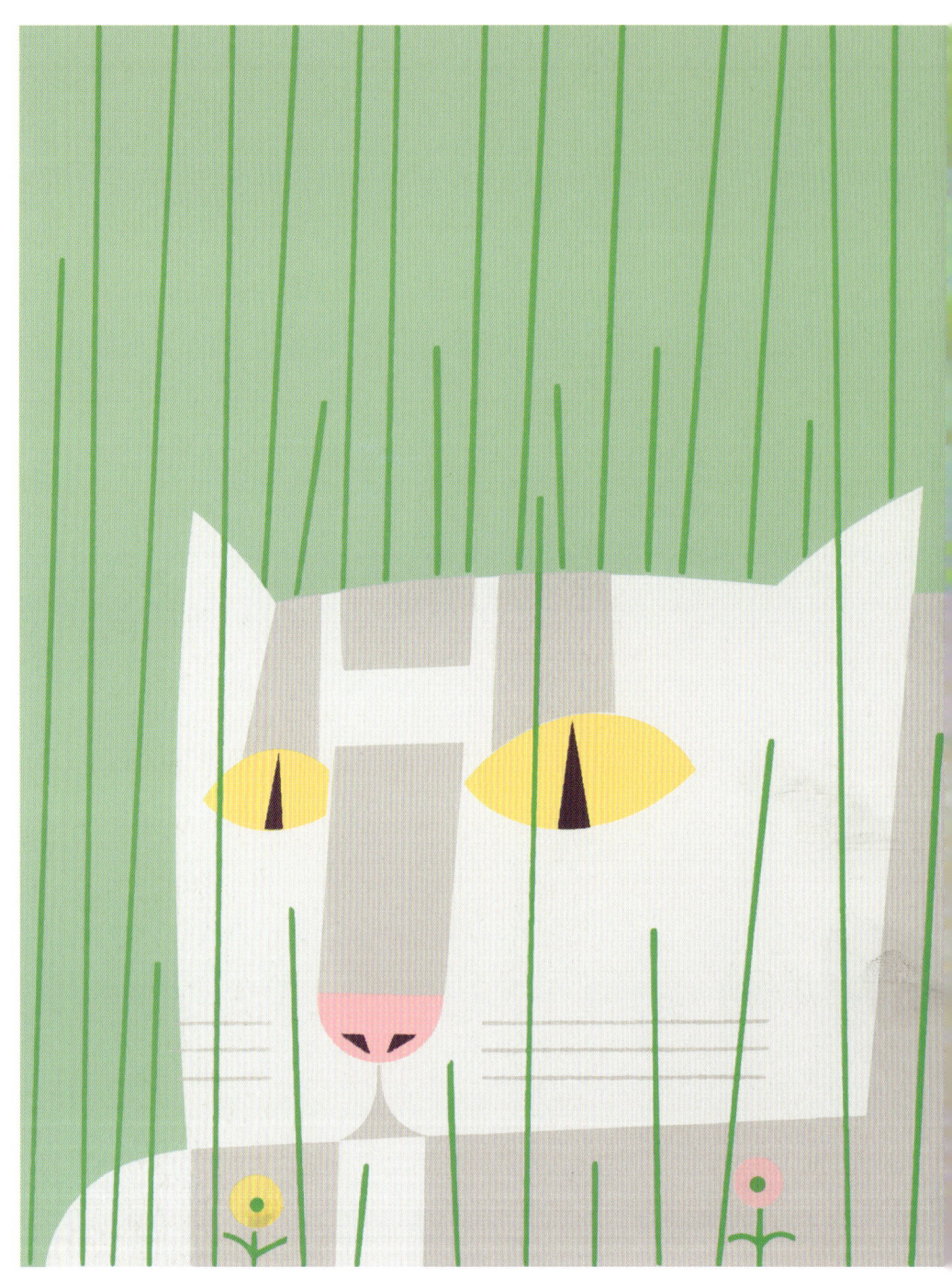

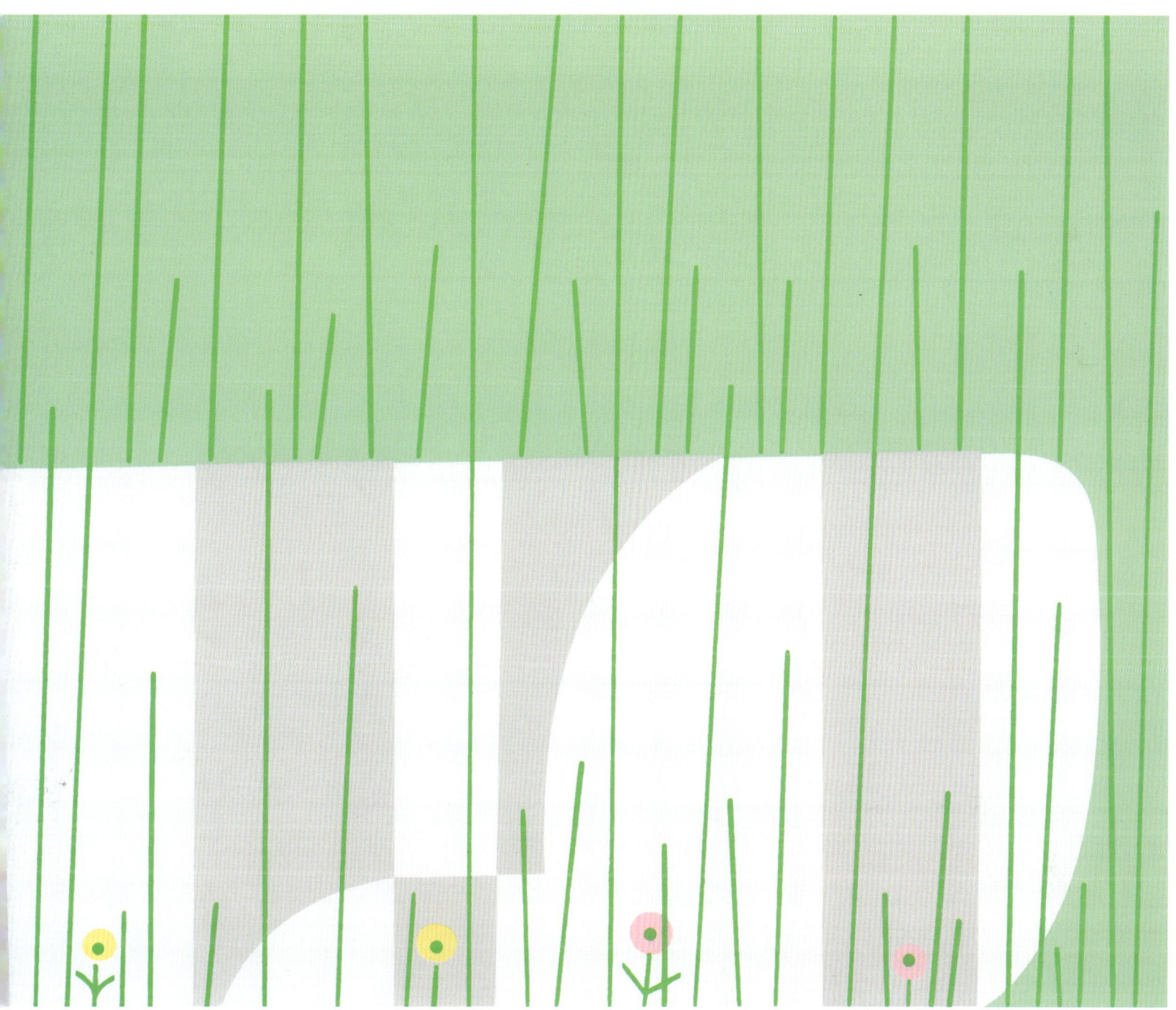

EDIE HARPER

Spring Creeper, 1980
Serigraph, 8 × 16 in. / 20.3 × 40.6 cm

Lying low in the long grass, this curious-looking cat is scaled up in size to occupy almost the entire length of the composition, with a bulky gray-and-white frame that towers over tiny flowers in the foreground. Although inconspicuous, a sense of timidity lingers in this gentle giant's bright yellow eyes, which, along with the artist's highly stylized aesthetic, connects to a playful narrative, encouraging the viewer to see the world in a more imaginative way. American artist Edie Harper (1922–2010), who was married to fellow artist and collaborator Charley Harper for more than sixty years, grew up in Missouri in the 1940s surrounded by an abundance of nature, which led to her lifelong love affair with animals. A multitalented creative, she excelled in many disciplines, including photography, printmaking, wood sculpture, weaving, jewelrymaking, and book illustration, working independently from Charley but also sharing a creative vision with him that was rooted in wildlife conservation. Together, they championed a reductive and geometric graphic style that has since been termed "minimal realism," using simple shapes and colors to convey a visual language full of charm, exuberance, and storytelling possibilities. In the 1980s, when the original acrylic version of *Spring Creeper* was created, Edie was particularly interested in unlocking childhood memories, gravitating particularly toward feline subjects, which she loved for their inquisitive and mischievous nature.

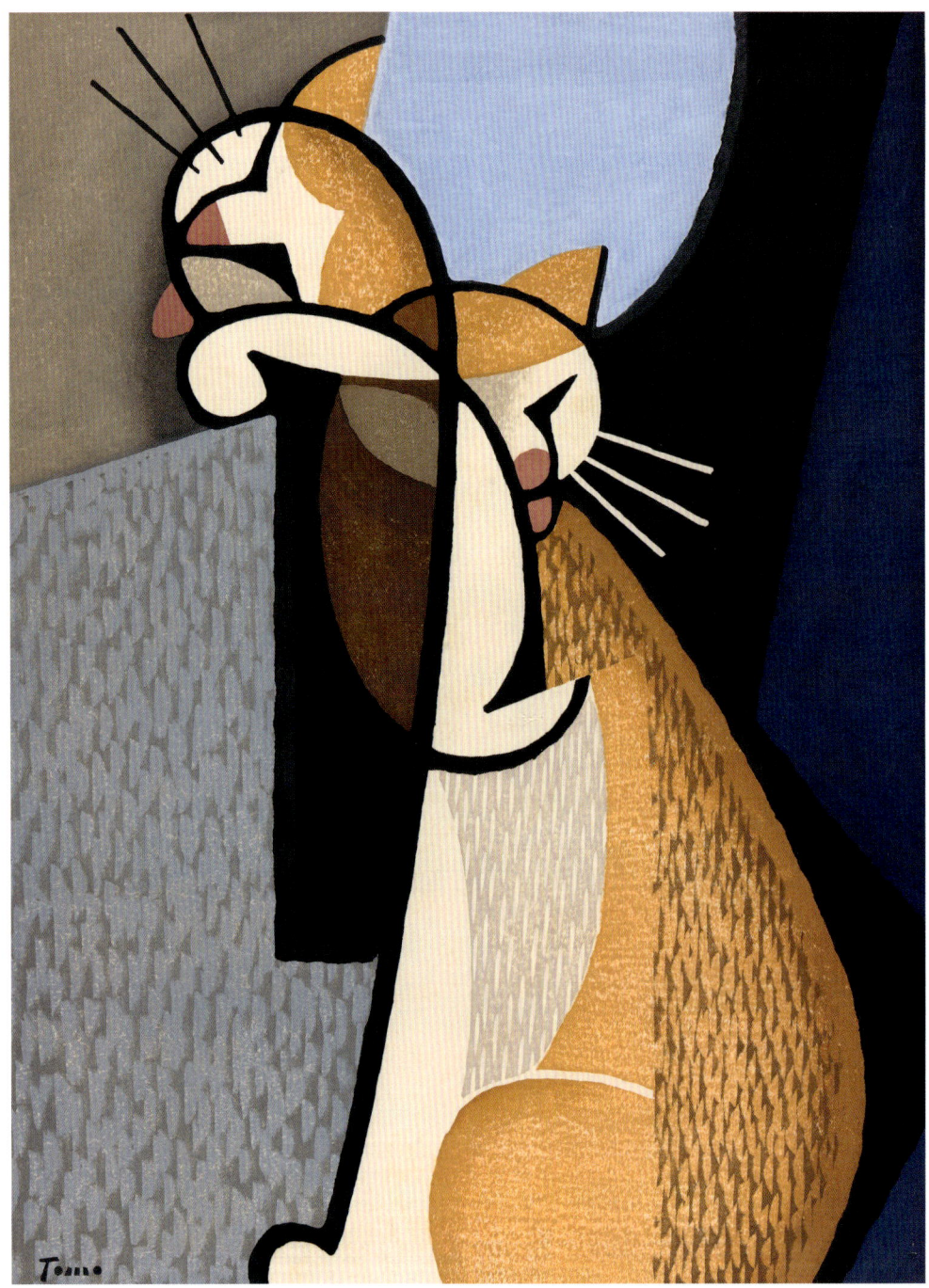

INAGAKI TOMOO

Cat Making Up, c. 1962
Woodcut, 25⅛ × 18¼ in. / 63.7 × 46.3 cm
Art Institute of Chicago

Inagaki Tomoo (1902–1980) was working as a steelmaker in his native Japan when he came across illustrations by the printmaker Koshiro Onchi in a poetry magazine that stopped him in his tracks. He left his job, enrolled in commercial art training, and began a career as an artist, running a successful studio in Tokyo until he was forced to close it during World War II. However, after the war ended, the presence of American GIs and businesses in the country created a demand for Japanese art and artists. Inagaki was heavily influenced by Onchi and Un'ichi Hiratsuka, both master printmakers in the *sōsaku-hanga* (creative print) movement who elevated traditional Japanese woodcuts from mass-produced commercial pieces to high art through the stylistic use of abstraction. After closing his commercial practice,

Inagaki began to develop the modernized style inspired by this movement that would become his signature. He published his first cat print in 1951, kicking off what would become a recurring theme in his work—and a highly sought-after commodity for collectors. His semiabstract prints share a common dynamism, deftly expressing the essence of the animals and their movement through simplistic shapes, typically in earthen tones accented by bright oranges and reds and heavy black line work. In this print, it may seem that two cats appear side by side, but there is actually only one feline present. The geometric shapes illustrate the classic motion of a bathing cat, washing its face with one paw and tongue out.

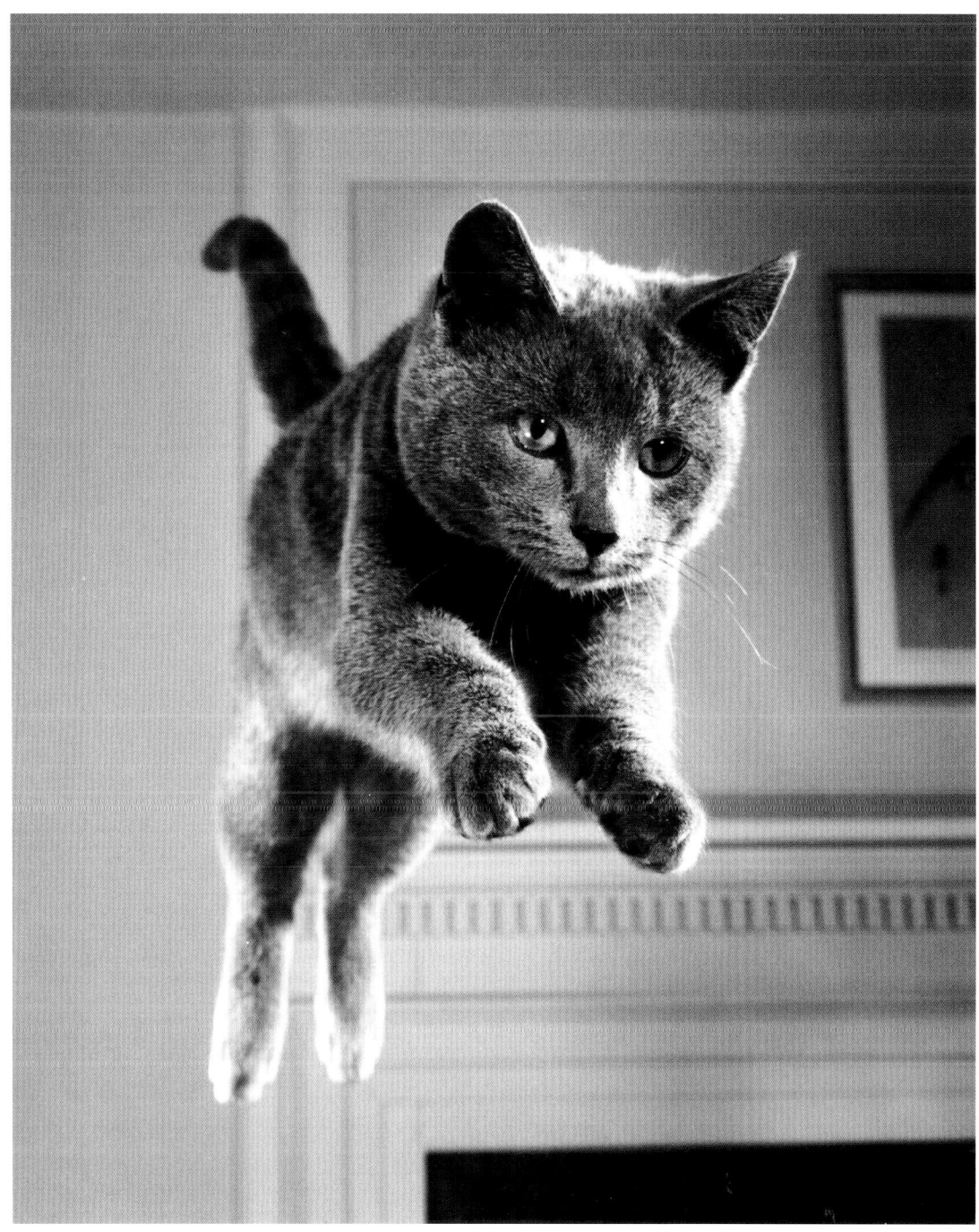

WALTER CHANDOHA

Loco, 1960
Photograph, dimensions variable

A gray cat soars through the air—body outstretched, eyes intensely focused on a spot beyond the photographer's lens. The feline in flight leaps through a nondescript domestic space in this image by American animal photographer Walter Chandoha (1920–2019). This shot is one of more than two hundred thousand photographs in Chandoha's archive—ninety thousand of which feature cats. Born in Bayonne, New Jersey, he fell in love with photography in high school and served as a combat photographer during World War II, but his passion for documenting felines can be traced back to a gray kitten he found in the snow in 1949, when he and his wife, Maria, were living in Queens, New York. He brought the kitten home, and they named him Loco in honor of his wild late-night sprints around the house. Loco was Chandoha's first feline muse (he is also the cat leaping in this photograph), and soon the photographer was submitting his images to contests and winning. *Woman's Home Companion* commissioned a Christmas-themed cover from Chandoha for its 1951 holiday issue, and other publications, publishers, and advertising firms started hiring him. Described as the "godfather of cat photography" and a pioneer of the genre, Chandoha created images for hundreds of magazine covers and thousands of advertisements in a prolific career that lasted seven decades. His legendary work was a family endeavor: his children frequently appear in the frames, while Maria was his art director, trusted cat whisperer, and, according to Chandoha, the secret to his success.

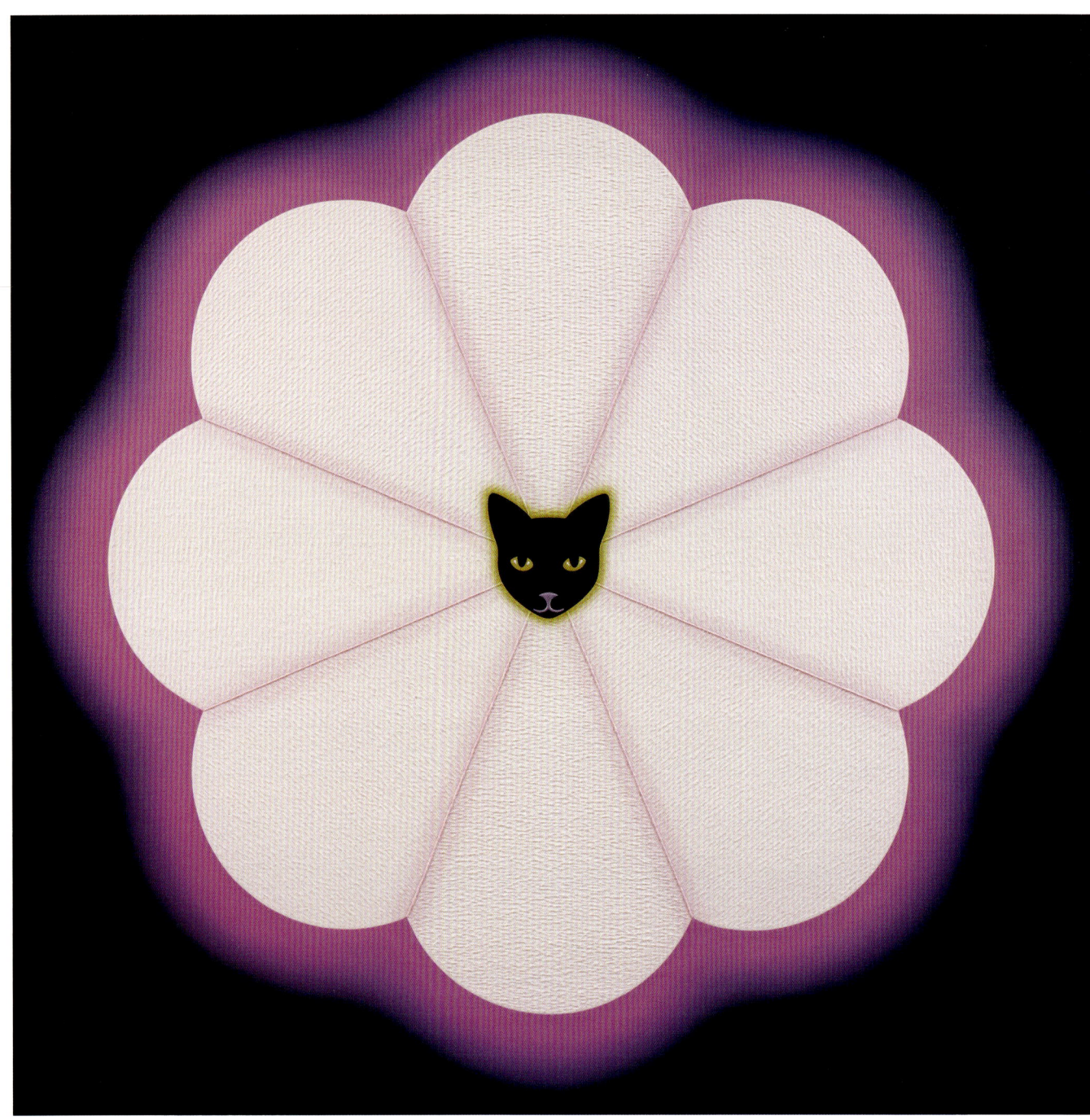

LINDA STARK

Samantha, 2005
Oil on canvas over panel
36 × 36 in. / 91 × 91 cm
Private collection

The apparent simplicity of this painting—which depicts the head of a black cat like an apparition at the center of what American artist Linda Stark (b. 1956) describes as "a flower of light"—belies its meticulous construction. Its intensely worked surface is made from layer upon layer of oil paint, which Stark applies with tiny brushes in a meditative and labor-intensive process. Over the course of months and sometimes even years, this results in richly textured, hard-edged pictures that combine a range of personal and cultural symbols rendered in a pared-back, graphic aesthetic. This painting is the first in a series of portraits portraying the Los Angeles–based artist's deceased feline pets, and although the square composition has charming and even humorous qualities, it is the product of grief. According to Stark, after her cat Samantha died, the animal appeared to her in a vision and, in painting this image, she found inner healing. Cats' heads also appear at the centers of luminous flowers in the paintings *Bastet* (2016) and *Tesla* (2018), while in *Self-Portrait with Ray* (2017), the head of her late gray tabby Ray is painted inside a rose-colored disk on the artist's forehead. In another, titled simply *Ray* (2017), the cat is painted in shades of blue within a glowing pink orb. Stark describes these works as "spirit portraits," functioning as portals through which, she says, she is able to have a "dialogue with the essence" of her former pets.

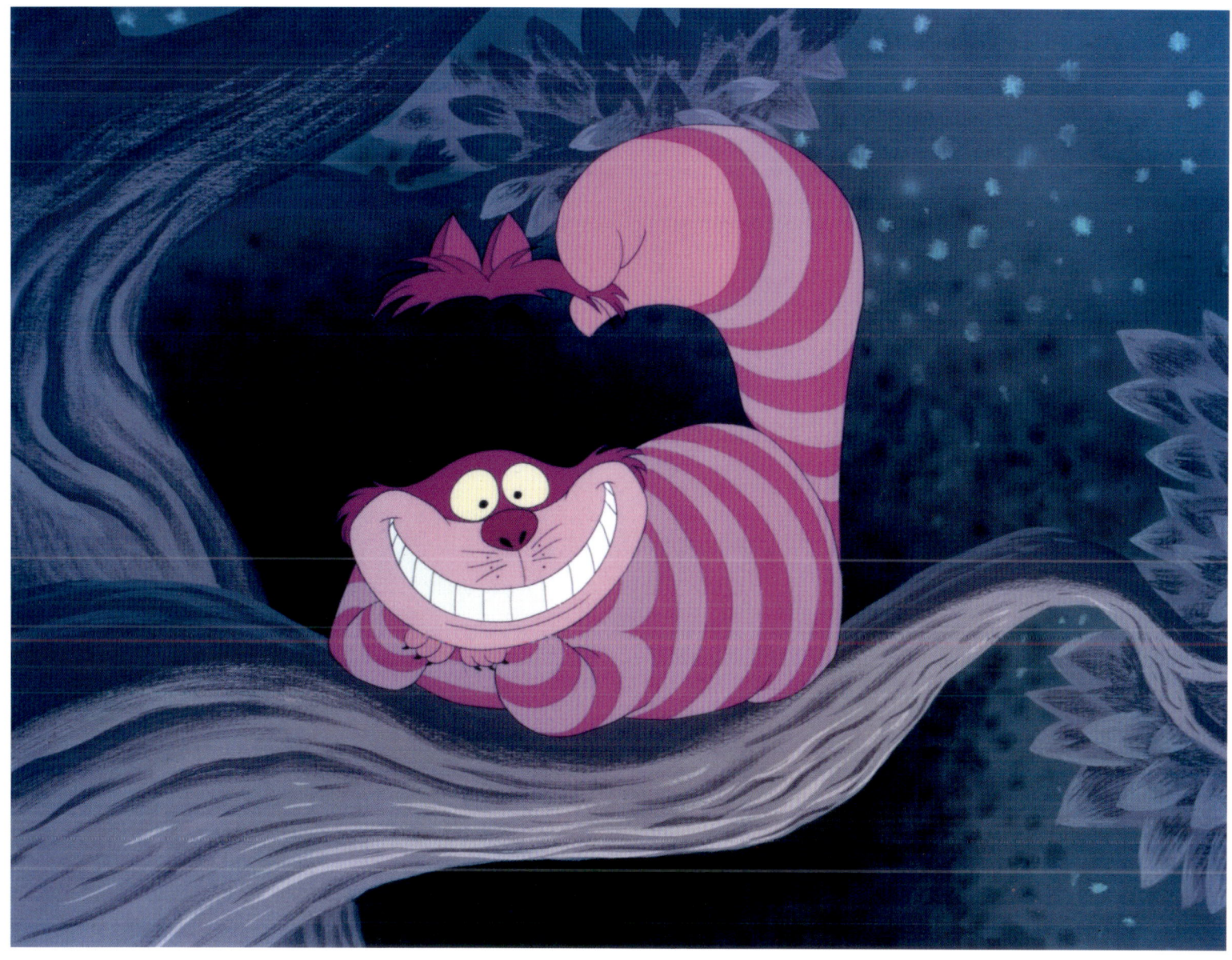

WALT DISNEY PICTURES

Alice in Wonderland, 1951
Film still, dimensions variable

Perhaps one of the most recognized cats in popular culture, the smiling Cheshire Cat from Walt Disney Pictures' 1951 animated classic *Alice in Wonderland* is an archetypal symbol of purposeful confusion. Although made famous by British author Lewis Carroll's novel *Alice's Adventures in Wonderland* (1865) and its accompanying illustrations by John Tenniel, the expression "grinning like a Cheshire cat" predates the children's books and can be found in various forms of early nineteenth-century literature, according to local writer Joseph Cox Bridge in *Cheshire Proverbs* (1917), a collection of the vernacular sayings of Cheshire, England. As Cox Bridge notes, the concept's origins remain unclear, but a whimsical explanation stems from the abundance of milk and cream in Cheshire, Carroll's birthplace, which boasted such a successful dairy industry that its local shorthairs were said to be constantly smiling with glee. In Disney's adaptation of Carroll's stories, a very lost Alice first meets the Cheshire Cat in a dark wood, perched on a tree with only his eyes and grin visible before his technicolor pink and purple stripes come into view. The Cheshire Cat reappears (and disappears) throughout the film, always leaving his grin as his last visible trace. A sphinx of sorts, this mischievous feline is unable—or unwilling—to give Alice anything but the most confusing directions to aid in her quest to find the Rabbit and leave Wonderland, a perfect representation of the enigmatic nature of cats.

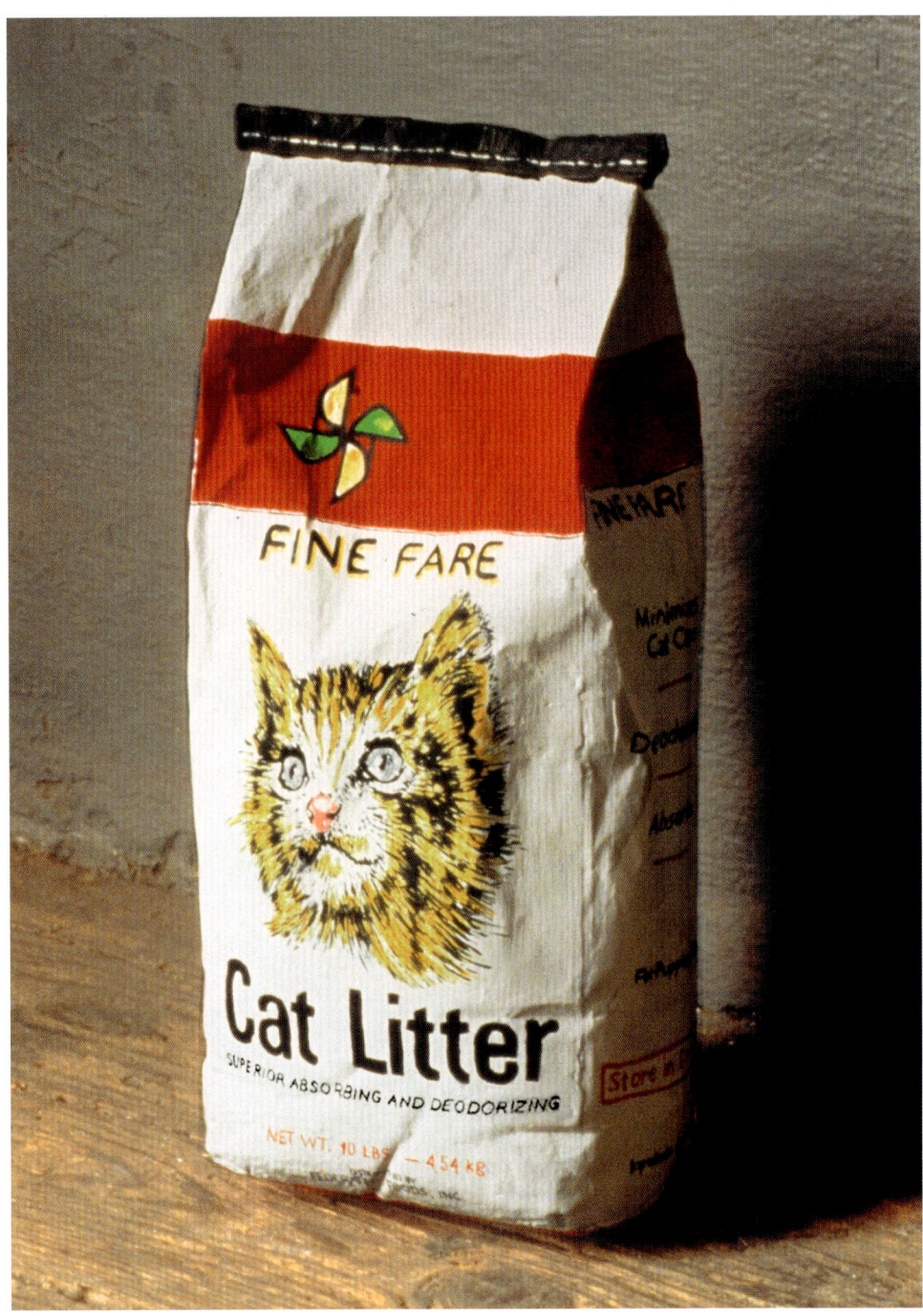

ROBERT GOBER

Cat Litter, 1989
Plaster, ink, and latex paint
17 × 8 × 5 in. / 43.2 × 20.3 × 12.7 cm
Edition of 7 + 2 AP

American artist Robert Gober (b. 1954) often evokes a vaguely sinister, off-kilter spirit lurking behind consumerism and domesticity in his work, imbuing commonplace objects with a multitude of meanings. The sunny yellow feline staring out from *Cat Litter* is no exception. This sculpture, like a good portion of Gober's art, is a copy, an uncanny resemblance in plaster of Fine Fare, a New York City supermarket's store-brand, 10-pound bag of kitty litter. The focus is the cat head, hand-painted with vacant eyes, wiry whiskers, and fur outlined in black. The bag's copy pledges superior absorption and no smell, repeating the brand's promise for a hygienic litter box, but it also ties back to thematic concerns with cleanliness and care in Gober's other sculptures, which include sinks and body parts. It should be innocuous, but something in the gaze and the off-color of the fur suggests the cat on this package is not so cuddly. *Cat Litter* was first shown in an installation at Paula Cooper Gallery in New York in 1989, where eight copies of the sculpture joined in conceptual conversation with other works by Gober in a room that he also designed, which included a wallpaper with a pattern that comprised a lynched Black man and sleeping white man and a sculpture of an empty wedding dress. Although disparate objects on paper, the three works and their subjects—men, alive and murdered; brides; and bags of litter for cats—are connected through questions of love, intimacy, and waste, highlighting the critical power of contemporary art.

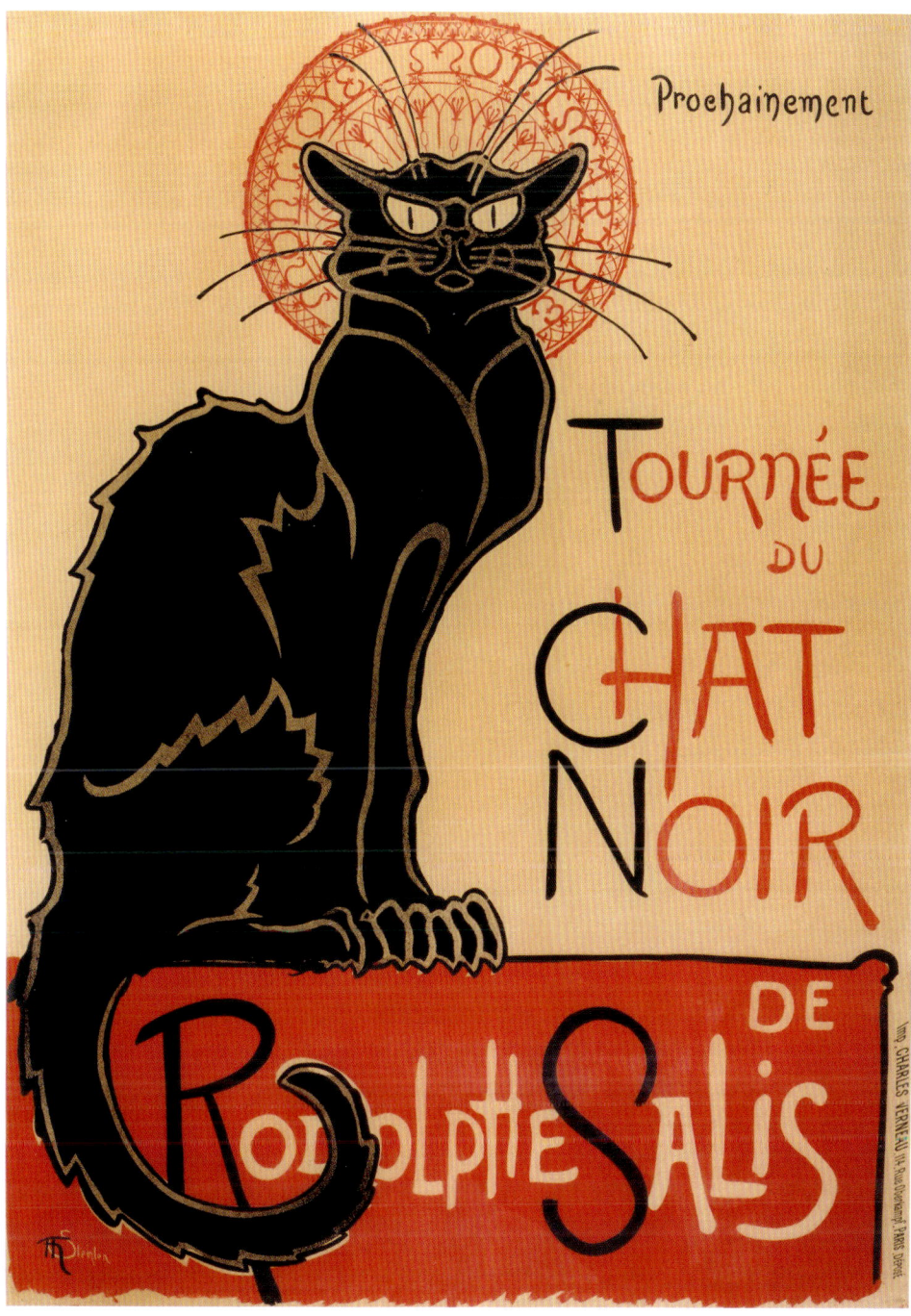

THÉOPHILE ALEXANDRE STEINLEN

Tournée du Chat Noir do Rodolpho Salis, 1896
Color lithograph, 53½ × 37¾ in. / 135.9 × 95.9 cm
Zimmerli Art Museum, Rutgers University,
New Brunswick, New Jersey

Nicknamed the "Cat Man," Théophile Alexandre Steinlen (1859–1923) was a preeminent artist during France's Art Nouveau period, legendary for his depictions of his animal companions. It was a cat that made him famous: this poster of the feline mascot of Le Chat Noir, a cabaret in Paris's Montmartre neighborhood, is his best-known work and a veritable icon of fin-de-siècle Paris. Opened by Rodolphe Salis in 1881, Le Chat Noir was the meeting place of literary and artistic bohemia in the French capital. In the 1890s Salis organized a company of performers from the cabaret to go on tour during the summer months and commissioned Steinlen to create an eye-catching poster that would advertise this traveling revue. The cabaret's name is said to have come from a lost black cat that was found on the sidewalk during the construction work of the building, but it could also be a reference to Edgar Allan Poe's 1843 short story of the same name (see p.79), translated into French by Charles Baudelaire, another great cat lover. For this design, Steinlen was inspired by the memory of one of his old feline friends from childhood, shining like the sun with its black fur gleaming. The void of the black cat also evokes the cutout silhouettes of shadow theater that were in vogue in cabarets at the time. Whatever the source, the crepuscular animal, whose color had long been associated with the devil in some cultures, was the perfect embodiment of the cabaret's rebellious spirit.

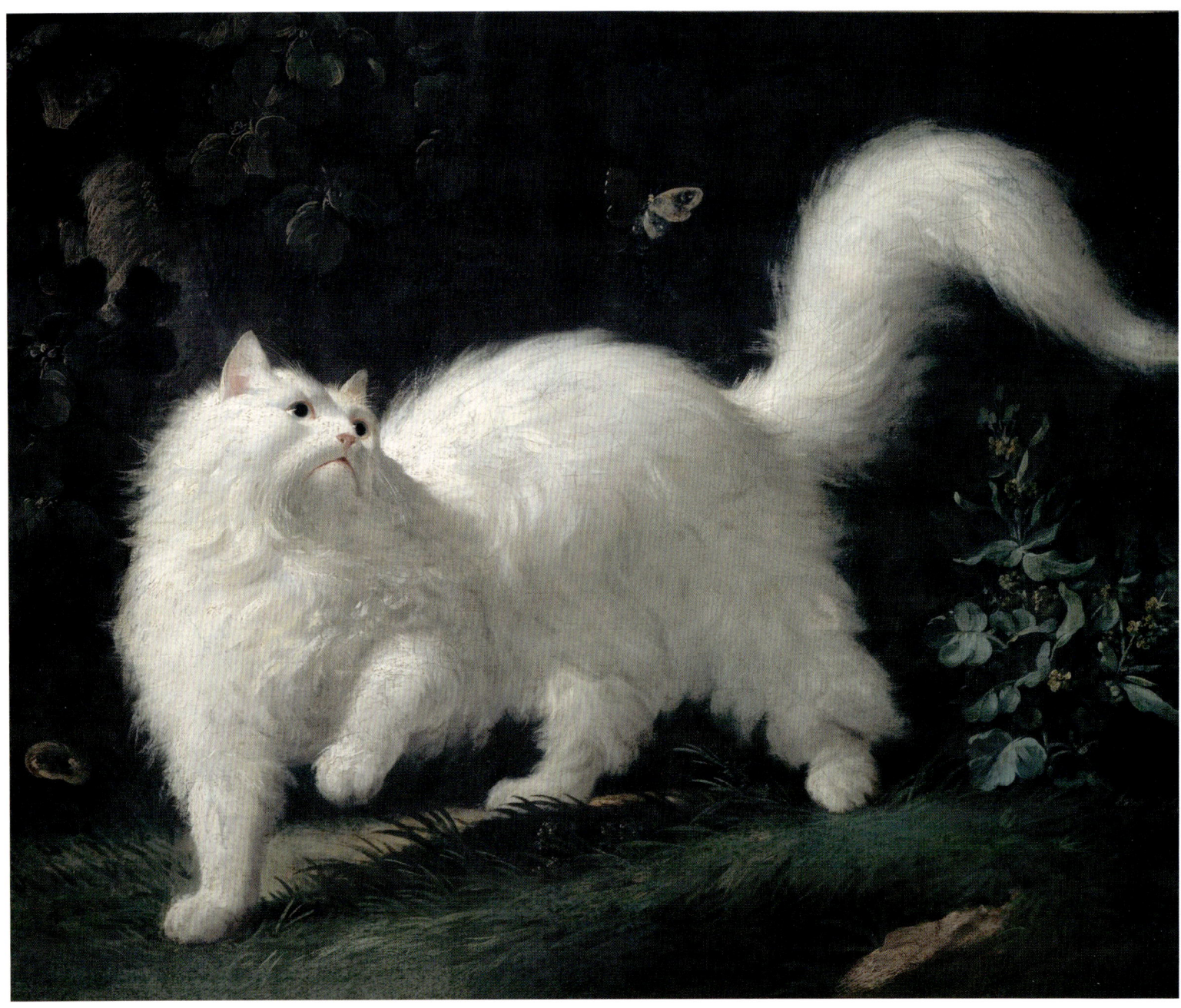

JEAN-JACQUES BACHELIER

White Angora Cat Chasing a Butterfly, c. 1761
Oil on canvas, 26 × 31⅞ in. / 66 × 81 cm
Musée Lambinet, Versailles, France

An impossibly white fluffy cat raises its paw, hoping to capture a lone butterfly in this Rococo painting by French artist Jean-Jacques Bachelier (1724–1806). The cat is an Angora, known for its flowing long hair, which Bachelier so convincingly paints, but also for its playful personality, which is equally evident. Originating in the Anatolian region of modern-day Turkey, Angoras are full of energy and easily bored. They were introduced into Europe at the end of the sixteenth century as luxury lap pets, and the breed was not distinguished from the equally furry Persian cat until it was recognized as separate during the following century. Known as a highly accomplished flower and animal painter, Bachelier was admitted to the Royal Academy in Paris in 1752. However, he is best remembered not for his association with cats, but with porcelain. When King Louis XV ordered a new factory to be built in Sèvres in 1756 (his mistress Madame de Pompadour was an enthusiastic patron of French porcelain), Bachelier, then the artistic director at the rival soft-paste porcelain manufacturer Vincennes, moved there to helm the innovative ceramics plant. While popular pets, cats were not so favored in porcelain design, so their appearance in French culture of the late eighteenth century was mostly in Baroque and Rococo paintings, such as this one. Little is known about the dreamy Angora in this portrait, but it is whimsical to think that it might be the fluffy companion of an aristocratic lady who is perhaps resting in a nearby grotto.

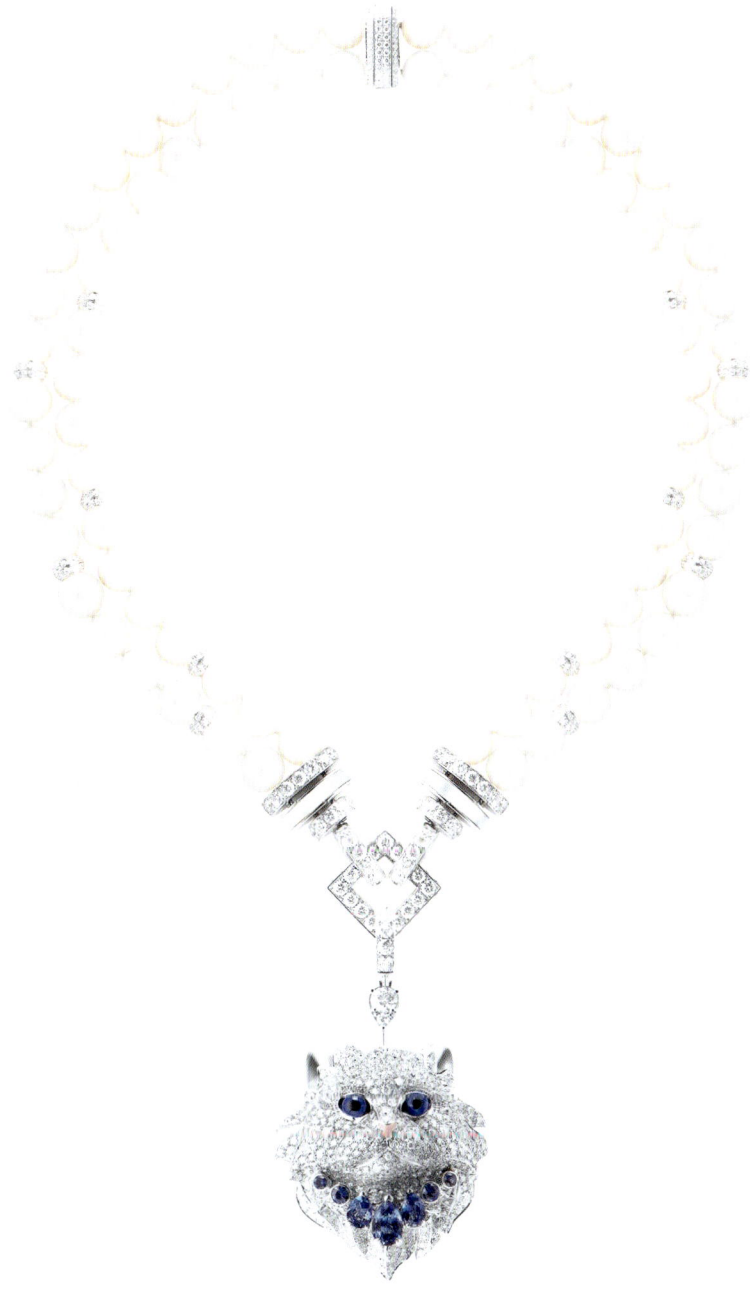

BOUCHERON

Wladimir necklace, Le Chat, from
Animaux De Collection, 2021
Diamonds, cultured pearls, tanzanites,
sapphires, and white gold

For the cat lover who has everything, this necklace from French jewelry house Boucheron is the perfect present. The decadent (and detachable) diamond, sapphire, and tanzanite feline brooch pendant, hanging here from a double row of cultured pearls, was inspired by the face of Wladimir the Cat, the maison's long-standing mascot. Legend has it that the gorgeous amber-eyed, long-haired black cat once watched over Boucheron's townhouse boutique in Paris on the Place Vendôme, which opened in 1893. Wladimir has featured in Boucheron high jewelry designs since the end of the nineteenth century, initially appearing on diamond brooches. In the 1970s and 1980s, he gained new fame as the star of advertising campaigns, wearing a luxurious diamond necklace around his neck

instead of a collar. Since its founding in 1858 by jeweler Frédéric Boucheron, the house has created exquisite high jewelry meant to be worn rather than to sit in bank vaults. Animals—including hedgehogs, snakes, hummingbirds, and cats—have consistently featured in its designs. In 2021 creative director Claire Choisne immortalized Wladimir's face once again, this time in diamonds, emphasizing the cat's position as a key member of the maison. Inspired by the bright-eyed cat's "elegant nonchalance," the pendant's jeweled face is predominantly made of diamonds, while his fur is sculpted from white gold. His striking eyes, comprising a profusion of sapphires, mother-of-pearls, and quartz, are complemented by the necklace he sports, a nod to the campaign that made him famous.

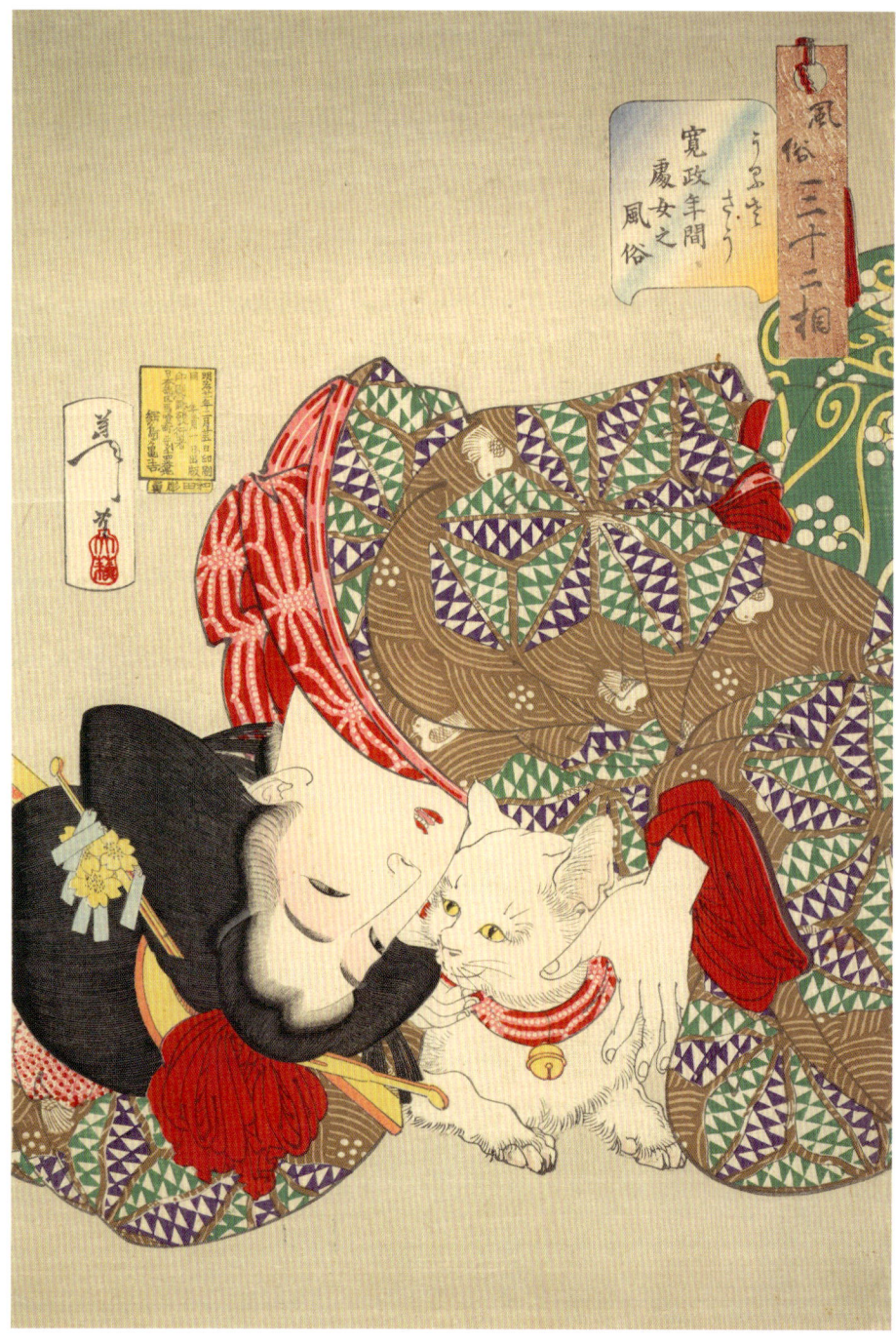

TSUKIOKA YOSHITOSHI

Teasing the Cat, 1888
Woodcut, 14⅝ × 10 in. / 37 × 25.4 cm
Metropolitan Museum of Art, New York

Wearing a pretty pink-red collar with a bell around its neck, this plump white cat has no means of escape as a young woman leans over and cuddles him in this somewhat disorienting composition by Japanese printmaker Tsukioka Yoshitoshi (1839–1892). The woodcut belongs to a series of thirty-two prints called *Thirty-two Aspects on the Customs and Manners*, which Yoshitoshi made in 1888, toward the end of his life. Inspired by the *bijin-ga*, or "beauty prints," that were then fashionable, he decided to create a survey of all types of women from the past century of Japanese history, from housewives and members of the imperial court to businesswomen and courtesans (the latter comprising almost half of the series). This print shows a young maiden from the Kansei era (1789–1800), who

is seemingly lavishing all her love and affection on her pet cat. Widely considered to have been the last great master of the *ukiyo-e* genre of the Edo period (1603–1868), which sought to depict the transient pleasures and beauty of life, Yoshitoshi disliked the modernization he saw in contemporary Japan. He longed for a return to the past that he portrayed in woodcuts with which he intended to keep *ukiyo-e* alive. These prints focused on feminine styles and activities were something of a departure for Yoshitoshi, an artist whose better-known works include *100 Aspects of the Moon* and a series of bloody images of samurai warriors, which made his early reputation as a "war artist."

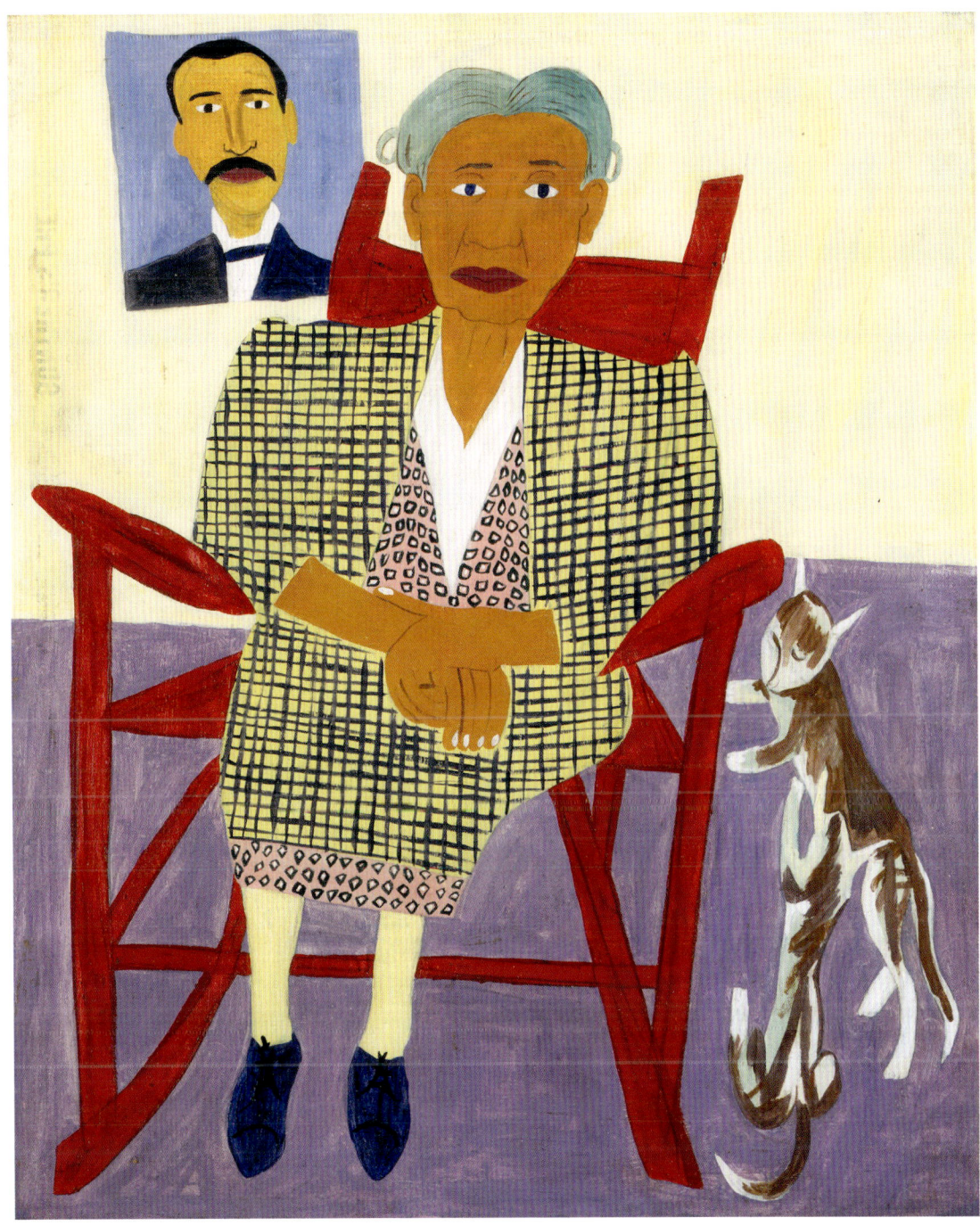

WILLIAM H. JOHNSON

Mom and Dad, 1944
Oil on paperboard, 31 × 25⅜ in. / 78.7 × 64.5 cm
Smithsonian American Art Museum, Washington, DC

In this innovative take on the family portrait by American painter William H. Johnson (1901–1970), the artist's mother, Alice, sits with her arms folded in a rocking chair beneath a likeness of his father, Henry. By Alice's side, a calico cat nurses its kitten, and the unusual perspective makes the animals seem almost an extension of the angular chair. The work is indicative of Johnson's style, which employed flattened perspective, simplified figures, and bright colors to document the lives of Black Americans. As part of the Great Migration, the post–World War II movement of Black Americans from the South to the North to escape Jim Crow segregation and racist discrimination, Johnson had moved to New York when he was seventeen, and worked odd jobs to pay for art school.

He relocated to Paris in the 1920s, where he fell in love with and married Danish artist Holcha Krake. The two moved to Scandinavia before settling in New York in 1938, although Johnson returned to his hometown of Florence, South Carolina, after his wife's untimely death. Created amid his grief, this portrait depicts Johnson's idea of home as well as a study of himself. The kitten nursing and the lighter skin of his father's portrait juxtaposed with his mother's darker coloring possibly refers to his own mixed racial ancestry. The domestic scene contains an added poignancy: Johnson never recovered from Krake's death, and this painting reflects his attempts to reconnect with his Southern family and life.

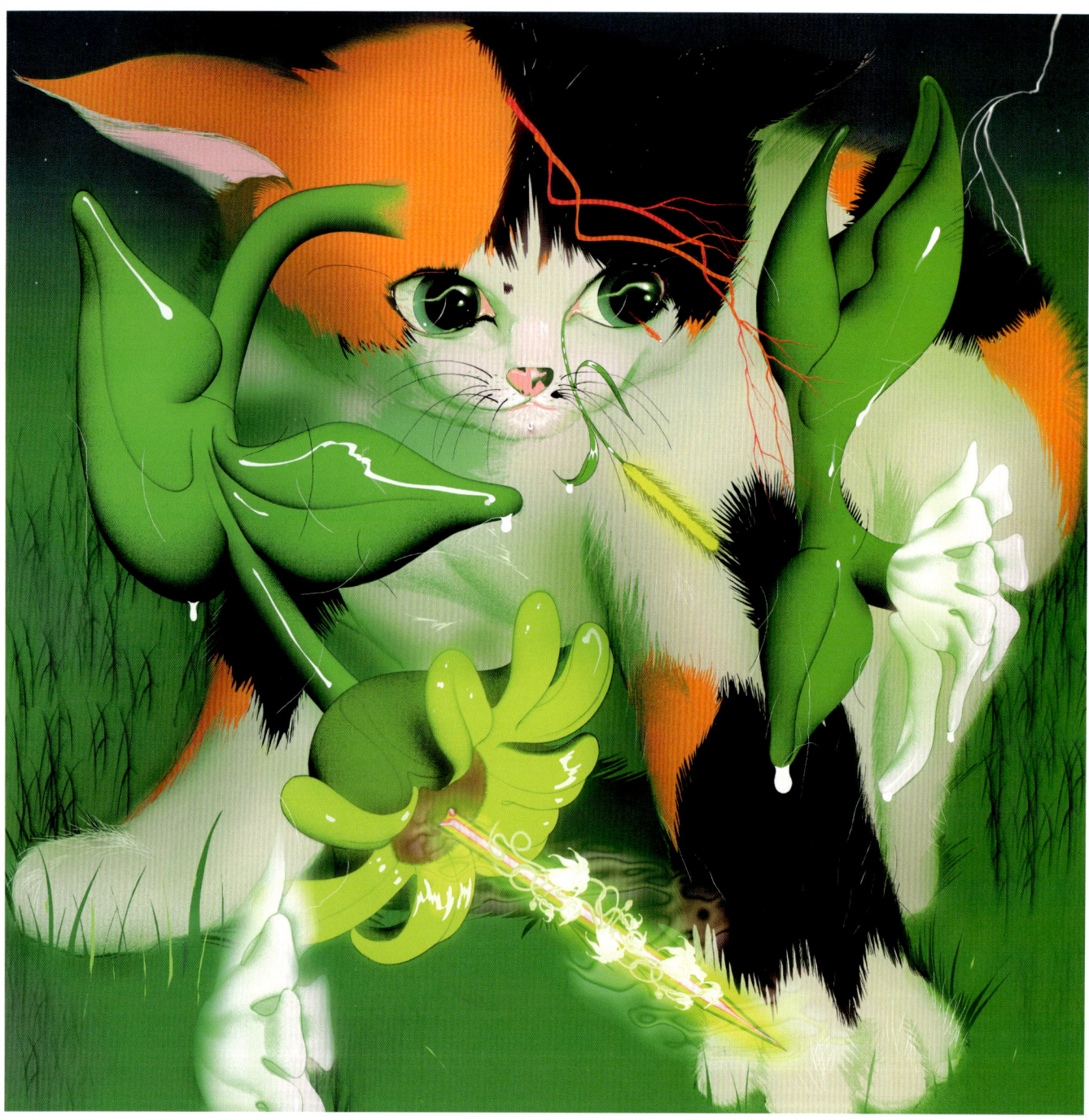

RAM HAN

disaster_cropped_02, 2019
Digital paint and light panel
27½ × 27½ in. / 70 × 70 cm

This kitty is drawn with the cutesy features of a typical cartoon cat—including wide eyes and Cheshire Cat smile (see p.21)—but the composition betrays a more sinister scene. Flower pods explode as if laser guns, while lightning strikes in the dark sky above. Does the cat, ears flattened, have anything to do with the disaster referenced in the title? Or does the fantastic setting evoke what is happening to our landscape? Korean artist Ram Han (b. 1989) remembers the watershed moment when she first saw painter Hieronymus Bosch's frenzied triptych *The Garden of Earthly Delights* (1490–1500), which opened up to her the possibilities of what art could be. Han's work presents a similarly highly stylized otherworldliness, meant to transport the viewer from modern reality and its terrors—a notion the artist describes as visual ASMR. Equal parts cyber dreamscape and psychedelic wonderland, her imagery is influenced by myriad aesthetic strands, including Surrealism, comics, anime, video games, and the larger technological landscape. Han's kinetic digital images are characterized by technicolor hues and a vivid textural quality. It is as if one could reach forward and feel the cat's bristling fur; cold, smooth objects; and glistening wet landscapes. Han's process is completely digital—she begins and ends on her computer in Adobe Photoshop. A young artist embracing the cutting-edge tools of her generation, she is a sought-after talent who has worked with numerous K-pop acts, themselves at the forefront of South Korea's cultural vanguard.

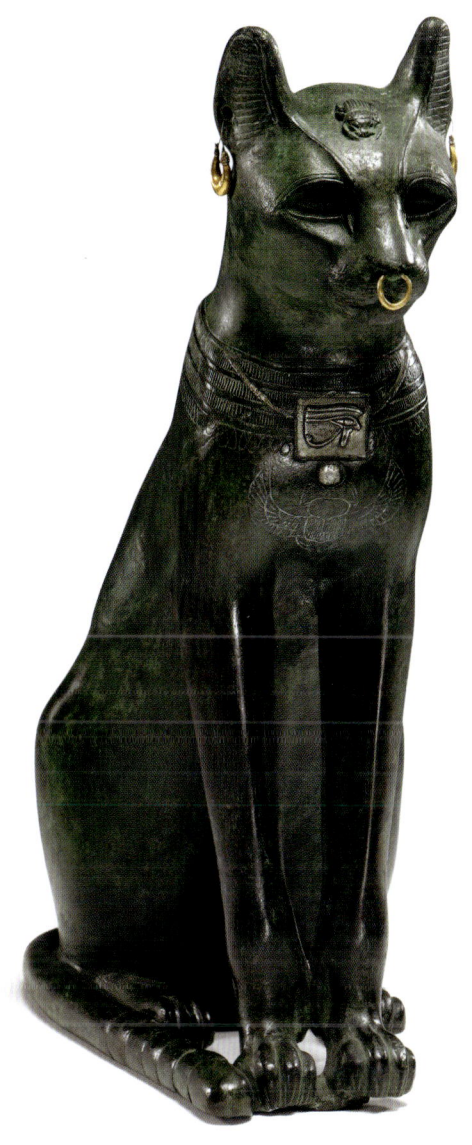

ANONYMOUS

Gayer-Anderson Cat, c. 600 BCE
Bronze, gold, and silver
13³⁄₈ × 5½ in. / 34 × 14 cm
British Museum, London

Probably domesticated in ancient Egypt, cats were venerated for their gentle care toward kittens and for their fierce hunting abilities that protected homes and granaries from vermin. The oldest feline goddess, Bastet, was believed to be a fearsome sentinel, with myths describing her as the sun god's daughter and a motherly guardian of the king. While Egyptians never worshipped cats themselves, divinities such as Bastet were frequently represented as felines, and worshippers offered bronze statues of cats to the goddess in hopes of health, safety, and fertility. Thought to be representing the goddess, this elegant bronze example—known as the *Gayer-Anderson Cat* in honor of its donor to the British Museum—is adorned with jewelry and endowed with symbolism. The cat's eyes were originally inlaid with rock crystal and semi-precious stones as well as other materials. The gold earrings and nose ring are complemented with a silver pectoral necklace, decorated with the so-called *wedjat* eye, a symbol of health and healing. A lavish beaded necklace and winged scarab beetle are incised around the cat's neck. Because scarabs represented rebirth and the morning sun, this beetle with a silver sun disk links the goddess with her father, the sun god Ra. Even minute details of the realistic-looking cat carry symbolism. The shape of a scarab between the cat's ears evokes the natural pattern of stripes on a cat's fur, while the tufts of fur in the ears are shaped like the hieroglyph that can be read as harmony or truth.

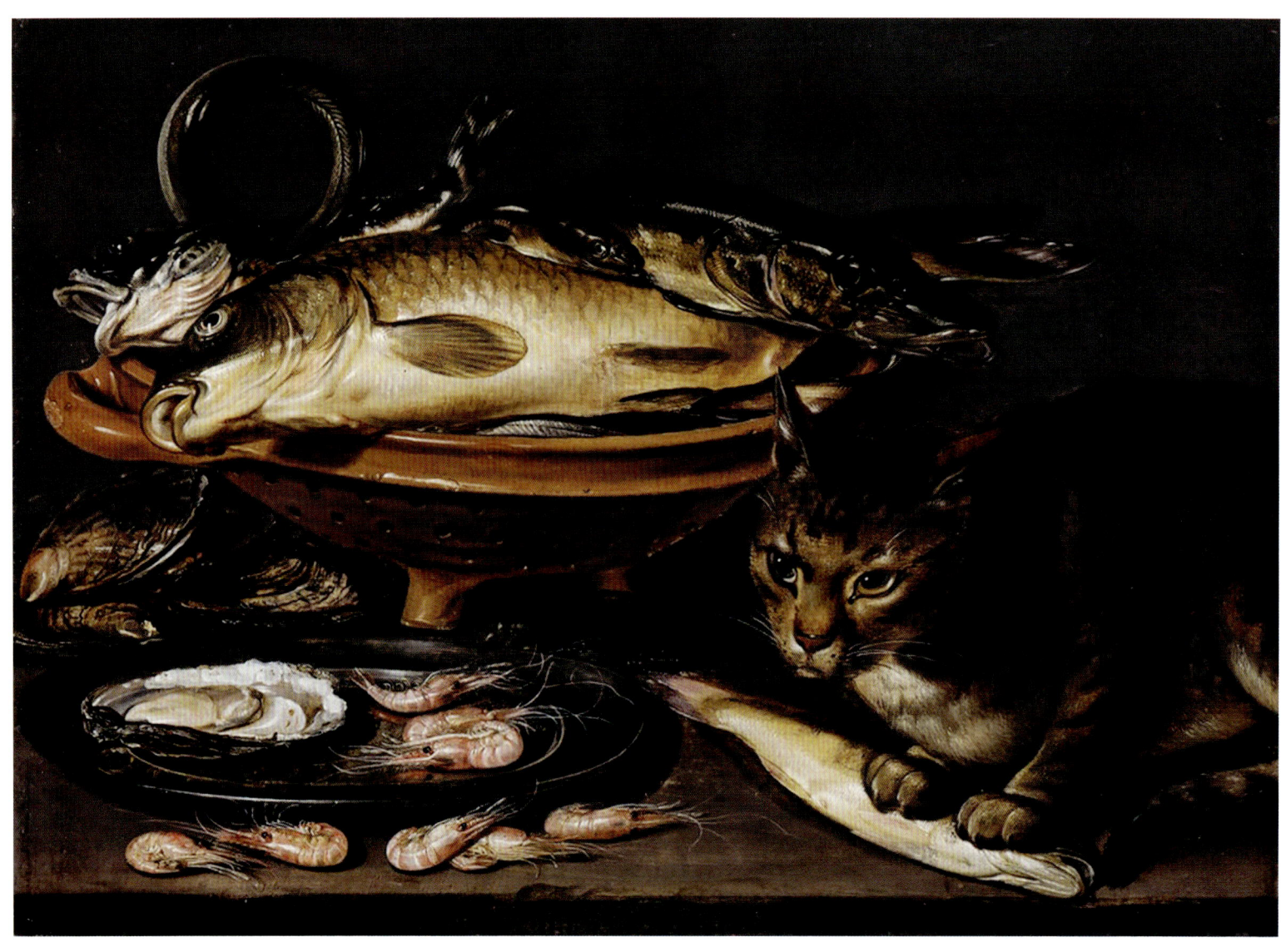

CLARA PEETERS

Still Life of Fish and Cat, c. 1620
Oil on panel, 13½ × 18½ in. / 34.3 × 47 cm
National Museum of Women in the Arts,
Washington, DC

With its front paws firmly placed on a dead fish, a tabby sits alert as it guards a bounty of seafood that also includes oysters and shrimp. Brought to life by Flemish painter Clara Peeters (c. 1594–1657), the cat's ears are pointed back as it prepares to defend its feast. One of the seventeenth century's few known women artists from northern Europe, Peeters is celebrated for her realistic still lifes that popularized so-called "banquet pieces"—artful displays of food and drink, plus flower arrangements and tableware, all rendered in precise detail. Here, Peeters captures the texture of the different fish scales; the glistening, freshly shucked oyster; and the pinkness of the shrimp with her fine brushwork. The feline's whiskers are clearly visible, as are the tabby markings of its fur. Peeters typically painted scenes from a low angle, so the viewer must look up at the tableau, allowing the light to capture the cat's whitish chest and the scales of the fish in the ceramic colander. Although the artist was one of the first painters to incorporate self-portraiture into her work—an approach later widely adopted by other artists in present-day Germany and the Netherlands— almost nothing is known about her life. It is assumed that she must have trained under a master, such is the sophistication of her technique. Here, Peeters presents an abundance of food without any attached moral value other than a cat that looks as though it might have got the proverbial cream.

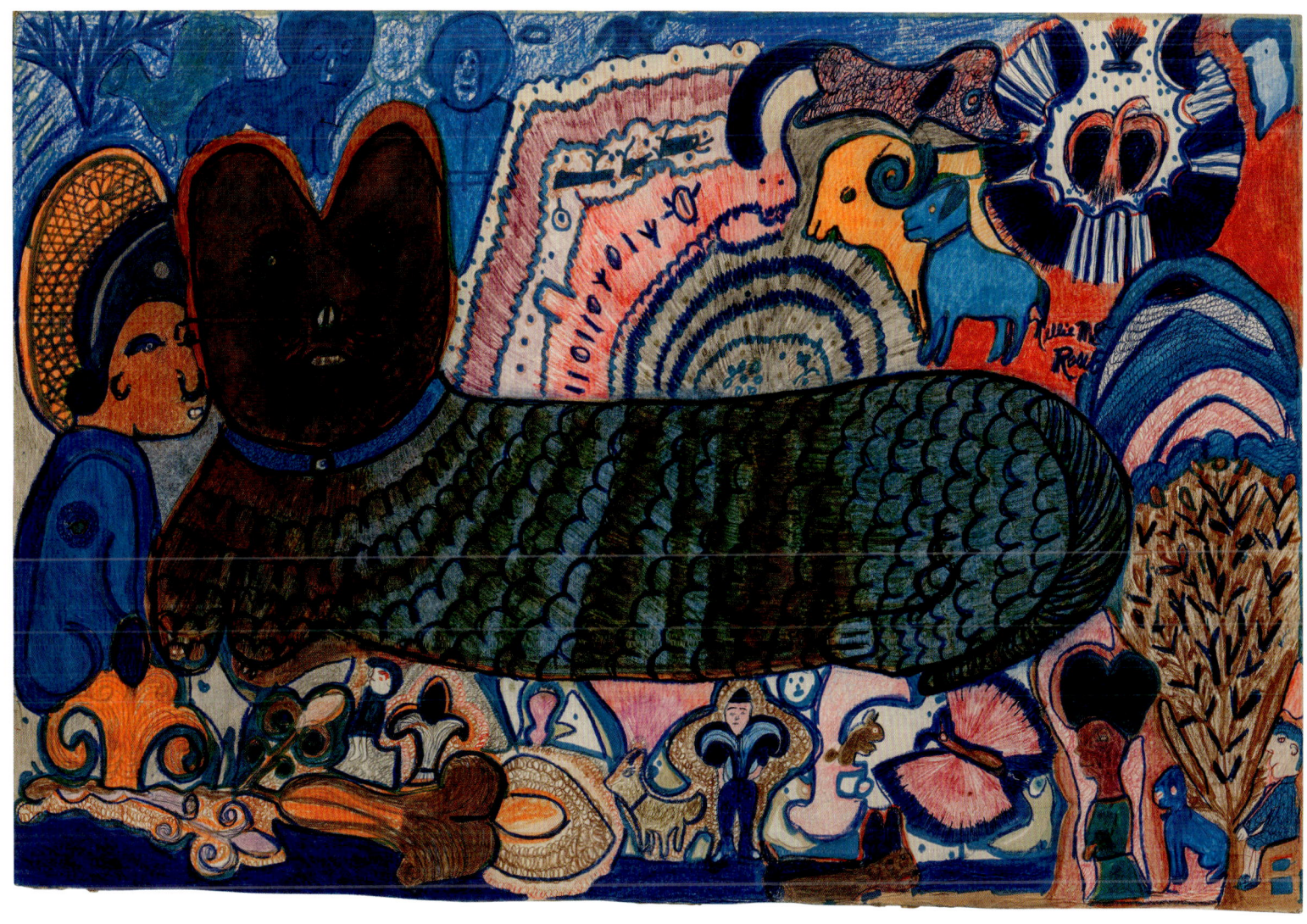

NELLIE MAE ROWE

Big Cat, c. 1980
Ballpoint and felt-tip pen on paper
20½ × 30 in. / 52.1 × 76.2 cm
Smithsonian American Art Museum,
Washington, DC

Big Cat exemplifies the unique signature of American artist Nellie Mae Rowe (1900–1982), its stylized feline holding court in a lush landscape jam-packed with flora and fauna, a crowned admirer kneeling at its feet. Today considered one of the most esteemed folk artists of the twentieth century, Rowe did not begin to create art in earnest until she was nearly fifty. She was born in the Deep South, the ninth of ten children to a formerly enslaved father and a mother born the same year as the Emancipation. It was not until the death of her second husband in 1948 that Rowe turned to making art, seeking in part to regain the joy of youthful exuberance lost to a life of labor as a domestic servant. She began hanging installations—soft dolls, chewing-gum sculptures, and ornaments made from household items—outside her home in Vinings, Georgia, which she called her "Playhouse." The eccentric attraction gained notice from locals, but she would not show her work in a gallery for decades more. A self-taught artist, she had displayed a knack for drawing from childhood and often turned to her friends and neighbors as subjects for her work. Believing her art to be divinely inspired, Rowe is particularly known for her densely populated illustrations on paper, which teem with vitality and color, such as the vibrant, larger-than-life house cat resting here amid a nearly psychedelic field of hues, people, and creatures.

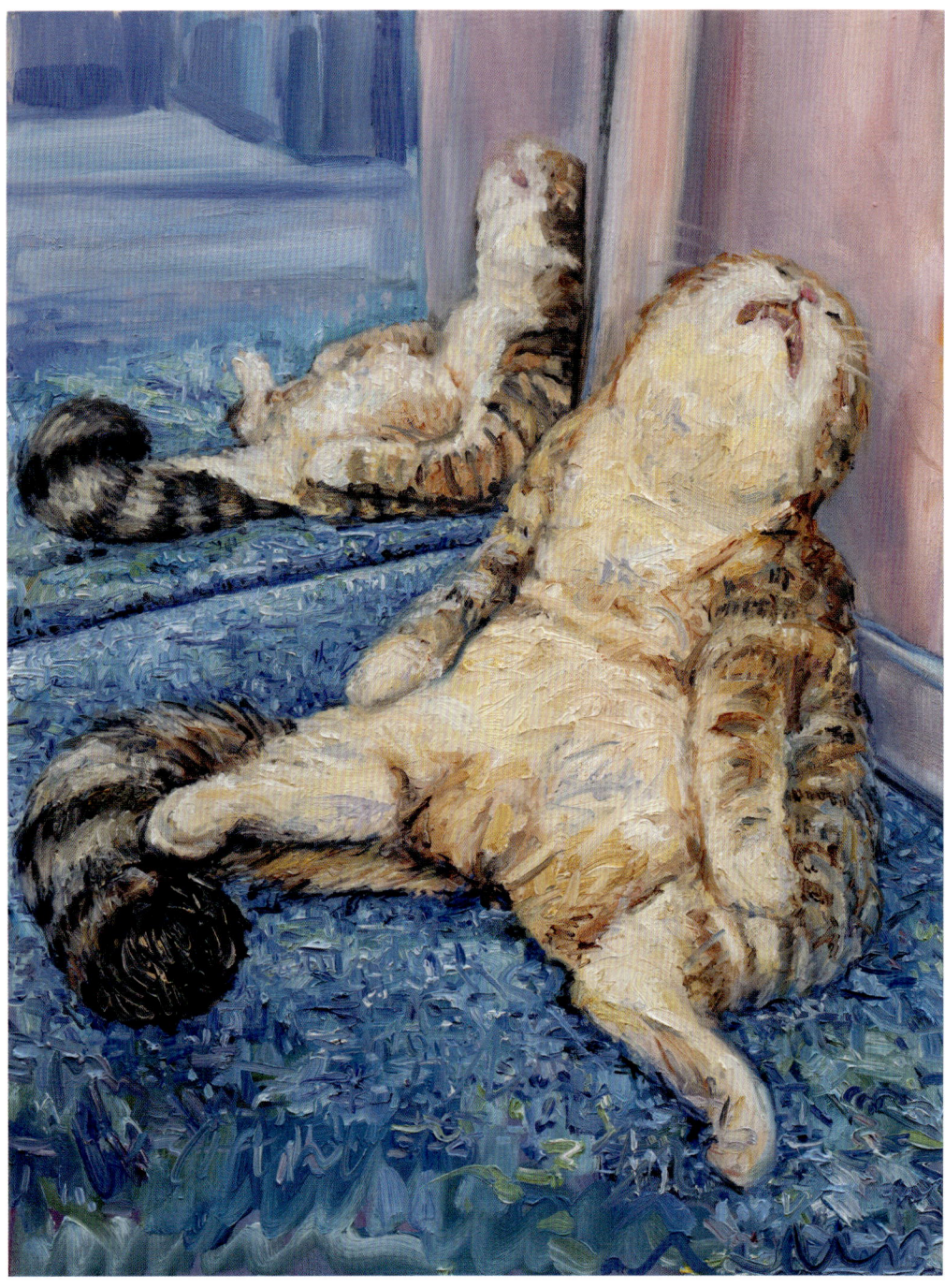

JODIE NISS

Untitled (#2), 2022
Oil on wood panel
16 × 12 in. / 40.6 × 30.5 cm
Private collection

It is common for people to ascribe human behaviors to animals, particularly their pets. In doing so, they strengthen the bonds they share by identifying commonalities. It is also a means of transference, a way to attribute feelings to an avatar outside of themselves. This anthropomorphized cat strikes a very human pose in American artist Jodie Niss's painting *Untitled (#2)*. The fluffy feline slumps against a mirrored wall, its legs hilariously splayed. It could be sleeping soundly, or one can even imagine it meowing loudly and despondently. What, the viewer must wonder, has caused this sudden collapse into slumber or hysteria? Niss, a New York–based painter and art teacher, typically works in oil paints and watercolors. Although animals are a frequent motif in her work, her cat paintings began somewhat by accident. She started by painting portraits of cat owners but over time realized that she was more drawn to the expressive abilities of the felines themselves, which possessed personalities that telegraphed both human emotion and a quixotic kind of magnetism. By using animals as proxies for people, she believes that viewers can more readily relate to the imagery and see themselves in it. Indeed, one can envisage being so bone-tired or upset as to collapse on the spot, mouth agape like the fat cat in this painting, either dreaming or howling, depending on the viewer's mood.

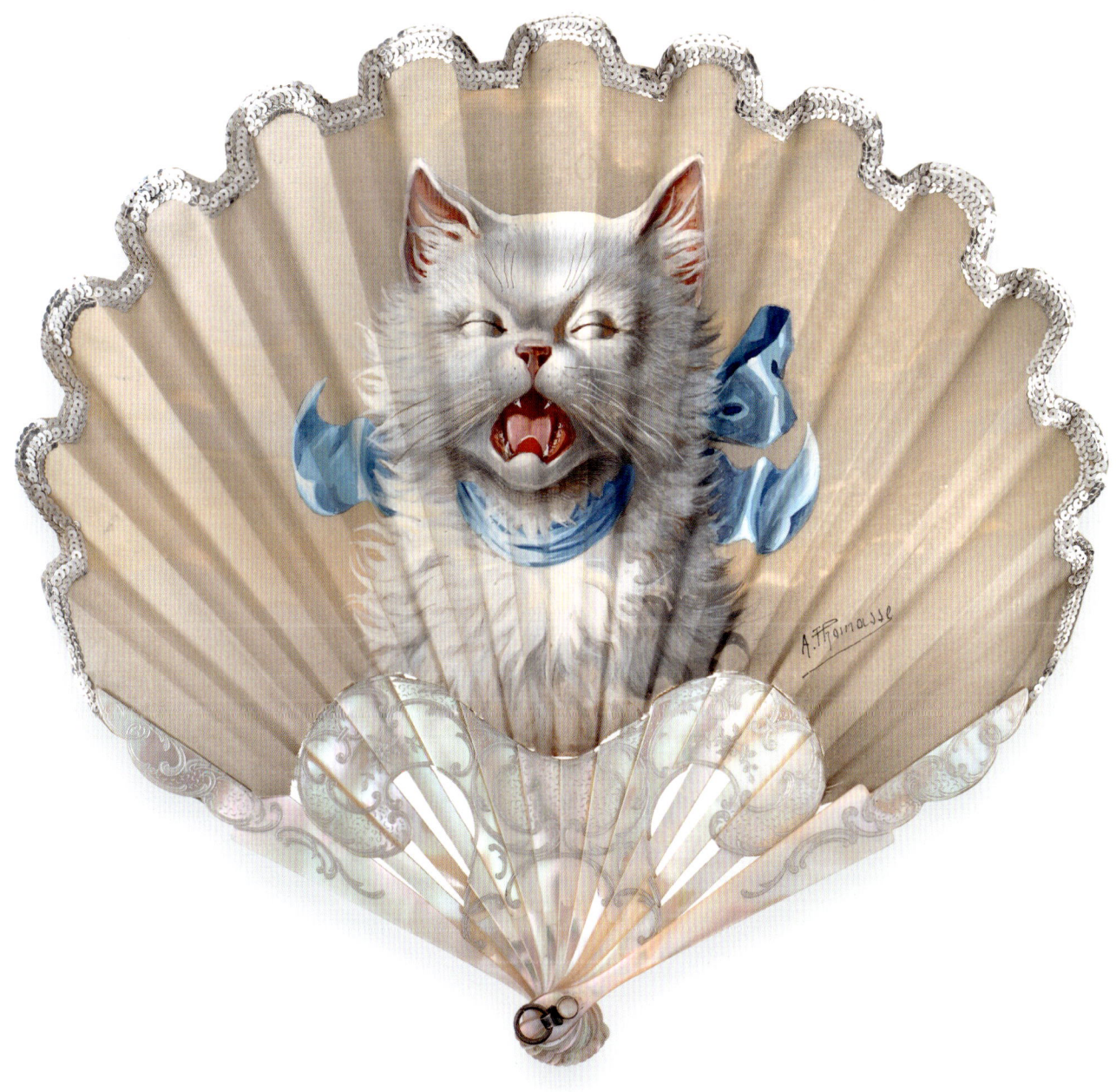

ADOLPHE THOMASSE

Fan, c. 1905
Paint on silk with sequins with a mother-of-pearl
monture, Diam. 5½ in. / 14 cm
Private collection

For centuries, the handheld fan was a status symbol and a mark of elegance and sophistication, enjoying its peak popularity in sixteenth-century Europe. This fine example was hand-painted on silk by Adolphe Thomasse (1850–1930) a few centuries later for the French maker of fans Duvelleroy, which catered to discerning clientele in Paris and beyond, counting Queen Victoria among its customers. The fan's scalloped edges are gilded with silver sequins and the central image is of a white cat festooned with a pale blue ribbon. Duvelleroy led a revival in the fan's popularity in the mid-nineteenth century when it published "The Language of the Fan," detailing the various ways in which a fan could be used by a woman to communicate messages nonverbally to her admirers. The leaflet was ostensibly a marketing gimmick, but the "secret" language caught fire among the wealthy partygoers of the day, who fluttered and flicked their fans to send messages across the ballroom. Drawing the fan across the eyes indicated an apology, while holding it against one's left cheek was an expression of love. Carrying it open in the left hand suggested an invitation to speak, but dropping it meant the man was fit to be a friend and nothing more. White cats were often symbols of innocence and purity, and the closed eyes of this one could telegraph a look of trust, or it could be singing, making this a fan for the opera. Conversely, the feline could read as overcome with fiery emotion, its mouth open mid-meow or in a potential hiss. A further dispatch for a would-be suitor?

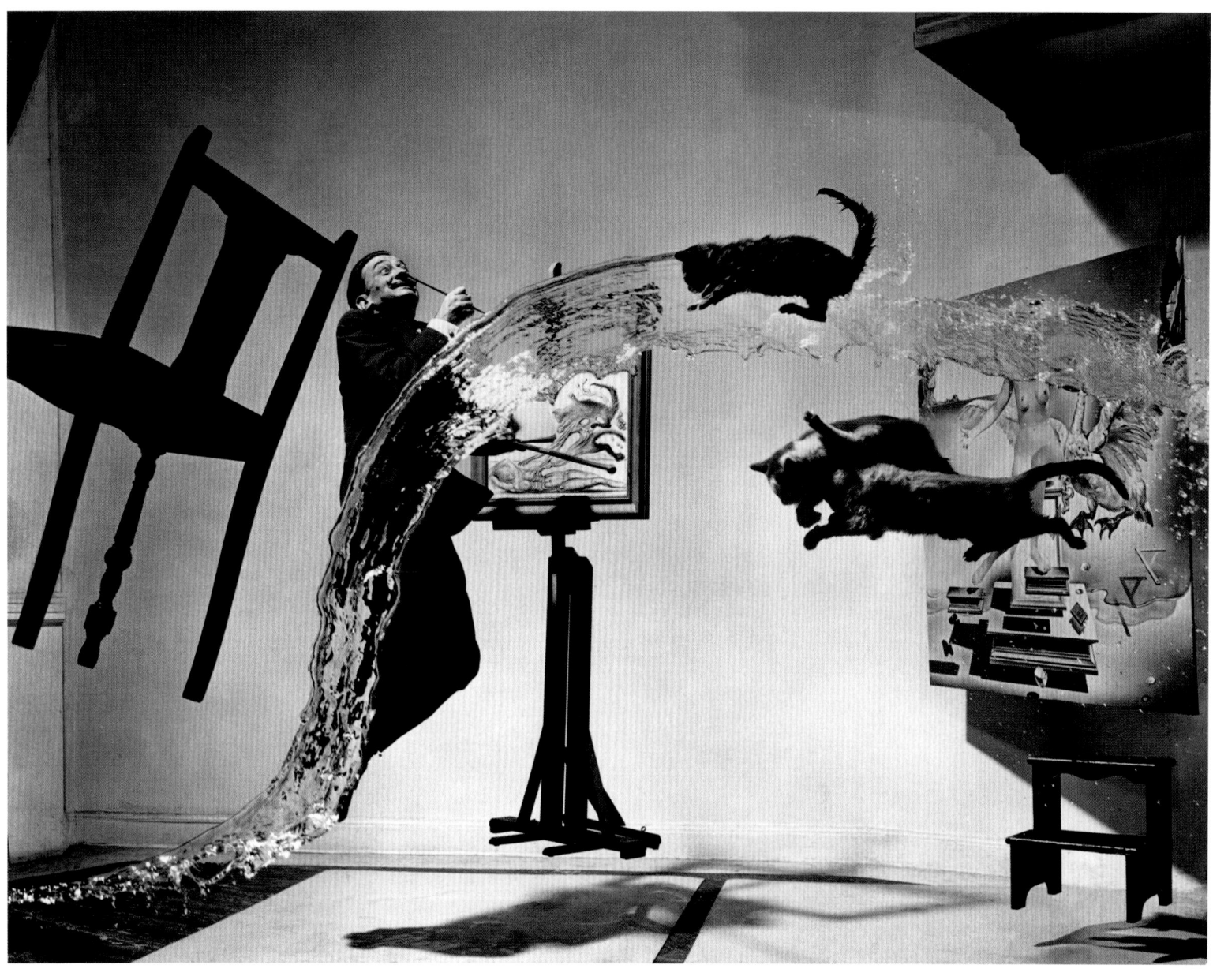

PHILIPPE HALSMAN

Dalí Atomicus, 1948
Gelatin silver print
10⅛ × 13⅛ in. / 25.8 × 33.3 cm

Described by *Time* magazine as one of the hundred most influential photographs of all time, *Dalí Atomicus* is an ingenious portrait of a man and an era. Captured by American photographer Philippe Halsman (1906–1979) for *Life* magazine, it shows his friend and collaborator, Spanish Surrealist Salvador Dalí, levitating together with three flying cats and an arc of water in a photographic attempt to illustrate the idea of suspension. Both men were fascinated by the Atomic Age and the successful detonation of the first nuclear weapon in 1945, and here they aimed to demonstrate how protons and electrons are suspended in an atom. To achieve the look of suspension, the cats and bucket of water were thrown by Halsman's assistants on a count of three for each take, while Dalí jumped on a count of four. The

chair, step stool, easel, and Dalí's painting *Leda Atomica* were hung on wires that were erased in the final print. It took twenty-eight attempts to get the photograph they wanted. The cats were dried between each failed take, before being tossed into the frame again in a process that took about five to six hours. The inclusion of the cats, although potentially not as important to the age of the atom, was paramount for the portrait. A confirmed cat lover, and true to his status as the leading Surrealist, Dalí later kept an ocelot as a pet during the 1960s, claiming that the cat, named Babou, was a gift from the head of state of Colombia.

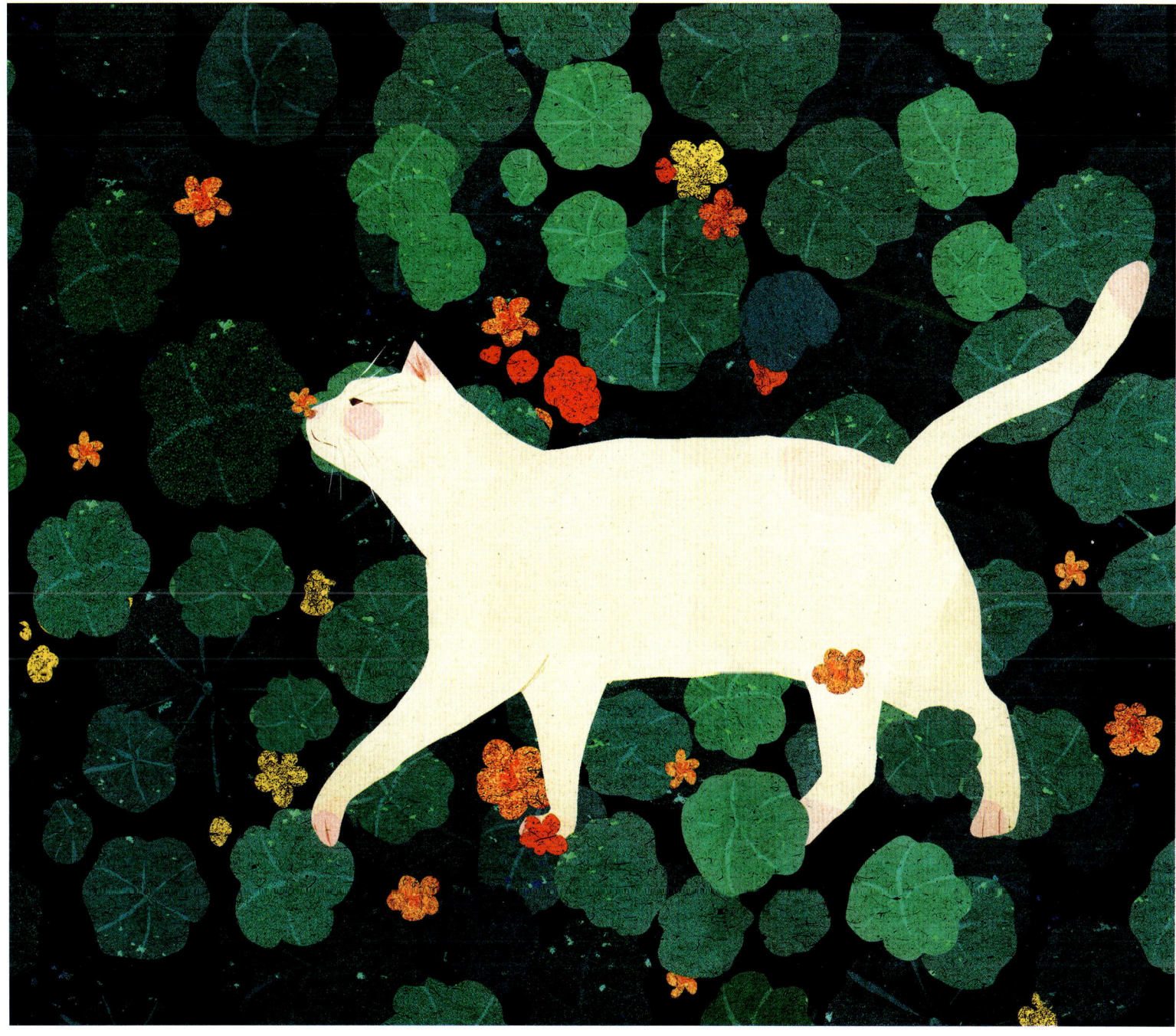

XUAN LOC XUAN

Nasturtium Cat, 2023
Digital painting, 9⅞ × 11⅜ in. / 25 × 29 cm

A cat with a cream-colored coat and pink cheeks, ears, paws, and tip of the tail saunters through a verdant patch of nasturtium leaves. The saturated background, with a scattering of bright red, orange, and yellow flowers, is a striking contrast to the nearly monochromatic cat. The illustrator of this minimalist work is Vietnamese artist Xuan Loc Xuan (b. 1989), who is based in Ho Chi Minh City. The youngest of a large family with busy working parents, Xuan spent long hours of her childhood drawing and dreaming of becoming an illustrator. For the artist, an introvert by nature, those early years were etched with loneliness, which she considers the most powerful and informative influence on her work. That sense of sorrow is infused in her art: her human subjects, typically strangers or individuals she conjures in her imagination, are often solitary figures situated in a range of settings, such as lying down, looking away, or standing with their back to the viewer. Her animal subjects, although also solitary, appear less isolated. She depicts a variety of animals, but cats are a recurring theme and bring a meditative and healing quality to her work. The vibrancy of this particular image—a feline moving calming through lush greenery, slowly enough to stop and smell a small orange flower—seems to break through the artist's deeply rooted feelings of sadness, instead communicating a sense of peace and resiliency in a sumptuous natural world.

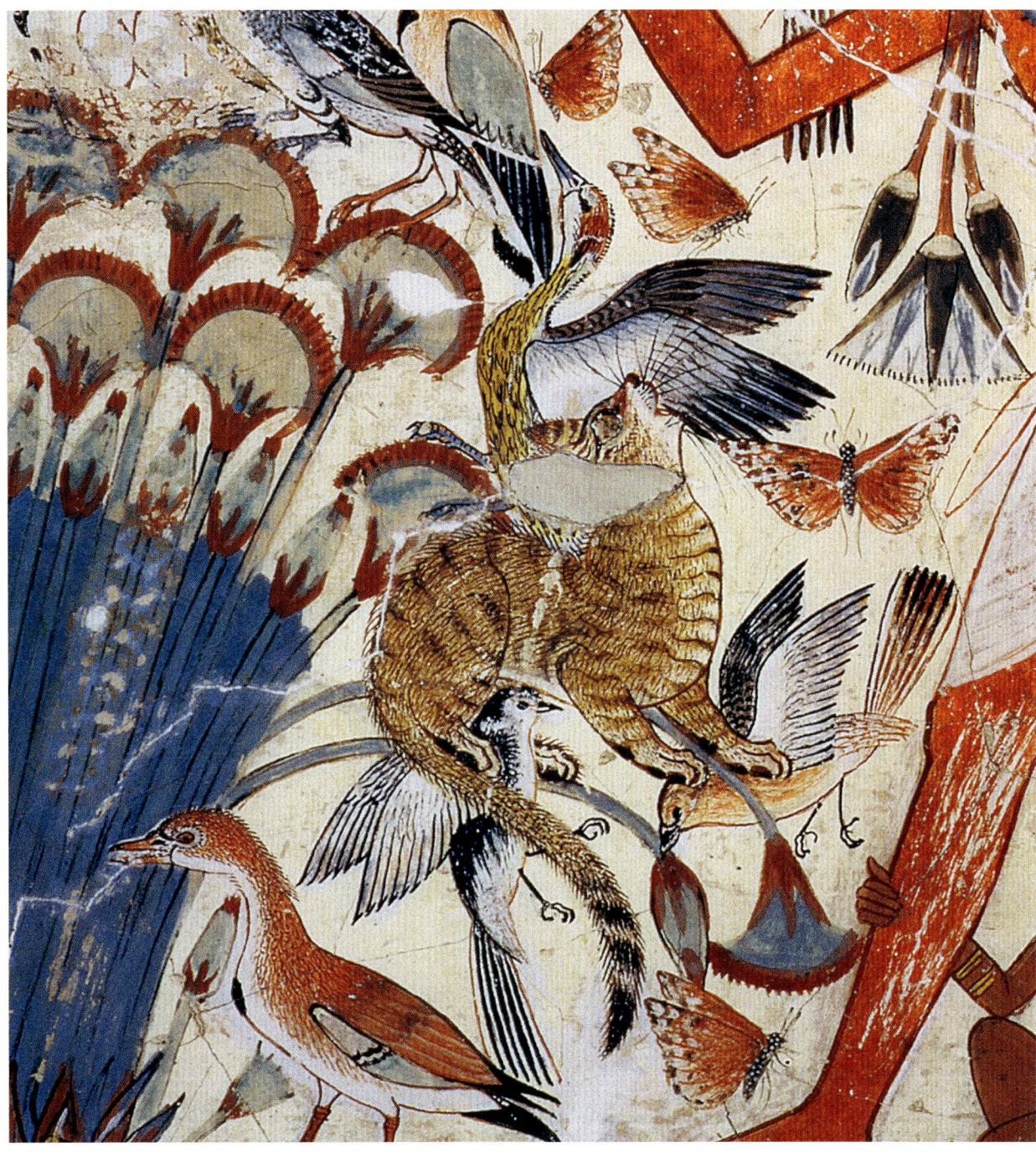

ANONYMOUS

Hunting cat (detail), from the Tomb of
Nebamun, c. 1350 BCE
Wall painting, 38½ × 45¼ in. / 98 × 115 cm
British Museum, London

With extreme agility, a tawny cat seems to hover in the air as it catches three birds, one in each paw and another in its mouth, while more fortunate fowl and tiger butterflies, flushed out of a thicket of papyrus plants, scatter through the air. This detail comes from an ancient polychrome painting in the Tomb of Nebamun, built about 1350 BCE for a wealthy Egyptian official responsible for collecting grain for the city of Thebes. Located in the tomb's chapel, the larger scene shows Nebamun and his family on a fishing and fowling expedition. It is one of several vignettes intended to both commemorate Nebamun's life and represent his aspirations for the afterlife—marshes were symbolic of rebirth and eroticism, while the vitality of the hunting cat represents Nebamun's victory

over the forces of death. Captured within this fragment are Nebamun's right leg and arm, draped with lotus flowers, as he stands in a small boat, his daughter beneath him holding onto his shin. His wife, Hatshepsut, is also depicted in the wall painting beyond this detail. Considered iconic animals in ancient Egyptian art and culture, cats were both beloved house pets and associated with gods who possessed feline traits (see p.29), including grace and swiftness, as well as the dual qualities of gentle care and powerful aggression. This golden-hued feline with a gleaming eye may be a representation of the sun god Ra, who was believed to hunt down the enemies of light and order.

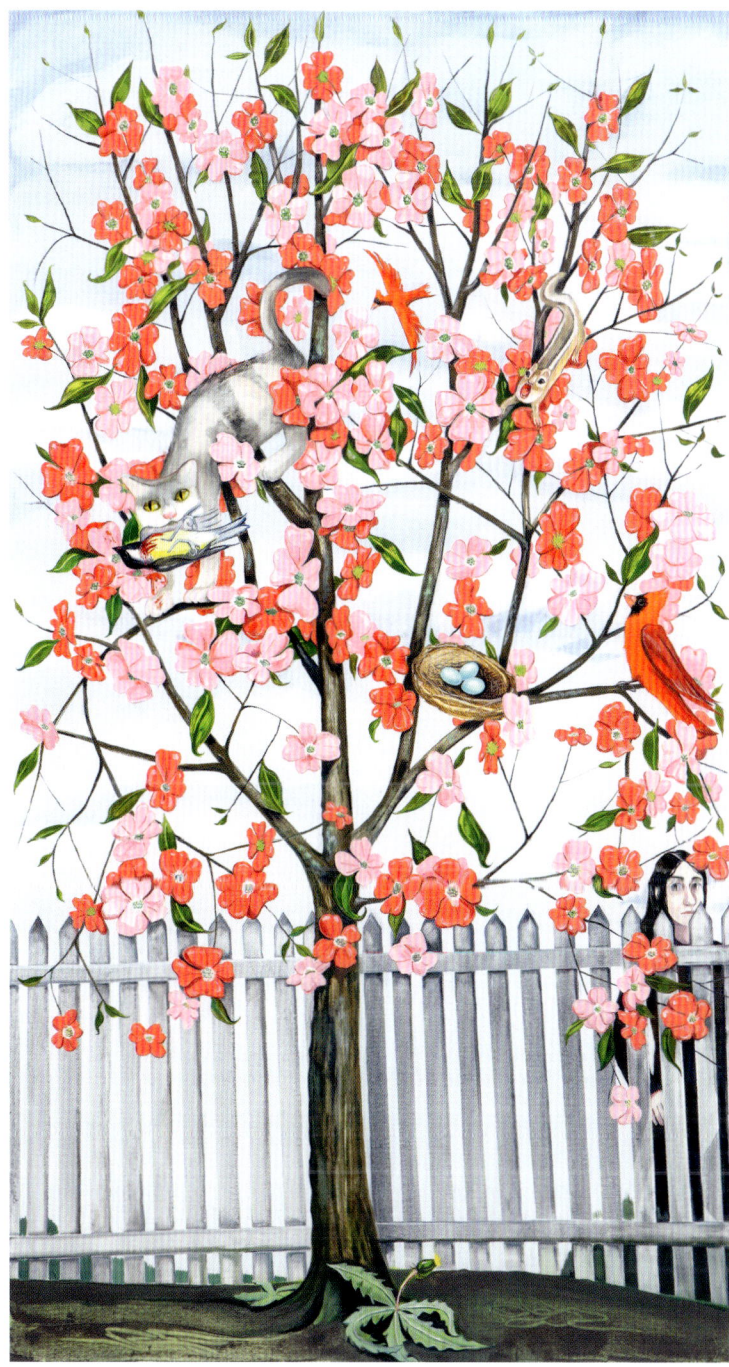

NIKKI MALOOF

Primavera, 2023
Oil on linen
71 × 40 in. / 188 × 101.6 cm
Private collection

American artist Nikki Maloof (b. 1985) favors interiors full of meticulous detail—including food, flora, and furnished rooms—in her paintings, capturing the quotidian with a tinge of the surreal or unsettling. She attempts to depict the reverberations of these rooms, objects, and outdoor landscapes in the real world in the hidden world of the mind. Like the Dutch Old Masters of the seventeenth century, she frequently employs the *vanitas* tradition and flowers as a motif, using them to express the somber transience of everyday life in all its messy glory. The stylized flowers of the tree in *Primavera* are in bright pink bloom, while its leaves are in a state of diverse growth. Not unusual for spring, the tree is teeming with animal as well as botanical life, home to a few birds, a chipmunk, and a bird's nest with bright blue eggs. Upon closer examination, however, death is also present, at the hands of a voracious gray cat that has climbed the branches and ensnared one of the songbirds. A woman at right glances up at the scene on her walk, but does not appear to be stopping as she moves out of frame. Maloof's characteristically bright palette and otherworldly composition add whimsy to the disquieting scene. The artist often favors using animals in her work, believing they are powerful symbolic proxies for humans. And, indeed, the viewers bear witness to the carnage, just as the animals in this painting do.

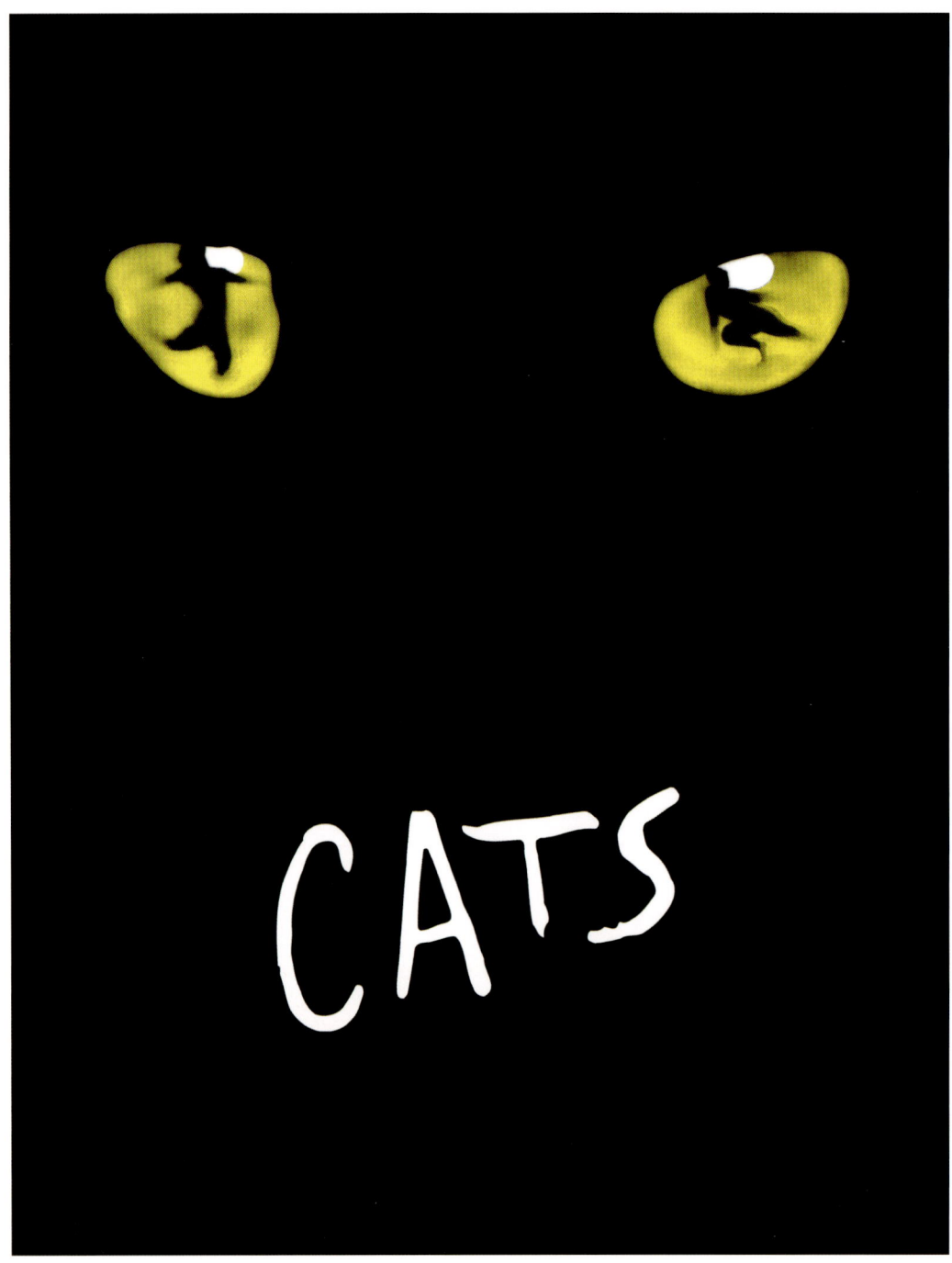

DEWYNTERS

Poster for *Cats*, 1981
Offset lithograph
20 × 12½ in. / 50.8 × 31.8 cm

Two yellow cat eyes peer out from a swath of solid black, the silhouettes of dancers replacing the slitted pupils. This original poster—now instantly recognizable—was designed by Dewynters, a London-based advertising agency for live entertainment, to promote what was then an unknown quantity: a brand-new West End musical by the composer Andrew Lloyd Webber. *Cats* went on to become one of the most successful musical theater shows of all time after its 1981 debut. The poster features the show's title in large handwritten white letters, a visual reference to its source material, T.S. Eliot's *Old Possum's Book of Practical Cats*. First published in 1939, the collection of nonsensical poems about cats by the British American poet was based on letters he wrote to his godchildren filled with the adventures of imaginary felines. An immediate hit, the poems have never gone out of print; the success of the musical led to the publication of a new edition in 1982, illustrated by Edward Gorey (see p.69). Lloyd Webber set the poems about a tribe of cats, the Jellicles, to music, and the story was brought to life by director Trevor Nunn, choreographer Gillian Lynne, and costume designer John Napier. The unusual subject matter initially deterred investors, but after positive reviews in London, the show transferred to Broadway in New York and became a commercial success in both cities. Translated into more than twenty languages, it ran on the London stage for 8,949 performances, closing on its twenty-first birthday.

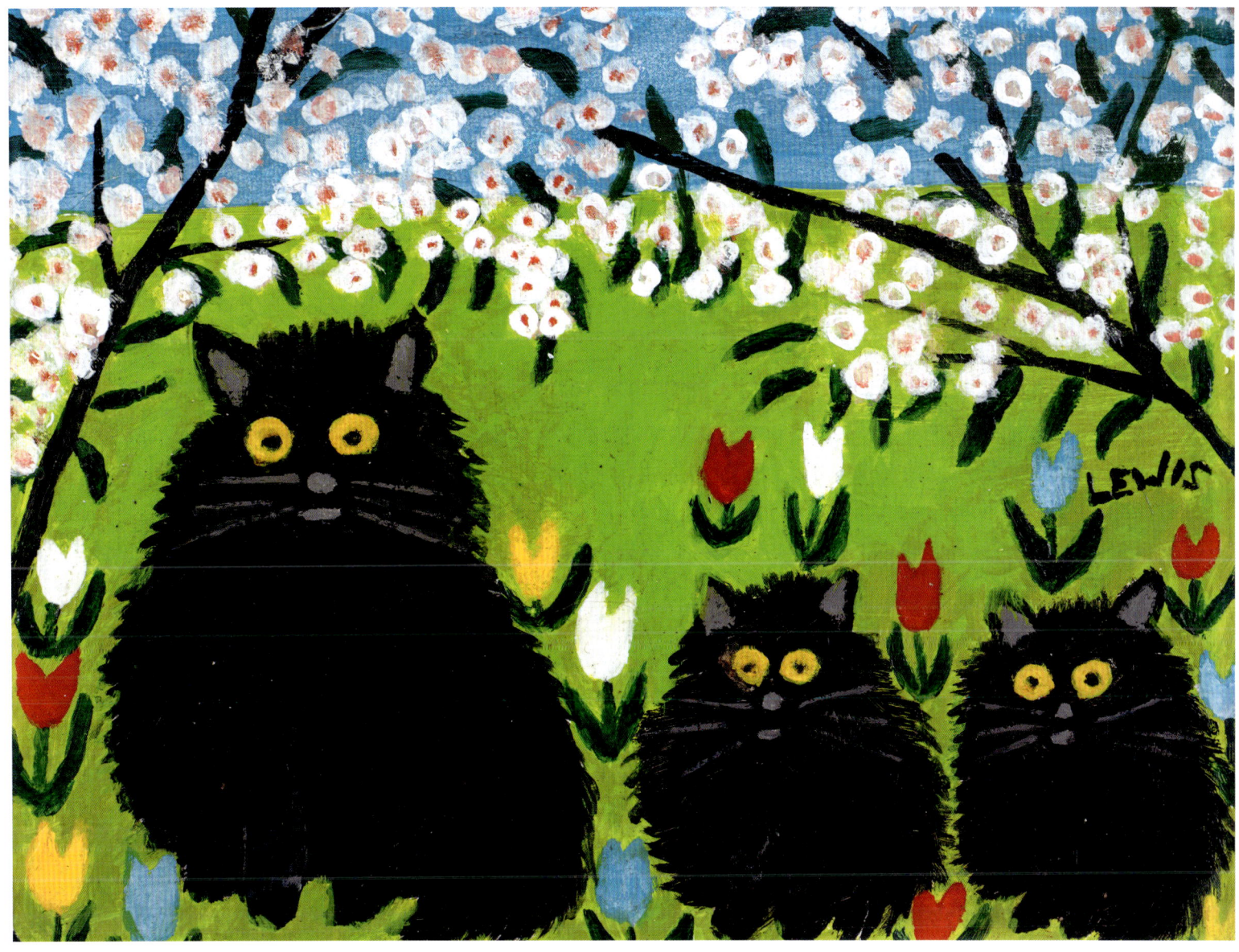

MAUD LEWIS

Untitled [Three Black Cats], c. 1960s
Oil on pulpboard, 8⅞ × 11¾ in. / 22.5 × 29.7 cm
Art Gallery of Nova Scotia, Halifax, Canada

Three stylized black cats—a mother and two kittens—sit in a row and stare ahead, wide-eyed and somewhat startled, in a spring garden filled with apple blossom and tulips. Painted by Canadian artist Maud Lewis (1901–1970), all three animals are probably based on Fluffy, Lewis's childhood black longhaired cat. Black cats were a favorite subject for the artist, whose flat, folk art paintings earned her a huge following. Born with a disability, now thought to be juvenile rheumatoid arthritis, that prohibited her from working outside the home, Lewis turned to painting to earn a living. Creating from her tiny house in Nova Scotia, where for decades summer visitors dropped in to buy a Maud Lewis painting as a souvenir, she saw her popularity soar in the mid-1960s. Barely able to keep up with the demand for her work, Lewis traced her cats from stencils made by her husband, Everett, then painted them in her distinct flattened style, which some critics have likened to traditional icon painting in Eastern Christianity. Here, Lewis's flattened cats sit against an equally flattened background of sky and grass; the apple blossom is created by stabs of color, while her tulips are each made from three strokes of paint in varying hues. The black cats are unique, with shaggy edges, clearly defined whiskers and ears, and round yellow eyes. She also painted white and gray cats, often as commissions. Despite her popularity, Lewis died in poverty, although she is remembered as a beloved Canadian icon and, of course, painter of cats.

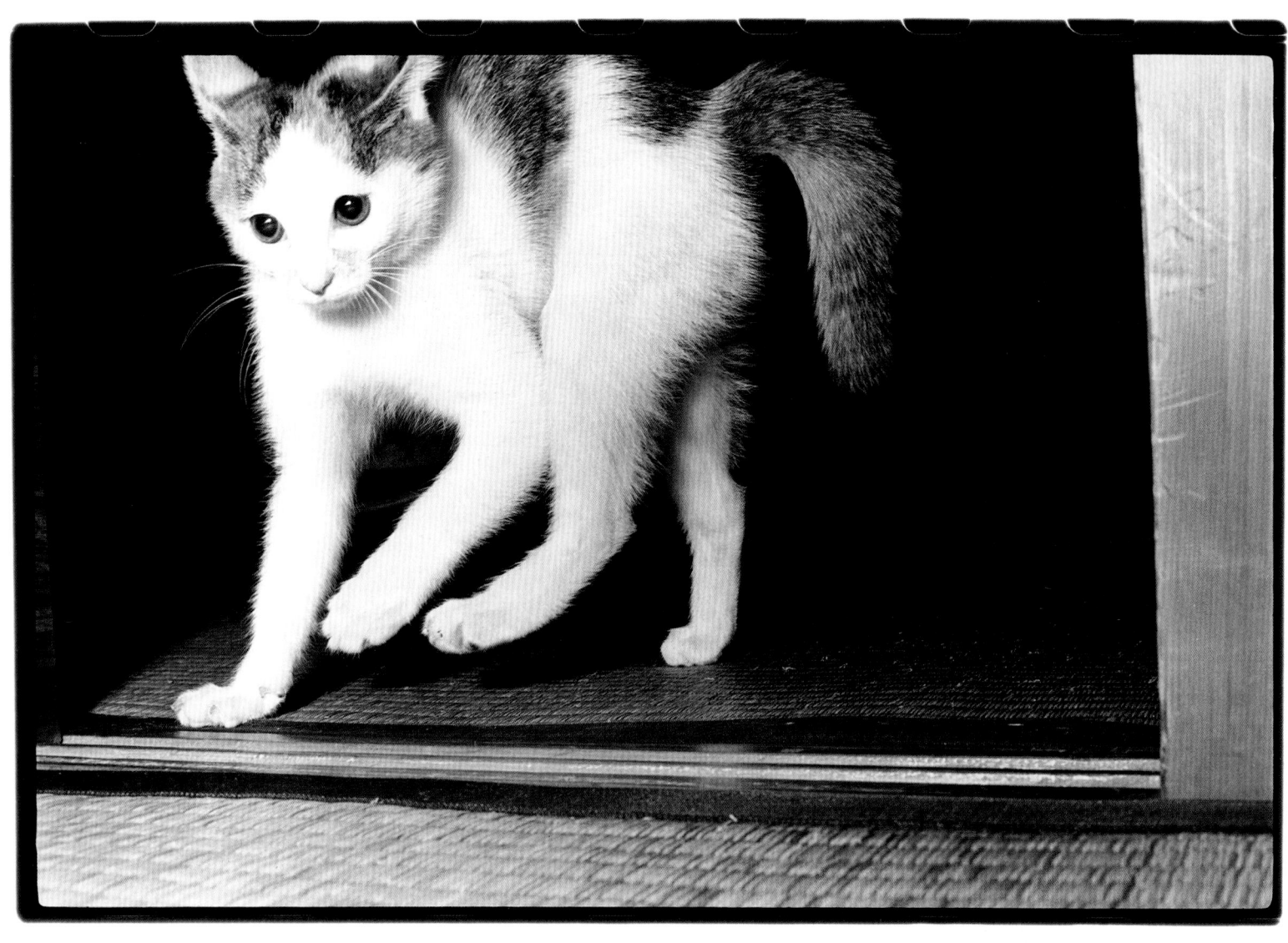

MASAHISA FUKASE

Untitled, from *Sasuke*, 1977
Photograph, dimensions variable

A wary cat named Sasuke springs back from a door-jamb, wearing a concerned expression that seems almost human in this image by Japanese photographer Masahisa Fukase (1934–2012). Alert and nimble, Sasuke, which in Japanese means "assistant" or "help," was named after a legendary ninja. Sasuke was one of Fukase's beloved cats, which he obsessively captured on 35 mm film and to which he devoted three books in the late 1970s. Fukase adopted Sasuke in 1977, but the kitten ran away, and when a helpful neighbor brought back a different kitty, he adopted it instead and gave it the same name. So close was their relationship, which developed in the wake of Fukase's second divorce, that Fukase took his cat with him wherever he went, identifying with his feline companion to such an extent that he considered images of Sasuke to be self-portraits. A self-declared ailurophile who claimed to be "mad for cats," Fukase was born into a family of photographers on the northern island of Hokkaido, and his father and grandfather ran a commercial photographic studio specializing in portraits. Familiar with the medium from a young age, Fukase studied photography in Tokyo and went freelance in 1968. Predominantly black-and-white, his oeuvre is characterized by extremes of transgression and violence, from graphic images of slaughterhouses to a celebrated series about ravens symbolizing lost love. His quiet, intimate scenes featuring his pets always eschew the trope of the "cute" cat in favor of depictions of soulful animals full of character.

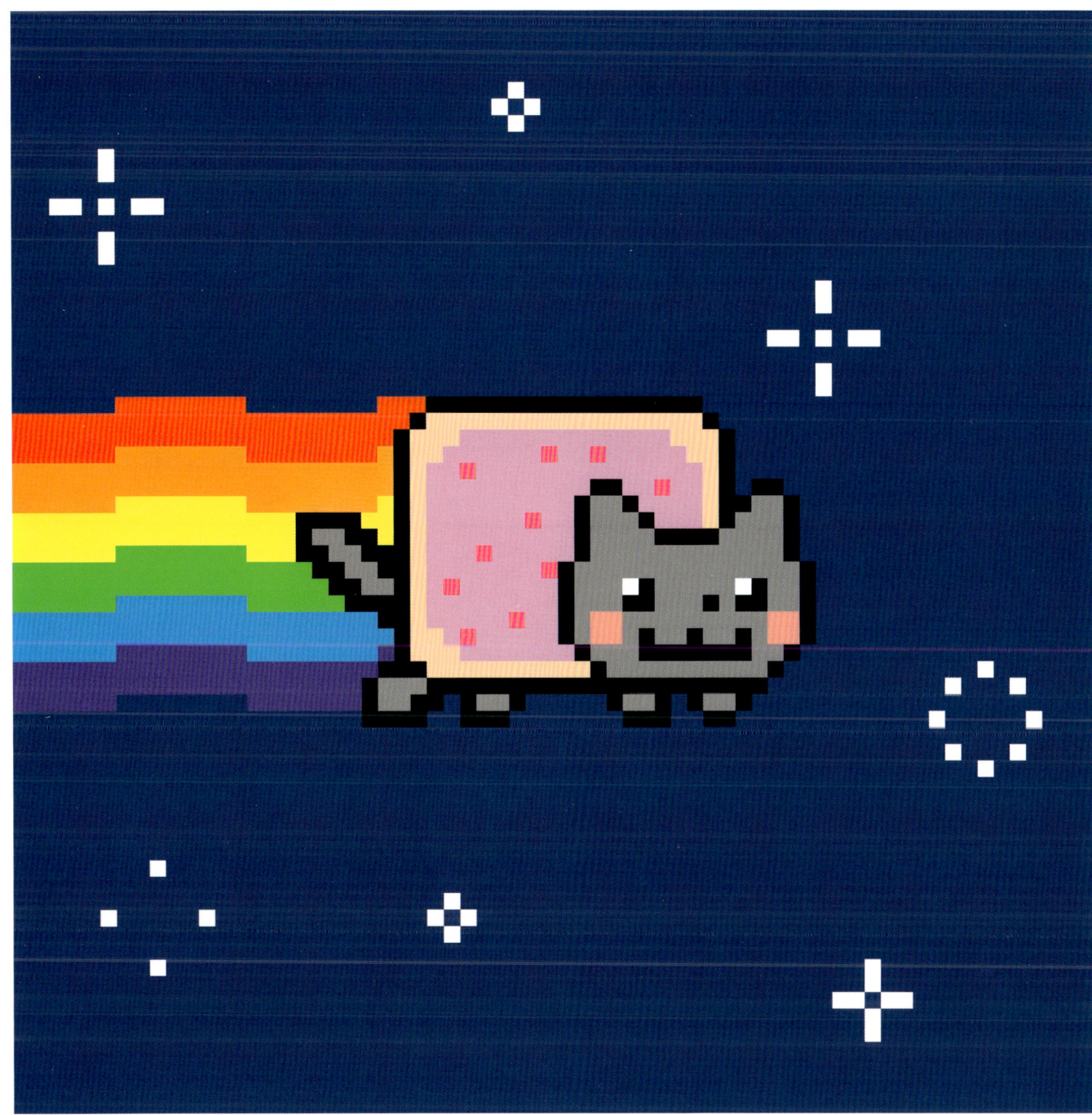

CHRISTOPHER ORLANDO TORRES

Nyan Cat, 2011
GIF, dimensions variable

Nyan Cat is an animated GIF (short for Graphics Interchange Format) created by American digital artist Christopher Orlando Torres (b. 1985) that became a viral sensation in 2011, widely credited for kick-starting the "meme economy" in the crypto world. Inspired by Torres's own cat Marty, Nyan has a gray head and a pink toaster-pastry body that is shown cheerily flying through space to a looped soundtrack of the Japanese pop song "Nyanyanyanyanyanyanya!" by daniwellP, emitting a rainbow trail along the way to mark his cute cosmic continuum. The Internet went so wild for Nyan that the surreal kitty inspired countless adaptations and merchandise ideas. The GIF even made its way into major advertising campaigns with Nike, Coca-Cola, McDonald's, Google, Playstation, Mentos,

and Honda. Eager to retain control of his digital work, Torres offered *Nyan Cat* up as a nonfungible token (NFT) in 2021 on the Foundation app, a digital art marketplace based on the Ethereum (ETH) blockchain. It was a shrewd business move that saw the flying feline reach new heights in the Web3 universe, achieving 300 ETH (roughly $590,000) at auction and igniting a craze for creature-themed memes as NFTs. Since the sale, Torres has created a slew of spin-offs, including a canine version called *Nyan Dogg* in collaboration with rapper Snoop Dogg, as well as an extensive NFT cat collection that features such zany delights as *Super Nyan Balloon*, *Biker Nyan Cat*, and *Vaporwave Nyan Cat*.

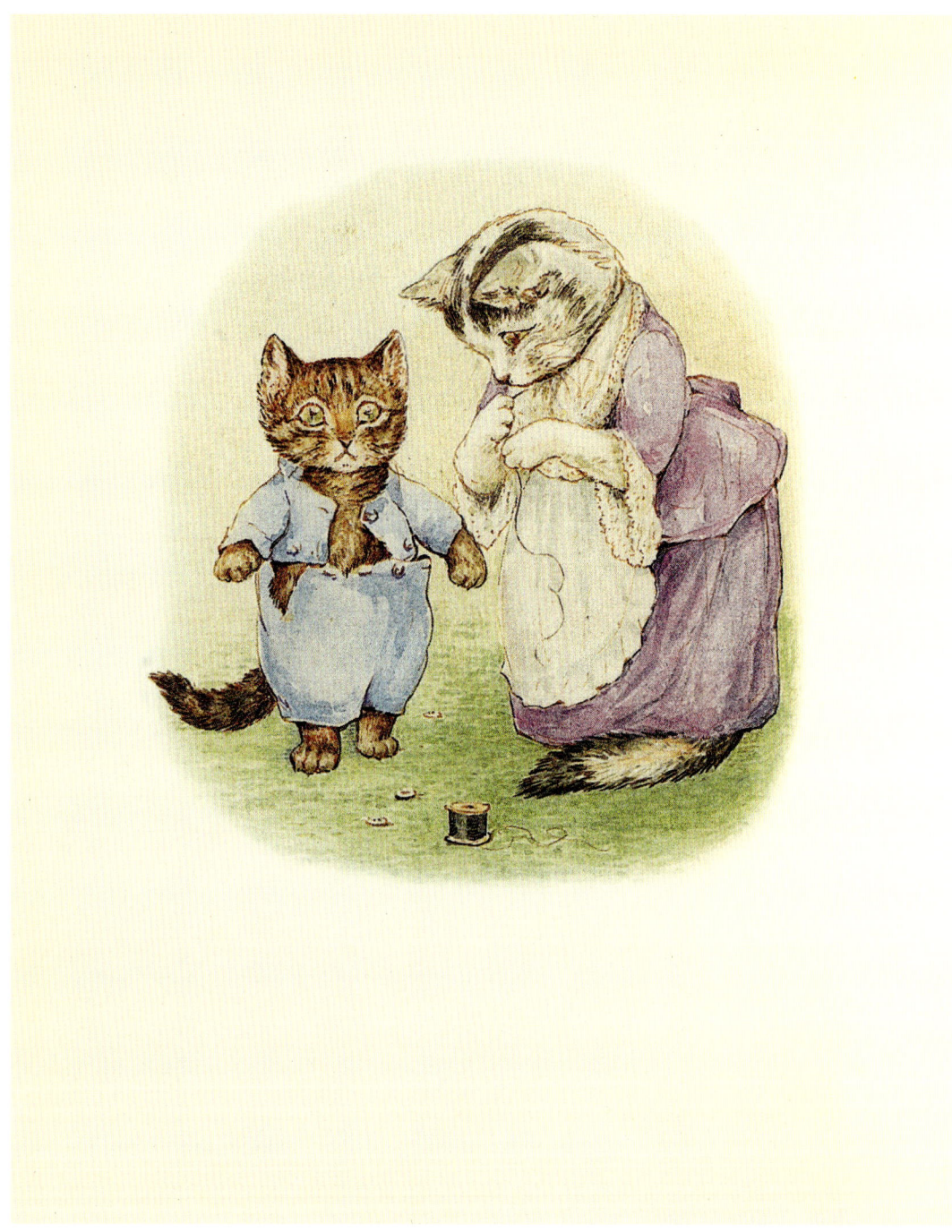

BEATRIX POTTER

Illustration from *The Tale of Tom Kitten* by
Beatrix Potter, 1907
Copyright © Frederick Warne & Co., 1907, 2002
Printed book, 5½ × 4⅛ in. / 14 × 10.5 cm

Capturing the playful and mischievous nature of kittens, this humorous children's book follows the adventures of Tom Kitten, Mittens, and Moppet as they become entangled in a series of mishaps, much to the irritation of their mother, Mrs. Tabitha Twitchit. With respectable guests expected for tea, the three little kittens are washed, brushed, and dressed in their best clothes before being admonished to stay clean while playing outside. However, their outfits soon become soiled and damaged and, after the kittens climb a garden wall and meet the Puddle-Ducks, they end up hilariously misplaced in a pond. Upon discovering that her children's antics have left them in a state unfit for company, Tabitha banishes the kittens to their beds, telling her friends that they have the measles. Yet the dignified tea party is soon disturbed by the sound of romping overhead, and, upon investigation, the kittens' bedroom is found in a state of disarray. The British author and illustrator Beatrix Potter (1866–1943) set this whimsical story in the cottage garden of her own beloved farmhouse, Hill Top in the Lake District, which she bought in 1905 with proceeds from her first successful children's stories, including *The Tale of Peter Rabbit* (1901). Between 1901 and 1913, she wrote and illustrated twenty-three books featuring anthropomorphic animal characters, with cats appearing several times. Whereas Tabitha Twitchit and her cousin Ribby are routinely presented as models of respectability, the same cannot be said of the impish Tom Kitten and his unruly siblings.

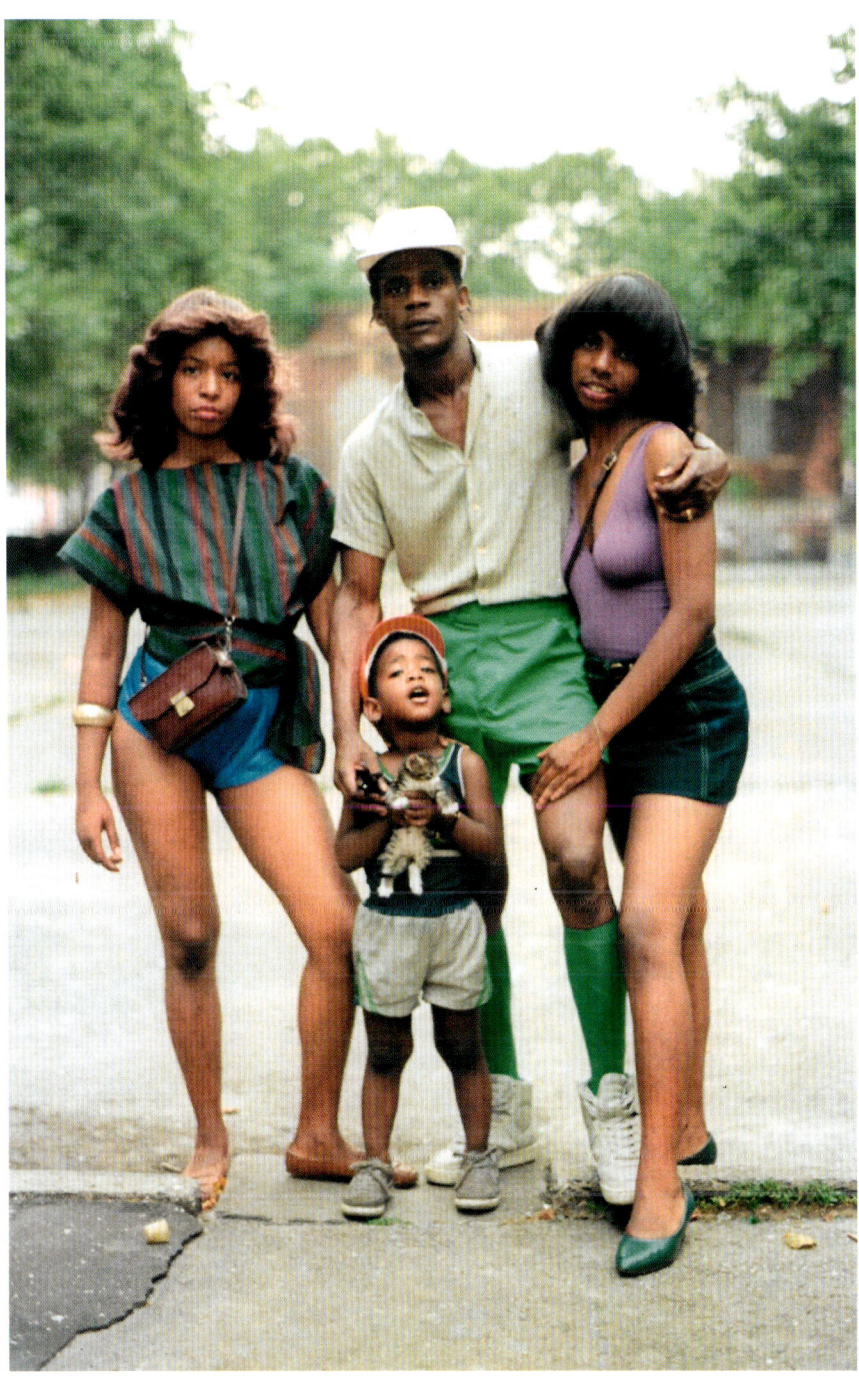

JAMEL SHABAZZ

Bittersweet, Lower East Side Manhattan, NYC, 1982
C-print, 30 × 24 in. / 76.2 × 61 cm

Brooklyn-born photographer Jamel Shabazz (b. 1960) is considered an icon of street photography, with a career spanning more than forty-five years. He often describes his camera as a kind of social connector — a tool that allows him to "engage people in a very unique way," helping him to convey the dynamic pulse of urban life, both in the streets where he was raised and beyond. Returning home from military service in 1980, Shabazz found inspiration in the Black- and Brown-majority neighborhoods of New York and felt compelled to reframe the experience of these places as he saw and felt it. His vivid, personal portraits capture the restless energy and hidden beauty of metropolitan life, while honoring the individuality of those living it, through a poignant mix of joy, excitement, tension,

and melancholy. A case in point is this arresting 1982 portrait taken on Manhattan's Lower East Side, titled *Bittersweet*, which highlights the bold stylish flair of its subjects, who model not only their fashion sense but their sense of togetherness. The man affectionately rests his hand on the child's shoulder, while the boy proudly holds up a tiny kitten—an intimate moment that introduces ambiguity to what may or may not be a family portrait. The "bittersweet" of the title is not explicitly stated, but it can be inferred through the family dynamic, subtly evoking the fleeting passage of time. What remains certain is the trust and affection shared between these young subjects, who are compositionally linked through touch. The kitten, without question, is in safe hands.

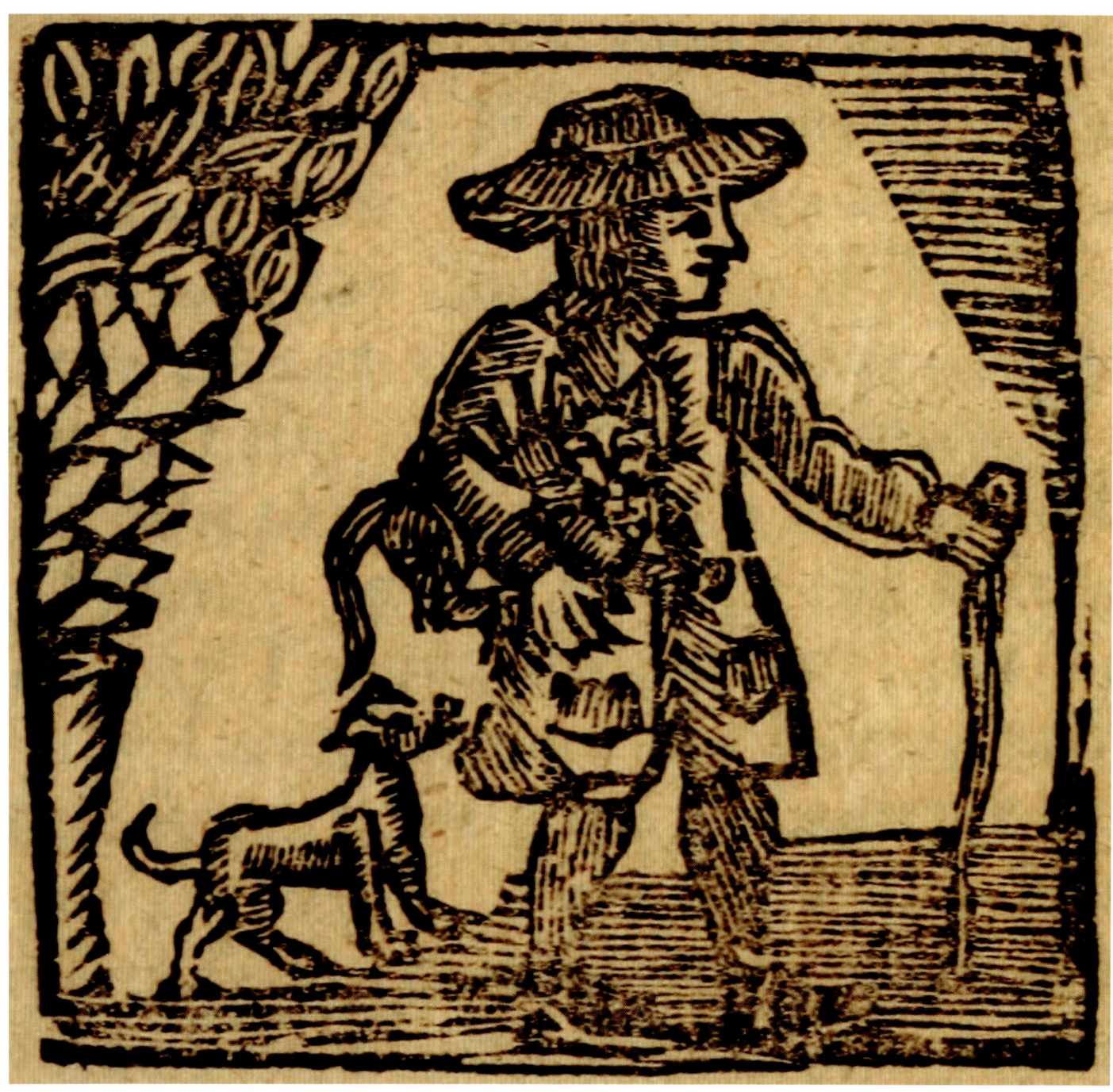

ANONYMOUS

*The Famous and Remarkable History of
Sir Richard Whittington*, 1770
Chapbook, H. 7⅞ in. / 20 cm
Boston Public Library

The rags-to-riches legend of *Dick Whittington and his Cat* is one of England's most famous folk tales. This illustration depicting Dick carrying his beloved cat comes from the frontispiece of a 1770 edition of the seventeenth-century story, which recounts the adventures of a poor orphan boy who travels to London to seek his fortune. Expecting the streets to be paved with gold, he instead finds work as a scullery boy in the house of a wealthy merchant. Plagued by the mice that infest his room, he buys a cat, which eradicates the vermin. When his master offers him a stake in a cargo bound for the Barbary Coast of North Africa, Dick gives him his feline friend as compensation, after which he decides to flee London. But, as he departs, he hears church bells chiming, which seem to say, "Turn again, Whittington, thrice Lord Mayor of London." Back in the city, he discovers that his master's ship has returned, and with it a change of fortune. While docked in Barbary, its captain found the Moorish king's palace overrun with rodents. Dick's cat swiftly dealt with the pests and, to show his gratitude, the king purchased the entire cargo, including the cat, for a fantastical sum. Thereafter, Dick prospered immensely and became mayor of London three times, just as the bells had foretold. The real-life Richard Whittington did not have humble beginnings: he was a wealthy merchant and mayor of London at the turn of the fifteenth century, and there is no evidence to suggest that he actually owned a cat.

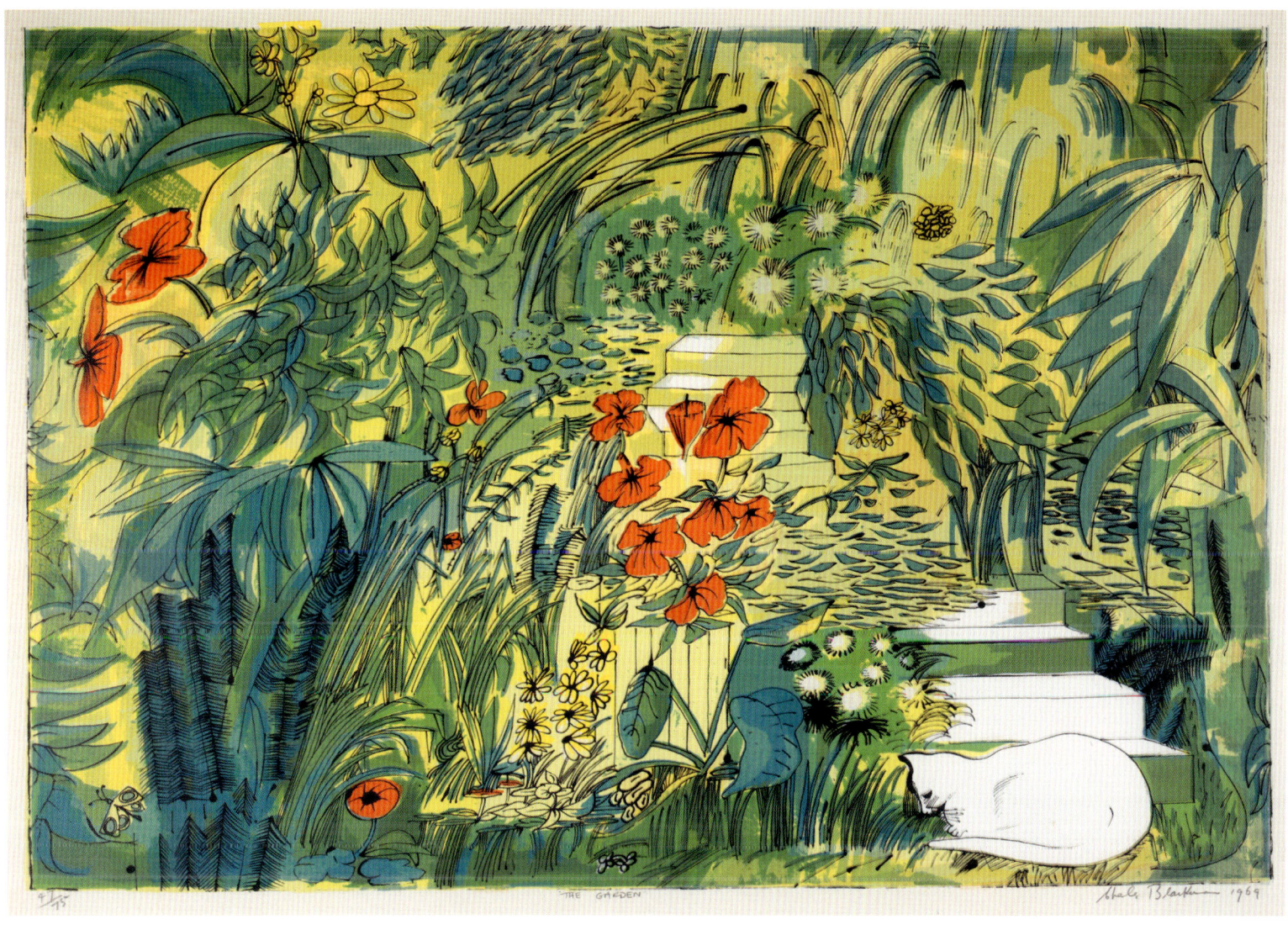

CHARLES BLACKMAN

The Garden, 1969
Screenprint, 26⅛ × 38¼ in. / 66.5 × 97 cm
Chau Chak Wing Museum, The University of Sydney

A white cat crouches in the bottom right corner of this lush tropical garden brought to life by Australian artist Charles Blackman (1928–2018). Seemingly oblivious to the verdant greenery all around, the cat may be staring at something it has seen in the grass, or it may be gazing at nothing at all. Gardens were a favorite subject in many of Blackman's paintings, prints, and tapestries from the 1950s onward, and he first depicted green spaces in a successful series of paintings based on Lewis Carroll's fantastical novel *Alice's Adventures in Wonderland*. Cats also became a recurring motif in Blackman's various works as important characters from his difficult peripatetic childhood. He had particularly fond memories of feeding stray cats in the Kings Cross area of Sydney. White cats featured as a symbol of childhood, memory, and innocence. Here, the lyrical beauty of the bright red flowers, green-blue foliage, and yellow sunshine feels almost secretive, enjoyed only by the cat. This was Blackman's view of his neighbor's garden from his studio window in Melbourne, where he moved in 1968 after five years in London. In another painting of the same garden, Blackman includes a Russian Blue instead of a white cat. A founding member of the Antipodeans art movement and a member of the Heide circle of artists, Blackman was one of Australia's most celebrated figurative artists of the twentieth century.

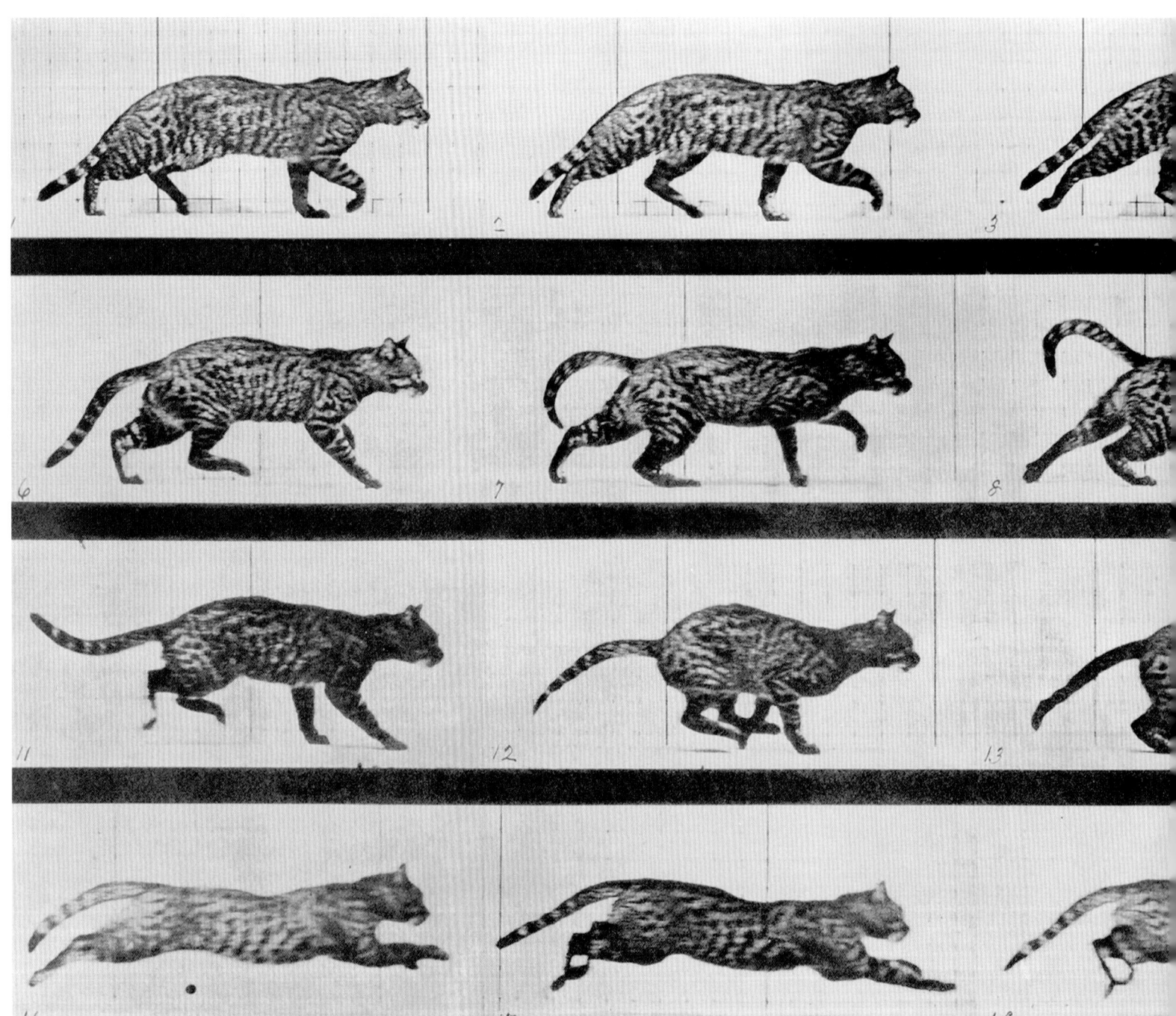

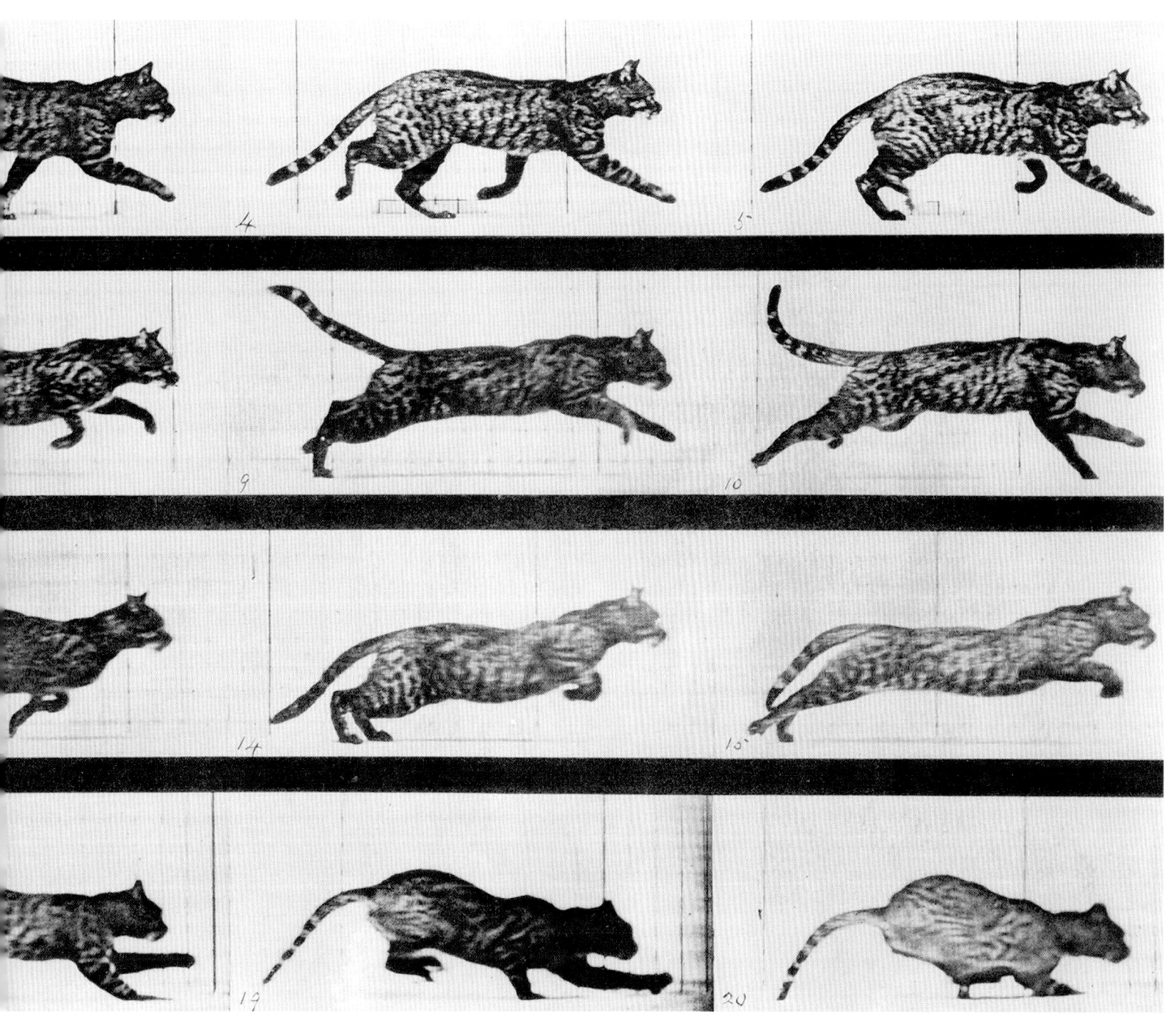

EADWEARD MUYBRIDGE

Cat Trotting, Changing to a Gallop, Plate 717,
from *Animal Locomotion*, 1887
Collotype, 6⅞ × 16¼ in. / 17.6 × 41.3 cm
Philadelphia Museum of Art

Recognized for their contribution to both photography and science, these images of a running cat were taken by American photographer Eadweard Muybridge (1830–1904) for his *Animal Locomotion* series, which he made to study motion in animals and humans. Comprising 781 plates, the series began when the railroad tycoon Leland Stanford commissioned Muybridge to prove that galloping horses momentarily lift all four hooves off the ground at once. Muybridge developed a system with multiple cameras, each placed 27 inches (68.6 cm) apart; as the horse ran past them, it successively triggered their shutters through trip wires. The same method was used for other animals, including the American shorthair here, which trots and then breaks into a sprint. Although cats walk by moving both legs of the same side together, they run with a diagonal gait, moving their front leg and the diagonally opposite hind leg simultaneously. Their powerful hind legs act like springs, propelling them forward with force. This enables them to cover more ground and be momentarily airborne, which reduces air resistance and increases their speed. The average house cat can sprint up to 25 miles per hour (mph; 40 kph), a speed they can maintain over short distances, although some have been known to reach 30 mph (48 kph)—faster than the fastest human. Muybridge went on to perfect his ingenious stop-motion technique, showing his images in quick succession using his patented zoopraxiscope, laying the foundation for motion pictures and cinematography.

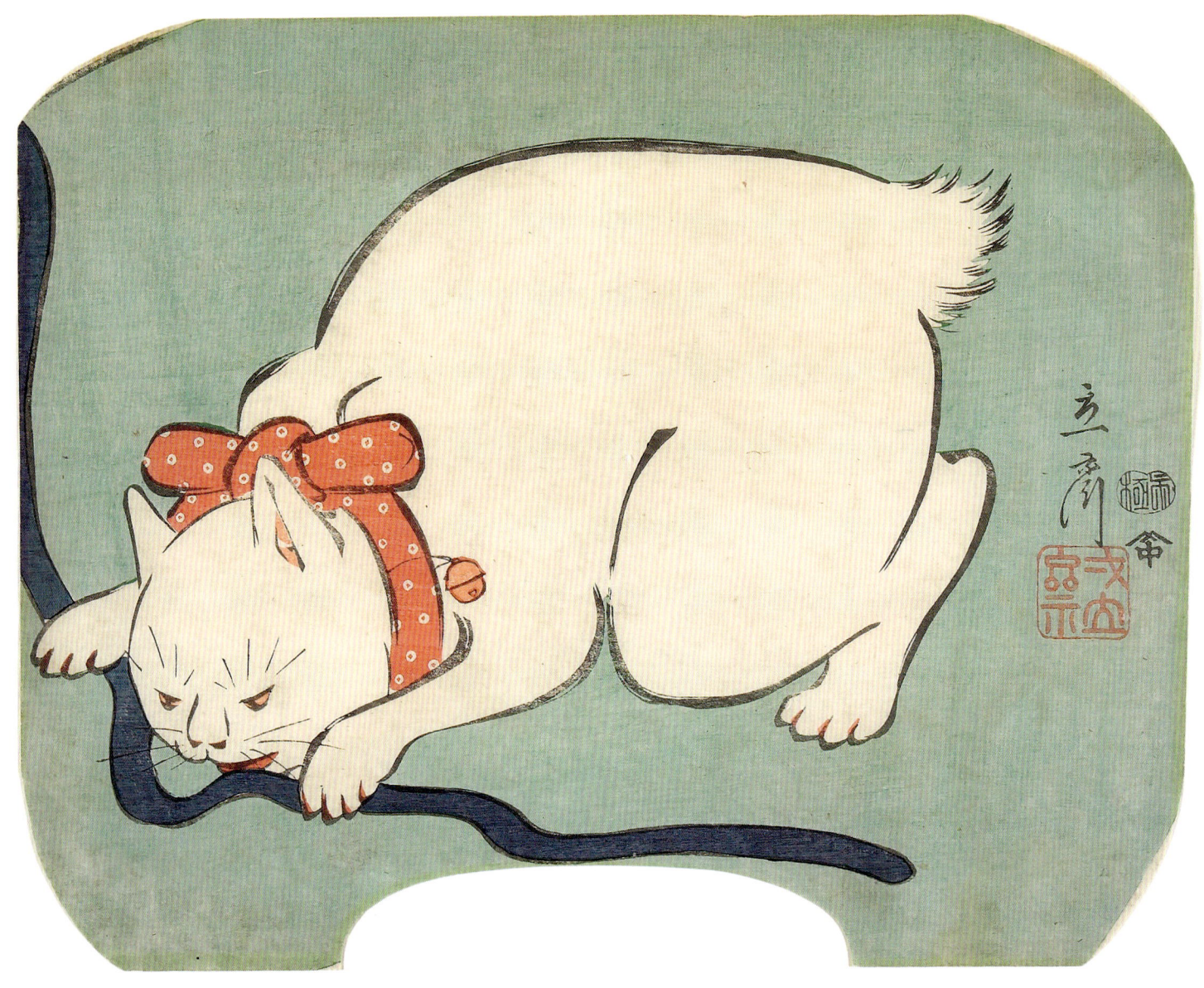

UTAGAWA HIROSHIGE II

A White Cat Playing with a String, 1863
Woodcut, 8⅜ × 10½ in. / 21.3 × 26.7 cm
Minneapolis Institute of Art

Since they were brought to the archipelago from China in the sixth century to protect migrating Buddhist monks' scrolls from rodents, cats have occupied a special place in Japanese culture and popular belief. From the *yōkai* (strange apparitions) *bakaneko* (changed cat), or *nekomata* (double-tailed cat; see p.78) to the lucky *maneki-neko* (beckoning cat; see p.185), Japanese artists have portrayed their beloved animal companions for centuries as more than just mousers. In the nineteenth century, Utagawa Kuniyoshi (see p.89) depicted them as mischievous, with anthropomorphic features, and drew so many that he was nicknamed the painter of cats. But he was not alone: many of his contemporaries, including Utagawa Hiroshige II (1826–1869), the artist of this work, were inspired by the animals, not only because of their grace and beauty but for their playfulness and many postures, as shown in the cute Japanese Bobtail toying with a ribbon here. In a design for a traditional fan, Hiroshige II imagined a bulbous cat that curves with the rounded shape of the object, its back legs poised as if ready to pounce. The feline's pink collar and bell were often worn by temple cats to distinguish them from strays and protect them from evil spirits. Perhaps more practical, the bell was also used to scare away birds from a hunting cat's approach. Both guardians and good-luck charms, cats like this one are still considered an integral part of the Japanese household and a true member of the family.

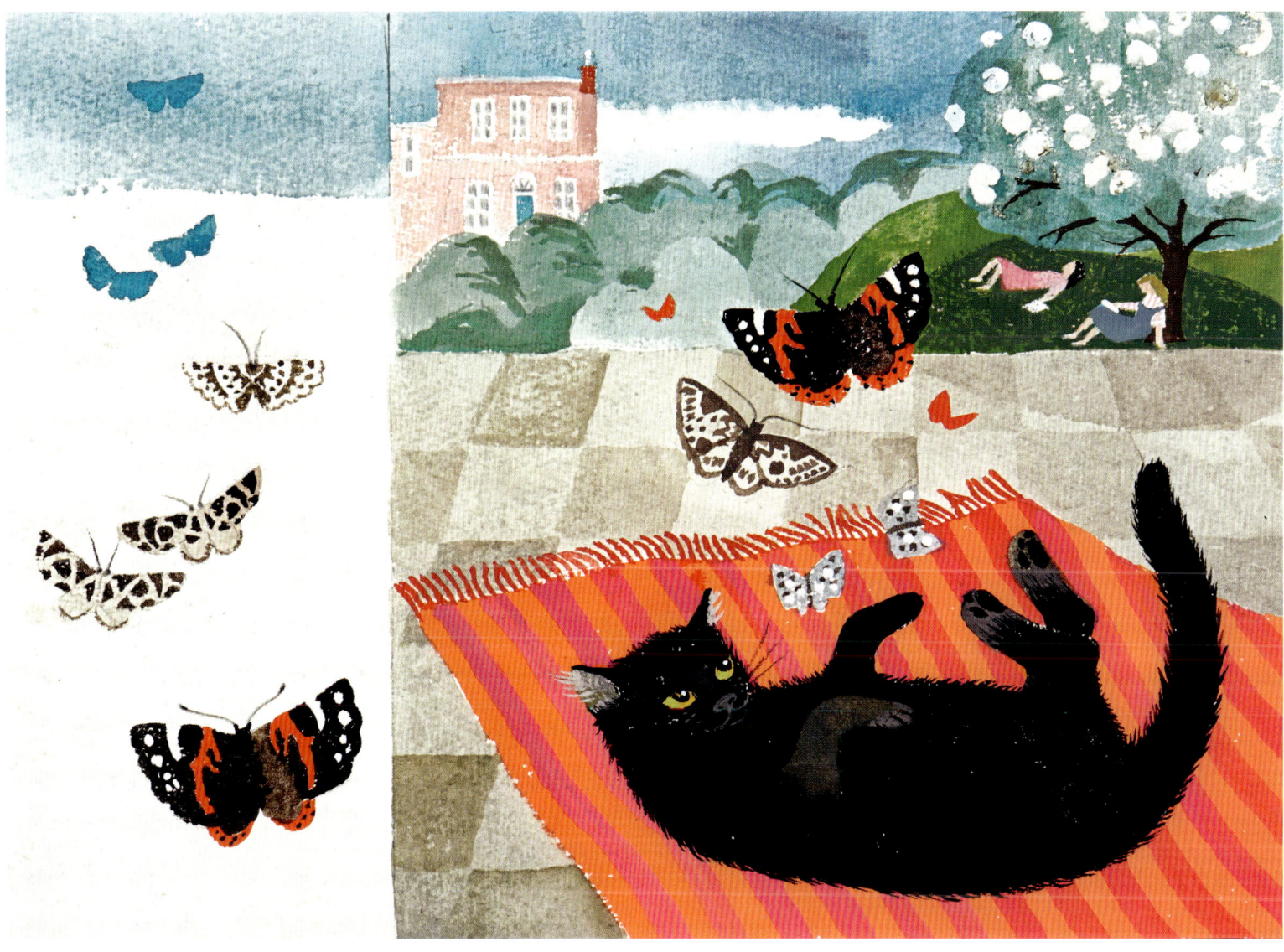

MARY FEDDEN

Darius and Butterflies, 20th century
Pencil, chalk, watercolor, and gouache
9⅝ × 13⅜ in. / 24.5 × 34 cm
Private collection

This charming watercolor seems like a simple scene, with a fuzzy black cat named Darius lounging on a vibrantly striped blanket, belly to the sky, gazing up at a cloud of butterflies that float above him. But look closer and the work starts to become less real: the watercolor seems to abruptly stop at the cat's left, with more butterflies funneling upward to a patch of blue sky that rejoins with the rest of the landscape. Two faceless girls lie in a meadow in the distance in front of some hedges and a red manse, but how close they are to the cat is unclear. Quietly surreal, this is the work of Mary Fedden (1915–2012), whose enigmatic still lifes and flower works made her one of Great Britain's best-loved artists. During her time at the Slade School of Art in the 1930s, she studied set design and painting under Vladimir Polunin, who had worked with Sergei Diaghilev's Ballet Russes. Although she did not make a career in the theater, the bold, sumptuous palette of her works, as well as their blurring of realism with the abstract, hearken back to this training. Cats are one of Fedden's most favored and recognized subjects, and she was fond of the animals and their eccentricities. Her most famous feline is the titular tabby in Susannah Amoore's 1997 children's book *Motley the Cat*, for which Fedden provided the illustrations. Rendered in her bold, expressive style, kitties like Motley and Darius are suffused with energy, making the still-life genre feel not so still.

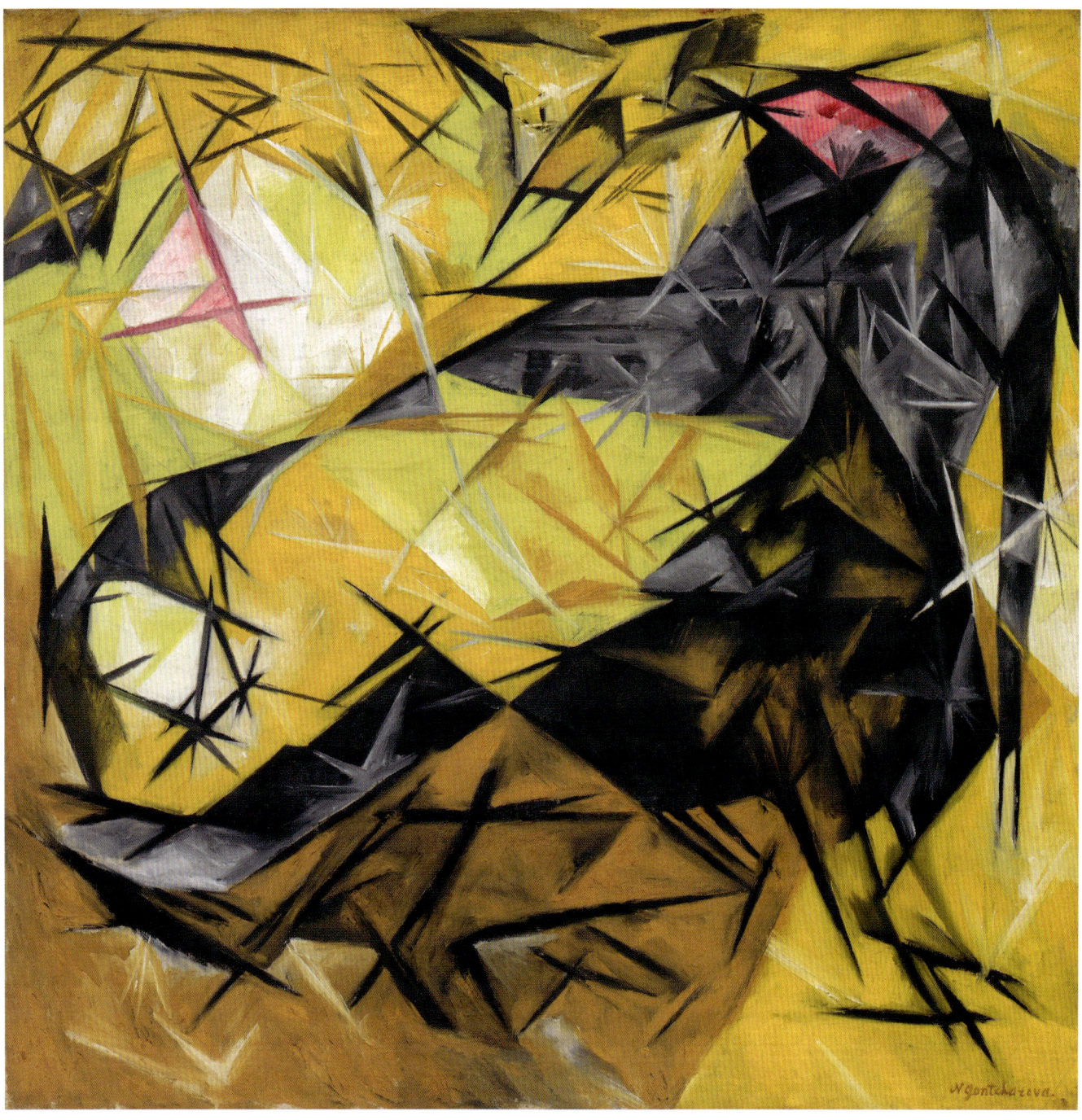

NATALIA GONCHAROVA

Cats (rayist percep.[tion] in rose, black, and yellow), 1913
Oil on canvas, 33½ × 33¾ in. / 85.1 × 85.7 cm
Solomon R. Guggenheim Museum, New York

After the development of photography in the nineteenth century enabled the movement of animals to be captured with scientific precision, as in the chronophotographs of Eadweard Muybridge (see p.47), avant-garde painters took different approaches to representing motion and speed. Most notable were the Futurists (see p.141), an Italian group launched in 1909 that became influential across Europe. It was one of three modernist movements, along with Cubism and Orphism, that fed into Rayonism, a concept devised by Russian artists Natalia Goncharova (1881–1962) and her lifelong partner, Mikhail Larionov. This painting by Goncharova of a clutter of cats exemplifies how Rayonist art captures energy and dynamism, while steering away from figurative representation. There is little in the composition itself to indicate the subject matter, yet the work's title enables a reconsideration of the abstract forms, revealing them to be felines engaged in a frantic rough-and-tumble. Rayonism also sought to depict how light reflects off solid objects, and as such, the glinting rays in this piece imply shiny coats of fur. The strong lines connect the work stylistically to Russian folk art, which was a major influence on Goncharova and an important aspect in the rejection of the exclusivity endorsed by European art academies of the day. Animals were a common subject in the folklore of her motherland, with cats symbolizing wisdom, mystery, mischievousness, and supernatural powers, demonstrating both the superstition and the affection for cats in Russian culture.

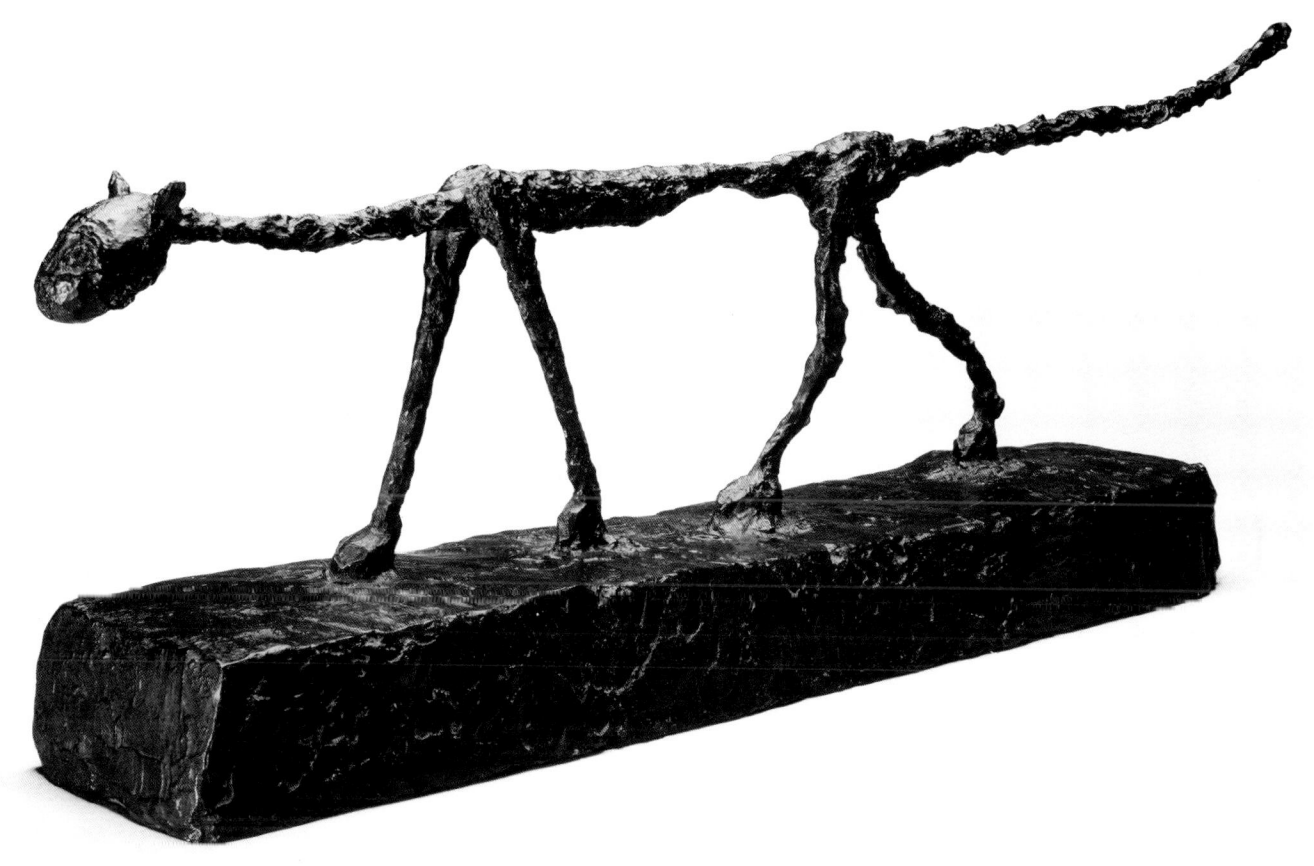

ALBERTO GIACOMETTI

The Cat, 1954
Bronze, 11 × 31½ × 5¼ in. / 27.9 × 80 × 13.3 cm
Metropolitan Museum of Art, New York

From the 1940s onward, Swiss artist Alberto Giacometti (1901–1966) devoted his work to the human figure, attempting to capture its fragile and fading presence on the verge of disappearance in the postwar era. However, there are a few exceptions to his human-centric oeuvre: horses, cats, and dogs, which the artist treated in the same elongated, stretched, and wiry manner as his people. Giacometti told his biographer James Lord how, after observing his brother Diego's pet, he came up with the idea of sculpting the animal: "I had seen Diego's cat so often when it walked through the bedroom toward my bed before I got up in the morning, that I had an exact picture of it in my mind. All I had to do was to make the cat. Yet only its head can claim to possess a certain trueness to life, because

when it came over to my bed, I only ever saw it from the front." It was an actual cat, with its own particular life and everyday presence, that inspired him, even if he could only truly capture the head. In this bronze sculpture, the animal appears as a long horizontal line, with a round, slightly elongated head that contrasts with its spindly body. A discreet and delicate tightrope walker of life, it is at once adventurous, curious, and cautious. Giacometti captures the muffled stretch of a walking cat, turning it into a line and sign in space. Beyond the particularity of Diego's cat, it is "the" cat, or every cat, in its calm, sharp movement.

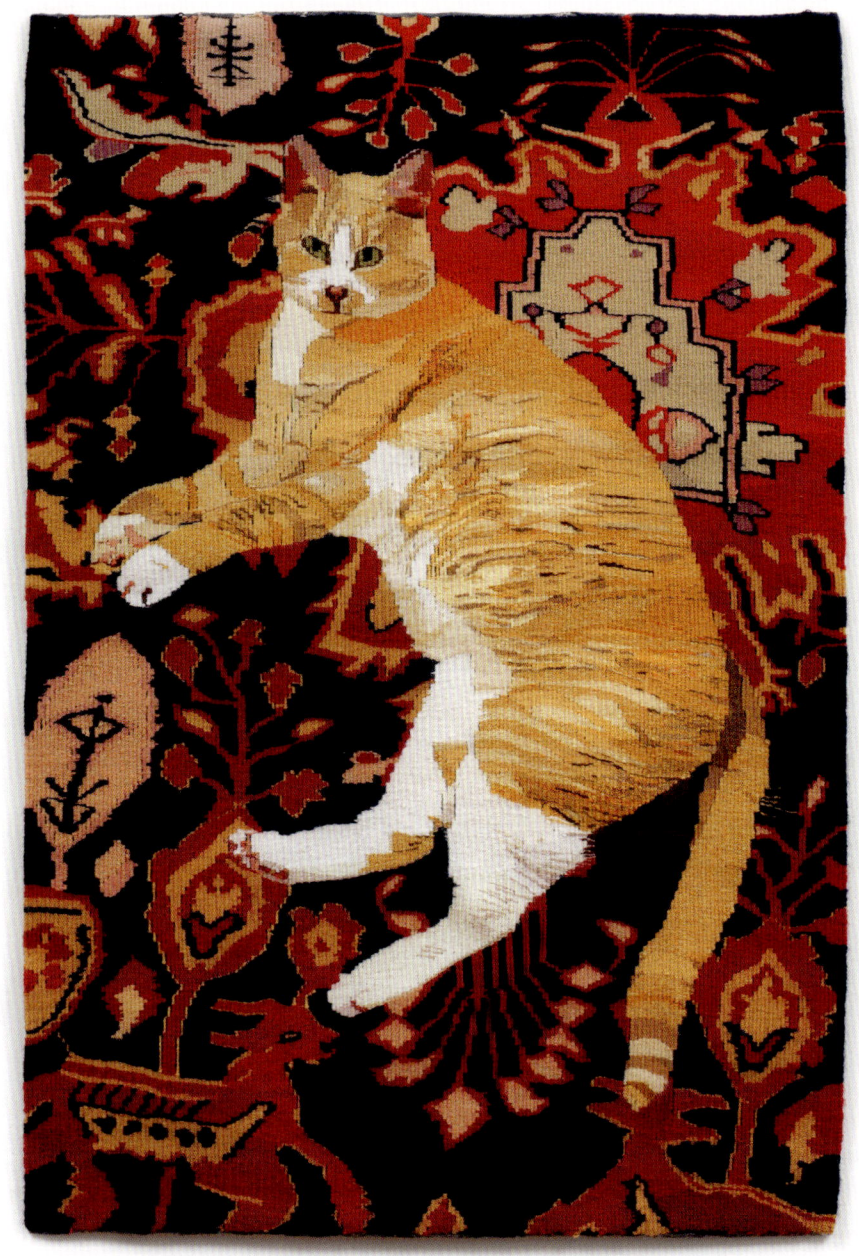

ELIZABETH RADCLIFFE

Algie, 2024
Wool and cotton warp
29 × 20 in. / 73.7 × 50.8 cm
Private collection

At first, this might seem to be a photograph of a cat lolling about on an Oriental rug. Look closer and the composition reveals itself: the work is actually, cheekily, a woven textile. Scottish artist Elizabeth Radcliffe (b. 1949) is intent on taking the ancient art form of tapestry into the modern day, particularly in her deployment of three-dimensional imagery into flat-woven panels. A trained artist who specialized in weaving as an undergraduate at Edinburgh College of Art, she spent most of her career as a high school art teacher but returned to her own practice full-time after retirement. Radcliffe's intricate, large-scale weavings often depict the human figure at life-size or details of clothing in shaped silhouette, so that they appear as if they have been cut out from the literal and metaphoric fabric of their surroundings. A man named Marc in plaid pants sitting in an armchair or just the shoulder of Marta wearing a tomato-red sporty jacket are recent examples. Another one of Radcliffe's favored subjects is animals, because she is especially interested in their interior lives, what lies behind their eyes. In this work, Algie the cat stares intently at the viewer, almost accusingly, as if it has just been awakened from a peaceful slumber. Locked into the animal's gaze, it is impossible not to feel a part of the scene. An original voice, Radcliffe pushes the boundaries of what woven art can be and will become.

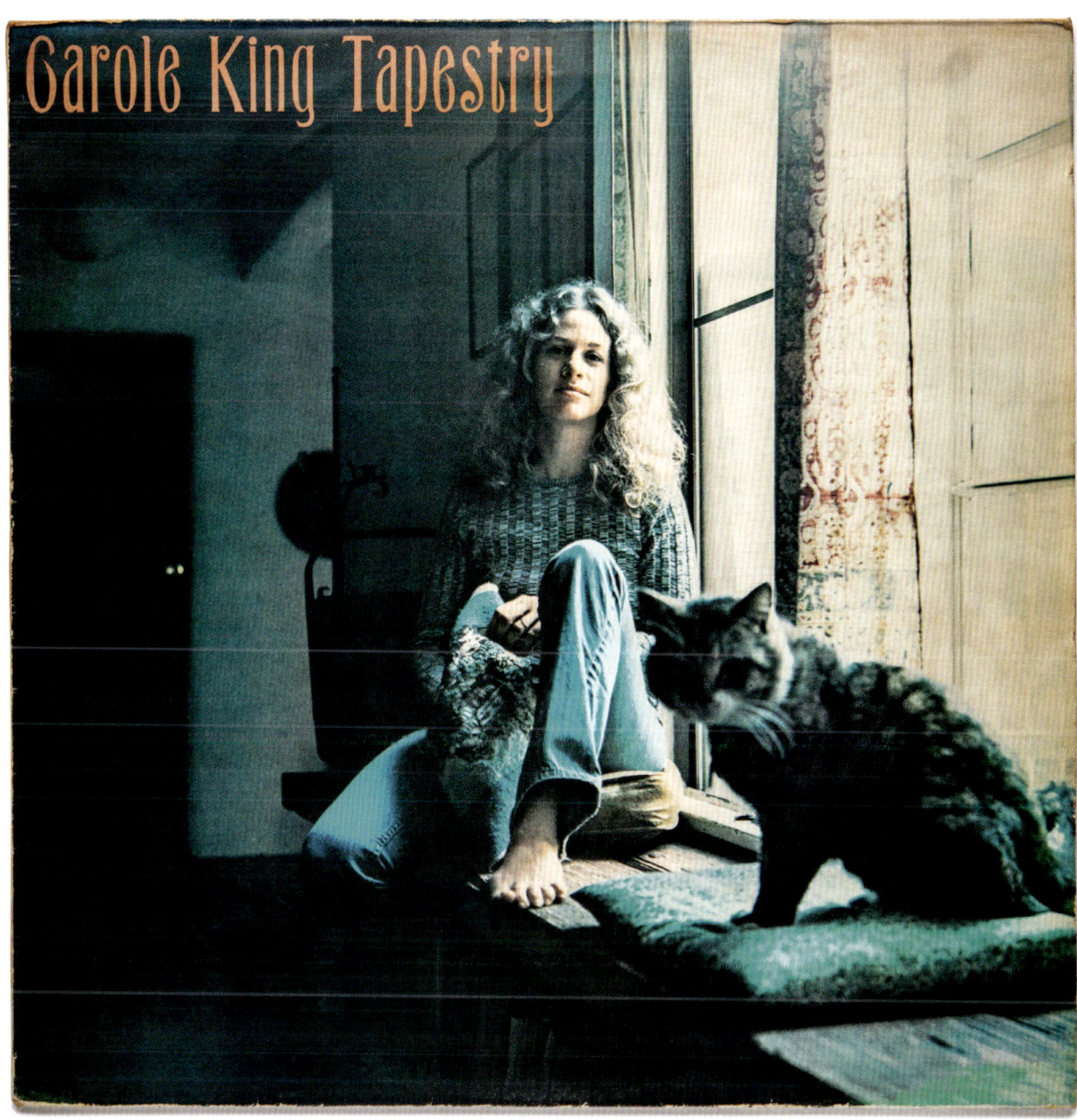

CAROLE KING

Tapestry, 1971
Vinyl record sleeve
12⅜ × 12⅜ in. / 31.4 × 31.4 cm
Photograph by Jim McCrary

An audiophile may not immediately think of cats when listening to *Tapestry*, the seminal 1971 record by American singer-songwriter Carole King (b. 1942), but the album artwork features one of the most iconic feline images in rock 'n' roll. Captured by photographer Jim McCrary, the cover image of King relaxing barefoot in the living room of her Laurel Canyon home became a symbol of the era's new sound. It also happened to feature her tabby cat, Telemachus, sitting next to her and peering out at the listener. McCrary was the chief photographer at King's record label A&M, tasked with shooting album covers, posters, and other music-related ephemera. He came up with the idea for including Telemachus in the images for *Tapestry* after he saw the cat asleep across the room. The sight of the cat reminded him of the results of a Kodak survey that revealed the two most popular subjects people photographed were their children and cats, so he asked the singer if he could include her pet. "I saw a cat," he remembered, "and I wanted to get something good." King liked the idea, so McCrary gently woke up the sleeping tabby and carried him into the frame, capturing him in three images before Telemachus decided he had better things to do. Three shots were enough, and McCrary had just taken what would become his most famous image and one of music's most indelible album covers, all thanks to the sweet presence of Telemachus.

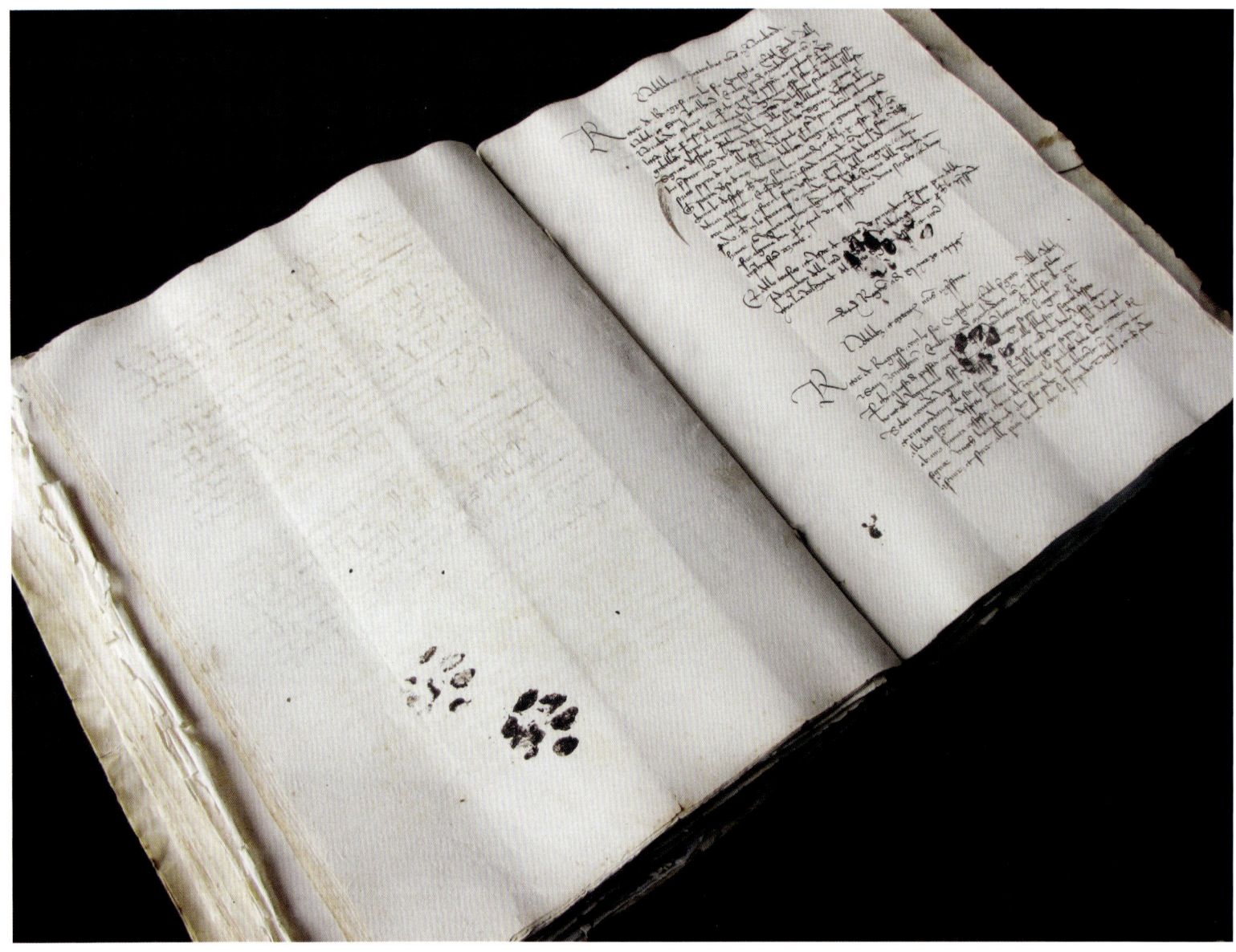

EMIR O. FILIPOVIĆ

Paw prints on a 15th-century manuscript
in the State Archives of Dubrovnik, 2012
Photograph, dimensions variable

The feline habit of nonchalantly walking across computer keyboards, often at the most inconvenient of times, is a familiar frustration for cat owners who work from home. But one can only imagine the sense of panic and indignation felt by the unfortunate fifteenth-century scribe when a cat pounced on his inkwell and traipsed blotchy paw prints across his freshly penned manuscript. The scribe's blemished page from 1445 was discovered in the State Archives of Dubrovnik by Emir O. Filipović, a professor of medieval history at the University of Sarajevo, Bosnia and Herzegovina. Although scribes across time and cultures have employed cats to help protect delicate papers from pests, the familiar shape of a cat's paws was the last thing Filipović expected to see as he waded through the large tome, which contains copies of letters sent to the envoys and merchants of medieval Dubrovnik in southern Croatia. The paw prints had laid hidden for nearly 570 years. Filipović's photograph of his unusual find quickly went viral after it was shared online, and people from around the world started contacting him to enquire about the provenance of the manuscript and other details that they wanted to include in their own posts about the historic paw prints. While the popularity of the image left him surprised, he was pleased that the actions of a medieval cat had inadvertently brought worldwide exposure to Dubrovnik's archives, which are an extraordinarily well-preserved source of information for historians researching life in the medieval Mediterranean.

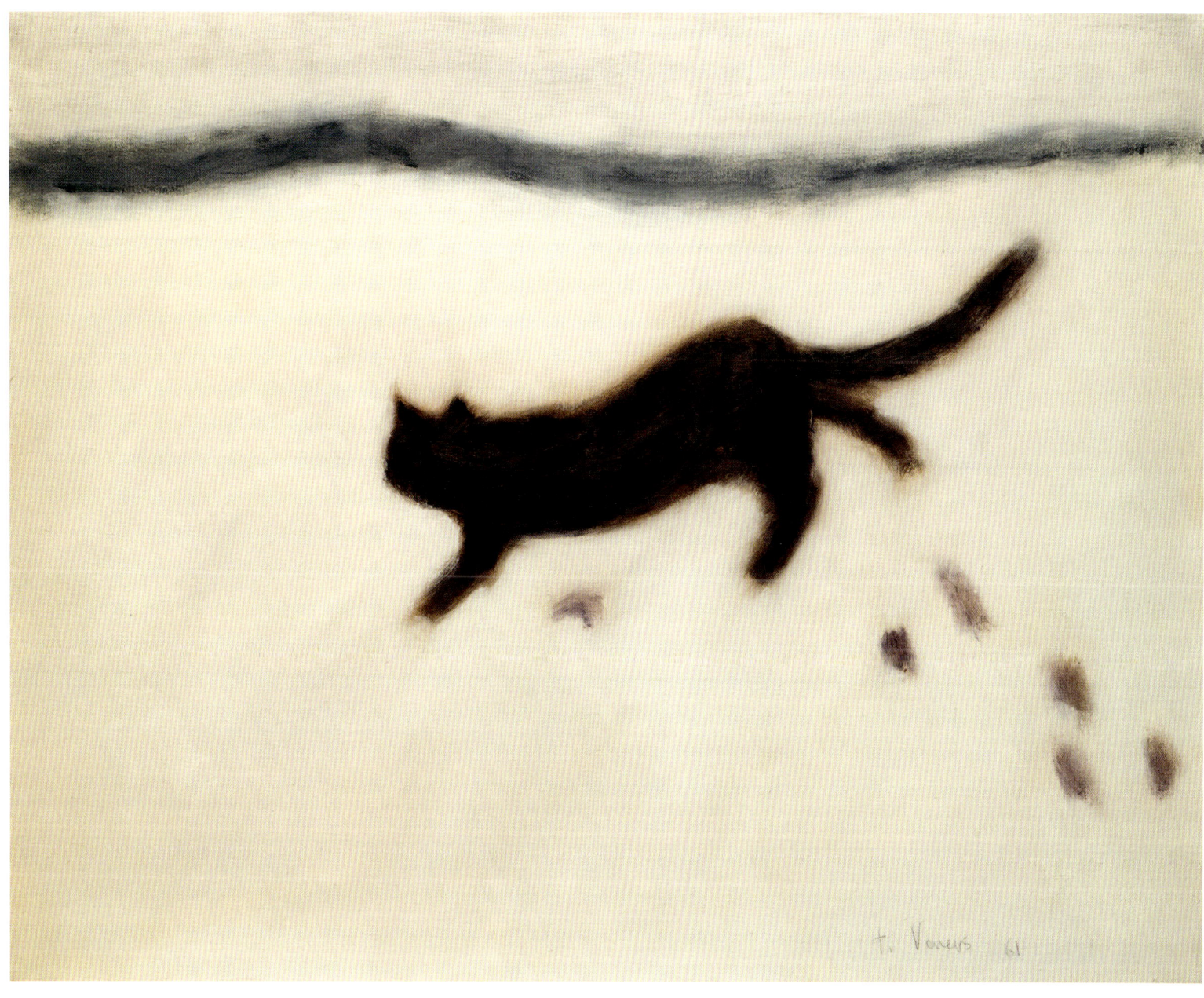

TONY VEVERS

Cat in Snow, 1961
Oil on canvas, 22 × 28⅛ in. / 55.8 × 71.3 cm
Hirshhorn Museum and Sculpture Garden,
Smithsonian, Washington, DC

Against a slightly fuzzy background, a brown cat makes its way across a landscape blanketed in deep snow. A trail of brown smudges in the off-white field of color suggests both the depth of the snow and the direction from which the cat has come in this painting by London-born American artist Tony Vevers (1926–2008). For more than five decades, Vevers was a key figure in the artistic colony that emerged in the Massachusetts seaside village of Provincetown. There, from the middle of the 1950s until the late 1960s, he produced a series of figurative narrative paintings, including *Cat in Snow*, which were in stark contrast to the then fashionable and popular Abstract Expressionism of friends, such as Mark Rothko, Robert Motherwell, and Franz Kline. In Massachusetts, Vevers found an escape from that

New York City art scene. He painted deliberately soft, blurry lines, inspired by his former teacher Hans Hofmann. Nature, particularly the changing seasons of Cape Cod and the Massachusetts coast, featured strongly in his work. The snow here captures the empty silence of the pretty town during the winter months, when the crowds of summer tourists have long since departed. The muted palette—just three colors feature here—suggests a transformed landscape where the only activity is the cat's tentative steps as it pulls its feet out of the deep snow, daintily making its way toward the gray winding line of a small stream.

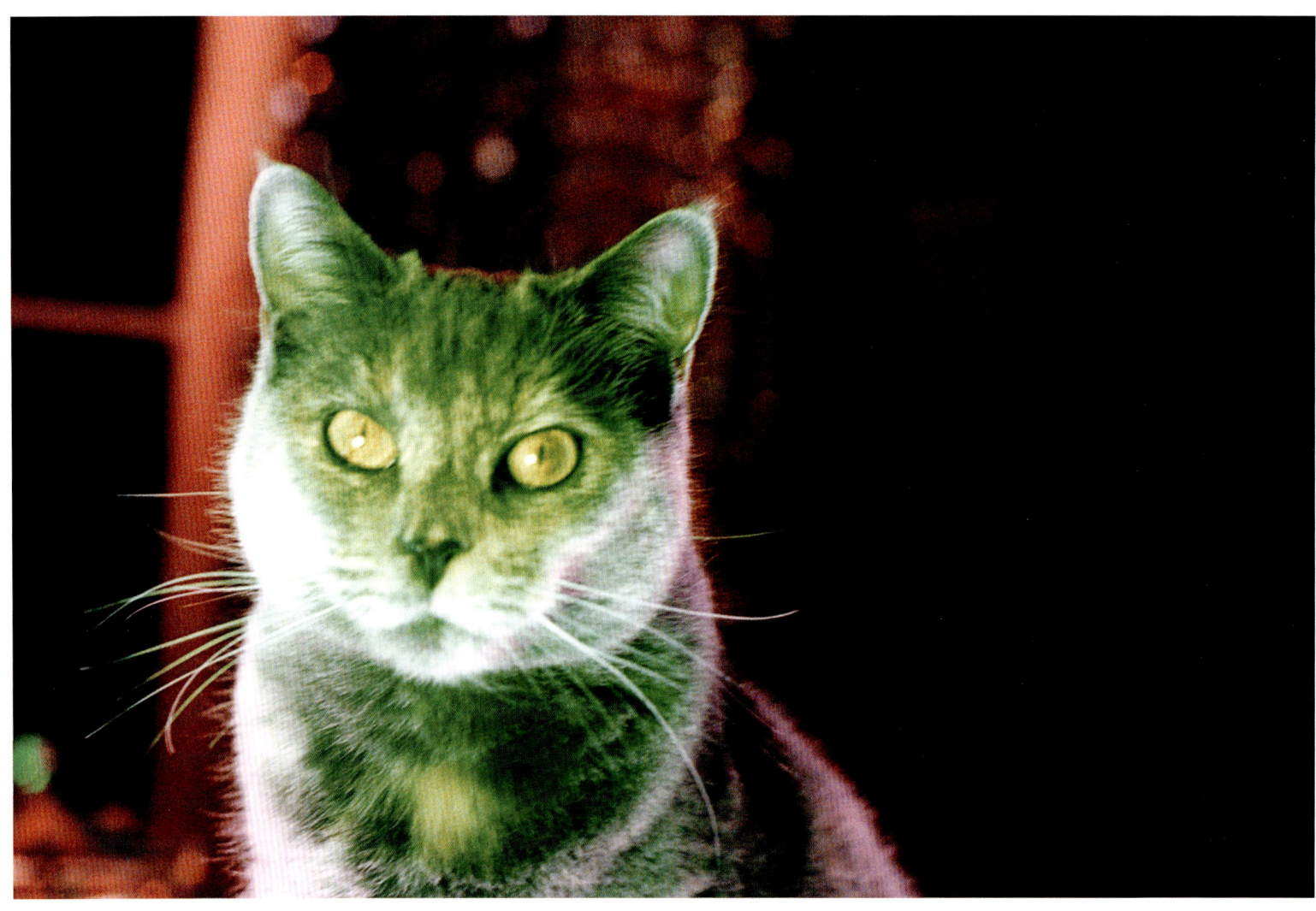

NAN GOLDIN

Electric Gaja, Paris, 2010
Dye sublimation print on aluminum
Dimensions variable
Private collection

When American artist and activist Nan Goldin (b. 1953) brought her cat Gaja home in 2000, she was known for capturing her friends and lovers in frantic, diaristic snapshots in their all-too-human complexities. Her subjects fought, danced, kissed, and stripped, wrestling with love, queerness, addiction, and AIDS, all while making art against the backdrop of a vibrant artistic scene in New York during the 1980s and 1990s. Gaja's arrival coincided, intentionally or not, with a change in Goldin's subject matter, of which this work is a slightly later example. Instead of people, she began to concentrate on landscapes, abstract scenes, and animals, including Gaja herself. In this era, Goldin also started experimenting with a new printing technique, dye sublimation prints on aluminum, which has a

smooth, shiny surface that adds to this image's nearly radioactive glow. Set off against a slightly blurred room with windows bathed in red light, Gaja's eyes are alienesque, her pupils slim black ovals surrounded by an almost neon green. Her fur, greenish brown at the top of her forehead and neck, is white at her mouth and the tips of her eyes, turning pink at the edges of her torso. The colors all mix with the red glow, casting Gaja in a powerful and otherworldly light and presenting her like a deity, as cats have been portrayed since ancient Egypt (see pp.29 and 36). After Gaja died in 2022, Goldin was asked if she would ever have another cat, to which the artist responded, "There's no other cat in the world."

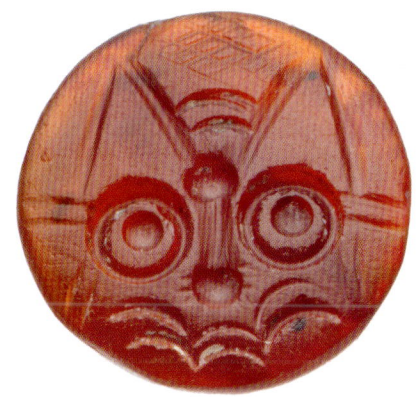

ANONYMOUS

Stamp seal, c. 1900–1600 BCE
Carnelian, ¼ × ⅜ in. / 0.8 × 0.9 cm
Metropolitan Museum of Art, New York

A small disk of carnelian—no bigger than a thumbnail—is carved with the head of a cat, complete with pointed ears, large eyes, and whiskers. The distinctive brownish red-colored stone was used to create this stamp seal as far back as four thousand years ago by an unknown Minoan artist. The Minoan civilization flourished on the island of Crete in the southern Mediterranean Sea from 3000 to 1100 BCE. Easily portable, the disk was used to seal and thus authenticate important documents by pressing it into a soft medium, such as clay or wax. The Minoans' use of such tools was probably inspired by the scarab seals of ancient Egypt, unsurprising given the proximity of Crete to the African coast. It was from Egypt that the cat originated, and the first felines arrived on Crete aboard a trade ship that sailed between the two states, while the island's earliest evidence of domesticated cats dates to between 1800 and 1700 BCE. Historians believe the Minoans were one of the first cultures to decorate their walls for pleasure rather than religious purposes, and cats appeared in frescoes there even before they were displayed on seals. In addition to being used to assert ownership, the seal might also have served, as in ancient Egypt, as a portable amulet or good-luck symbol. A cat's head is even a symbol in the Minoan writing system, its pointy triangular ears standing in for the value "ma." Although the Cretan hieroglyphs have yet to be deciphered and what the cat's head symbol means remains a mystery, "ma" does not seem that far off from "meow."

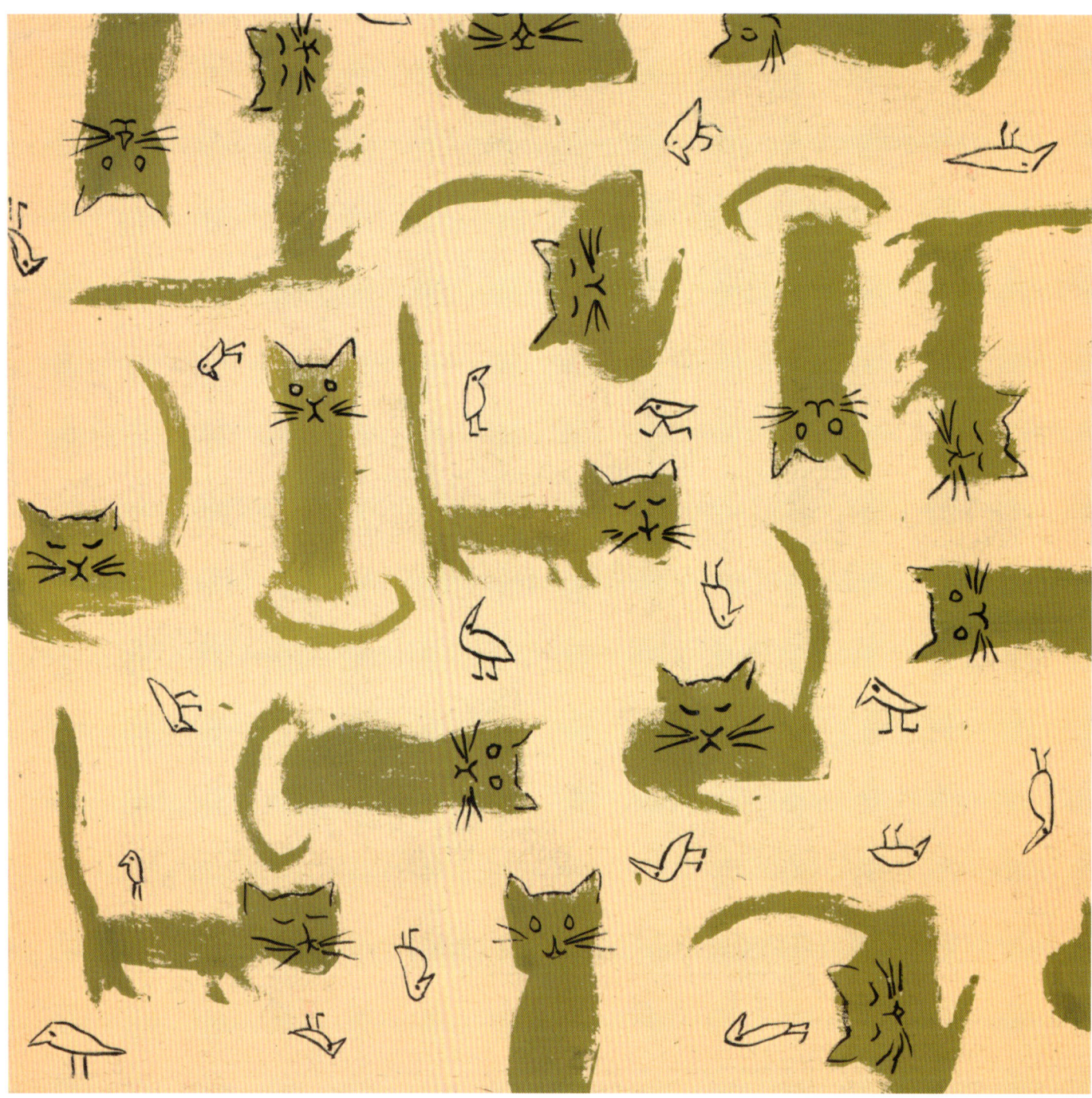

LULU KRALIK

Textile Design: Cats and Birds, 1957
Brush and green, black gouache on beige wove paper
laid down on white wove paper
7¼ × 7⅜ in. / 18.3 × 18.7 cm
Cooper Hewitt, Smithsonian Design Museum, New York

Anyone who has a cat knows all too well the way it behaves when a bird is nearby: tensed, on high alert, ready to pounce at any moment. Not so the cats in American artist Lulu Kralik's mid-century textile design. They appear contented, listless, and grumpy by turns, but not one of them seems to be paying any attention to the birds in this composition. What is more, the birds, for their part, show no inclination toward self-preservation themselves. Instead, the animals form a pleasing mosaic, the spare black linework of the tiny, dynamic birds punctuating the smudged pea greens of the felines' bodies and sharp curvatures of their exaggerated tails. The 1950s were fervent times for industrial design, because factories devoted to the war effort were able to pivot once again to making consumer goods. Innovations in materials and manufacturing processes led to an explosion of creativity, along with a riot of color and pattern for both private and public spaces. Although not much is known about the artist herself, it is clear that Kralik's design is imbued with the exuberance of those boom times, when consumers were eager to shake off the austerity of the war years. The color story and gestural geometry, in particular, are quintessentially atomic. And the pattern's playfulness speaks to the times, happy as a cat that does not need to go hunting for its dinner.

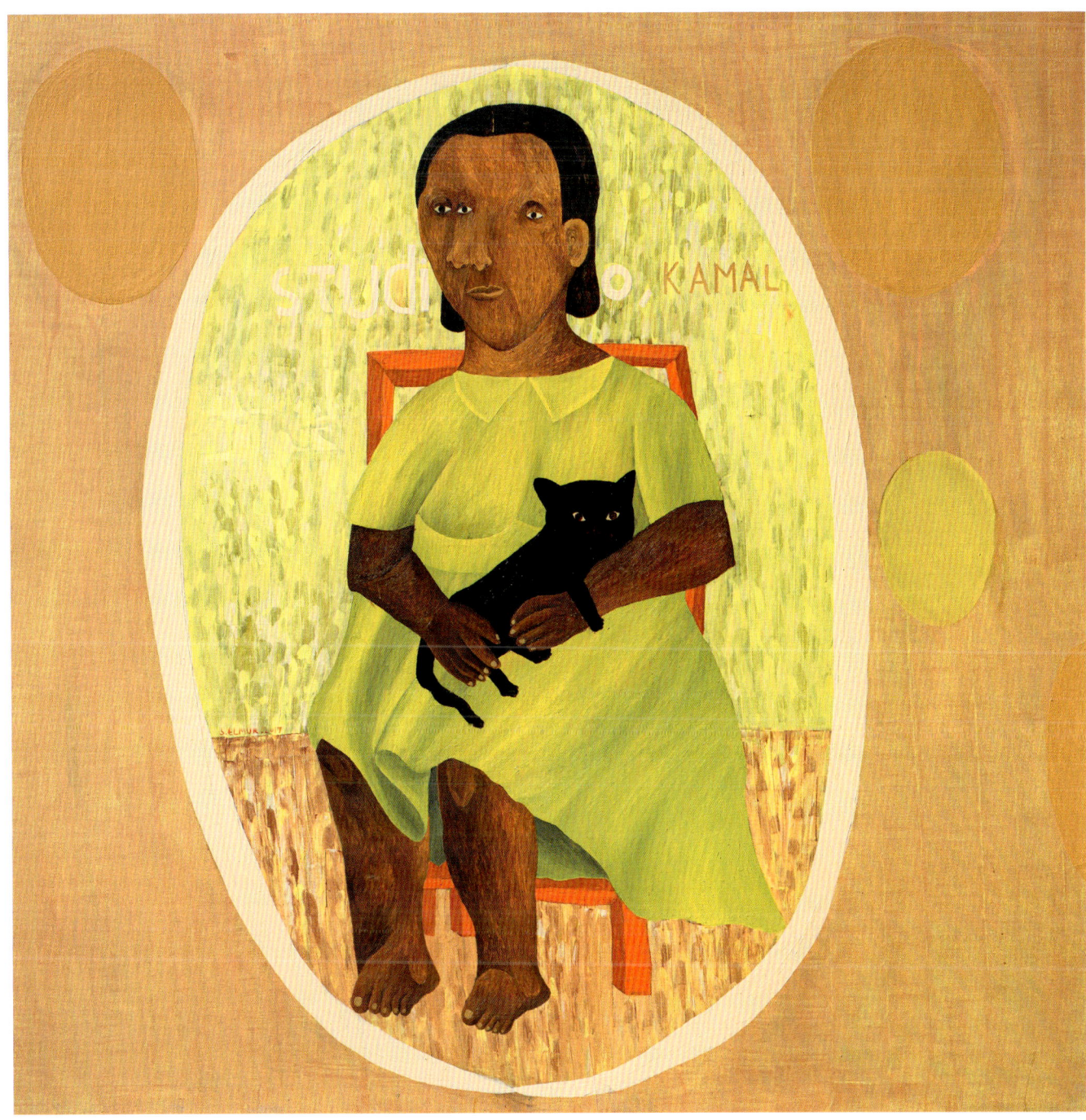

SALAH ELMUR

With the Wild Cat, 2017
Acrylic on canvas
72⅞ × 72⅞ in. / 185 × 185 cm
Private collection

If the black cat on the lap of the young woman really is wild, as the title of this painting suggests, it must be being held tightly to stop it from escaping. In fact, the scene is comfortably tame. Wearing a short-sleeved chartreuse dress, with bare feet, the sitter snuggles her animal companion as it stares contentedly into the distance. A work by Sudanese artist and filmmaker Salah Elmur (b. 1966), the painting mixes figurative abstraction with themes of familial intimacy, reflecting Elmur's inspiration from his upbringing in a family of fishermen near the Blue Nile River in Khartoum. A pioneering member of the Khartoum School, Elmur infuses his paintings with nostalgia for 1960s Sudanese portrait photography, hence the frequently bold colors, which are a conscious reminder of the strength of the sun and the colorful clothes worn by the people in Sudan. In his portraits, Elmur is not concerned with capturing the precise likeness of his sitters. Instead, they are distorted—this young woman has three eyes—and they are rarely alone, often accompanied by pets or other people. Cats appear regularly in the artist's work, as a reminder of his childhood and family life. Following a military coup in Sudan in 1989, Elmur fled first to Nairobi, Kenya, then to Cairo, Egypt, where he now lives and works, making frequent trips to his native country but relying on his portraits to relive the Sudan of his youth.

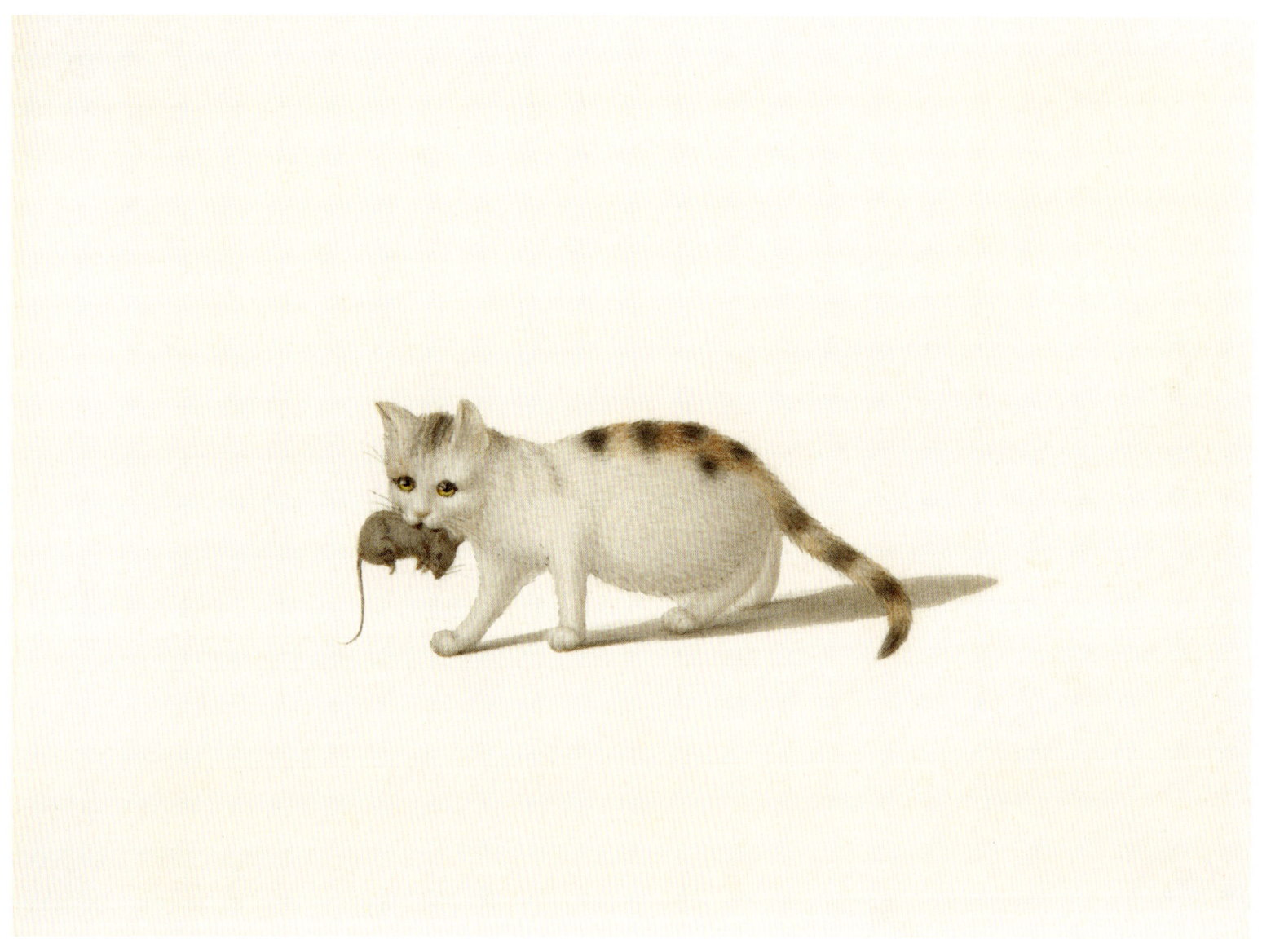

GOTTFRIED MIND

Katzen, c. 1800–14
Watercolor on paper, 3⅛ × 4⅜ in. / 8 × 11 cm
Swiss National Library, Bern

Set against a clean white background, a young cat with an expression of innocence grasps a freshly caught rodent between its jaws. This skillfully rendered watercolor by Gottfried Mind (1768–1814) demonstrates the Swiss artist's masterful observation of feline behavior and anatomy, which earned him the nickname "The Raphael of Cats." Mind was born in Bern and, as a child, was described as having "a weak constitution." He struggled with formal education and, due to severe learning difficulties, was cruelly labeled as a "cretin" and "imbecile." Yet, his savantlike artistic abilities won him an apprenticeship with Sigmund Freudenberger, a Swiss artist well known for his depictions of peasant life. After Freudenberger's death, Mind began creating his own watercolor paintings and prints, primarily of animals, with cats becoming his best-known subject. Celebrated for their realism and fine draftsmanship, his pictures portray his favorite creatures doing everything cats do, such as lounging, hunting, arching their backs, and cleaning themselves. Mind's biographer, the English collector George Fairholme, reported that the artist regularly worked with a cat curled up on his lap or shoulder, and, although he gained recognition across Europe, he lived in poverty. His cat drawings remained popular for decades after his death, influencing a generation of French artists in the nineteenth century after the art critic and novelist Champfleury included several in his 1869 illustrated book *Les Chats*, a series of essays about cats in culture.

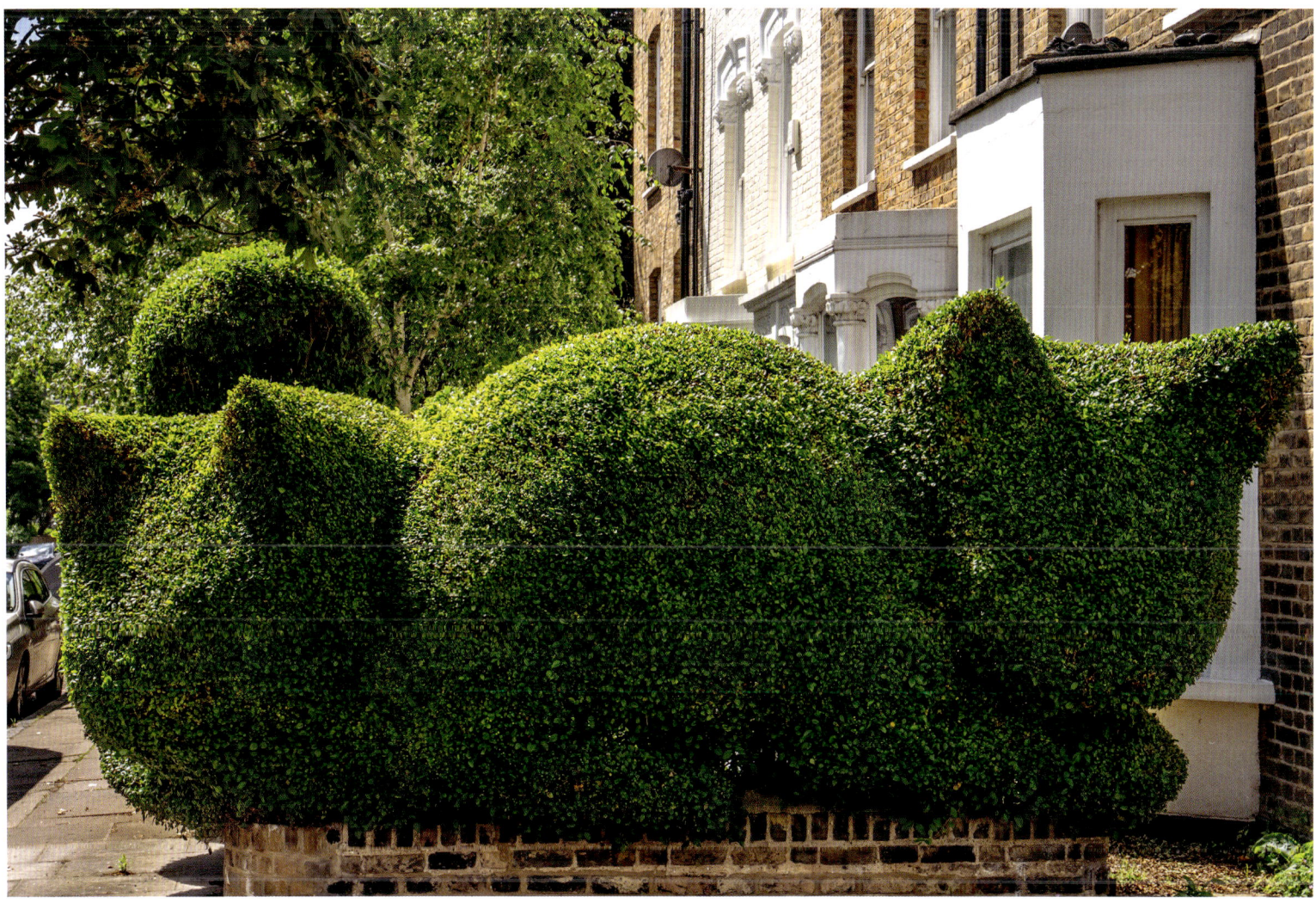

TIM BUSHE

Cats sculpted from a hedge, London, 2024
Photograph by Andrew Testa

There is nothing remarkable about two dozing cats happily nestled together, but when they are sculpted from a hedge in a leafy north London suburb, they become a local talking point. This eye-catching topiary was created by Tim Bushe, an architect of more than thirty years who, in 2011, turned his hand to sculpting bushes after his wife requested that he cut the hedge outside their terraced home into the shape of a cat. To his wife's disappointment, he instead sculpted a locomotive but, as his confidence with the electric trimmer grew, he soon progressed to felines. Bushe's topiary creations delighted his neighbors, who began commissioning him to transform their own privet hedges. He is now a master of the medium and, besides cats, he has cut elephants, fish, hippos, squirrels, dragons, and even a reclining nude inspired by the sculptures of Henry Moore, all of which are located in front yards and other suburban locations. It can take three to four years for his sculptures to properly form their shape, and each one requires regular maintenance. The business of hedge-cutting can therefore be a lucrative one, although Bushe donates all of his earnings to charity, including a Down syndrome organization that cares for his sister. Bushe's cat-loving wife, Philippa, died from cancer in 2017; the shaped hedges, which brought great joy and happiness to her and to local communities across north London, stand as her legacy.

61

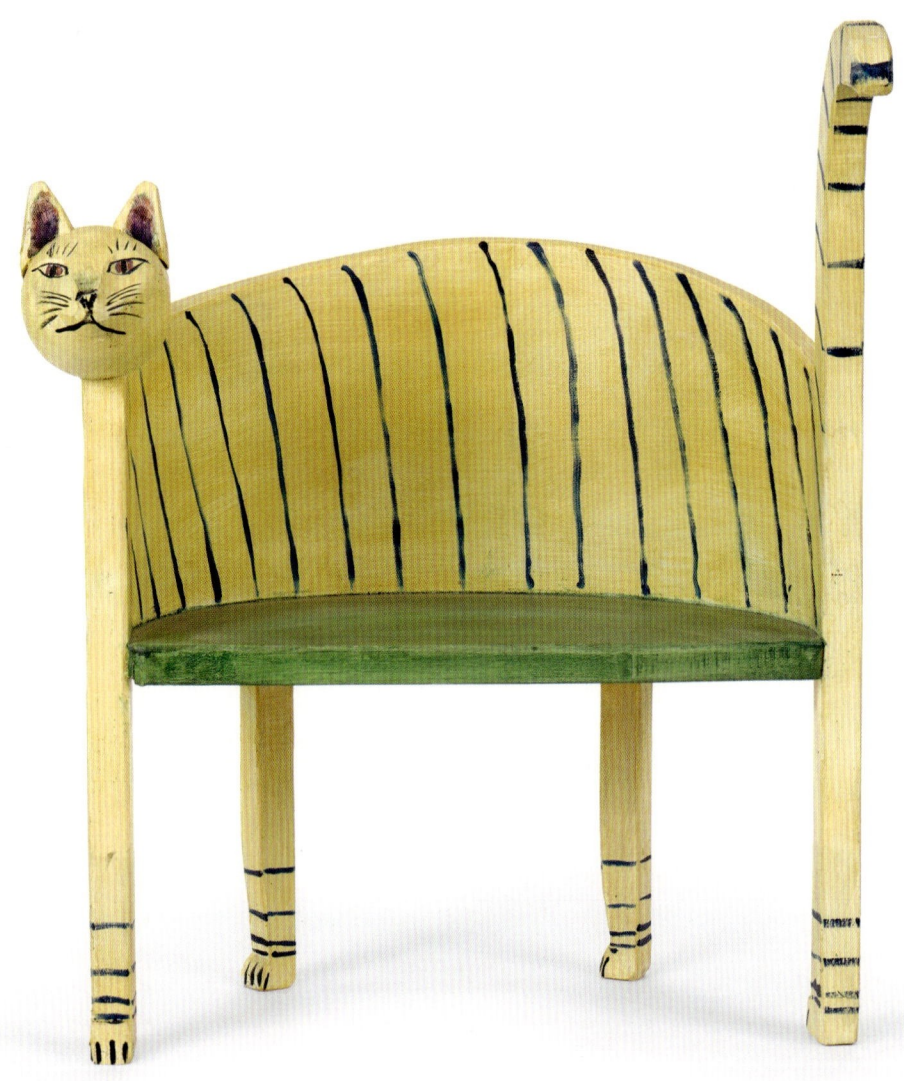

GÉRARD RIGOT

Animeubles Child's Chair, 1980s
Softwood, probably pine, alder, ash, birch,
or hornbeam, painted in oils
25⅝ × 18⅞ × 13⅜ in. / 65 × 48 × 34 cm
Victoria and Albert Museum, London

This quirky children's chair playfully reimagines the concept of a lap cat with its inviting green seat set within a yellow, feline-themed frame. It is part of an extensive collection of zoomorphic furniture pieces created in the 1980s and 1990s by French artist Gérard Rigot (b. 1929), known as *animeubles*. Rigot hand-carved each work from wood—sometimes incorporating papier-mâché—and painted it in a naive, expressive style. The artisan sculpted his forms in such a way that he captured the grace, charm, and agility of his favorite creatures. A cat-shaped chair is believed to be Rigot's first design in the form of an animal, lovingly made in his Toulouse home for his daughter, Marie, and inspired by his own farmhouse cat. It marked the beginning of a whimsical menagerie of silhouettes, which

include a dragonfly table, a pair of tiger benches, a hippopotamus chest, and a flamingo dresser. Notable chair designs from the collection also include an adult-size curving seat shaped like a sleek whippet and a throne inspired by the plumage of a peacock. Rigot's bold and imaginative use of color often deviated from naturalistic tones, favoring creativity over realism. For example, a toy box shaped like a standing sheep was painted in acid green and yellow. His use of vibrant hues was influenced by the vivid landscapes and colors of Algeria, where he once worked as a teacher. The result is a joyful collection of fantasy furniture that looks like it has wandered straight out of a storybook.

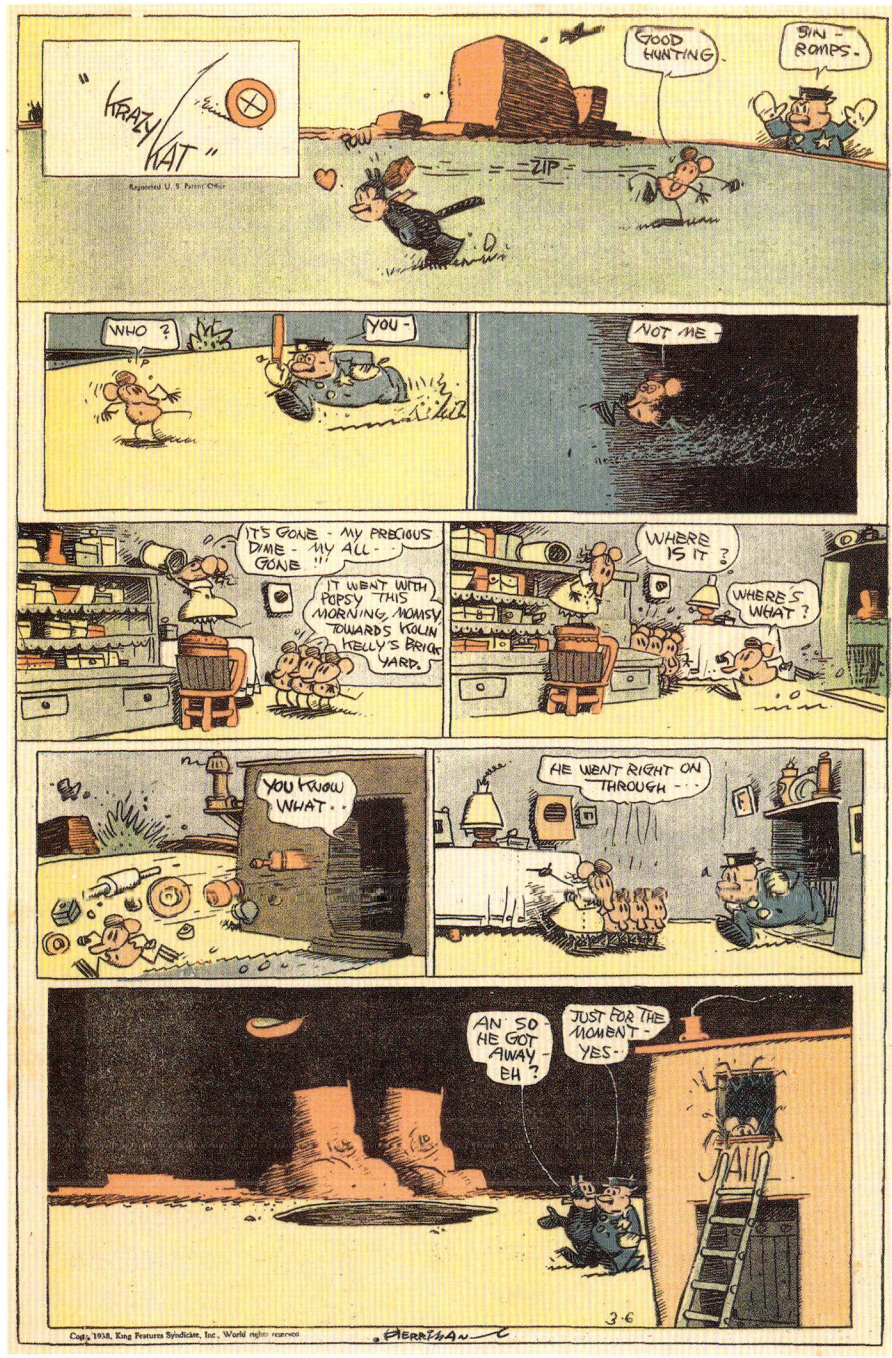

GEORGE HERRIMAN

Krazy Kat, March 6, 1938
Comic strip, 20 × 17 in. / 50.8 × 43.2 cm

"Pow." A brick thrown by a short-tempered mouse named Ignatz flies through the air and smacks Krazy Kat square on the back of the head, sending him plummeting to the ground. Yet, instead of an angry response, a small heart appears above the cat's head. Krazy perceives Ignatz's sustained campaign of violence as a declaration of love—a view not shared by the law-enforcing bulldog Officer Pupp, who attempts to arrest the mouse after each attack. This is the basic premise of every *Krazy Kat* comic strip, which was created by American cartoonist George Herriman (1880–1944) in the early 1910s and first appeared in black and white in the *New York Evening Journal*. By 1935, the strip was published in color across the United States, filling entire pages of the Sunday newspapers owned by American media magnate William Randolph Hearst. The violent action is set in a fictional and somewhat surreal version of Coconino County, Arizona, complete with dusty landscapes, adobe buildings, and distant mesas. Here, an unlikely love triangle unfolds as Krazy's unrequited love for Ignatz is mirrored by Pupp's own affections for the "heppy go lucky kat." In addition to its zany slapstick, the strip is known for dense wordplay, wry commentary, and Krazy's thick dialect, which readers must carefully decipher. A dark satire of abusive relationships, *Krazy Kat* is widely considered to be among the greatest American newspaper strips of all time, with many subsequent cartoonists citing it as an influence.

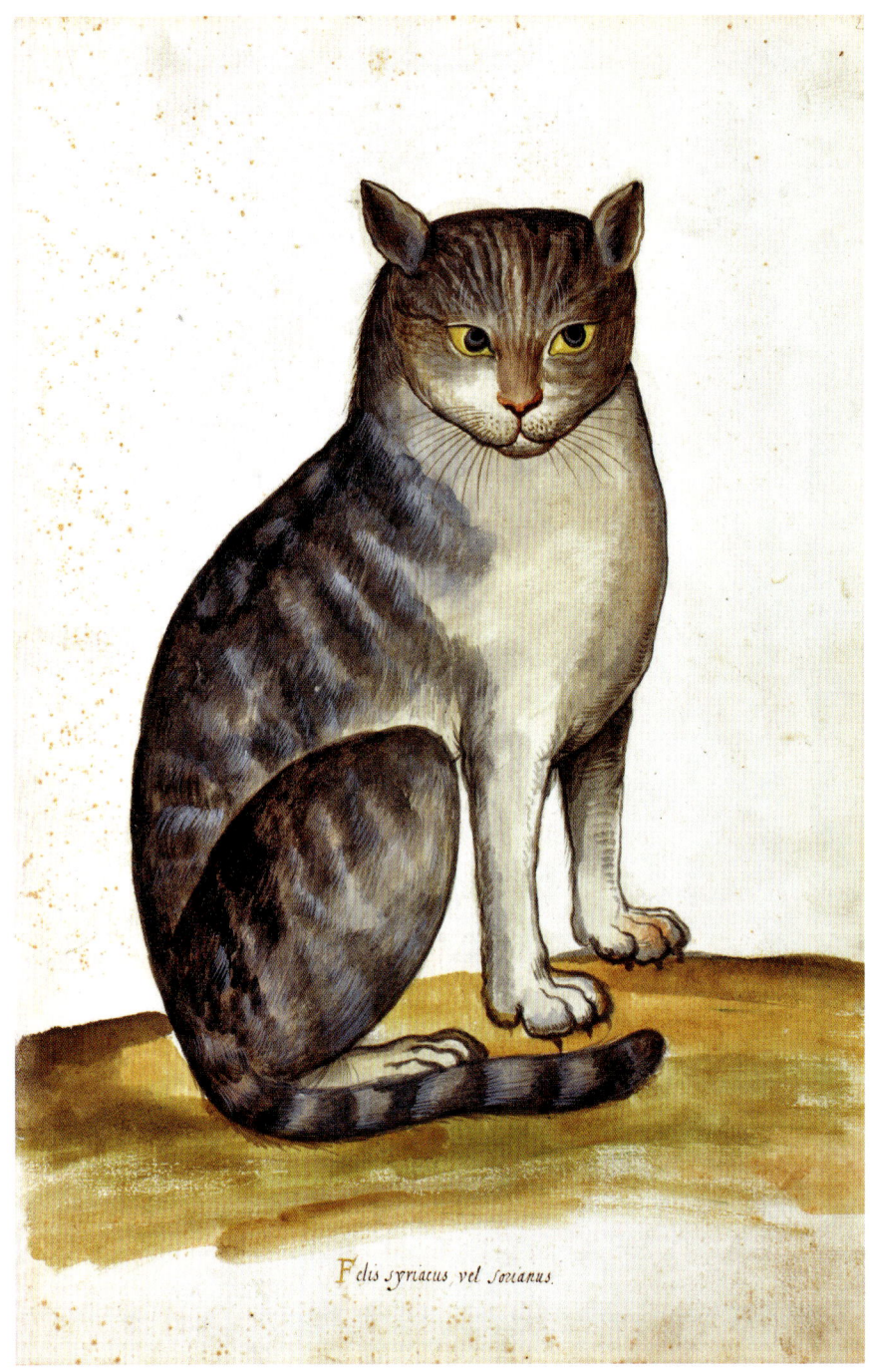

Felis syriacus vel sorianus.

ULISSE ALDROVANDI

Felis Syriacus (Plate 15), from *Tavole di animali*, vol. 5, c. 1603
Engraving, H. 14⅛ in. / 36 cm
University of Bologna Library, Italy

A stalwart tabby stares down the viewer in this manuscript illustration from the Italian Renaissance. The text at the bottom helpfully identifies this fearsome feline as *Felis syriacus vel sorianus*, or a "Syrian cat," which is how Western Europeans referred to striped cats during this period, because they were often imported from Damascus. The word "tabby" itself did not come into use until the end of the eighteenth century, thanks to increased textile trade with the Muslim world; it probably stems from the Arabic *al-'Attābiyya*, a district in Baghdad known for its striped silk fabrics. Although "tabby" is the more common way to refer to this familiar coat pattern today, *soriano* remains the translation for "tabby" in modern Italian. This image was included in a twelve-volume encyclopedia of natural history by Italian Renaissance polymath and academic Ulisse Aldrovandi (1522–1605), dubbed the father of natural history by Carl Linnaeus. Aldrovandi dedicated his later career to classifying and studying the natural world, collecting mineral, vegetable, and animal specimens to create a "microcosm of nature" at the University of Bologna, where, in 1568, he founded one of the world's first botanical gardens. Aldrovandi received financial support from Pope Gregory XIII to publish the results of his studies in his encyclopedia, with specimens illustrated by local artists and engravers. The encyclopedia was considered the most comprehensive of its day, including not just this tabby and the black cat (*Catus niger*) but also more exotic species, such as crocodiles and puffer fish.

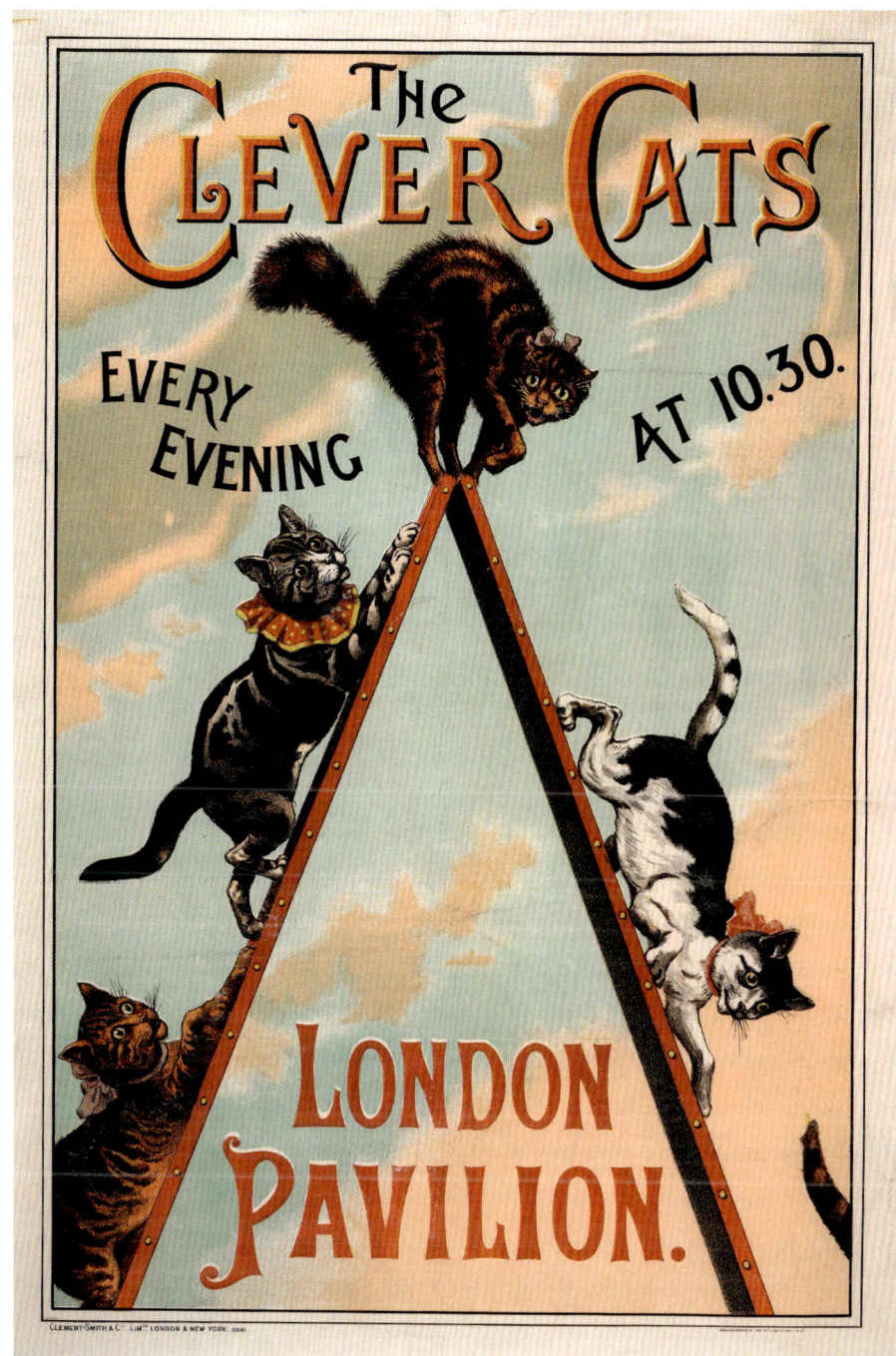

ANONYMOUS

The Clever Cats, 1888
Poster, 30 × 20 in. / 76.2 × 50.8 cm
British Library, London

Frolicking felines dexterously climb a circus ladder in this Victorian poster for what promises to be an entertaining show. Cats of all colors, decorated with fanciful collars and ribbons, are so high up they appear at the same height as cotton-candy clouds. After the explosion of Cat Fancy showcases at London's Crystal Palace (see p.208) in late nineteenth-century England, other kinds of feline performances became popular forms of mass entertainment, such as the tricks and flips of these "clever cats" at the London Pavilion in Piccadilly. This poster comes from the Evanion Collection at the British Library, a compendium of almost five thousand items of Victorian ephemera related to popular entertainments and pantomimes in variety theaters, circuses, and music halls, as well as advertisements, tickets,

and catalogs. Evanion was the stage name of Henry Evans, also known as "The Royal Conjuror," a ventriloquist and entertainer who sold his vast collection to the library in 1895. His archive was so passionately collected that, when the magician Harry Houdini first saw it, he said he felt "dazzled by a sudden shower of diamonds." *The Clever Cats* poster was not the only feline-related ephemera in Evanion's possession; he also collected countless advertisements related to performances of *Dick Whittington and His Cat* and *Puss in Boots* (see pp.44 and 94), two of the most popular pantomimes of the era. Although *The Clever Cats* promises a fun night out, it is hard to imagine any cat voluntarily performing tricks for a raucous crowd.

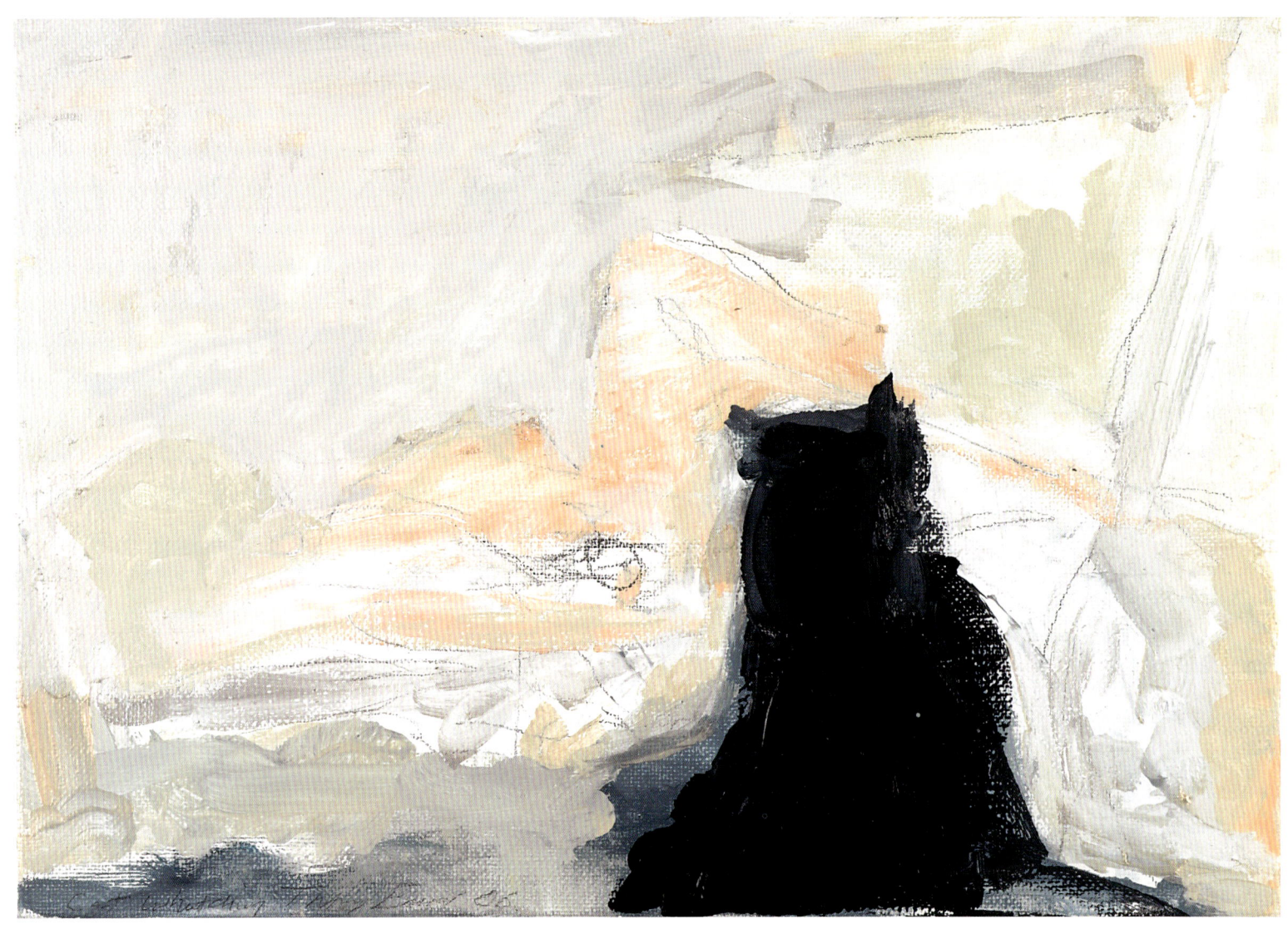

TRACEY EMIN

Cat whatching, 2006
Acrylic and pencil on canvas
8¼ × 11¾ in. / 20.8 × 29.7 cm
Private collection

A black cat is watching something, but what exactly? In this painting by British artist Tracey Emin (b. 1963), the shadowy cat sits motionless, seemingly transfixed as it watches, or maybe it is being watched by its human owner. Emin's reputation has been forged largely by her examination of the female body, and she has interrogated what it means to be a woman through diverse, sometimes sexually provocative works since the 1980s, from paintings and quilts to installations and neon signage. But cats have also played a significant role in her life and oeuvre. Emin paints and sculpts cats, because, as she says, "I really love animals. My cat is my little soulmate, he's not just a cat, he's my friend." Her beloved pet Docket—a gift from her then partner, the artist Mat Collishaw—was one of the loves of her life alongside

her art. For more than nineteen years, Docket was her muse and her constant companion. Both artist and cat made international headlines when Docket went missing from her East London home in 2002. Emin put posters of the lost gray-and-white cat on lampposts across her neighborhood, but many were removed by passersby who thought the pieces were works of art, selling them for prices reportedly as high as £500. Docket was fortunately found safe after a week. In 2022, two new cats, Teacup and Pancake, came into the artist's life. As with Docket, Emin continues to immortalize them in sculpture and painting.

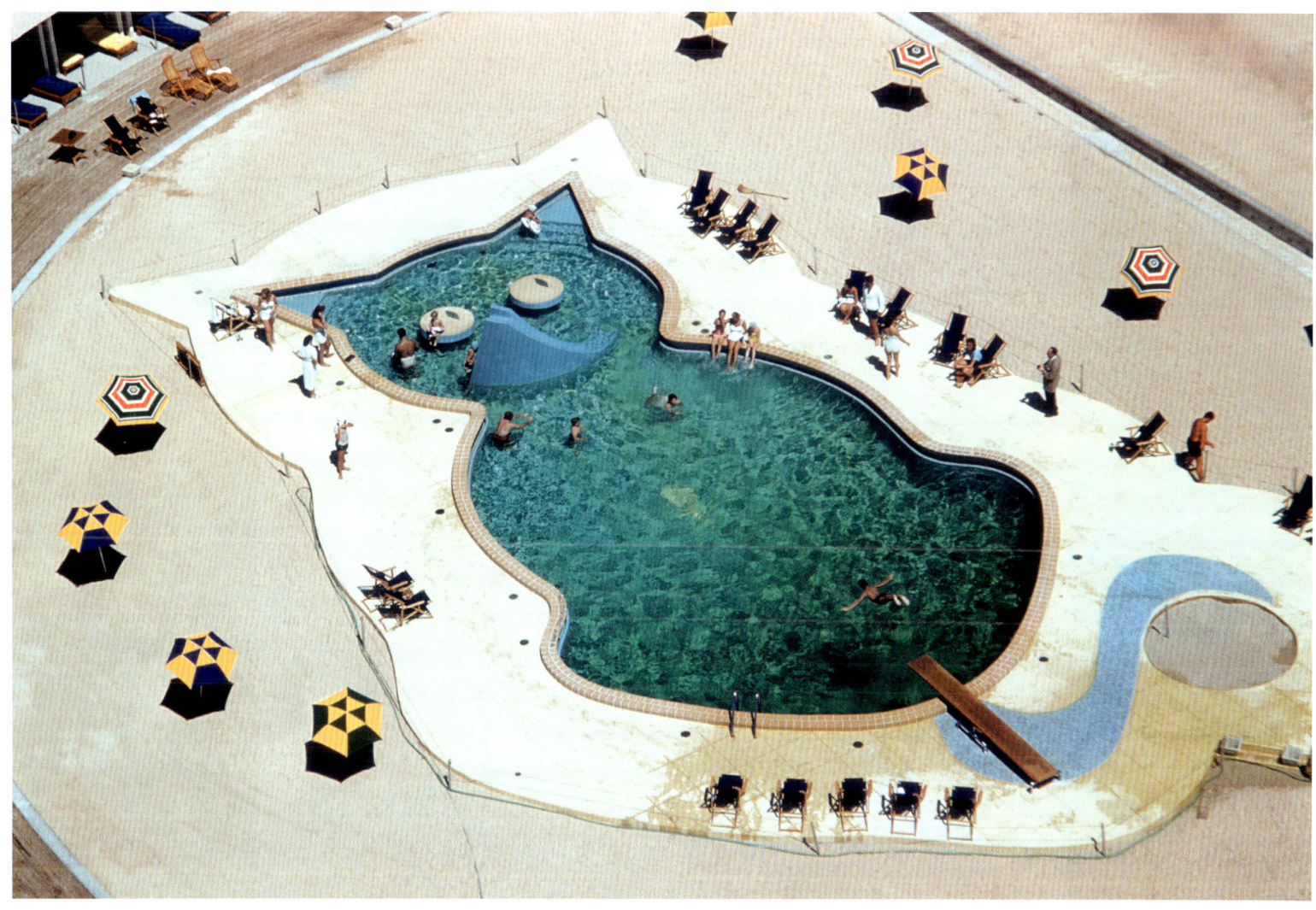

SLIM AARONS

Cat-Shaped Pool, c. 1955
C-print, dimensions variable

Cats might be afraid of water, but this feline-shaped pool at Miami's iconic Fontainebleau Hotel captured by American photographer George "Slim" Aarons (1916–2006) is an aquatic paradise. A fixture of glossy magazines from the 1960s to the 1990s, Aarons chronicled the lives of the post–World War II elite. His camera captured them all, from bohemian artists and celebrities to socialites and politicians for magazines such as *Life* and *Town & Country*. After years of loss and violence during his wartime army service, Aarons swore off those themes in his work, favoring, as he frequently said, "attractive people who were doing attractive things in attractive places." His saturated, sun-drenched photographs exude ease and leisure. Eschewing flash photography and utilizing available light, his frames

are filled with palm trees, sparkling blue pools, colorful dresses, and sharp suits. He also photographed animals, from the exotic ones usually seen in zoos to pampered pets. A different kind of animal, this pool, with its pointy triangle ears and little stone islanders in place of cat eyes, comprised a major part of the Fontainebleau's Miami Modernist architecture. This style often includes playful, nautical details, such as porthole windows; bright, bold colors; and asymmetrical facades constructed out of materials that include concrete and glass. Although the cat shape may have been hard to appreciate while swimming, Aarons's innovative aerial snap reveals the full feline effect, allowing the viewer to enjoy the cool cat's blue waters by proxy.

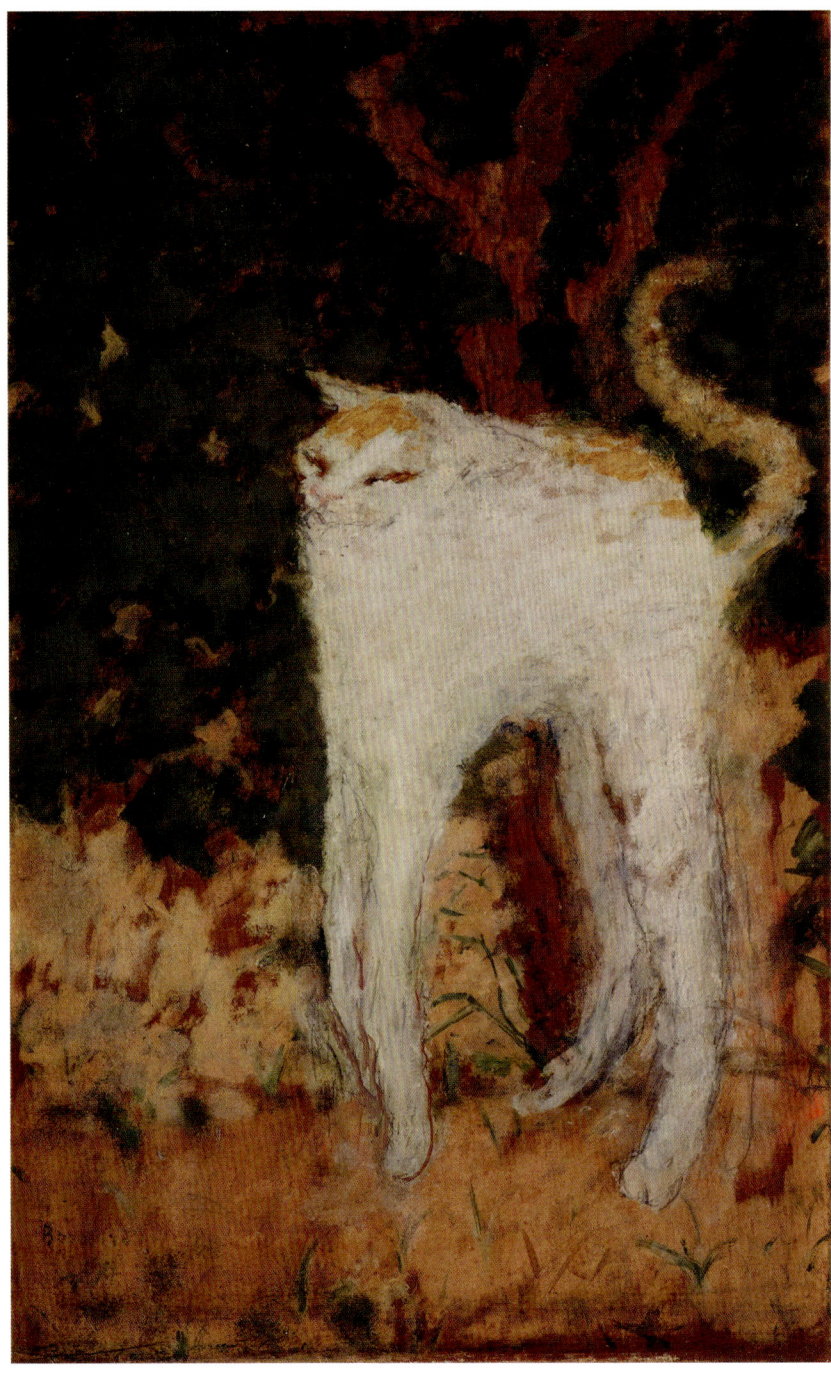

PIERRE BONNARD

The White Cat, 1894
Oil on board, 20⅜ × 13⅛ in. / 51.9 × 33.5 cm
Musée d'Orsay, Paris

Cats often hide in the works of French painter Pierre Bonnard (1867–1947), revealing themselves only after long observation. This is definitely not the case for *The White Cat*, a somewhat eccentric painting by the Post-Impressionist. Here, the cat is the subject in its own right, occupying almost the entire surface of the unquestionably vertical painting. Against a tree with twisted branches that echo the animal's sinuous tail, the feline stands with oversize paws. The artist's aim is not realism, but expression: he accentuates the cat's elongated legs stretching out and eyelids wrinkled with joy, giving an impression of bliss and slightly mannered refinement. These are key characteristics of this elegant animal, whose leg shape gives the impression that it is always walking on tiptoe, as ethereal as a dancer. Early in Bonnard's career in the 1890s, he was a member of The Nabis (Hebrew and Arabic for "prophet") artist group, along with Maurice Denis, Félix Vallotton (see p.166), Édouard Vuillard, and others, who decompartmentalized the arts, practicing painting as well as photography and graphic and decorative arts. Within the group, Bonnard was nicknamed the *nabi très japonard* (the very Japanese *nabi*), because his art was so influenced by Japanese prints. The elongated, highly stylized format of *The White Cat* and its winding lines with no illusionist perspective is indicative of this influence. As in the feline Japanese prints that inspired him, cats feature prominently in Bonnard's work: to him, they were the joyful and sensual companions of intimacy and everyday life.

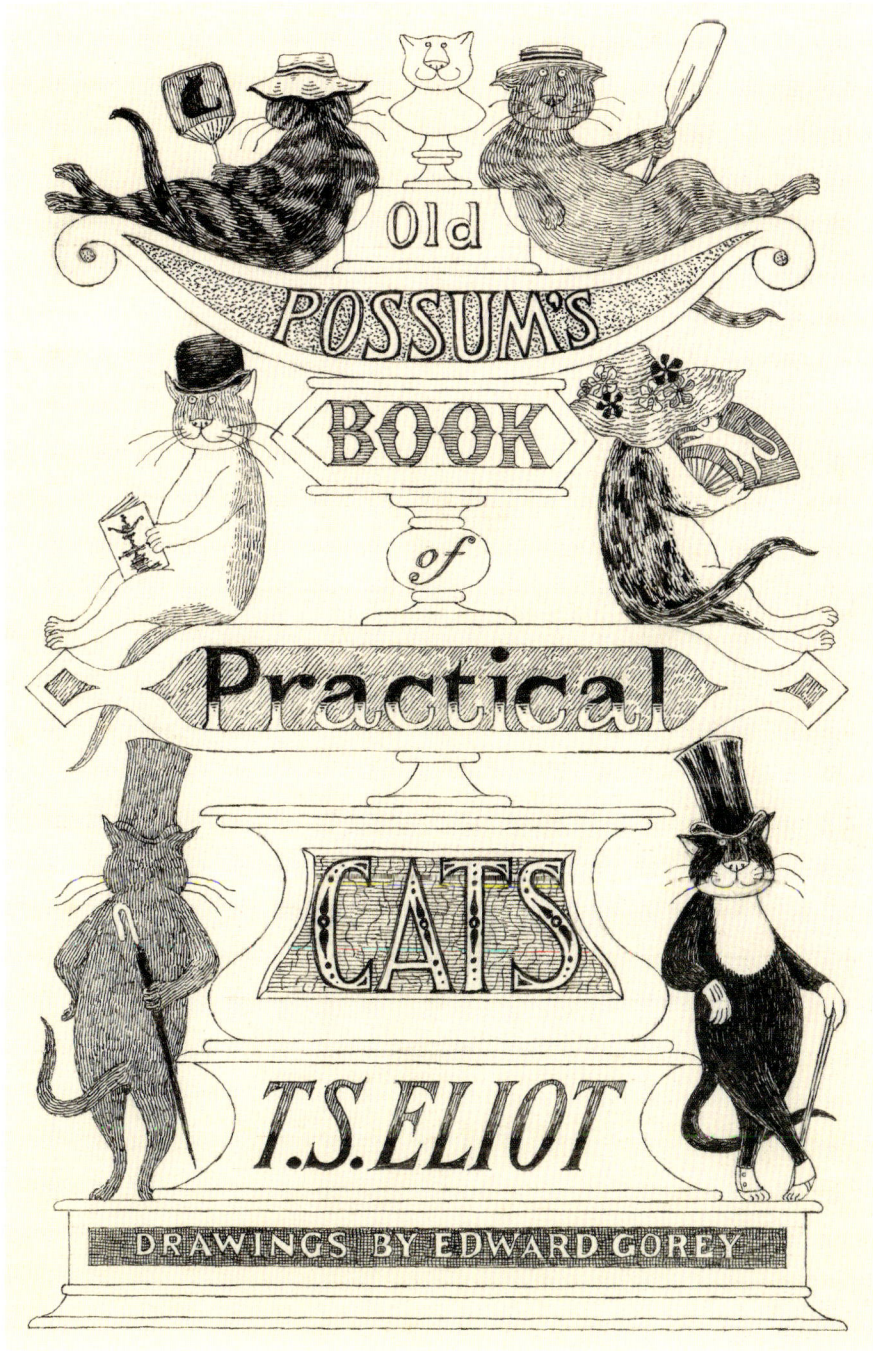

EDWARD GOREY
AND T.S. ELIOT

Old Possum's Book of Practical Cats, 1982
Original cover art for printed book
8 × 5¾ in. / 20.3 × 14.7 cm

The retro feel of this cover of *Old Possum's Book of Practical Cats* encapsulates the creative minds of three major cat lovers across time. This new edition of humorous poems by writer T.S. Eliot (1888–1965) was illustrated by American artist Edward Gorey (1925–2000), who succeeded in capturing the sheer fantastical silliness of the original verses in his whimsical black-and-white portraits of various felines, from Macavity the Mystery Cat to the Jellicles, which he drew as slightly crazy, nocturnal jumping creatures. Gorey was known for his eccentric Victorian- and Edwardian-inspired illustrations, especially owing a debt to another notable feline supporter, Edward Lear, the nineteenth-century caricaturist and writer. Fixated with the simultaneous darkness and playfulness inherent to cats, Gorey loved

the animals, having always owned at least one since childhood. First published in 1939, Eliot's poems were a surprising departure for the "serious poet," who was best known for his epic modernist poem *The Waste Land*, but Eliot himself was a confirmed cat lover. He originally wrote his nonsensical verses of feline psychology and social order during the 1930s as a series of letters to his godchildren, signing himself as "Old Possum." The publication of this new edition followed the 1981 adaptation of the book into the musical *Cats* (see p.38). The theater production created a newfound popularity for *Old Possum*, which, although commercially successful, had initially been criticized as a creative failure but is now a beloved example of cats in culture.

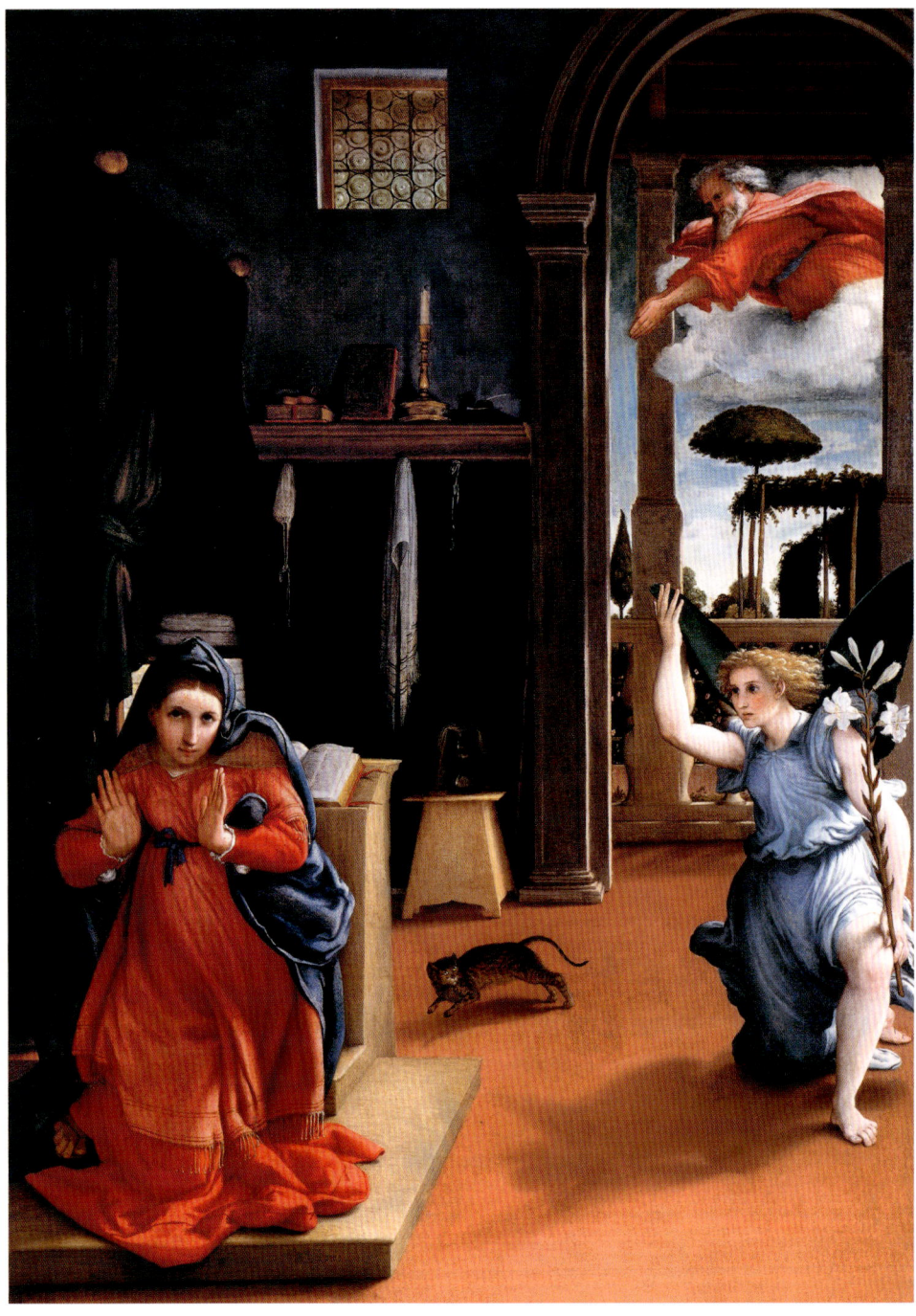

LORENZO LOTTO

Recanati Annunciation, c. 1534
Oil on canvas, 65 × 45 in. / 166 × 114 cm
Villa Colloredo Mels, Recanati, Italy

A startled cat flees in terror at the sight of the archangel Gabriel, who has supernaturally materialized in the Virgin Mary's bedchamber to announce that she has been chosen to be the mother of Jesus Christ, the Son of God. The *Recanati Annunciation*, painted by Lorenzo Lotto (1480–1556), is one of the Italian Renaissance master's most renowned works, celebrated for its innovative treatment of a traditional theme. Originally executed for the oratory of the church of Santa Maria sopra Mercanti in Recanati, a commune in the eastern region of Marche, where it remained until 1953, the painting is set in an orderly bedroom and captures a quiet moment of domestic life shattered by a divine intervention. Unlike in conventional Annunciation scenes, Mary, distracted from her devotions, turns away from Gabriel, gazing directly at the viewer with an expression of shock and her hands raised. In the top right of the composition, floating on a cloud, God the Father stretches his hands toward the Virgin, bestowing his favor upon her. Outside, a well-kept garden, with a large white lily held by the kneeling archangel, alludes to Mary's virginal purity. The inclusion of a frightened cat with its back arched is highly unusual; there is no mention of a cat in the Gospel of Luke from which this story originates, nor, indeed, are cats found anywhere in the Bible. Its ambiguous presence here is probably a symbol of evil that cannot endure the holy presence of God.

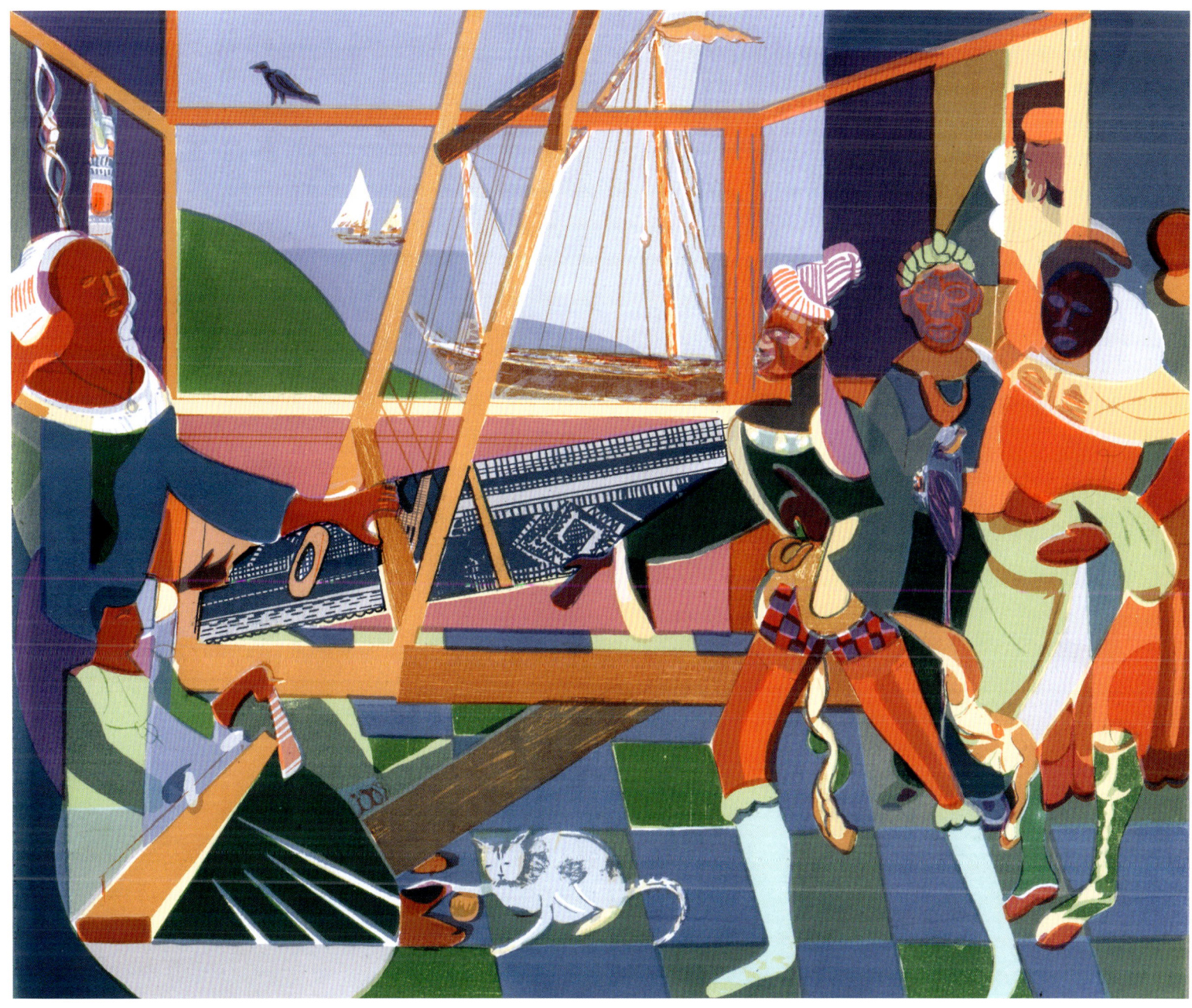

ROMARE BEARDEN

The Return of Ulysses, 1976
Screenprint, 18½ × 22½ in. / 47 × 57.1 cm
Smithsonian American Art Museum, Washington, DC

In a busy room, a woman works at a loom as her husband enters, addressing her in front of a window that reveals a sailing ship in the harbor, with another on the horizon. This is no everyday greeting, but a momentous return: the striding warrior is the Greek hero Odysseus, coming home to his wife, Penelope, after a decade of wandering, as described in the ancient Greek epic *The Odyssey*. An oblivious cat plays beneath the loom in this reimagining of the reunion by American artist Romare Bearden (1911–1988). Inspired by the everyday life of Black America, Bearden attempted to give full value to the individuals of his communities in his bold expressionist style and use of collage over a forty-year artistic career, redressing what he saw as an imbalance in art history. In this screenprint—one

of twenty collages and watercolors based on both Homer's poem and a sixteenth-century painting of the same moment by Italian artist Pintoricchio—Bearden depicts the characters of the legend as Black figures. His inclusion of a playful pet cat in the significant scene hints at the everyday domesticity of Penelope's life while she awaited her husband's return from his journey. Although there is not actually a feline character in *The Odyssey*, Bearden may have included one here, unobtrusively toying with a ball of yarn, because cats were integral parts of his own family. One of his pets, Gippo, went on an odyssey himself, accompanying the artist and his wife on a Caribbean cruise in the late 1960s, making for an unusual tourist tabby.

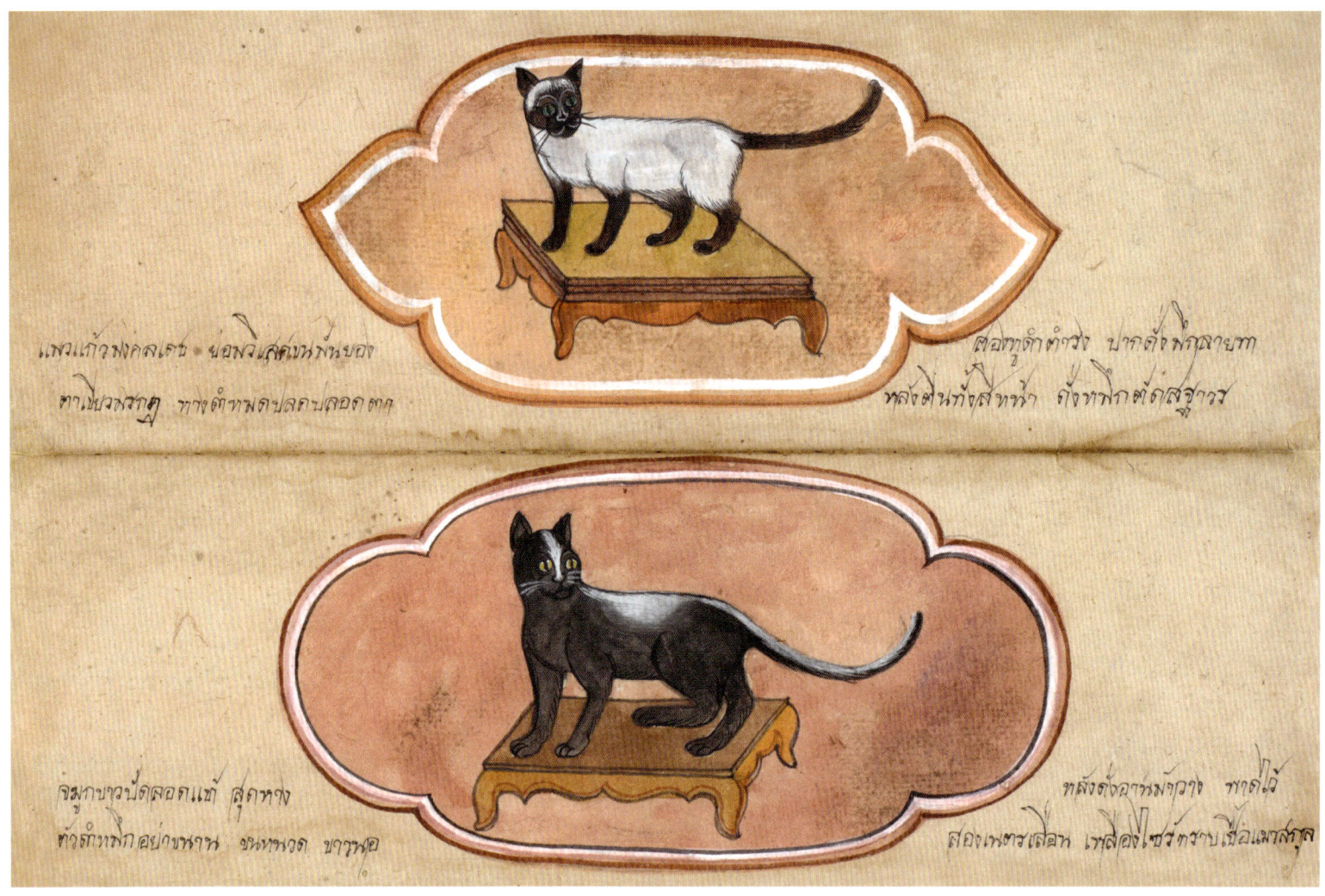

แมวแก้วมงคลเคร่ง ย่อมวิเศษยิ่งกว่าพันยอง
ตาเป็นวงพรกตู ทางดำทมดปลคบลอด ๆ

สองทุกติกำวัง ปากตั้งพกุลายุก
หลังงนทั้งสทหนำ ตั้งทพักตดัสฐำวร

จมุกบาวบัดลอดแท้ สุคหาง
ทั่วกำหนำก อย่าบขนๆๆ ชนทหวด ขาวูพฮ

หลังตั้งอาหมๆวำง ทาดไว
สองเพชรเสือท เหลื่องโซร์ทวาบเนื่อแมวสกุล

ANONYMOUS

Page from a treatise on cats, 19th century
Paper folding book with 12 folios
4⅝ × 14¼ in. / 11.9 × 36.1 cm
British Library, London

Two cats appear on this page from a *samut khoi*, or "folding book," from Siam (present-day Thailand). Standing on a small podium in the top half of the page is a Siamese cat, above a grayish black cat with a white stripe on its nose. Produced by an unknown artist in the nineteenth century, the book was designed to open from top to bottom and consists of twelve folios. Each page features a delicate painting of two different cats found in Siam accompanied by captions describing the feline's features. More unusually, the texts also explain how possession of a particular cat might affect its owner. For example, owning a white cat with green eyes and nine spots on its fur was auspicious and would bring good fortune, while the presence of other combinations of colors and spots was considered unlucky.

The Siamese cat—notable for its distinctive blue eyes, triangular-shaped face, and large ears—was originally thought to be bred only by the royal family of Siam. Animals, from the elephant to the horse, played an important role in the royal and religious life of the devout Buddhist nation, with cats being particularly revered and well cared for, because the Siamese believed they were the "keepers" of temples. The first documented Siamese cats in the United Kingdom, Pho and Mia, were imported in 1884 by the British Consul-General in Bangkok as a gift for his sister. They became the talk of the town at the Cat Fancy show at London's Crystal Palace (see p.208) in 1885.

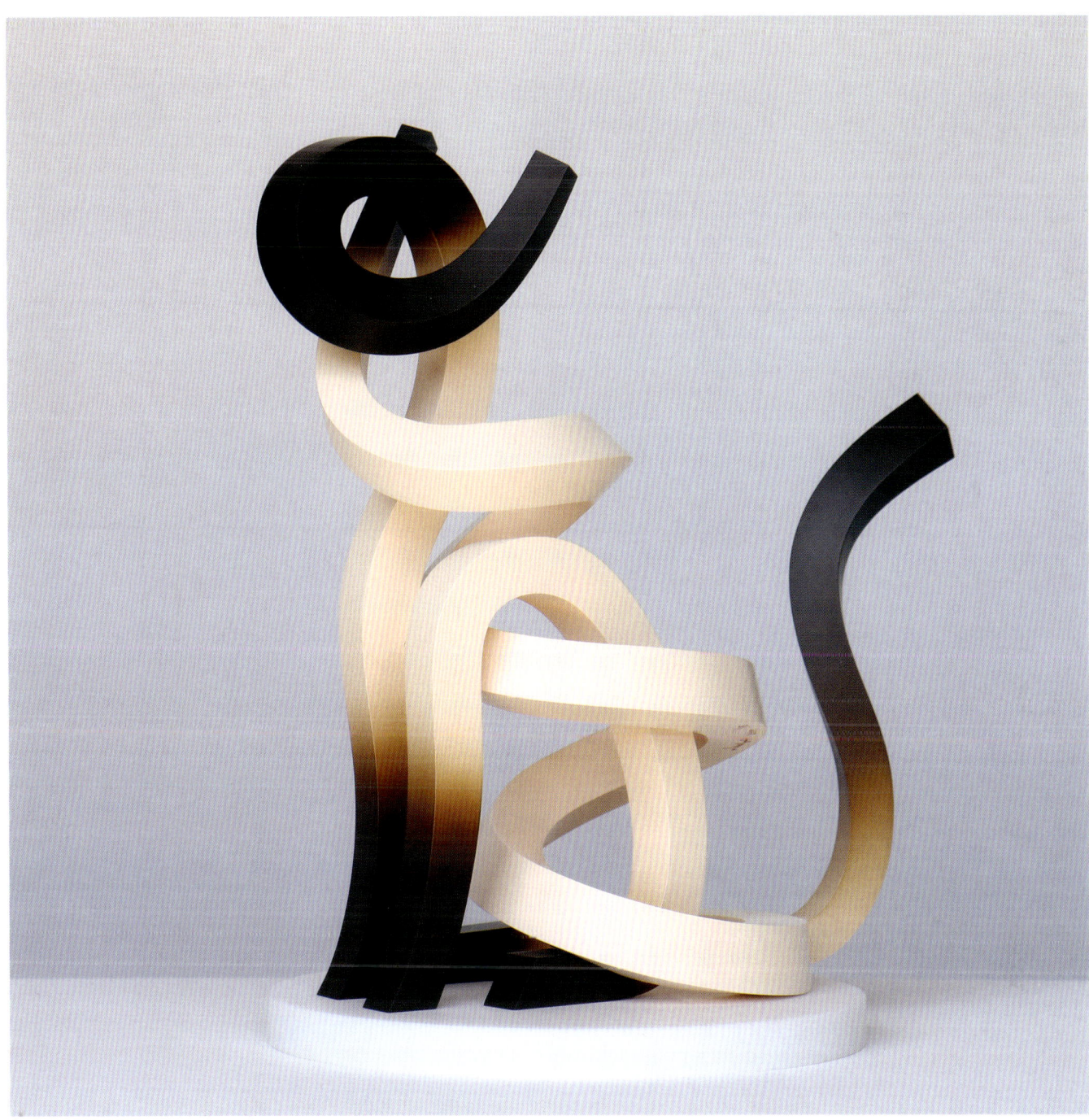

LEE SANGSOO

Sitting Cat (Siamese), 2024
Paint on resin
15¾ × 13¾ × 10¼ in / 40 × 35 × 26 cm
Private collection

The elegant posture of a seated Siamese cat is deftly evoked by the entwined forms of this sinuous resin sculpture. South Korean artist Lee Sangsoo (b. 1983) is renowned for the refined simplicity of his three-dimensional animals, which find their inspiration in the small semiabstract drawings of Pablo Picasso (see p.204), an artist famed for his masterful ability to capture the essence of his subjects with just a few simple lines. The Spanish artist was a great lover of animals and kept three Siamese cats as pets. Lee is similarly fond of these sleek creatures and, here, he economically balances line, plane, and color to reveal the enigmatic beauty of the feline form. As with all the artist's works, which he describes as "drawings in the air," this minimalist sculpture began life in his sketchbook, where he worked to capture the essence of the cat before digitizing his drawing, further developing it in software and finally realizing the piece with a 3D printer. The raw resin was then painted in light cream and chocolate brown hues to re-create the distinctive point coloration typical of Siamese cats, where darker extremities appear on a pale body. The Siamese cat is one of several breeds native to Thailand (formerly Siam), where they were once associated with royalty. As a result of their highly social nature, they became one of the most popular pedigree pets in Europe and North America after their introduction there in the late nineteenth century.

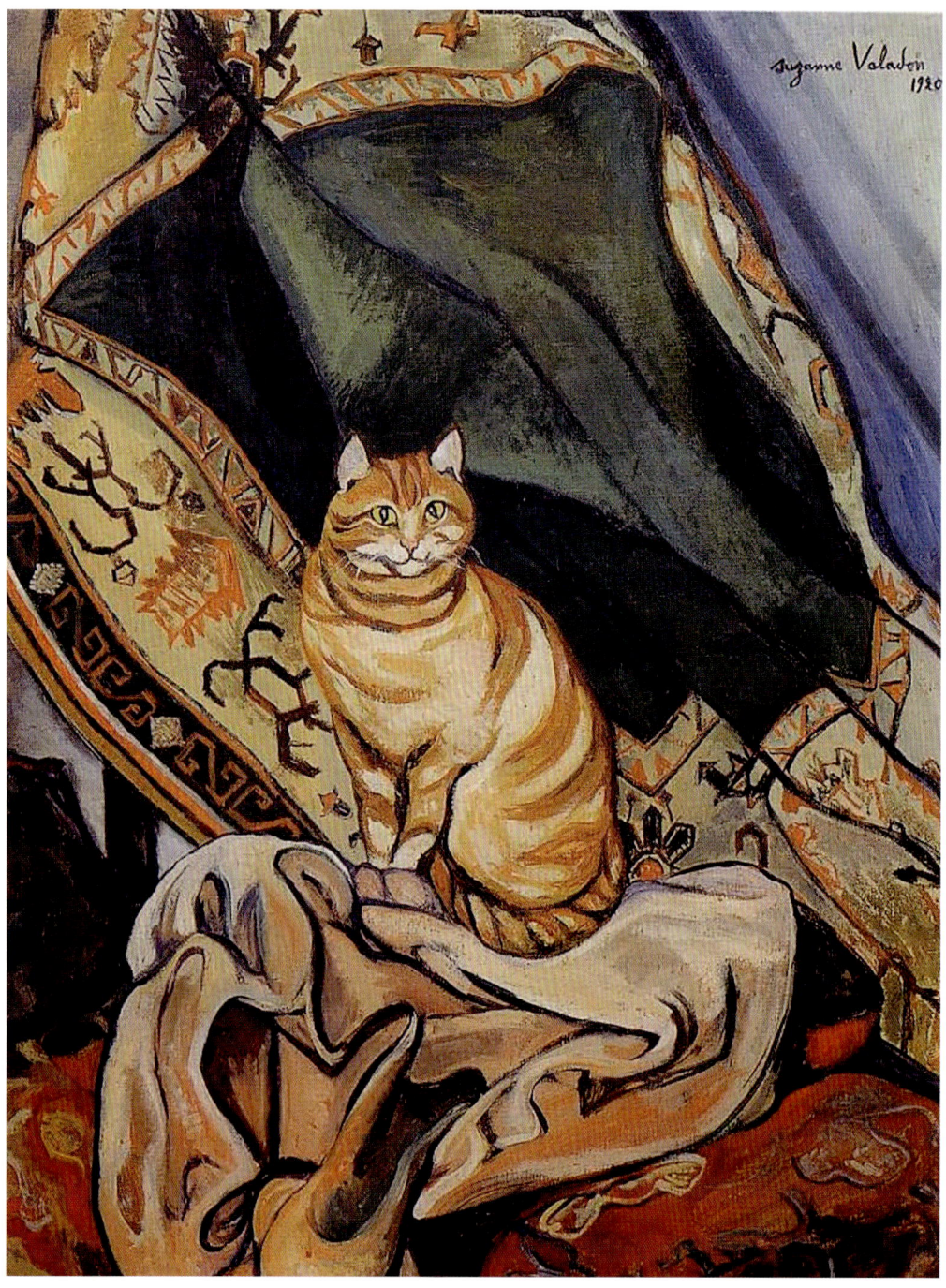

SUZANNE VALADON

The Cat Raminou Sitting on a Cloth, 1920
Oil on canvas, 31½ × 23⅝ in. / 80 × 60 cm
Private collection

Sitting upright, staring straight ahead is Raminou, the beloved pet cat of French painter Suzanne Valadon (1865–1938), the first woman admitted to Paris's prestigious Société Nationale des Beaux-Arts. An animal lover—she once kept a goat in her studio to eat her bad drawings—Valadon had a particular affection for her cats, particularly the orange Raminou, whom she often painted, reportedly feeding them caviar instead of fish on Fridays. Valadon started her career as a life model for her friends, Henri de Toulouse-Lautrec and Pierre-Auguste Renoir (see p.108), two of the most important painters of the day. She was unable to afford art school, but Toulouse-Lautrec and Renoir trained her in painting, while one of her closest friends, Edgar Degas, taught her to draw and etch when she was in her forties.

For the rest of her life, Valadon frequently painted Raminou and domestic scenes of floral still lifes, female nudes, and the gardens of her home in Rue Corot, as well as other animals. In this work from 1920, when Valadon was at the height of her fame, Raminou's calm demeanor belies the eccentricity and turbulence of the life he shared with his mistress. The unmarried mother of the painter Maurice Utrillo, Valadon conducted many passionate affairs, including with the composer Erik Satie and with much younger men. She began to paint only in 1909, when she was forty-four years old, staging her first solo show just two years later, but during her lifetime she held no fewer than four acclaimed retrospective exhibitions.

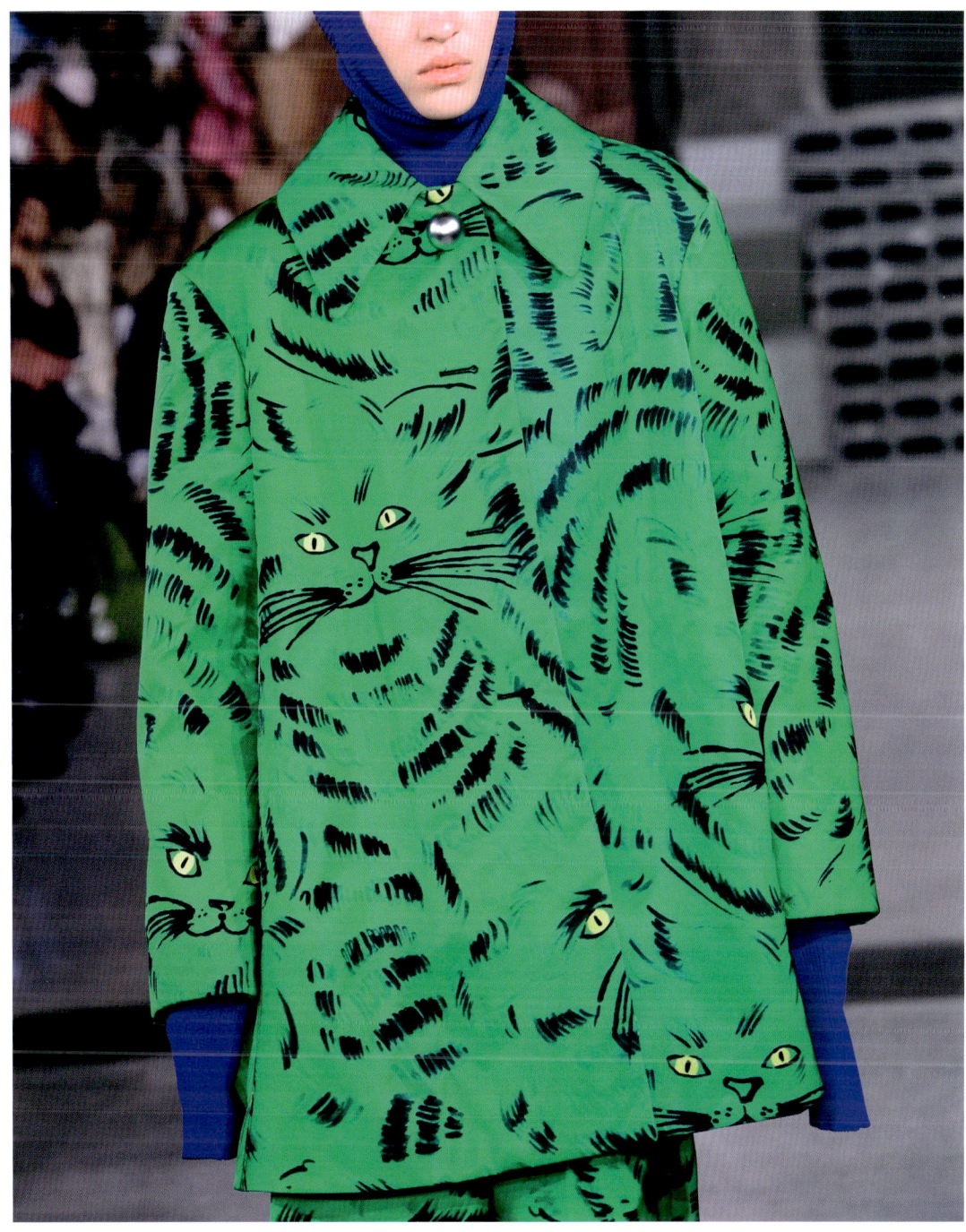

MARNI

Cat Print Swing Coat, 2018
Cotton, polyester, and silver-toned button

For the contemporary cat lady who does not take herself too seriously, look no further than this graphic green coat from Italian fashion brand Marni. Covered in floating feline faces with yellow eyes that peek out from a swirl of whiskers and fuzzy lines, the garment takes the mid-century trapeze silhouette and innovates it for the 2010s. Founded in 1994 by Consuelo Castiglioni in Milan, Marni established itself as a luxury brand that embraces the quirky and alternative, from the use of clashing colors and unusual shapes in its clothing range to its eclectic collection of bags and funky homeware. Since 2016 Marni has been led by Italian designer Francesco Risso, the imaginative and irreverent creative force behind the modern-day brand that has reached new audiences among the hippest

eccentrics and fashion misfits. This coat, which Risso designed for the Fall 2018 Ready-to-Wear collection, comes in three outrageously bright colors—fuchsia, lapis, and, as here, emerald—and has all the trappings of his hallmark aesthetic. Risso played with the juxtaposition between technology versus nature for this collection, with many of the garments being constructed from synthetic and natural fabrics spliced together, such as in the cotton and poly blend of this coat. The innovative creative director's colorful approach is working for cat lovers and fashionistas alike: contrary to many luxury brands who have experienced drop-offs in revenue in recent years, Marni enjoyed a 29 percent increase in business between 2021 and 2023, with no signs of stopping.

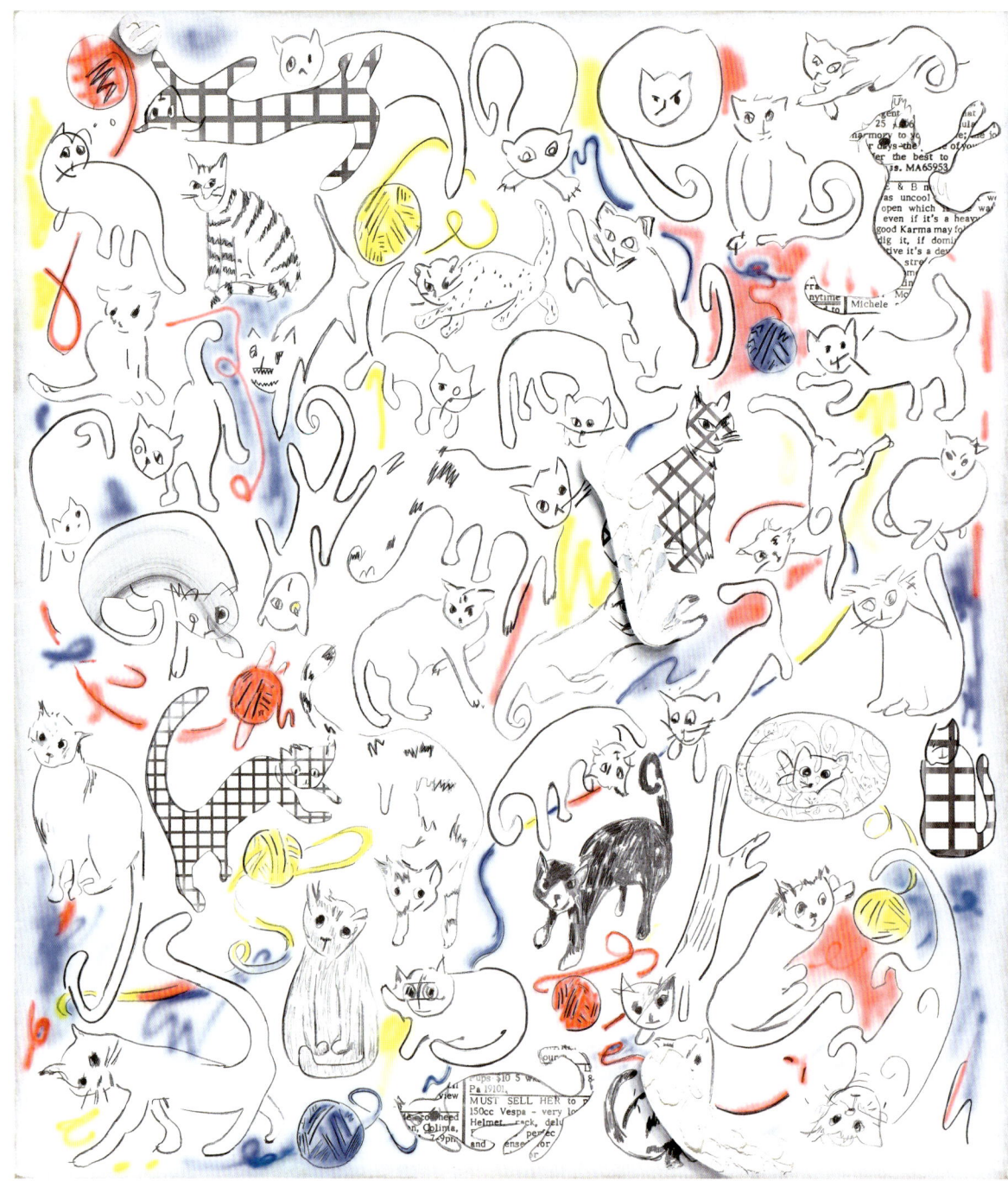

LAURA OWENS

Untitled, 2013
Acrylic, oil, Flashe, and charcoal on linen
137½ × 120 in. / 349.3 × 304.8 cm
Private collection

Dozens of cats drawn in charcoal fill this monumental white canvas. Caught in various poses, the cats tumble, sit, stretch, and play alongside colorful markings, unfurling balls of string in yellow, red, and blue. Most of the cats appear to have been composed quickly, drawn with provisional lines and gridded patterns. Some of the bodies are blank, but others are filled with traditional tabby stripes, graphic cross-hatching, newspaper print, and even more drawings of cats. The cats themselves stand in for a varied lexicon of brushstrokes. The original and playful approach of American artist Laura Owens (b. 1970) is clear to see. Taking inspiration from other artists and using a variety of media and techniques, such as sketching, embroidery, screenprinting, and collage, Owens experiments with painting, absorbing a vast range of references into her works. *Untitled* was one of twelve large-scale paintings the artist created for an exhibition at 356 Mission, a nonprofit gallery and arts organization she cofounded in Los Angeles, all showcasing her unique blend of abstraction with figuration and use of color. Owens's works are bold statements on the potentialities of paint, but they also remind us of the endless inspiration that can come from our feline companions.

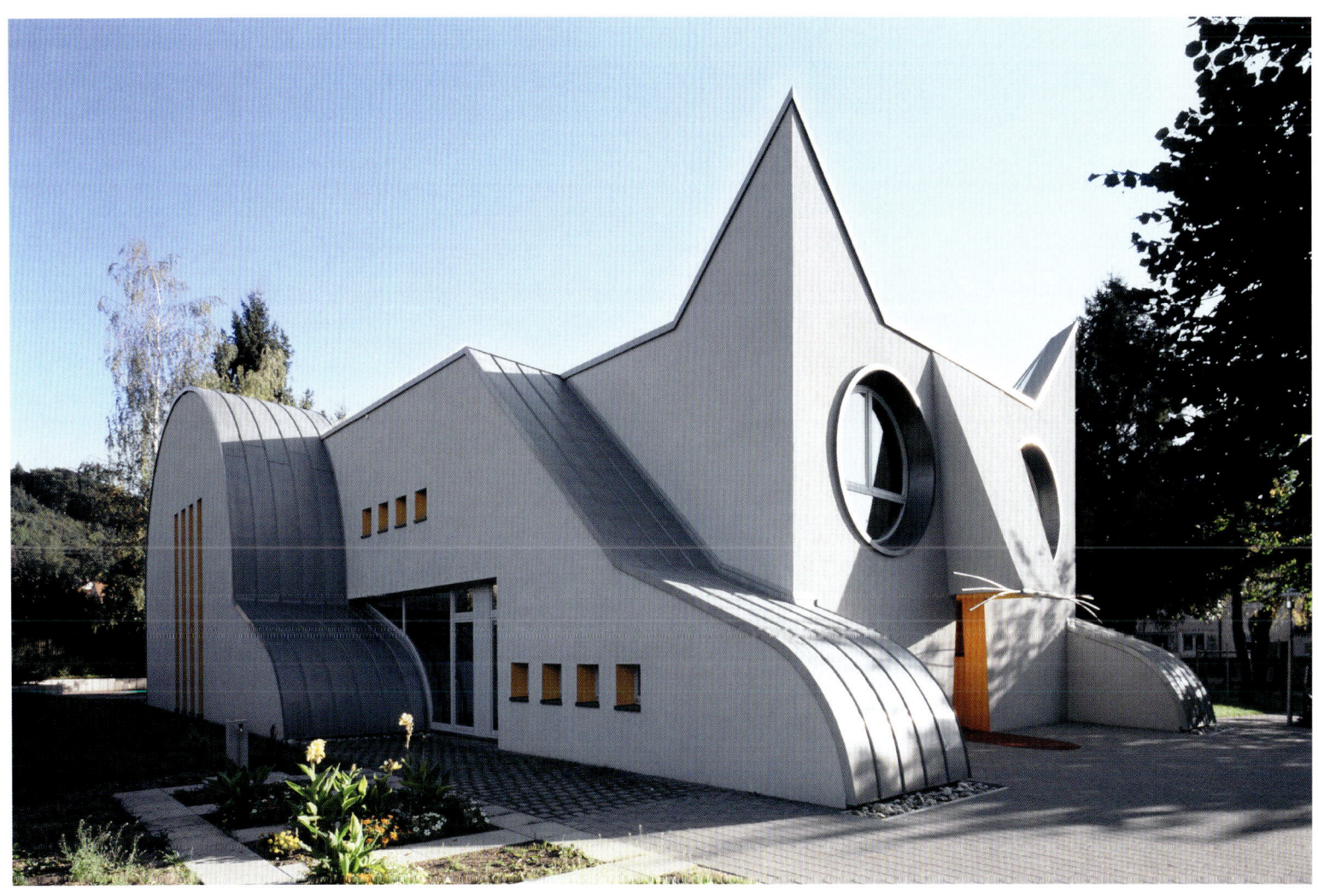

TOMI UNGERER AND AYLA SUZAN YÖNDEL

Kindergarten Wolfartsweier, 2002
Building, dimensions variable
Wolfartsweier, Germany
Photograph by Dirk Altenkirch

Most know the nursery rhyme about the little old lady who lived in a shoe, but what about the kindergartener who goes to school in a cat? This contemporary cat-shaped building is straight out of a storybook, built to ignite children's imagination and create lasting memories connected to friendship and play. Erected in 2002 and designed by French artist Tomi Ungerer (1931–2019) in collaboration with German architect Ayla Suzan Yöndel, Die Katze (the cat) Kindergarten is located in the German village of Wolfartsweier and built as a symbol of Franco-German friendship. Like all felines, this gray cat is wonderfully agile, with a structure that serves simultaneously as a shelter, an educational facility, and an interactive discovery zone equipped with a series of imaginative indoor and outdoor learning spaces that promote movement, multisensorial experiences, and social engagement. Designed to look as though it is crouching and ready to pounce, the building is also a statement about the importance of fostering curiosity in children. As such, preschoolers actively engage with the building: they enter through the cat's mouth, look out through windows shaped like big round eyes, and play around giant silver paws. Best of all, they can whiz out of school through the kitty's tail, which doubles as a steel tube slide, ensuring that every day ends with a thrill. The perfect combination of animal magic and avant-garde architecture, the kitty kindergarten creates a sense of anticipation around schooling (and feline friends) from an early age.

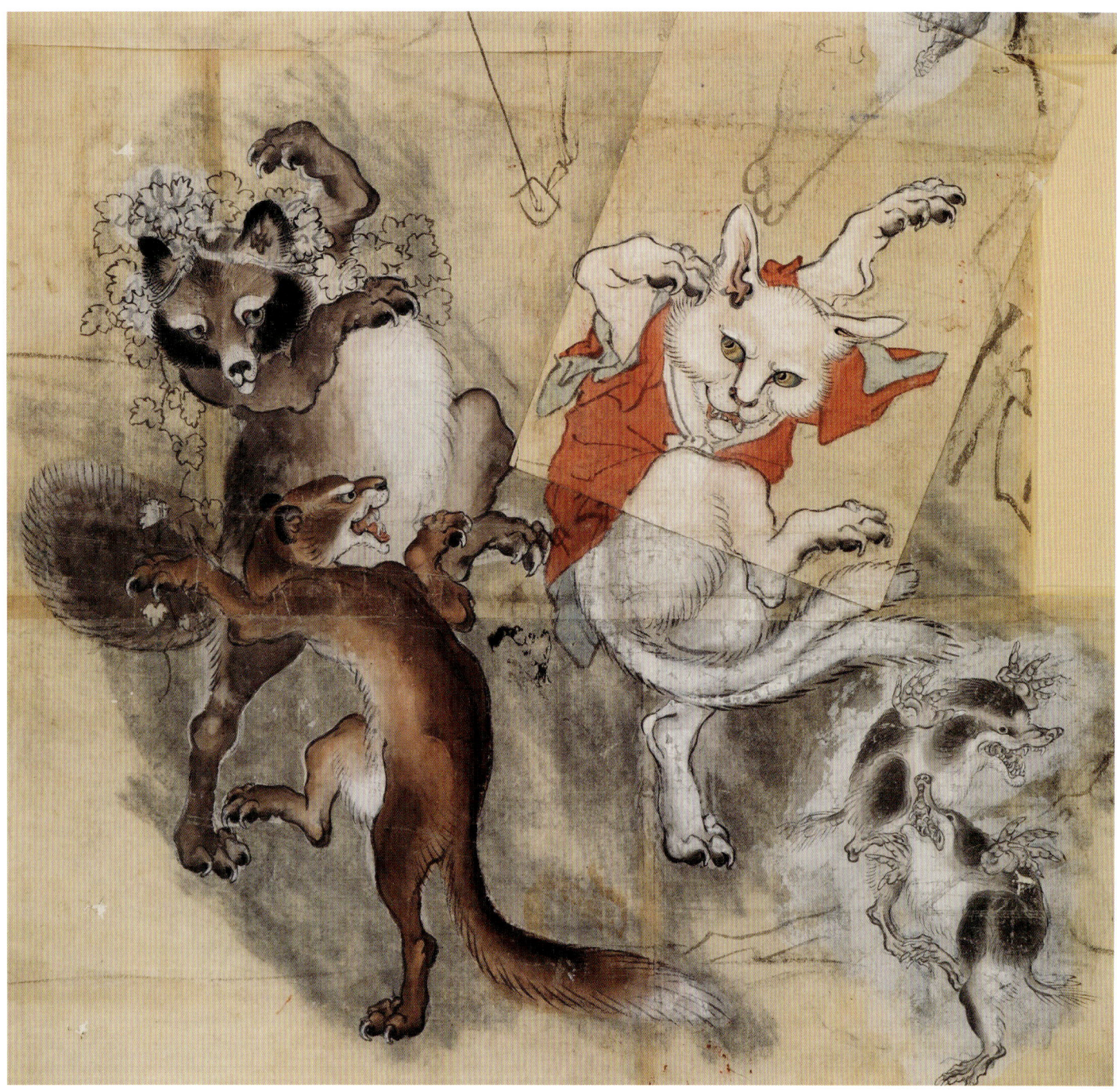

KAWANABE KYŌSAI

*Frolicking Animals, Nekomata and
Tanuki Badger*, 19th century
Drawing, dimensions variable
Kawanabe Kyōsai Memorial Museum,
Warabi, Japan

Considered by some to be the father of manga and the inspiration for traditional Japanese tattoo designs, Japanese artist Kawanabe Kyōsai (1831–1889) had a varied and prolific output during the Meiji period (1868–1912). This playful yet unsettling drawing depicts two frolicking animals who are not the average woodland creatures, but *yōkai*, or supernatural beings from Japanese folklore. Surrounded by weasels and moles, a concerned *tanuki* badger (also called a Japanese raccoon dog) is engaged in a whirling dance with a feisty feline creature known as a *nekomata*, a double-tailed demon cat. *Nekomata* have appeared in Japanese myths from as early as the thirteenth century and are notorious for their malicious behavior. Kyōsai's artwork is probably a *sekiga*, or an improvised drawing he created as a performance at a social gathering, which would account for its medium of two to three sheets of paper pieced together and sketchlike quality. Following the restoration of imperial rule in 1868, Kyōsai became Japan's first political caricaturist as he witnessed the country's transformation from a feudal to a modern state. Known as *kyoga* (which is also the inspiration for his chosen name, Kyōsai), or "crazy pictures," the artist's style hybridized influences from folklore with Japan's contemporary political turmoil. In work that moved from the terrifying to the cute, Kyōsai often revealed an intuitive understanding of animals' inherent mystery. Prized for his independent spirit, he depicted cats sleeping, hunting—frogs, mice, even humans—playing, and, as here, dancing.

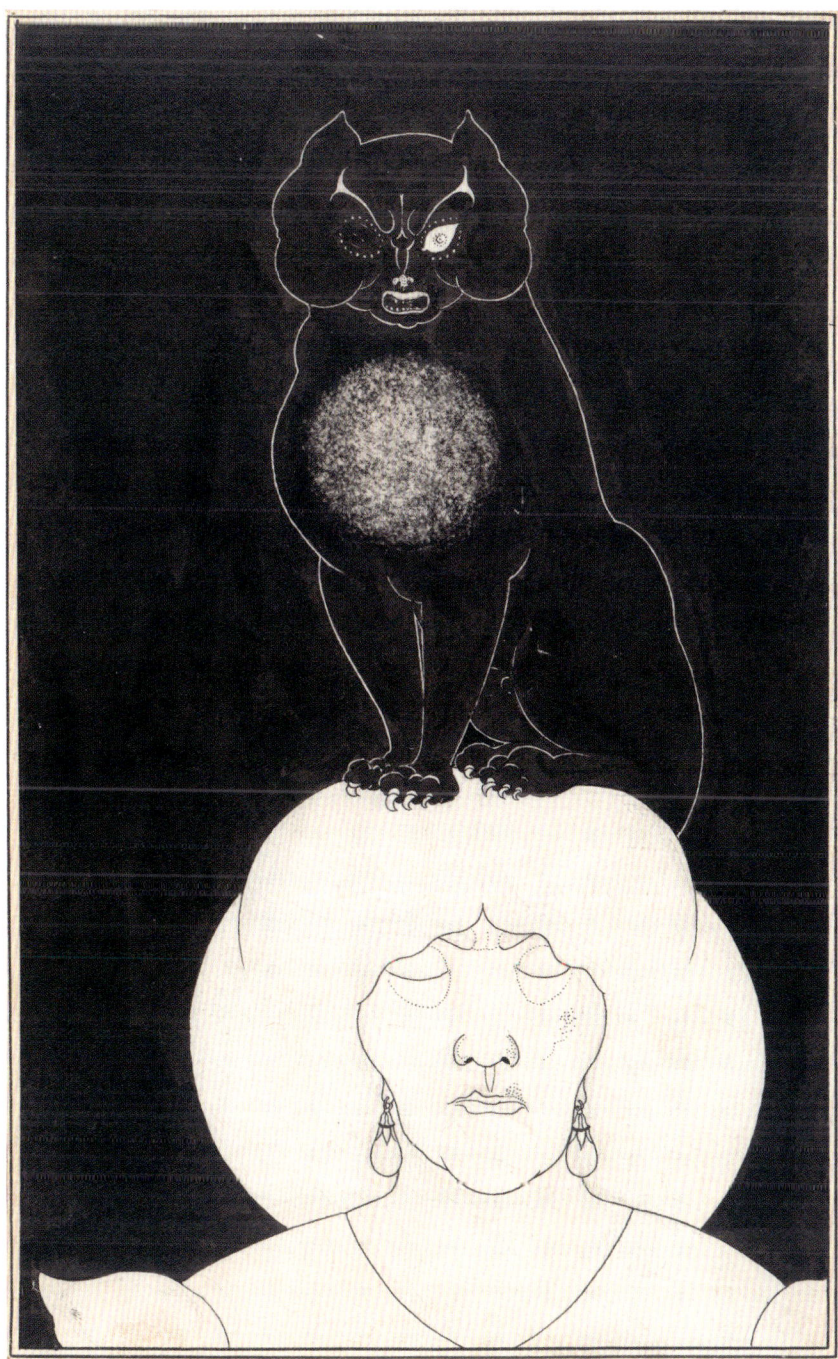

AUBREY BEARDSLEY

The Black Cat, from *Tales of Mystery and Imagination*, 1894
Pen, brush, and India ink over graphite
10 × 6⅜ in. / 25.4 × 16.2 cm
Metropolitan Museum of Art, New York

A black animal that looks more like a demon than a cat sits on the head of a woman, its claws extended and one eye open in a glare, the other missing. This unsettling ink drawing is the work of British artist Aubrey Beardsley (1872–1898), a leading and provocative illustrator of the Art Nouveau style. In the early 1890s, Beardsley was commissioned to illustrate a new edition of Edgar Allan Poe's *Tales of Mystery and Imagination*, a successful collection of the American author's gothic horror fables. First published in 1843, "The Black Cat" follows an increasingly unreliable alcoholic narrator, who reveals that he has killed his wife with an ax blow meant for a one-eyed black cat, which he believes is haunting him. The man has walled up her corpse in his cellar, accidentally trapping the cat, too. Beardsley chose to depict the horrifying final scene when the police break through the makeshift crypt only to come upon the corpse's head "with red extended mouth and solitary eye of fire . . . the hideous beast whose craft had seduced me into murder." In contrast with the white corpse, Beardsley's cat fuses into the drawing's deep black background, with only thin lines of negative space separating the eerie animal from the composition. Even before Poe revolutionized the scary story for the Victorian age, black cats in some cultures had long been symbols of the devil, bad luck, and witchcraft. Although contemporary black cats have largely shed their demonic associations, unfortunately, they are still less likely to be adopted from animal shelters.

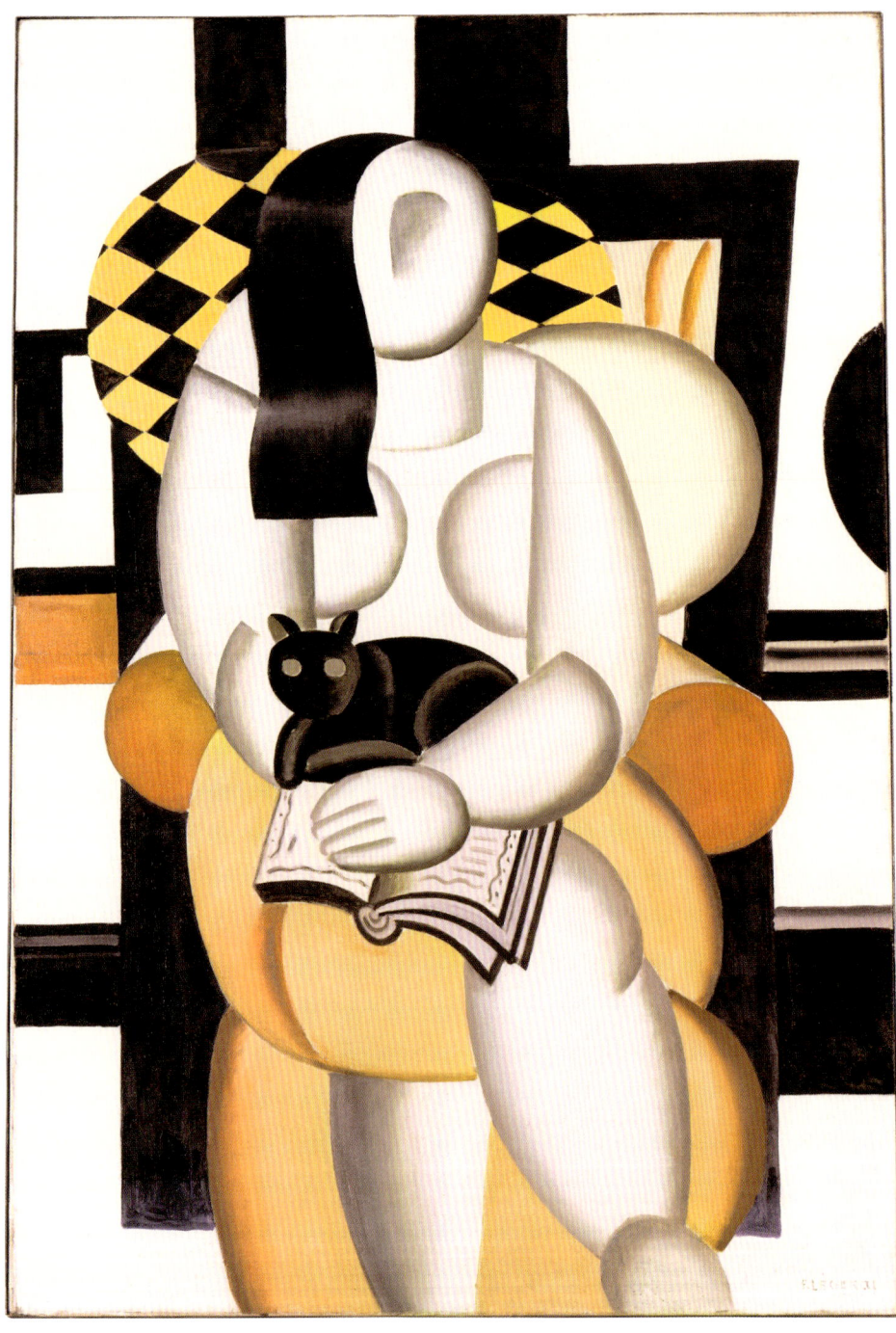

FERNAND LÉGER

Woman with a Cat, 1921
Oil on canvas, 51½ × 35⅝ in. / 130.8 × 90.5 cm
Metropolitan Museum of Art, New York

It is often remarked that dogs look like their owners, but here is a cat that matches the rounded sculptural proportions of its companion, with silky black fur to complement the woman's glossy cascade of undulating locks. More than just a simple scene of quiet domesticity, this painting by French artist Fernand Léger (1881–1955) is also telling of his passion for Purism, an art movement that, unlike the sharp and fragmented look of Cubism, is characterized by simple unified shapes and interlocking planes devoid of decoration and texture. Purism was also a reaction against the devastations of World War I, which resonated with Léger, whose experiences on the front line had a significant effect on his work. Pioneered by architect Le Corbusier and artist Amédée Ozenfant, the movement drew inspiration from Classical forms as well as mechanical and industrial themes, fusing the authenticity of a distant past with the optimistic spirit of a new machine age. As such, both lap cat and sitter are rendered in a soft reductive style that combines these expressive qualities, at once statuesque and futuristic, meditative and alert. Tiny and ball-like, Léger's lucky black cat is snugly shielded by this idealized vision of a strong and stoic woman, a symbol perhaps of how new positive narratives can pave the way toward brighter beginnings.

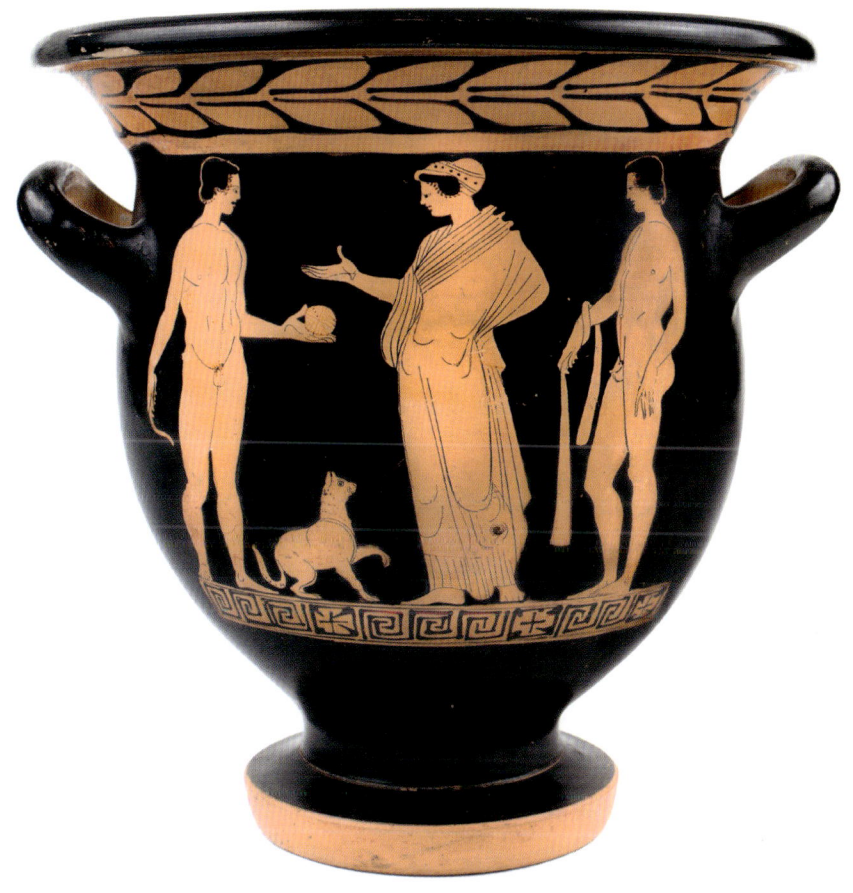

CYCLOPS PAINTER

Bell krater, c. 425–400 BCE
Clay, 12¾ × 12⅝ in. / 32.4 × 32 cm
Chau Chak Wing Museum, The University of Sydney

In the fifth century BCE, the Greek historian Herodotus wrote extensively of the ancient Egyptians' reverence for cats in his *Histories*, with vivid descriptions of entire families shaving their eyebrows in mourning of their dead pets and people rushing into burning buildings to save their beloved felines. Archaeologists believe it was around this same time that cats were introduced to Greece and southern Italy by Phoenician traders, who had smuggled the animals out of Egypt as effective pest controllers on their ships. Both the Greeks and Romans considered the creatures omens of good fortune and readily adopted them into their homes, as shown by this vase. On one side, a young woman stands between two naked young men, with an inquisitive cat looking up at her. Although the meaning behind the scene is unknown, it is evidence that by 400 BCE there were domestic cats in Greek-colonized *Magna Graecia* (Great Greece) in Lucania, the "instep" and "toe" of modern Italy's boot. The vessel is a krater, a large bowl for mixing water and wine, and bears the typical hallmarks of red-figure painted pottery in form and color, including the region's deep red clay. It is believed to be the work of an artist known only as the Cyclops Painter, so named by historians at the British Museum after his surviving vase depicting Odysseus blinding the cyclops Polyphemus. A slightly mysterious object, this krater is an excellent example of the curious cat even in the ancient world.

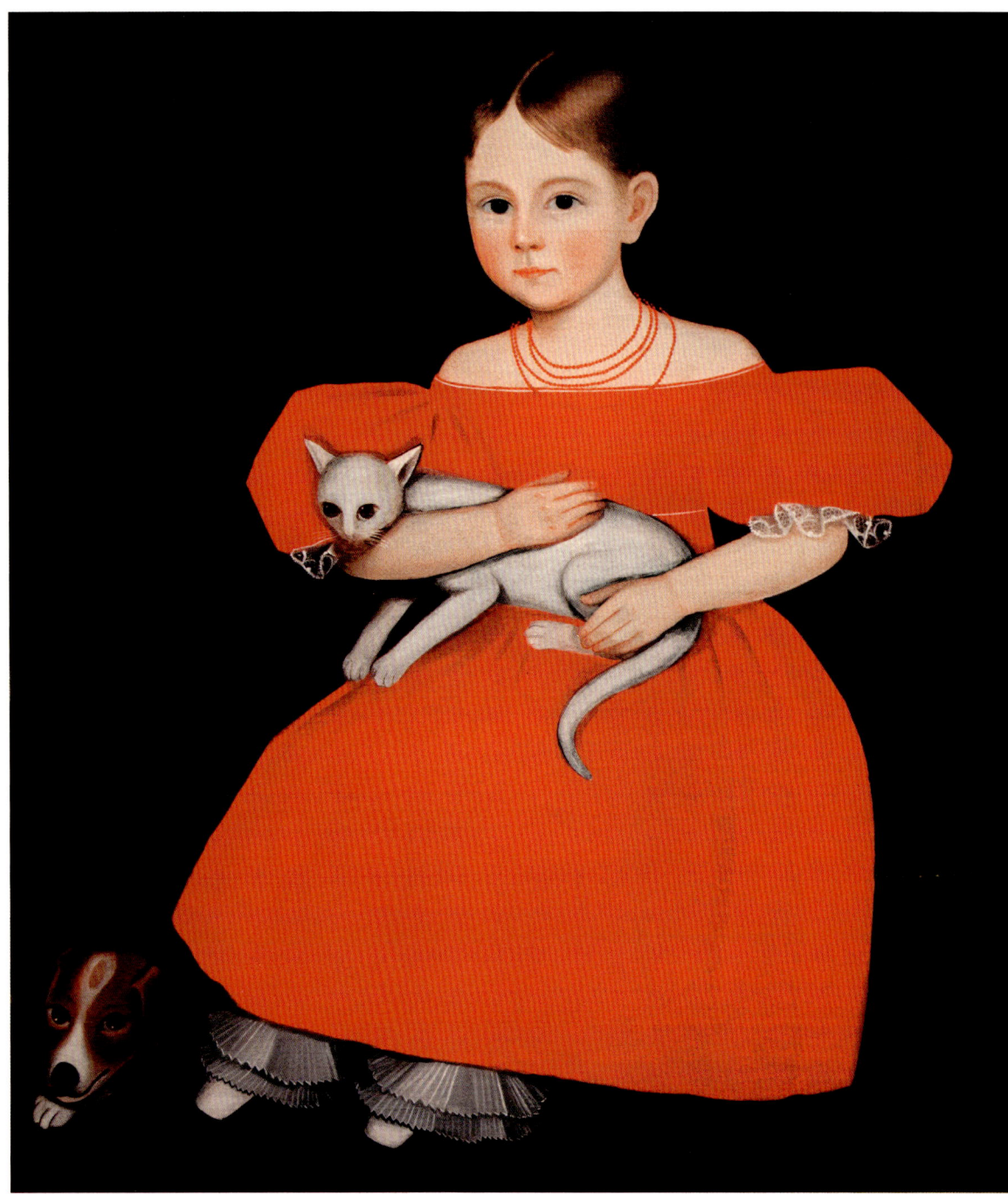

AMMI PHILLIPS

Girl in Red Dress with Cat and Dog, 1830–35
Oil on canvas, 30 × 25 in. / 76.2 × 63.5 cm
American Folk Art Museum, New York

With a white cat on her lap and a dog by her feet, a young girl sits dressed in a highly starched, vibrantly red, off-the-shoulder dress with a string of red beads around her neck. Her large blue eyes gaze resolutely ahead. When an anonymous donor purchased this painting by American artist Ammi Phillips (1788–1865) in 1985 and then donated it to the American Folk Art Museum, it was the first work in the genre of folk art to sell for a million dollars. In a career that spanned fifty years, Phillips, who was probably self-taught, produced perhaps as many as two thousand paintings, working chiefly as an itinerant portrait painter—known at the time as a "limner"—in the villages of New England, along the Massachusetts and Connecticut borders. A limner moved from town to town, fulfilling commissions for local people who wanted their likenesses painted. This is the most famous of all of Phillips's surviving works: frequently reproduced, it appeared on a US postage stamp in 1998. It is known that Phillips painted it while living in upstate New York, and the girl was one of four children he painted wearing red. The plain dark background is typical of his style, which often contrasted light and dark. Here, the black velvety field behind the sitters contrasts with the brilliant red of the dress and the stark whiteness of the cat. Unlike the dog that seems happy to sit at the girl's feet, the cat looks as if it might jump the minute she relaxes her hold.

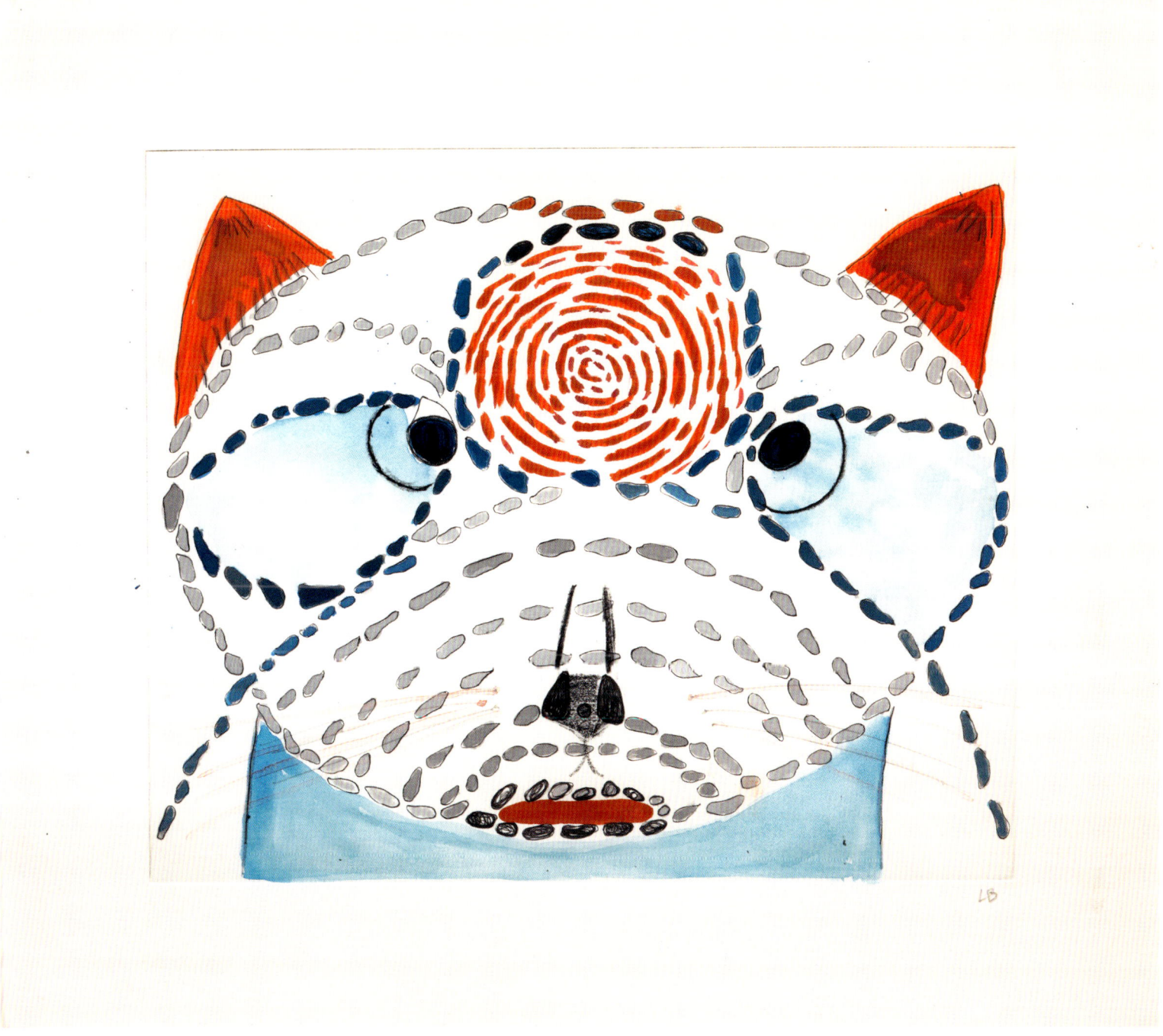

LOUISE BOURGEOIS

Champfleurette #2, variant of *The Angry Cat*, 1999
Drypoint with red and gray gouache, blue watercolor,
black crayon, and black ink additions
9⅞ × 11⅞ in. / 25.2 × 30.3 cm
The Easton Foundation, New York

During the 1950s, French American artist Louise Bourgeois (1911–2010) and her family shared their New York home with two pet cats, Champfleurette and Tyger, and their weekend home in Connecticut with a whole menagerie of animals. Decades later, Champfleurette starred in a series of seven prints by Bourgeois, of which this is the second. Each iteration features the same fierce-looking feline face, but with slight differences to suggest the cat's thoughts. In this variant, red swirls in her brain suggest she is angry; in other versions, she is thinking of mice or of nothing at all. On closer inspection, the furious cat is, perhaps, not that angry and also not entirely catlike, having a half-filled glass of red wine for a nose and drawn with a childlike quality that belies a certain vulnerability. Bourgeois often anthropomorphized animals and insects, but she had a particular lifelong fascination for felines, which appeared in her sculptures as well as her drawings. Champfleurette once was even depicted as a temptress in high heels. The cat's unusual name is probably a feminization of Jules Champfleury, the nineteenth-century art critic, novelist, and champion of the Realist movement in France. Over a remarkably long career—she worked well into her nineties—Bourgeois concentrated on the inseparability of the body and mind, most notably in monumental sculptures, such as *Spider* (1996). Here, the cat's face is the gateway to a subconscious where memory, humor, and trauma coexist.

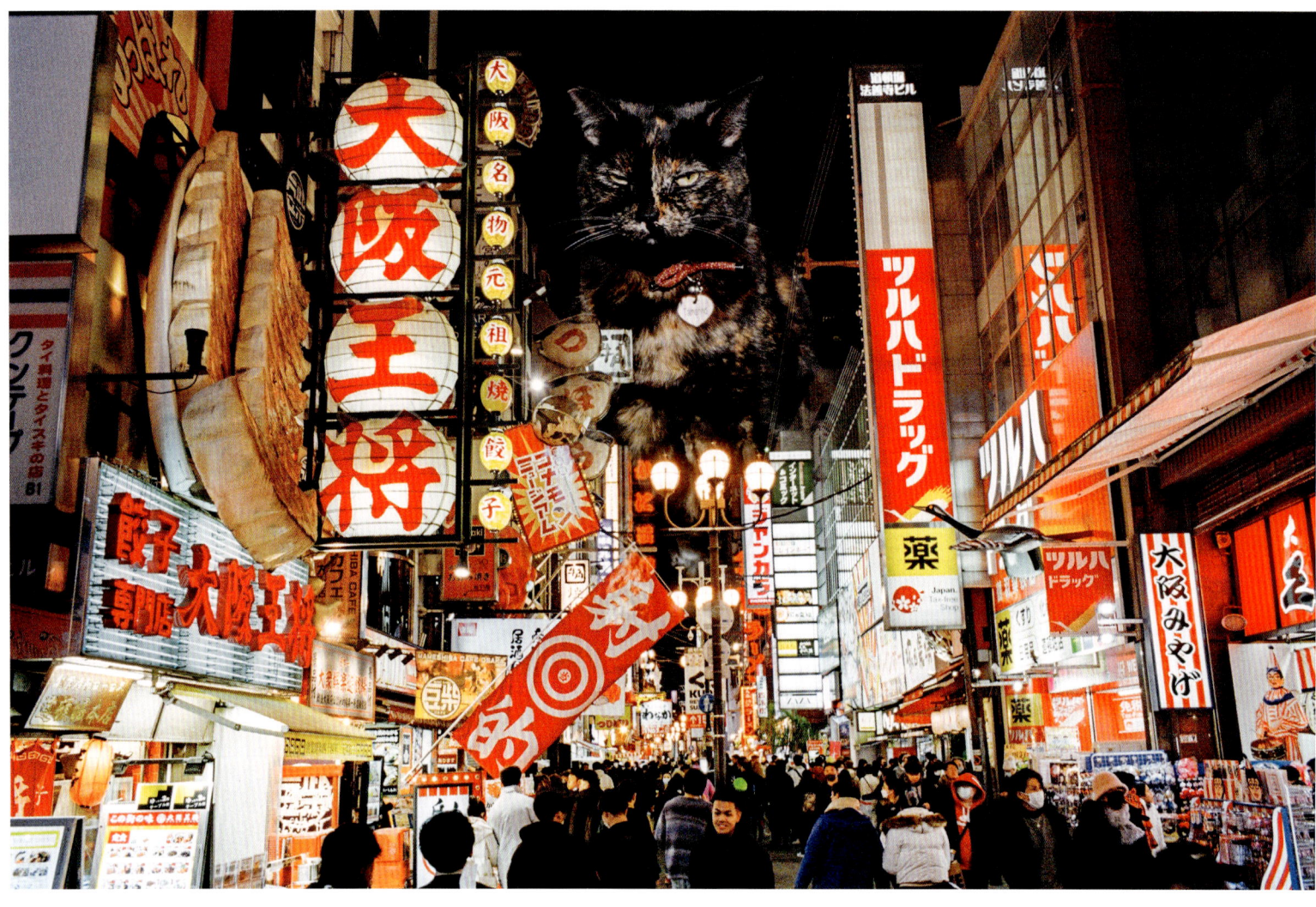

SATOMI SUGIYAMA

Queen of Osaka, 2022
Photograph, dimensions variable

A humongous tortoiseshell cat, complete with collar and bell, looms over Osaka's celebrated Dotonbori entertainment district in a photograph that recalls the reptilian monster Godzilla's attack in the eponymous 1954 horror movie classic. Although the kitty's name is actually Tamarind, she has been nicknamed "Tamazilla" here in honor of the movie monster. She is one of a pair of cats—the other is Bandit—that belong to the Japanese-born, Los Angeles–based photographer Satomi Sugiyama (b. 1978). Tamarind may live in the United States, but thanks to technology, Sugiyama is able to transport her loyal sidekick to Dotonbori by fusing two photographic images together. Working with a 35 mm film Leica M3 analog camera, Sugiyama uses in-camera double exposure techniques to enlarge her pet to giant proportions while the cityscape remains to scale. Obsessed with old movies, Sugiyama pays homage to the classic Japanese *kaiju* films of her youth, while also referencing the Japanese love affair with cats as exemplified by the work of feline photographers, such as Walter Chandoha, Masahisa Fukase, and Satoru Tsuda's infamous *Namennayo* delinquent cat gang of the 1980s (see pp.19, 40, and 145). Dotonbori is a popular tourist hotspot in Osaka, famous for its towering neon signs that attract countless travelers each year—here, all of them are oblivious to the looming Tamazilla. Sugiyama's witty photograph is part of her mission to raise cat art to a new level and to express her affection for her pets: "The project was born purely out of the love for my cats," she says.

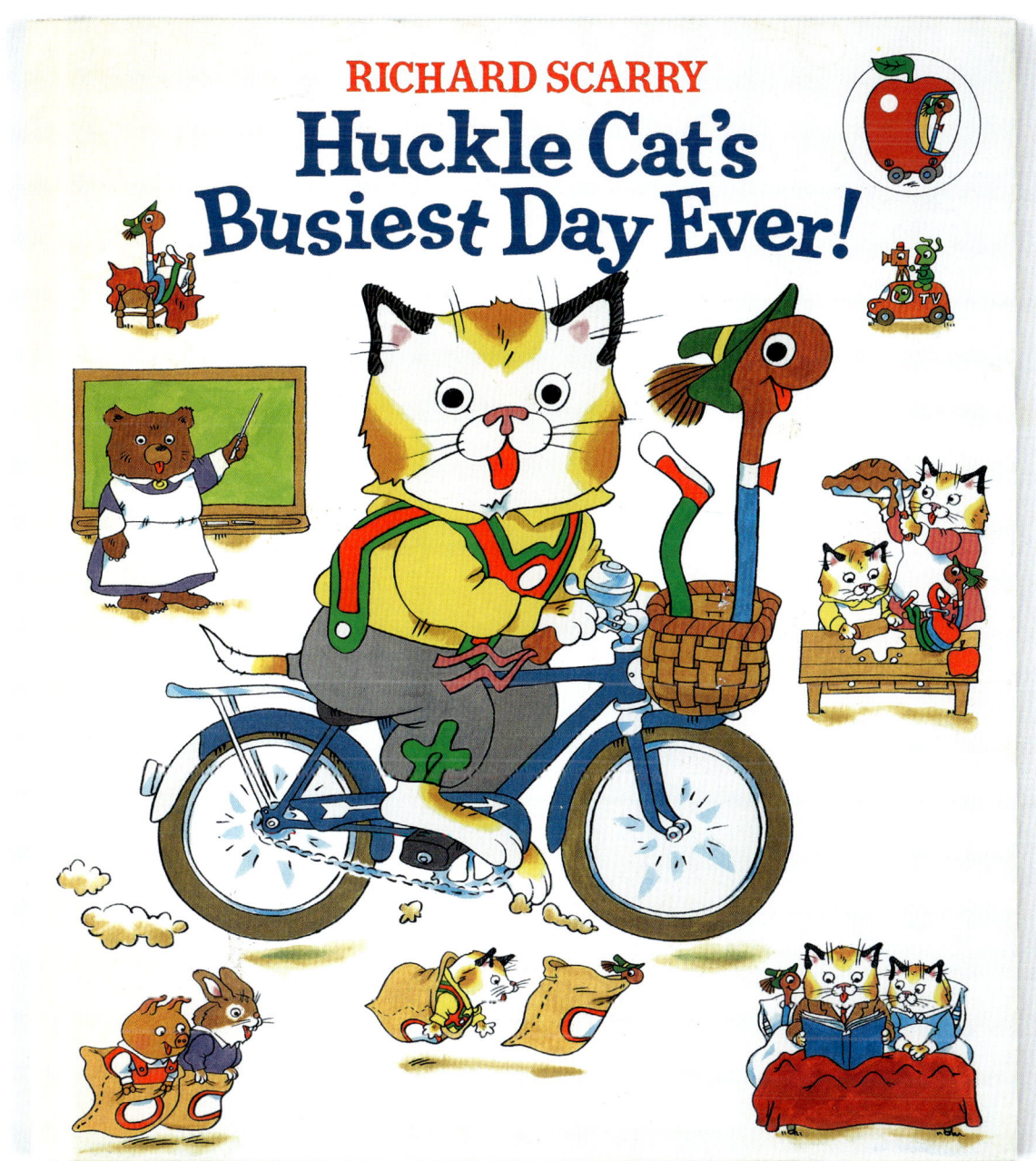

RICHARD SCARRY

Huckle Cat's Busiest Day Ever, 1992
Printed book, 12 × 10½ in / 30.5 × 26.7 cm

The fictional world of Richard Scarry (1919–1994) is full of sprightly animal characters. The American children's author and illustrator released over three hundred books in his lifetime, but he is best known for his *Best Ever* book series, set in Busytown, where anthropomorphic residents include Sergeant Murphy, a cocker spaniel cop who drives a motorcycle; Mr. Fixit, a DIY-loving fox with a flair for invention; and Lowly Worm, a jolly earthworm who wears a green Tyrolean hat and drives an apple car. Lowly's best friend is the kind and ever-curious Huckle, an orange tabby cat-cum-mystery-solver, inspired by the author's own son, Huck. He is often dressed in a yellow shirt and lederhosen, a nod, like Lowly's hat, to Scarry's adoptive hometown of Gstaad, Switzerland, where he and his family lived from 1972 onward. In *Huckle Cat's Busiest Day Ever*, Huckle Cat and Lowly Worm go on various adventures in Busytown, from baking an apple pie to flying a kite with Father Cat. Charming, nostalgic, and eternally popular, Scarry's books have been translated into more than thirty languages and have produced many spin-offs, including toys, apparel, and an animated series. Most recently, luxury Italian fashion house Bottega Veneta created a capsule collection of accessories inspired by the *Best Ever* series, which included an apple-shaped coin purse and a wallet in Huck's lederhosen hues, all crafted in the brand's signature *intrecciato* woven leather—which is proof that Scarry's animal magic has enduring cross-generational appeal, from kindergarten to catwalk.

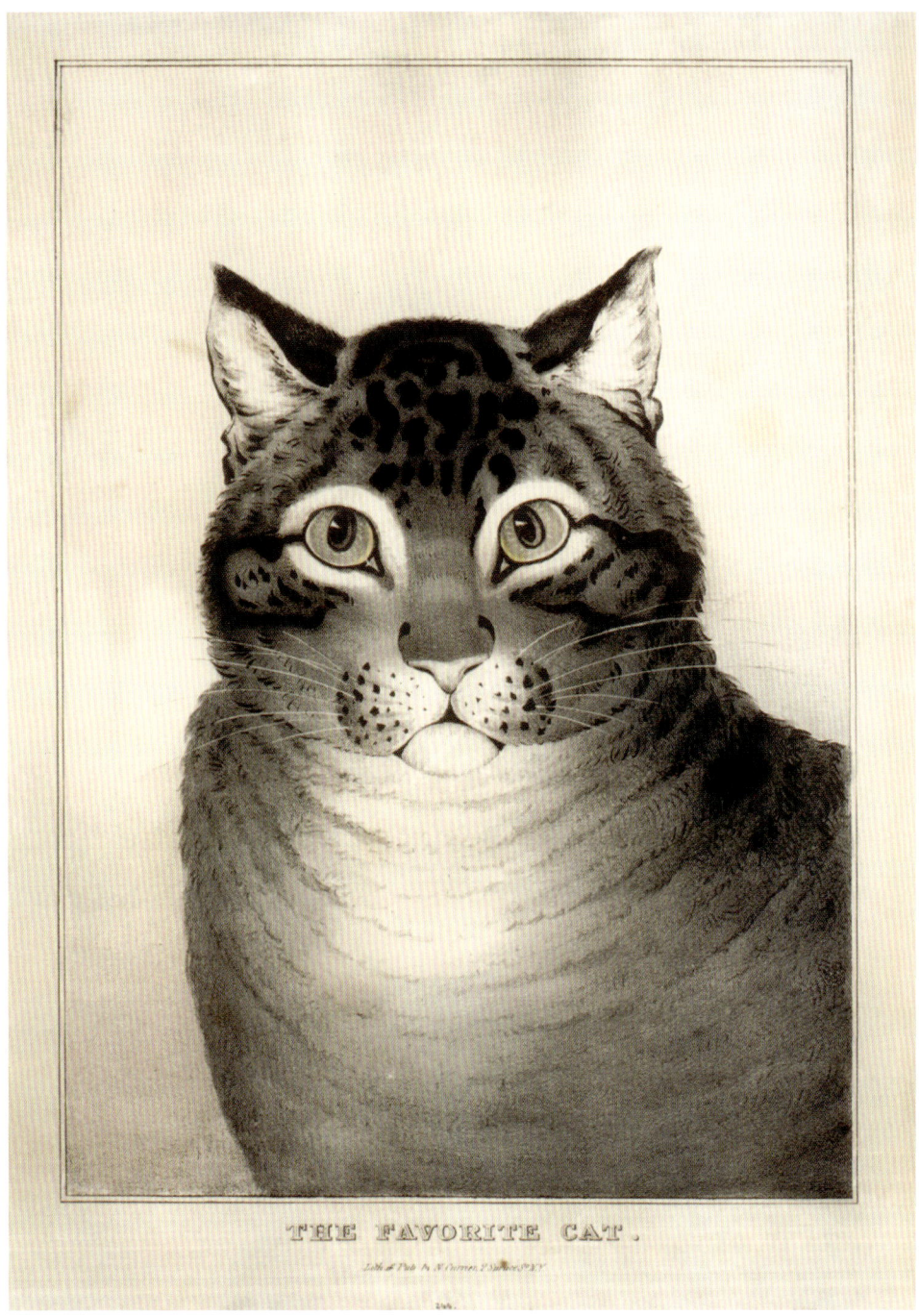

THE FAVORITE CAT.

Lith. & Pub. by N. Currier, 2 Spruce St. N.Y.

NATHANIEL CURRIER

The Favorite Cat, 1838–48
Hand-colored lithograph
12¼ × 8⅝ in. / 31 × 22 cm
Metropolitan Museum of Art, New York

A handsome cat stares straight ahead in this hand-colored lithograph cleverly titled *The Favorite Cat*—and this large-eyed feline does look every inch the idea of somebody's beloved pet. Produced in the mid-nineteenth century by Currier and Ives, a celebrated New York City printmaking business started by American artisan Nathaniel Currier (1813–1888), the illustration was part of an innovative series of affordable hand-painted lithographs. With these works, Currier and Ives took advantage of improved printing technology to sell what the company called "cheap and popular pictures" to decorate the homes of the growing US population. From printing letterheads and sheet music, Currier moved on to create, among other things, popular views of the changing American landscape, urban bridges, views of Christmastime, sentimental scenes, and images of pets, as here. Before photojournalism became established, the company produced images of new events, such as the Civil War (1861–65): its prints of the Battle of Gettysburg, for example, became some of the definitive images of the conflict. Currier and Ives insisted on high quality and, to that end, used the best lithographic materials. In-house staff created most of the images and an assembly line of around a dozen women hand-colored each print: one color per worker. Between 1840 and 1890, the company published more than seven thousand prints, but as technology changed with the advent of photography, the era of colored prints disappeared.

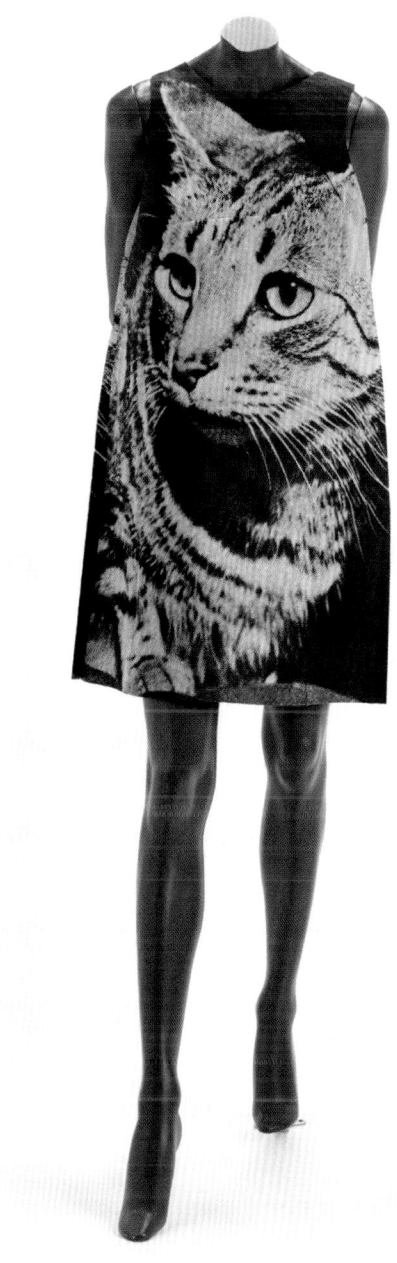

HARRY GORDON

Cat Poster Paper Dress, 1968
Screenprinted tissue, wood pulp, and
rayon mesh, with polyethylene and
card packaging, 34 × 24 in. / 86.4 × 61 cm
Indianapolis Museum of Art

A blown-up, black-and-white photograph of a tabby cat is screenprinted on this sleeveless minidress. Originally retailing for $2.98, this is one of several paper dresses created by American graphic designer Harry Gordon (1930–2007) in the late 1960s. The series was part of a fashion-forward trend, when artists, companies, and even political campaigns adopted the disposable paper dress as a moving billboard for Pop art images or messaging. Scott Paper Co. initially sparked this trend in 1966, when the brand advertised paper dresses to promote a new line of products. Other companies released their own designs, including Campbell's "Souper Dress," while politicians—Richard Nixon, Eugene McCarthy, and Robert Kennedy among them—employed the trend for campaign advertising (women supporters wore them at rallies). An artifact of the era's sexual politics, this fashionable but impractical ready-to-wear article of clothing was a playful, risky statement: while the dresses were flame-retardant, a nearby lit cigarette still must have posed a serious threat. Gordon encouraged wearers to repurpose the garment if they ever became tired of it by opening the seams and tacking it to the wall as a poster, or by sewing several together to create curtains, a bedspread, or a tablecloth. Thankfully, some customers did not listen to his suggestions. Coveted today, Gordon's still intact screenprinted paper dresses can be found in the collections of prestigious institutions, including the Indianapolis Museum of Art, which holds this version.

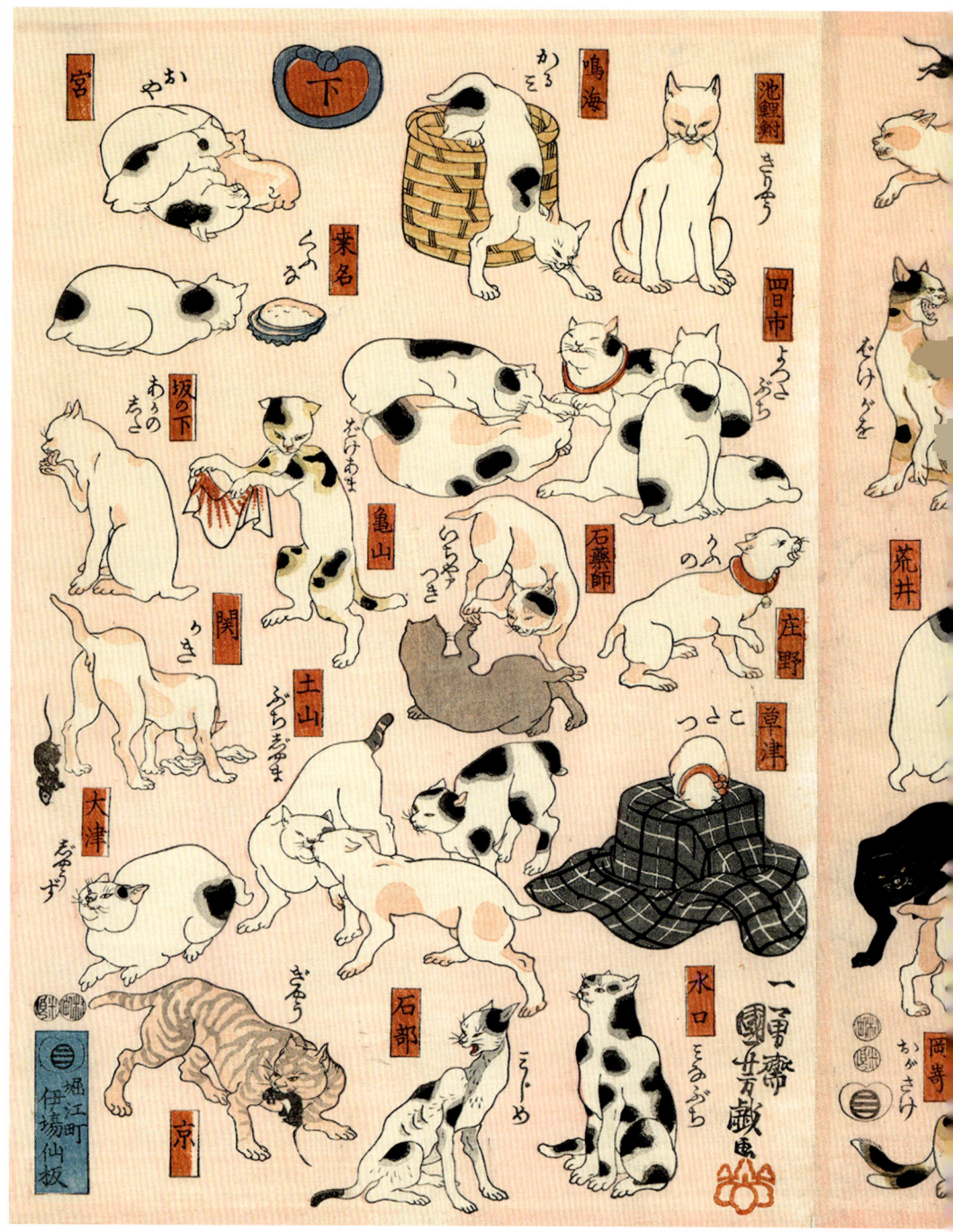

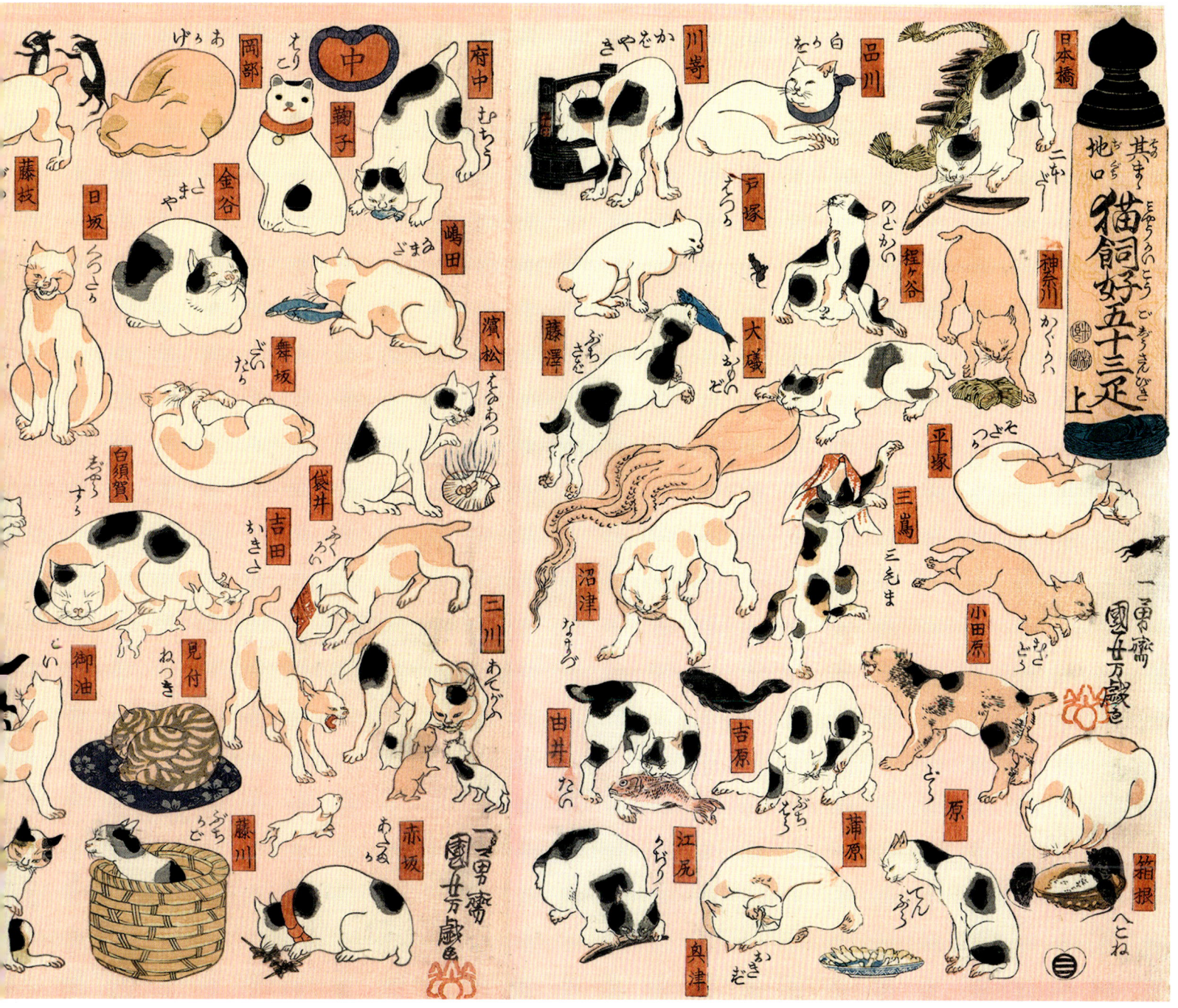

UTAGAWA KUNIYOSHI

*Cats Suggested as the Fifty-three Stations
of the Tōkaidō*, 1850
Woodcut, 14¾ × 30⅝ in. / 37.4 × 77.8 cm
Private collection

Washing, feeding, and fighting—all manner of cat behavior is captured across this triptych by Japanese artist Utagawa Kuniyoshi (1798–1861). The Edo-period printmaker was, as the work suggests, a major cat lover. Cats wandered through his studio, and he would frequently have one cuddled into his kimono when he painted. So devoted was he to his pets that he honored them by inscribing their names on a Buddhist altar at his home when they died. Kuniyoshi's fascination with felines echoed Japan's long reverence for cats. Cats were introduced to Japan by Buddhist monks in the sixth century, who brought them aboard their ships as lucky charms and to safeguard their scriptures from nibbling mice. Kuniyoshi was one of the final masters of *ukiyo-e*, a genre of popular Japanese art that had

flourished from the seventeenth century and is characterized by its bold, flat color and everyday subject matter. In this work, Kuniyoshi wittily referenced another grand master of *ukiyo-e*, Utagawa Hiroshige (see p.102) and his woodcut series, *Fifty-three Stations of the Tōkaidō* (1832), which depicts the stopping places along the road from Edo (present-day Tokyo) to Kyoto. Kuniyoshi substitutes Hiroshige's picturesque landscapes for cat-themed puns that ingeniously evoke each location. For example, at the forty-first site, Miya, which sounds like the Japanese word for "parent," Kuniyoshi shows a mother cat with her small kittens. Although this wordplay may be understood only by an audience fluent in Japanese, an appreciation for the colorful and characterful cats is universal.

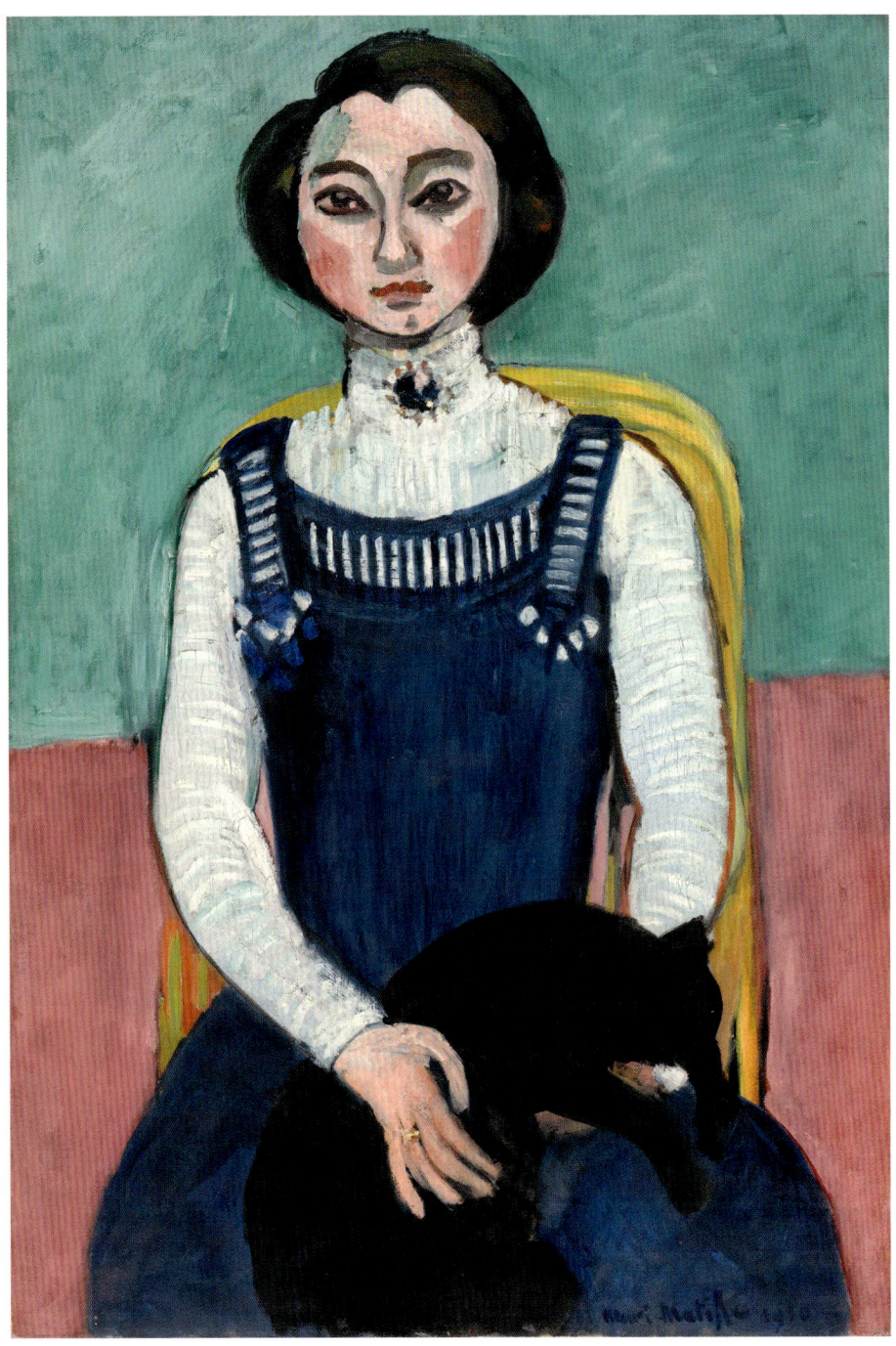

HENRI MATISSE

Marguerite with a Black Cat, 1910
Oil on canvas, 37 × 25¼ in. / 94 × 64 cm
Centre Pompidou, Paris

In 1910 French artist Henri Matisse (1869–1954) painted his daughter, Marguerite, with a large black cat curving around her lap. Although it seems like a straightforward portrait to modern audiences, this colorful painting was deemed radical upon its first exhibition. While the cat's sinuous form echoes the bulbous dress, they both provide contrast to the otherwise austere presentation of the young woman, whose stiff frontal pose and halo of dark hair are reminiscent of Byzantine icons. This style is a harbinger of Matisse's visit to Russia in 1911, where he was deeply impressed by the collections of religious icons from the Byzantine era, and these inspired his flat, simplified, decorative portraits from this period. The presence of the cat in this earlier work suggests influences closer to home. The philosopher Henri Bergson was highly fashionable in Parisian circles after the publication of his iconic text *Creative Evolution* in 1907, which heralded a dynamic organic world that was constantly evolving. Inspired by Bergson, Matisse began to include plants in his portraits, suggesting his sitters were part of nature's rhythm, although here the organic world is represented by the feline in dynamic repose. Its twisting, continuous movement resonates with Bergson's concept of a world in unceasing motion. This fluid ink spill of a cat anticipates Matisse's later more abstract work, especially his monumental frieze *The Swimming Pool* (1952), with aqueous blue figures that leap and unfurl with the same graceful effortlessness.

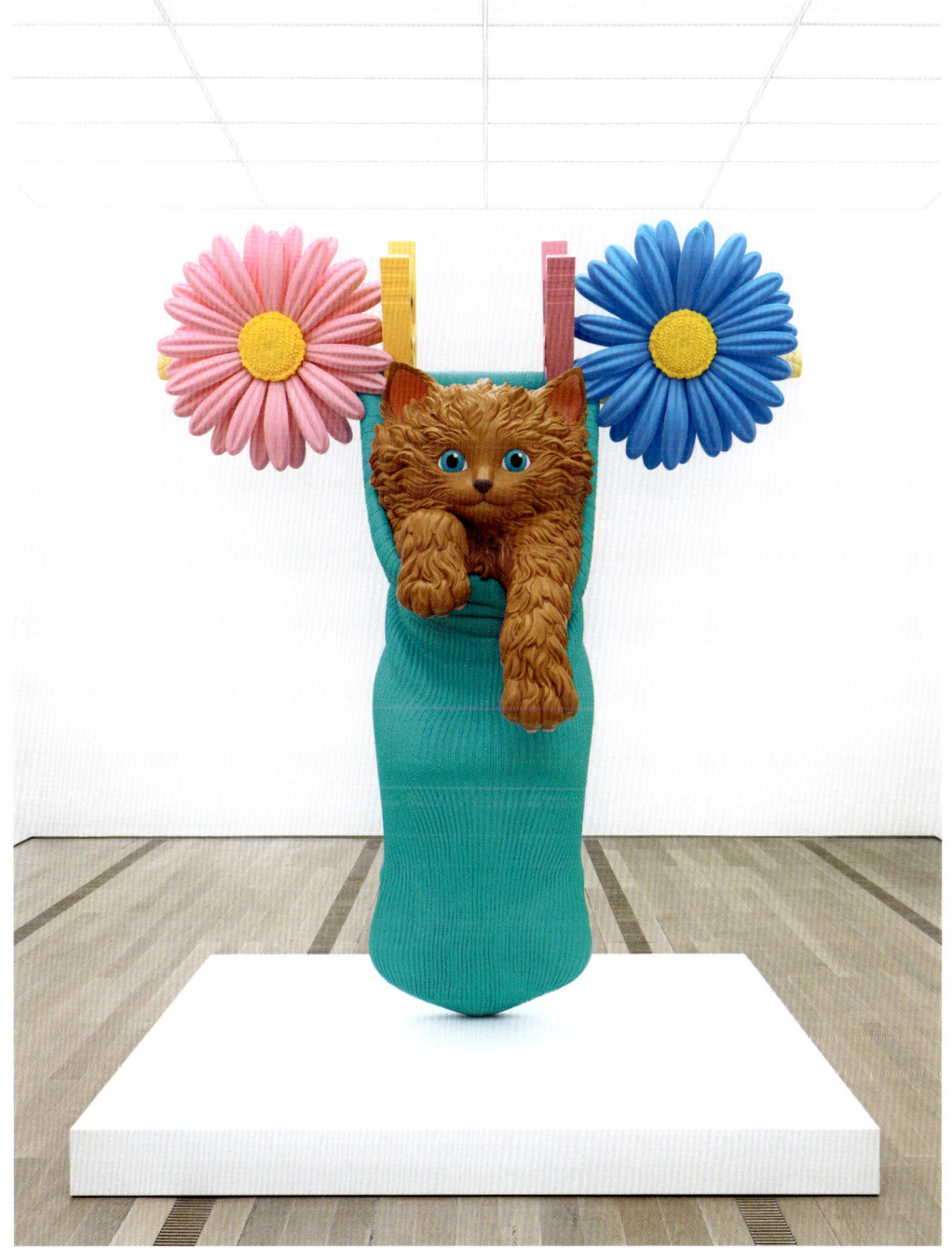

JEFF KOONS

Cat on a Clothesline (Aqua), 1994–2001
Rotationally molded polyethylene
123 × 110 × 50 in. / 312.4 × 279.4 × 127 cm
One of five unique versions

A whimsical representation of a ginger cat, snagged in a sock on a clothesline, is brought to life in realistic detail. But there is something slightly repellent about it, the sweetness offset by the unlikely scenario, larger-than-life proportions, and unnaturally bright colors. A playful riff on the concept of "cute," *Cat on a Clothesline (Aqua)* was created by American artist Jeff Koons (b. 1955). The giant sculpture may have been inspired by a photograph of a kitten in a sock, but it looks more like a toy one would find in a McDonald's Happy Meal, pushed to the limits in terms of scope and size. A member of the post-Pop generation, Koons expanded the use of commercial culture, Readymades, and color in art that had been pioneered by creatives, such as Andy Warhol (see p.95). He translates this fascination with

consumerism into provocative work that ranges from the kitsch to the pornographic or mundane, developing a distinctive style composed of smooth, mirrored surfaces in technicolor. Household items are common motifs in his shiny, oversize sculptures, with objects that include basketballs, vacuum cleaners, and balloon animals being faithfully reproduced. In this looming polyethylene piece, Koons has invited deeper interpretations into what may at first seem to be a mundane image. The layers of reference are seemingly limitless—Internet memes, Jesus on the cross, cheap kitsch, actual kittens, and actual clotheslines—so much so that art critic Blake Gopnik has declared this "an adapted-imagined-enlarged readymade" and the "apotheosis of Koons's career."

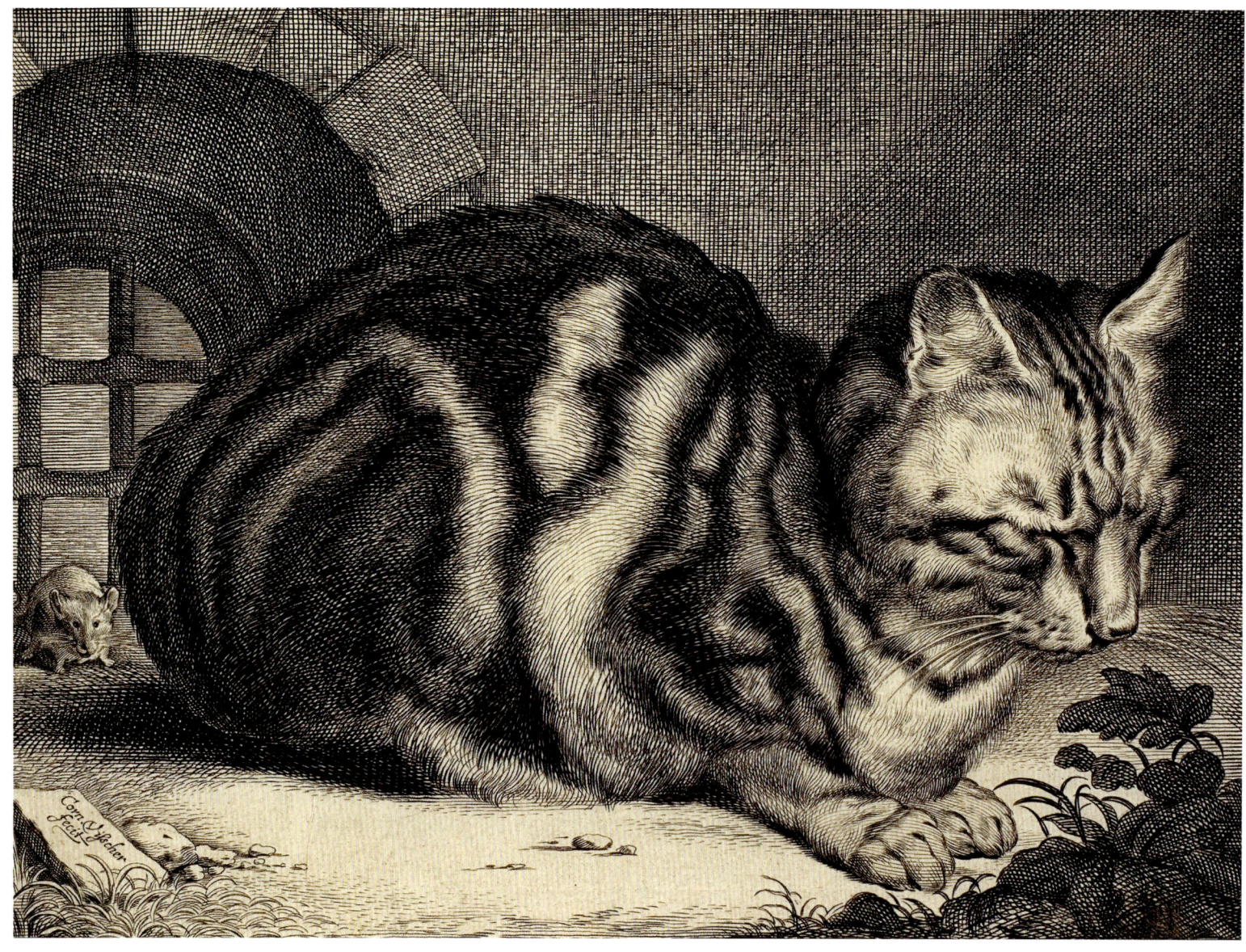

CORNELIS VISSCHER

The Large Cat, 1657
Engraving on ivory paper
5⅝ × 7¼ in. / 14.3 × 18.5 cm
Art Institute of Chicago

A downy coat ripples across a striped feline's body in what the Art Institute of Chicago calls "one of the softest, most tactile renditions of a cat ever printed." Viewing this work engraved by Dutch printmaker Cornelis Visscher (c. 1629–1658), one can almost imagine the restful kitty's body undulating with each sleeping breath. A curious mouse lurks in the background, deliberating whether it dares chance an escape. Cats were effective dispatchers of vermin in Haarlem, where Visscher was born, so a scene like this one was commonplace. Although history says Johannes Gutenberg invented the printing press in Germany in the mid-fifteenth century, there are some who say that the Dutch Republic city of Haarlem was its true birthplace and Laurens Janszoon Coster its creator. Whether that is accurate

or not, Haarlem was indisputably the center of Dutch printmaking, particularly during the seventeenth century's Golden Age, an explosion of creativity and trade in what is now the Netherlands. A prolific artist who created more than two hundred known works during his short lifespan, Visscher was one of the city's leading engravers. His subjects include everything from landscapes and allegorical prints to animal studies, such as the one seen here. But he was particularly gifted in portraiture, where his skilled hand was able to convey a heightened sense of luminosity and realism in his compositions—no small feat for the medium. The attention to detail is readily apparent in *The Large Cat,* one of Visscher's later works.

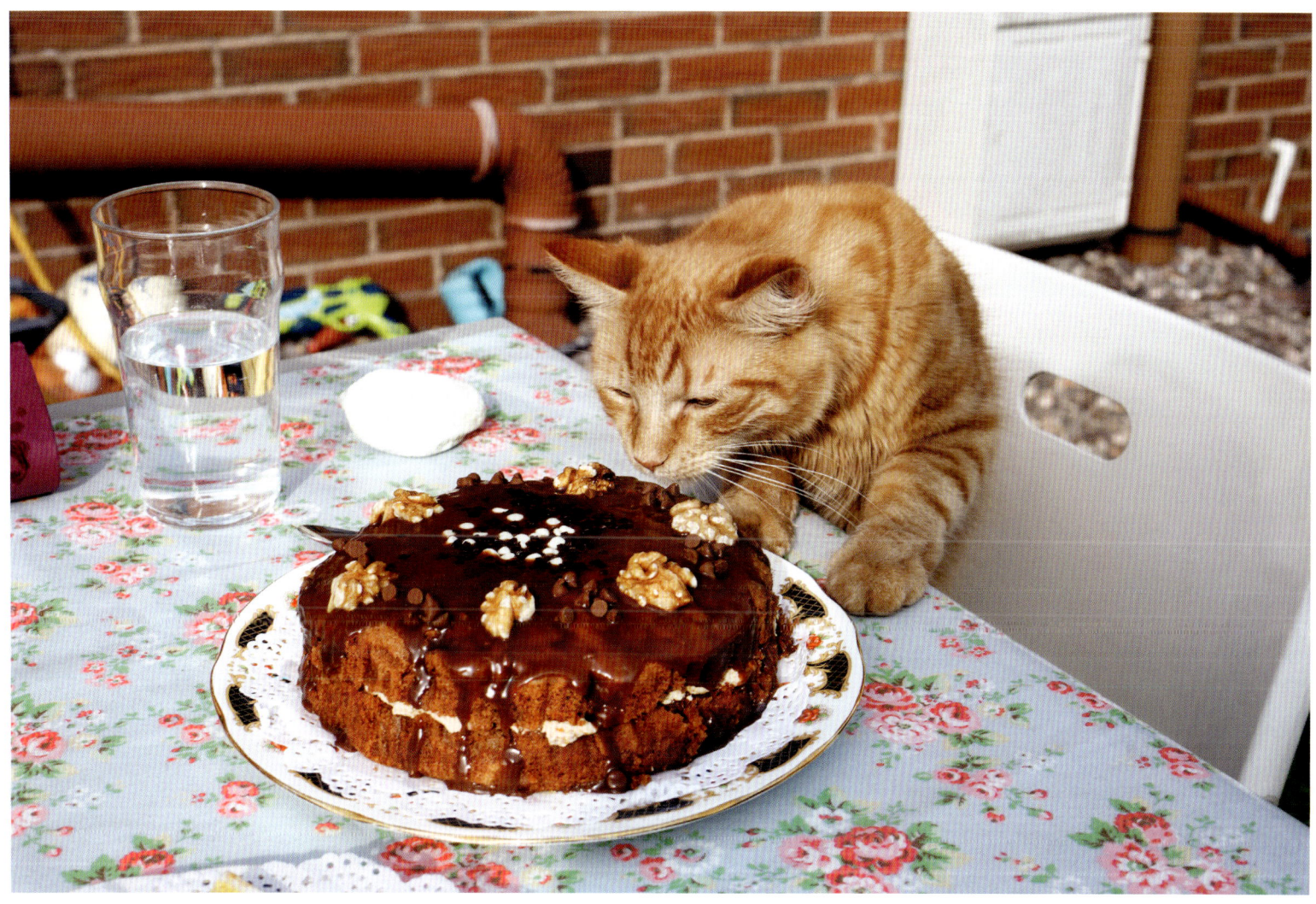

MARTIN PARR

GB. England. Southport, 2014
Photograph, dimensions variable

A real-life Garfield (see p.219) gets uncomfortably close to a teatime cake in this charming shot by legendary British photographer Martin Parr (b. 1952). Known for his satirical and anthropological images, Parr is one of the world's best known documentary photographers capturing everyday British life everywhere, from tennis courts, beaches, and the Chelsea Flower Show to the dining room and, as here, the garden party. This mischievous feline was the star of a photograph from Parr's 2014 exhibition *A Bird's Eye View*, where he was commissioned by frozen food company Birds Eye to capture ordinary mealtimes from across the United Kingdom, illustrating the important role they play in people's lives. Over the course of four months, Parr traveled to areas in Cornwall,

Yorkshire, Norfolk, and Liverpool, where the Atkinson family's afternoon snack—including their neighbor's hungry orange cat—was immortalized. Other photographs included a couple eating TV dinner, a family digging into a big pot of curry, and friends preparing a feast while camping. As Parr declared, "My aim was to champion the many food traits and behaviors Brits have in a way that makes us appreciate each other for our different and wonderful ways of living." Although an orange tabby may not be the first kind of Briton that comes to mind (or a chocolate walnut cake might not be demonstrative of a kitty's standard fare, for that matter), Parr's straightforward and humorous photographs showcase the extraordinary ordinariness of British culture.

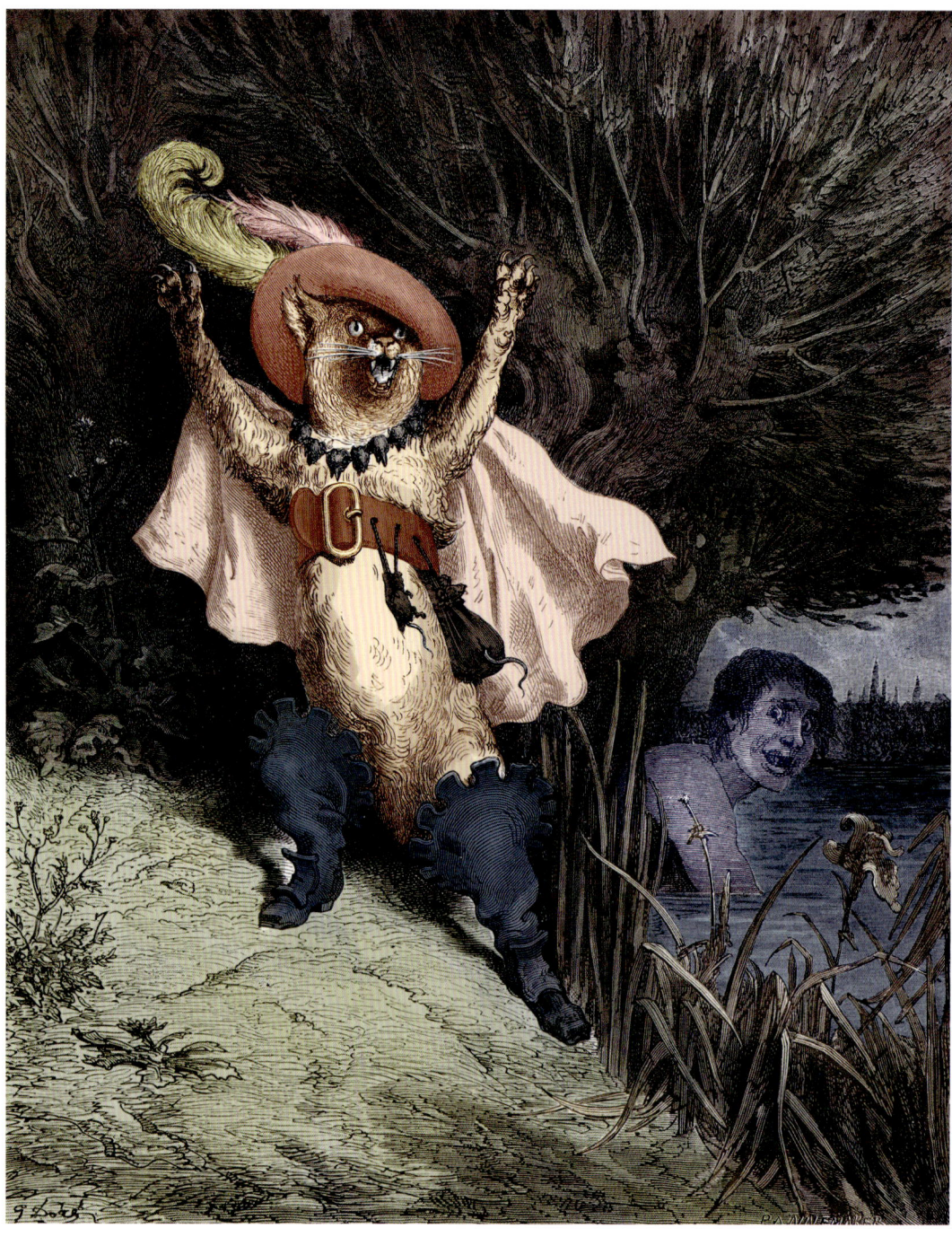

GUSTAVE DORÉ

Puss in Boots, from *Les Contes de Charles Perrault*, 1862
Engraving from printed book
17⅜ × 13¼ in. / 44.2 × 33.1 cm
Hand-painted by anonymous artist from the original
in the Bibliothèque nationale de France, Paris

The prolific French illustrator Gustave Doré (1832–1883) tackled the great classics of Western literature: Cervantes, Dante, Shakespeare, and, perhaps most famously, the fairy tales of Charles Perrault, originally published in 1697. The fin-de-siècle artist's version of the book brings together nine "stories or tales from days gone by," taken from popular culture and passed down orally throughout Western Europe. The most famous of these vignettes included Cinderella, Little Red Riding Hood, and—long before *Shrek* (2001) brought him into contemporary consciousness—Puss in Boots. For the latter, Doré imagined a romantic cat dressed as a musketeer, a gallant seventeenth-century soldier, hailing the king's retinue from the riverbanks, tricking them into thinking his master, the miller's son,

is drowning. Whereas Perrault's original text describes the cat as simply wearing boots, Doré caps the anthropomorphic feline with a Baroque feathered hat and dresses him in a cape, a wide belt, and extraordinarily refined boots. He adapts the human costume to the cat's reality: the animal wears a collar made of bird skulls and a *gibecière* (purse) full of mice. Puss, however small, is no less a ferocious predator than a man, and his elegance does not hide his trickster nature as he uses deceit to gain power for himself and his lowborn master. Doré brings together realism and wonder, while sharing one of the tale's possible morals: in the end, are not humans, behind their elegance and malice, also ferocious beasts who make the law of the strongest reign?

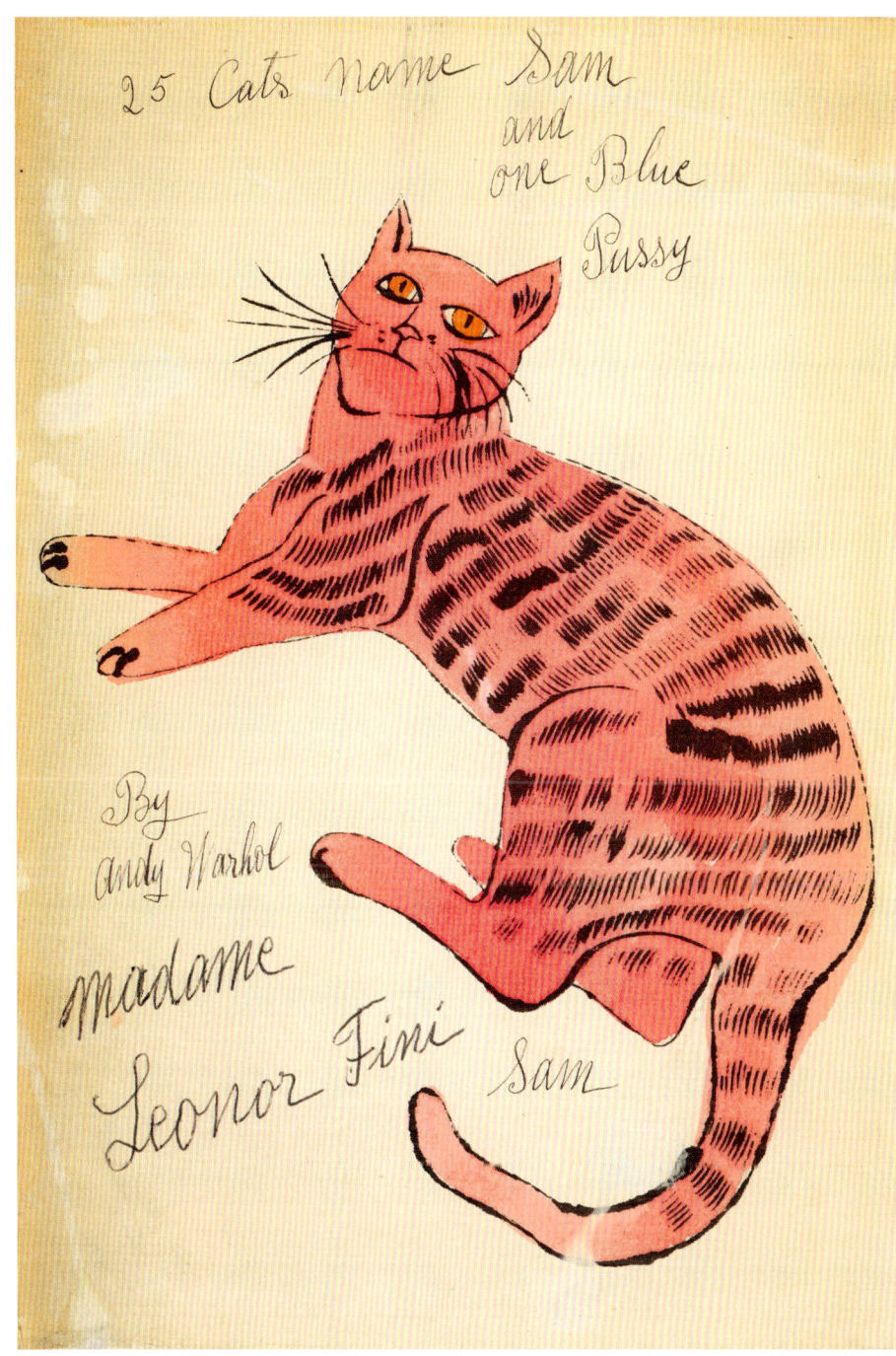

ANDY WARHOL

25 Cats Name(d) Sam and One Blue Pussy, c. 1954
Offset lithograph with hand-coloring in watercolor
9¼ × 6⅛ in. / 23.5 × 15.6 cm
Private collection

In the decade before Andy Warhol (1928–1987) became synonymous with Pop art, the American artist produced a small—but colorfully mighty—book devoted to cats. Composed of a series of drawings that he then reproduced in lithographs, the album is an early example of Warhol's affinity for compiling collections of prints and offers a glimpse into his developing artistic style. In the early 1950s, Warhol lived in an apartment on Lexington Avenue in New York with his mother, Julia, where they owned twenty-five cats, all named Sam, who inspired this work. Despite the book's name, it only contains sixteen Sams, plus "One Blue Pussy" and an extra cat on the cover, making for eighteen works in total. Each cat, thoughtfully drawn, reveals Warhol's love for his feline subjects, a tenderness slightly absent from later works depicting familiar symbols of consumerism or celebrity, such as Campbell's soup cans. The thick outlines and bold, unnatural colors of those famous works are present here, alongside the delicate line techniques he had learned in his first jobs as a commercial illustrator. *25 Cats Name(d) Sam and One Blue Pussy* encompasses Warhol's distinctive collaborative approach to artmaking, where Julia provided the calligraphy and friends filled in the lines of his prints, giving the cats their vibrant hues at "coloring parties." Warhol self-published fewer than two hundred copies of this book, most of which he gave away to friends, including another famous cat lover, the artist Leonor Fini (see p.189).

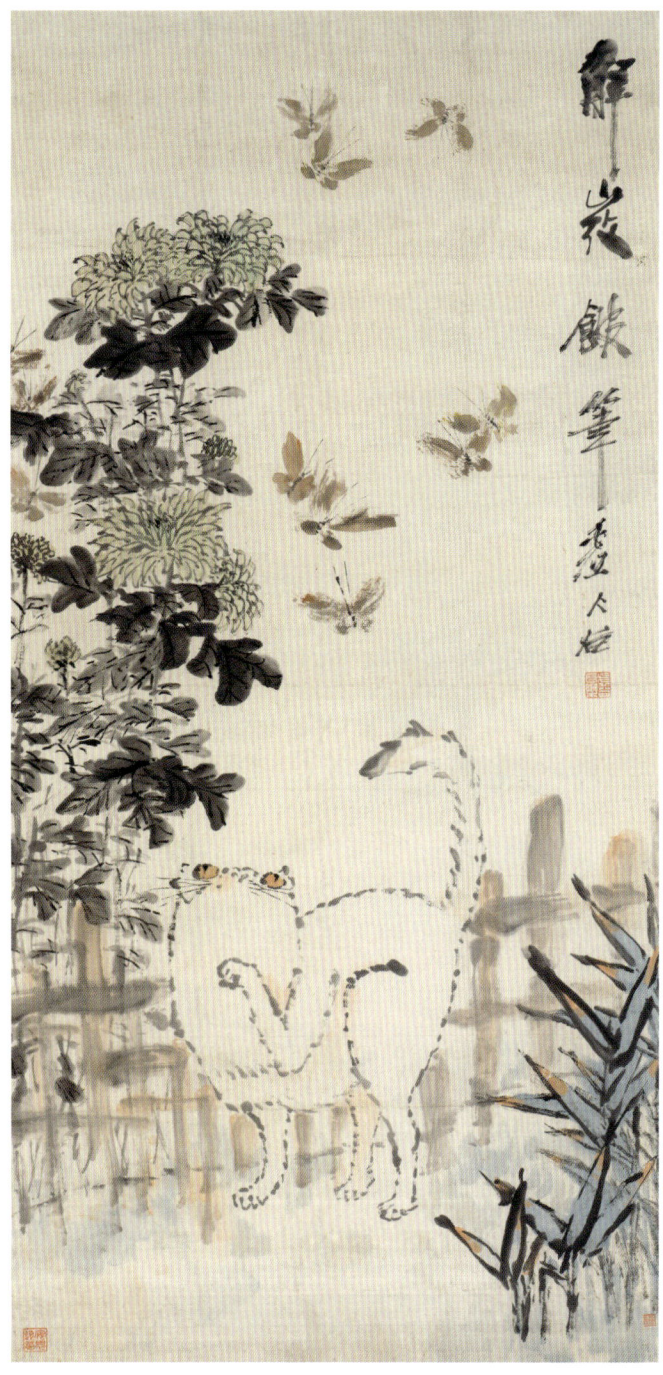

XUGU

Cat and Butterfly, 19th century
Ink and color on paper
52¾ × 25¾ in. / 134 × 65.4 cm
Metropolitan Museum of Art, New York

A lightly sketched outline of a hilariously shaped cat stands with its front left paw raised, its head thrown back, and its tail up, poised to strike at the butterflies delicately fluttering high above it. While the cat's body, tail, and limbs are suggested by a series of short lines, in contrast, its bulging eyes are fully drawn as they concentrate on the butterflies in this paper scroll by the Qing dynasty–era (1644–1911) Chinese artist Xugu (1823–1896). Born Zhu Xubai or Zhu Huairen, he initially joined the Imperial Army in 1851 only to desert to become a monk, taking the name Xugu, before becoming a wandering painter. Within an impressionistic landscape, Xugu tells the story of the cat goddess, Li Shou, whom farmers worshipped in return for her protection for their crops. According to the Chinese creation myth, cats were originally intended by the gods to run the world, but they preferred to enjoy themselves, chasing butterflies, as here, or sleeping under cherry trees. When the gods realized this, they took away cats' power of speech and gave the job to humans—but allowed the cats to carry on enjoying themselves. Given that felines were their first choice, the gods also determined that humans would always be able to tell the time just by looking at a cat's eyes: at morning and night, the eyes were pools of black, but at midday they were black slits in disks of gold, which is helpfully indicated in the hanging scroll here.

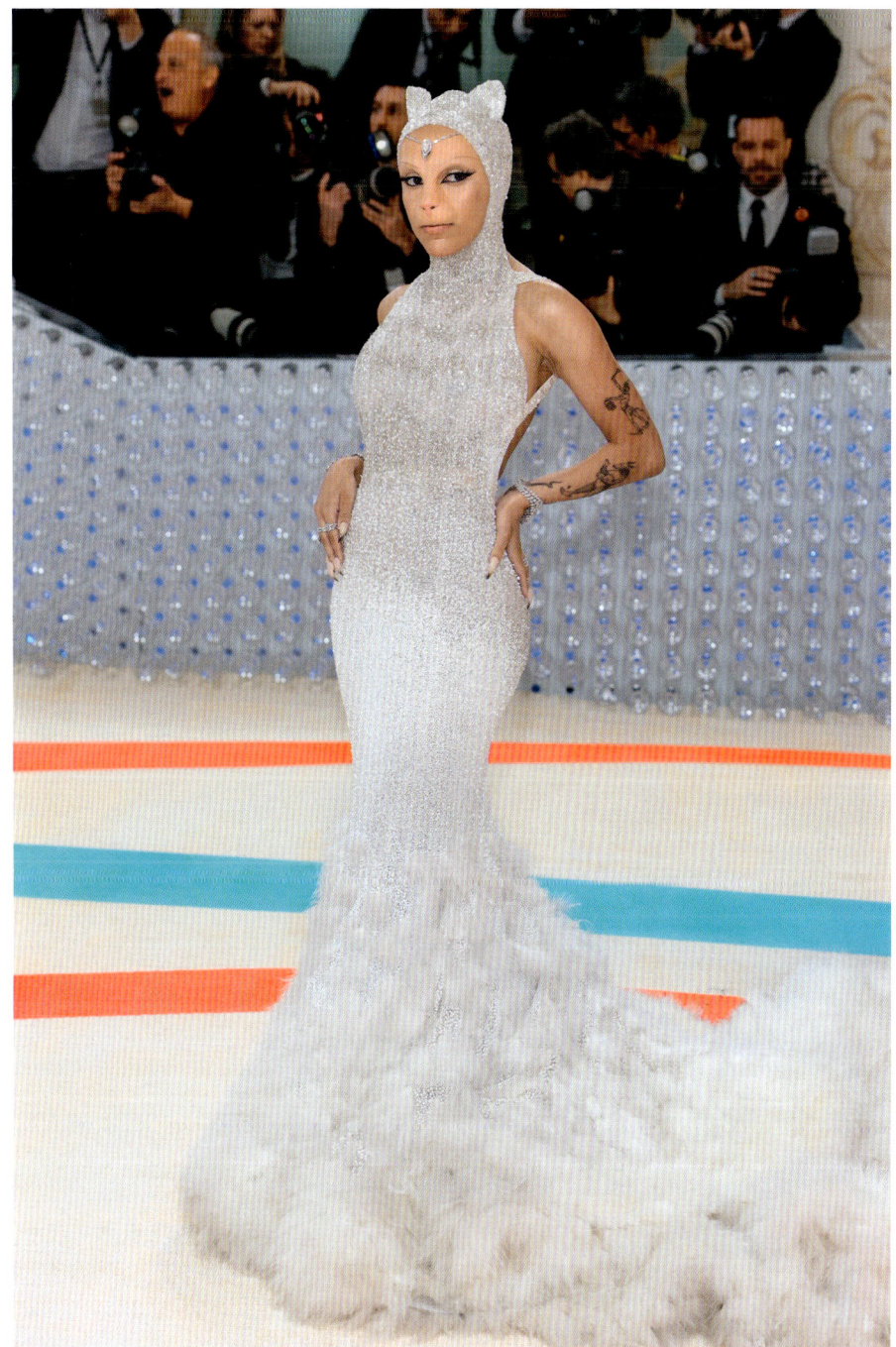

OSCAR DE LA RENTA

Doja Cat as Choupette at the Met Gala, 2023
Prosthetics by Malina Stearns

The first Monday in May, the date of the annual Met Gala, is the most important date of the fashion calendar. Celebrating the Costume Institute of the Metropolitan Museum of Art in New York, it is when the fashion world takes its biggest risks and enjoys its most viral moments. This Oscar de la Renta look, worn by American rap and pop superstar Doja Cat, accomplished all three. The theme of the 2023 gala was *Karl Lagerfeld: A Line of Beauty*, honoring the legacy of the late designer, who was best known as the creative director of Chanel. Lagerfeld's work was characterized by its uncompromising luxury and elegance married with edge. He was an unmistakable presence, always dressed in a sharp black suit with a starched collar, dark sunglasses, and fingerless gloves, his silver hair swooped back into a neat ponytail. In his final years, however, his most notable accessory was his beloved white Birman cat, Choupette, to whom he left a portion of his estate in 2019. Doja's look is an homage to Choupette, among the world's most famous—and most pampered—felines. The hand-beaded, hooded dress was a six-month collaboration between Doja Cat's stylist, Brett Alan Nelson, and Oscar de la Renta co-creative directors Laura Kim and Fernando Garcia. The coup de grâce—feline-inspired prosthetics created by Malina Stearns—were suggested by Doja Cat herself. Although Choupette declined to attend, this eccentric nod to Lagerfeld's feline companion was a fitting tribute to the man whose six decades in fashion altered the trajectory of modern design.

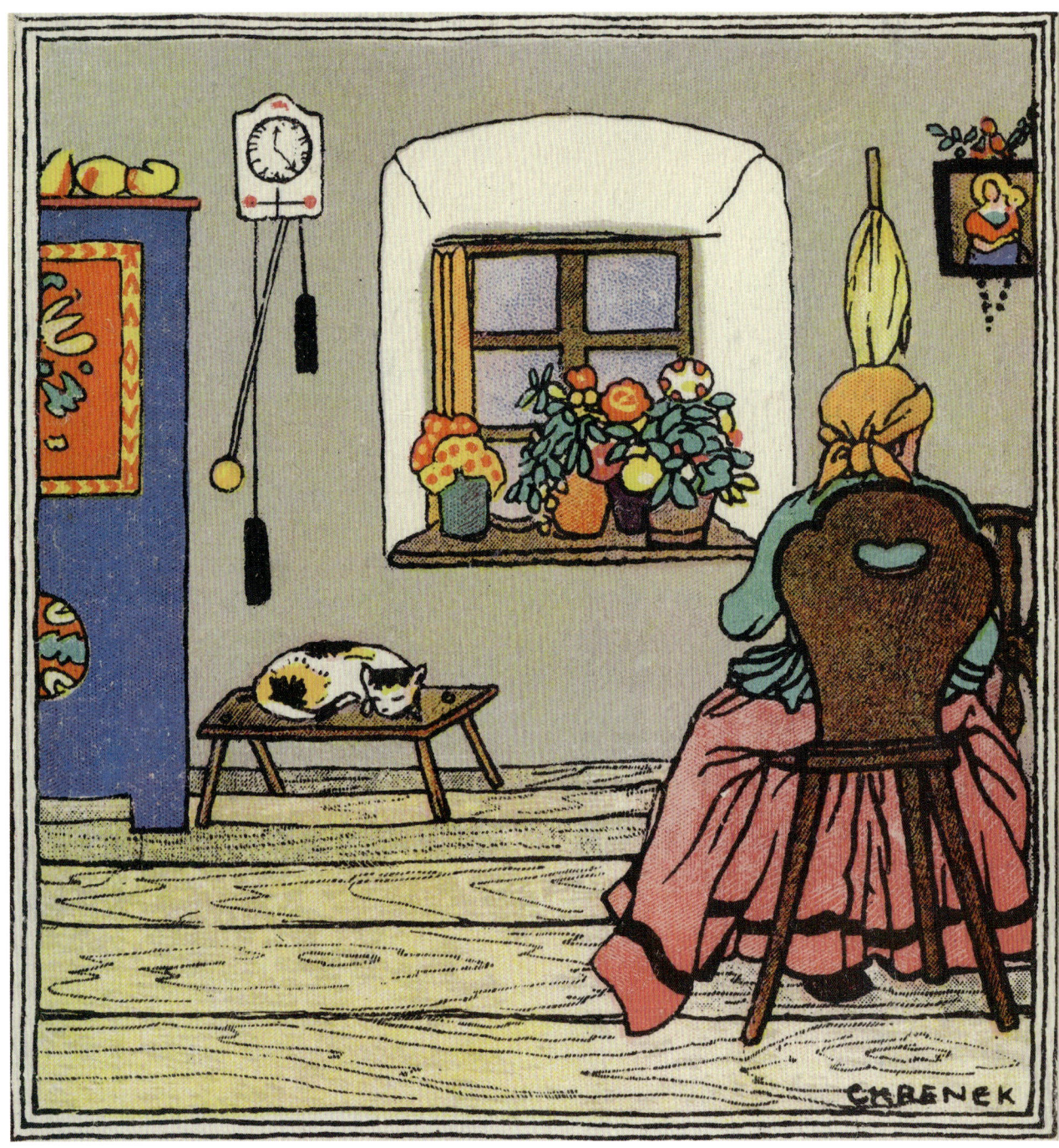

CARL KRENEK

Farmhouse Parlor (detail), 1912
Color lithograph, 5½ × 3½ in. / 13.9 × 8.9 cm
Metropolitan Museum of Art, New York

This postcard celebrates pastoral domesticity, complete with a flower-filled windowsill, a kerchiefed woman working, and a sleepy calico. Created by Austrian artist Carl Krenek (1880–1948), who is best known for his stylistic woodcuts, it is part of a series of nine postcards depicting seasonal vignettes from everyday life in turn-of-the-century Austria. Prolific in everything from printmaking and illustration to ceramics and stained glass, Krenek was a member of the Wiener Werkstätte (Vienna Workshop), a collective of artists, architects, and designers founded in 1903 in the Austrian capital, which published this woodcut in an accessible and reproducible format. The Werkstätte was established on the principle of *gesamtkunstwerk*, meaning that utilitarian items, not just paintings or sculptures, should

also be produced as "total works of art." During the collective's three-decade run, formally trained artists, such as Krenek, Gustav Klimt, and Egon Schiele, produced artworks and a range of objects, including decorative arts, furniture, jewelry, and clothing, according to the movement's tenets, which inspired later design enterprises, such as the Bauhaus. Graphic prints like this postcard provide a snapshot into the bucolic home life of regular Austrians at the beginning of the twentieth century and showcase new developments in aesthetic trends. While its feminine and feline subject matter may borrow from traditional folk art, the square composition, saturated hues, and graphic, almost cartoonlike, linework are indicative of the period's Art Nouveau style.

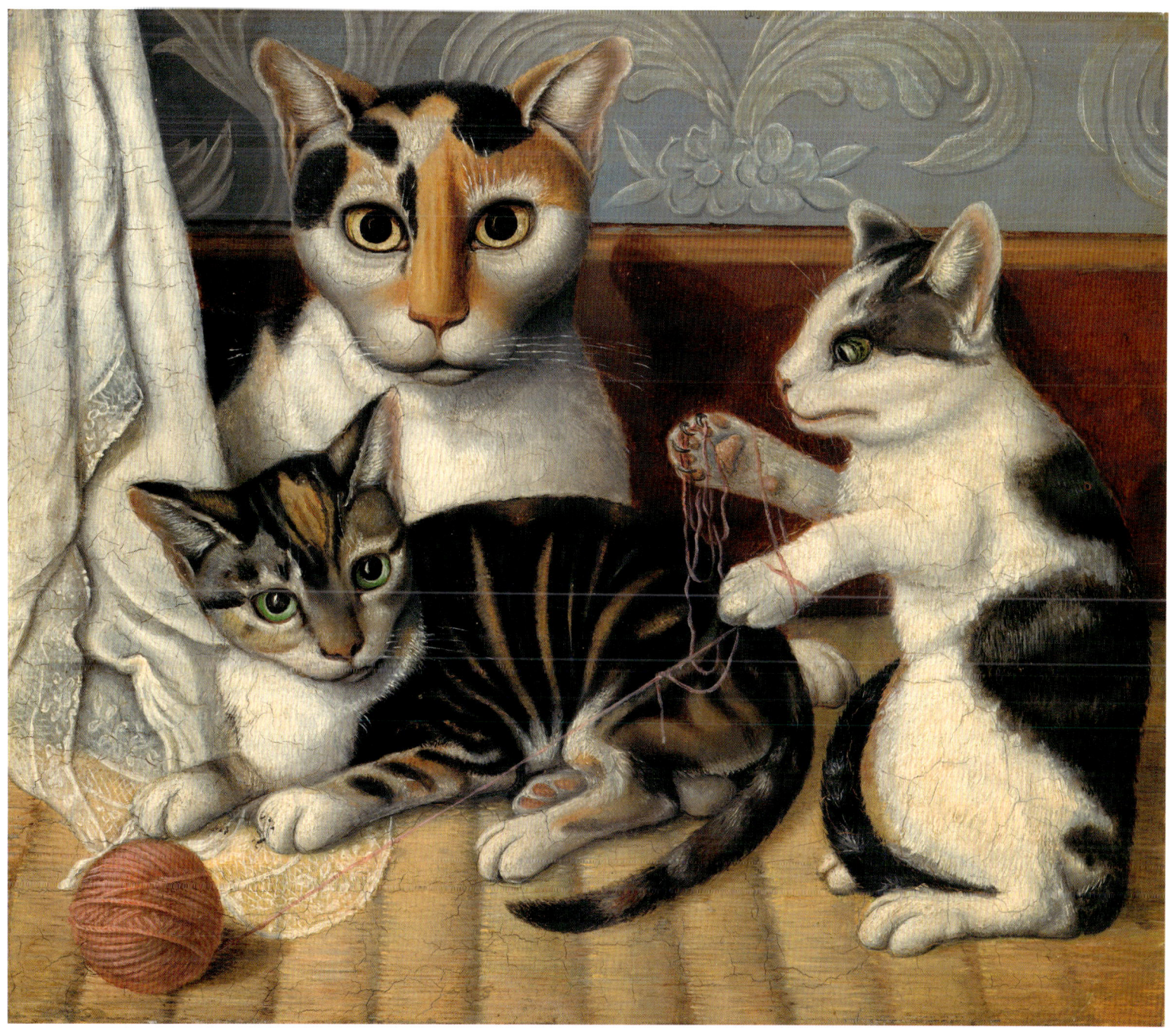

ANONYMOUS

Cat and Kittens, c. 1872/83
Oil on millboard, 11¾ × 13¾ in. / 30 × 34.9 cm
National Gallery of Art, Washington, DC

A calico mother cat stares sternly out of this feline family portrait as her two rambunctious kittens toy with a ball of yarn in a classic scene of domesticity. Although not much is known about the anonymous American painter who created this work, *Cat and Kittens* is a jewel of American naïve art and one of the most popular cat-centric canvases in the National Gallery's collection. Also known as folk, primitive, or provincial art, naïve art is defined by the flat and two-dimensional yet brightly colorful and highly individual painting style employed by self-taught artists in the United States from the seventeenth to nineteenth centuries. The planar forms and vibrant color palette here are markers of naïve art, even if *Cat and Kittens* is a later example of the American school. Many folk artists were itinerant, traveling around the countryside to paint on commission, usually creating portraits of well-to-do farmers or townspeople and their families (see p.82). Naïve painters were less likely to make still lifes, landscapes, or other kinds of genre scenes, so this feline portrait is also unique for its subject matter. The cats here are rendered almost realistically, with the tabby kitten on the left appearing more true-to-life than its awkwardly standing sibling tangled up in yarn. The work also boasts intricate details, from the uniform pattern of the blue wallpaper to the delicate rendering of embroidery on the curtain. For a final elevated touch, the anonymous artist emphasized the powerful mother cat's gaze by encircling her pupils in shimmering gold leaf.

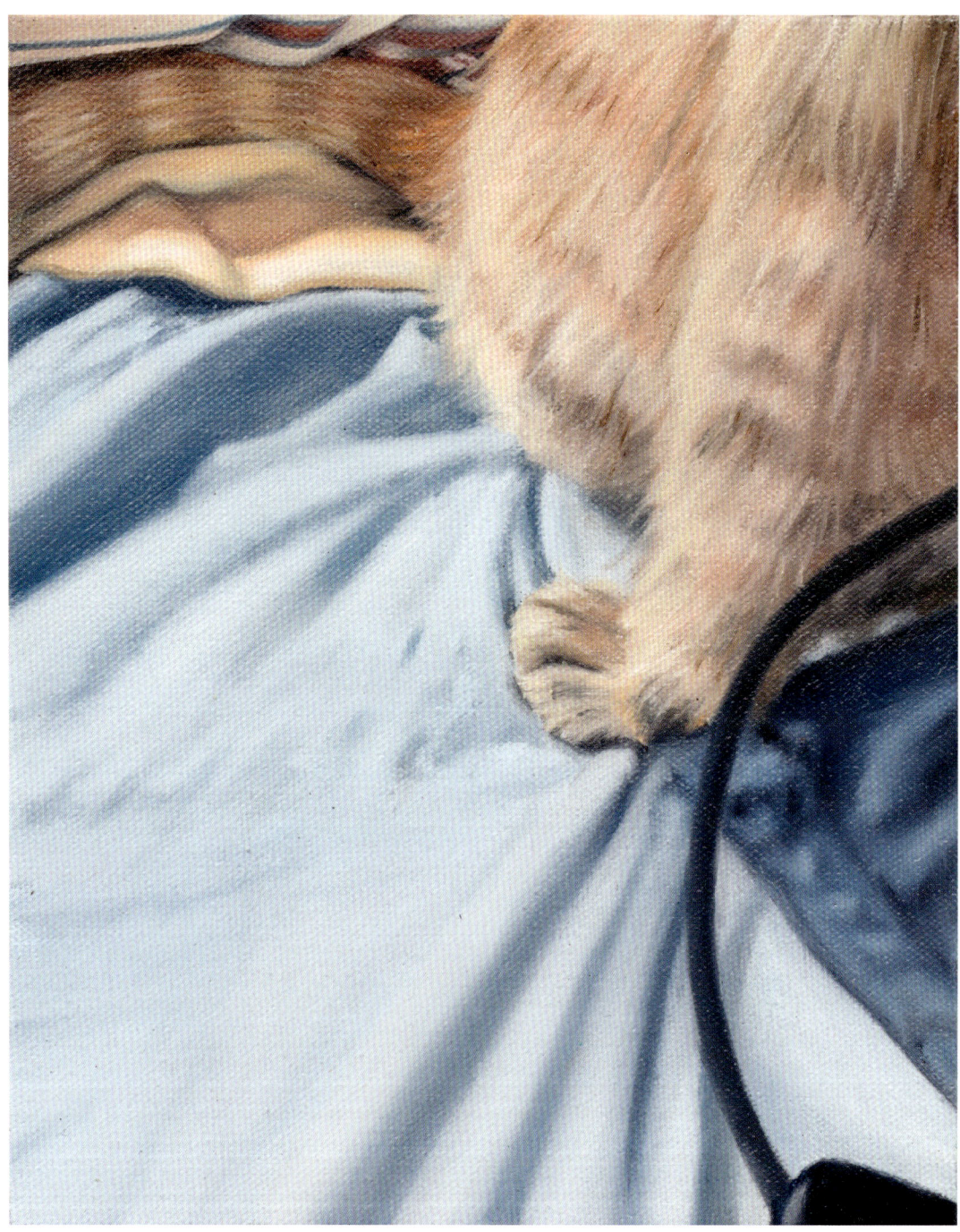

CAIT PORTER

Wheezie with Blue Sheets, 2022
Oil on linen, 10 × 8 in. / 25.4 × 20.3 cm
Private collection

A tabby's paw pushes firmly into icy blue sheets, with only its tail, lower body, and front right leg visible, in this close-up painting by New York–based artist Cait Porter (b. 1985). Slightly out of frame and partly obscured by a black object—perhaps a charger cord or book light—Wheezie the cat is claustrophobically close, filling the viewer's gaze. It is a position all too familiar to cat owners who, while trying to relax or read in bed, are distracted by their pet's looming presence, creeping into their peripheral vision and silently demanding attention. (The feline's name makes one wonder if we should also be imagining some heavy nearby breathing.) This delicate depiction of a singular cat paw is indicative of Porter's other work, which comprises tightly framed, highly realistic paintings of the details that are often missed in already over-looked everyday objects and phenomena, ranging from bubbles dissolving in a bathtub to a freshly peeled orange sitting next to a crumpled can of hard seltzer. The artist has said that she is drawn to these quiet moments of normal objects for the "kind of weight that they can carry of things within our daily lives that are avoided, or pushed away, or left unsaid." Suffused with this emotional weight, Porter's works, which she paints from photographs, are so true-to-life that they become almost abstract, the granular elements distorting into the canvas upon long reflection. This, then, is not just a painting of Wheezie's paw, but an intimate flash between cat and human captured in time.

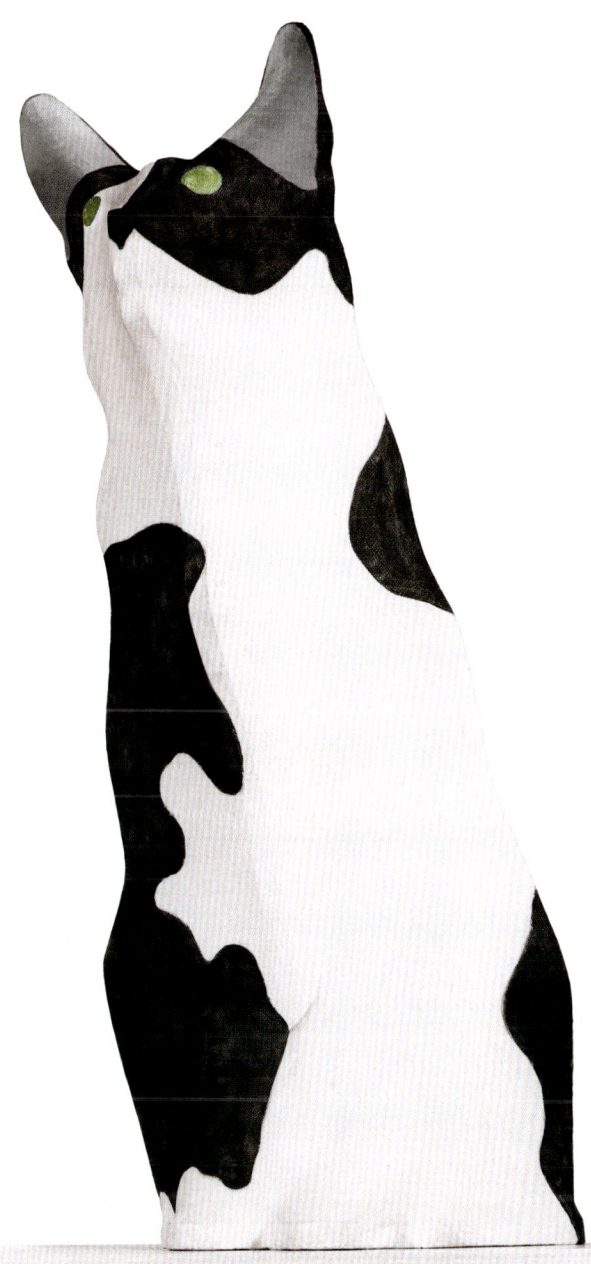

ANNE ARNOLD

Charlie, 1969
Acrylic on canvas over wood
49 × 23 × 27 in. / 124.5 × 58.4 × 60.6 cm
Buffalo AKG Art Museum, New York

In the mid-1950s, American sculptor Anne Arnold (1925–2014) began to create the oversize animal sculptures for which she became famous. This large black-and-white cat is *Charlie*, named for one of Arnold's pets, whom she modeled by stretching canvas over a wooden frame before painting it to reproduce the colors and pattern of Charlie's fur. Unlike the real Charlie, however, Arnold's sculpture has been both elongated to give the animal a stretched-out leanness and significantly enlarged, so he stands more than 4 feet (1.2 m) tall. In the era of Abstract Expressionism, when nonrepresentational art was fashionable—Arnold's husband, Ernest Briggs, was an abstract painter—the artist's figurative zoological sculptures were unlike anything else on the scene. With his green eyes fixed into the distance,

the cat is highly realistic as he perhaps tracks a bird or tries to peer over a windowsill, although abstract elements creep in. *Charlie* the sculpture, for instance, has no discernible limbs. Arnold and Briggs lived in Montville, Maine, where they kept a menagerie of cats and dogs, as well as pigs, cows, and chickens, which feature in many of Arnold's sculptures. Working from a photograph of her chosen animal, she selected her material—bronze, clay, wood, or fabric soaked in resin—according to the personality of the creature and how she could best distill its unique characteristics. Her wooden *Charlie* sculpture, which combines both a folk tradition and a modernist interpretation, captures the spirit of her much-loved pet.

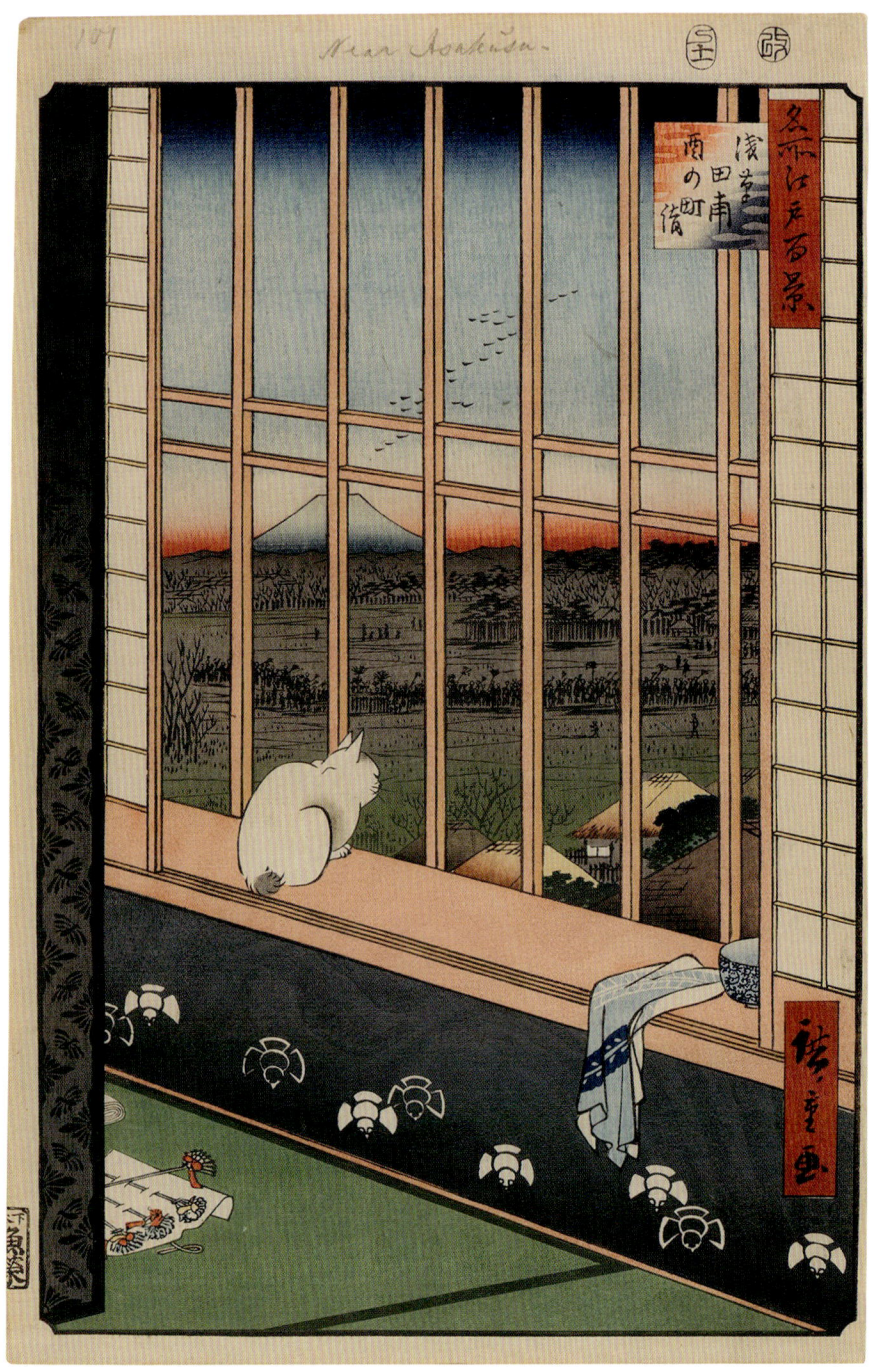

UTAGAWA HIROSHIGE

Asakusa Ricefields and Torinomachi Festival, No. 101,
from *One Hundred Famous Views of Edo*, 1857
Woodcut, 14⅛ × 9¼ in. / 36 × 23.5 cm
Brooklyn Museum

A white Japanese Bobtail cat, a breed known for its naturally short, curly tail resembling a pom-pom, gazes out the window as the sun sets over Mount Fuji in this woodblock print by Japanese artist Utagawa Hiroshige (1797–1858), a master of *ukiyo-e*, or "pictures of the floating world." Known for views of nature and birds, which feature here in the sky above Mount Fuji but also in the pattern on a standing screen and on the wall beneath the window, Hiroshige also depicted erotica and settings associated with courtesans and prostitutes. Set in the Yoshiwara pleasure quarters, a famous red-light district in Edo, now Tokyo, this scene takes place on the second floor of a brothel during the Torinomachi Festival, the busiest day of the year in the area. Visible in the distance are the silhouettes of people taking part in the festival procession through the Asakusa rice fields to the Washi Daimyojin Shrine. Although the serene cat is the focus of the image, the presence of a courtesan is evident in items scattered about the room, including a blue-and-white china bowl and used towel; a set of ornate *kumade* hairpins on the floor, probably a gift from her customer; and just visible behind a decorated screen, a roll of *onkotogami*, or tissue papers used during the act of sex. On this special day, known as a *monbi*, each courtesan was required to take a customer or to pay the fee to the brothel owner herself if she was not able to.

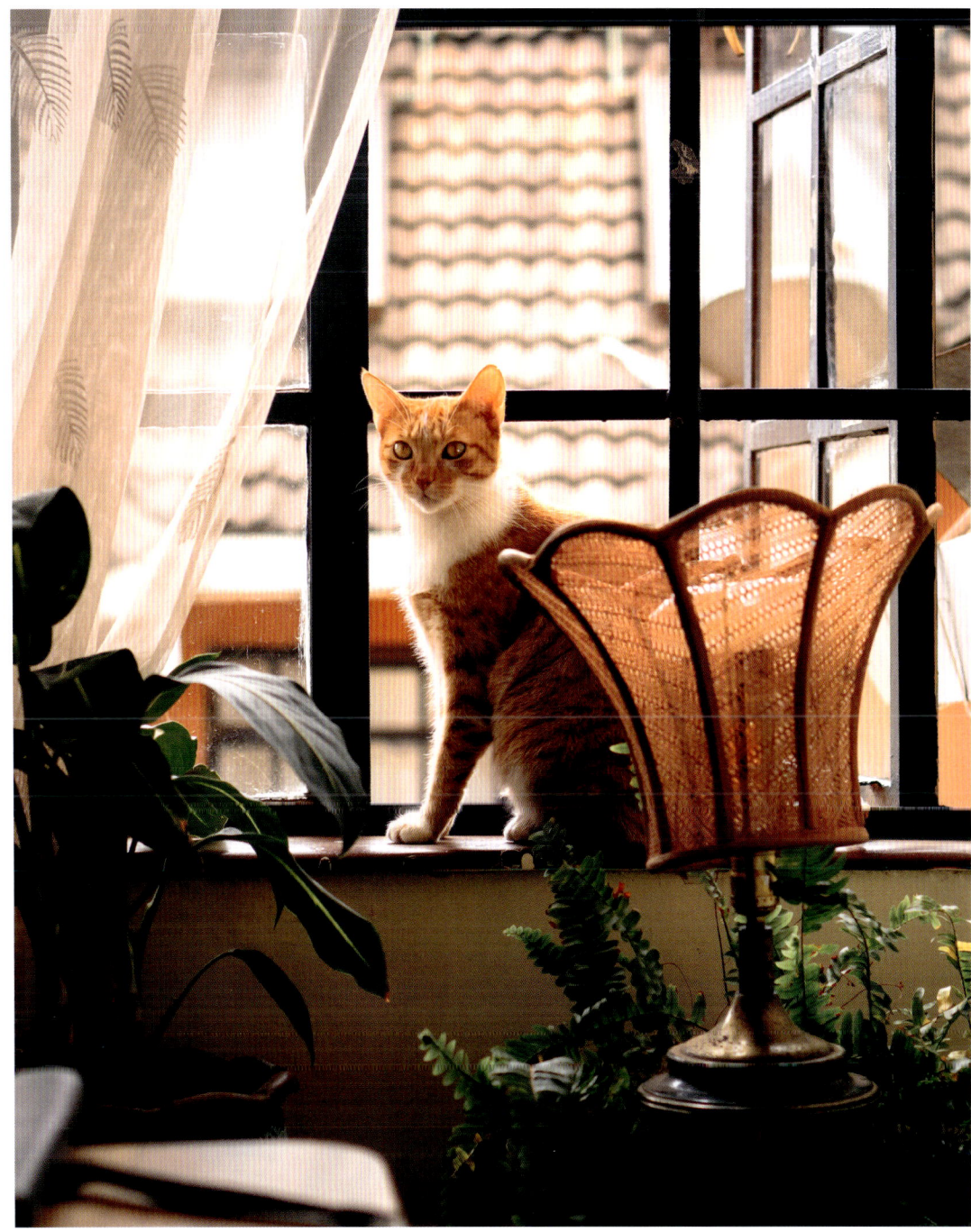

BILL MUGANDA

*By the window, she thought of what the
human will have for dinner, 2023
Digital photograph, dimensions variable*

Nairobi-based photographer Bill Muganda is an avid reader and a self-proclaimed cat dad, two attributes that contributed to the genesis of his Instagram account, @kenyan_library. The images on his page reflect the quotidian pleasures of curling up at home with a good book and a furry friend. Yet there is a heightened quality of surreality in his images, soaked in a golden radiance and seemingly staged with an element of theatricality. Take, for instance, the diffused light permeating the upside-down and off-kilter wicker shade in this composition. Not always a fan of cats, Muganda fell in love with his two feline companions, a white Maine Coon and the orange tabby seen here, after rescuing them and beginning to observe their unique behaviors. It is no small feat to capture such evocative images when the subject possesses an obstinate feline mind. Muganda's companions seem willing participants, however, connecting with the photographer and his lens to create moments of quiet beauty, such as this one. Here, the cat's gaze is not trained outside, where birds and sundry other distractions could surely entice it; instead, the action is interior. The photographer captions it thus, "By the window, she thought of what the human will have for dinner," solving the mystery of what has captured the cat's attention. Always beautifully composed and serene, Muganda's images are a worthy addition to perhaps the most irresistible milieu on social media: the cats of Instagram.

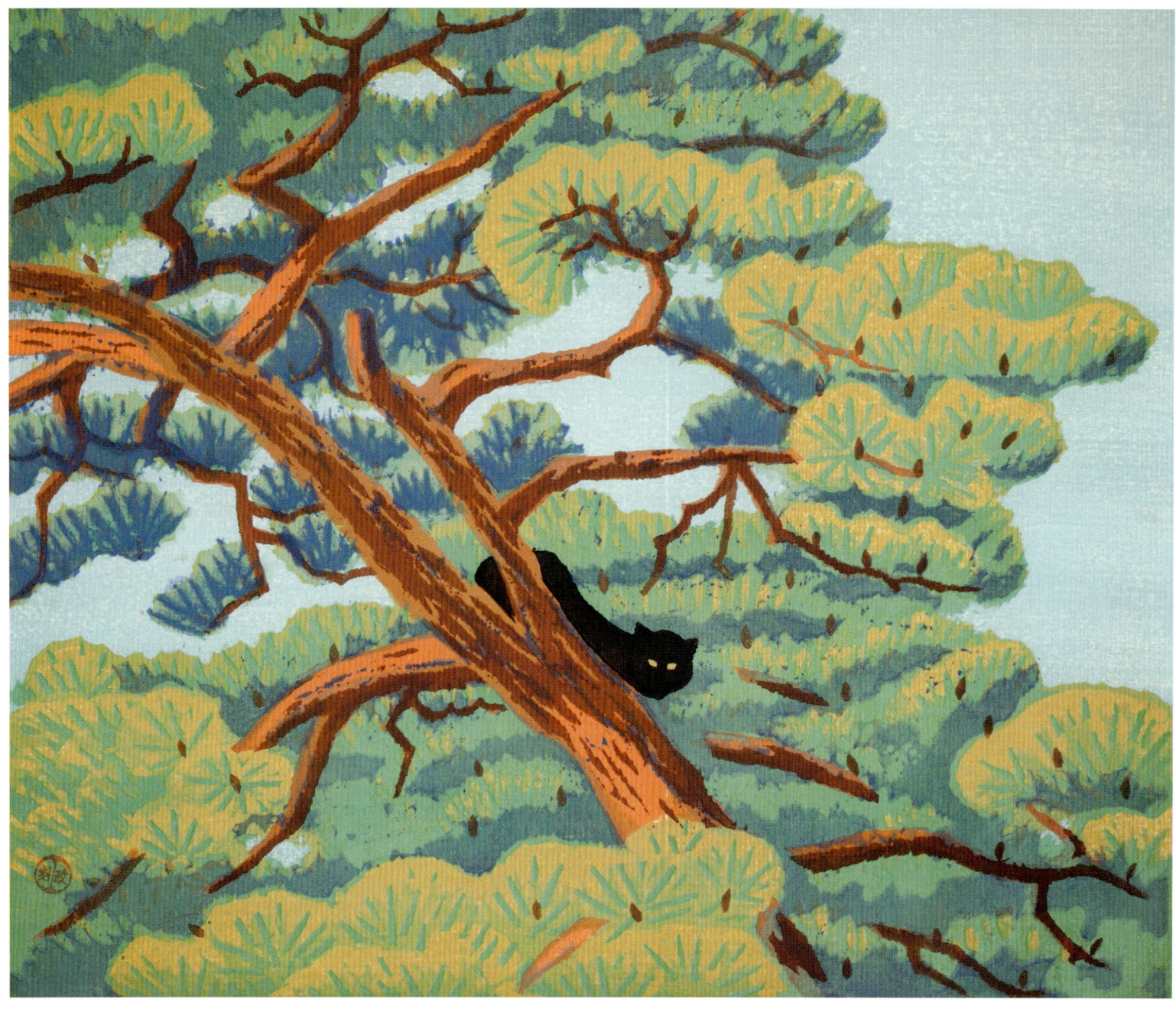

MAEDA MASAO

Black Cat in Tree, 1940
Color woodcut, 15⅝ × 18½ in. / 39.7 × 47.1 cm
Art Institute of Chicago

Crouching halfway down a great pine tree, a black cat balances on the thick trunk and stares ahead, its eyes fixed on unseen prey. The inspiration for this woodcut print by Japanese artist Maeda Masao (1904–1974) was his neighbor's cat, which he often saw climbing a tree. Here, Maeda imbues his version of the cat with a cool sleekness as it pauses its climb. The pine is a traditional symbol in East Asia of stability, strength, and wisdom, its verdant and colorful stalwartness contrasting with the dynamic, furtive, and fully black cat. Born on the island of Hokkaido, Maeda originally trained as a painter at the Kawabata Painting School in Tokyo, where he studied in the Western style known as *yōga*, working in oils before turning to woodcuts in the 1930s and becoming a member of the *sōsaku-hanga* (creative print)

artist group. The composition of this print suggests the influence of his earlier training, but the solid shapes of the defined boughs lend themselves perfectly to the graphic woodcut technique. By the time of this 1940 print—originally intended to be one of fifty, although it is unclear whether the edition was completed after Japan joined World War II—he was working exclusively with woodcuts, producing a diverse range of subjects, from landscapes, particularly mountainscapes, to traditional Japanese scenes and urban vistas. An enthusiastic mountain hiker, Maeda believed that the best views were to be found halfway down—exactly where he positioned his cat in the tree—as he once declared, "The finest panoramas are down in the middle heights."

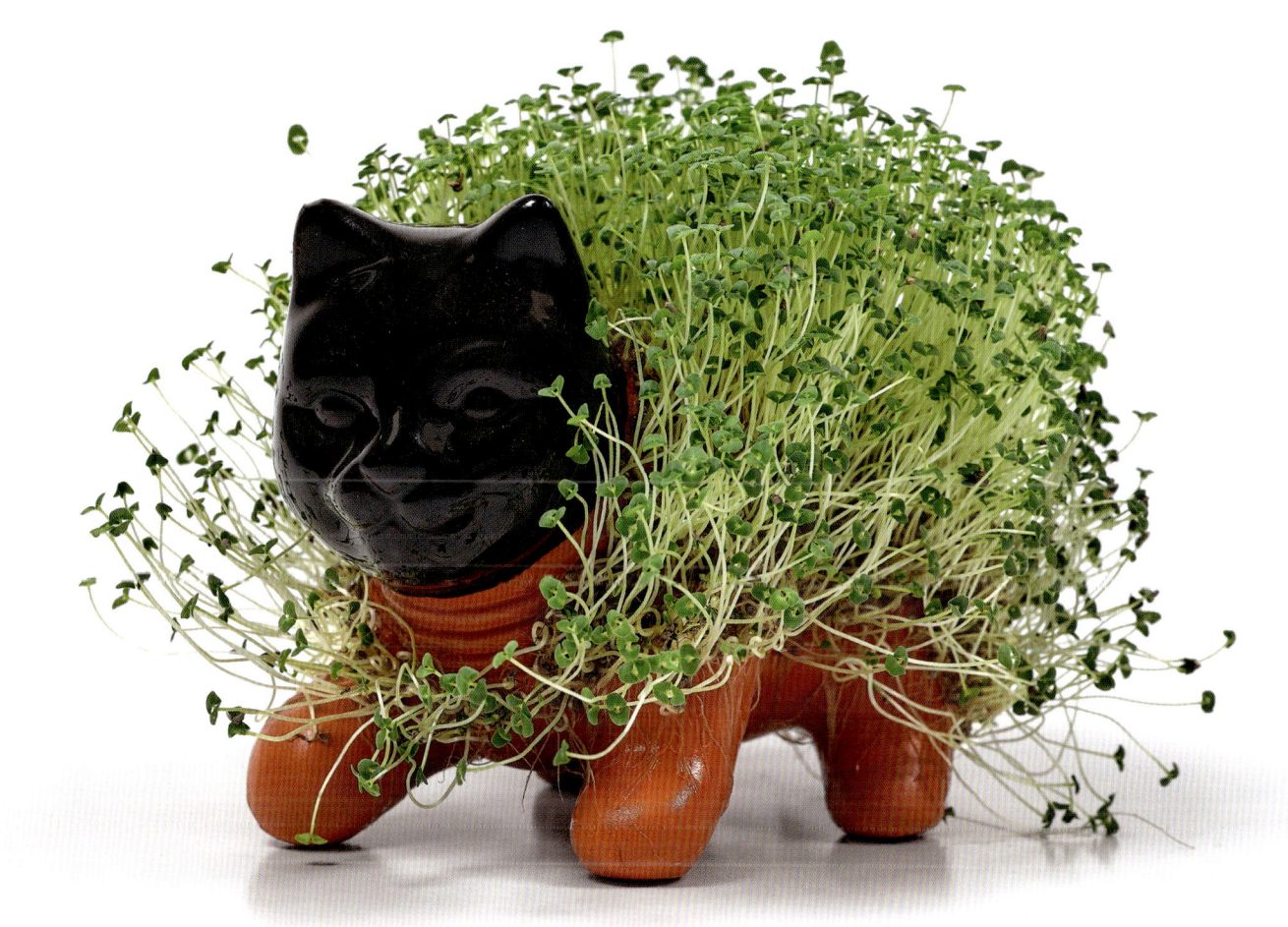

JOSEPH ENTERPRISES

Kitten Chia Pet, c. 1980s
Terracotta planter with chia seeds
6 × 6 × 6 in. / 15.2 × 15.2 × 15.2 cm

In 1977 San Francisco advertising executive Joe Pedott was attending a trade show in Chicago and asked a retailer there about his best-selling holiday item. Surprisingly, it turned out to be a terracotta ram that grew "hair" when chia seeds (*Salvia hispanica*) were planted onto the grooves in the pottery's exterior. He tracked down the man who was importing them from Oaxaca, Mexico, and bought the rights on the spot. Joseph Enterprises was soon established and the Chia Pet was born. The tiny planters became an instant sensation, thanks in no small part to its marketing scheme and, in particular, its unforgettable television jingle, "Ch-ch-ch-chia!" By 1982, the Chia Pet was available in multiple forms, including dogs, turtles, rabbits, and the kitten seen here. Over the decades, countless variations of the product have been made. The brand began licensing partnerships in the year 2000, offering a variety of *Looney Tunes* and *Simpsons* characters. Today you can grow chia sprouts on pottery versions of everyone from Ice Spice and Willie Nelson to Baby Yoda and *The Golden Girls*. An iconic American product, it has been lampooned by *Saturday Night Live* (the riotous Chia Head), is held in the Smithsonian National Museum of American History, and was even included in a *New York Times*–sponsored time capsule in 2000, alongside a Purple Heart medal and a can of Spam, naturally. It is estimated that more than twenty-five million Chia Pets have sold to date.

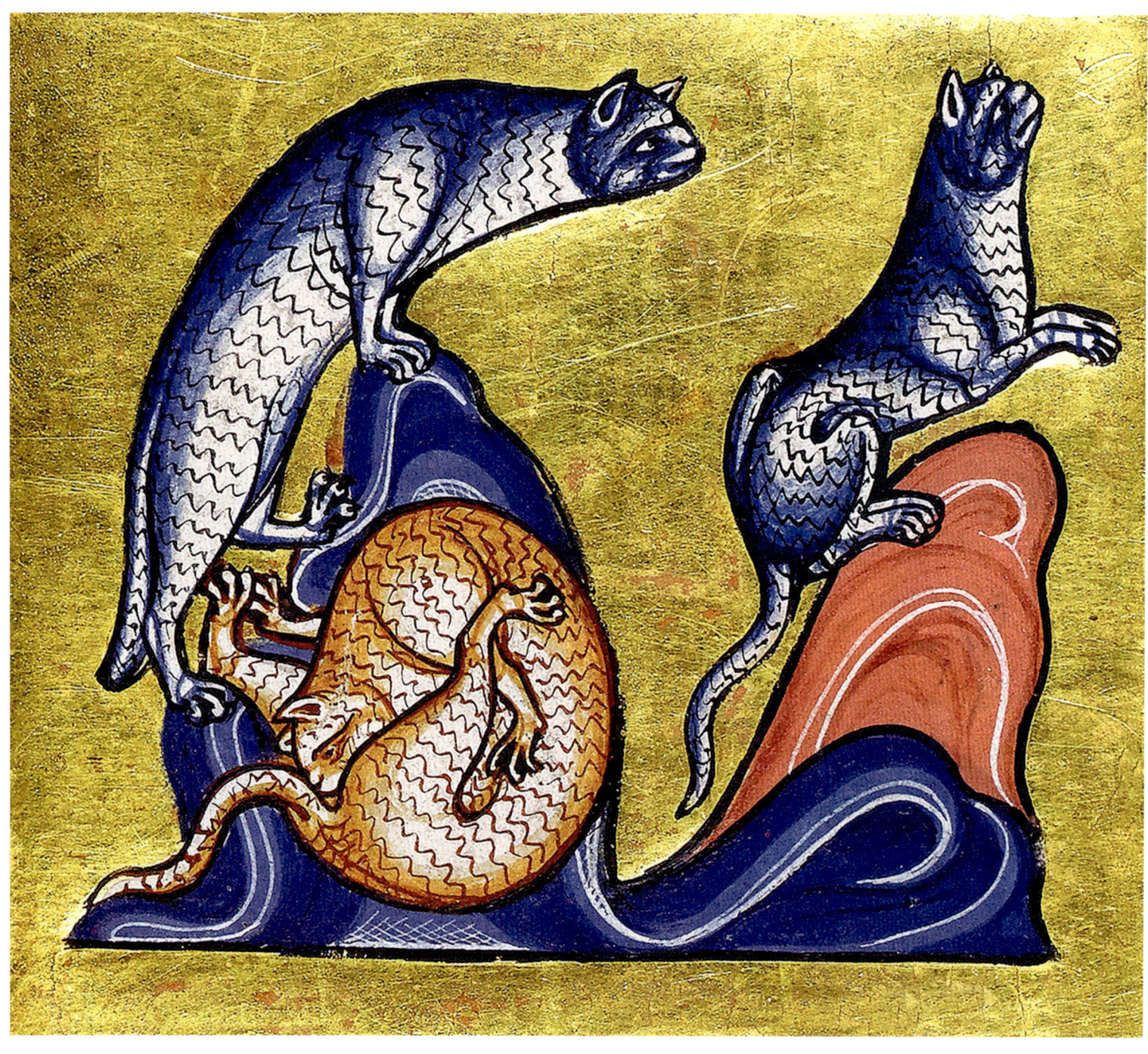

ANONYMOUS

The cats gambol and hunt, fol. 23v (detail), from
The Aberdeen Bestiary, c. 1200
Illuminated manuscript, 11⅞ × 8¼ in. / 30.2 × 21 cm
University of Aberdeen Library, Scotland

Although anatomically improbable, the three creatures perched on rocklike formations in this medieval illumination are immediately recognizable as cats. Two seem to be begging for tidbits, while a third is preoccupied, contorted as it licks its backside. These svelte felines, illustrated in vibrant hues and gold leaf, are found in *The Aberdeen Bestiary*, an English illuminated manuscript from the turn of the thirteenth century. Bestiaries, which were popular throughout northern Europe during the Middle Ages, are compendiums of animals—from wild and domesticated to fantastic beasts of myth and legend—with descriptions typically derived from classical texts about the natural world intermingled with Christian theology. With its lavish illuminations, *The Aberdeen Bestiary* is considered

to be one of the best examples of its type and, due to similarities, is believed to be the sister manuscript of *The Ashmole Bestiary* in the Bodleian Library at the University of Oxford. Offering a didactic account of nature with the primary purpose of Christian moral teaching, it was probably commissioned by a high-ranking member of society, such as a king or eminent churchman. Reflecting its medieval author's worldview, the accompanying script recounts that the cat is "the enemy of mice" and derives its name from the Latin word *captura*, meaning "to catch." The cat is praised for its piercing eyesight, by which it hunts and "overcomes the dark of night with the gleam of light from its eyes," a gleam reinforced by the exquisite background rendered in gold leaf.

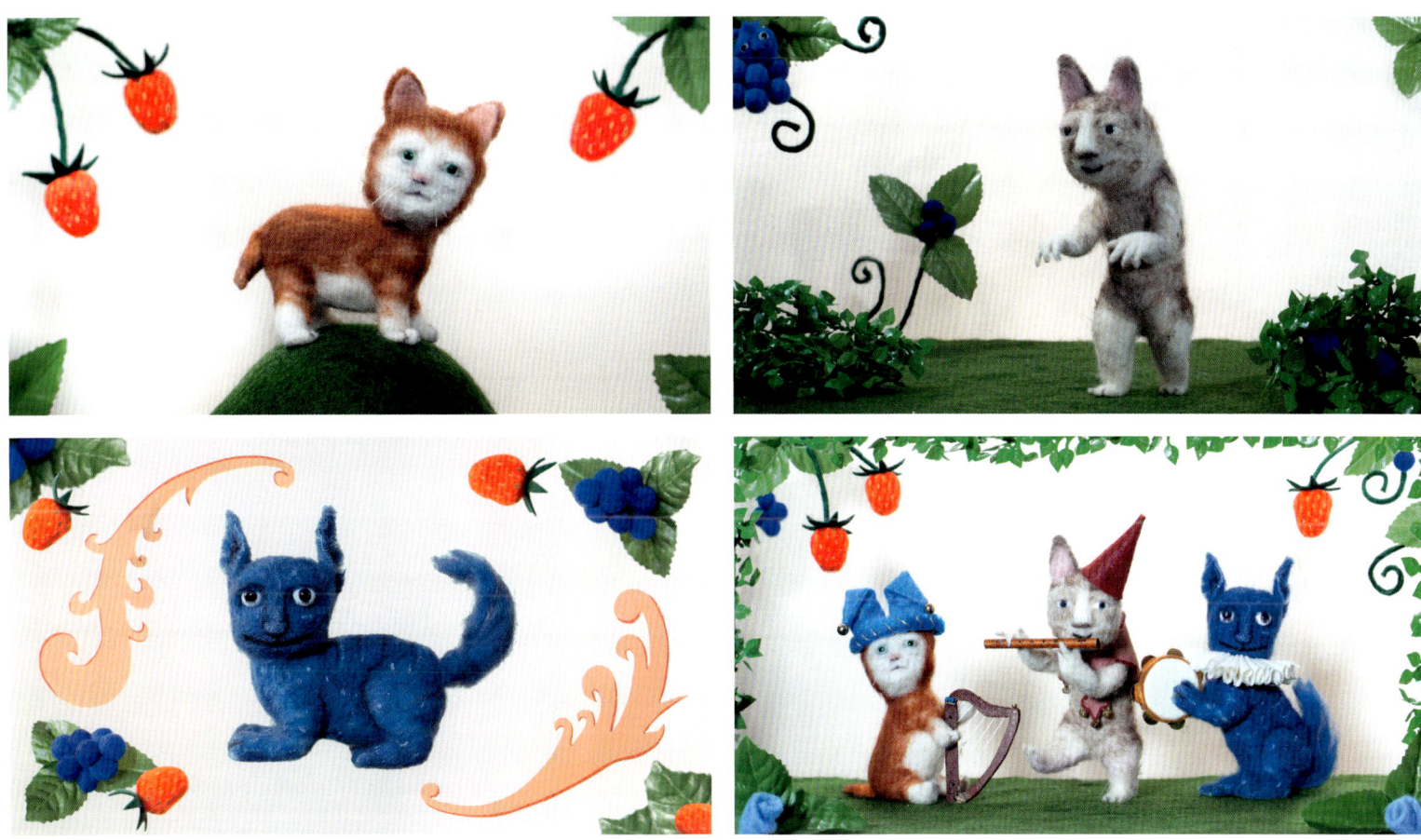

LAURA VENDITTI

Medieval cats having a good old medieval time, 2024
Animation, 30 secs

With their oddly proportioned bodies and anatomically questionable features, the cats of medieval art proved irresistible for Montreal-based stop-motion animator Laura Venditti, whose humorous, needle-felted characters are derived from centuries-old books and paintings. Venditti discovered the bizarre-looking creatures through social media, where hilarious images of cats plucked from old prayer books and illuminated manuscripts were being shared as viral memes. Medieval artists did not paint felines in a realistic way, portraying them instead with exaggerated features and expressive humanlike faces to convey their playful and mischievous nature. In illuminated manuscripts, they are variously seen skulking in gardens, sitting by fireplaces, or even accompanying the Virgin and Child. The renowned religious manuscript *The Book of Kells* (c. 800 CE) features cats with wide eyes entwined within Celtic knots, while the *Queen Mary Psalter* (c. 1310–20) includes a cat playing a drum. Drawing from these sources and others, Venditti's quirky thirty-second film, *Medieval cats having a good old medieval time*, comprises a series of whimsical vignettes in which three felt cats engage in different scenarios. One prowls on its hind legs in a garden while another is set upon by rats; later, a saintlike feline complete with halo prays to the Almighty as another takes a swipe at a goblet of wine. At one point, all three assemble to play their instruments but, soon after, one is punished in the stocks before meeting its end by being burned at the stake.

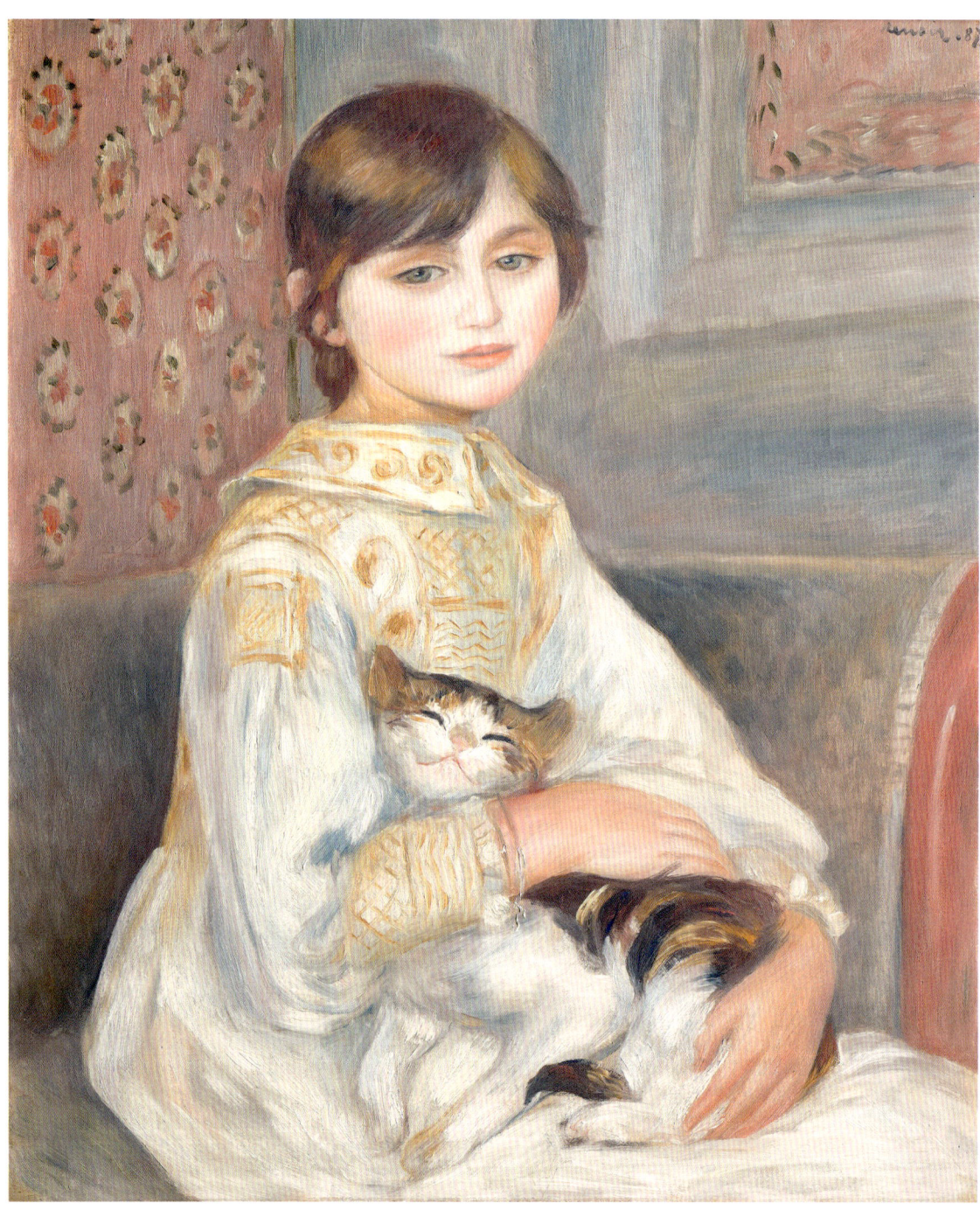

PIERRE-AUGUSTE RENOIR

Julie Manet, 1887
Oil on canvas, 25⅞ × 21⅛ in. / 65.6 × 53.5 cm
Musée d'Orsay, Paris

A smiling calico lies back contentedly in the arms of a young girl in this portrait by French painter Pierre-Auguste Renoir (1841–1919). The sitter is Julie Manet, then nine years old, the daughter of Impressionist painter Berthe Morisot and her painter husband, Eugène Manet (brother of Édouard, the father of Impressionism; see p.147). Morisot and Manet commissioned the portrait from their old friend in 1887, and Renoir chose to depict the mademoiselle with her cat to add an air of informality and fun. The sweet smile on the recumbent cat's lips adds to the sense of ease and comfort. Later, Julie recalled that Renoir painted her portrait "in small sections, which was not his usual way of working," adding, "I thought it was a good resemblance." The painting, which involved at least four preparatory drawings, marked a development in Renoir's style as influenced by the French Neoclassical artist Jean-Auguste-Dominique Ingres, whose portraits of women were less realist than doll-like, as reflected in Julie's flat, oval-shaped face and placid expression. Renoir's new approach involved more vivid colors and close attention to both the line and drawing. Morisot was a big fan of his Ingres style but another contemporary, Edgar Degas, complained: "By doing round faces, Renoir produces flowerpots." Over the years, Julie was painted by many of the other leading Impressionists including Degas, Claude Monet, Alfred Sisley, her uncle, and, frequently, her mother.

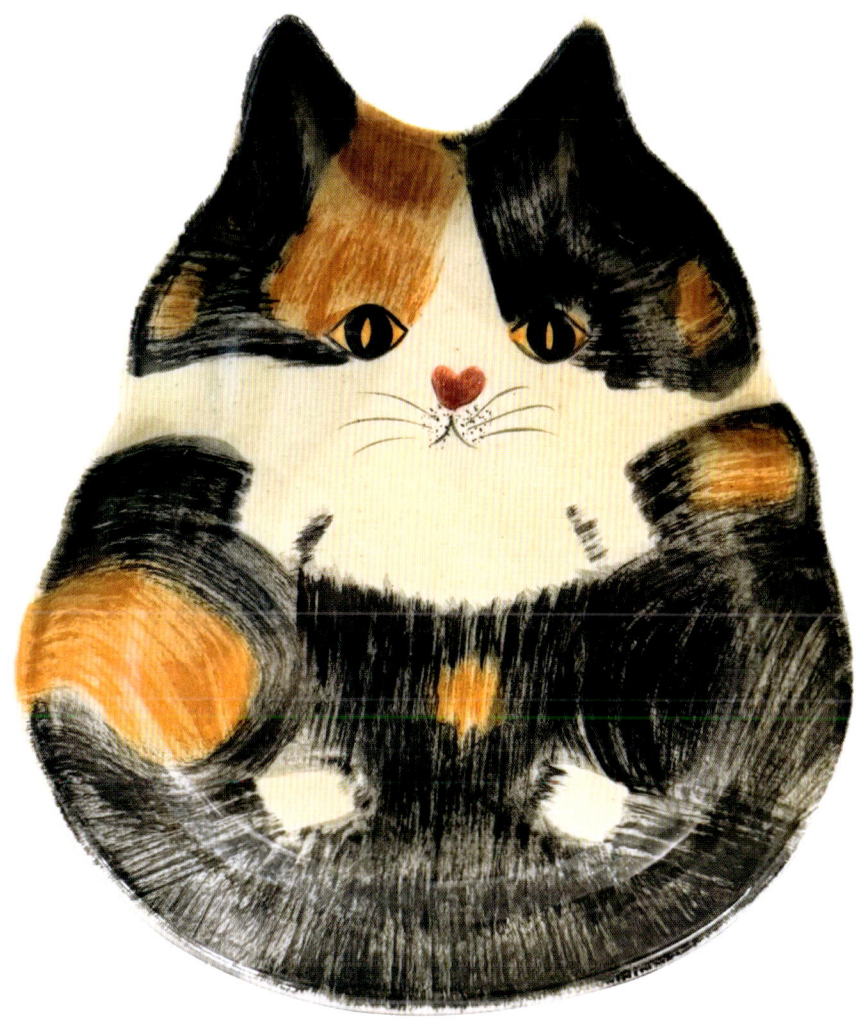

N. S. GUSTIN CO.

Dish, c. 1950–80
Ceramic, H. 7½ in. / 19 cm
Private collection

Kitschy and irresistibly cute, this round little calico cat dish looks ready for a belly scratch. The delightful piece of pottery was manufactured by N. S. Gustin Co., a Los Angeles–based ceramic workshop that operated from the 1950s through the 1970s. Known for its fun, folksy collection of hand-painted, animal-inspired homewares, Gustin produced everything from tabby cat bookends to duck-shaped planter pots. Today, these vintage pieces remain affordable, but this particular kitty dish comes with serious rock and roll credentials. One just like it once belonged to the late music icon Freddie Mercury, a passionate cat lover and insatiable collector of decorative objects, especially anything feline-themed. His version of the dish was kept in his London home, Garden Lodge, which housed more than 1,400 personal possessions featured in the landmark auction at Sotheby's London in September 2023, *Freddie Mercury: A World of His Own*. The sale drew a record-breaking 140,000 visitors to the exhibition at Sotheby's New Bond Street location, all eager for a glimpse of the star's extraordinary collection of art, furniture, fashion, and cherished curiosities. A blockbuster event, with almost all items selling above their high estimate, this modestly valued dish—originally estimated at £40 to £60—fetched an astonishing hammer price of more than £12,000. For those less concerned with provenance, the same piece can still be found online for its original estimate.

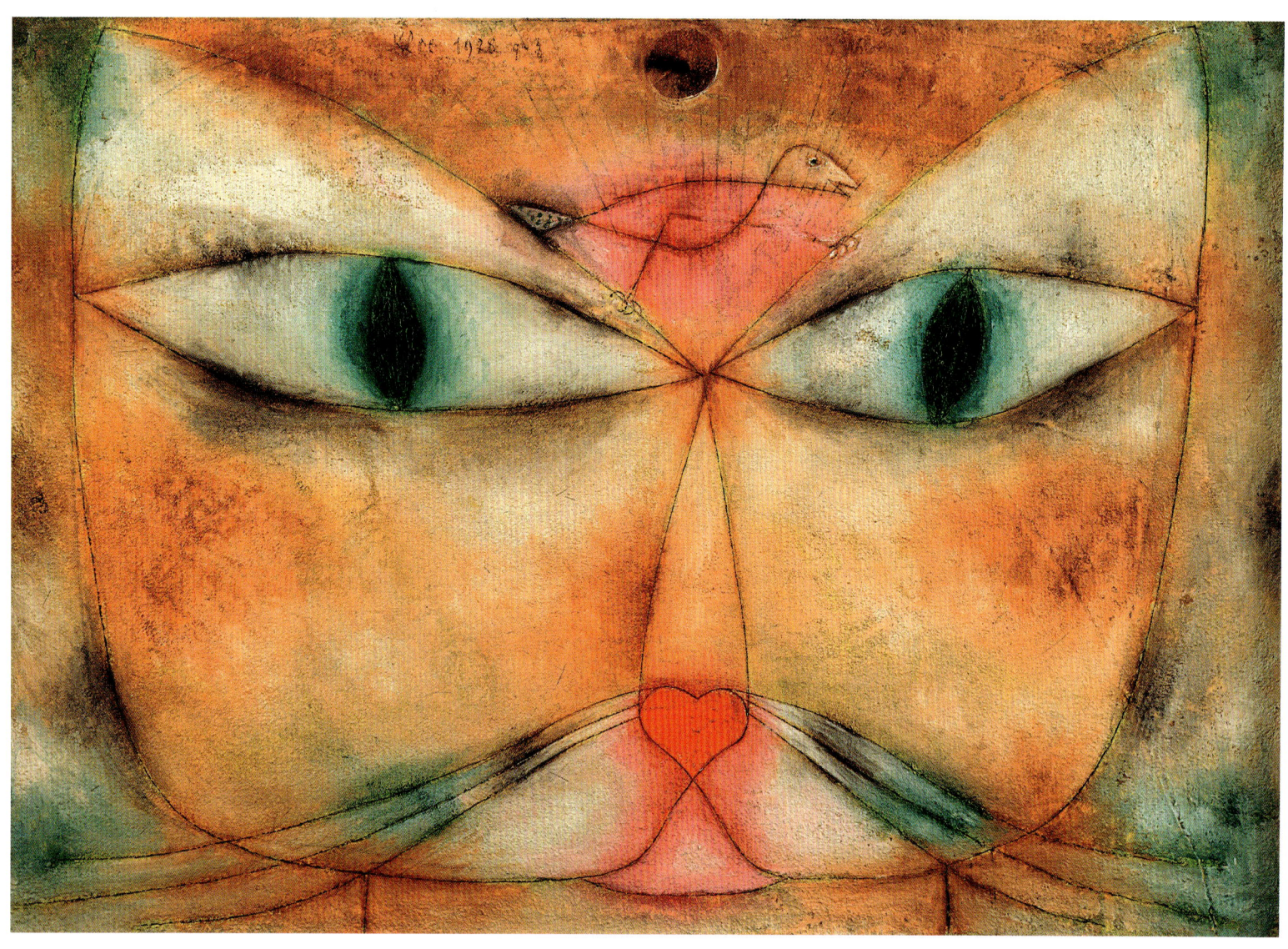

PAUL KLEE

Cat and Bird, 1928
Oil and ink on gessoed canvas mounted
on wood, 15 × 21 in. / 38.1 × 53.2 cm
Museum of Modern Art, New York

"Art does not reproduce the visible, rather it makes visible." So declared French artist Paul Klee (1879–1940) in his *Creative Credo* from 1920. A modernist, Klee developed a personal, poetical style, trying to find signs that would express the inner essence of things. Although the format of this painting is small like most of his works, this cat—or rather this cat's face—takes up the entire frame. Its almond-shaped eyes fill its visage from ear to ear and its pink nose takes the form of a heart. The animal hypnotizes viewers with mysterious green eyes, looking more like a wise man than a domestic animal, even with its long whiskers. The artist expresses the cat's ambivalence in this close-up: it is both cute and scary. Instead of a *bindi* on its forehead—a good-luck mark usually worn by Hindi, Jain, and Buddhist women—this cat has a bird. The creature is wingless, suggesting that it might be a prisoner of the cat and symbolizing the feline's lust and hunter's nature. Klee manages to convey so much expression with great simplicity and enhances the main features of the cat in a straightforward manner, with black lines and vibrant complementary colors. For Klee, childlike expression was the purest form, because it is sincere and free. As he wrote in his diary, "There are still primordial origins of art. . . . Children are no less gifted, and there is wisdom at the very source of their gifts."

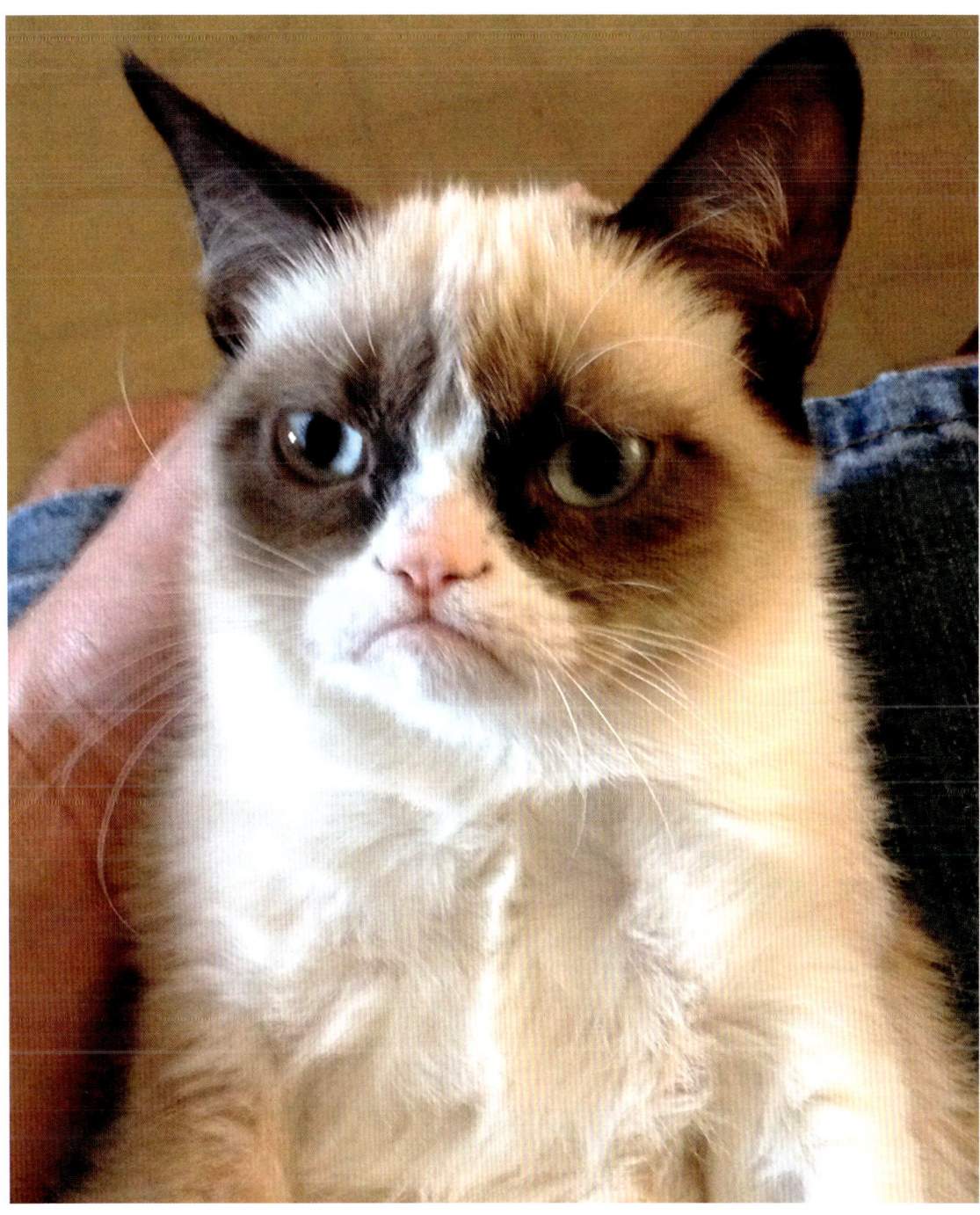

GRUMPY CAT

Original Grumpy Cat meme, 2012
Photograph, dimensions variable

Grumpy Cat and her frown, what *The New York Times* has dubbed "a piercing look of contempt," were everywhere online in the 2010s. This permanently scowling pet—whose sullen visage was probably a consequence of feline dwarfism—changed the face of the Internet, literally. Grumpy Cat first rose to fame in 2012 after her owner shared a photo to Reddit with the caption, "Meet grumpy cat." In response to commenters who exclaimed the photo was digitally altered, Grumpy's owner, Tabatha Bundesen, posted a video to YouTube to prove the expression's veracity, racking up more than 1.5 million views in thirty-six hours and leading to the creation of a digital star. Grumpy Cat became a viral meme used to illustrate any number of perennially online posters' grievances, with bold text placed above or below her frowning face, including the pithy "I had fun once. It was awful." After being named Meme of the Year at the 2013 Webby Awards, Grumpy Cat turned into a full fledged sensation, landing movie and book publishing deals, securing the top job at Friskies as the brand's official "spokescat," and having her likeness appear on almost one thousand items in her official shop. After building her media empire, Grumpy Cat sadly passed in 2019, but her uncanny ability to make people smile with a frown continues to be one of the Internet's most powerful and longest-lasting memes.

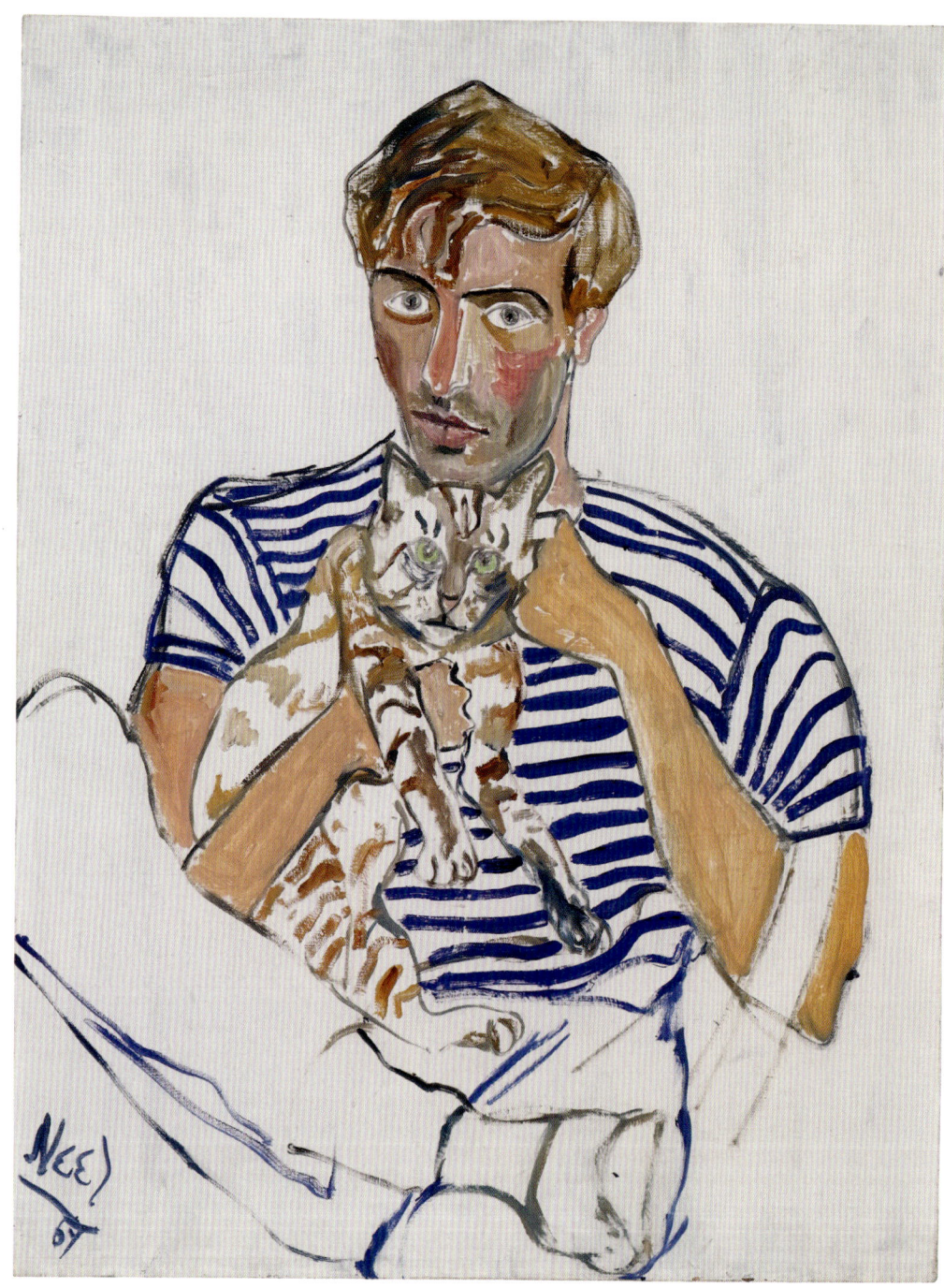

ALICE NEEL

Hartley with Cat, 1969
Oil on canvas, 40⅛ × 30⅛ in. / 101.9 × 76.5 cm
Private collection

Considered a master of figurative painting, American artist Alice Neel (1900–1984) was committed to representation when abstraction was the rage. Over her six-decade career, Neel interpreted her subjects expressionistically—playing with line, color, and other techniques to distort, exaggerate, or otherwise showcase their personalities and inner life—instead of sticking to photorealistic depictions of their physical appearance. In her work, she also captures pets as sensitively and intimately as she did people, revealing their souls and eccentricities. In this portrait, Neel's son Hartley wears a vibrant blue-and-white striped shirt and clutches an equally striped tabby. Both Hartley and cat gaze directly at the viewer, with Hartley holding onto the cat as if for comfort or protection, the feline's stare aligning with ancient Egyptian representations of the animals as guardians (see p.29). It is Hartley and the cat against the world. In a later painting from 1980, Neel depicts her granddaughter Victoria lifting a fluffy calico, with the cat nearing the little girl's own size, perfectly encapsulating a child's awkward yet well-meaning love toward an animal companion. Curator Courtenay Finn was so taken with Neel's portraits with pets that she included many in a 2023 exhibition at the Orange County Museum of Art in California. As Finn noted to *Hyperallergic*, she was drawn to the power Neel gave these animals, declaring that they "aren't props to say something larger about [her subjects]: they're characters in their own right."

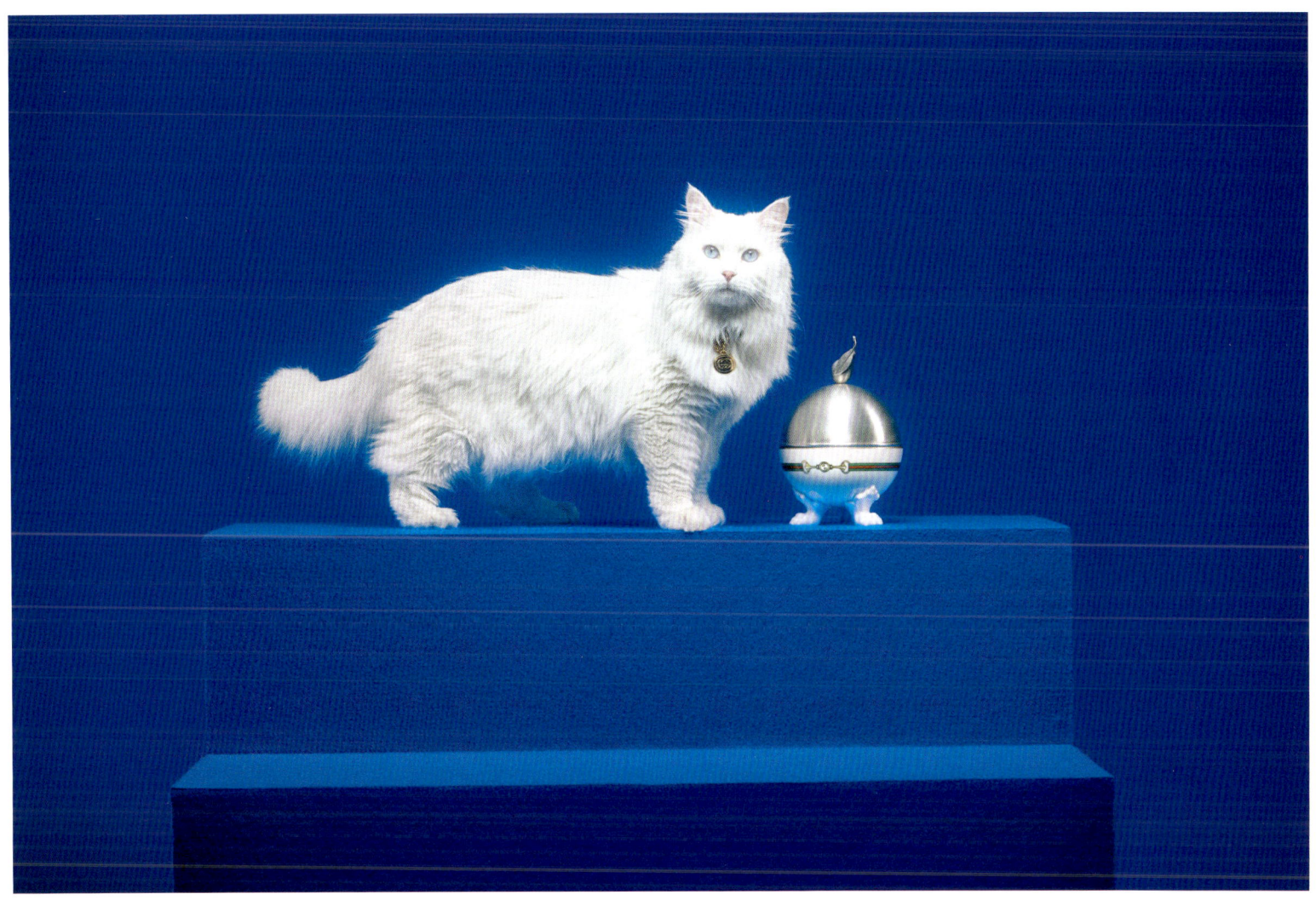

MAX SIEDENTOPF
FOR GUCCI

Bowl and Cloche, from Gucci Pet Collection, 2022
C-print, 15¾ × 23⅝ in. / 40 × 60 cm

From businesswoman Leona Helmsley's dog Trouble, the canine heiress to a cool twelve million dollars, to Karl Lagerfeld's beloved Choupette (see p.97), the Birman that inherited some of the Chanel designer's estate, the wealthy have spared no expense in pampering their pets. The Italian fashion house Gucci became the latest in a line of high-end designers—including Prada and Saint Laurent—to cross into the pet business when it unveiled its Pet Collection in 2022. Designed by then creative director Alessandro Michele, the offering features everything from couture harnesses and leashes to sweaters, raincoats, and T-shirts. There is even a claw-footed pet sofa for luxurious lounging. The advertising campaign was art directed and shot by Namibian German artist, photographer, and longtime Gucci

collaborator Max Siedentopf (b. 1991), who envisioned refined portraits set against a series of sparse yet brightly colored backgrounds, each one intended to let the pet's individual personality shine. A stately Weimaraner sits rigidly upright, as if a soldier at attention, while a cocker spaniel happily stands at its food bowl, tongue lolling out. The fluffy Persian pictured here sports a collar with Gucci's interlocking double-G logo in a gold-toned brass. This feeding bowl has a silver-toned brass cloche atop a ceramic basin with the brand's signature horsebit detail and red-and-green-striped motif. Featuring more than one hundred luxury items for cats and dogs, Gucci's Pet Collection proves that providing one's pet with the very best never goes out of style.

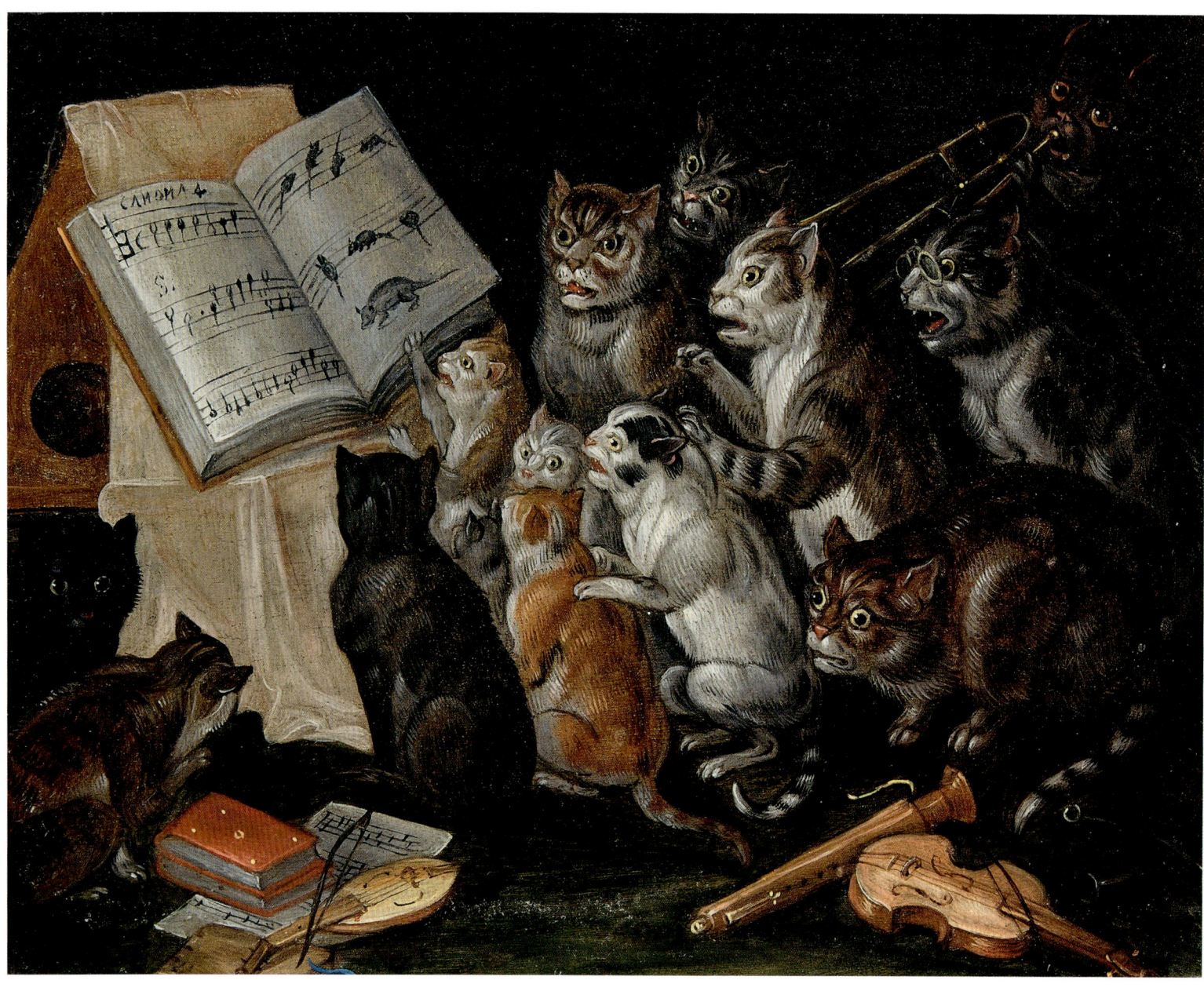

JAN VAN KESSEL THE ELDER

Concert of Cats, c. 1650–60
Oil on copper, 5¼ × 6½ in. / 13.5 × 16.5 cm
Private collection

A clowder of cats sings from a musical score on which tiny images of mice and rats take the place of notes, surrounded by instruments and more sheet music scattered across the floor. Their collective effort and concentration are evident from the kitties' intent frowns and brightly shining eyes. As in many Baroque group paintings, each figure in this assembly has a personality: one tomcat wears a pince-nez, while another mouser accompanies the feline choir on the trombone, and a black pussycat to the left appears aloof. The Flemish painter Jan van Kessel the Elder (1626–1679) was accomplished in numerous genres and specialized in studies of insects and flowers, as well as more imaginative subjects, including allegories featuring animals and elysian landscapes. Influenced by his grandfather, the

illustrious painter Jan Brueghel the Elder, Van Kessel was popular across Europe, with his work collected by merchants, nobles, and his artistic peers, and in 1644 he was made master of the guild of painters in his native Antwerp. Painted in oil on copper, allowing individual hairs to be delineated, this work is an example of the trend of *singerie*, which translates to "monkeying around," in which monkeys were depicted adopting human behaviors in humorous scenes. This anthropomorphizing genre also extended to other creatures, including birds and cats, and anticipated a lineage of kitsch scenes featuring animals engaging in human activities. Here, one can only imagine the shrill cacophony of this caterwauling concert!

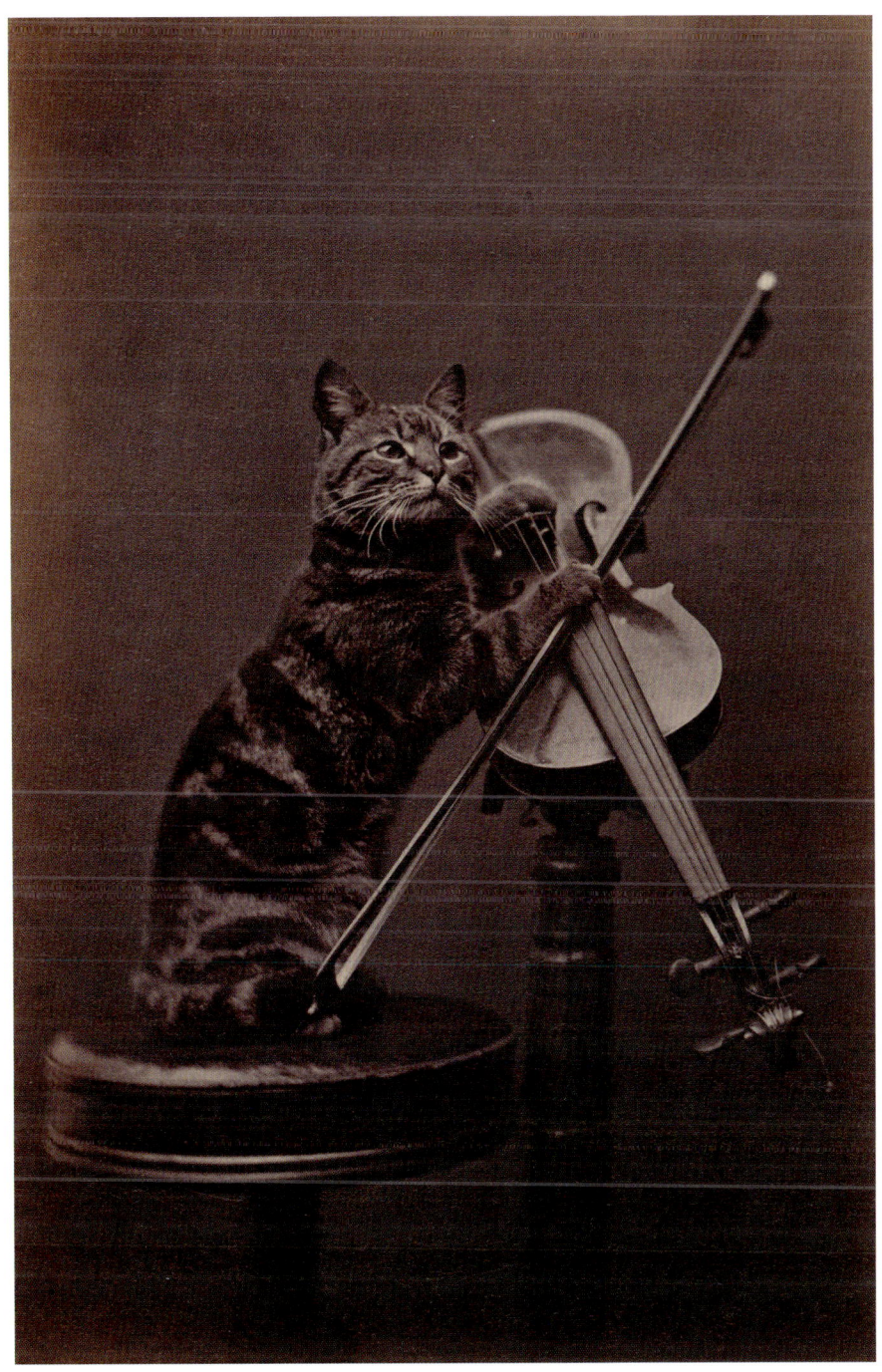

HARRY POINTER

Cat on a stool "playing a violin," 1872
Albumen silver print, 4⅞ × 2½ in. / 12.4 × 6.4 cm
J. Paul Getty Museum, Los Angeles

A violin placed on a stand is being "played" by a cat that stands—alarmingly—upright on a stool with its right paw placed on the bow. The tabby was captured by English photographer Harry Pointer (1822–1899), who made a reputation for himself in the 1870s for his so-called "Brighton Cats," named after the seaside town where he lived. Pointer created a series of quirky and highly popular photographs of his pet cats performing myriad human activities, such as roller-skating, riding a tricycle, and even taking a photograph themselves. Pointer began his career taking conventional photographs of his pet cats sleeping, sitting in baskets, and drinking milk for *cartes de visite*, a souvenir format introduced from France in 1857, in which images were reproduced on small cards that were the same size as a conventional visiting card (a little larger than a credit card). These had grown in popularity after the British royal family appeared on them and Pointer was eager to cash in on the demand for these inexpensive gifts. He began to add written captions, such as "A Happy New Year," to his cat photographs, and the resultant greeting cards became more popular when he placed his cats in more anthropomorphic poses. Known for his ability to train his cats, Pointer featured more than two hundred unique cat poses on his cards. So popular were the "Brighton Cats" that they were mentioned in the leading art journals of the day and shown at photographic exhibitions in London and Dublin.

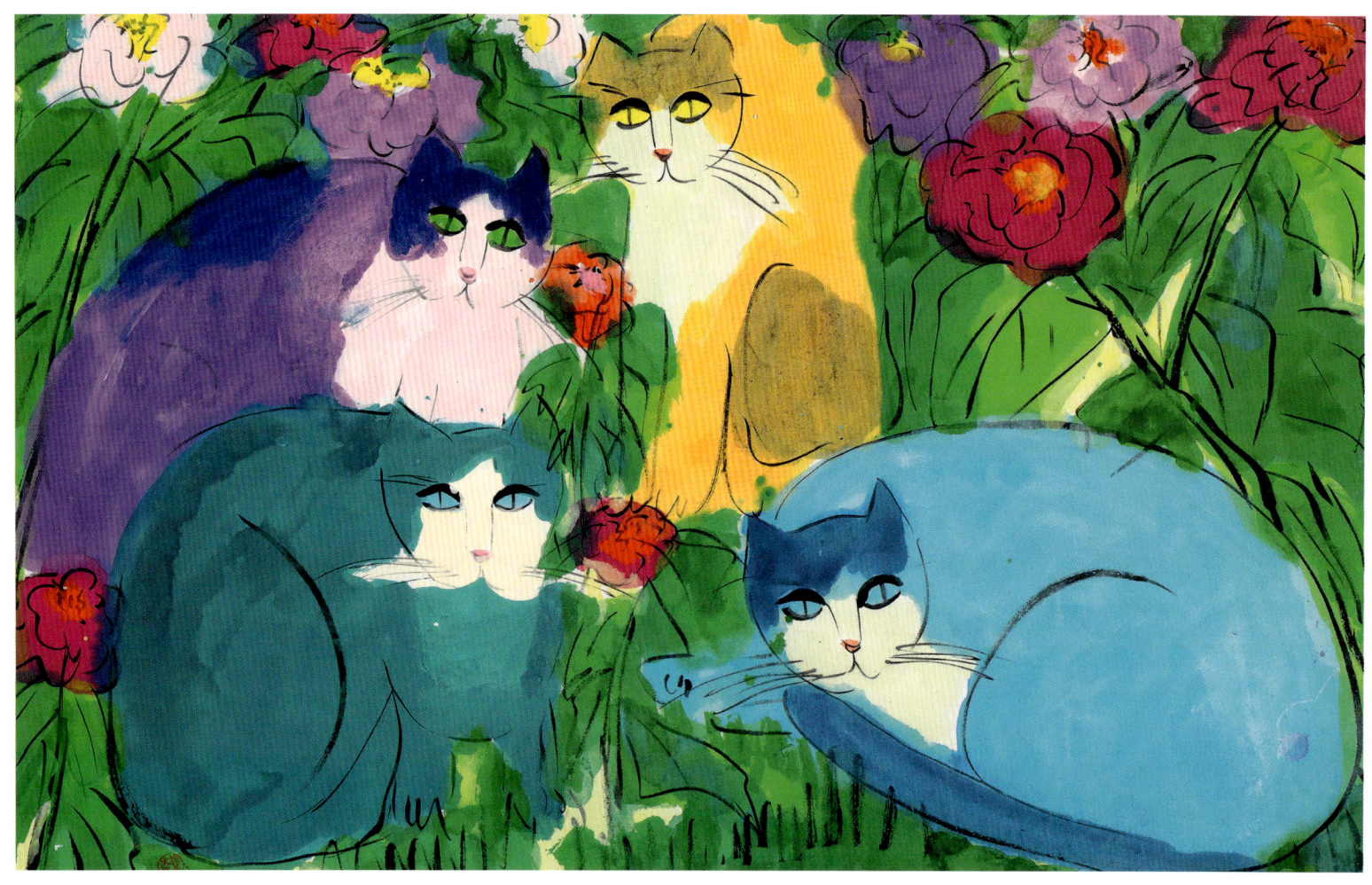

WALASSE TING

Colorful Cats, date unknown
Watercolor on paper
26¾ × 42⅜ in. / 68 × 107.5 cm
Private collection

These vibrant *Colorful Cats* amid a field of flowers in bloom come from the mind of self-taught Chinese American painter and poet Walasse Ting (Ding Xiongquan, 1928–2010). Ting began his artistic career in Hong Kong in 1946, combining Chinese calligraphic techniques and ink painting. He moved to Paris in 1952, where he joined in with the CoBrA art collective that held spontaneity as its central conceit. In the late 1950s Ting relocated to New York, where he would live for most of his life, and encountered firsthand the major aesthetic trends of the era, including Pop art, Action Painting, and Abstract Expressionism. These influences, along with his gravitation toward certain artists, such as Pablo Picasso (see p.204) and Henri Matisse (whose "-sse" was adopted for Ting's own Western

name; see p.90), coalesced into the artist's inimitable, exuberant style. Female nudes, parrots, horses, and cats were among his most favored motifs, all wrought in an aggressively psychedelic palette: acid yellows, vivid pinks, electric blues, and fluorescent oranges, that resulted in compositions teeming with wild energy. Yet his most famous work is a volume of his poetry, *1¢ Life* (1964), for which Ting, along with friend and fellow painter Sam Francis, managed to wrangle artworks from twenty-eight leading artists of the day, including Andy Warhol (see p.95), Roy Lichtenstein, Robert Indiana, and Joan Mitchell. The creatures inhabiting *Colorful Cats* hearken to Warhol's own watercolor cats: here, as there, the cats' varied technicolor hues are their defining characteristic.

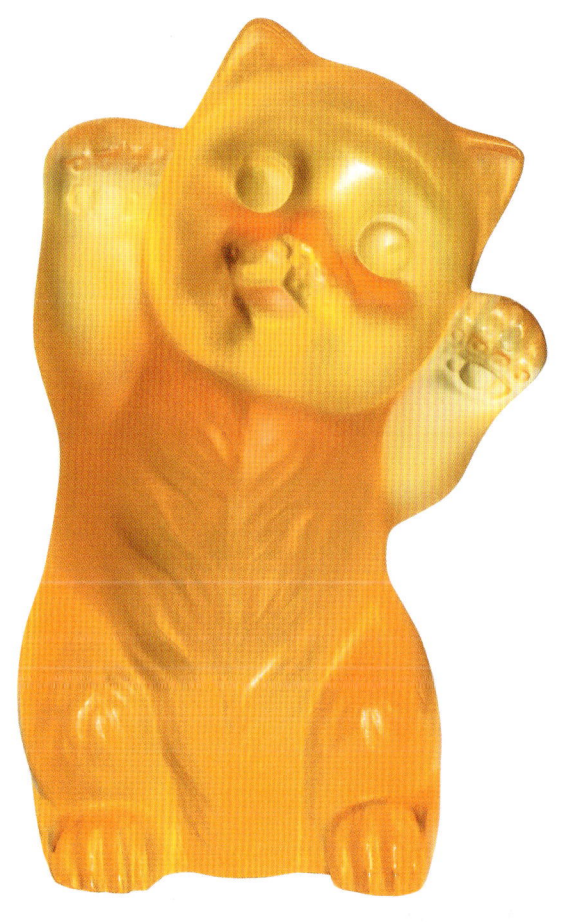

LALIQUE

Lalique Kitten Sculpture, 2021
Amber crystal
3⅝ × 2½ × 2¼ in. / 9.1 × 6.3 × 5.7 cm

This adorable neon orange kitten might not be the first object associated with a storied century-old design house, but the tiny feline objet d'art provides a lesson in aesthetic reinvention. A contemporary offering from the French glassmakers at Lalique, this miniature sculpture has its roots in the innovative techniques the house has used since its founding by René Lalique in 1887. Beginning his career as an apprentice for Parisian goldsmith Louis Aucoc and designing for some of the finest jewelers of his day, including Boucheron (see p.25) and Cartier, René Lalique's refined taste and fresh approach established him as a leading avant-garde jeweler with an impressive roster of clients among Paris's intelligentsia. He made his name by eschewing precious gems and instead employed semiprecious stones and unconventional materials, such as ivory, horn, and glass. By the first decade of the twentieth century, Lalique's interest in glassmaking overtook his jewelry practice and he built a dedicated glassworks to reach a wider audience with his work. Helping to define the Art Deco aesthetic in glass, he favored the three F's in his designs—flora, fauna, and the feminine form—and experimented with many techniques, including relief sculpture and iced glazing. The house of Lalique continues to use many of these approaches today, such as in the satin-finished crystal kitten seen here. Widely considered the "haute couture of glass," Lalique is still in business after nearly 140 years, expanding the medium's possibilities, from crystal candlesticks to cute cats.

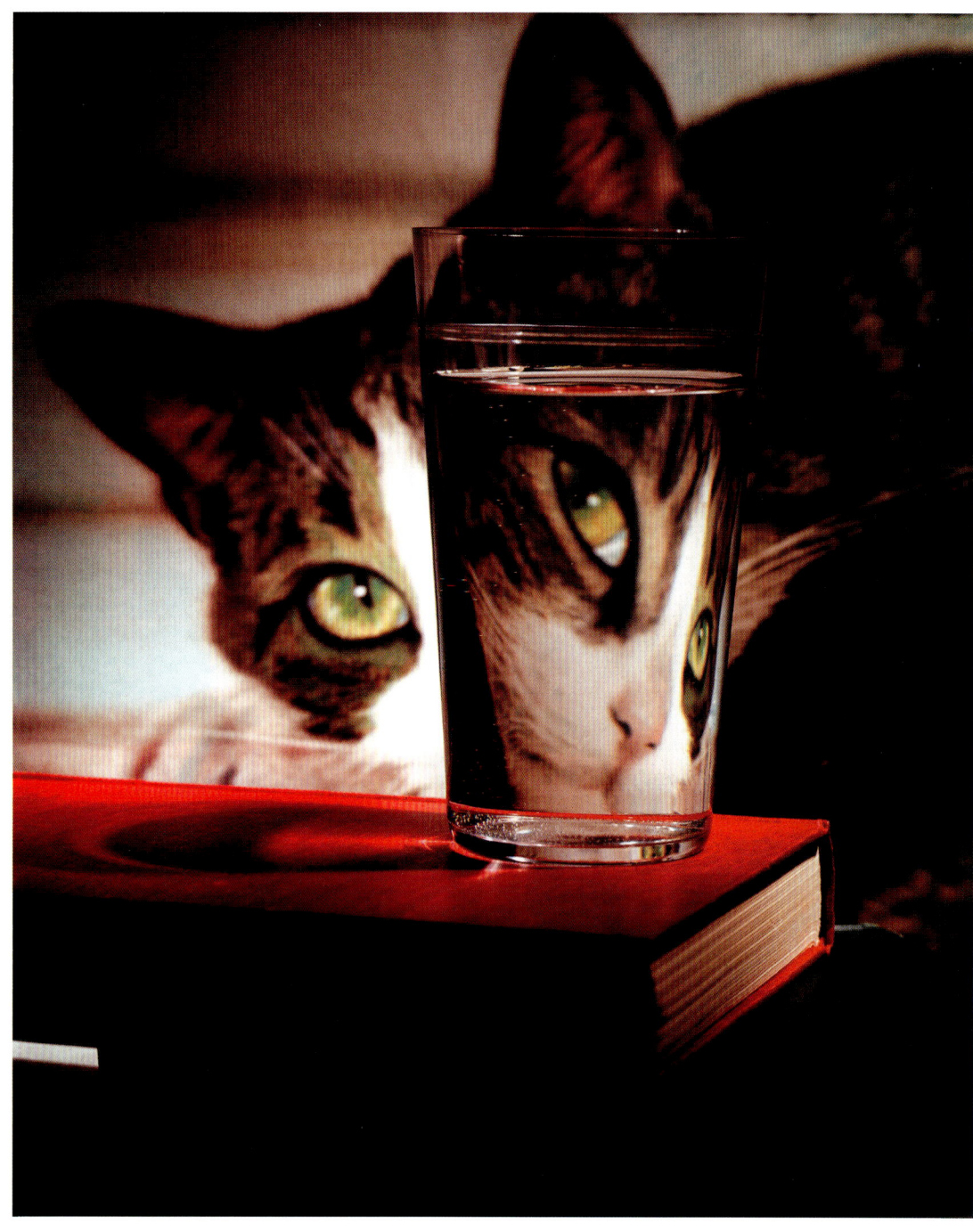

NINA LEEN

Close-Up of a Glass with Water Reversing a Cat's Reflection, United States, 1963
Photograph, dimensions variable

A handsome tabby cat with a white snout, its face partly reversed, crouches as it peers through a glass of water placed on top of a book in this surreal image by American photographer Nina Leen (c. 1914–1995). The cat's reflection in the glass provides a textbook demonstration of the physics of light refraction: as light moves through the water, its wavelength changes, making it appear to bend and causing the cat's face to look distorted. Leen's love of animals, particularly her dog, Lucky, cats, and bats (which she called "flying kittens"), was legendary—as was the photographer herself. Born in Russia in the early twentieth century (she refused to say exactly when), she lived in Europe before emigrating to the United States in 1939. For the next three decades, she worked as a contract photographer for

Life magazine, producing thousands of images, including more than fifty covers, only ceasing to work for the publication when it folded in 1972. Leen's passion for animals was behind much of her work for *Life*—her first published photograph was of two tortoises in New York's Bronx Zoo in April 1940—and later collections of her work in books. In addition to her animal photography, her subjects were typically everyday people living everyday lives, primarily American women and adolescents in the United States and abroad, as well as a group of artists known as the "Irascibles," which included Willem de Kooning, Jackson Pollock, and Mark Rothko.

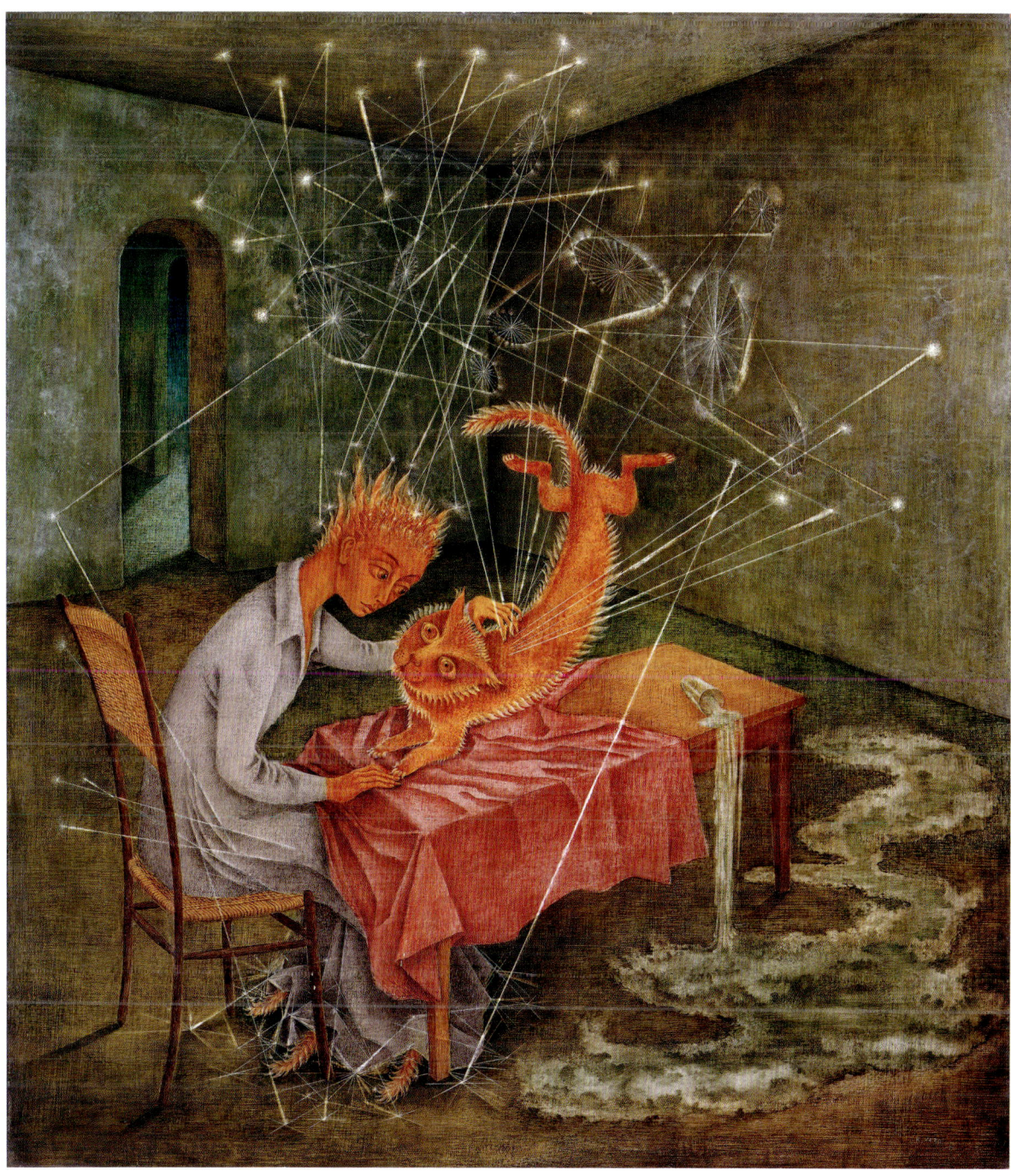

REMEDIOS VARO

Simpatía (La rabia del gato), 1955
Oil on Masonite, 37¾ × 33½ in. / 95.9 × 85.1 cm
Private collection

Cats are both everyday pets and mysterious creatures associated with metamorphosis and the supernatural. Companions of scientists, witches, and alchemists, they are emblematic of the artist's ambiguous universe. Like many of her fellow Surrealists, Spanish artist Remedios Varo (1908–1963) was fascinated with the esoteric, especially as embodied by her pets, and included them along with alchemical symbolism in her work. Executed in Varo's unique figurative style, which she honed after relocating to Mexico in 1941 to flee the war in Europe, *Simpatía* (*Sympathy*) was originally titled *La rabia del gato* (*Madness of the Cat*) thanks to its central orange animal. The feline jumps on the table, engendering chaos in the otherwise bare room by wrinkling the tablecloth and spilling a glass of liquid. The stream

pouring out seems to create a river of sludge on the floor. Varo described her painting simply: "This lady's cat jumps onto the table, producing the sort of disorder that one learns to accept if one likes cats (which I do). Upon caressing it, so many sparks fly that they form a very complicated electrical current. Some sparks and electricity go to her head and rapidly make a permanent wave." Varo depicts the electricity with constellations of lines and dots that sometimes resemble the gears and spokes of bicycle wheels, another common motif in her art. Both the cat and the woman are the same auburn hue, and their hair stands on edge as if they were communicating their identity to each other, alchemically converting themselves from one matter to another.

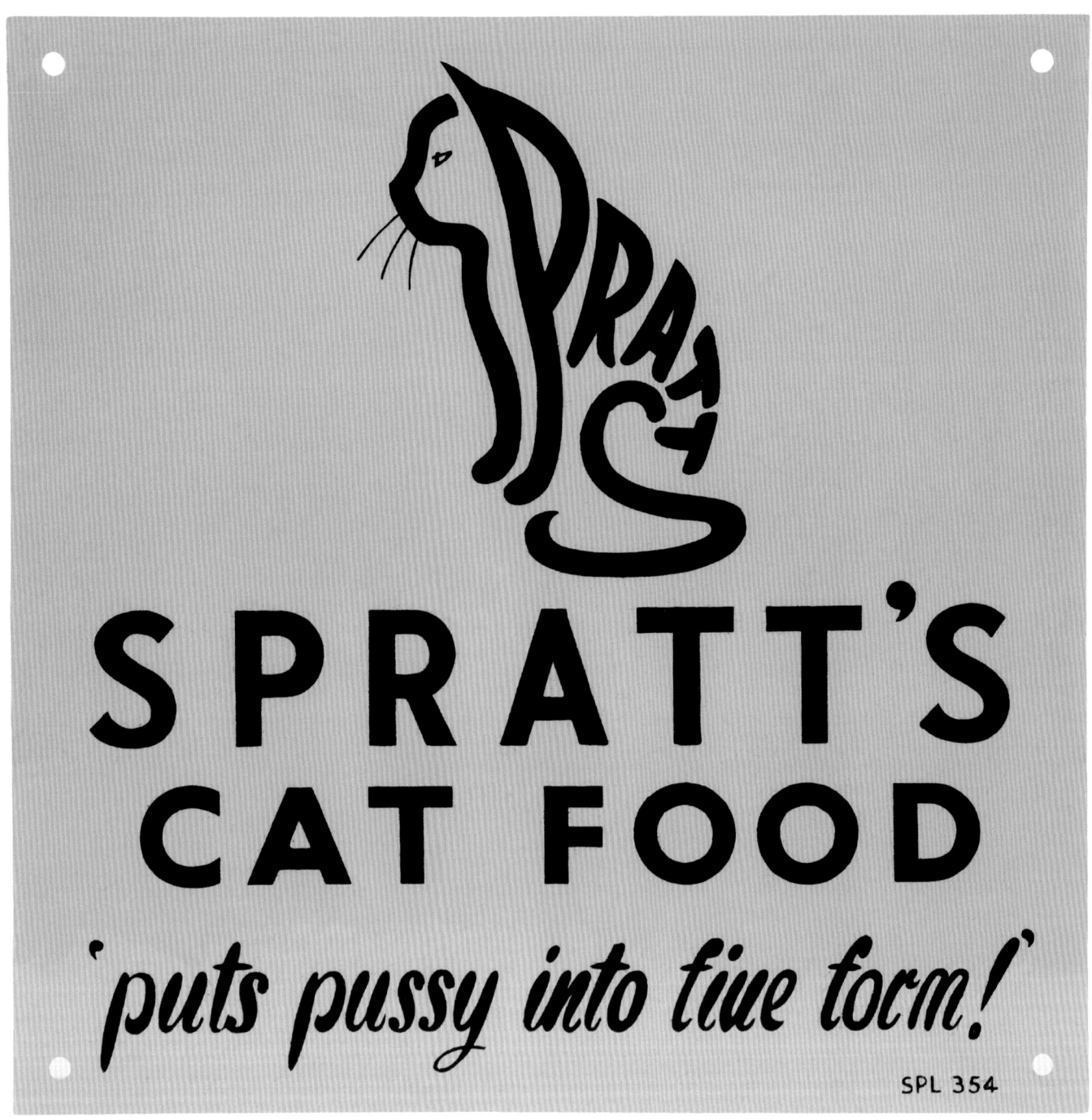

Spratt's Cat Food sign, c. 1930s
Enamel, 11¾ × 11¾ in. / 30 × 30 cm
Private collection

SPL 354

SPRATT'S

Spratt's Cat Food sign, c. 1930s
Enamel, 11¾ × 11¾ in. / 30 × 30 cm
Private collection

Appearing on the streets of London in the 1930s, this strikingly modern enamel sign advertised cat food for the British pet food manufacturer Spratt's. Conceived by British designer Max Field-Bush in 1936, the cat advertisement used a series of clever calligrams—visual devices whereby the letters create an image related to the meaning of the words—to promote the product. The black cat logo was created by using the first two letters, *S* and *P*, to make the animal's head and legs, while the letters *RATT* taper to create the body and the tail is made up of the final possessive *S*. Below the logo is the slogan, "Puts pussy into fine form!" with none of the word's modern connotations, dating the advertisement to a more innocent era. Spratt's, which had numerous factories in east London, was started by the

electrician James Spratt, who originally emigrated to London from the United States to sell lightning conductors before being inspired to make biscuits for dogs. After seeing the chewy gristle meat that London porters fed to dogs, he realized the commercial possibilities of canning and baking his own animal products. The success of the dog chow led to food for cats and fish, and even birdseed, and Field-Bush replicated the witty calligram design in the shape of each relevant animal for Spratt's advertisements. The 1930s were a golden age for logos in both Great Britain and the United States: Coca-Cola and Warner Bros. both created logos at the time that are still in use today.

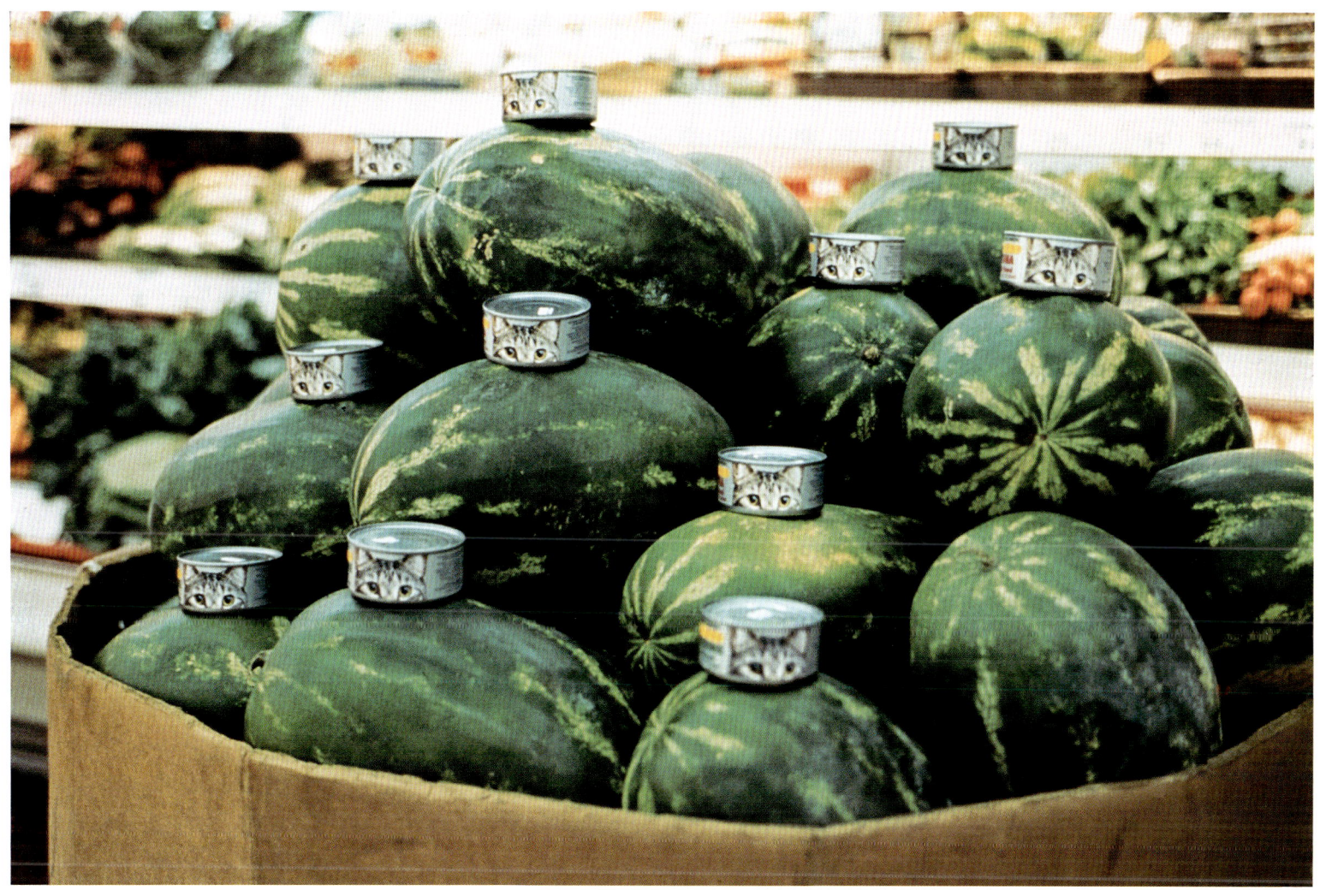

GABRIEL OROZCO

Cats and Watermelons, 1992
C-print, 16 × 20 in. / 40.6 × 50.8 cm

Eleven cans of cat food carefully balanced on a pile of green watermelons create the impression of a clowder of felines peering out from the ripe fruit, which doubles up as rudimentary bodies. Each can is printed with a cat's head cropped at the nose, forming an unintentionally comical image that Mexican artist Gabriel Orozco (b. 1962) exploits with characteristic whimsy. Perhaps only a handful of bemused shoppers ever saw this mischievous assemblage in a New York grocery store before the tins were returned to their shelf. Yet, as with Orozco's other impromptu sculptures in public spaces—including oranges arranged in the windows of apartments neighboring the Museum of Modern Art in New York (*Home Run*, 1993) and a patch of condensed breath evaporating from the surface of a piano (*Breath*

on Piano, 1993)—this surreal, transitory action was recorded for posterity by the artist's camera. A master of the appropriated object, Orozco is known for his subtle transformations of everyday objects into quirky and often humorous works of art that extract poetry from the mundane. As the artist said in an interview with *Bomb* magazine, "I think the smallest gestures that we make in our lives can have much greater repercussions than some things we might consider to be more forceful." Working across a range of media, Orozco takes an eclectic approach that resists straightforward categorization, drawing inspiration from the streets, his apartment, cats, or wherever in the world he happens to be.

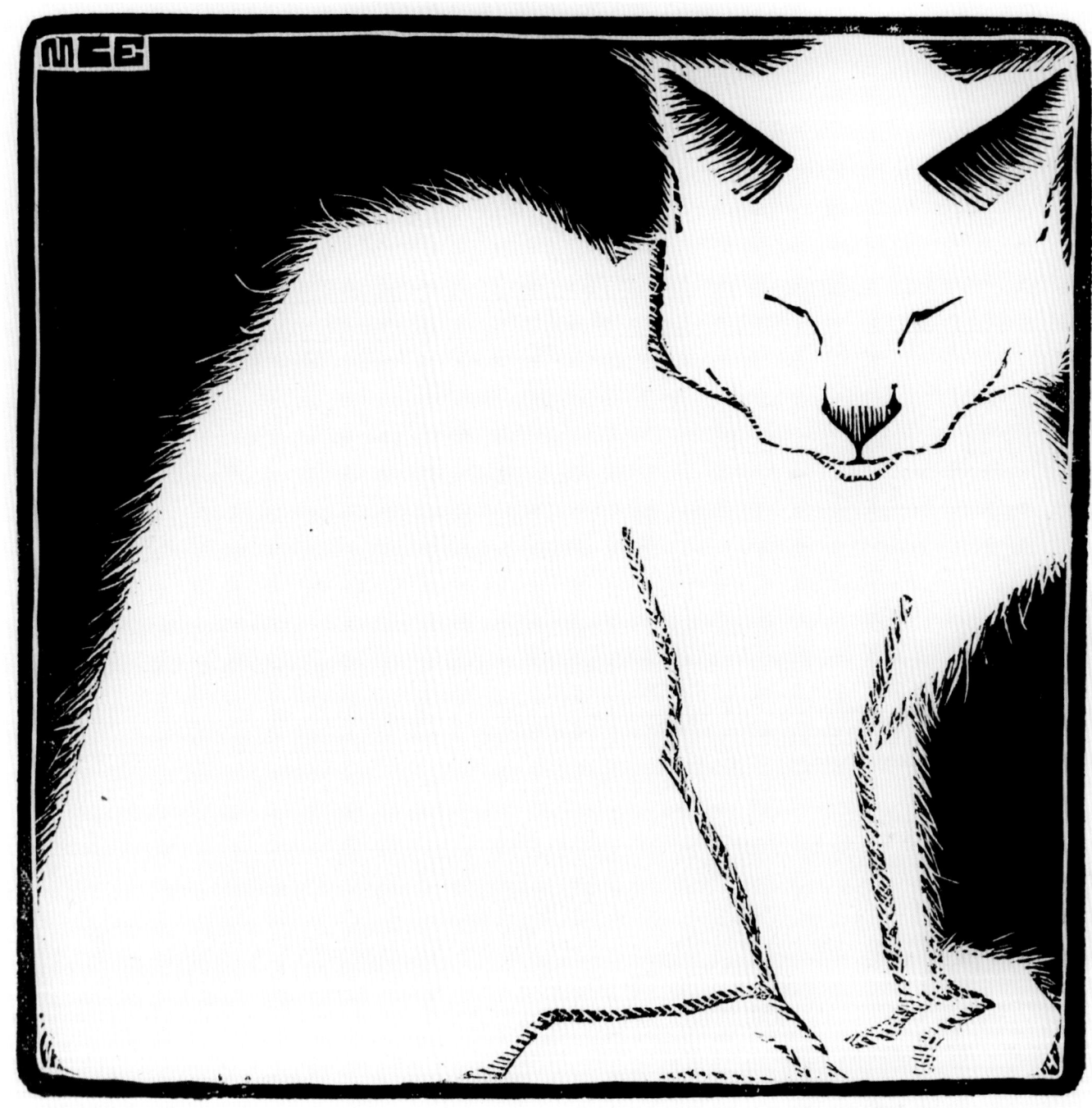

M. C. ESCHER

White Cat, 1919
Woodcut, 6½ × 6½ in. / 16.6 × 16.6 cm

Dutch artist Maurits Cornelis Escher (1898–1972) is best known for his innovative optical art, which combines the precision of both mathematics and draftsmanship to produce "impossible drawings" and metamorphic tessellations that push the very limits of graphic art. Yet despite being a household name worldwide, the breadth of Escher's work is largely unknown. This early woodcut was produced by the artist in 1919, when he was a young man studying at the School of Architecture and Decorative Arts in Haarlem, the Netherlands. The image is of Escher's own cat, serenely perched—perhaps alongside her companion while he worked or soaking up sun from a windowsill—a picture of contentment. She was a gift from his landlady and a frequent subject in his early woodcuts and sketches. For a typical woodcut, a printmaker carves a design onto a block of wood, then inks and presses it to paper to reveal the mirror image of the carving. In a reversal of that process, this woodcut is a counterprint. Escher wanted to capture a truer version of the image by restoring it back to its original; he believed that in portraying a subject with asymmetrical features its likeness was lost when reversed. By placing another paper atop the page with wet ink and applying extreme pressure through an etching press, a mirror image of the mirror image could be achieved. The reversal is indicated clearly by his signature in the upper left corner, where the initials "MCE" are legible from left to right.

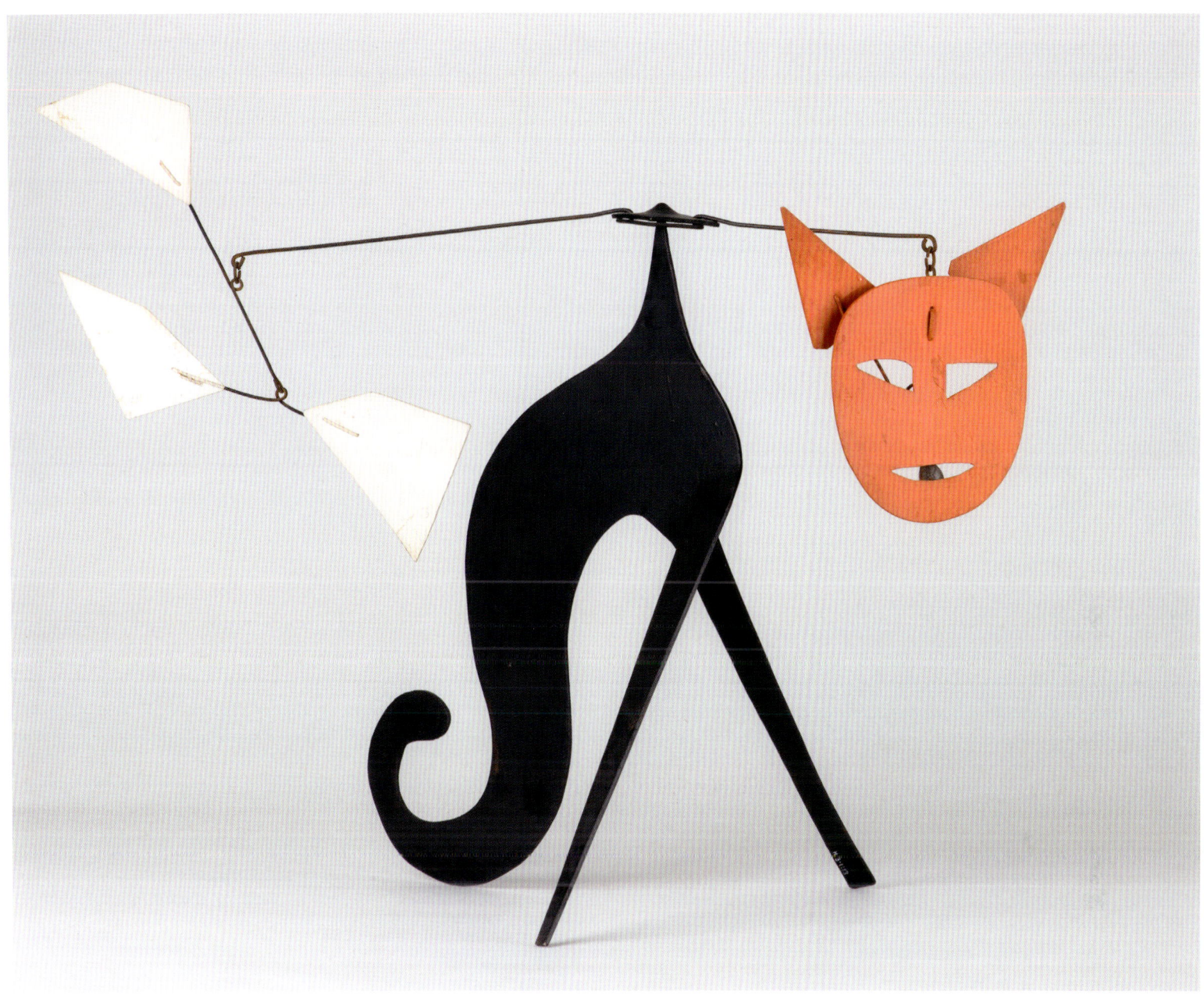

ALEXANDER CALDER

Chat-mobile, 1966
Sheet metal, paint, and steel wire
20 x 26 x 26 in. / 50.8 × 66 × 66 cm
Museum of Contemporary Art Chicago

Quietly surveying its territory, American artist Alexander Calder (1898–1976)'s *Chat-mobile* captures a feline's sense of enigmatic wisdom, with its devilish red head, wide cutout eyes, and pricked ears. The kinetic sculpture is made of thin, painted metal components that are activated by the air and can be viewed from any angle. The masklike face and white geometric shapes gracefully bob on a thin wire suspended from a black base that is the picture of felinity, underscoring a theatrical theme that is central to Calder's practice, particularly his famous mobiles, which explore motion as an active part of artistic expression. Dynamic and thought-provoking, the work is part of a family of creature-themed standing mobiles that Calder created in the mid-1960s, which evolved from his earlier wire sculptures of the mid-1920s, as well as his miniature traveling circus, *Cirque Calder* (1926–31), a portable body of performance art composed of tiny mechanized figures and animals, activated by the artist. Today, Calder is best remembered for his large-scale abstract mobiles and monumental static sculptures (known as *stabiles*), but he was less interested in the impact of volume and weight on the viewer's gaze than the spatial relevance of an artwork and its ability to spark the imagination. This slinky cat, whose tail resembles the curl of a treble clef, certainly has its own unique rhythm thanks to its shape-shifting silhouette that casts dancing shadows on the wall, resulting in a mesmerizing display of movement and light.

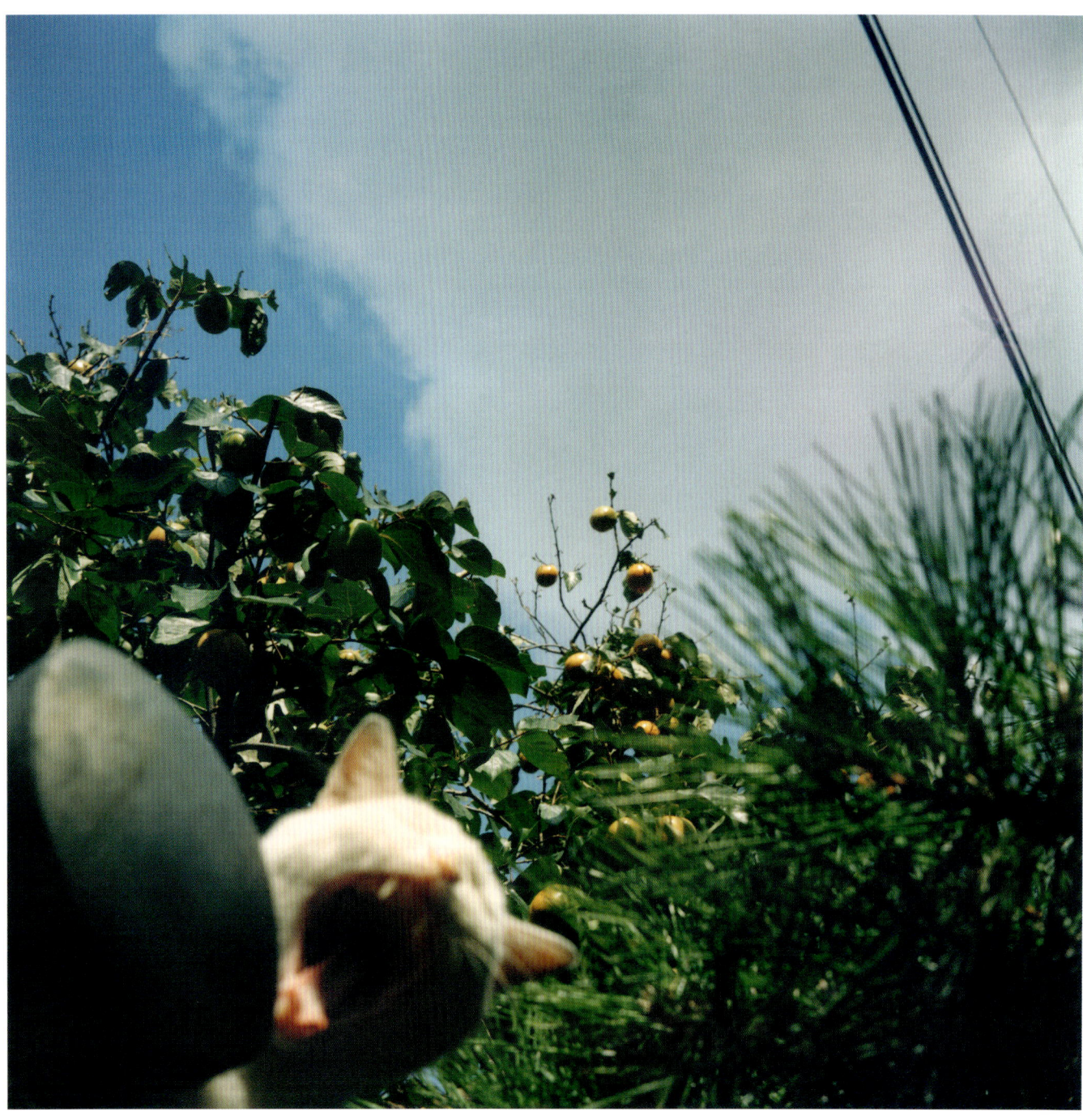

MIKIKO HARA

Untitled, from Is As It, 1996
C-print, 14 × 14 in. / 35.6 × 35.6 cm
Private collection

The cat in *Untitled* by Japanese photographer Mikiko Hara (b. 1967) resembles a globe with ears more than the familiar domestic animal. The feline's open mouth is covered in shadow, with only a hint of fangs, pointy triangles on each side of its head almost resembling ears, and a hazy suggestion of fur, thanks to the bright natural light. It is hard to tell whether someone is holding the cat (perhaps the reason for its agape expression), if it jumped out of the bushes in the middle ground of the frame, or if it fell from the cloudy blue sky that fills the top of the composition. A black circular shape is in the foreground, just to the left of the animal's face. The viewer wonders whether the form is photo equipment, a trick of the light, or something entirely different. The cat could be the focal point, but Hara's practice gently disrupts the expected elements of a photograph. She uses a medium-format camera to capture snapshots of fleeting moments. Holding the camera at chest level instead of at her eyes, Hara relinquishes the control over composition, focus, and subject that looking through the viewfinder usually gives. This adds an element of risk—the resulting photograph might be blurry, lack focus, or be otherwise askew—but it is also an opportunity for serendipity to take effect. The inclusion of the feline is also unusual for the photographer, who does not often feature animals in her work. The uncertainty—and unexpected subject—makes the picture feel almost furtive, as if a secret message between Hara and the cat.

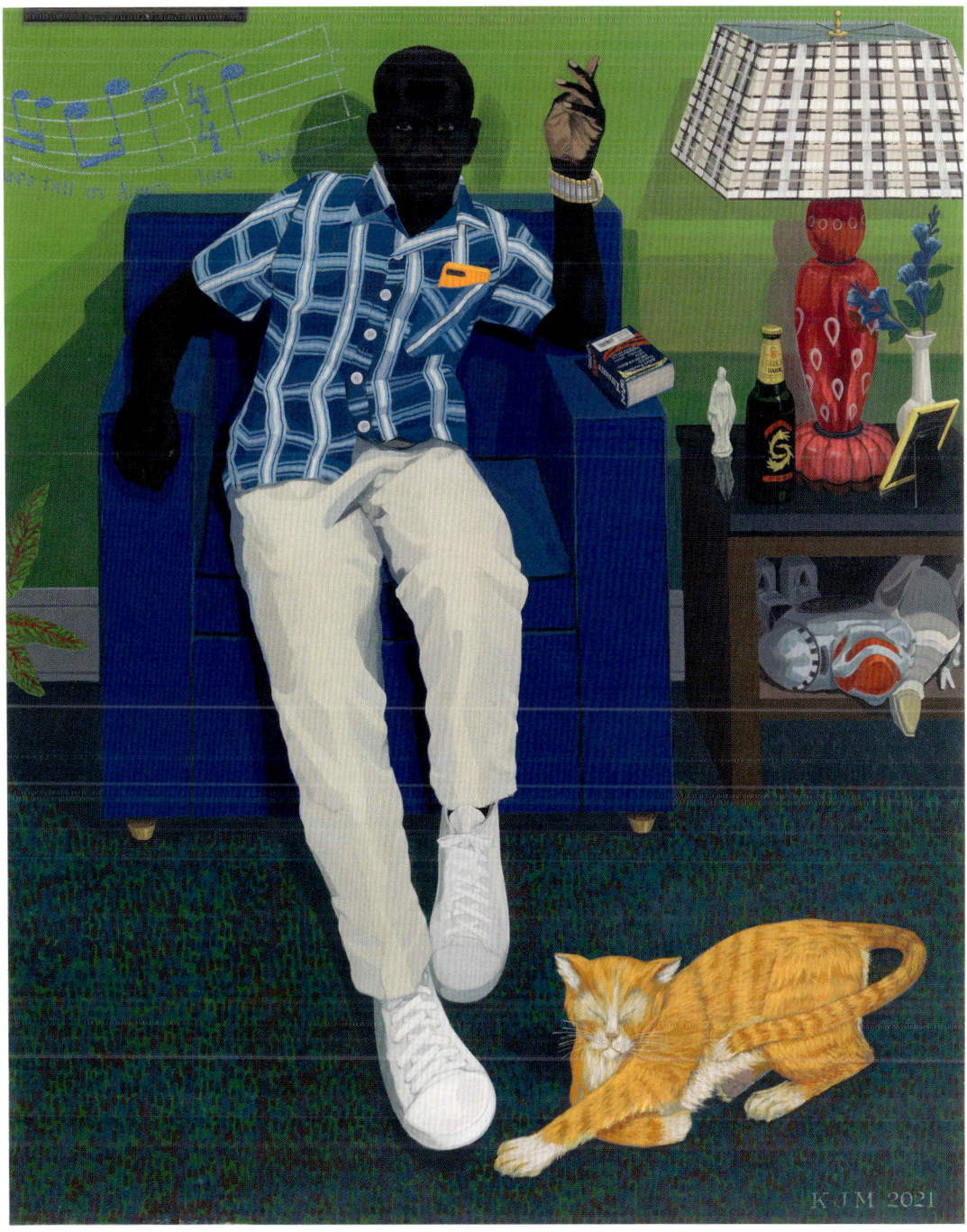

KERRY JAMES MARSHALL

A lithe young man . . ., 2021
Acrylic on PVC panel in artist's frame
60½ × 48 in / 153.7 × 121.9 cm
Glenstone, Potomac, Maryland

An orange-and-white striped tabby cat stretches luxuriously in the bottom right corner of this painting by American artist Kerry James Marshall (b. 1955), effortlessly stealing the spotlight from the portrait's ostensible subject, a young Black man relaxing in a blue armchair. The graceful poses of both beg the question of just who is the lithe young man indicated in the work's title. Marshall created this painting for the 2022 exhibition *Toni Morrison's Black Book* at David Zwirner gallery in New York. Curated by writer and critic Hilton Als, the show brought together works inspired by *The Black Book*, a 1974 publication of collected writings and imagery about Black American life edited by writer Toni Morrison. Marshall's painting takes its title from Morrison's novel *Song of Solomon*

(1977), which follows Macon "Milkman" Dead III, the scion of a wealthy Black family in a town in the Midwest. Milkman shares the same name as his father but yearns for one of his own, dreaming of a "lithe young man with onyx skin and legs as straight as cane stalks, who had a name that was real." Marshall's young man, although nameless, is surrounded by the items of a real life, from the Oxford thesaurus at his elbow and the music floating into the room to the cat sitting with him in content contemplation. Like Morrison's Milkman, this man acts as a snapshot, a portal through which to view a moment of rest in an otherwise complex existence.

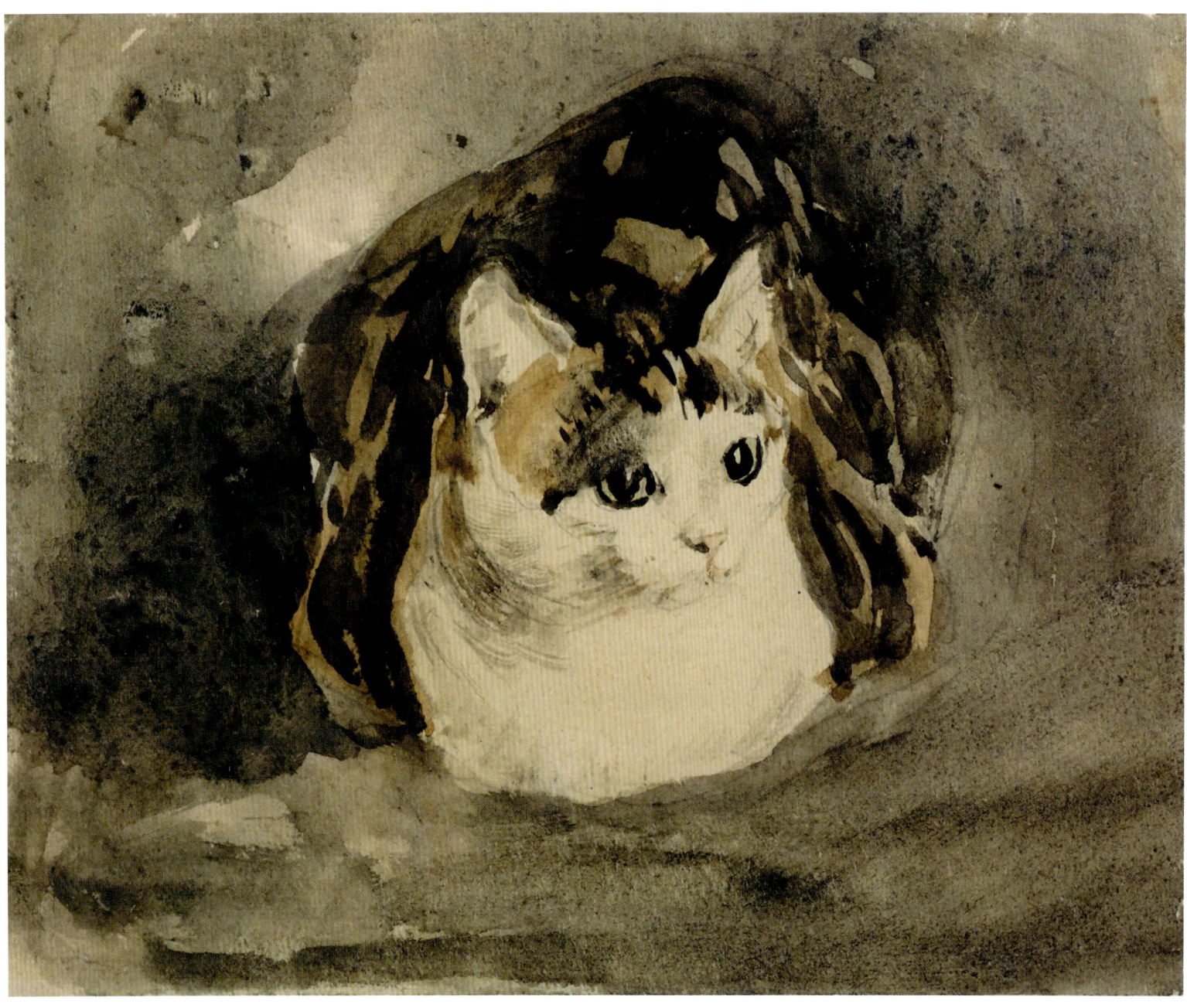

GWEN JOHN

Cat, c. 1904–8
Graphite and watercolor on paper
4⅜ × 5⅜ in. / 11.1 × 13.7 cm
Tate, London

Painted shortly after she first moved to Paris from her native Wales, this small feline portrait by British artist Gwen John (1876–1939) is rendered in pencil and watercolor. As such, it is a more informal work than the oil-painted portraits and interiors for which the artist is best-known. This quiet work is one of numerous studies John made of her beloved pet—the tortoiseshell Edgar Quinet, named after the street where she lived at the time—which she captured in a variety of poses: stretching, washing, sleeping, or, as here, sitting open-eyed with front paws tucked under the body. This position has come to be described as the "classic cat loaf," where with limbs out of view and head raised, a cat resembles a loaf of bread. In 1908 Edgar Quinet disappeared, and John expressed her sadness in a letter to a friend and in a poem she sent to her then lover, the artist Auguste Rodin. Cats also appear in a number of her later portraits, sitting in the laps of her subjects, including two paintings of young women with a black cat, both made between 1918 and 1922, which are now in the collections of Tate, London, and the Metropolitan Museum of Art, New York. The subdued palette and melancholy expressions of her models have led some writers to make a connection between John's works and the evolution of the cliché of the lonely spinster who has only the love of her cat, which endures even today.

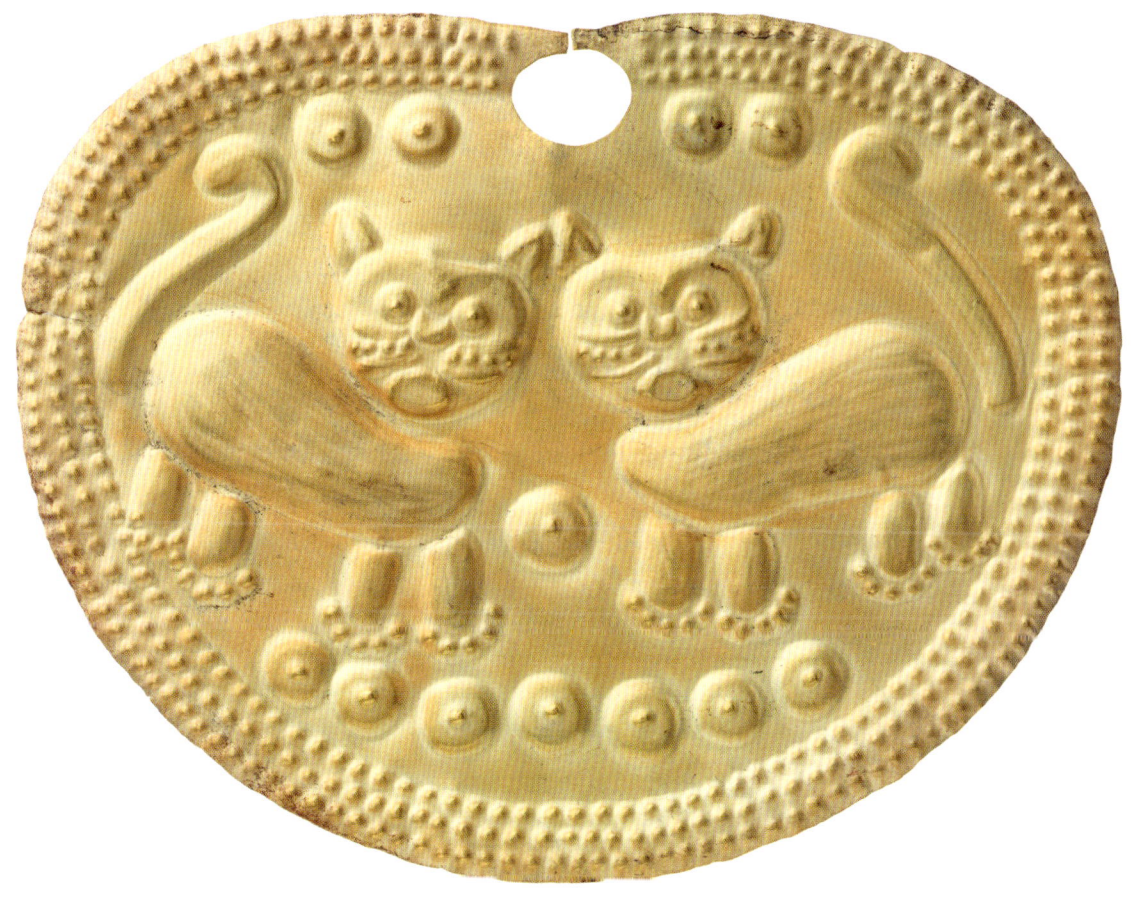

ANONYMOUS

Nose ornament, c. 100 BCE–500 CE
Gold, 3⅜ × 4⅜ × ¼ in. / 8.6 × 11.1 × 0.6 cm
Metropolitan Museum of Art, New York

A pair of cats look slightly startled as they stare out from this gold nose ornament made by an unknown Vicús artisan around the turn of the millennium. The Vicús culture flourished in the Pacific region in the far north of Peru, close to the border with present-day Ecuador, between the third century BCE and seventh century CE. This design is notable for its execution, because Vicús metalsmiths were highly skilled at the repoussé technique, whereby metal was cut and then hammered from behind to create a raised design on the front. Although the Vicús probably never domesticated the wild cats depicted here, birds and cats frequently appeared in their designs as representations of the hunt. Nose ornaments were popular with the coastal cultures of northern Peru, and this ornament would have attached to the septum by the oval opening at the top to cover the lower half of the face. While neighbors of the Vicús, such as the Moche, featured highly ferocious cats on their ornaments, this pair of felines more closely resemble contemporary pussycats: they have rounded toes rather than claws and lack sharp fangs. Vicús culture was patriarchal, and only men of high rank wore jewelry such as this. They prized precious metals, expending great effort to source them, and silver, gold, and copper objects featured prominently in their material culture. However, despite a shiny appearance that suggests a high gold content, metallurgical analysis of this ornament showed that copper was its largest component.

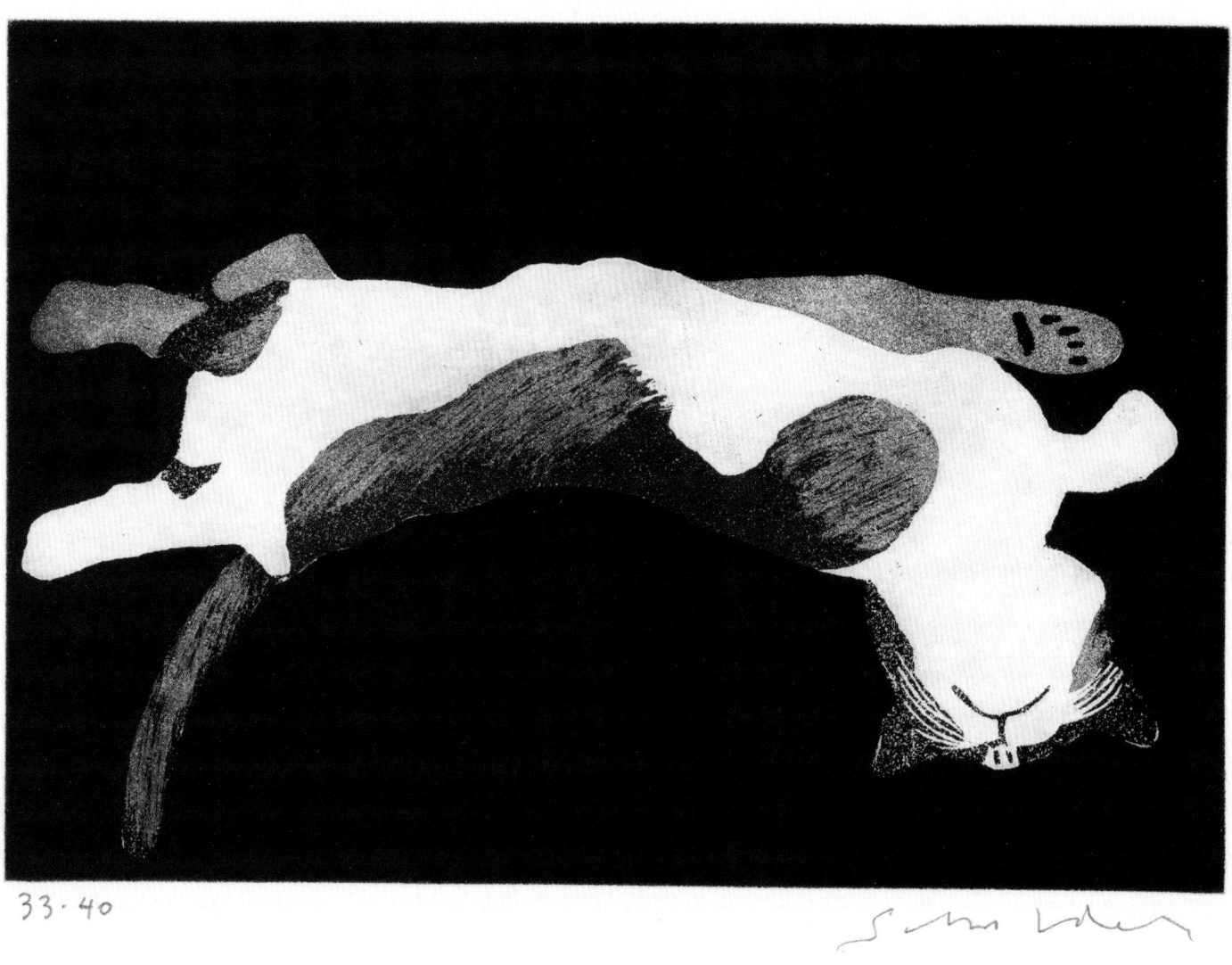

33·40

FRITZ SCHOLDER

Rolling Cat, 2003
Lithograph, 14½ × 17⅜ in. / 37 × 44 cm
National Museum of the American Indian,
Smithsonian, Washington, DC

Against a stark black background, a black-and-white cat lies in a familiar feline pose, stretched out in a position of total relaxation, belly up, with its paws and face turned upside down. This dramatically composed lithograph is by American artist and teacher Fritz Scholder (1937–2005), who was an enrolled member of the La Jolla Band of the Luiseño tribe, the Indigenous people of southern California. Best known for his controversial and colorful expressionist paintings and etchings of Native Americans that show, in his words, "the real Indian," Scholder was the first artist to portray Native Americans with mundane objects from everyday life, such as the American flag and beer cans. But he also worked with traditional motifs from art history, such as portraits, myths, and, of course, contemplative cats.

His intention was to destroy the stereotype of an "Indian artist" and provoke debate by relocating American Indians to the contemporary world instead of keeping them in the ersatz romanticism of the past. Scholder was not brought up in Luiseño culture, and his split identity gave him a unique perspective that he examined through his art, although he once observed, "I never called myself an Indian artist. Everyone else has." This lithograph of a cat, which is among the last prints the artist signed before his death, reveals a different side of his work. It is more relaxed and intimate—the cat seems to be waiting for its stomach to be tickled—and a change from Scholder's vibrant canvases to a calmer black, gray, and white palette.

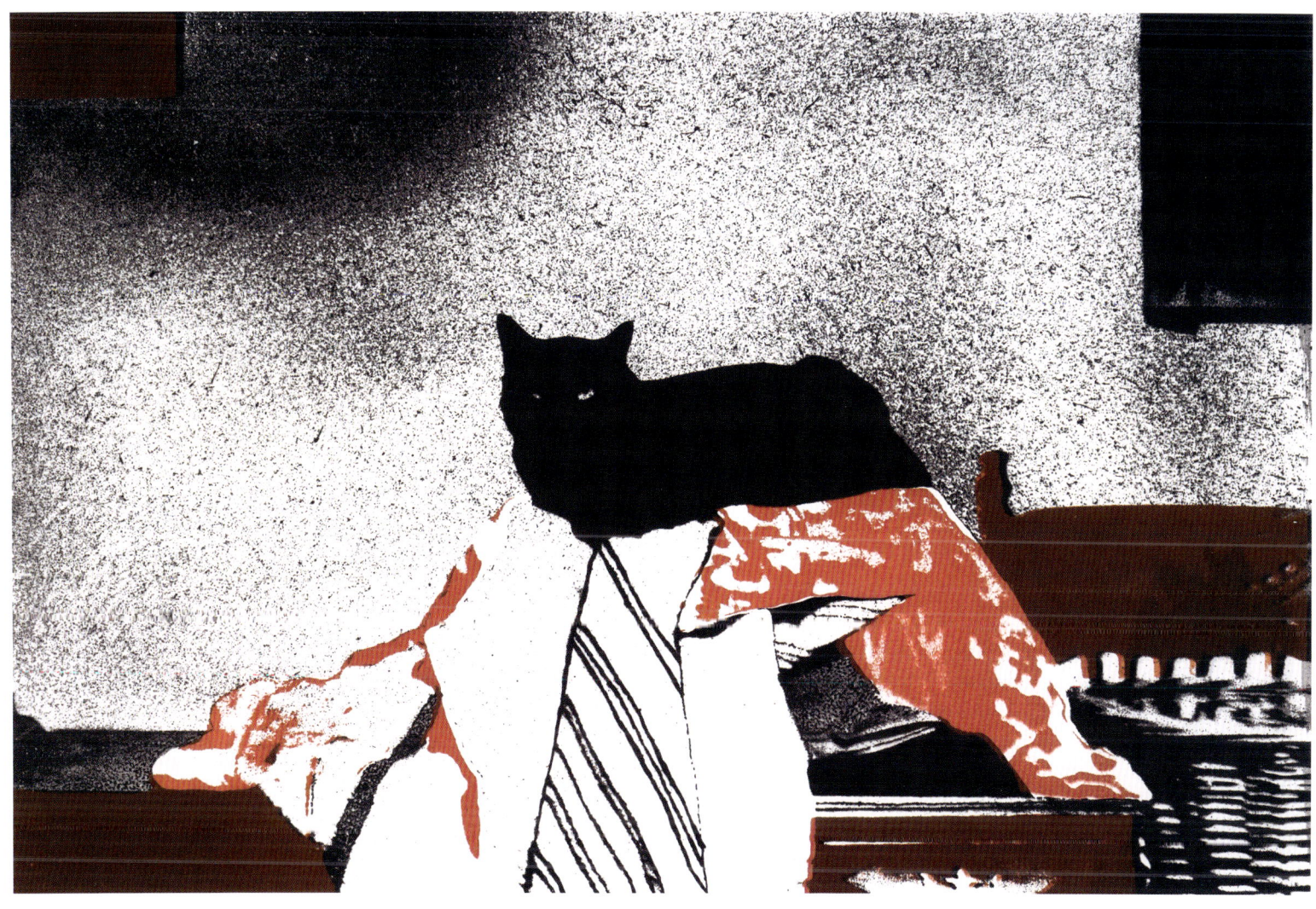

MAVIS PUSEY

Untitled, date unknown
Lithograph, 9⅛ × 14 in. / 23.2 × 35.7 cm
Petrucci Family Foundation, New Jersey

With a striking economy of graphic line and form, Jamaican-born American artist Mavis Pusey (1928–2019) conjures the unmistakable silhouette of a black cat lounging on a pile of bed linen. In taking a domestic pet as its subject, this figurative print is highly unusual in the artist's oeuvre, which was overwhelmingly committed to abstraction. Nevertheless, each element of the composition, from the distinctive feline shape to the fabrics, bed, and room, is reduced to simple shapes and patterns, reflecting the artist's formal concerns as well as her longstanding interest in textiles (her first job was at a clothing factory and, before studying art, she pursued a fashion degree at Traphagen School of Fashion in New York). Pusey was best known for her hard-edge, nonrepresentational paintings and prints responding to the urban environment and the restless energy of New York City. She studied at the Art Students League under Will Barnet (see p.202) and, later, worked at Robert Blackburn's Printmaking Workshop (1969–72), which was frequented by artists, such as Romare Bearden (see p.71), Emma Amos, Jacob Lawrence, and Melvin Edwards, among others. Although she earned a degree of critical recognition for her rich abstract pictures during her lifetime, Pusey has remained largely overlooked. Unlike the artist's works inspired by demolition and construction sites, which are typically filled with hard lines and sharp angles, this homey scene displays an uncharacteristic softness and charm.

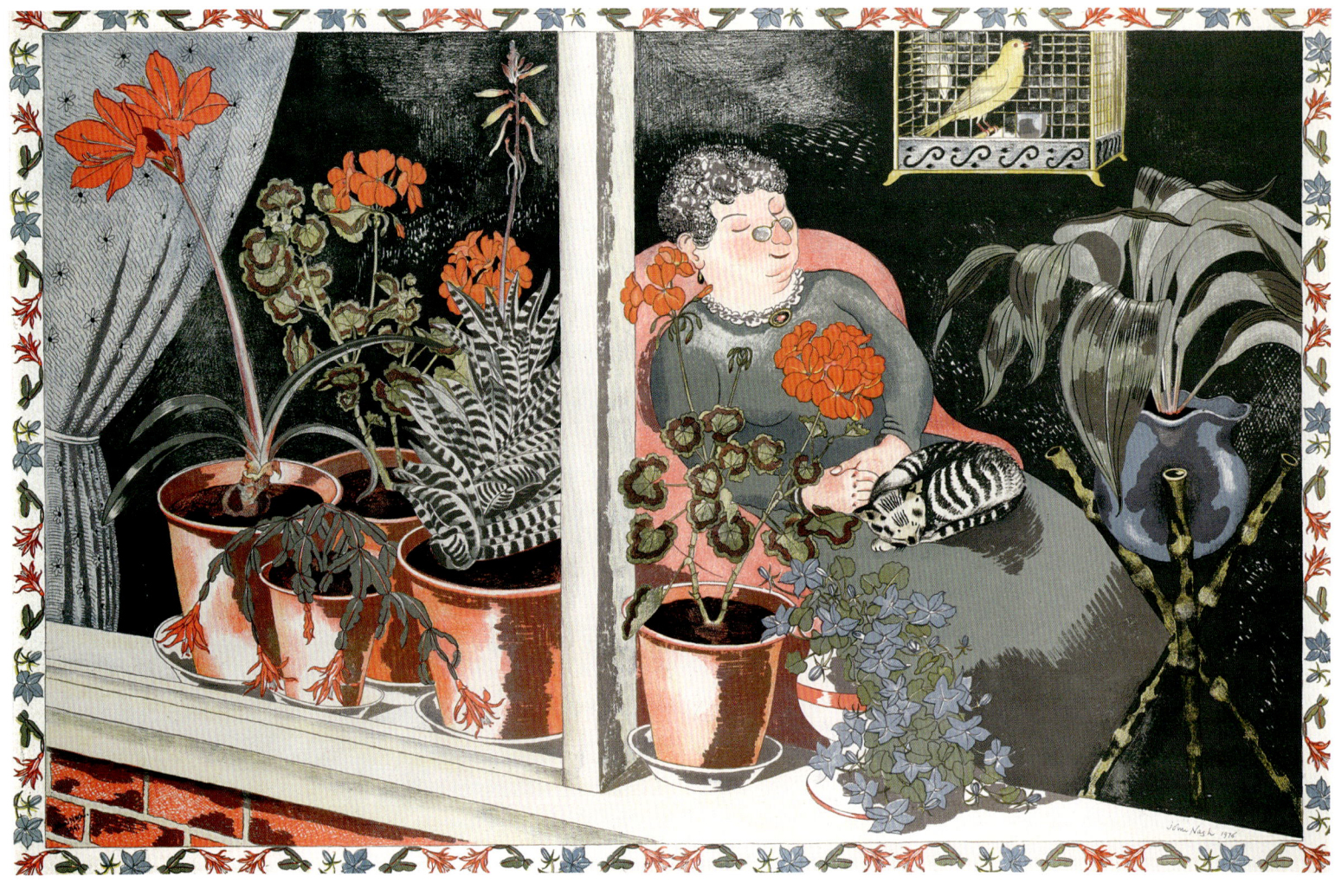

JOHN NASH

Window Plants, 1945
Lithograph on paper
19⅝ × 30 in. / 49.8 × 76.2 cm
Tate, London

Seen through a large window, an older woman dozes in her armchair, her spectacles perched on her nose, while her tortoiseshell cat is fast asleep on her lap, in this lithograph by British artist and printmaker John Nash (1893–1977). Colorful plants, including geraniums, lilies, and a striped cactus that matches the cat's fur, are clustered on the windowsill. In this idyllic image of urban calm, the only creature awake is the yellow canary in its cage. Nash was self-taught: his older brother, the artist Paul Nash, advised him against formal art school training, fearing it might take away "that special thing" John possessed. Over a lengthy career, which included service as an official war artist during both world wars, Nash painted mainly landscapes and made illustrations of humorous subjects and plants.

A founding member of the Society of Wood Engravers, he spent much of the 1920s and 1930s working in woodcuts, before abandoning the medium in favor of lithographs, etchings, and metal engravings, often of rural landscapes of the Gower peninsula in Wales and the countryside around his home on the Suffolk/Essex border. An interior landscape of sorts, *Window Plants* showcases Nash's deftness at representing greenery, as well as the artist's ability to capture the tender moments that can happen among plants and flowers. Studies have argued that cats can help senior adults overcome feelings of loneliness or depression by acting as sources of company and affection, a phenomenon that is apparent in this heartwarming lithograph.

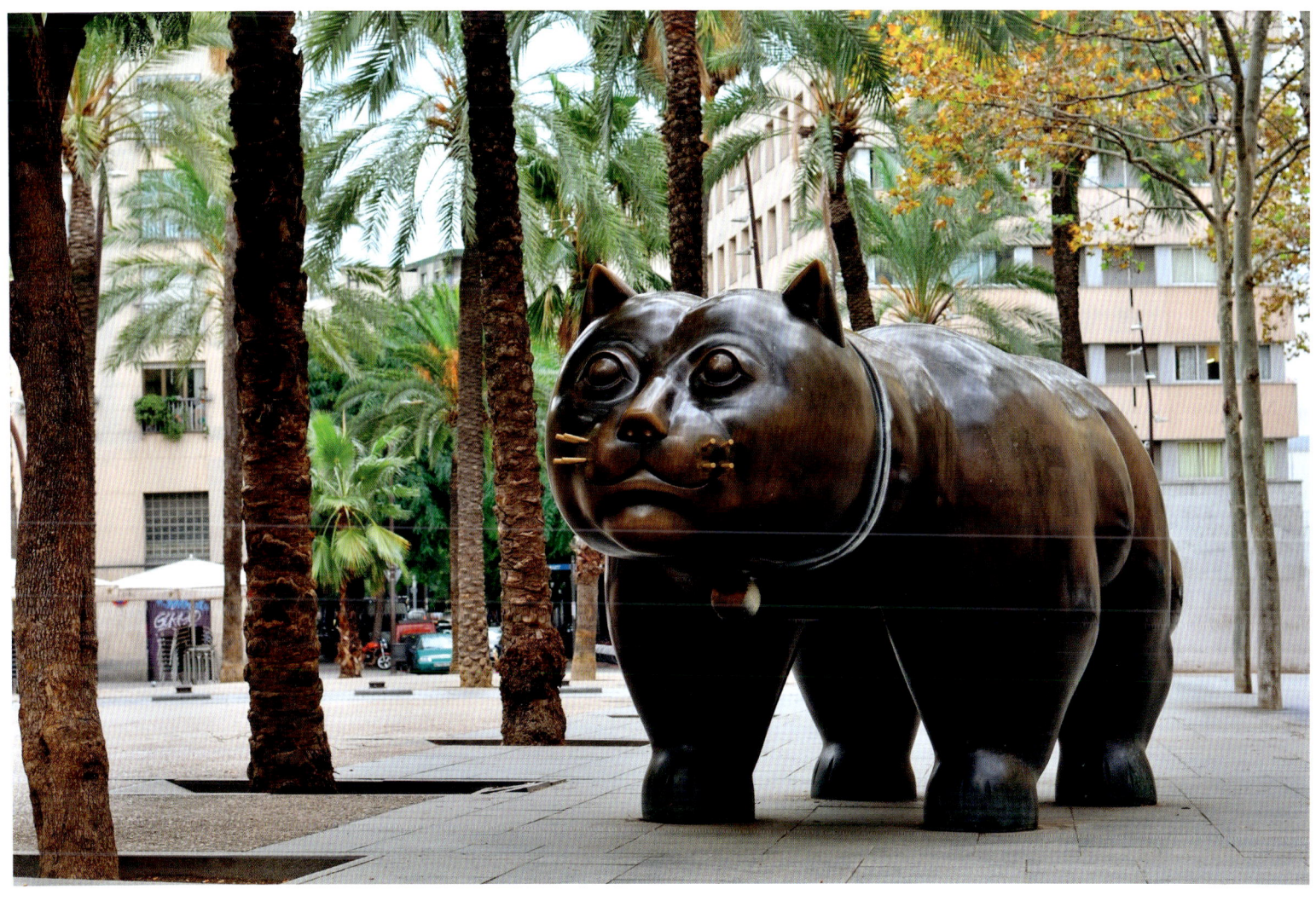

FERNANDO BOTERO

El Gato, 1987
Bronze, 11. 8 ft. 3 in. / 2.5 m, L. 23 ft / 7 m
Rambla del Raval, Barcelona

Measuring more than 20 feet (/ m) long and 8 feet (2.5 m) tall, and weighing in at more than two tons, this oversize bronze cat is appealingly plump, a body type characteristic of the sculptures of Colombian artist Fernando Botero (1932–2023). Although as a child Botero dreamed of becoming a bullfighter, he decided to study art in Spain after moving to Madrid in the 1950s. He focused on painting for the early part of his career, but, after living in New York for more than a decade, he returned to Europe, moving his studio to Paris in 1973, and began working in sculpture. His distinctive style is sometimes labeled *Boterismo* and features sculptures of voluptuous women and animals with exaggerated proportions. With its neck outstretched in a gesture of friendly curiosity, this city kitty wears a collar with a bell that has been polished to a high shine by the hands of countless passersby. Purchased by Barcelona City Council in 1987, *El Gato* (Spanish for "the cat") has resided in different locations around the popular Spanish tourist destination and is beloved by locals and visitors alike. After spending time in the picturesque Parc de la Ciutadella near Barcelona's zoo, it was relocated near the Olympic Stadium, then to a small square close to Barcelona's medieval-era shipyards. Finally, in 2003, this peripatetic puss settled into his permanent home on the Rambla del Raval, where it has become a popular meeting place.

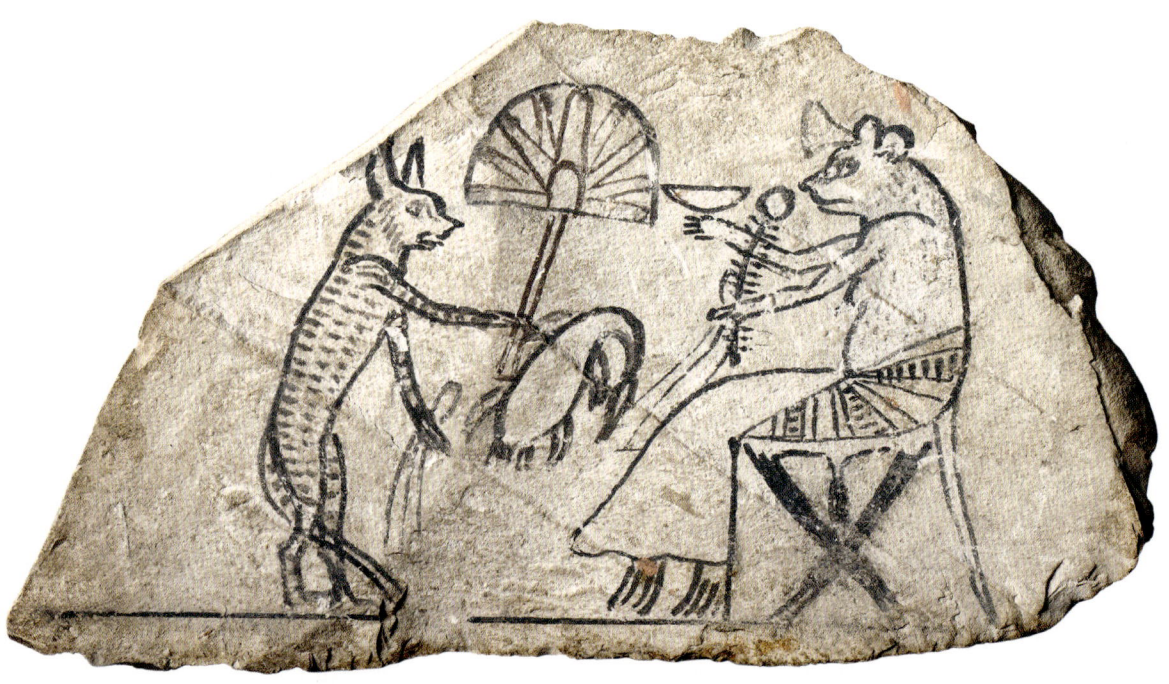

ANONYMOUS

Cat and Mouse, c. 1295–1075 BCE
Limestone and ink, 3½ × 6¾ in. / 8.9 × 17.3 cm
Brooklyn Museum

An ancient example of the comedic power of the doodle, this ink drawing on a rough flake of limestone depicts two animals imitating human behavior. A cat, with striped fur and pointed ears, stands on his two hind legs at left. He performs the role of a funerary priest, holding a fan and a roast duck in one paw and a piece of linen in another. In a reversal of prey and predator, the subservient feline offers these to a large, enthroned mouse, who is represented as an elite person of high status, sitting on a chair and holding a cup. This privileged rodent wears a long kilt and a lotus flower on his head. Egyptian artists used limestone flakes, as seen in this jagged example from the New Kingdom, to practice their drawing skills or sketch scenes. Although cats usually hunt mice in nature, depictions of a cat serving a mouse are surprisingly the most common motif in drawings of this type. At first glance, the charming picture appears to be humorous satire poking fun at the banquet scenes that frequently occur in tombs of Egyptian nobles. In reality, ancient Egyptian drawings with anthropomorphic animals are based on ancient myths and animal fables and are not usually related to the artist's own feelings about nobles' fancy feasts. Unfortunately, the exact story referenced by these anthropomorphic characters remains a mystery.

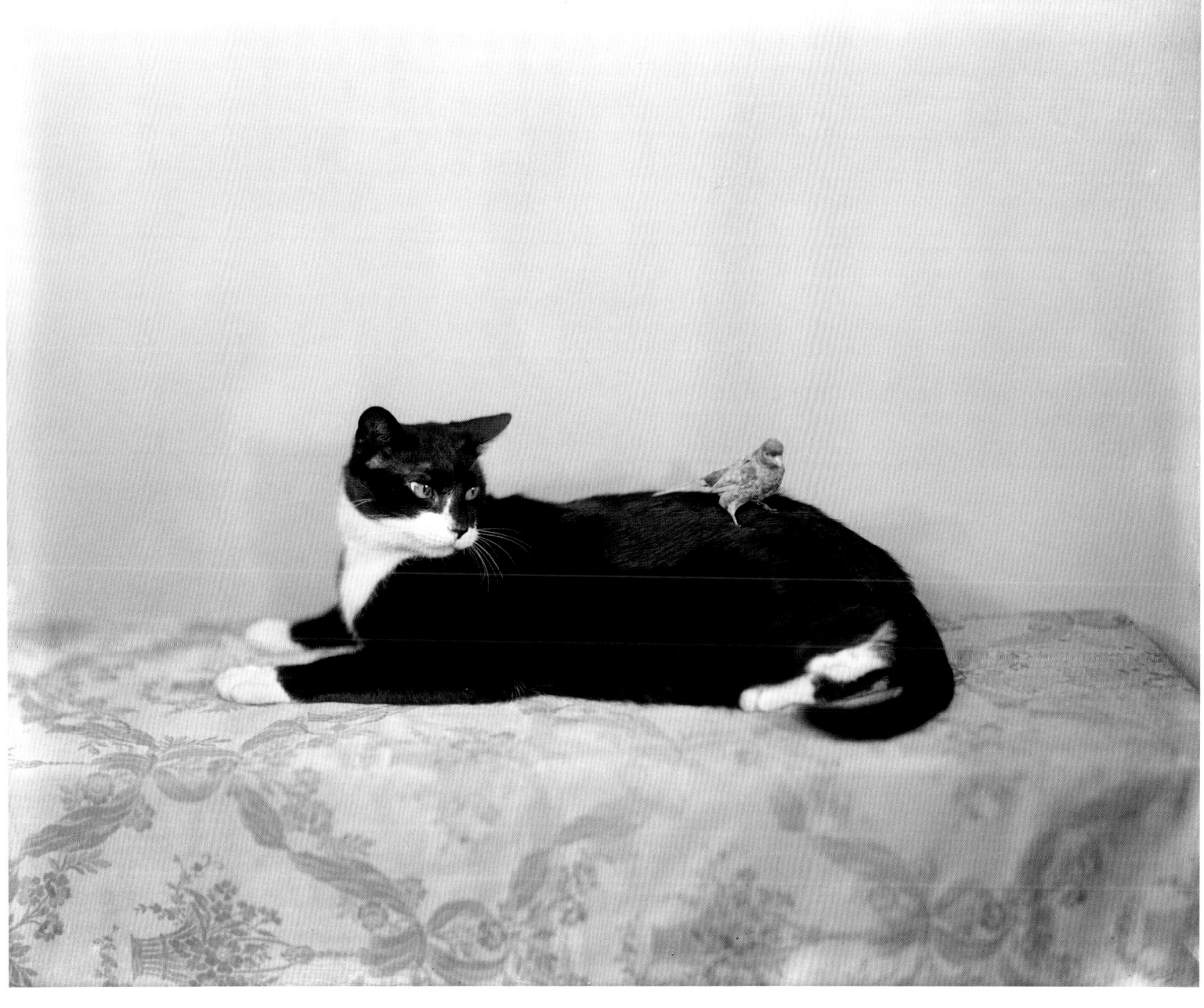

HARRIS & EWING

TIMMONS, MRS. BASCOM N., c. 1928–36
Gelatin silver print, 8 × 10 in. / 20.3 × 25.4 cm
Library of Congress, Washington, DC

Fear not. The daring little canary, Caruso, is quite safe perched on the back of his furry companion, Timmie. Despite Timmie's sharp gaze—one that might suggest he's eyeing Caruso up as a potential meal—he is, in fact, vigilantly guarding his feathered friend in a striking display of loyalty. This bond mirrors the strong rapport shared by their owners: Timmie belonged to Bascom N. Timmons, the prominent Texan political correspondent and president of the National Press Club, who also served as an advisor to President Calvin Coolidge, owner of Caruso. When Coolidge observed the unique kinship between the two animals, he graciously gifted the bird to Timmons, who was a cat lover, amassing more than one hundred during his lifetime. Timmie was one of a kind, known for his peaceful habit of quietly observing birds. More docile dog than killer cat à la the cartoon Sylvester, who was forever scheming to catch Tweety Pie, Timmie reportedly loved car rides and often traveled with his human on business trips. The two animal companions were photographed sometime between 1928 and 1936 in a shot attributed to the famous Washington-based photographic firm Harris & Ewing, known for its high-quality portraits and topical news photographs, including a number of memorable feline moments, such as a young Walt Disney (see pp.21 and 209) presenting a picture of Mickey Mouse to a kitten, and a portrait of Hattie Caraway, the first woman elected to the US Senate, looking determinedly at the camera with a Russian Blue on her lap.

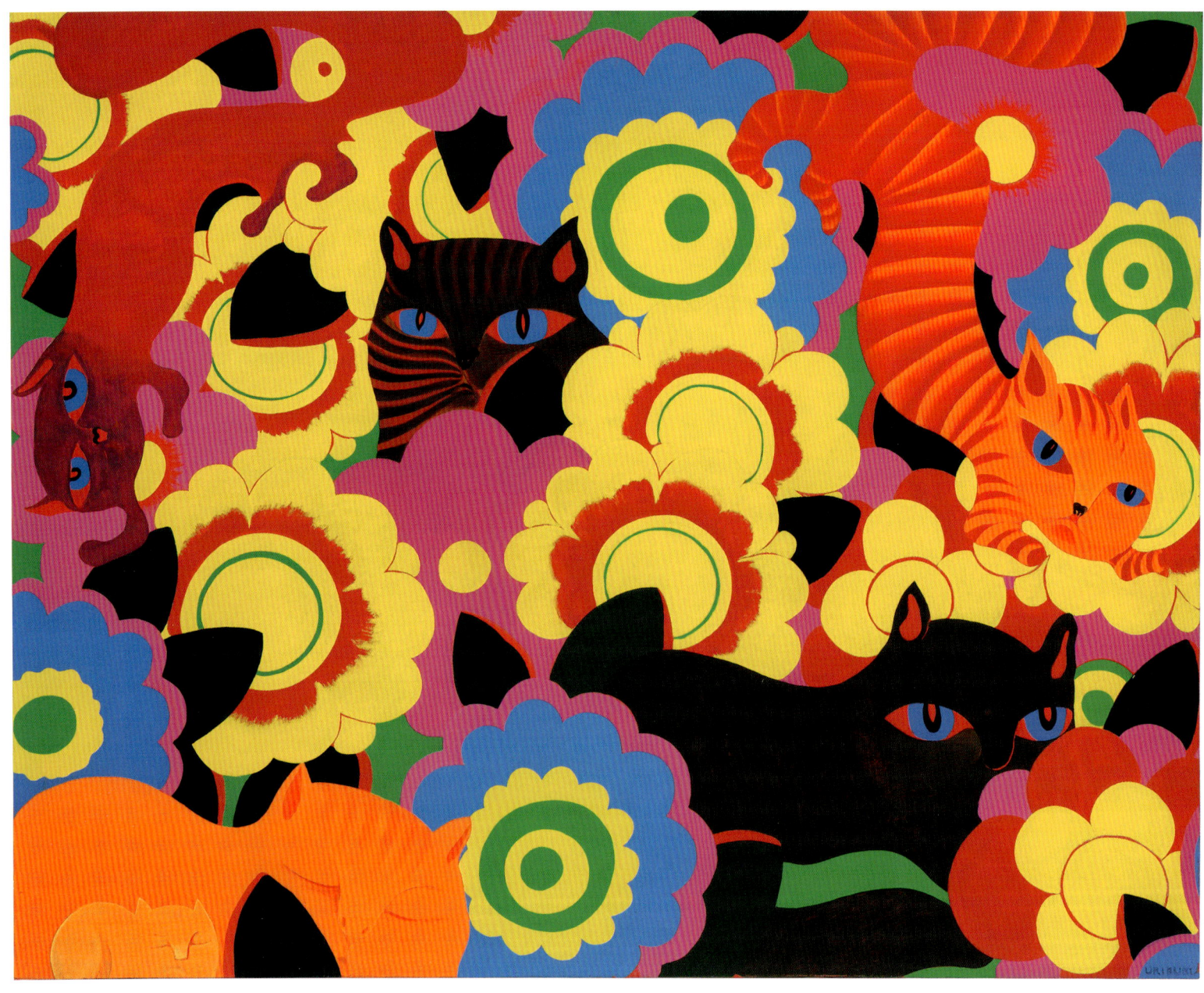

NICOLÁS GARCÍA URIBURU

Untitled (Cats), c. 1967
Oil on canvas
51¼ × 63½ in. / 130.2 × 161.3 cm
Private collection

How many cats can you spot in this vibrant homage to mischievous felines? A work of pure sunshine, the colorful tableau captures everything we know and love about these creatures: their playful energy, their wide-eyed nonchalance, and their fondness for napping in unpredictable places. In this case, see if you can find the striped orange cat and kitten nestled together in the foreground, oblivious to the chaos around them as their fellow pusses run riot among the flowers. There is also a deeper message at work here that relates to the regenerative powers of nature, communicated not only through the vivid hues but through shape and movement. This coterie of cats seemingly travels clockwise around a garden saturated with circular spinning forms, adding a dynamic and rhythmic element to the composition. In fact, action within art was a source of inspiration for Argentinian artist Nicolás García Uriburu (1937–2016) in more ways than one. An environmental activist and early pioneer of land art, he was as adventurous with his ideas as he was with his palette, famously dyeing Venice's Grand Canal fluorescent green in 1968 to protest water pollution. During the 1970s and 1980s, García Uriburu also helped to plant more than fifty thousand trees in his native Buenos Aires, promoting environmental sustainability and biodiversity. In this little world of multicolored cats, every corner is bursting with life and vitality, reminding us that even the smallest patches of land can be vital sanctuaries for wildlife.

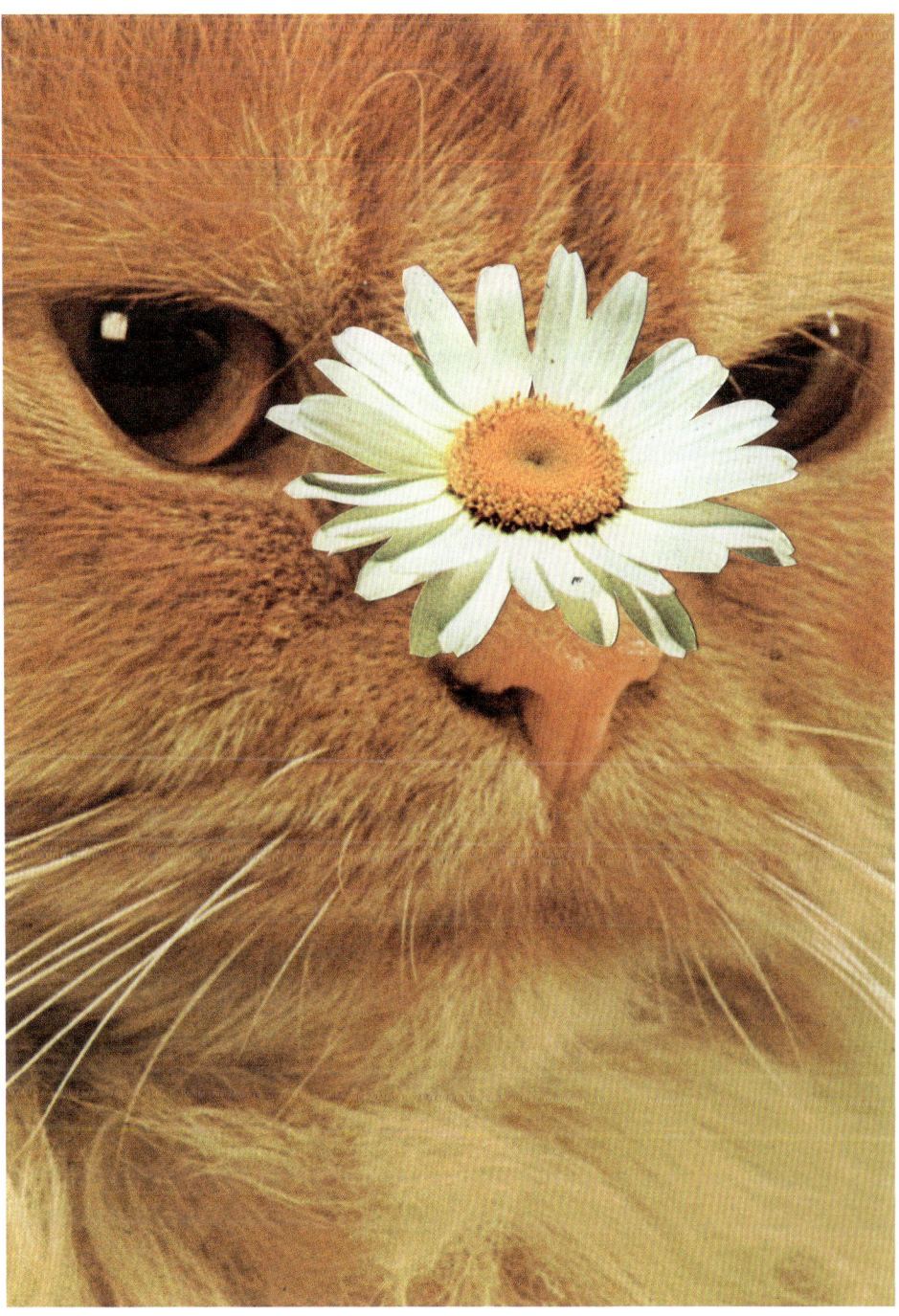

STEPHEN EICHHORN

Orange, 2009
Hand-cut collage
13½ × 10 in. / 34.3 × 25.4 cm
Private collection

This adorable daisy-dappled kitty appears in the 2017 book *Cats and Plants* by Chicago-based multimedia artist Stephen Eichhorn (b. 1984). A collector of vintage printed ephemera, Eichhorn noticed a shared visual language in old guidebooks for houseplants and cats. He remembers, "There was a quirkiness and humor to the . . . compositions of the houseplants that the cat photos shared, like the cat and plants were both domestic objects." That kernel of an idea blossomed into a series of collages combining the two elements as still lifes. These explorations culminated in whimsical works, such as this one, where a close-up of a smug orange tabby is made surreal by the bright white aster somehow balancing on its nose. The artist's deft hand and sharp eye are on full display, and his attention to

detail shows in his ability to render the most intricate cuts to his source materials so that they combine seamlessly into one image. The practice of collage is a decidedly modernist art form, developed in the early twentieth century by Cubist and Dadaist artists who embraced paper collage techniques, such as Pablo Picasso (see p.204), Georges Braque, and Hannah Höch. While Eichhorn's work contains Surrealist elements, it echoes more modern influences, such as the mid-century collagist Ray Yoshida—himself a Chicago artist—who similarly sourced his images from mundane materials, such as catalogs, newspapers, comic books, and calendars. Both artists' works exude an offbeat humor and an inviting familiarity due to the commercial images employed in their compositions.

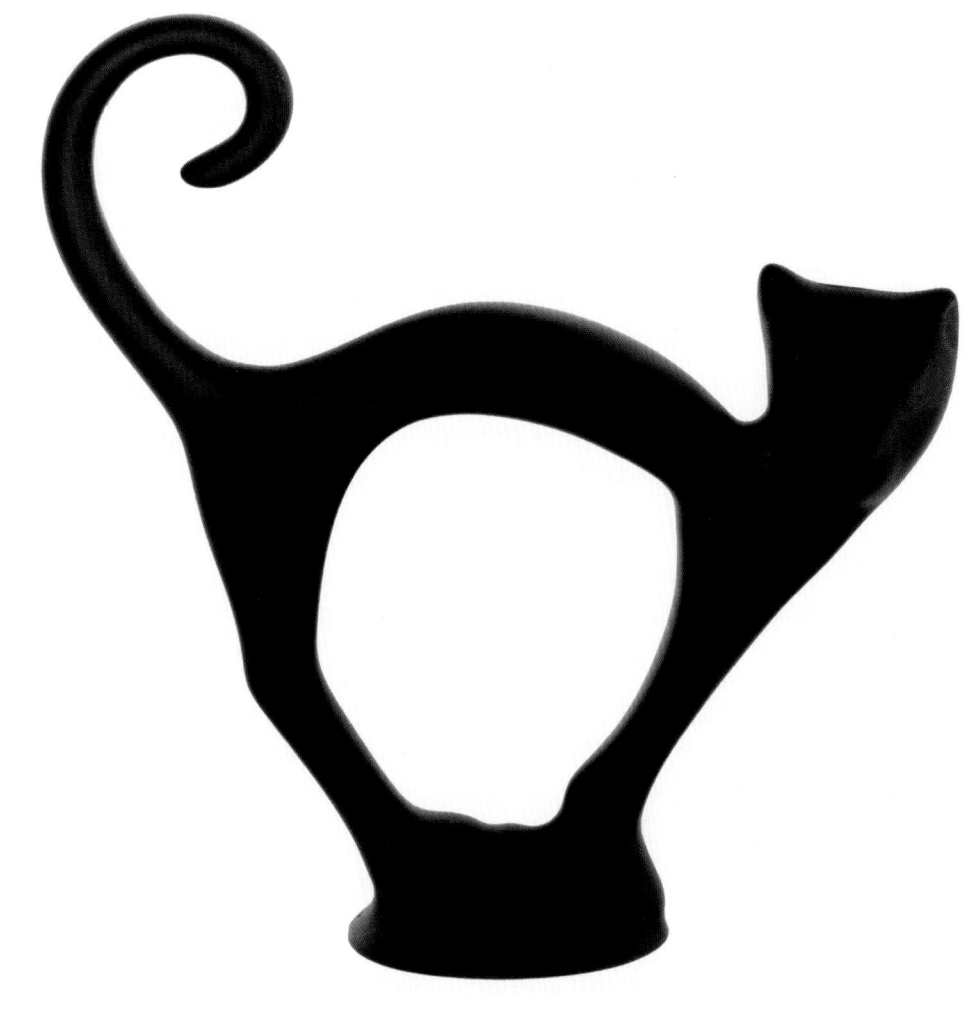

KATHARINA FRITSCH

Katze (Cat), 1981–89
Synthetic material
6⅝ × 6⅝ × 2⅜ in. / 17 × 17 × 6 cm
Private collection

With its back arched and tail curled, this stylized statue is clearly a black cat—yet its overexaggerated, elongated form reimagines the animal, playing with the recognizable shape of a witch's familiar. This plastic sculpture is an early work of German artist Katharina Fritsch (b. 1956), who gained widespread recognition for the giant blue cockerel (*Hahn / Cock*) she created to occupy the fourth plinth in London's Trafalgar Square between 2013 and 2015. Fritsch's uncanny approach takes everyday objects and animals, as disparate as cats and octopuses, and manipulates their scale and color. Here, the common black cat is made slightly unfamiliar, and its stretched body creates the large emptiness that makes up much of the sculpture. As Fritsch says, "I think everything can be a

sculpture for me. From the beginning, I wanted to create a kind of middle world . . . a world that really surprises people like they haven't seen the object before." The artist's process is involved: she first sketches the object and molds it by hand, before sculpting it in plaster and reworking it to its final shape. Fritsch then casts the new being in her material of choice—bronze, copper, stainless steel, or, as here, plastic—before finishing it with matte paint, often mixed by the artist to achieve specific saturated colors. Inspired by her own experiences and by folklore, Fritsch creates unsettling and enigmatic creatures as in *Katze,* the sleek form and dark material of which hint at the cat's true nature.

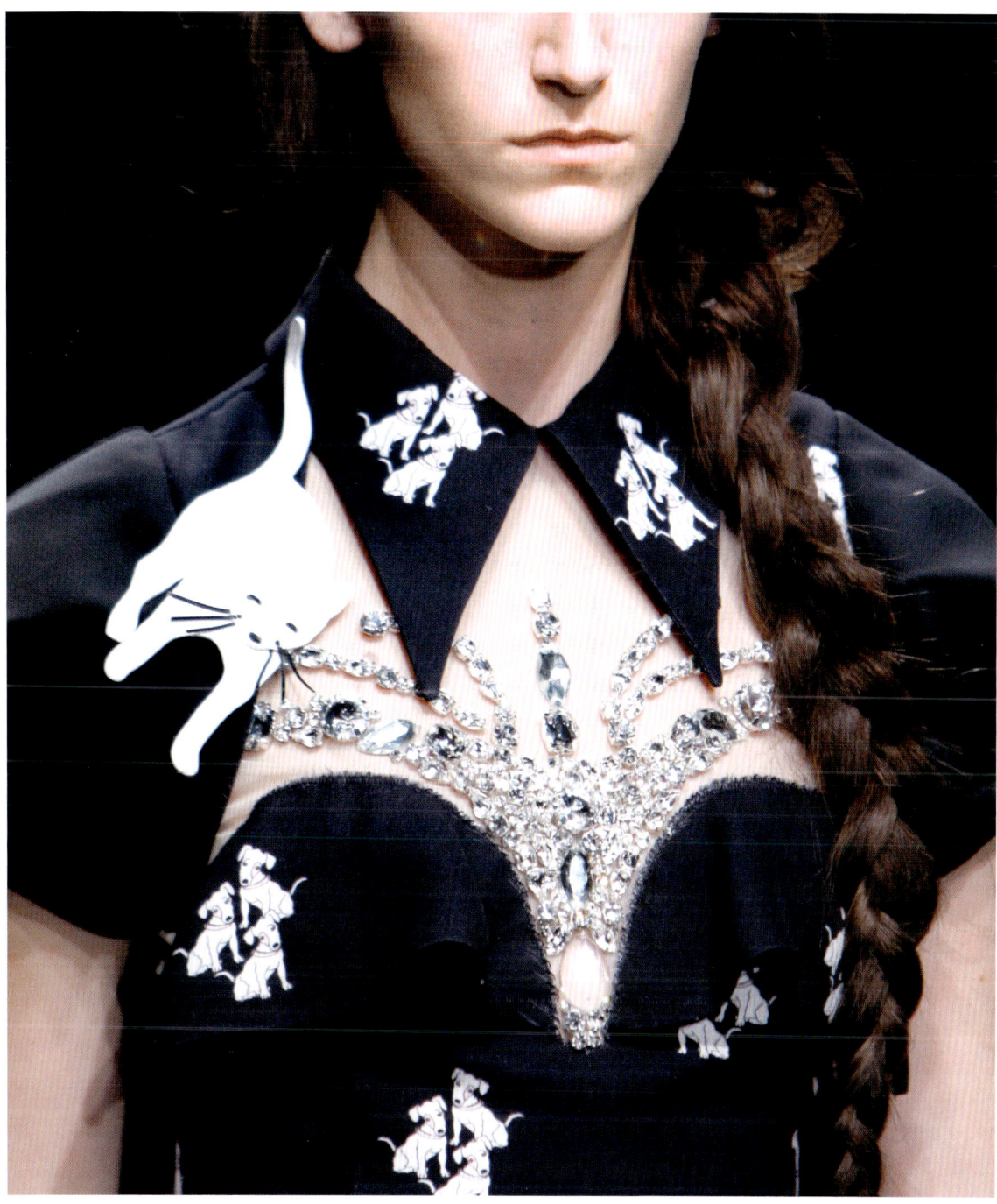

MIU MIU

Look 29, from Spring/Summer collection, 2010

The sister brand of Italian high fashion house Prada, Miu Miu takes its name from the childhood nickname of founder Miuccia Prada, which evokes the sound of a cat's meow when spoken aloud. It is then no surprise that feline motifs frequently appear in Miu Miu collections. Notably, the label's first kitty print to capture the fashion world's attention was the *chats à la mode* pattern, featured on its Spring/Summer 2010 runway, which also showcased fabrics emblazoned with tiny swallows, puppies, budding flowers, and reclining nudes. With its sleek, sophisticated form, long whiskers, and gracefully curving S-shaped tail, this posh pedigree was replicated in delicate shades of white or pale blue on a variety of luxury, highly tailored fabrics. Blurring the line between doll and woman,

this coquettish ready-to-wear line included baby-doll dresses, silk blouses, bandeau tops, and platform shoes that set the stage for indie, twee 2010s fashion and are all now highly coveted vintage finds. Here, the svelte feline takes the form of a leather pin brooch playfully tilted next to an oversize beaded collar. This quirky touch captures the essence of Miu Miu, a brand synonymous with fresh and fun designs that celebrate craftsmanship and inspire imaginative styling, synthesizing opposites from vintage and contemporary to girly and edgy. True to its name, Miu Miu is like an affectionate cat seeking attention, offering whimsical glamour in every carefully designed piece.

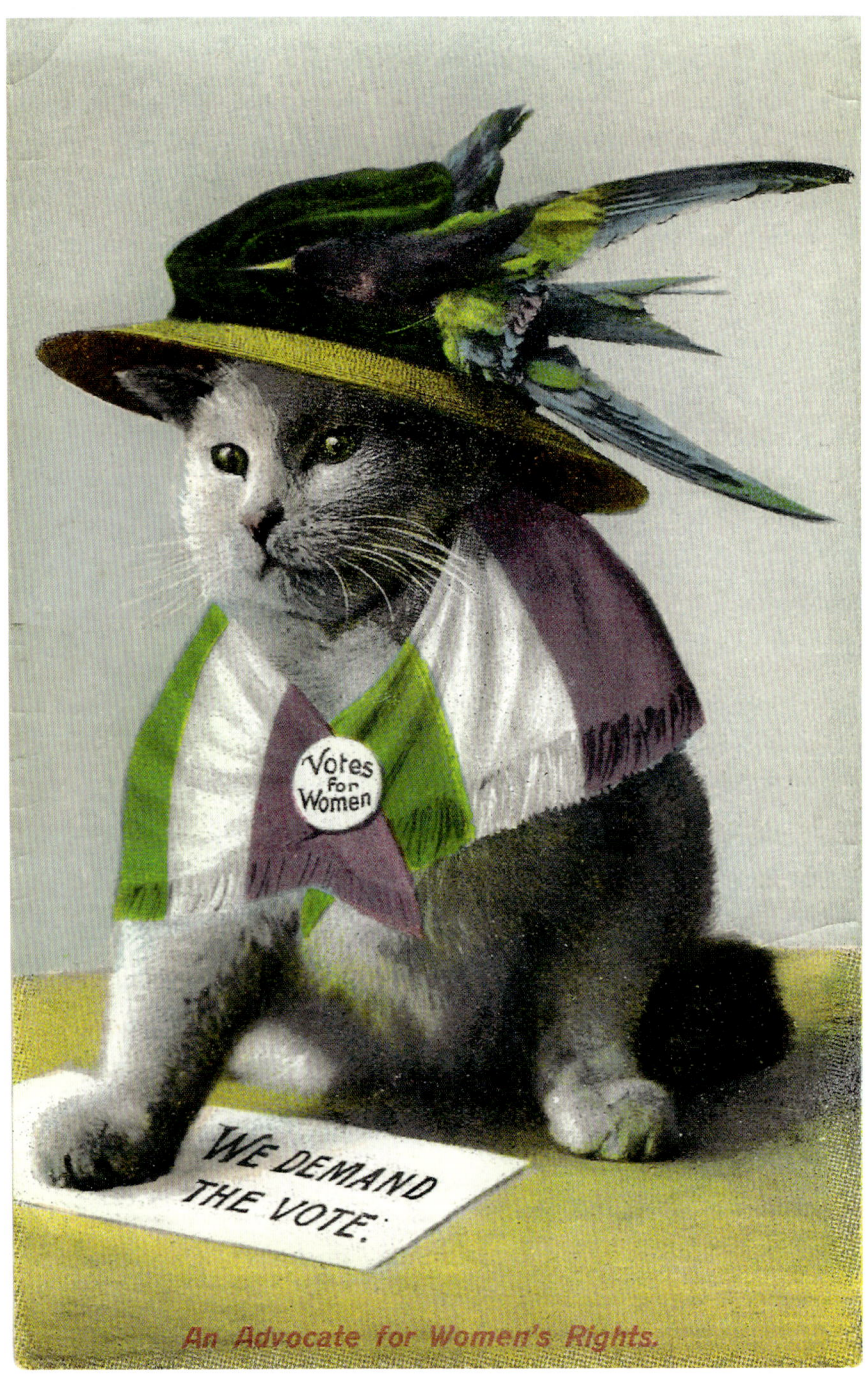

An Advocate for Women's Rights.

ANDREW AND GEORGE TAYLOR

An Advocate for Women's Rights, c. 1910–13
Postcard, 5½ × 3½ in. / 14 × 9 cm
Ann Lewis Women's Suffrage Collection

A large gray cat sits on a table, wearing a straw hat decorated with a few bird feathers—or possibly a whole canary—dressed in a shawl with purple, white, and green stripes held in place by a badge that reads "We Demand the Vote." The colors in this propaganda postcard are those of the English women's suffrage movement, the Women's Social and Political Union (WSPU), founded by activist Emmeline Pankhurst in 1903. Photographic postcards were a popular propaganda and advertising medium in Edwardian London, where dozens of private photography studios set up to produce them, including "photographers to the Queen" Andrew and George Taylor, holders of a Royal Warrant, who produced this tinted half-tone example. Cats often featured on both pro- and anti-suffrage postcards.

In popular culture, cats had become symbols of stereotypes about women: the indoor cat represented passive domestic space while the outdoor cat was feral and lawless. In the struggle over voting rights for women, anti-suffrage postcards frequently set out to suggest that giving women the vote was as absurd as giving cats the vote. When the WSPU's initial peaceful protests failed, its members turned to militant tactics, such as going on hunger strikes when they were imprisoned. The British government's response to these tactics was the so-called Cat and Mouse Act of 1913. Hunger strike protestors were released from jail when they were on the point of starvation, then rearrested once they had gained sufficient weight.

MOG
the Forgetful Cat

Judith Kerr

JUDITH KERR

Mog the Forgetful Cat, 1970
Printed book, 10¼ × 7¼ in / 26 × 18.4 cm

A portly, confused-looking tabby cat with a round face and white paws and chest sits in a patch of greenery in this beloved, best-selling British children's book. Written and illustrated by Judith Kerr (1923–2019), *Mog the Forgetful Cat* was originally published in 1970. The now classic story features a feline protagonist named Mog (a shortened version of "moggy," a Britishism for a cat of unspecified breed), who is a member of the Thomas family—Mr. and Mrs. Thomas and their two children, Nicky and Debbie. Mog is a nuisance without realizing it, sitting on Mr. Thomas's flowers or eating Nicky's egg at breakfast. Most frustrating is her habit of forgetting about the cat flap, her own private door that allows Mog to spend time in the garden, then return home at her leisure. Routinely convinced that she is locked out, she meows loudly for reentry. One evening, this maddening pattern leads to unlikely heroism. Sitting in the flower box outside the kitchen window—forgetting, yet again, about the cat flap—Mog spots a burglar in the kitchen. She hopes he will let her in, but scares him with her relentless meowing, an accidental act of bravery. A policeman arrives, calls her a "remarkable cat," and gives her a medal. As a token of appreciation, she is served an egg for breakfast every day thereafter. Mog was a legend of her time, and Kerr went on to write more than a dozen books about this endearing cat's absent-minded and lovable, if exasperating, antics.

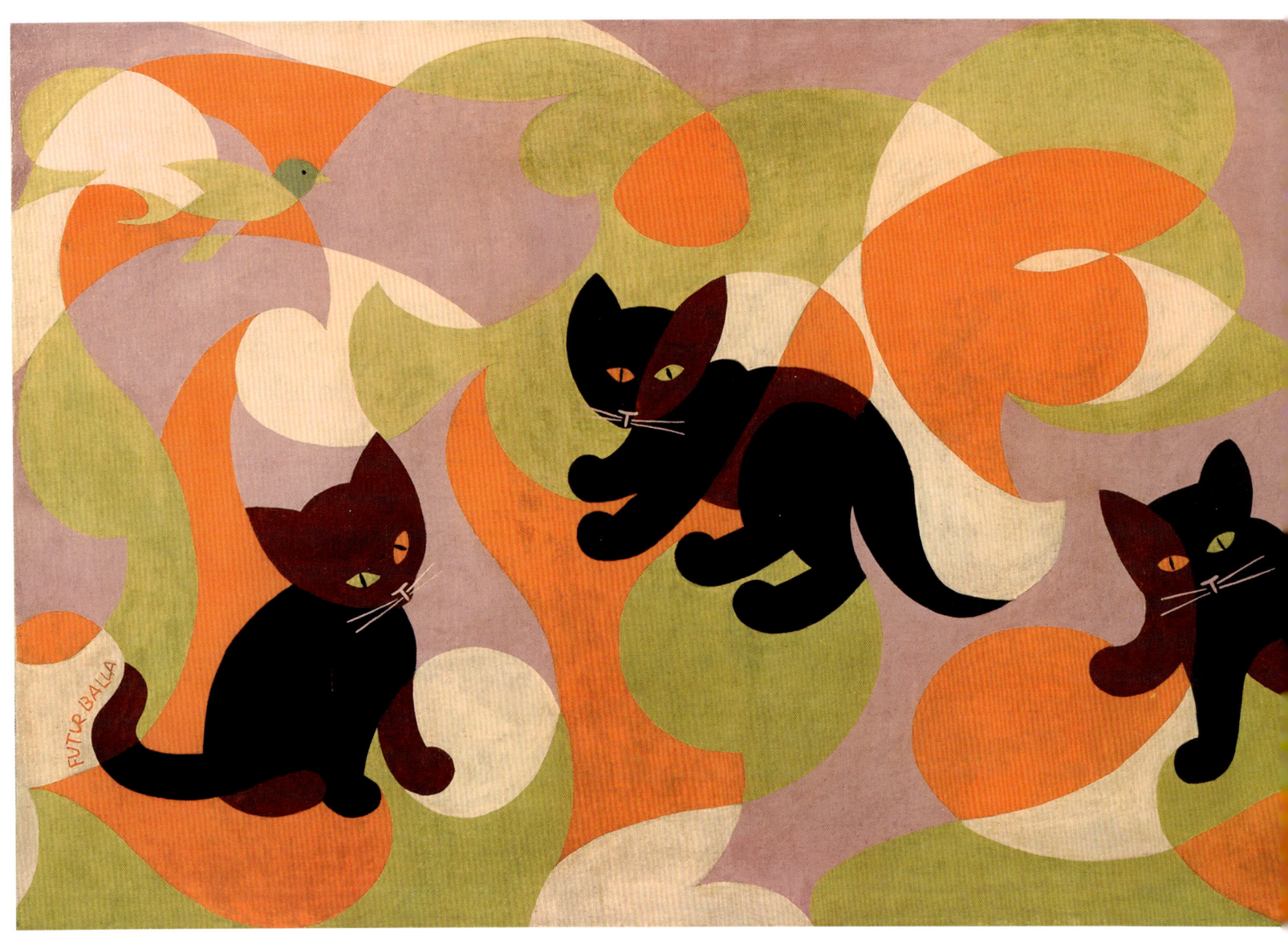

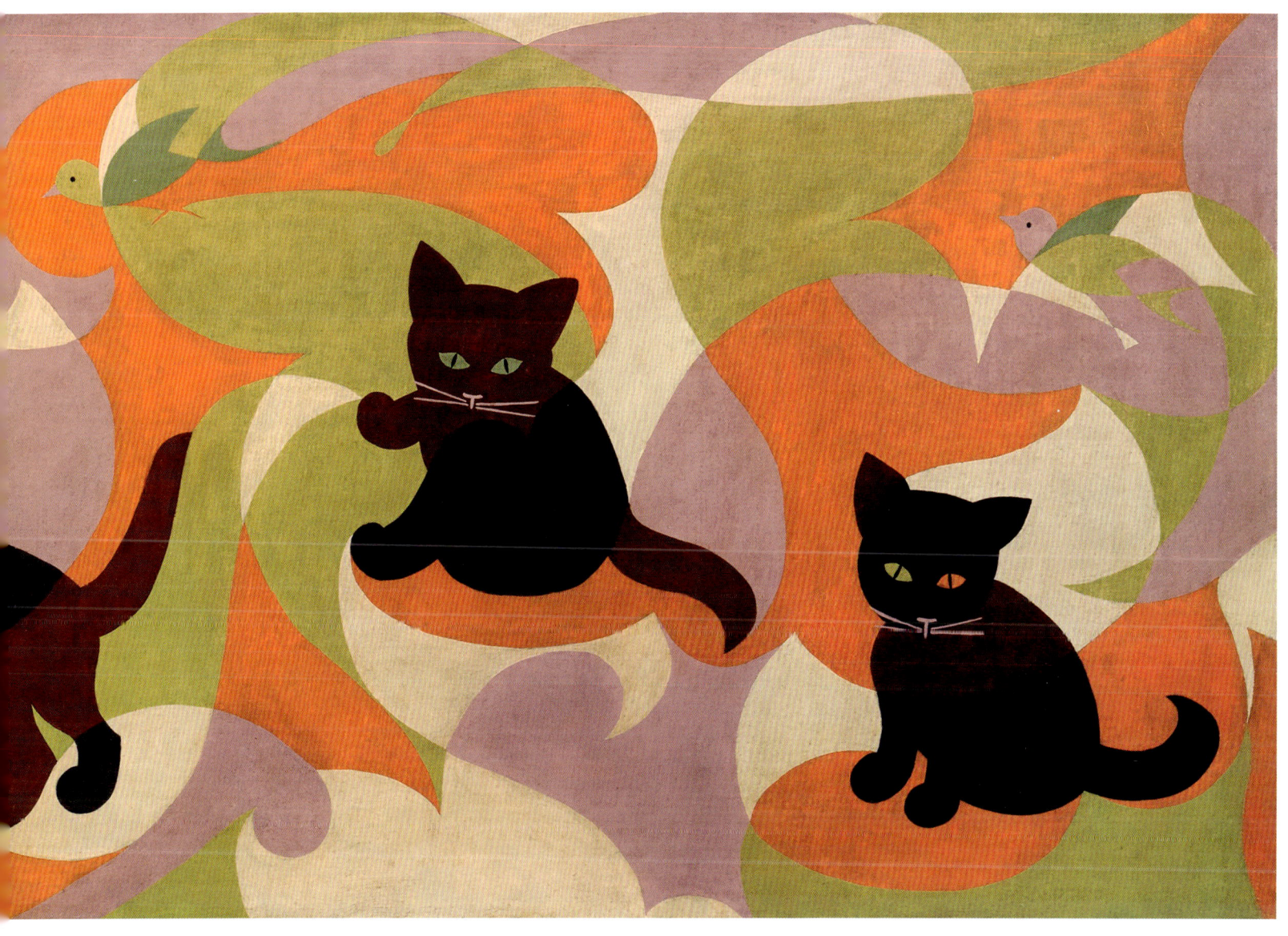

GIACOMO BALLA

Canaringatti—Gatti futuristi, c. 1925–26
Oil on canvas, 25¾ × 74⅞ in. / 65.5 × 190.3 cm
Galleria d'Arte Maggiore, Bologna, Italy

This colorfully horizontal painting is an oddly cat-centric work for the artist perhaps best known for his depiction of a dog in motion. But the five black cats here are also expressions of dynamism, flitting across the groovy, lava-lamp background of raspberry, chartreuse, cream, and burnt orange, with tiny canaries hidden among the shapes at the top. The work of Italian artist Giacomo Balla (1871–1958), *Canaringatti—Gatti futuristi* (*Canary Cats—Futurist Cats*) is, as its title suggests, a prime example of the avant-garde movement known as Futurism. Founded in the early twentieth century by a group of Italian artists, Futurism explored speed, light, movement, and technology in abstract art, grappling with the rapid innovations of the period, especially in regard to warfare, youth culture, airplanes

and automobiles, and living in an industrial city. Unlike other key Futurists, who included Umberto Boccioni and Gino Severini, Balla was less concerned with violence or technology and more interested in capturing the expression of movement in his works, which make many of his paintings more whimsical examples of the style. His most famous work, *Dynamism of a Dog on a Leash* (1912), features a dachshund on a walk, with both the dog's legs and owner's feet represented as whirling windmill-like shapes to suggest the fast-paced movement of a city stroll. Regardless, Balla liked his *Futurist Cats* so much that he made a blue-and-green version and repeated its colorful black cat motif in a few designs for Futurist lampshades.

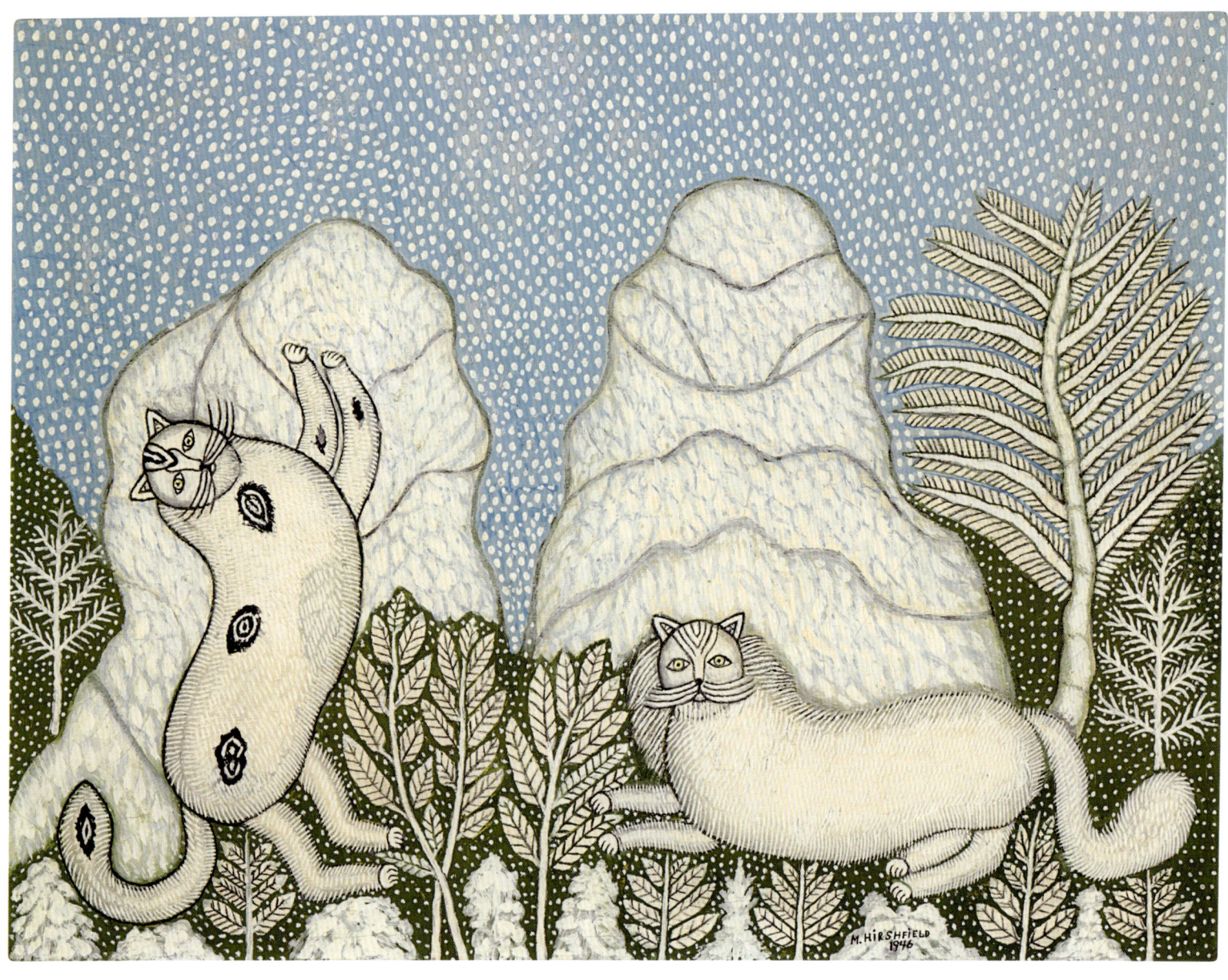

MORRIS HIRSHFIELD

Cats in the Snow, 1946
Oil on canvas, 26 × 34 in. / 66 × 86.4 cm
Private collection

Polish-born American artist Morris Hirshfield (1872–1946) began to explore art as a means of creative expression in his sixties, after poor health spurred him to retirement. A garment worker for most of his life, he immigrated to New York at eighteen and ultimately started a slipper company, becoming a successful entrepreneur. After learning how to paint in 1937, Hirshfield was selected by his gallerist Sidney Janis for a 1939 group show he was curating at the Museum of Modern Art's "members room," spotlighting contemporary unknown American painters. Four years later, Hirshfield had his own solo show at MoMA, the first self-taught artist ever to do so, and later exhibited in the first official American exhibition of Surrealist art alongside Marcel Duchamp, Max Ernst, and Yves Tanguy. It was

a stratospheric rise for an artist who had taken up painting later in life. Although he was mocked by some as "the master of two left feet" for his unusual depiction of the human form, he was critically celebrated during his lifetime. *Cats in the Snow* captures the energy and intricacy of a typical Hirshfield composition, bursting with fine detail stretching to the edges of the canvas. His linework and flat, repetitive patterns recall the motifs of textiles that were at one time the clothing manufacturer's stock-in-trade. Here, two cats cavort through a geometric landscape of stripes and polka dots, themselves festooned with paisley accents, gazing directly at the viewer, as if suddenly interrupted in their frolic.

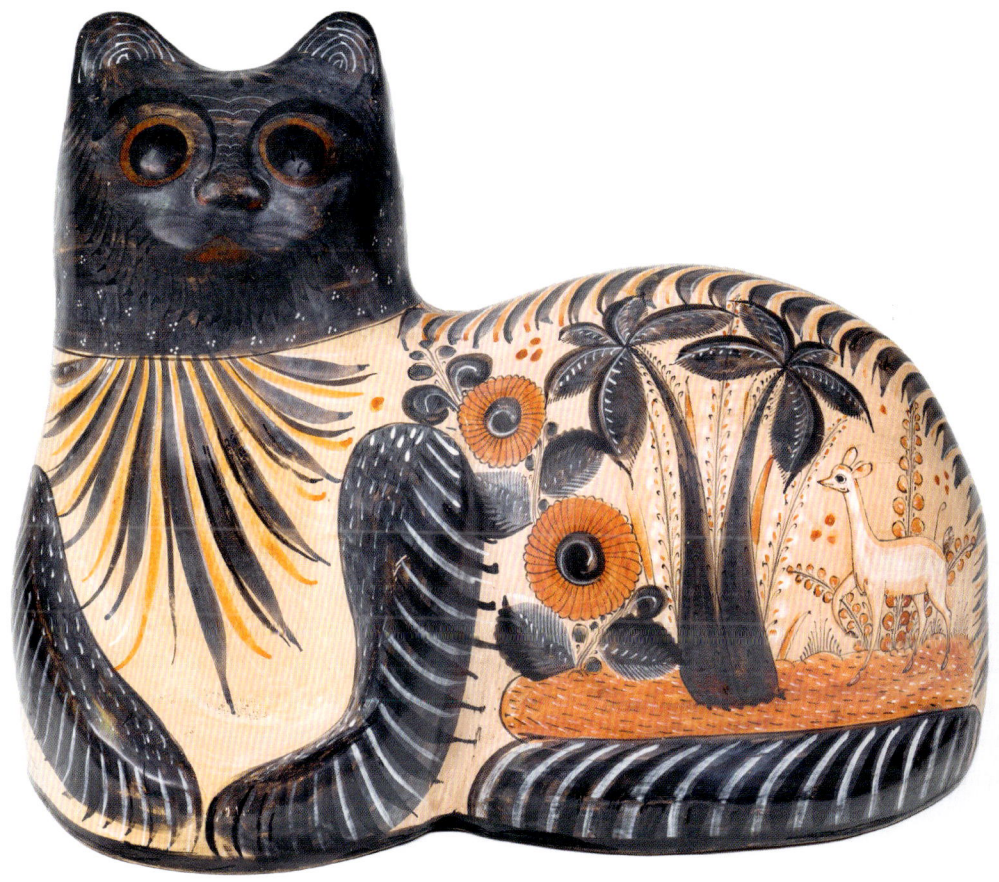

ANONYMOUS

Seated Cat, 20th century
Earthenware, slip, and glaze
13 × 9⅛ × 15½ in / 33 × 24.1 × 39.4 cm
San Antonio Museum of Art

The navy blues, reds, and whites of this hand-painted ceramic cat mark it as typical Tonalá pottery. The earthenware is so named for its place of origin, the Mexican town of Tonalá in the state of Jalisco, northwest of Mexico City. Made by an anonymous artisan using the aromatic clay (*barro de olor*) for which the region is known, the cat belongs in a pottery tradition that predates the arrival of the Spaniards in the sixteenth century. In pre-Hispanic Mexico, cats were an important example of a Mesoamerican *nahual*—a guardian angel and shamanic shape-shifter that can move between the human and animal worlds. These spirits are typically associated with an animal and their significance continues to this day in Tonalá art, where they take the ceramic form, as here, of a sitting cat, whose rounded eyes and button nose are more human than feline. This undated figurine is highly decorated, with energetic strokes along the arms, chest, back, and tail to indicate the animal's fur. The sides feature intricately painted botanical scenes; two large white birds, maybe a pair of the chachalacas or guans endemic to the country, amid dense foliage grace the animal's back, while a dainty creature, perhaps a mule deer, under two palm trees appears on the front. The bright hues used to decorate the cat are made from local colored powdered clay. Originally intended to be displayed in homes in Tonalá, the ceramics are so popular that they are often bought by visiting tourists from elsewhere in Mexico.

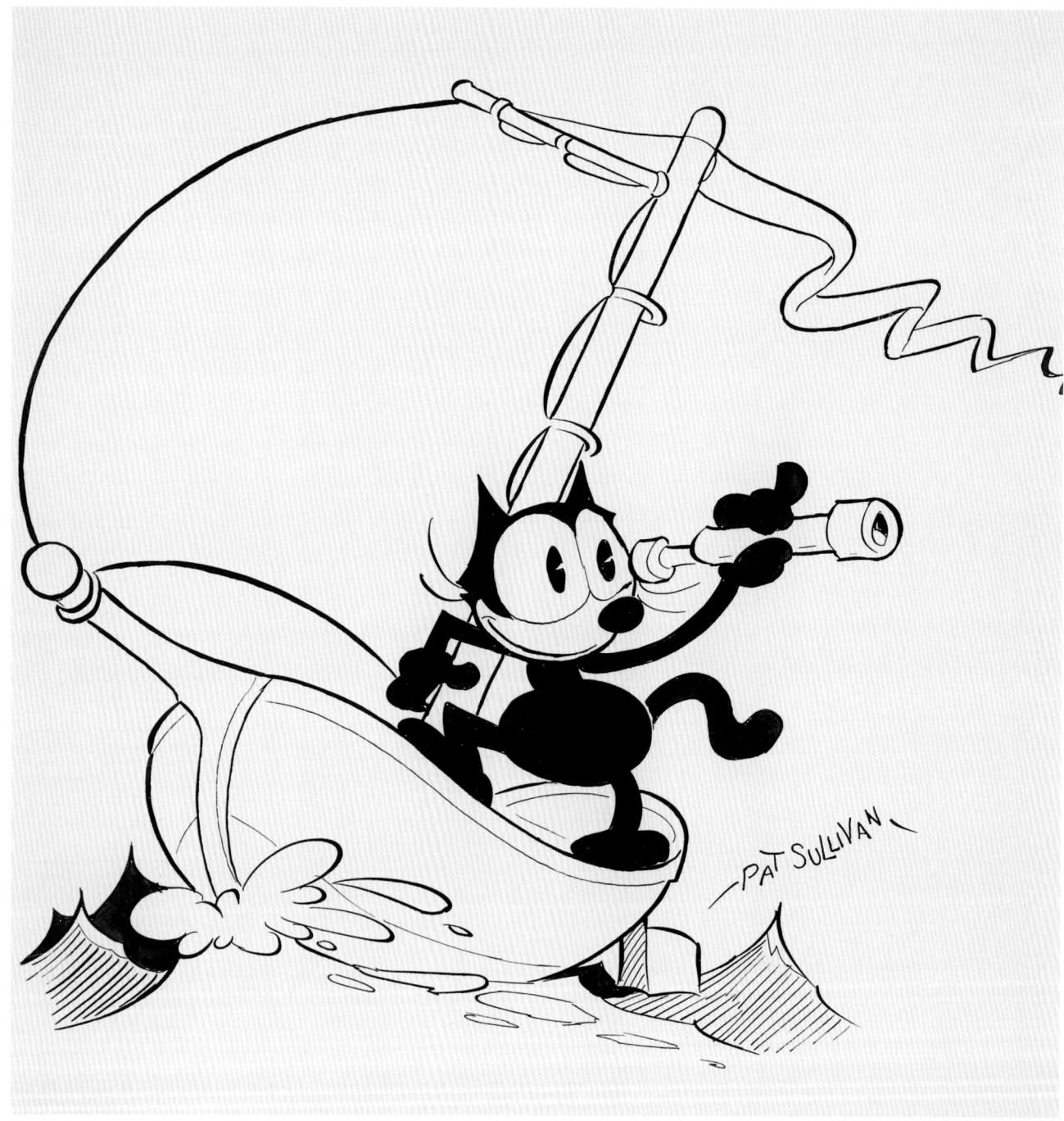

PAT SULLIVAN

Felix the Cat, c. 1930s
Pen and ink on paper
11 × 10 in. / 27.9 × 25.4 cm
Private collection

Before there was Mickey Mouse, there was Felix the Cat. Created by Australian cartoonist Pat Sullivan (1887–1933) in 1917—a full eleven years before Walt Disney's (see pp.21 and 209) *Steamboat Willie* catapulted Mickey to fame—the lithe and big-eyed Felix is considered the world's first cartoon star. He made his debut in the animated short *The Tail of Thomas Kat* and became a mainstay of movie palaces during the silent film era, appearing in more than seventy animated shorts by the end of the next decade. With Felix, Sullivan originated the classic cartoon archetype—an anthropomorphized animal with an oversize head and exaggerated facial features. This feline typifies the so-called "rubber ball on legs" that became the stock-in-trade of animators, a formula allowing for maximum expressiveness and

ease of execution in drawing. Felix was nothing short of a sensation, spawning a comic strip and mass merchandising. In 1927 the black cat was the first-ever balloon to appear in the Macy's Thanksgiving Day Parade, when organizers began to replace live animals with the now-iconic floating attractions. With the advent of "talkies" in the late 1920s, interest in Felix began to fade and his last short was released in the 1930s. Subsequent revivals would follow, including a 1950s television series and two feature films, but they were met with substantially less fervor. Felix's original creator is still subject to debate: Was it producer Sullivan or his studio's lead animator Otto Messmer? Regardless, his legacy in the annals of animation history cannot be denied.

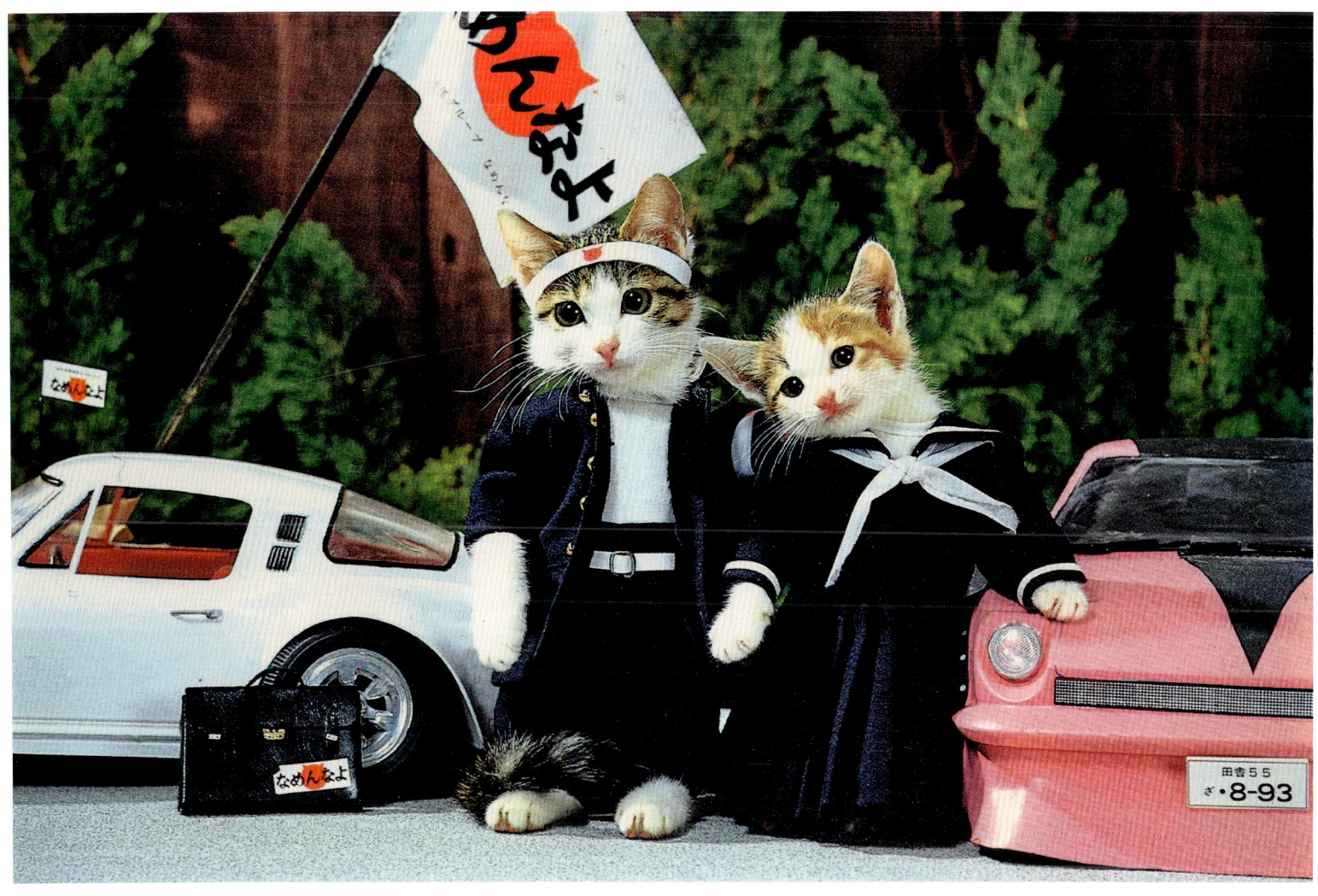

SATORU TSUDA

Namennayo Matakichi No Kattobi Album, 1981
Photograph from printed book
10 × 8¼ in / 25.4 × 21.1 cm

Two cats, dressed as what a Japanese audience would recognize as juvenile delinquents, pose defiantly between two sports cars in this photograph, which started a cultural phenomenon. The briefcase propped against the white car and the Japanese flag both bear the slogan "All Japan Fast Feline Federation: You Won't Lick Us!" This quirky image struck a nerve, selling eight million copies in the early 1980s. The message it conveys of rebellion—albeit a playful one—against social norms launched a craze for what Japanese photographer Satoru Tsuda branded *Namennayo* cat photography (in the United States, it was marketed under the name Perlorian). Although Tsuda had once disliked cats because they preyed on the birds he enjoyed feeding, he changed his mind after rescuing four abandoned

kittens, which he fell in love with as he nursed them back to health. The idea to dress up the kittens came when he saw one of them playing with doll's clothes: this resulting image was the first of a series. To make each photograph, Tsuda created a cat-size diorama, encompassing scenes from camping sites to kitchens, before dressing the models in costumes designed for comfort and ease of movement. Most important, he used only cats that were happy to be dressed up, and each shoot lasted for only ten minutes to avoid stressing the animals. The *Namennayo* phenomenon spawned more than five hundred cat-themed products, including video games and trading cards, and the brand remains popular today.

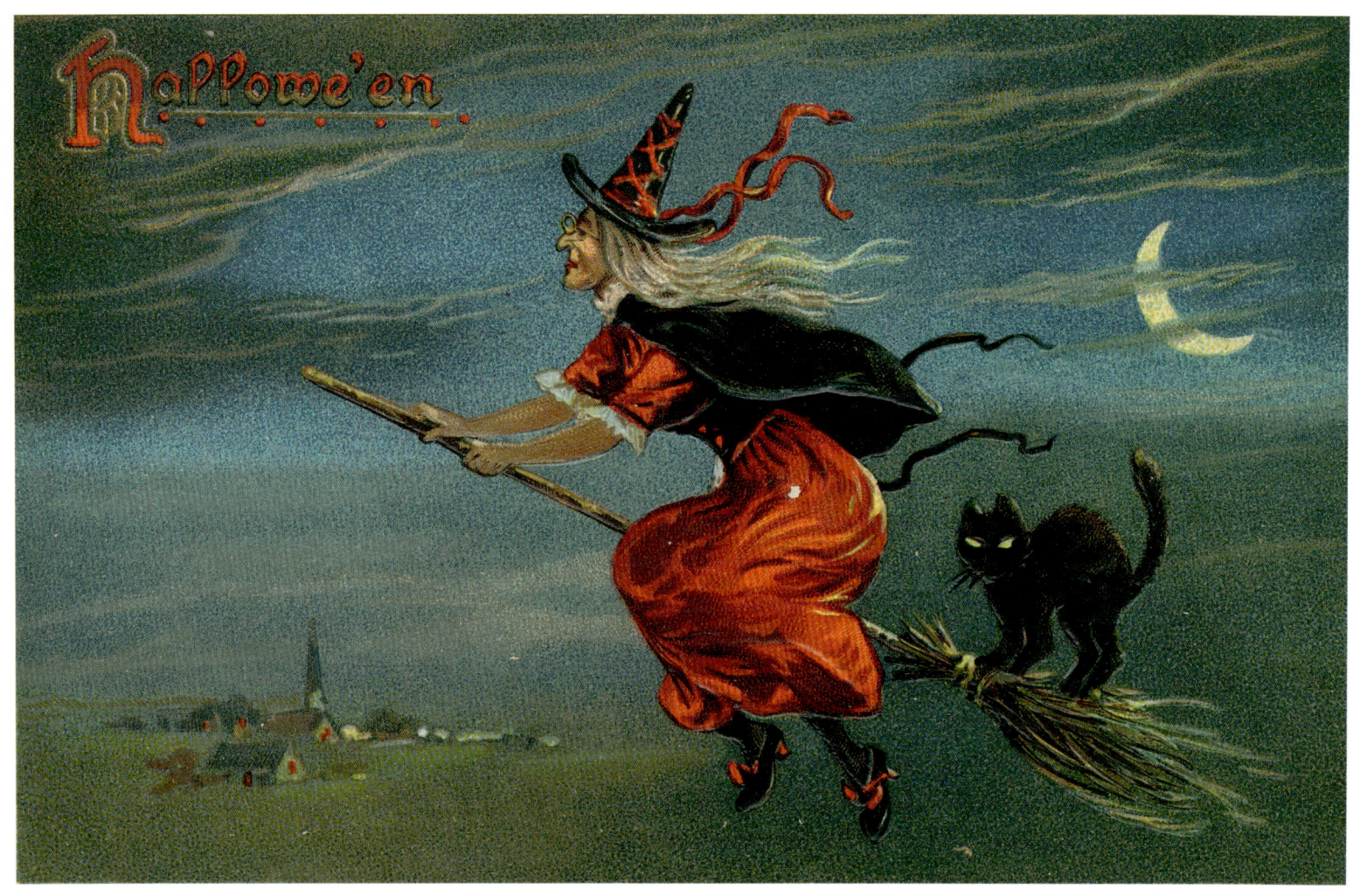

ANONYMOUS

Hallowe'en, c. 1908–10
Postcard
Missouri History Museum, St. Louis

With a quaint village depicted in the distance and a crescent moon hanging in the sky, a quintessential Halloween witch soars through the air on her trusty broomstick, her black cat at her side. The association of black cats with both witches and Halloween has a long history. In the Middle Ages, black cats were considered to be signs of the devil, and during the witch hunts, which lasted from the fifteenth to the eighteenth centuries, women (and some men) accused of being witches were believed to have cats as familiars. The animals were thought to have been involved in the practice of dark magic, and black cats, in particular, were believed to be witches in disguise. The holiday of Halloween has its origins in the ancient Celtic festival of Samhain (see p.188), which celebrates the harvest

season in advance of winter's arrival. At that time of year, the veil between the living and the dead is thought to be especially thin and porous. Communities lit bonfires and people wore costumes to ward off evil ghosts and spirits, and these traditions were also associated with the occult practices of witches. This benevolent-looking witch, wearing a blood-red dress and fancy shoes, might be on her way to a Halloween party. Her black cat rides shotgun on her flying broomstick, its back arched in the "scaredy-cat" symbol that became one of the archetypal icons of modern Halloween. The image features on a postcard, which could have been used to send a spell to its recipient.

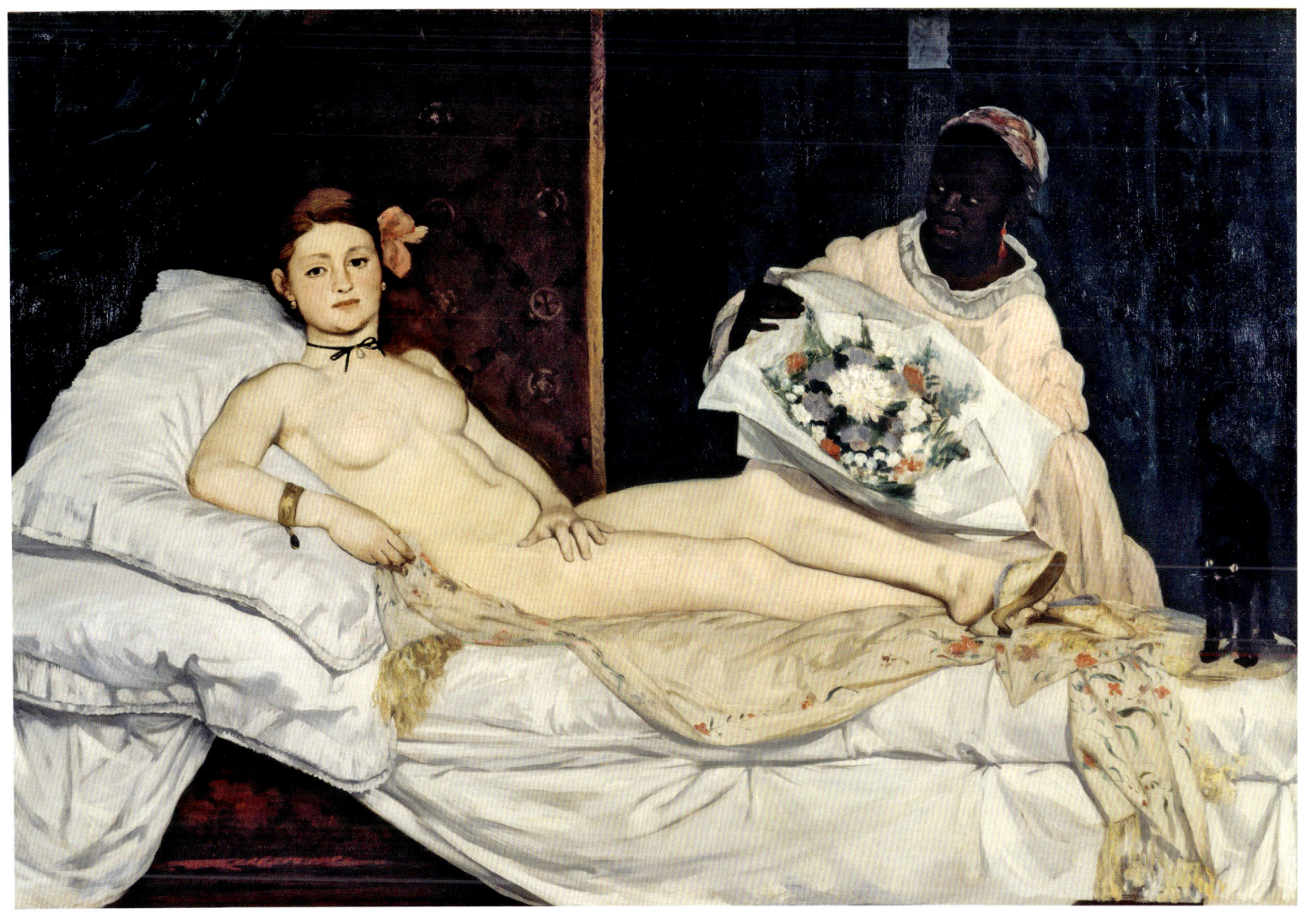

ÉDOUARD MANET

Olympia, 1863
Oil on canvas, 51⅜ × 75¼ in. / 130.5 × 190 cm
Musée d'Orsay, Paris

Édouard Manet (1832–1883), a leader of French Impressionism, is considered one of the masters of modern painting, and *Olympia* is one of his most famous canvases. Revolutionizing the possibilities of paint for subsequent generations, it was a scandalous success when it was first exhibited at the 1865 Salon in Paris, not only because of its subject but for the harsh, realist way it was depicted. Manet clearly represents a prostitute in her boudoir, ironically called Olympia in reference to Greek mythology. She is not naked, but stripped—she has kept her shoes on, which accentuates the eroticism—and the flowers brought to her by her maid are a gift from a client. Although the names of Manet's human models are known—Olympia was embodied by Victorine Meurent, herself an artist,

while a woman named Laure posed as the maid—the identity of the black cat at Olympia's feet remains a mystery. Manet's *Olympia* echoes classic paintings from the art historical canon, including Titian's Renaissance painting *Venus of Urbino* (1538) and Francisco Goya's *The Naked Maja* (1795–1800). The black cat stretching at the foot of the bed replaces the lap dog curled up at the feet of Titian's *Venus*. While the dog is a symbol of faithfulness, the black cat had satanic connotations and represents sexuality—its erect tail is phallic, while the diminutive in both French (*chatte*) and English ("pussy") can also be associated with female genitalia. A noted cat lover, Manet played with these connections in art and life, even naming his own cat Zizi, French slang for "willy."

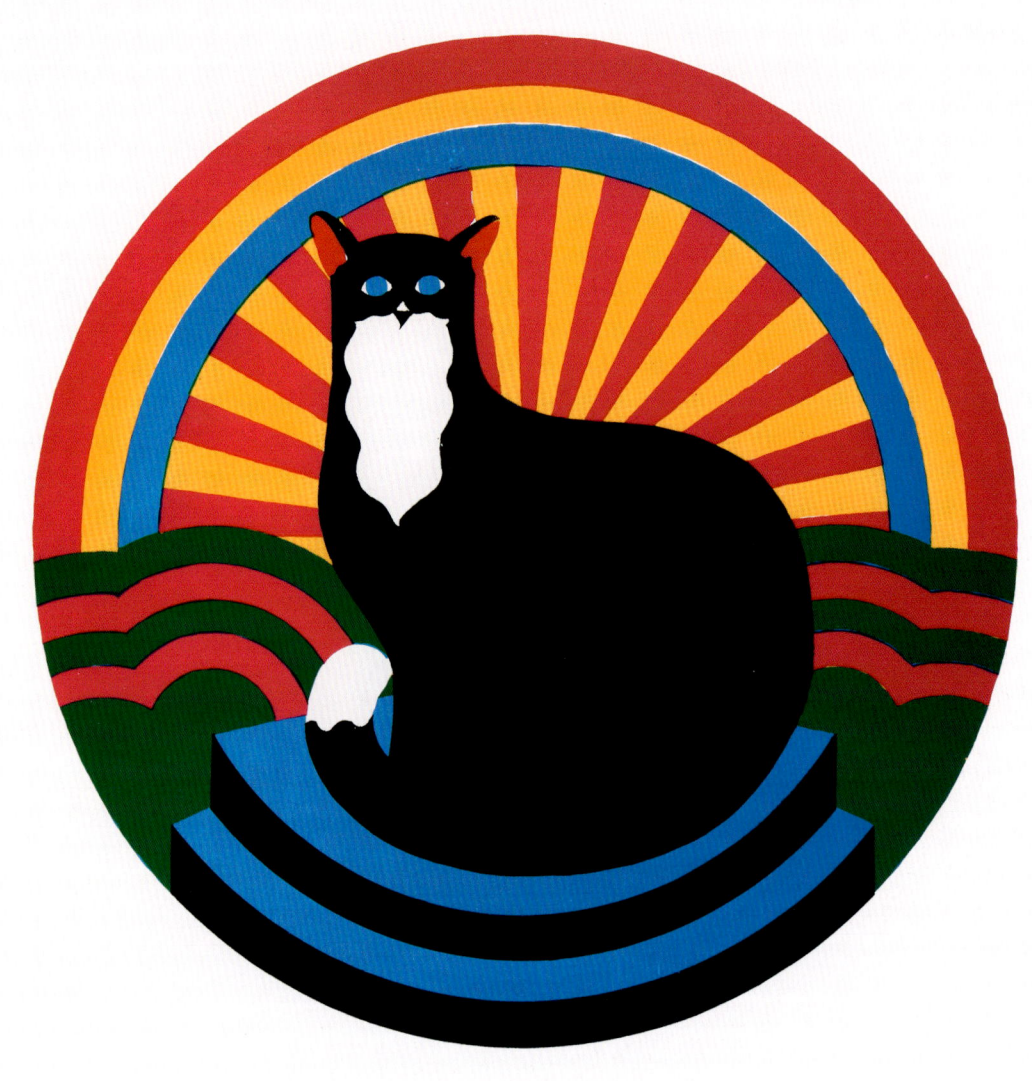

EDGARDO GIMÉNEZ

untitled (cat), 1970
Offset lithograph
10⅜ × 9⅛ in. / 26.4 × 23.2 cm
Private collection

A smiling cat with its long tail curled neatly around its body sits on a bright blue podium, ensconced in a psychedelically striped circular vignette. The funky background might be suggestive of a setting sun or a rainbow over a field, or it might be purely abstract. Although not related to any artist or event, this print by Argentinian polymath Edgardo Giménez (b. 1942) is the same poster format as many of his other Pop-influenced graphics. Self-taught and prolific, Giménez began his career in advertising and created innovative photomontage posters that appeared all over Buenos Aires, reflecting his belief that "Art should come to the viewer, and not the viewer to art." Nearly impossible to categorize, Giménez worked across media, including architecture, performance art, and sculpture. A key

member of the counterculture and experimental movement of Argentina's capital city during the 1960s and 1970s, before the military dictatorship of 1976 led to the widespread repression of artists and other creators, Giménez and other artists formed *La Siempreviva* (Always Alive), a collective that coordinated spaces for creatives to show their work. His own graphic designs reinterpreted contemporary art movements from the United States and Europe, such as Pop art and New Abstraction, for the Argentinian sensibility, featuring bold clashing colors, clean lines, and odd juxtapositions of subject matter. Whatever Giménez's cat might ultimately signify in this design, it is very much a symbol of its era.

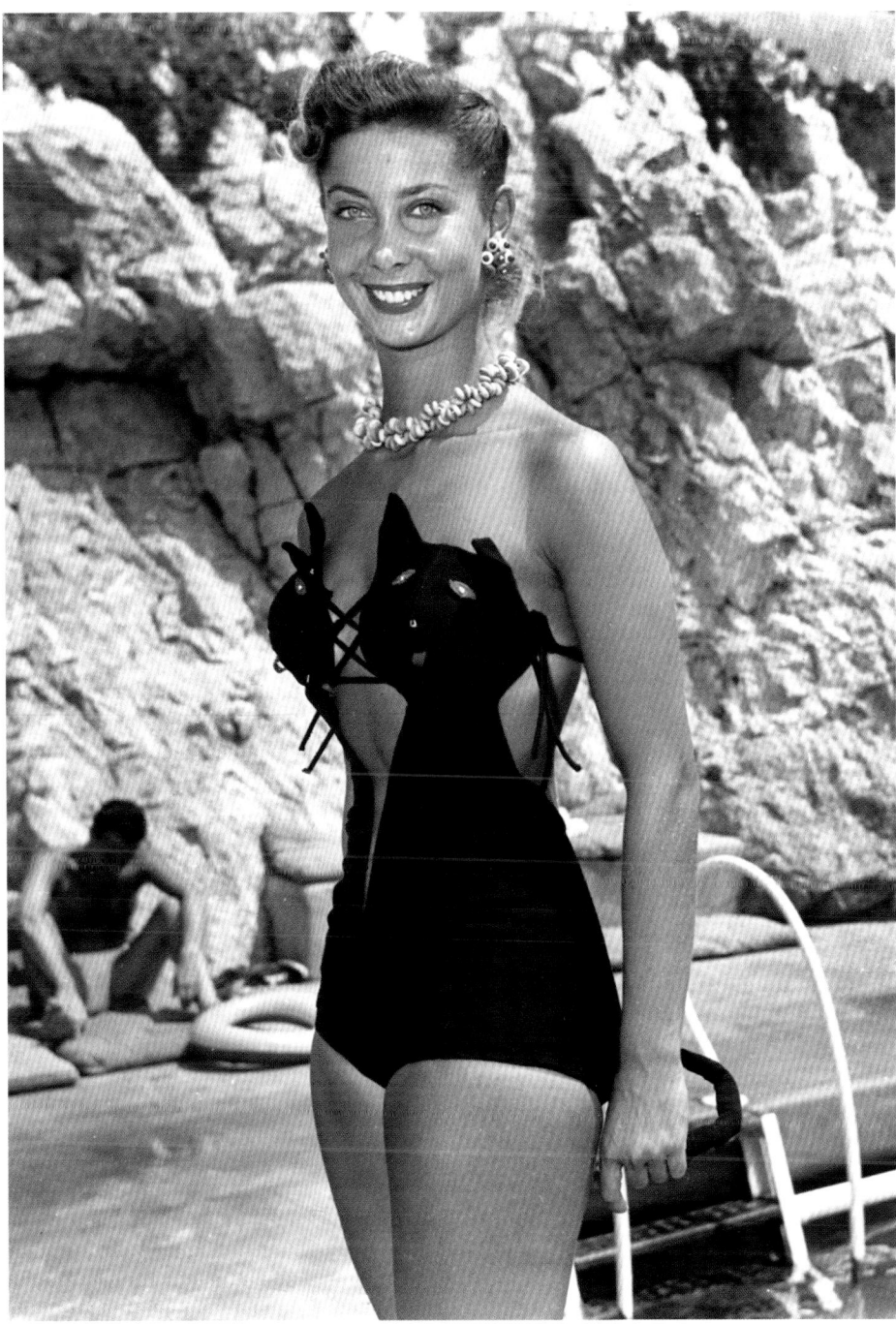

ROBERT COHEN

"Le Chat" Swimsuit, 1952
Photograph, dimensions variable

Not much is known about this photograph or its stylish subject, but one thing is for certain, the bathing suit pictured is the cat's meow. Taken on the stunning beaches of the French Riviera, this 1952 glamour shot shows a woman ready for a swim in a fashionable black swimsuit. Innovatively—and suggestively—cut to give the impression of two cats sitting across the front, complete with pointed ears, slit pupils, and stuck-out tongues. One can only hope that the eyes are bright green and the tongue a rosy pink to complete the picture of feline fashion, but the black-and-white print leaves that to the viewer's imagination. The sleek shape and campy motif of the cat has inspired fashions over the years from graphic handbags to bejeweled necklaces, and both sleekness and camp are invoked in this vintage suit. This image was one of millions captured by Robert Cohen, a Greek photojournalist who founded the photography agency AGIP in 1935 to comprehensively document significant events and notable personalities in France. Cohen snapped this photograph on the beach of the Hôtel du Cap-Eden-Roc in Antibes, a historic luxury resort that has been in operation since the 1880s. Long a haven for creatives, the hotel has welcomed many esteemed guests, including a young John F. Kennedy, Orson Welles, Marlene Dietrich, Conan O'Brien, and, of course, the wearer of this incredible cat-inspired swimsuit.

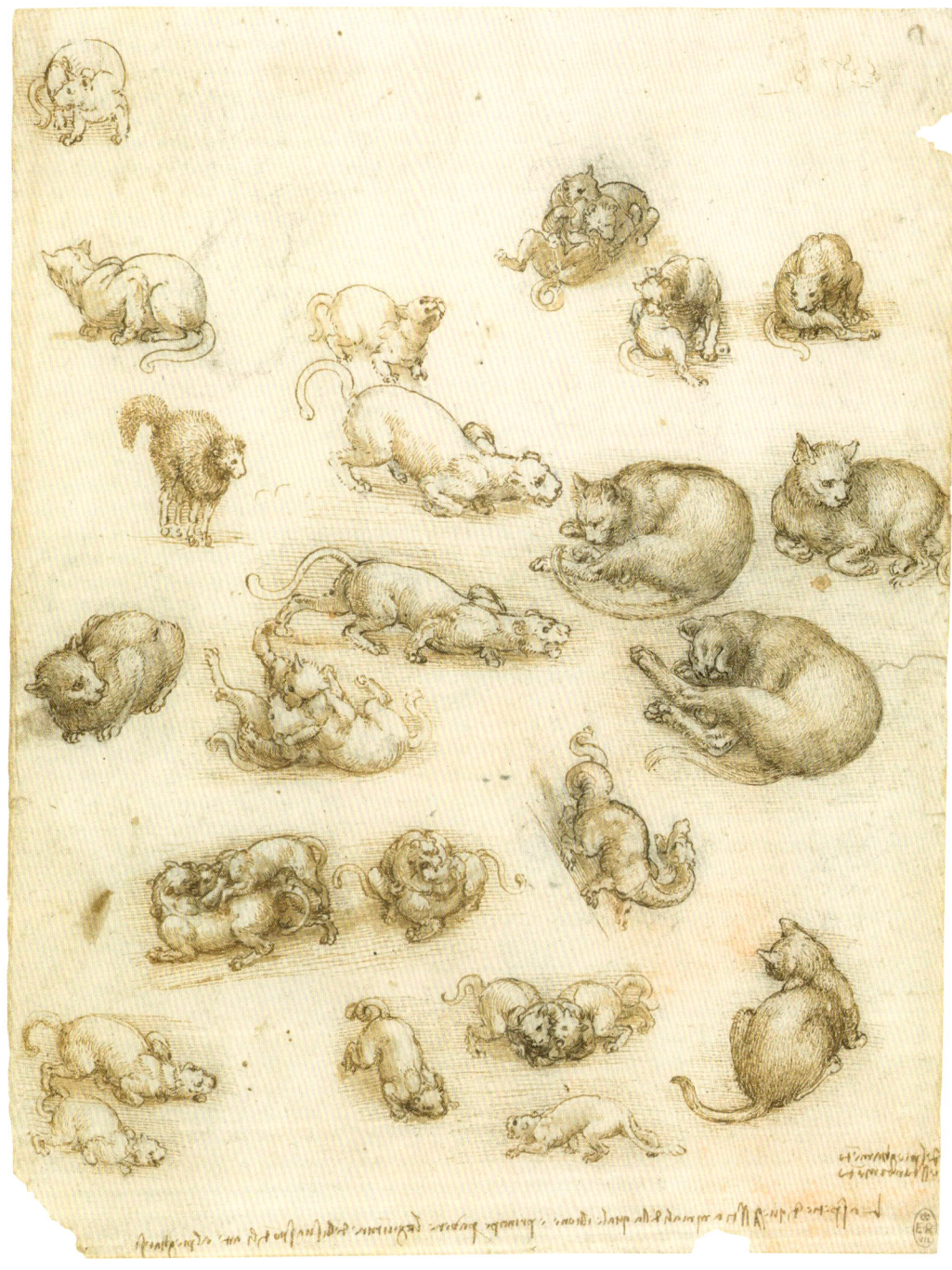

LEONARDO DA VINCI

Cats, Lions, and a Dragon, c. 1517–18
Black chalk and pen and ink wash on paper
10⅝ × 8¼ in. / 27 × 21 cm
Royal Collection Trust, UK

A collection of more than twenty cats, a lioness, and a single dragon appear in this black chalk and ink drawing by Italian Renaissance artist Leonardo da Vinci (1452–1519). Sketched onto a background approximately the same size as a sheet of notebook paper, the drawings show Leonardo's virtuosic style, capturing the rich variety of feline movements, behaviors, and poses, as well as their lithe, undulating bodies, with accurate anatomical details and proportions. Through different styles of drawing, the sketches reflect the intensity, precision, and self-absorption of humanity's feline companions, as they crouch, poised to leap on their prey; perform acts of personal hygiene; play and fight; loll around and sleep; and prowl stealthily across the page. One of the greatest artists of all time, Leonardo was born in the Republic of Florence and grew up to become a polymath. Scientist, artist, engineer, and architect, Leonardo had an enduring interest in the study of movement, in particular, that of animals with four feet, including horses, humans—who crawl on all fours in infancy—and, of course, cats. His handwritten text at the bottom of the sheet notes the species of cats "of which the lion is the prince, because of its spinal column, which is flexible." One kitty arches its spine, its fur standing on end, perhaps startled at the presence of the dragon, which seems to exist on a wholly different plane, purely a product of the artist's imagination.

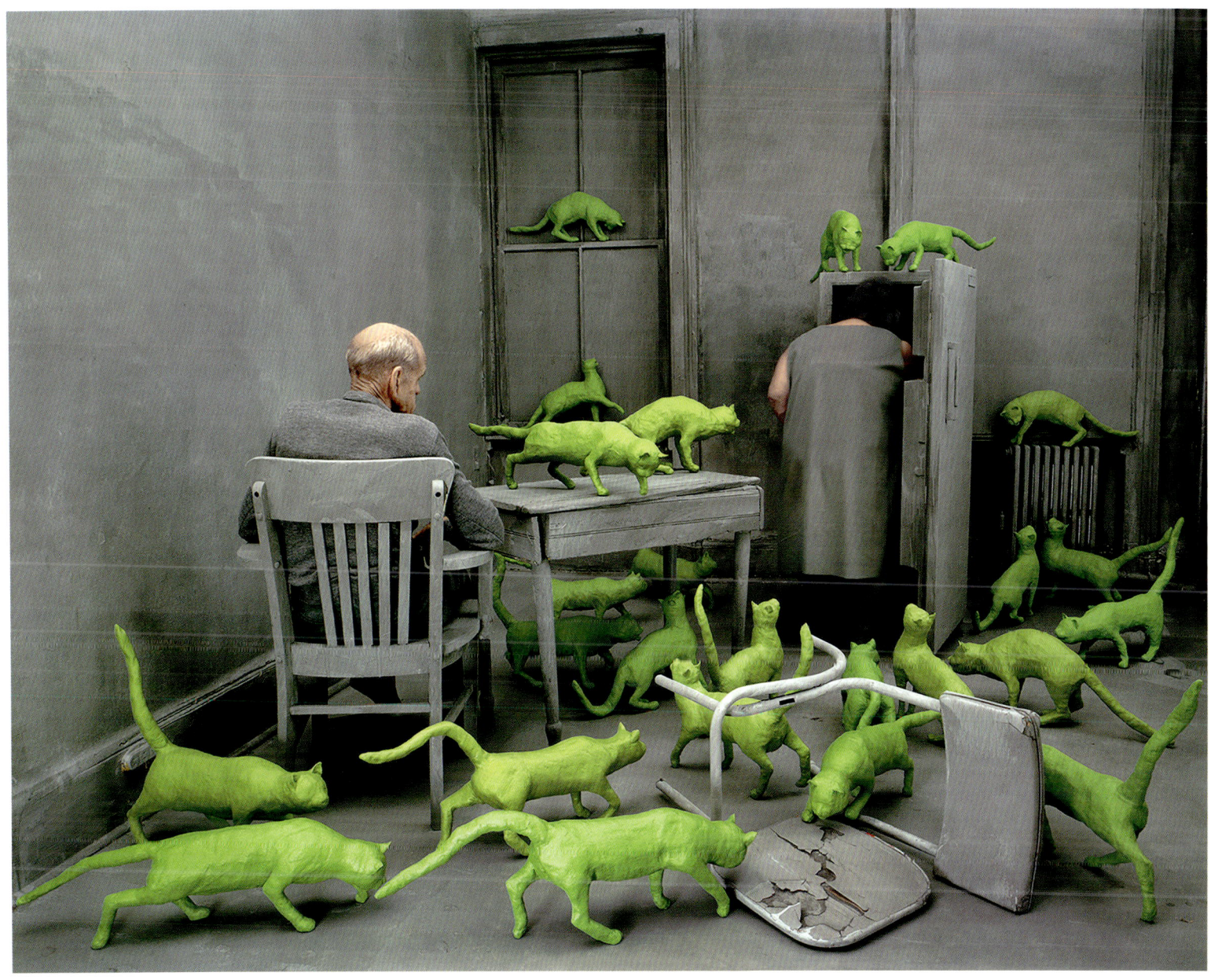

SANDY SKOGLUND

Radioactive Cats, 1980
Dye destruction print
30 × 37¼ in. / 76.2 × 94.6 cm
Saint Louis Art Museum

A gang of slimy green cats swarm upon an aged couple and their gray apartment in this photograph by American artist Sandy Skoglund (b. 1946). Skoglund began her career in New York in 1972, focusing on conceptual, process-based art that led to experiments with photography. The approach for which she became best known combines sculpture, installation, and photography to craft completely immersive worlds, as seen in the cat-infested setting here, constructed and staged completely by Skoglund. *Radioactive Cats* is a companion piece to another photograph, *Beyond the Door*, and both images combine scenes of domesticity with monotone interiors overrun by animals, such as in her renowned Whitney Biennial entry, *Revenge of the Goldfish* (1981). Skoglund knew she could not rely on actual cats to pose as needed, so she sculpted twenty-five out of plaster, clay, and chicken wire before painting them. In her own words, the artist aimed "to undermine the stereotype in our culture of the cute, domesticated pet," exaggerating these cats as ferocious leftovers of a cataclysm. Their radiant green color also certainly nods to the palpable threat of the era; the meltdown at the Three Mile Island nuclear power plant had happened just a year before, and the Cold War tension between the Soviet Union and United States was at its peak in 1980. Apart from the cats, the tableau is a picture of banality; there is an overwhelming feeling of powerlessness, with the couple seemingly resigned to the radioactive new normal in which they find themselves.

151

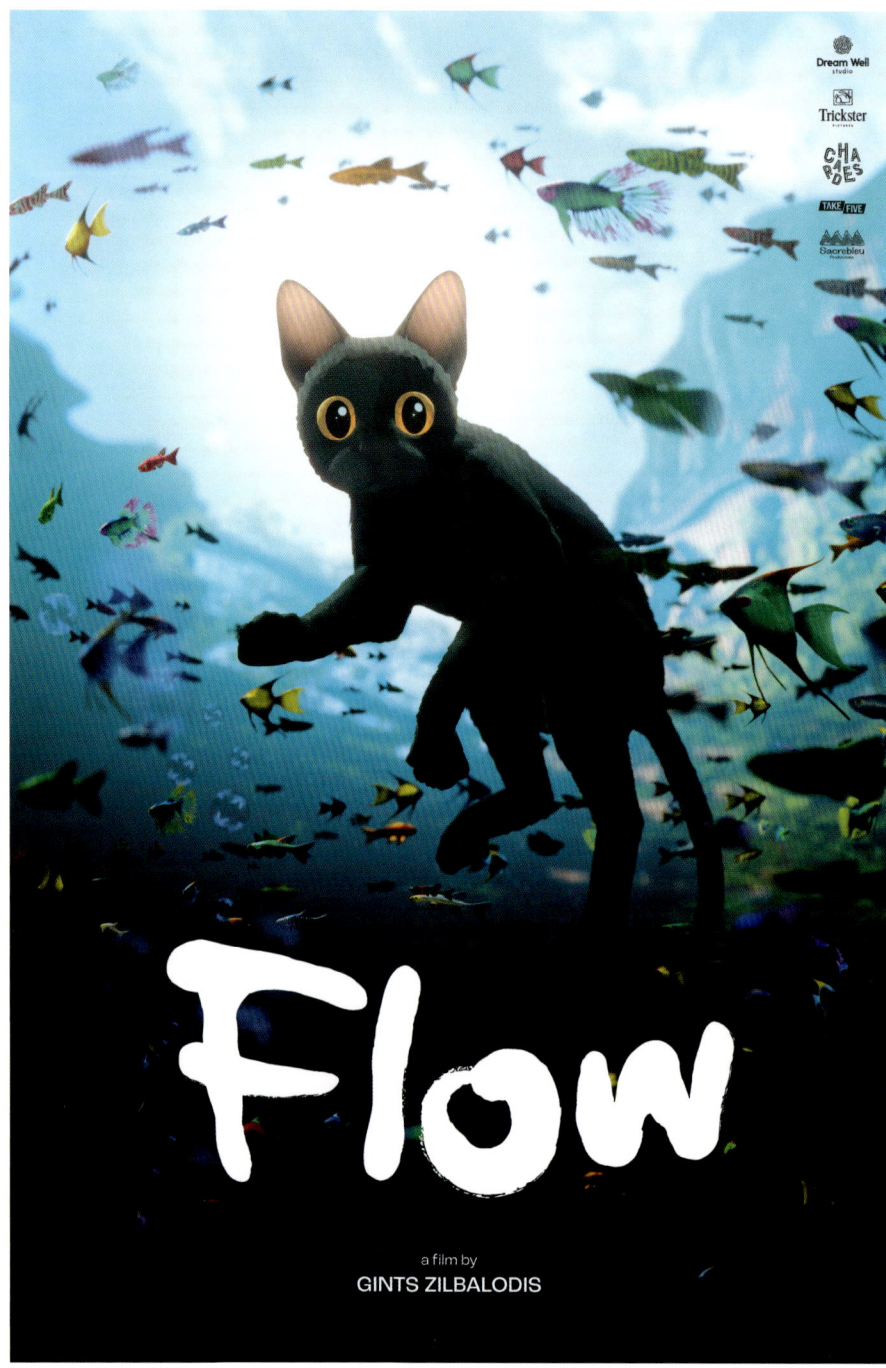

GINTS ZILBALODIS

Flow, 2024
Poster, 40 × 27 in. / 101.6 × 68.9 cm

A nameless, dark gray cat with large amber eyes stars in this beguiling and charming animated film that tells the story of a disparate group of animals who learn to cooperate in order to survive an apocalyptic flood. Told from the cat's perspective, *Flow* does not reveal the source of the deluge, which could be natural or human-induced. Against a backdrop of uninhabited ancient cities, the cat searches for higher ground in a small boat, teaming up with a capybara, lemur, Labrador retriever, and secretary bird. The stirring, Oscar-winning tale of survival against the odds took visionary Latvian director Gints Zilbalodis (b. 1994) and his small production team five years to develop, but only one year to create. Remarkably, its crisp, computer-generated world was made with the free, open-source animation software Blender, with every aspect of the film designed and modeled on the computer without the use of story-boards. Unlike other animated films with animals as characters, *Flow* mostly eschewed anthropomorphism, with Zilbalodis letting his creatures act as they would naturally (the cat instinctively knocks objects off ledges and swats at the lemur's dangling tail). Accordingly, with no dialogue, sound designer Gurwal Coïc-Gallas used real animal sounds for each character, employing recordings of his own pet cat for the protagonist. *Flow* has won fans the world over since its release in 2024, and its enormous popularity in Latvia, where it broke box-office records, has led to a statue of its feline hero being installed in the nation's capital, Riga.

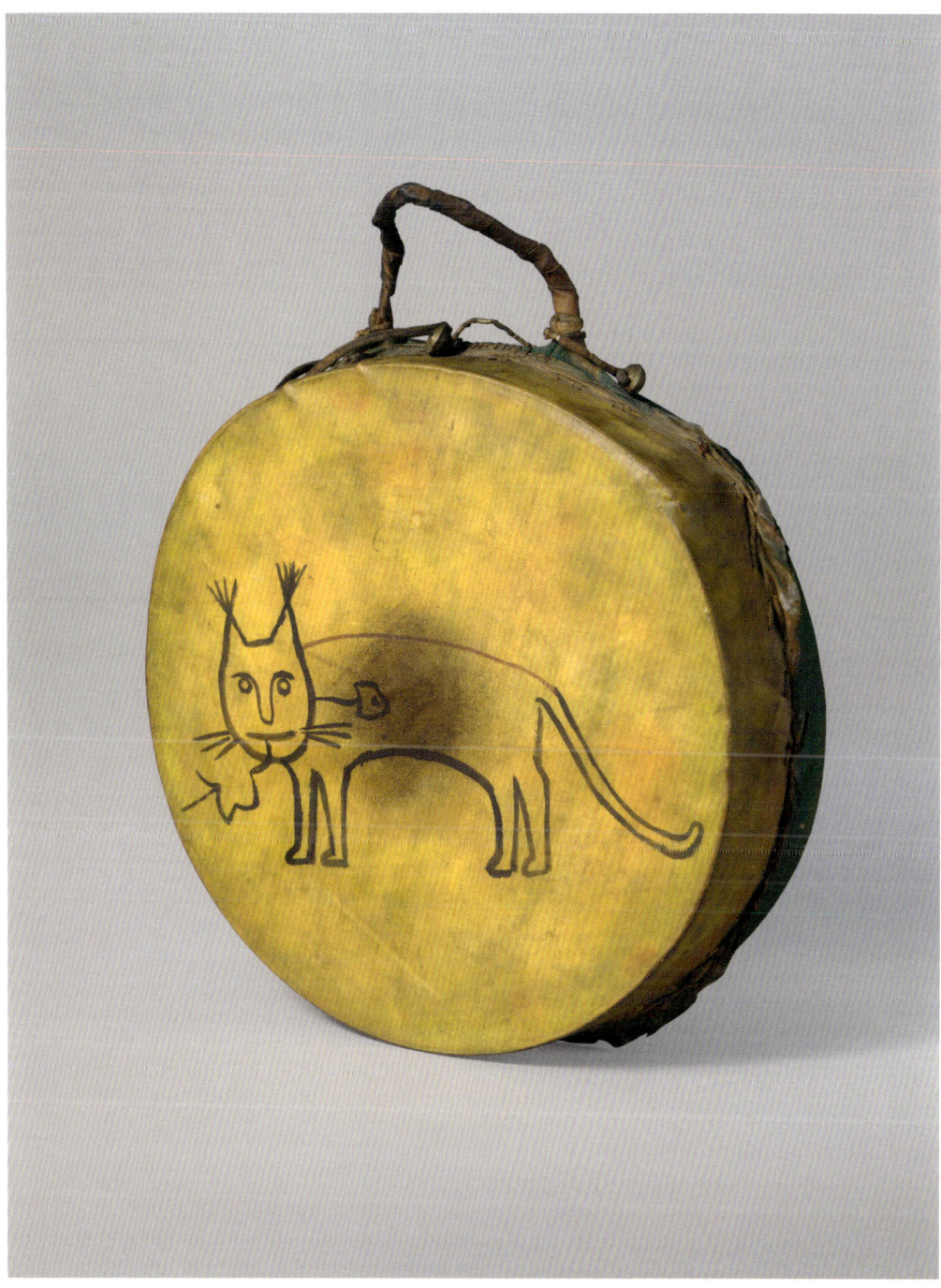

ANONYMOUS

Wakan-chan-cha-gha (frame drum), late 19th century
Wood and skin, Diam. 10⅝ in. / 27 cm
Metropolitan Museum of Art, New York

This round-frame drum probably belonged to the Dakota band of the Sioux, one of the largest of all Native American peoples, who lived on the Great Plains of North America in the late nineteenth century, in an area that covered the present-day states of the Dakotas, Montana, Wyoming, and Nebraska. Like the other Sioux, the Dakota were mobile, moving around the Great Plains to live by hunting, fishing, gathering, and horticulture. The large cat drawn on one side of this drum—created by stretching animal skin across a wooden frame—is mirrored on the reverse by an image of a bird with a lightning-arrow symbol, probably a thunderbird. Called *wakinyan* in Sioux languages, the thunderbird was revered for its supernatural qualities, specifically its ability to protect the honorable from evil and even

control stormy weather. Used during ceremonies and rituals, such drums were considered sacred, because they connected the Sioux with their spirits. The depiction of the cat shows the skeleton of a fish just visible in its stomach, suggesting that it must have had a symbolic meaning, although it was probably not as widespread among the Plains peoples as the thunderbird. Early Native Americans respected wildcats, including the bobcat and cougar, as sacred parts of nature but were not familiar with domestic cats until European settlers introduced them to the Americas. By the time this drum was made in the late nineteenth century, the animals had become part of everyday life on the Great Plains, where they were used to control pests and traded for their fur.

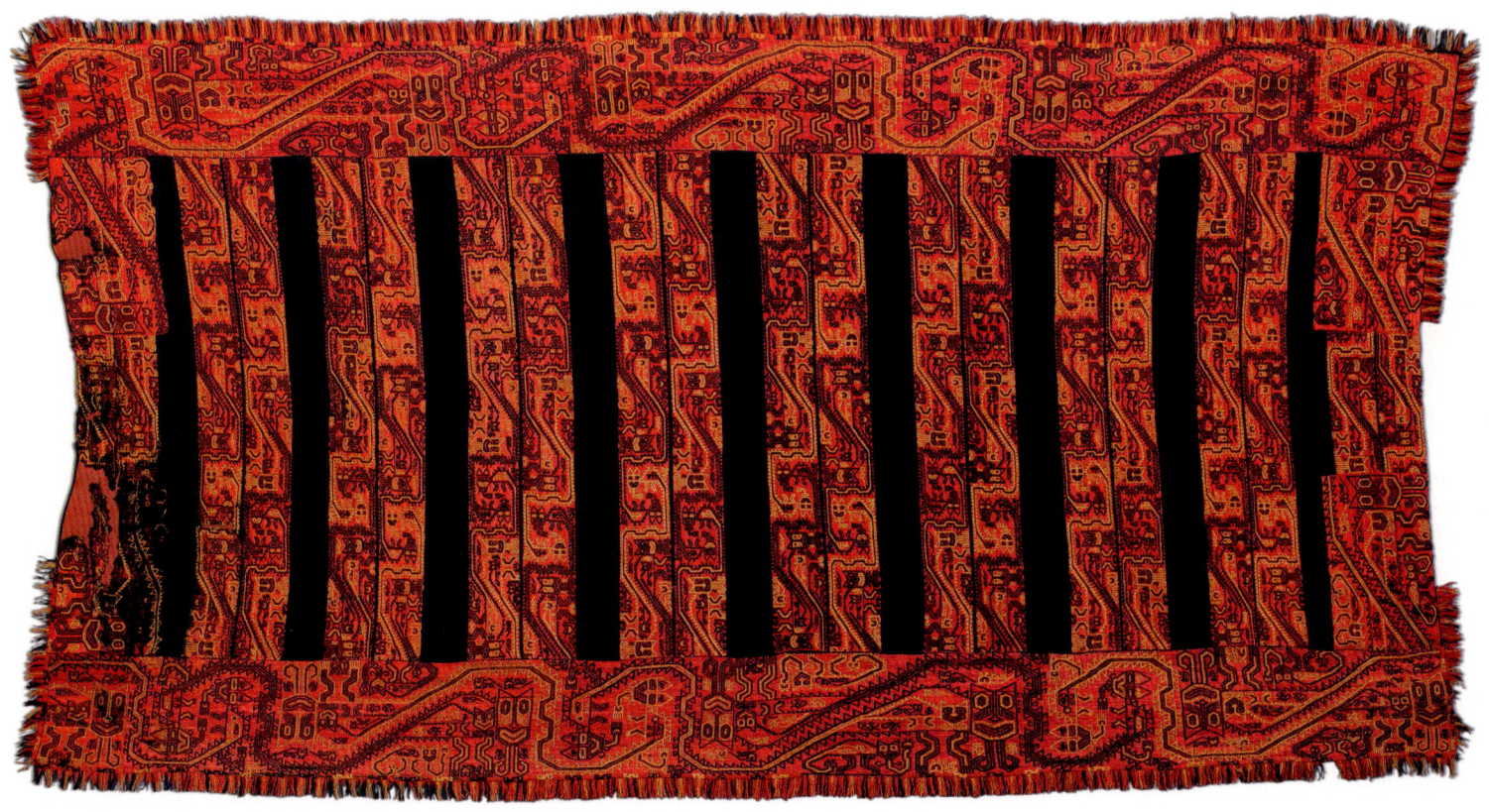

ANONYMOUS

Mantle, c. 200 BCE–100 CE
Camelid fiber
50 × 102⅜ in. / 127 × 260 cm
Saint Louis Art Museum

The motifs in this weaving may seem purely geometric, but look closer and there is a pure panoply of cats. Smiling felines trail one another in linear formation, while others morph together into two-headed creatures. Elsewhere, the angular rise and fall of a cat's tail gives way to another's form to make an elaborate border. This mantle, or a sleeveless cloak or shawl, was created by an anonymous artisan during the Early Horizon period (c. 900–200 BCE) of the ancient Paracas culture, one of the earliest complex societies in South America in what is now southern Peru. The camelid wool is probably from llama or alpaca, both native to the coastal Andean region. Given the lack of wear and the vibrant coloration, the textile is probably a funeral shroud recovered from one of the underground grave

sites that were discovered in the early twentieth century. Known for its elaborate textiles, the Paracas culture had intricate burial rites; members of the highest caste were dressed in finely embroidered cloth, provisioned with food and gold for the afterlife, and then mummified. Based on surviving artifacts, archaeologists surmise that the Paracas people practiced a totemic religion, believing animals to be their divine ancestors. The universe was considered a trinity of earth, air, and water, with snakes and cats, condors, and orcas representing each realm, respectively. The divine cat—based on the wild Pampas cats that the Paracas never fully domesticated but lived among—is beautifully represented in this artifact, and the skill of the ancient artisans is on full display.

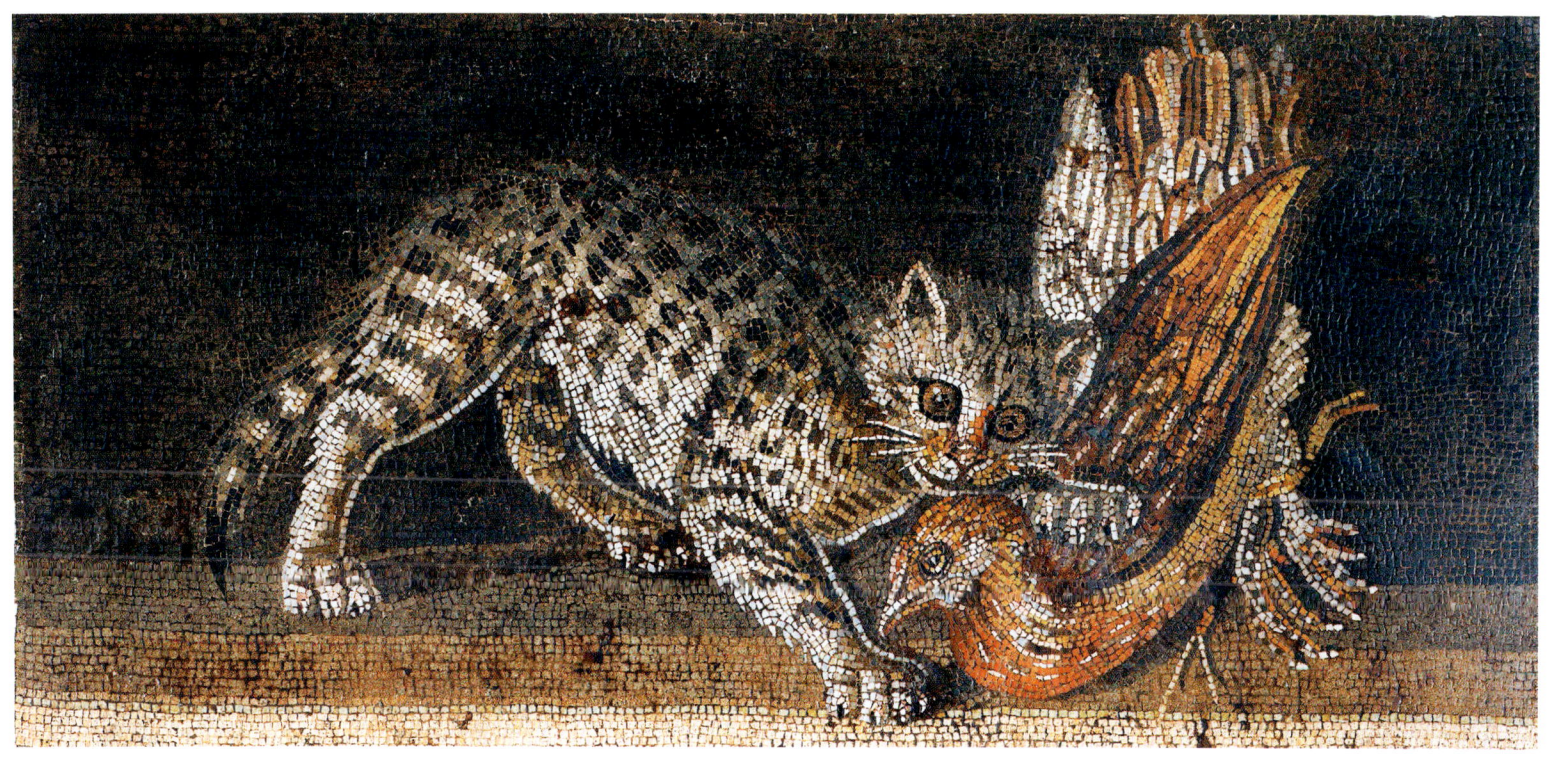

ANONYMOUS

Cat clawing a partridge (detail), from
the House of the Faun, Pompeii, c. 180 BCE
Mosaic, H. 20¾ in. / 53 cm
Museo Archeologico Nazionale, Naples

A young tabby cat, its fur bristling and stripes marked out with geometric precision, claws a partridge, the hunter's ancient gaze piercing that of modern viewers. This detail comes from a floor mosaic in the grand House of the Faun, a Hellenistic palace built during the second century BCE in Pompeii, Italy, and the source of many of the finest mosaics from ancient Rome, which were preserved under ash after the eruption of Mount Vesuvius in 79 CE. In Roman times, the technique of making mosaics went from being a special art form reserved for places of worship to a popular domestic decoration. This mosaic captures one of the cat's primary instincts: to hunt. Rendered in meticulous detail using thousands of tesserae, or small square tiles, the cat has gleaming eyes, alert whiskers, and claws curling over the edge of the shelf on which it stands. The work anticipates the still-life genre of the late Middle Ages, in which food—often game birds and other animals—is laid out in all its visual splendor, but it also provides a lively portrait of one of ancient Romans' favorite pets. Although Roman households traditionally used ferrets, polecats, and even snakes to root out rodents and pests, about the time this mosaic was created, cats were preferred, because they were deemed cleaner than other animals. Plus, it is harder to snuggle with a snake.

MYCHAEL BARRATT

Yves Klein's Cats, 2022
Mezzotint, 8⅝ × 8⅝ in. / 22 × 22 cm
Eames Fine Art, London

A brilliantly blue canvas seems to be marred by the paw prints of a mischievous cat who has sauntered across its surface when the paint is still wet. A fantastical creation by Canadian artist Mychael Barratt (b. 1961), this work is actually a print, a humorous—and probably accurate depiction—of what it might look like if the French conceptual artist Yves Klein had a cat. Barratt is a London-based painter, printmaker, and cartographer whose narrative artworks blend fact with fiction, imbued with the visual culture of art history, literature, and theater. A Renaissance man, Barratt is a past President of the Royal Society of Painter-Printmakers and was an artist-in-residence for Shakespeare's Globe Theatre during British actor Mark Rylance's reign as Artistic Director in the early 2000s. *Yves Klein's Cats*

comes from an imaginative series of prints called *Artists' Dogs and Cats* in which Barratt adopts the aesthetics and styles of famous creatives from the art historical canon to showcase how they might depict their beloved animal companions. *Cy Twombly's Cat* is a thick red scrawl with hints of triangles for ears, while *Yayoi Kusama's Dog* is a spotted pup in an infinite field of her signature black-and-yellow pumpkins. For *Yves Klein's Cats*, Barratt riffs on International Klein Blue, the French artist's famous shade of ultramarine that he developed in 1960. A nod to Klein's monochrome canvases, Barratt's own cats, Jigsaw and Marmalade, are the proud artists whose paw prints dot the field of Yves Klein blue seen here.

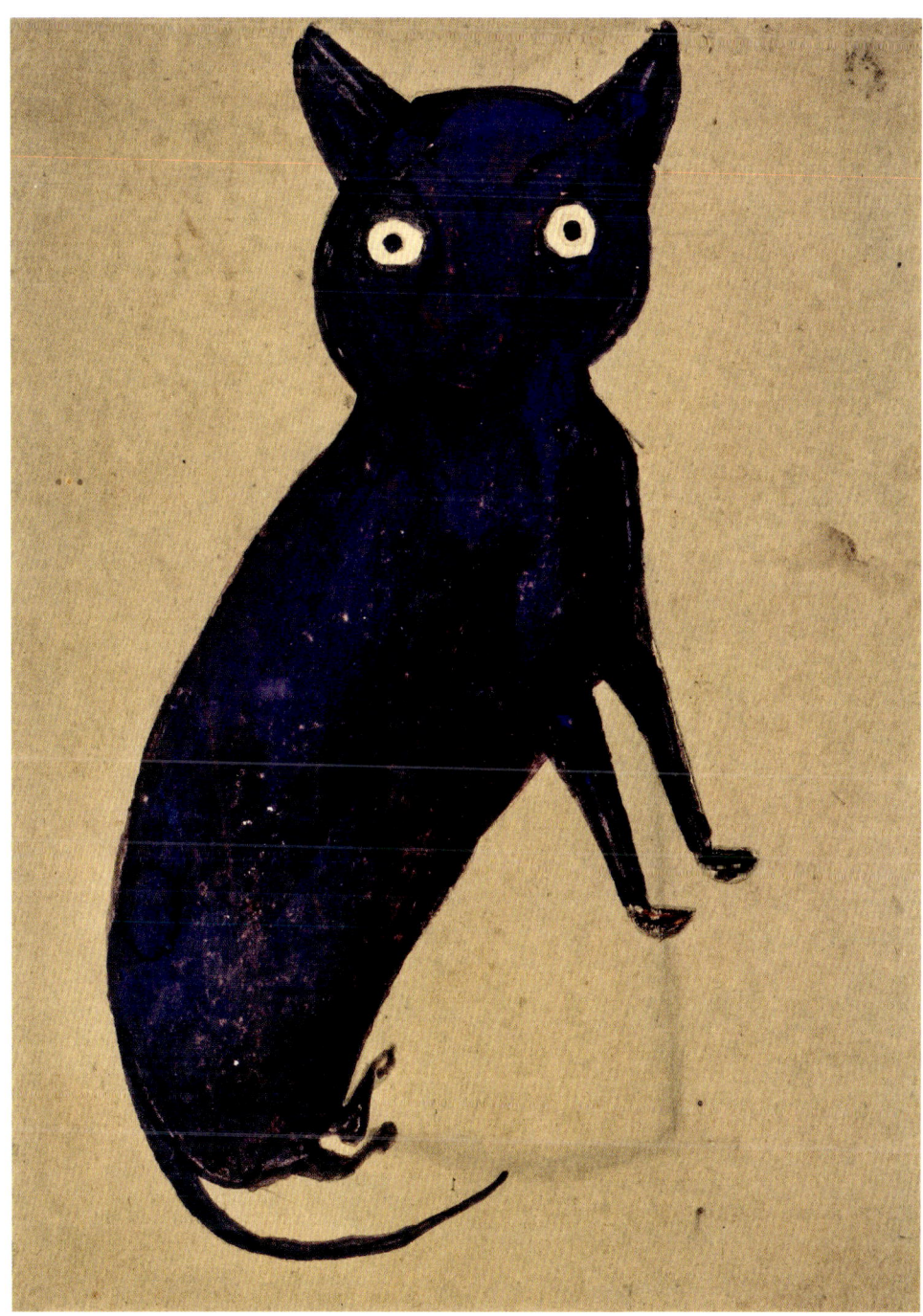

BILL TRAYLOR

Untitled (Midnight Blue Cat), c. 1939–42
Poster paint on found cardboard
11 × 8 in. / 27.9 × 20.3 cm
Private collection

This bold cat has both eyes wide open and all four legs at the ready, perhaps in order to look out for its own safety. The poster paint used to depict the animal is deep cobalt blue, a signature color for American artist Bill Traylor (c. 1853–1949) and one that in African American culture is associated with protection from harm and malevolent spirits. Born into slavery on a plantation in Alabama, Traylor saw his life marked by some of the most significant events of American history. He was about twelve years old when the Civil War ended and was emancipated in 1865, after which he remained a sharecropper on the same plantation for another forty-five years, living through the era of Jim Crow segregation. A self-taught artist, Traylor started to make art when he was in his late eighties, encouraged by a younger artist, Charles Shannon, who provided him with materials. He worked outdoors, setting up a table on a street corner in Montgomery, Alabama, where he would draw and paint on found scraps of paper or cardboard. Traylor's art relates personal stories, memories of life on the plantation, and changes within Black American culture in the first half of the twentieth century, but it also functions symbolically, with objects and figures, including men pointing rifles, representing the oppression and violence he witnessed during his life. When he died, he left more than one thousand works behind, but his oeuvre did not begin to receive public recognition until the 1980s.

The Charles Mingus CAT-alog

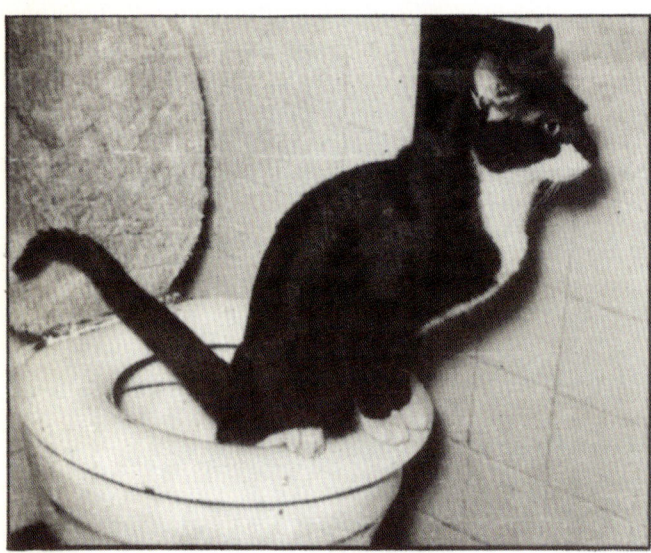

for Toilet Training Your Cat

CHARLES MINGUS

The Charles Mingus CAT-alog for
Toilet Training Your Cat, 1972
Printed trifold pamphlet
Folded 7½ × 4½ in. / 19 × 11.4 cm

An unlikely treatise by a surprising creator, this quirky but enlightening pamphlet teaches owners to toilet train their cats. The author of this step-by-step guide is Charles Mingus (1922–1979), the legendary American jazz bassist, composer, pianist, and band leader—and the black feline with the white chin is his cat, Nightlife. In the 1950s, while Mingus was establishing himself as one of history's most gifted jazz musicians, he was also toilet training Nightlife and taking time to diligently outline those steps for other cat caretakers. In his step-by-step instructions, he advises first training your cat to use a cardboard box instead of a litter box and torn-up newspaper instead of kitty litter. The several-week process involves moving the box closer and closer to the toilet while gradually trimming the cardboard sides.

Eventually, place the box on top of the toilet seat, securing it for safety. Let the cat use it, but stay patient. The last two steps are more technical and can take a week or two: they involve cutting a hole roughly the size of a plum, which the cat will start aiming for, trimming what's left of the sides of the box, and sliding the flat cardboard bottom (with hole) under the seat—then, pray. If all goes well, you can eventually remove the cardboard. "Don't be surprised," the jazz great writes, "if you hear the toilet flush in the middle of the night. A cat can learn how to do it, spurred on by his instinct to cover up."

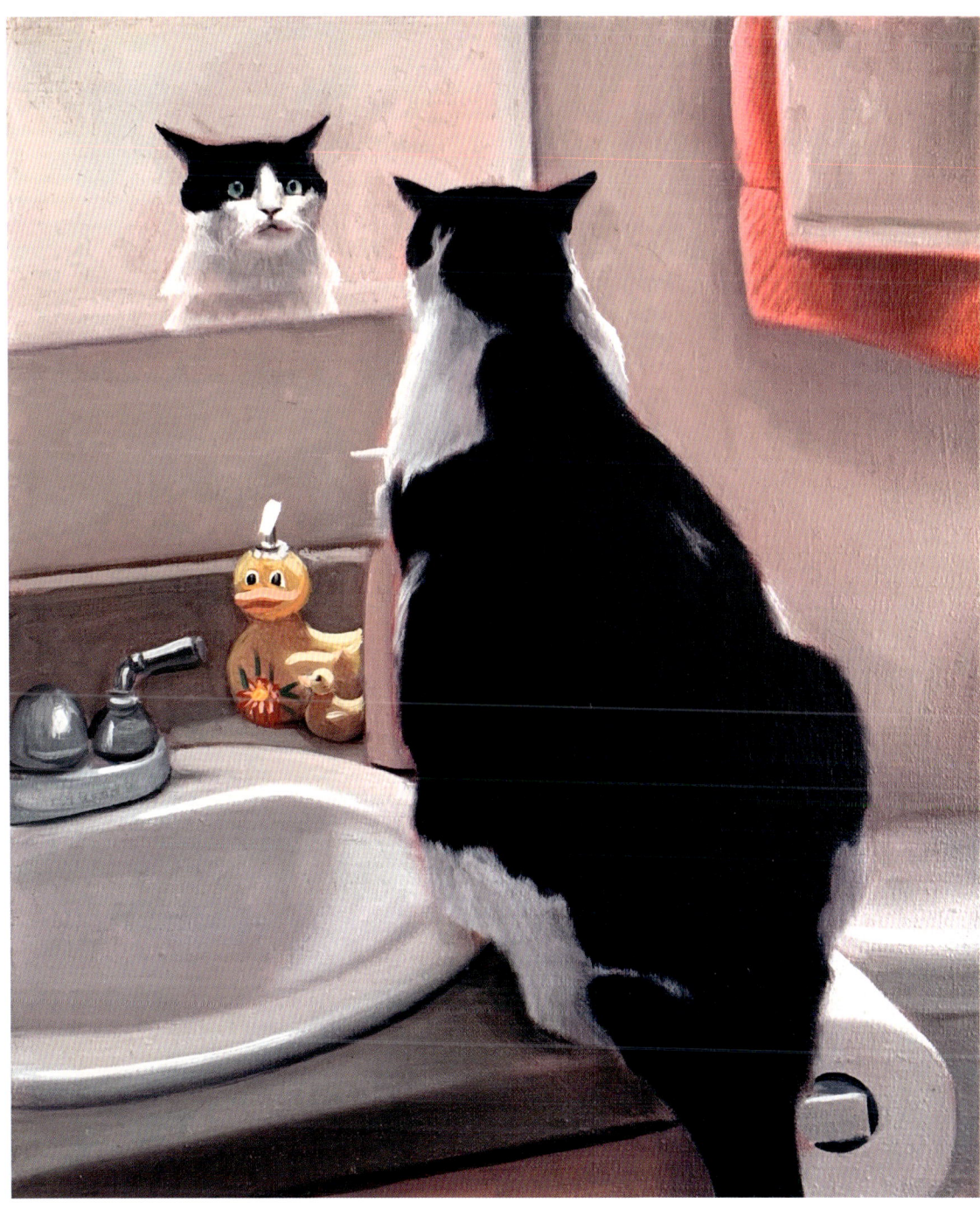

LYDIA BLAKELEY

Reflections 3 (Chonky), 2021
Oil on linen, 11¾ × 9⅞ in. / 30 × 25 cm
Private collection

Pet owners worldwide know the routine: despite the lack of evidence that people's treasured animals understand human languages, they still wonder if their companions know what they look like and how much they are loved, constantly asking the rhetorical "How did you get so cute?" and "Do you know how adorable you are?" The subject of *Reflections 3 (Chonky)* by British painter Lydia Blakeley (b. 1980) takes the investigation into its own hands, courtesy of a bathroom mirror. The titular Chonky, a perhaps slightly overweight black-and-white cat, sits on a bathroom sink and stares directly into the mirror. In Blakeley's hyperrealistic oil, Chonky looks slightly bewildered but not unhappy. If cats had eyebrows, theirs would be raised. A duo of yellow rubber ducks sits on the pet's left, and there is a small patch of pink peeking out from what might be a window frame, the only flashes of color in an otherwise beige bathroom. Blakeley's work depicts and is inspired by the environment and the screens around her, and she bases her paintings on her collection of screenshots and memes, often referencing desires for idealized lifestyles and bodies, streetwear and fashion, and even the dog-eat-dog world of pet shows. It is unclear whether Chonky is in pursuit of trendiness or physical perfection. *Reflections 3 (Chonky)* was, in fact, based on a pandemic-era meme of various cats and dogs looking in the mirror, contemplating their cuteness and their fate.

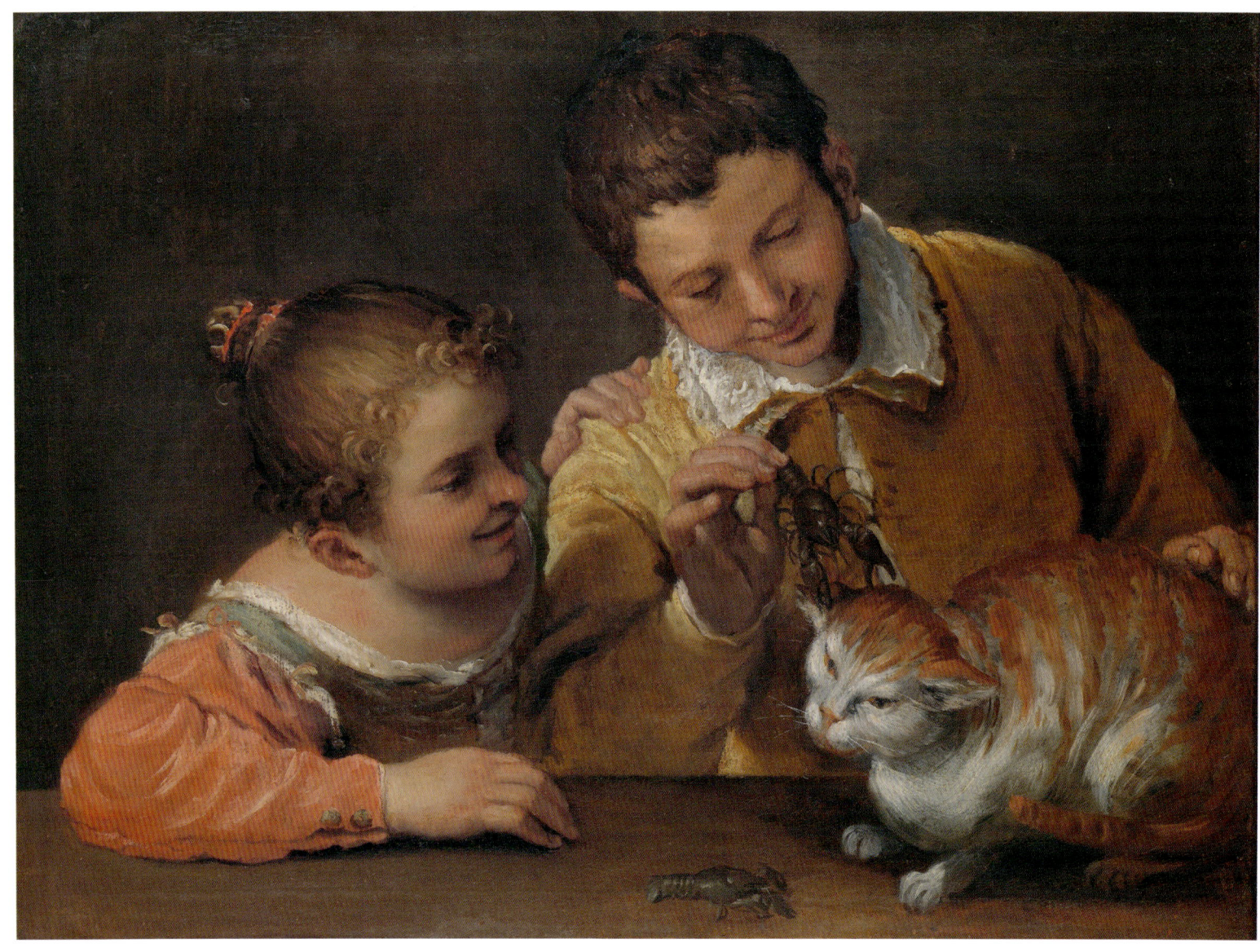

ANNIBALE CARRACCI

Two Children Teasing a Cat, late 16th century
Oil on canvas, 26 × 35 in. / 66 × 88.9 cm
Metropolitan Museum of Art, New York

The young boy and girl in this work by Italian Baroque painter Annibale Carracci (1560–1609) are about to learn a valuable lesson. An orange-and-white cat looks angrily at the boy, its patience clearly tested as he taunts the animal with the pincers of a crayfish, holding it in position to stop it from escaping. The girl, perhaps his sister, eggs him on, her hand on his shoulder. Both children are clearly enjoying what they see as a great game, but one imagines that it will only be a few seconds until the feline expresses its annoyance by lashing out at them. The sentiment behind one of the earliest known genre paintings, or paintings of everyday life instead of grand scenes, appears to be not to cause trouble if it can be avoided. Carracci, who frequently worked with his less talented brother and cousin, was one

of the most significant painters of his age, credited with transforming Italian painting in the sixteenth century with the creation of a new style now known as Baroque. He painted directly from nature and introduced a technique of breaking up his brushstrokes to create a sense of movement on the canvas. Here, the cat's incipient escape is hinted at by the position of its head. The Baroque style is also evident in the lighting of the painting: the boy's ruff appears illuminated in contrast to the shadow on his forehead. This painting was something of an outlier among Carracci's work, much of which had a religious theme.

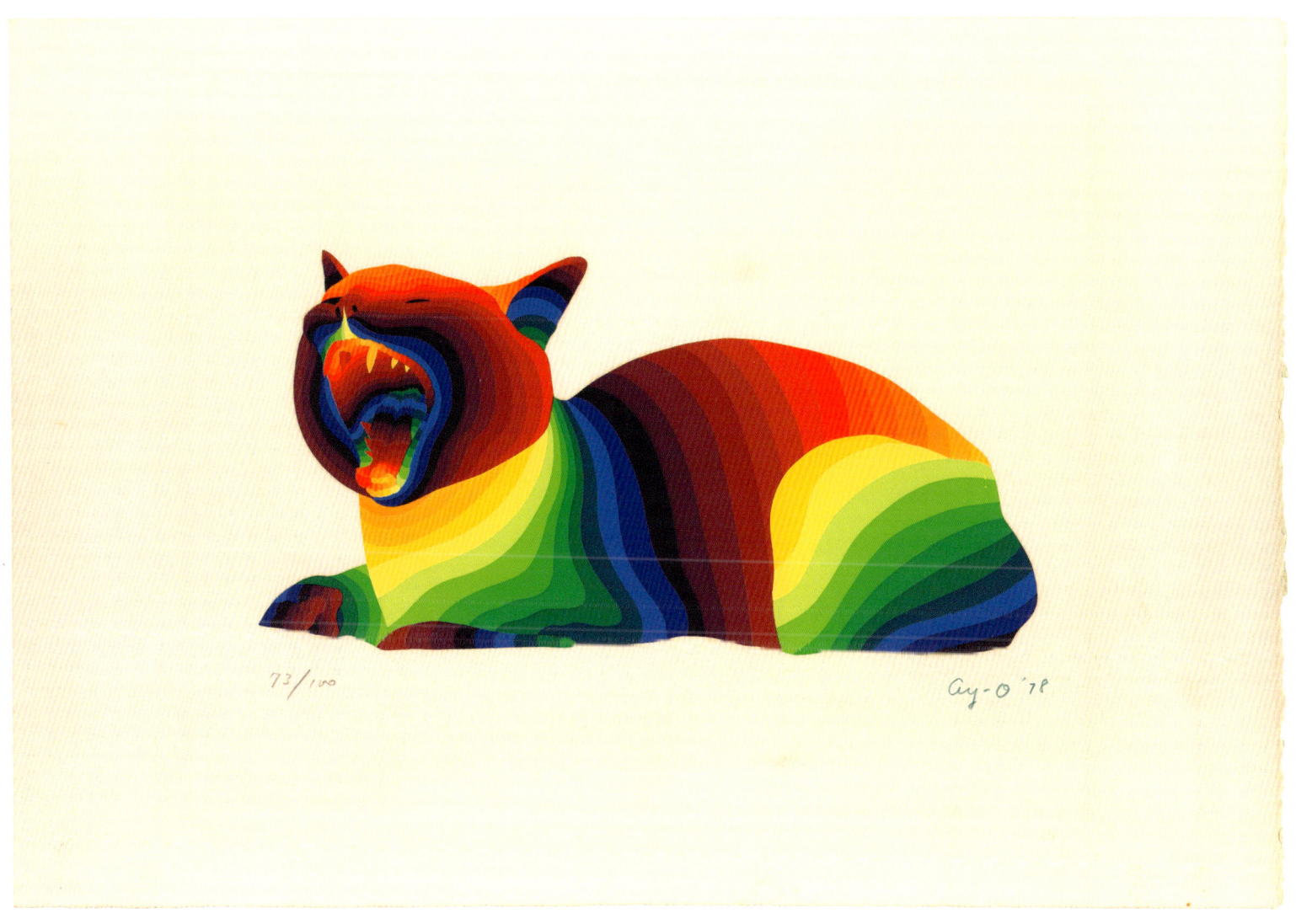

73/100   ay-O '78

AY-O

Yawn (Akubi), 1978
Ink on paper, 6⅞ × 13⅜ in. / 17.5 × 34 cm
National Museum of Asian Art, Smithsonian,
Washington, DC

A visual paradox, this languid cat is dynamically rendered in vivid rainbow stripes by Japanese artist Ay-O (Takao Iijima, b. 1931), bringing a fantastical element to a familiar feline pose as it sits loaflike, comfortably yawning to its heart's content. Ay-O is known internationally as the "rainbow artist," because of his effusive palette, often applied to everyday objects and commonplace situations. His fascination with color began with the vibrant paintings he made when he was part of the Demokrato Artists Association in Japan during the 1950s. After moving to New York, he joined the avant-garde Fluxus art movement in the early 1960s, alongside experimental artists, musicians, and creatives, such as Yoko Ono, Nam June Paik, and John Cage, who sought to dismantle the rigid traditions of high art and transform it into something more interactive, playful, and socially engaging. Breaking from the traditional linework of printmaking, Ay-O instead infused his works with various colors, eventually incorporating the whole spectrum of the rainbow and applying it to subjects as disparate as moving figures to abstract color-fields. Although Ay-O has termed this impulse his own "rainbow hell," his trademark color palette instantly connects people to the shared experience of an intense optical journey, one that encourages the eye to travel deep "inside" a simple two-dimensional surface, allowing silhouettes like this cat to come alive, fangs and all.

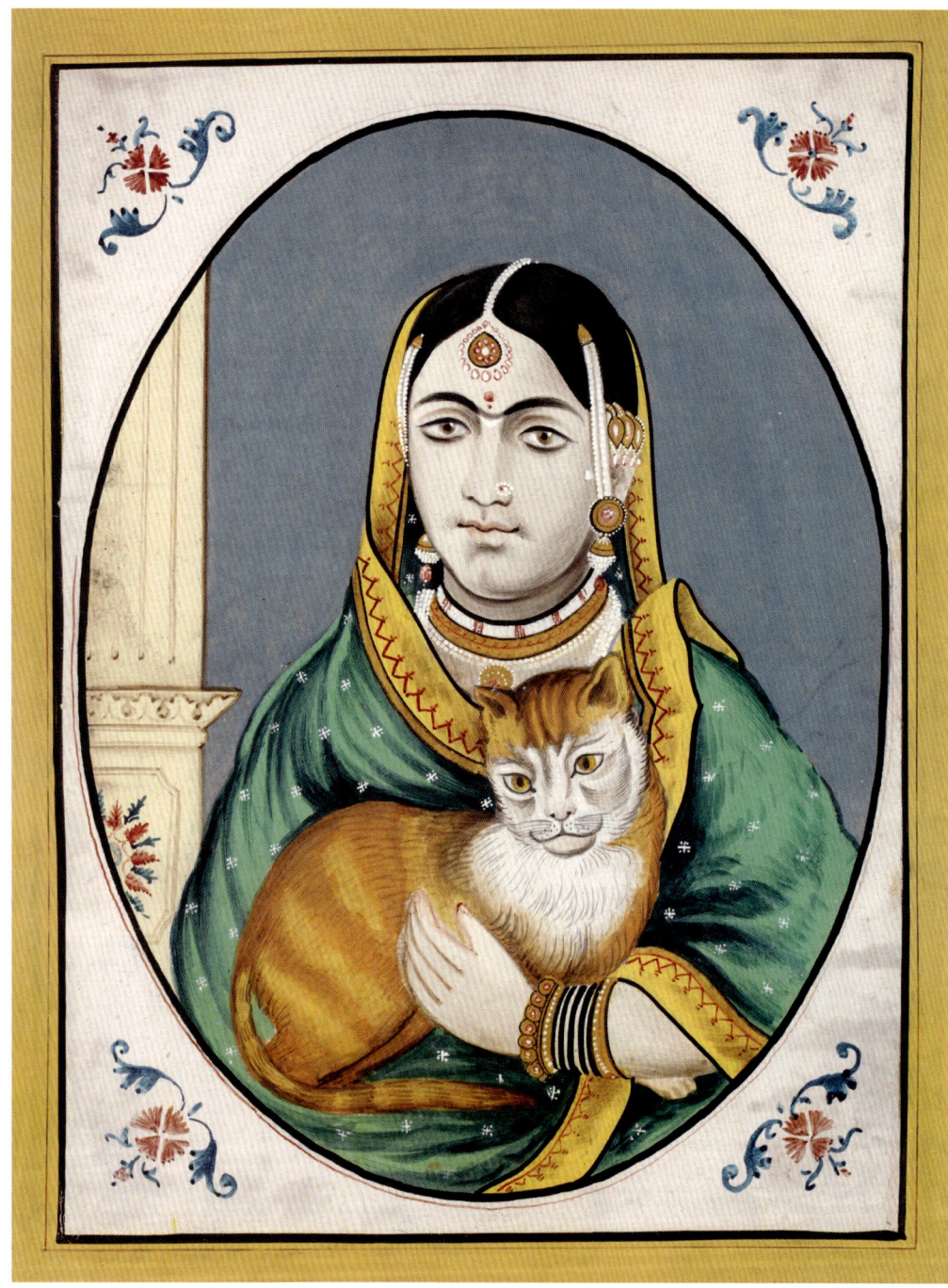

ANONYMOUS

Painting, c. 1890
Opaque watercolor and gold on paper
Victoria and Albert Museum, London

With a somewhat baleful expression, a woman looks straight ahead as she holds an orange-and-white cat in her left arm. This delicate watercolor is the creation of an unknown nineteenth-century artist from India, working in a style known as the Jaipur School of painting. The portrait depicts the sitter in all her finery: her sari is trimmed with gold and she is dripping with jewels. Her cat is equally well drawn: its striped auburn body contrasts with a bright white chest and face. This woman probably belonged to the royal court of Jaipur, one of many independent kingdoms of Rajasthan in present-day northwest India. The region's cultural tradition was inherited from the school of Amer, so named for the capital city where it originated in the early seventeenth century. When Jaipur became the new capital in 1727, the kingdom's creative activities shifted to the metropolis and were affected by the Islamic art of its Mughal neighbors. Although this painting was made more than a century later, the Mughal influence is clear in the work's attention to detail, vibrant colors, and liberal use of gold leaf. However, the subject matter is unusual, because cats were rarely depicted in Indian art, perhaps due to occupying an ambivalent position in both ancient and modern India. That being said, there are some positive references to felines in Indian culture. The Sanskrit word for "cat" is *marjara*, and Hinduism describes a path of devotion to the god Vishnu known as *marjara-nyaya*. It suggests that a follower must submit to the deity as a kitten does to its mother.

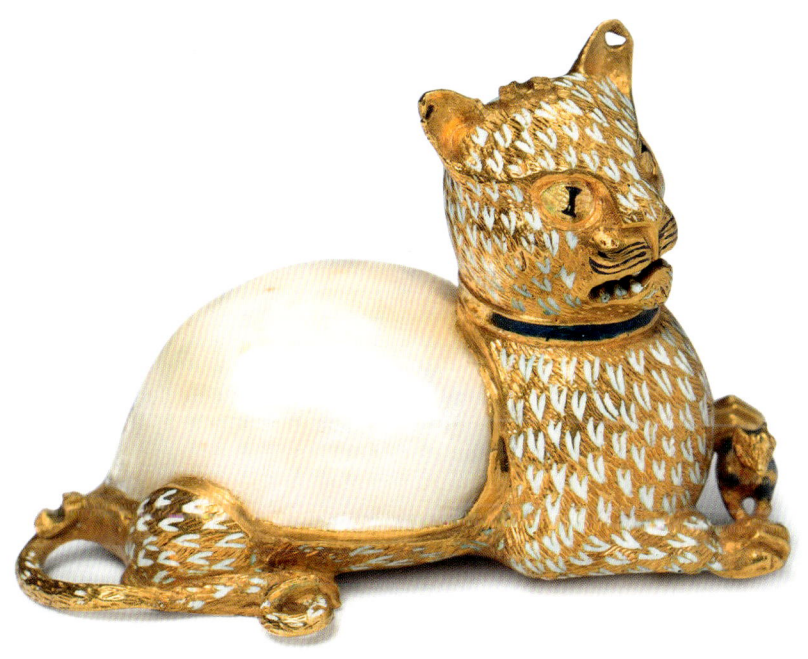

ANONYMOUS

*Baroque Pearl Mounted as a Cat
Holding a Mouse*, 17th century
Gold, enamel, and baroque pearl
1⅛ × 1½ in. / 2.7 × 4 cm
Art Institute of Chicago

A crouching cat, its gold body flecked with white enamel to suggest the texture of fur, keeps its left paw firmly on the tiny gold mouse it has trapped. Forming the cat's back and hindquarters is a large, irregular-shaped baroque pearl—a pearl that is not perfectly round—its translucent iridescence providing a contrast with the enameled metal. Both the feline's upright ears contain holes suggesting that, at one time, it wore miniature golden earrings or, more likely, was intended to hang from a chain as a pendant around the wearer's neck. Made by an unknown European artisan in the seventeenth century, the golden cat once had blue eyes that matched its translucent blue collar. While its precise provenance is also uncertain, it is known that this type of jewel was popular in Habsburg Spain at the time,

when white enameling was often used on jewelry. Baroque pearls were also fashionable then, initially as a symbol of motherhood and fertility, but later in the seventeenth century they were increasingly associated with expressions of love. As the pearls became more expensive when the rich supply from the American colonies began to dry up, they became a status symbol favored by the royal family and nobility. Many of the pearls seen in surviving Spanish portraits of the period are fake, but this charming cat combines inventiveness and originality with a real pearl.

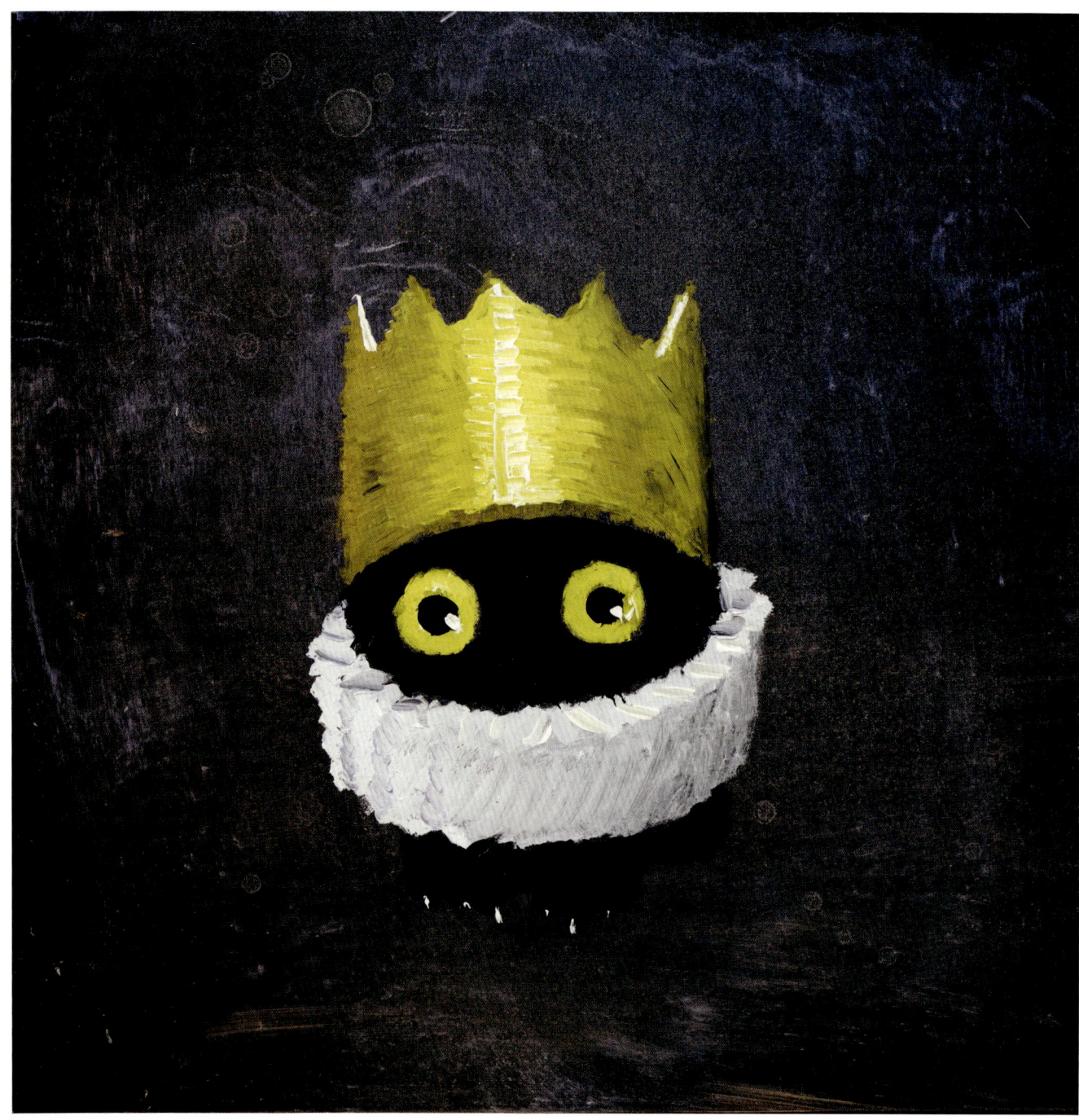

VANESSA STOCKARD

Kevin the Kitten, 2023
Oil on Dibond
16 × 16 in. / 40 × 40 cm
Private collection

Adorned with a golden crown and frilly neck ruff, this wide-eyed little ball of black fur, otherwise known as Kevin, is a regular protagonist in the humorously surreal paintings of Australian artist Vanessa Stockard (b. 1975). The mischievous kitten crops up in all manner of unexpected places, from lounging on regency furniture and sitting like a fly atop mushrooms to catching a ride on a giant rubber duck and steering a rowboat through stormy seas. Kevin also appears regularly in Stockard's versions of historical masterpieces. He can be spotted, for instance, in the water with John Everett Millais's Ophelia, or seated on the lap of Whistler's mother. Elsewhere, he hangs from the footbridge over Monet's water lily pond and perches on the turban of Vermeer's girl with a pearl earring. The character

was born when Stockard noticed a rolled-up black sock on her studio floor that reminded her of a kitten. She gave the sock a name and personality and decided to use it as an avatar in her paintings. Since then, Kevin has enjoyed adventures wherever Stockard's imagination has chosen to take him. The artist has always had a fondness for cats, finding them endlessly entertaining. As a child, she had a black Manx, which she loved despite its aggressive temperament. In homage to this pet, Stockard sometimes features a scowling black cat called Satan in her paintings, who appears alongside Kevin as a malicious counterpoint to his anxious and jittery character.

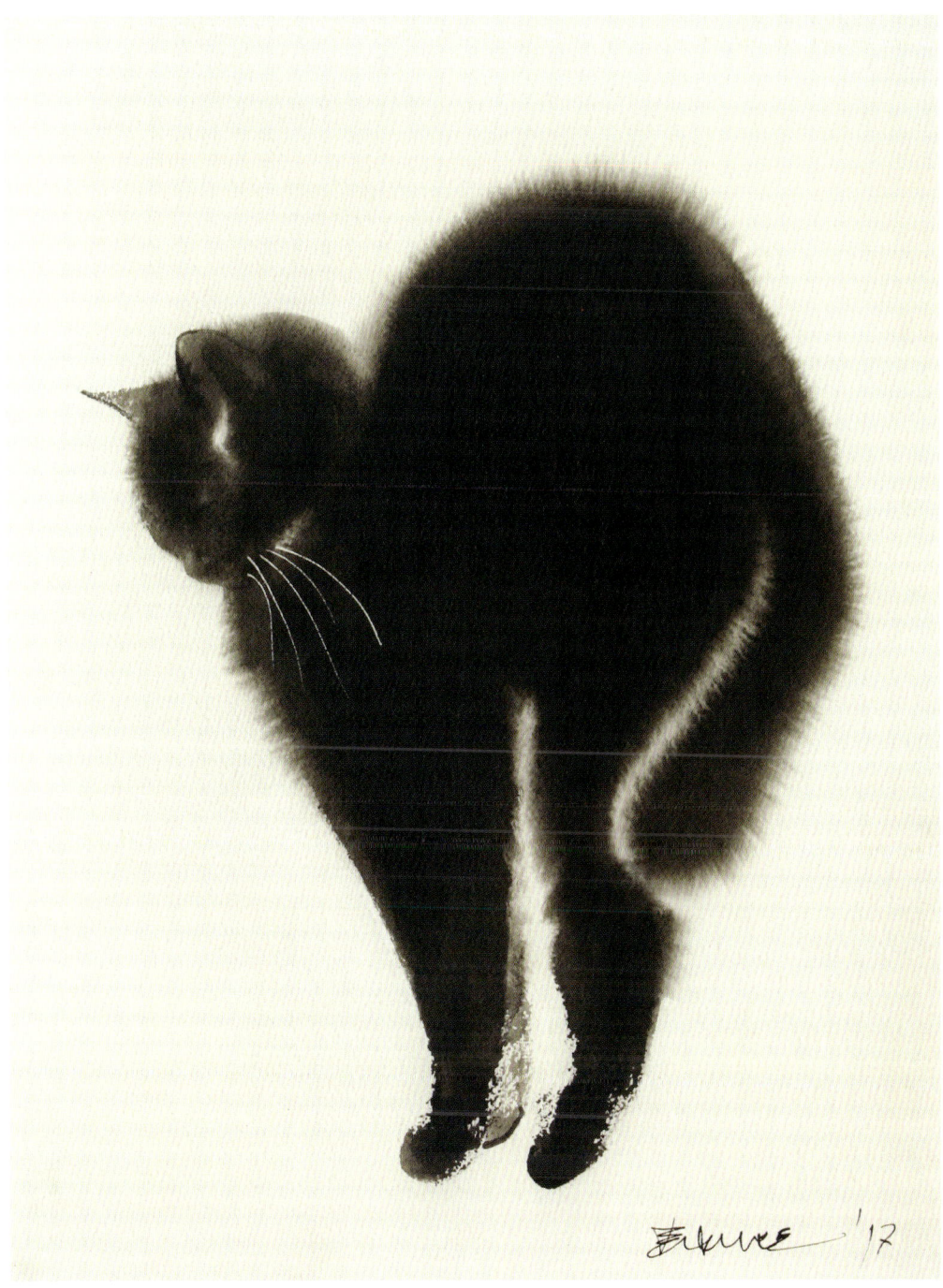

ENDRE PENOVÁC

Morning Stretch, 2017
Watercolor, 15 × 11 in. / 38 × 28 cm

Every cat loves a good stretch, and how well that unique combination of release and readiness is captured in this delightful contemporary watercolor of an arched black cat by Serbian artist Endre Penovác (b. 1956) Penovác is famous for his delicate feline portraits that capture the silent and secretive qualities of these stealthy creatures through gentle brushstrokes and subtle changes in tone. Although his cats all appear black, they are invariably composed from a mix of two or three paint colors, such as browns, purples, and blues, applied on blank paper with no background, similar to the Chinese calligraphy art that inspires these works. This gives the animals a fuzzy, layered look that ineffably conveys life, vitality, and mischief with remarkably little definition, as if they are fleeting apparitions, ready to scamper off the page. Indeed, even when his fluffy subjects are curled up in a ball, there is a sense of impermanence to Penovác's work that emphasizes the idea of time's whispered moments, encouraging the viewer to enjoy the important transient experiences that make up daily life. Penovác's soft yet sharply evocative technique exists not only on the page, but in three dimensions on the T-shirts he designs and sells himself under the brand Zendre. The artist's most frequent muse is his own beloved black cat called Boszi, a play on the Hungarian word for "witch" or "hellcat," *boszorkány*—a name that he aptly brings to life in his hazy and ethereal paintings.

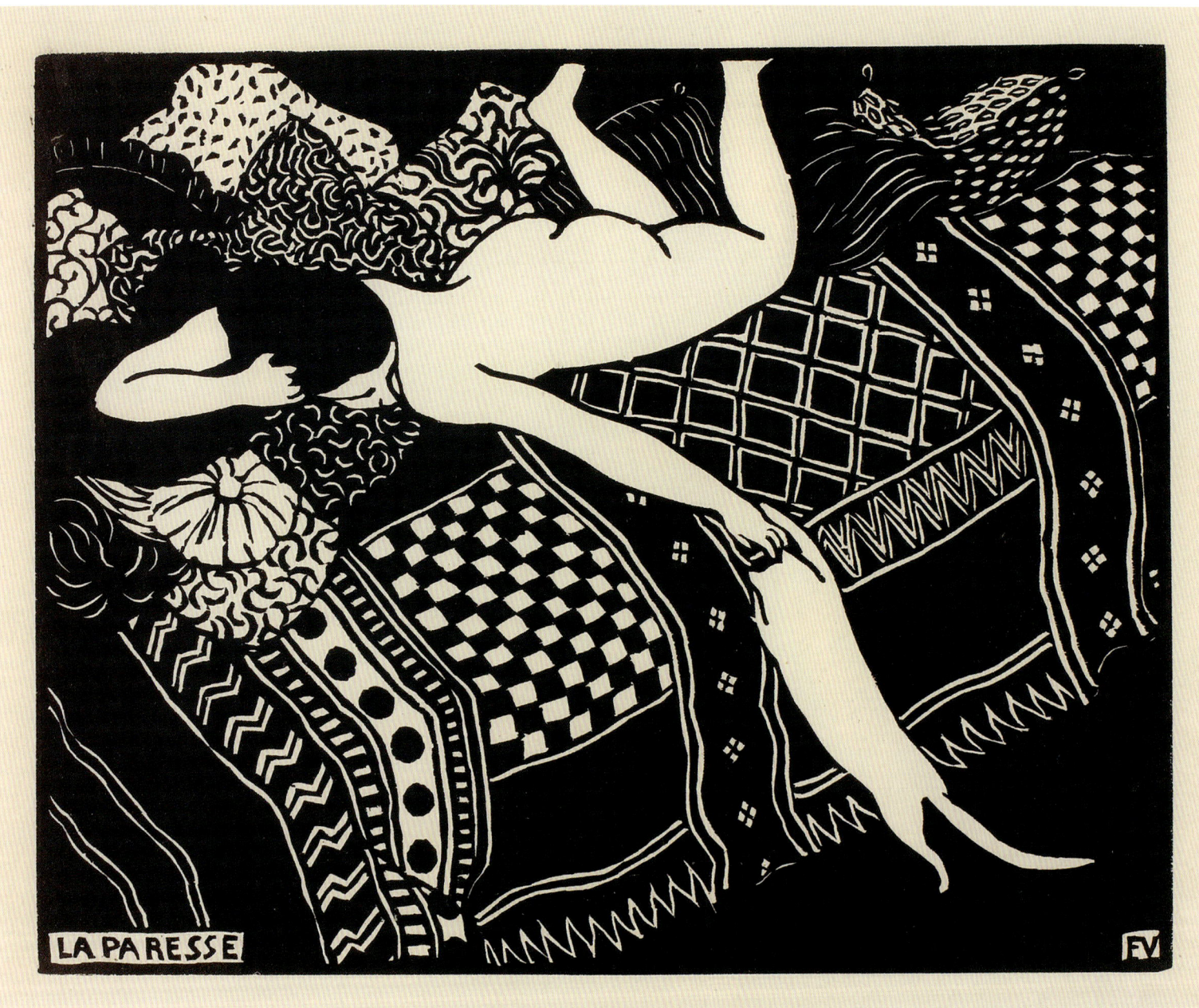

LA PARESSE

FV

FÉLIX VALLOTTON

Laziness, 1896
Woodcut printed in black on ivory
wove paper, 7 × 8¾ in. / 17.8 × 22.2 cm
Art Institute of Chicago

A nude woman lies face down on a quilt-covered bed; her right hand props up her head while her left hand scratches the head of a white cat, which, in turn, stands on its hind legs to be greeted. As the title suggests, this elegant and graphic woodcut is the epitome of a delicious moment of languor and rest. It is the work of Swiss-born Parisian artist Félix Vallotton (1865–1925), who used the medium of printmaking to capture both the appearance and the spirit of Parisian life. In the early 1890s, Vallotton became involved with The Nabis (Hebrew and Arabic for "prophets"), a group of artists, including Pierre Bonnard (see p.68), who sought to convey emotion instead of the mere appearance of the physical world. Inspired by the ethnographic art of Paul Gauguin and the stylistic approach of Japanese prints, which became popular in Paris in the 1890s, Vallotton took up woodcuts, enjoying their ability to create depth, shape, and form using solely monochrome contrast. He played a key role in the modernist revival of the oldest printmaking technique in Europe, which had been used by important artists throughout history, including Albrecht Dürer. Vallotton's works have a voyeuristic quality tinged with ironic humor: here, the viewer wonders whom this wholly modern and independent woman is waiting for, or who might have just left . . . while there is an implication that the feline companion on which she lavishes her affection has seen it all.

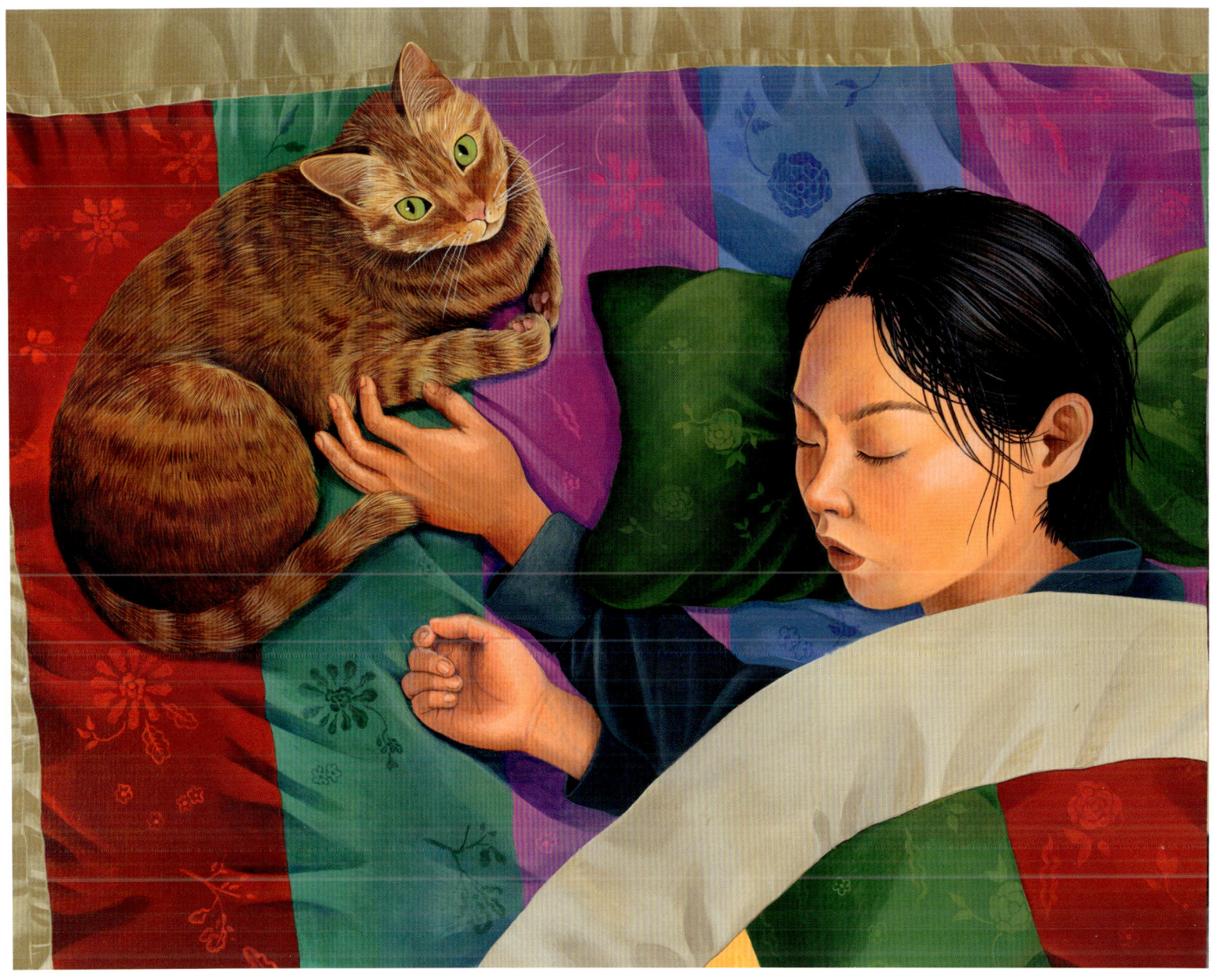

SALLY J. HAN

Nap, 2022
Acrylic paint on paper mounted on
wood panel, 24 × 30 in. / 61 × 76.2 cm
Private collection

This painting captures an enviable moment of peace and quietude shared between pet and owner, evoking emotions related to comfort, security, loyalty, and love. A work by Korean and Chinese American artist Jingmei "Sally" Han (b. 1993), the painterly style bursts with color and texture. The atmosphere of cozy cocooning is enhanced by the composition's unusual bird's-eye view, with the orange cat staring up as if a sentry, on duty while its companion snoozes. Han is known for her uncannily realistic depictions of everyday life and interiors that explore the human condition and universal emotions. Cats and birds are often present, as are figures in Korean and Western dress, usually paused in the middle of some action, such as playing a game of mahjong or allowing a cup of coffee to cool. Through nuanced narratives, subtle symbolism, and a vibrant color palette, Han conveys her own experiences as well as explodes them out, attempting to create some sense of universality through her intimate scenes. Poignant as they are, her paintings are intended as platforms for individual thought, as the artist explains: "Personally, I want my paintings to speak for themselves, so I don't usually explain my work in detail. However, no matter what I paint, I aim to create art that, like the simple actions of a cat, can easily captivate people and leave a lasting memory."

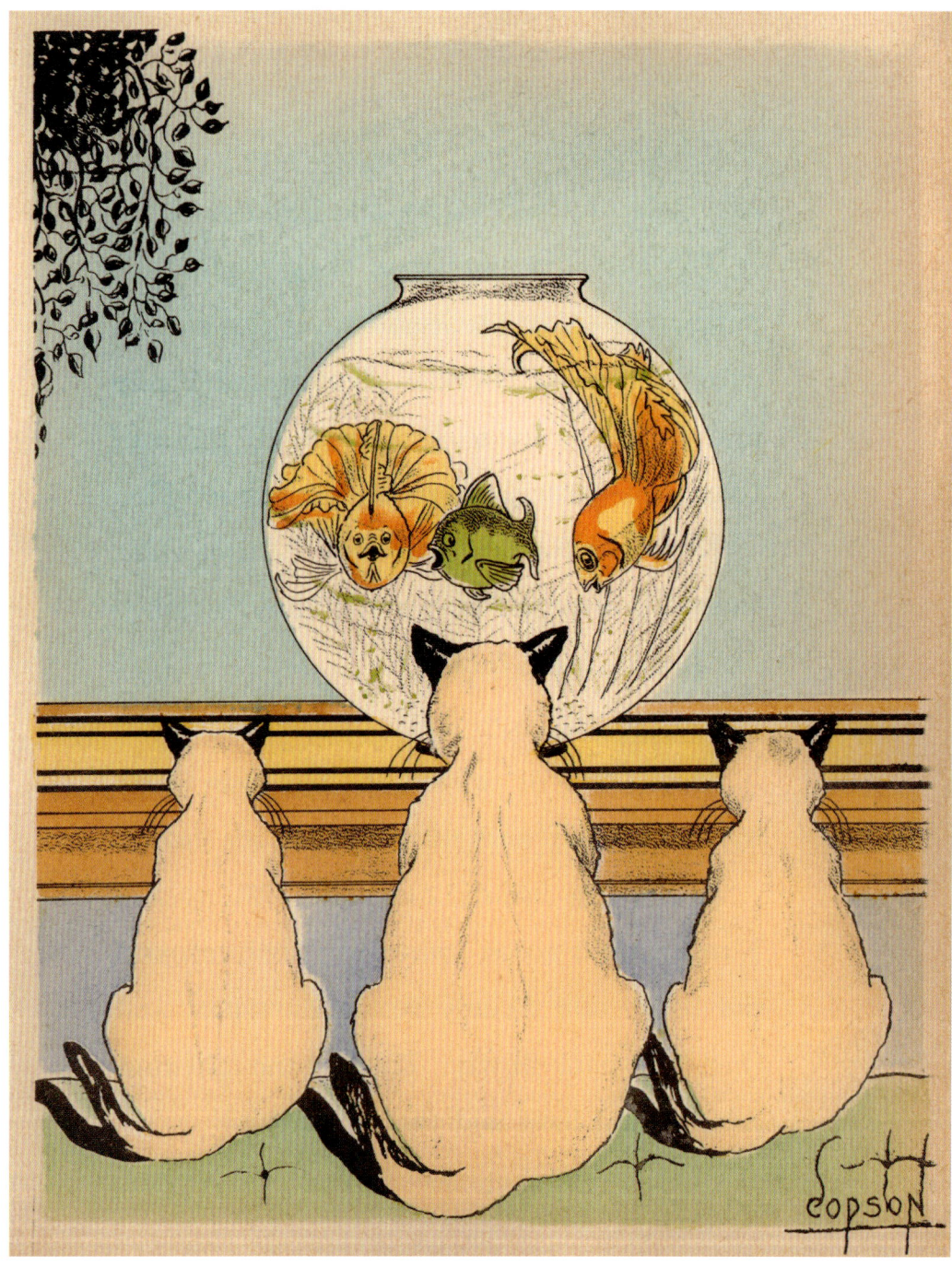

CLYDE A. COPSON

Three Cats Watching Fish in an Aquarium, from
A Day with Bum and the Smart Little Fish, 1938
Print, 11⅜ × 9⅞ in. / 29 × 25 cm
New York Public Library

Domesticated cats have long counted fish as a favorite food, which may be surprising given their sandy origins eight to ten thousand years ago. Fresh fish were probably hard to come by in the deserts of North Africa and the Middle East, but as the species evolved and spread over the world, so did their taste for these salty snacks. By 1500 BCE, there is evidence in an ancient Egyptian tomb painting of a cat delightfully tearing into a fish, and stories abound of medieval fishermen in Western Europe besieged by feline thieves. Today, more than 6 percent of all fish caught in the wild goes into cans of cat food, and it seems there is a biological explanation to cats' famous love for fish. In 2023 scientists discovered that cats' tastebuds include the special receptors needed to detect the taste sensation known as umami, a meaty flavor usually found in cheese, mushrooms, meat, and fish. Unlike dogs, carnivorous cats do not have the receptors that help them detect sweet, and they boast fewer taste receptors for bitter than humans, absences that help explain why your cat might be such a fussy eater. This delightfully colorful print, which features three Siamese cats, tails wagging with hunger as they stare greedily at a full fishbowl, speaks to the age-old feline hankering for umami-rich fish. Illustrated by Clyde A. Copson, the page comes from a Depression-era reading primer, *A Day with Bum and the Smart Little Fish*, which taught American schoolchildren about the concept of responsibility, although it is unclear if that moral code extended to these cats.

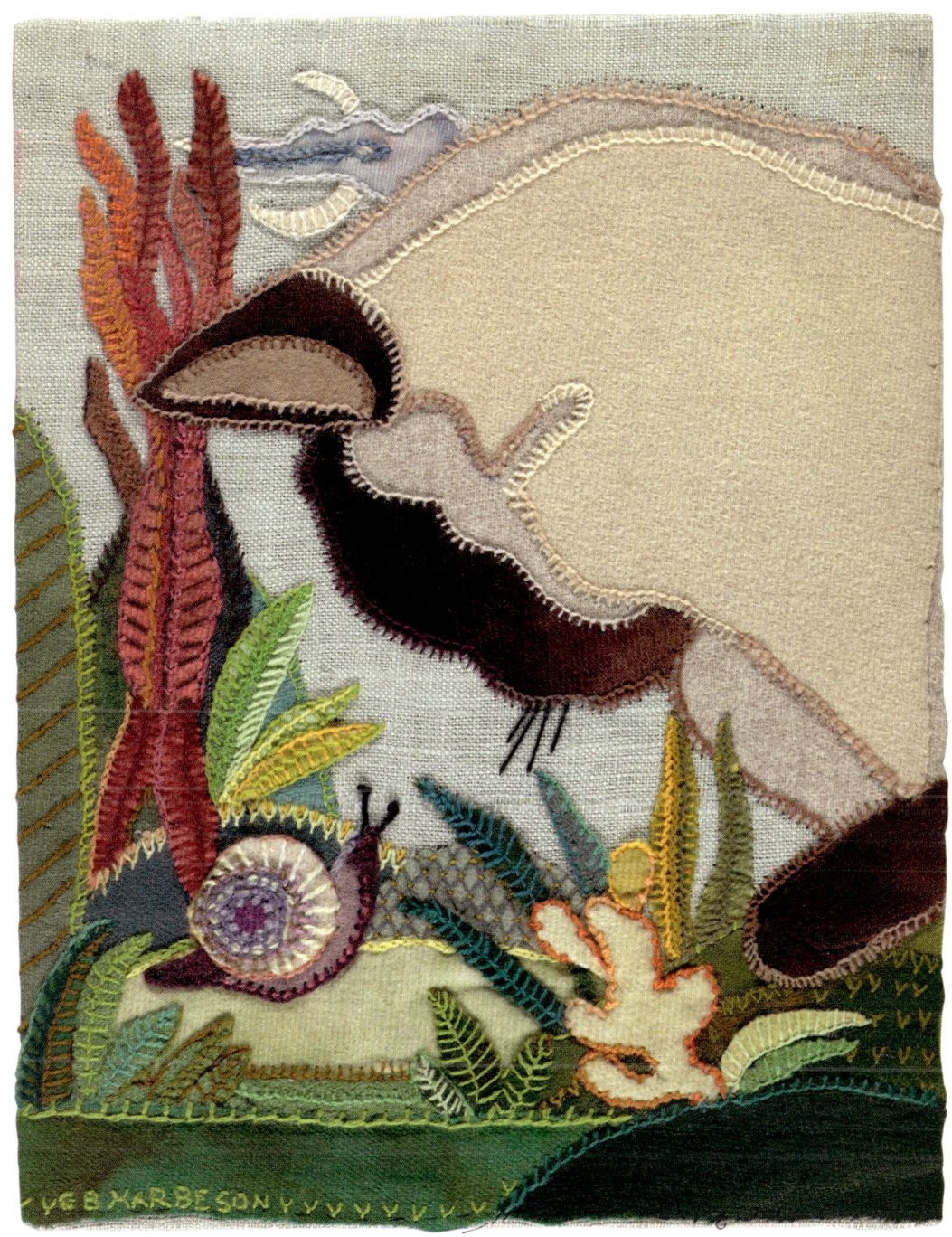

GEORGIANA BROWN HARBESON

Cat and Snail, 1961–62
Linen with wool and velvet appliqué and wool embroidery in buttonhole, stem, chain, and couching stitches, 13 × 10 in. / 33 × 25.5 cm
Cooper Hewitt, Smithsonian Design Museum, New York

Only slightly larger than a sheet of paper, this richly detailed embroidery was created by American artist Georgiana Brown Harbeson (1894–1980). Weaving storytelling into fabric, this garden scene is more than mere decoration—it is a tribute to the often-overlooked natural wonders beneath our feet. The right side of the piece is dominated by the profile of a cat, peering down at a cheerful little snail gliding along a path surrounded by colorful plants that resemble a vibrant coral seabed. There is no sign of danger or threat in this charming tableau; instead, the artwork radiates a quiet joy, evoking a scene of peaceful coexistence and tender curiosity within this miniature patch of verdant splendor. Widely regarded as one of the foremost needlework talents of the twentieth century, Harbeson saw her creations grace numerous magazine covers throughout the 1920s and 1930s, and today her work is featured in prominent collections, including the Metropolitan Museum of Art and the Cooper Hewitt in New York. A passionate member of both the Embroiderers' Guild of America and the American Needle Arts Society, she wrote the genre-defining 1938 book *American Needlework*, which charts the history of decorative stitchery and embroidery from the late sixteenth century to the modern period. Harbeson painted with stitches, using what she referred to as a "palette of wool" to create evocative pieces that elevated embroidery from a quaint domestic pastime to a respected form of fine art.

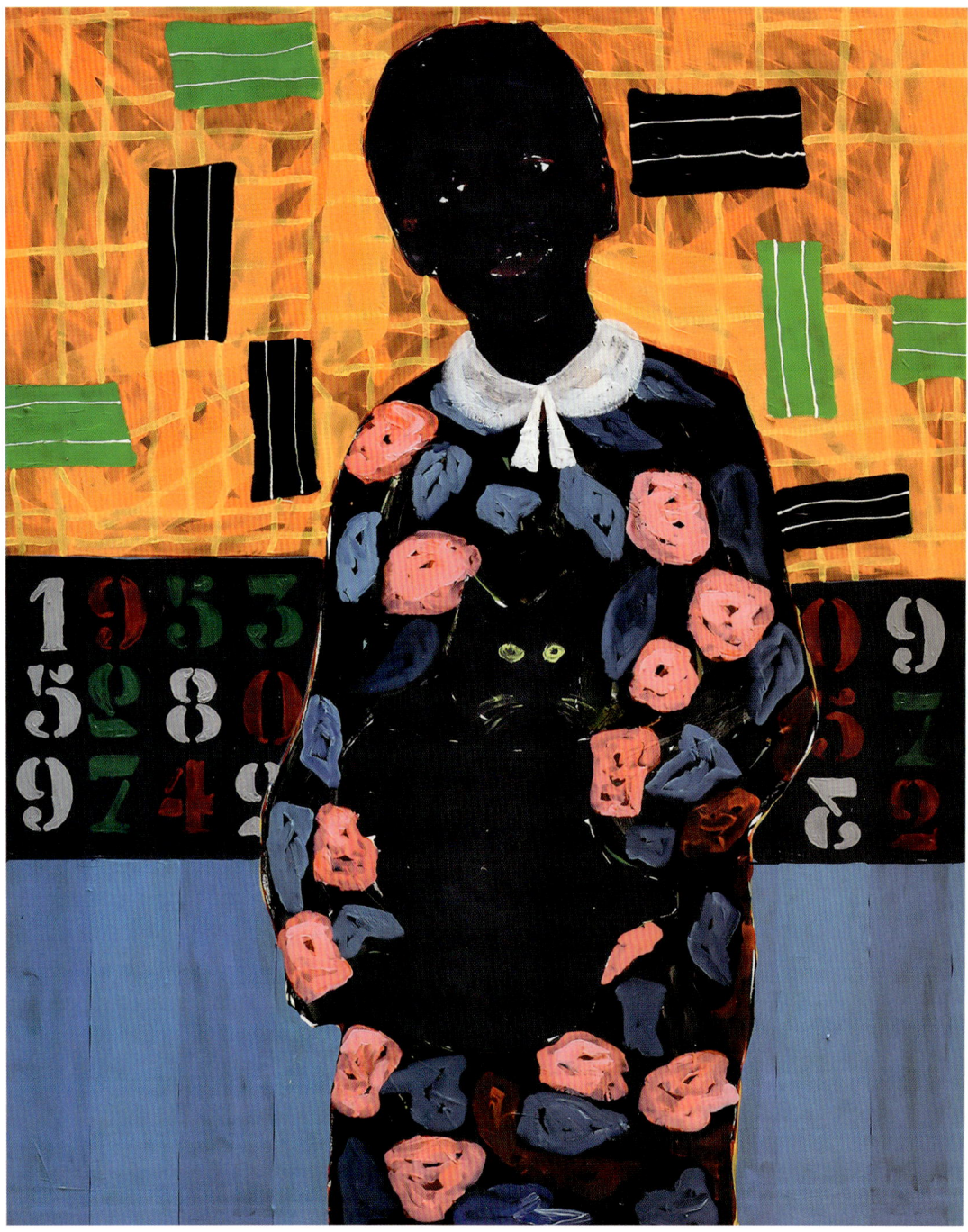

GODWIN CHAMPS NAMUYIMBA

Cat Girl, 2021
Mixed media on canvas
52½ × 42⅞ in. / 133.5 × 108.8 cm
Private collection

Despite the title, viewers must gaze intently to find the animal in *Cat Girl* by Ugandan painter Godwin Champs Namuyimba (b. 1989). The black cat is rendered abstractly in the arms of an equally impressionistic girl, wearing a patterned dress with a round pussy-bow collar. The girl's expression is as inscrutable as the pet she carries: her eyes look straight ahead, giving nothing away, and her mouth is faintly visible in a straight line. She stands against a brightly flat background that plays with perspective and motifs from modern art, including lines, numbers, and color fields. This depiction aligns with much of Namuyimba's work, in which Black semiabstract figures pose in front of boldly graphic backgrounds engaged in diverse postures, modes, and activities. The artist combines his astute

skills of observation with a knowledge of form and art history to reveal the fantastical in the everyday, forcing the viewer to inhabit the painting and look at common people and objects with a new pair of eyes. One wonders how this girl and cat know each other and whether this cat likes being held or, as most felines are wont to do, will inevitably squiggle itself out of her grasp just as the viewer looks away. The mystery is slightly unsettling, and yet Namuyimba's painting still captures the sweetly transcendent camaraderie between a girl and her cat.

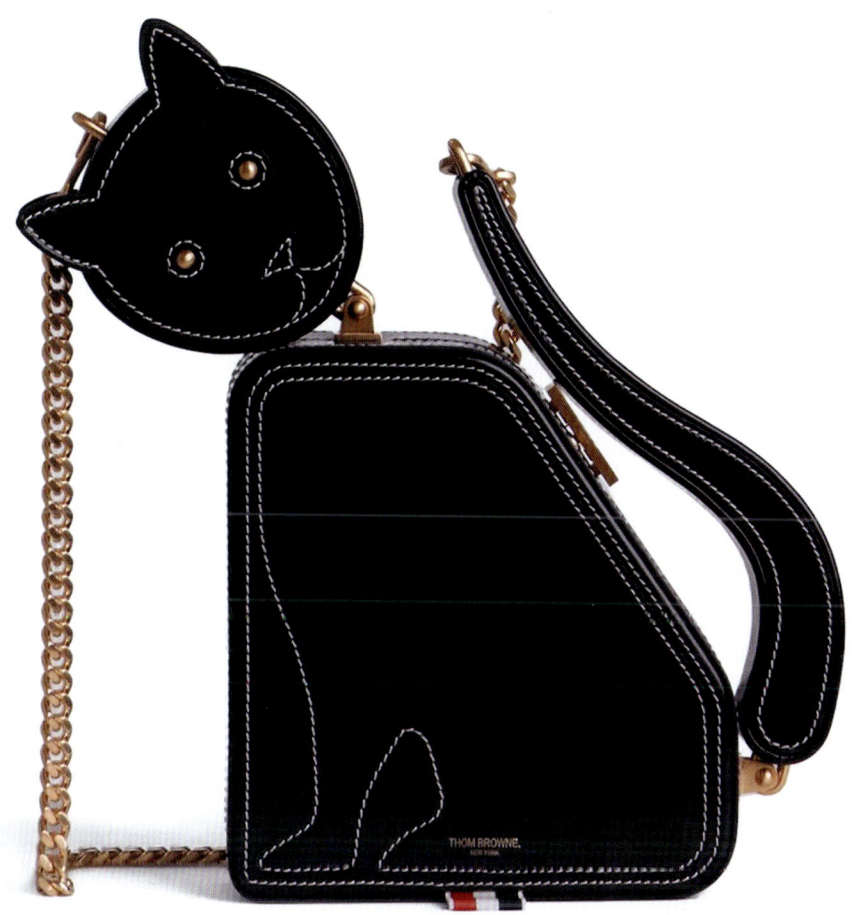

THOM BROWNE

Cat Bag, 2018
Leather and brass

No one plays at the intersection of playful and preppy like Thom Browne (b. 1965). Originally a tailor before joining brands, such as Giorgio Armani and Club Monaco, the American fashion designer launched his own menswear business in 2001. He created made-to-measure suits by appointment only, and just two years later he presented his first collection at New York Fashion Week. His reinterpretation of men's suiting, featuring modernized cuts and revamped proportions while staying committed to traditional colors—especially his favored gray and navy—helped him find his footing early. Browne started his first full women's collection in 2011 and rose to national prominence when Michelle Obama wore one of his designs to her husband's presidential inauguration in 2013. The designer introduced what would become his best known hand-bag, the Hector—a dachshund-shaped purse named and modeled after Browne's own pooch—in 2016. Animal bags, carried by fashionistas of all genders, have been a mainstay in Browne's runway presentations, where the menagerie of creatures adds a fanciful note to his crisp, tailored silhouettes. This black cat bag, introduced in 2018, is crafted from calfskin with a brass chain and details. It also features a surprise: both the neck and tail of this kitty are hinged, making this accessory wearable—and posable—art. Superb quality of crafts-manship and forward thinking are hallmarks of the Thom Browne brand, and many of his pieces, including this one, carry his unmistakable red-white-and-blue-striped signature.

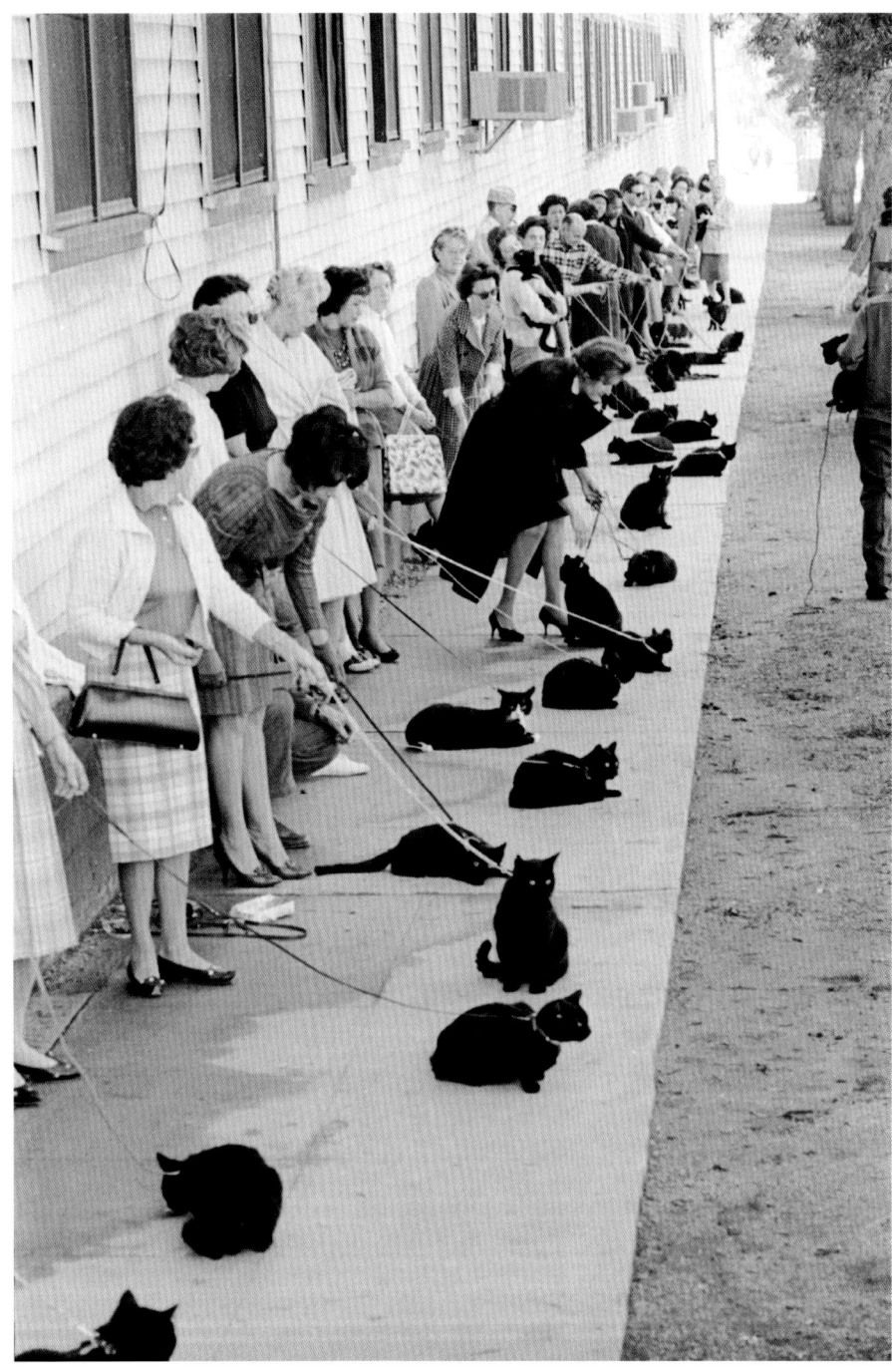

RALPH CRANE

Auditions for Tales of Terror,
Hollywood, California, USA, 1961
Photograph, dimensions variable

While some might consider black cats unlucky, the owners of these kitties were hoping to get lucky and see their pet become a Hollywood star. In 1961 producers for a new movie version of Edgar Allan Poe's 1843 short story "The Black Cat" (see p.79) advertised a casting call in the local papers, seeking "a sagacious black cat" to act alongside stars Joyce Jameson, Vincent Price, and Peter Lorre. On assignment for *Life* magazine, American photographer Ralph Crane (1913–1988) captured the 152 hopeful felines who showed up with their "managers" to try out for the part in what became one segment of the 1962 gothic horror movie trilogy *Tales of Terror*. Born in Germany, Crane moved to the United States in 1941 to work with the Black Star photography agency and also began creating images for *Life*, whose

staff he joined in 1951. Famous for his sonorous laugh, which earned him the nickname "Whooping Crane," here, he captures the absurdity of putting a cat, an animal known for its independent spirit, on a leash. One seemingly disgruntled black-and-white cat toward the middle of the photograph would have been disqualified from the auditions because of its markings, but the bona fide black cats were judged based on which one had the "meanest" face and on their ability to cooperate with their human costars. Ultimately, the part went to a professionally trained cat, with seven additional mousers hired as understudies and for promotional purposes.

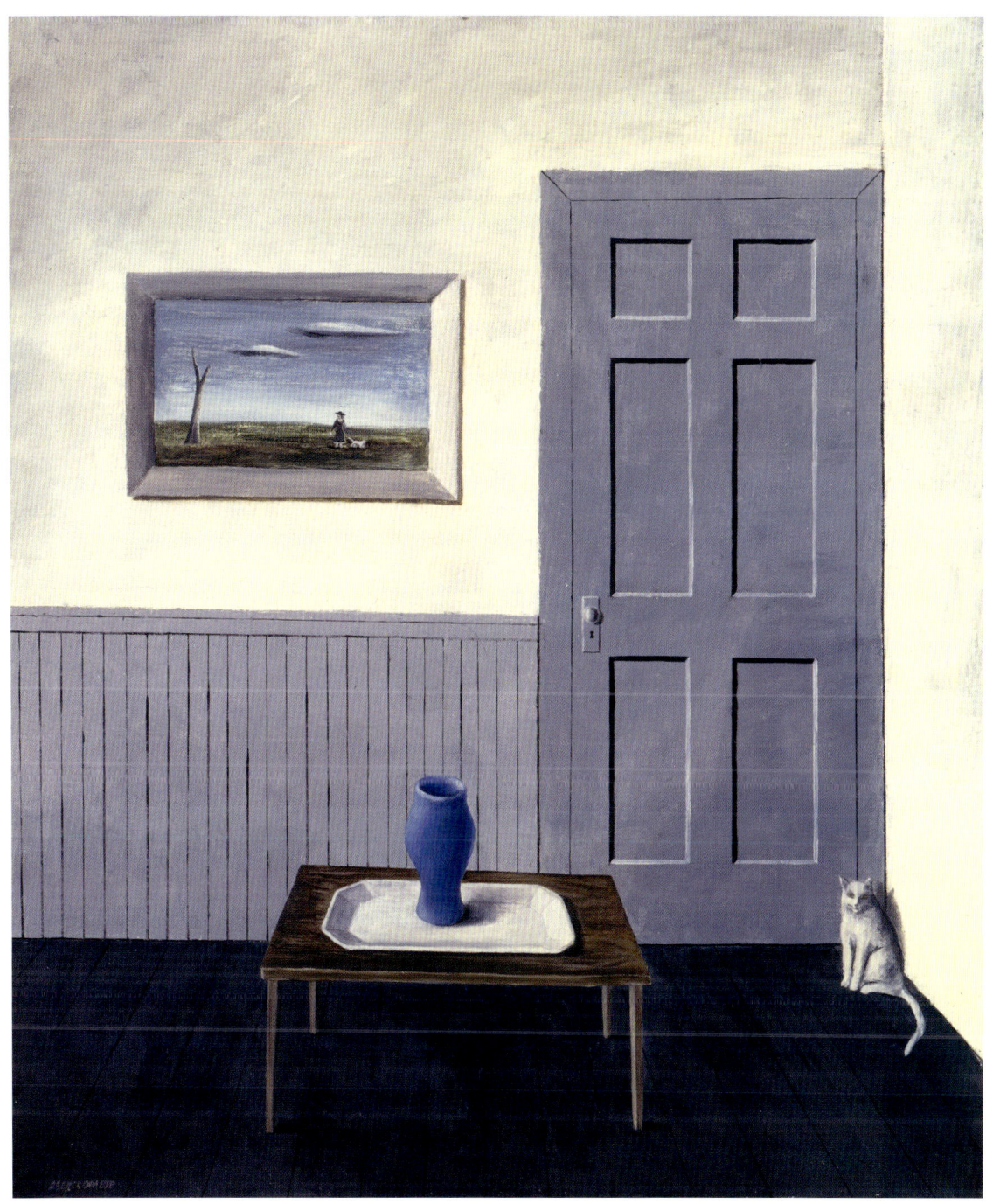

GERTRUDE ABERCROMBIE

White Cat, c. 1938
Oil on canvas, 36 × 30⅛ in / 91.5 × 76.5 cm
Smithsonian American Art Museum, Washington, DC

A small white cat sits by the door of a sparsely decorated room, as if waiting for its owner to return. A similar feline appears in a picture on the wall, where, in a barren landscape populated only by a dead tree, it accompanies a female figure, most probably a self-portrait by American artist Gertrude Abercrombie (1909–1977). Cats were of great importance to Abercrombie, a critical figure in the mid-twentieth-century Chicago art scene, who made this painting while working for the Works Progress Administration's Federal Art Project, an American government program designed to provide jobs to unemployed artists during the Great Depression of the 1930s. She kept several cats in her apartment in the city's Hyde Park neighborhood, which acted as a lively gathering place for literary figures, progressive artists, critics, and jazz icons, such as Charlie Parker and Miles Davis. Yet, despite her active social life, she often painted solitary women in lonely settings, accompanied only by a cat or sometimes an owl. Employing a restrained palette and concise visual vocabulary of personal emblems across her landscapes, still lifes, and interiors, Abercrombie also painted many portraits of the cats she owned. These creatures were not only beloved pets, but often served as alter egos. Indeed, the artist identified so closely with them that, when pregnant with her daughter Dinah, she commented that she could imagine giving birth to a kitten more than a human baby.

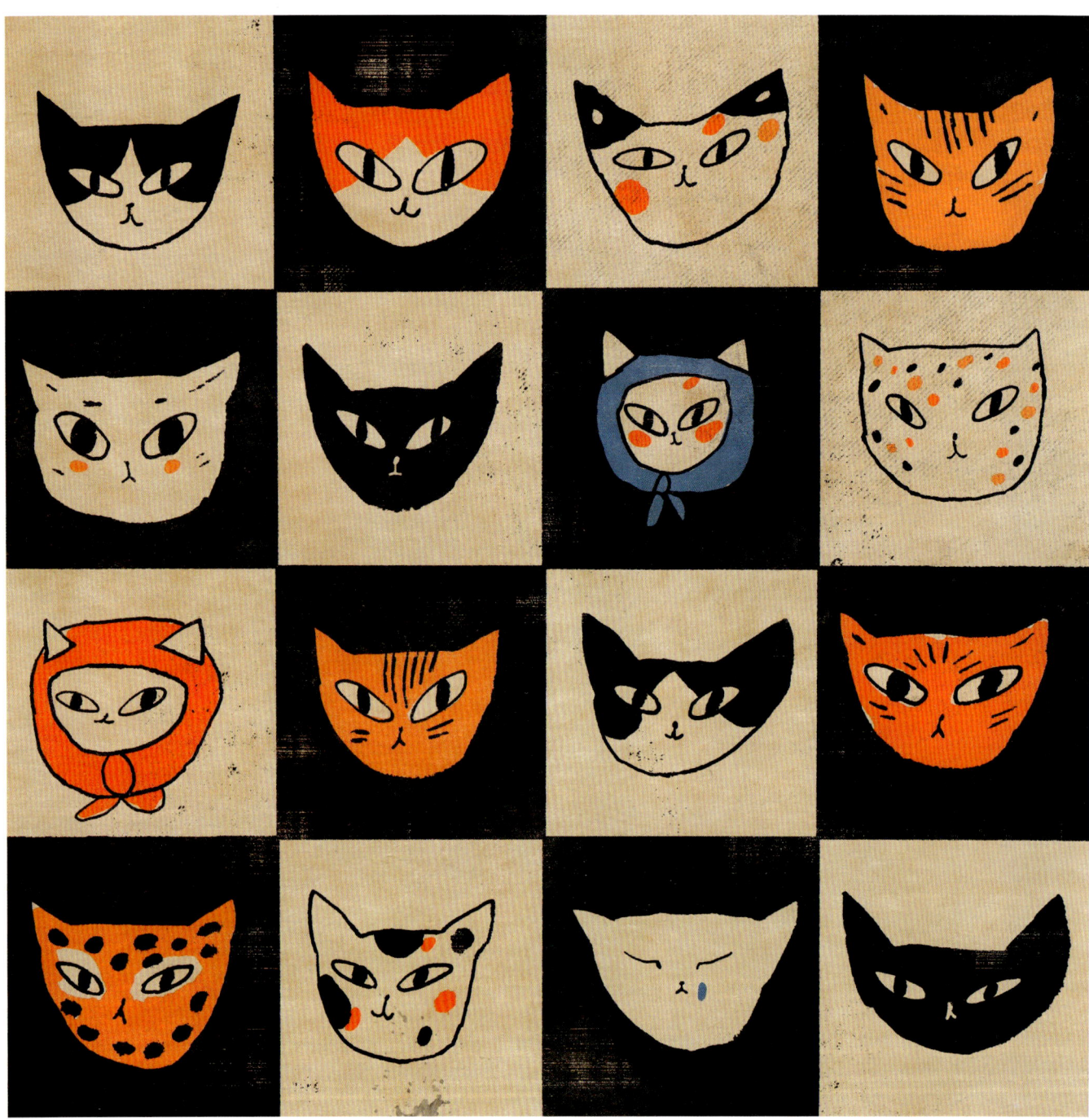

ENIKŐ EGED

Monday Cat Bingo "choose your fighter," 2023
Digital, 8¼ × 8¼ in. / 21 × 21 cm

This stylized bingo board comes from the mind of Hungarian artist Enikő Eged, who specializes in illustration, prints, and pattern design. Inspired by the animal world and aesthetics of traditional Eastern European folk art, Eged's whimsical and joyful illustrations depict dogs and cats, as well as lobsters, horses, and even humans. Eged takes influence from a variety of artists, especially women painters, such as Frida Kahlo (see p.193), Ilona Keserü, Judit Reigl, and Baya Mahieddine. She also takes cues from Asian folk art, particularly the floral and geometric patterns seen in *ukiyo-e* prints. Eged's illustrations are commercially available in a wide range of products and applications—everything from art prints to apparel to home goods. Her works begin as paper-based sketches in pencil or ink before being brought into the digital realm. From there, her drawing is saturated with the bold colors she often turns to, such as the vibrant tangerine orange and cobalt blue seen here. Despite the static expression on all of the faces of the cats on this bingo board, they evoke a wide range of emotions through their accoutrements, coloration, and proximities to one another. House cats are a frequent motif in Eged's art, as is the grid design that tips the patternmaker's hand. There is a wit and a wink to all of her designs, and a supreme confidence evoked from her simplistic yet deeply evocative images.

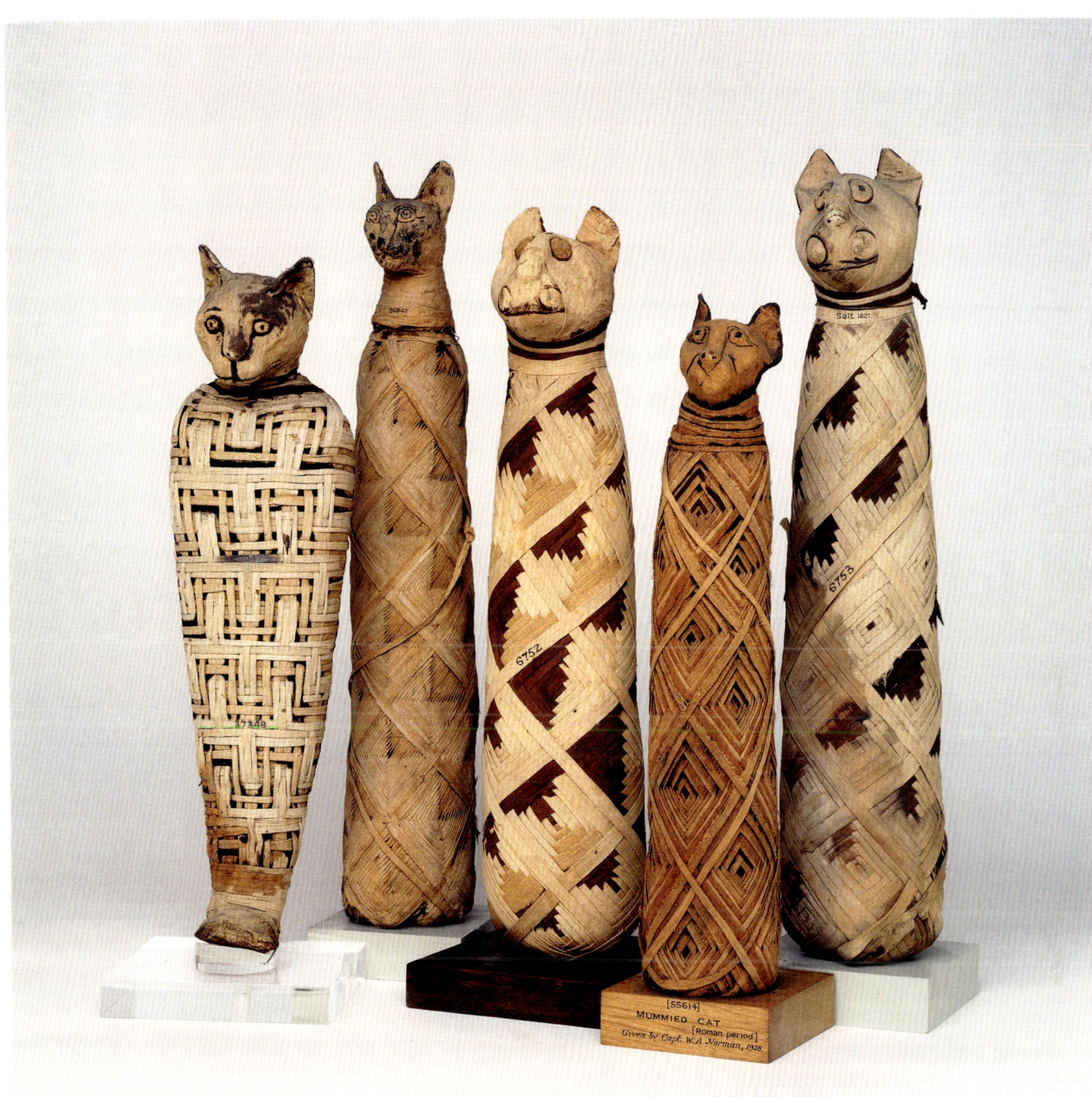

ANONYMOUS

Cat mummies, c. 30 BCE
Linen, cat remains, plaster, and pigment
Dimensions variable
British Museum, London

Cats were buried in human cemeteries as early as Egypt's Predynastic period (c. 5000 to 3000 BCE), suggesting that the animals had already been domesticated by the beginning of Egyptian civilization. While the ancient Egyptians did not worship cats themselves, they believed that felines had a special link with several divinities. Of the numerous feline goddesses, Bastet, who was often represented as a cat or a cat-headed woman, is most commonly linked with the beloved pets (see p.29). The Greek historian Herodotus visited Egypt in about 450 BCE and described huge crowds of worshippers gathering at festivals in order to commune with Bastet in wild celebrations. It was possibly during these festivals that pilgrims would offer sculptural manifestations of the goddess back to her. Millions of cats

(and other animals) were bred and embalmed in temple complexes during the later stages of Egyptian history. The purchase and burial of a cat mummy allowed worshippers to convey a prayer to the gods. Dedicatory inscriptions found alongside some animal mummies request health, life, and protection for the worshipper. These five mummified cats were wrapped in elaborate patterns of multicolored linen bandages, their facial features modeled in linen with eyes, noses, and mouths emphasized in linen and brown paint. The patterns created by alternating light and dark strips of thin linen skillfully arranged to create a geometric design are typical of the so-called Roman period, when Egypt was under the rule of the Roman Empire.

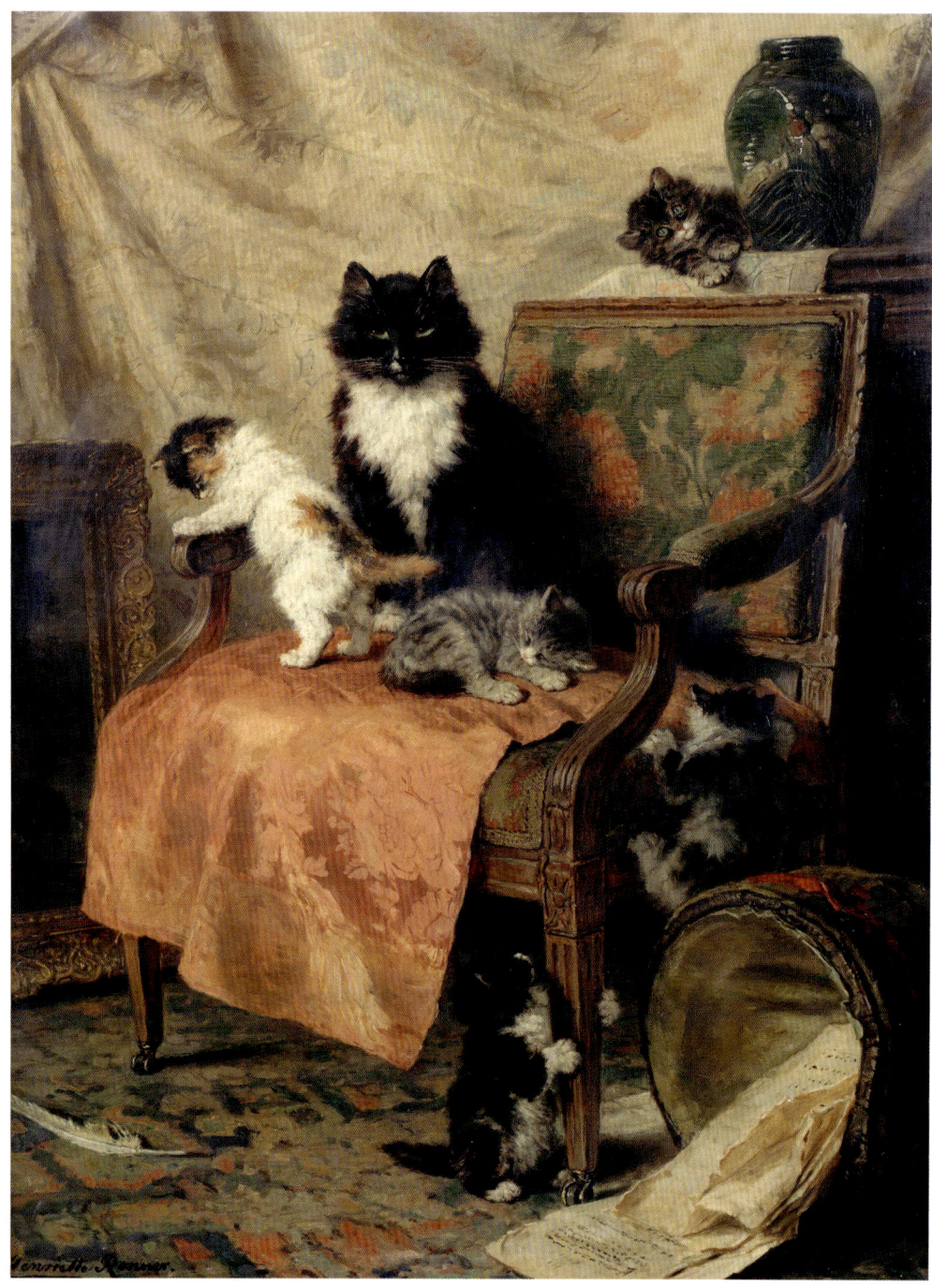

HENRIËTTE RONNER-KNIP

Kittens at Play, 1897
Oil on canvas, 44½ × 33½ in. / 113 × 85 cm
Private collection

Sitting imperiously on a chair, a mother cat is seemingly oblivious to the havoc her kittens wreak around her in this oil painting by Dutch Belgian artist Henriëtte Ronner-Knip (1821–1909). Having overturned a bin of papers, three of the kittens play around the chair, while one sleeps and the other lolls next to a vase, which may or may not be the next casualty of their inquisitiveness. Ronner-Knip, whose talent was clear from childhood, began her artistic career when she was fifteen, painting farms, forests, and animals directly from nature. In 1848 she became the first woman admitted to the Dutch artists' society founded in 1839, Arti et Amicitiae. In 1870 a stray cat moved into her home, and her fascination with her new companion's behavior led her to concentrate her work exclusively on cats. Ronner-Knip's highly realistic feline depictions showed both her prodigious talent and an understanding of the animals' individual personalities. Her specialty of producing dark canvases with kittens at play was well-timed, because keeping cats as pets had become more popular among the late nineteenth-century middle class, and the middling sort could also afford to buy paintings. As she sold more work, she started to prepare watercolor or oil sketches to avoid repetition and to deter forgers. Although Ronner-Knip was a successful artist during her career, her saccharine and realist portrayals of cats later fell out of fashion as modernism took hold.

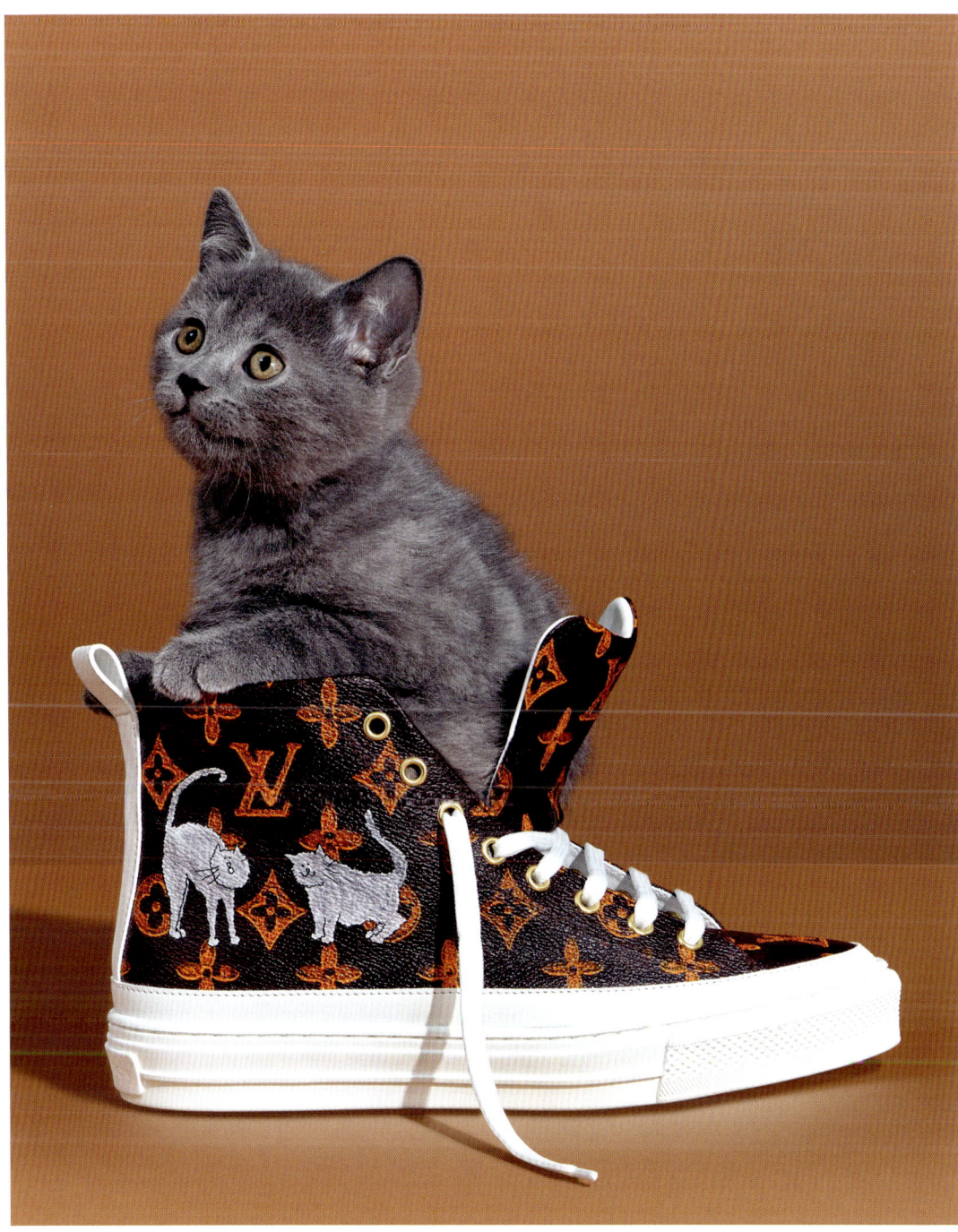

LOUIS VUITTON AND GRACE CODDINGTON

Stellar Sneakers, from *Catogram*, 2018
Canvas, rubber, and gold hardware

Two hand-drawn Persian cats adorn a high-top sneaker covered in the iconic Louis Vuitton monogram, while a gray Persian kitten sits inside, modeling the footwear appealingly. The sneaker belongs to a 2018 collaboration between the French couture house Louis Vuitton and the British-born, New York–based fashion stylist Grace Coddington (b. 1941), best known for her long career as the creative director of *Vogue*. Famed for her style, flaming red hair, and love of cats, Coddington worked with the artistic director of Louis Vuitton—her friend, frequent collaborator, and dog lover Nicolas Ghesquière—to immortalize their pets in a capsule collection called *Catogram*. Pumpkin and Blanket, Coddington's Persians, appear here in sketches done by their proud owner, contrasting with the orange monogram (a nod to Coddington's hair) and the brown that is immediately recognizable as the classic Louis Vuitton shade. On other pieces in the collection, playful cats, as well as dogs and mice, are scattered across leather handbags, woven into blankets and scarves, and printed onto silk pajamas. For the *Catogram* launch, Pumpkin and Blanket also took over Louis Vuitton's store in New York's Meatpacking District, with an oversize Blanket greeting shoppers from the building's roof. Coddington's cat sketches have also appeared in other collaborations, including teapots for the London store Liberty and a mural for the San Vicente Bungalows in Hollywood in 2023. As Coddington describes the inspiration behind her work, "It's all my cats living their lives and having fun."

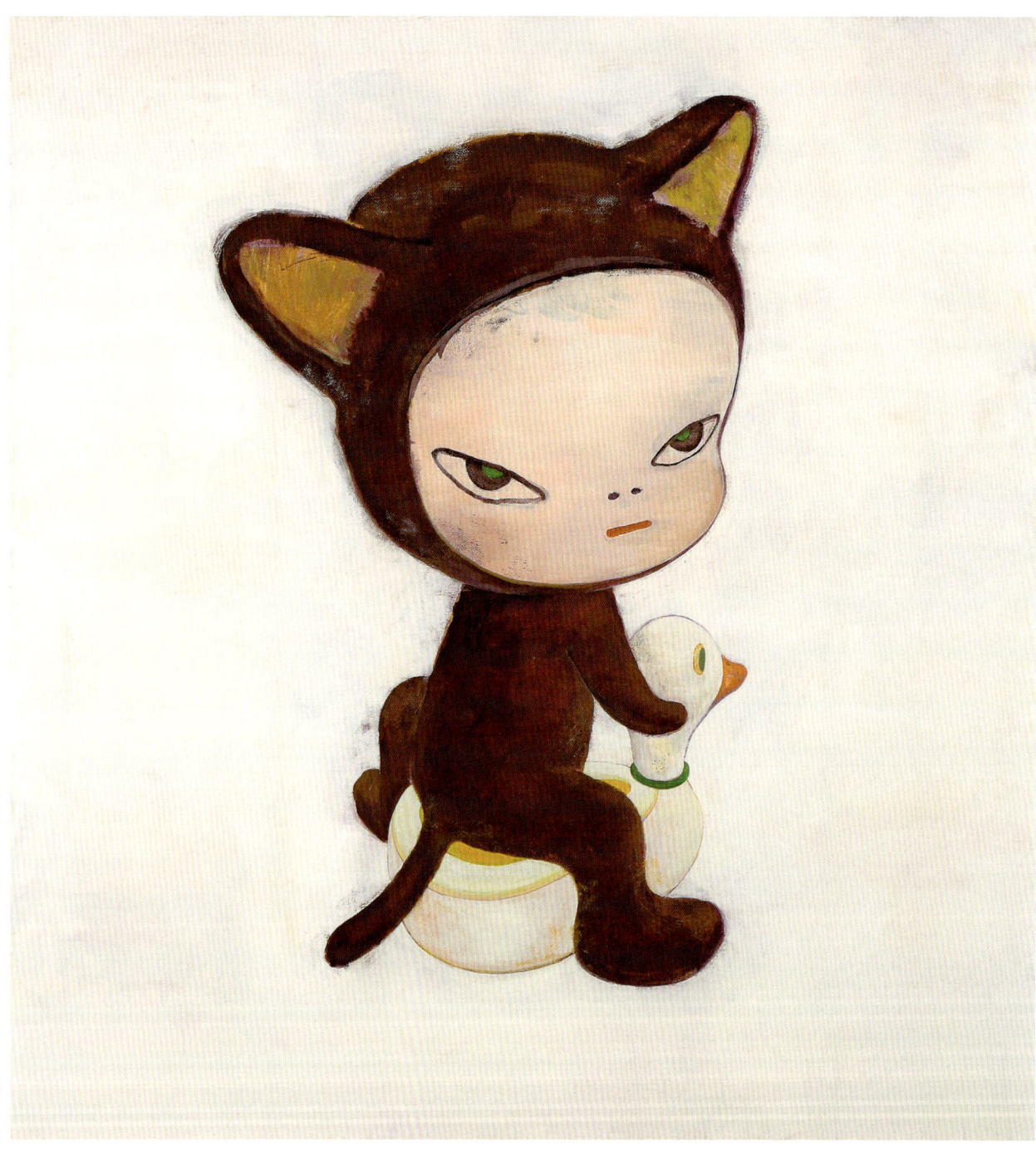

YOSHITOMO NARA

Harmless Kitty, 1994
Acrylic on canvas, 59 × 55⅛ in. / 150 × 140 cm
National Museum of Modern Art, Tokyo
© Yoshitomo Nara

Painted by Japanese artist Yoshitomo Nara (b. 1959), *Harmless Kitty* is characteristic of his large-headed, wide-eyed children, who combine apparent innocence with knowing looks and an edge of menace. Dressed up in costume as a cat, this child takes on the animal's attributes: independent and curious, soft but with sharp teeth, domesticated but wild. Nara considers his figures to be self-portraits, which primarily draw on his childhood memories and sensibilities. His approach is further influenced by sources from literature, modern art, and folk music that express individual humanity. As a latchkey kid from a remote, rural part of northern Japan, he experienced a solitary childhood, in which friendships with animals held great importance. He spent afternoons drawing and

listening to music on the radio, accompanied by his pet cat, Chape. As an adult, Nara moved to Germany to study. Unable to speak the language, he felt transported back to the loneliness of his early years: "I recalled myself as a child who was talking to the cat and rediscovered that sensitivity." Cats symbolize a connection with Nara's past and add to the continuity of memory that lies at the core of his artistic development. His linear style, derived from a deep-rooted commitment to drawing, is evident in *Harmless Kitty*, but this painting does not share the graphic flatness of comics. Even beneath the seemingly monochrome background, Nara uses multiple layers of paint in a complex interweaving of colors and brushstrokes, to create depth and texture across the canvas.

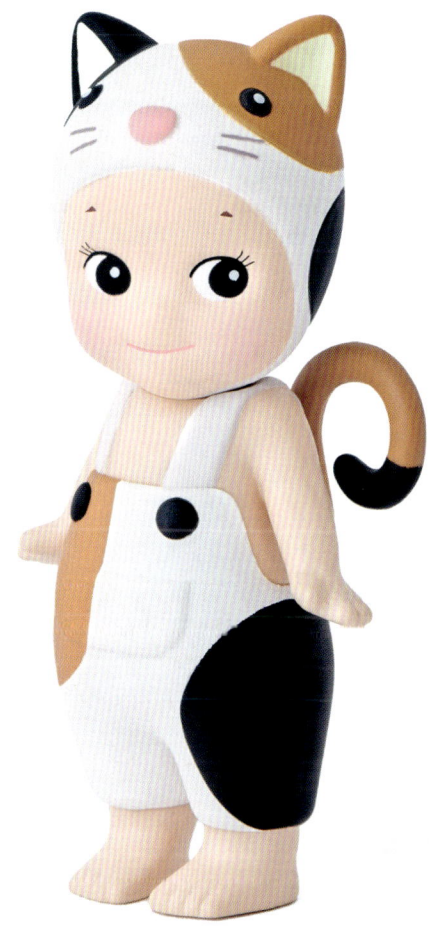

DREAMS INC.

Calico Sonny Angel, from Cat Life, 2023
Figurine, H. 3 in. / 7.5 cm

Sonny Angel is a highly collectible blind-box toy figure with a cult following, counting among its celebrity fans Bella Hadid, Rosalía, and Victoria Beckham. So far, there have been more than 650 permutations of this three-inch-tall cutie across many series, each centered on a different theme that showcases Sonny's impressive range of adorable headgear, from food and flowers to circus and Halloween. Produced by Japanese toy manufacturer Dreams Inc. since 2004, Sonny is the brainchild of company founder Toru Soeya, who named the cherub after his own childhood nickname. Inspired by an American Kewpie doll, the product was never intended for children but for adult women as a good-luck charm designed, according to the brand's motto, "to bring you happiness," aligning him with protective qualities and positive energy like a portable talisman for the modern age. This calico version is part of the Cat Life collection, comprising fourteen figurines, including tabby and Siamese editions, as well as three "lucky figures" produced in much smaller batches in orange, purple, and pink feline-inspired costumes. Most desirable of all are two ultrarare "secret figures": Sonny as a pink cat holding a golden fish and his pal Robby Angel—a mystery creature that could be a dog, mouse, or bunny—also cast in pink, positioned on a teeny can of cat food. While either of this pair can reach up to $500 on the resale market, this *kawaii* cat is also sought after, selling for up to eight times its original $10 retail price on auction platforms.

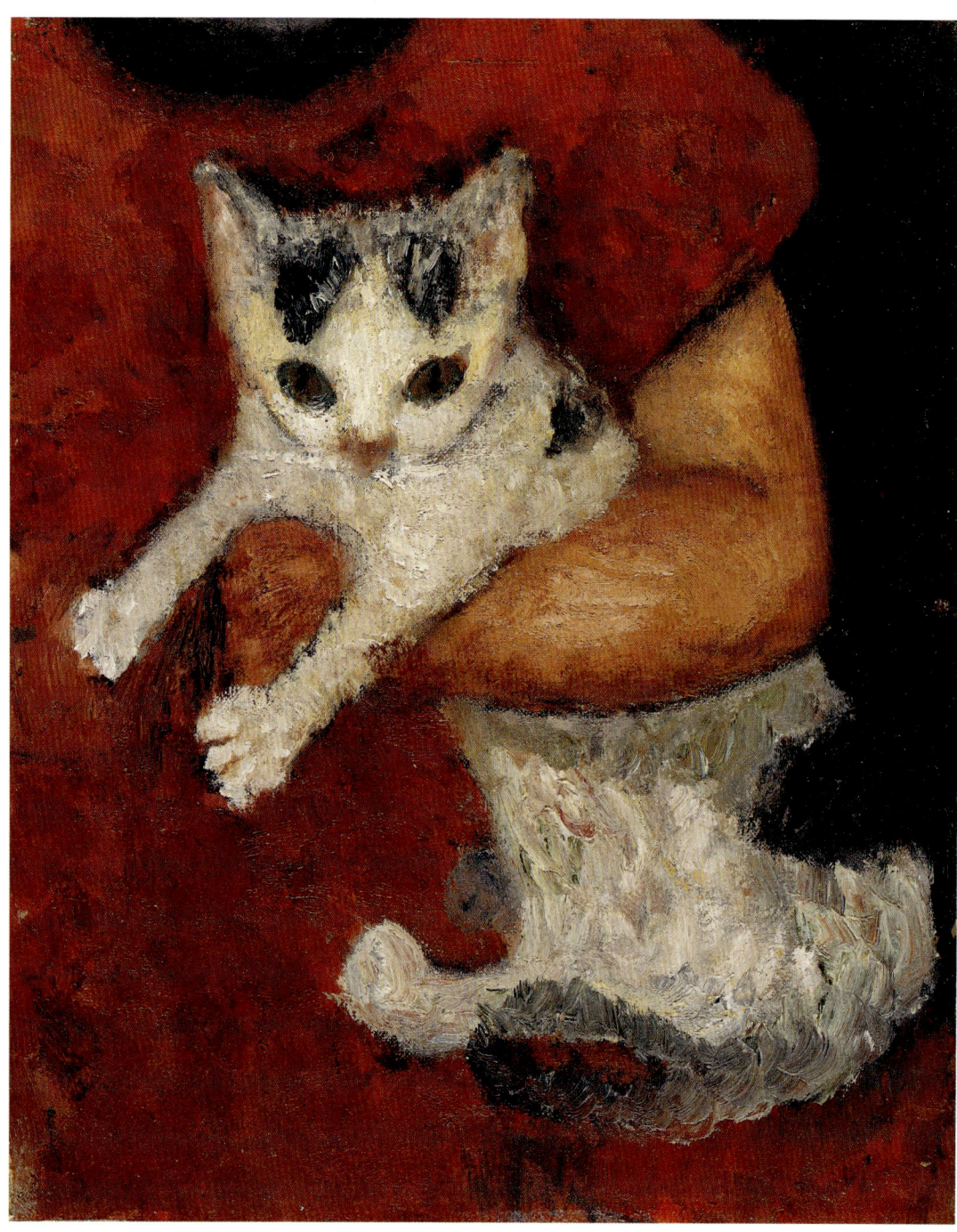

PAULA MODERSOHN-BECKER

Cat in a Child's Arms, 1903
Oil on canvas, 12¾ × 10⅛ in. / 32.5 × 25.6 cm
Kunsthalle Bremen, Germany

As is the case for several women artists, German painter Paula Modersohn-Becker (1876–1907) was not recognized during her short career (she died at just thirty-one, following complications from childbirth), selling only three paintings during her lifetime. Thanks to recent scholarship, she is now understood as one of the most important artists of the early twentieth century, known for her intimate portraits of women and children, as well as her remarkable self-portraits. This small work from 1903 depicts a large-eyed kitten, looking at the viewer head-on, letting them into its interior world the same way the human figures in her paintings do. Striking for its unusual framing, the canvas is also the portrait of a relationship between a cat and a child, with the head and face of the child missing from the composition. The child, who is probably a girl due to her red dress, appears only through her arm. Her small, closed fist holds the cat tightly against her, a shape mirrored by the kitten's two little paws. In her primitivist style and straightforward manner, the artist shows this special bond between the little girl and the little animal, achieving great expressivity and emotion in both subject and form. It does not matter if they have one fist or two paws—they are not so different after all. Even with such a small, simplified space, the artist succeeds in expressing the mysterious and marvelous tenderness between two species, the human and the cat.

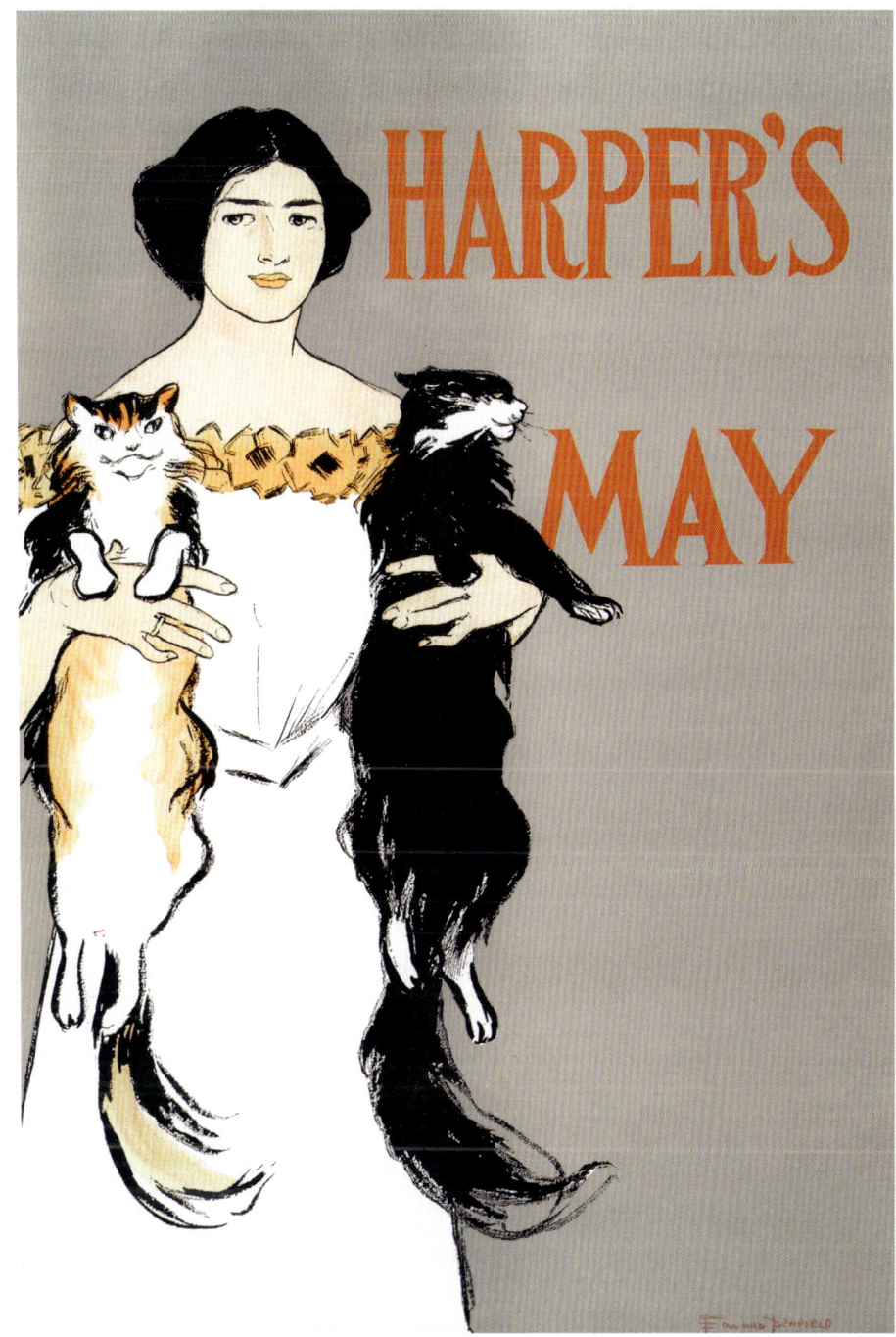

EDWARD PENFIELD

Harper's May, 1896
Lithograph, 17¾ × 11⅞ in. / 45.1 × 30.2 cm
New York Public Library

A fashionable turn-of-the-century girl wearing a white dress trimmed with flowers holds an Angora cat in each arm in this poster advertising the May 1896 edition of *Harper's Magazine*. It is the work of Edward Penfield (1866–1925), considered one of the most influential American poster artists of all time. Penfield originally joined the publishing house Harper and Brothers as a staff artist and editor before being promoted to artistic director in 1893, when he created his first lithograph for its monthly general-interest title, *Harper's Magazine*. It was so successful that he began to design the posters that would advertise every issue of the magazine for the next seven years. This May iteration is notable for its informality and simplicity, making it one of the most popular of all his posters. Penfield had myriad influences, including the French Art Nouveau artists Henri de Toulouse-Lautrec and Théophile Steinlen (famous for his love of cats, see p.23), the *ukiyo-e* woodblock prints of Japan, and paintings from early Egyptian sarcophagi. These inspirations translated into a style that was notable for its strong shapes pared down to simple, graphic forms that caught the eye of passersby. Maine Angora cats—here, one tortoiseshell and one black and white—originated in Turkey and are known for their silky fur and their long, tapering furry tails. Considered highly intelligent and playful, they were popular in 1890s America and were often given as gifts during the holiday season.

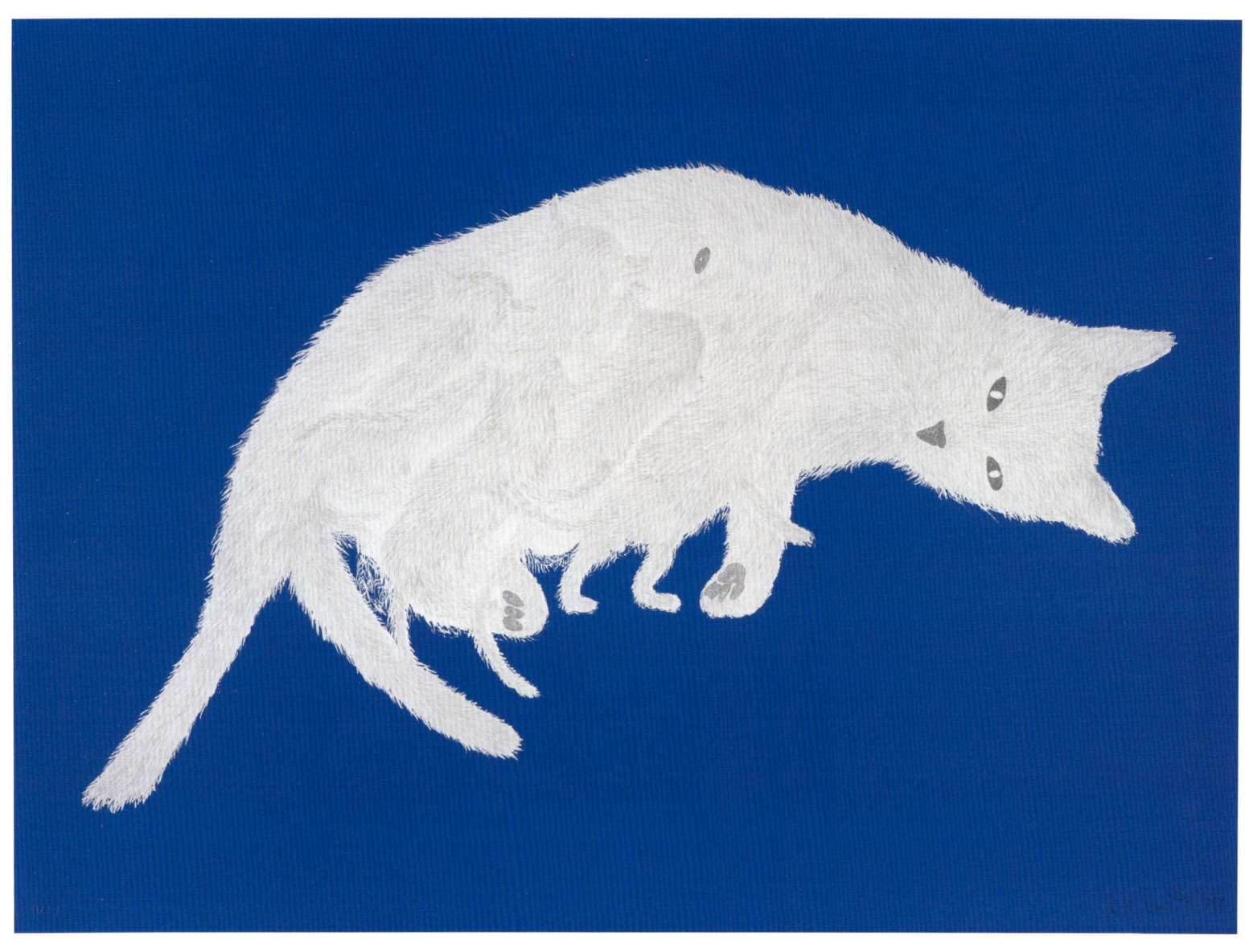

KIKI SMITH

Litter, 1999
Lithograph with hand-applied platinum
leaf, 22⅛ × 29⅞ in. / 56.2 × 75.9 cm
Edition 13 of 15, Printer: Universal Limited Art
Editions, Inc., Publisher: Fireplace Editions
Metropolitan Museum of Art, New York

In her varied, multidecade practice, American artist Kiki Smith (b. 1954) has consistently interrogated the themes of sex, birth, life, and death, exploring their entanglements with not only humanity but the entire animal kingdom. Although Smith's earlier work of the 1980s focused more on the human body, she began to represent animals' bodies in an expansion into nature in the 1990s. *Litter*, a four-color lithograph from this period, depicts a stark white cat lying prostrate against a deeply saturated cobalt background, the fur of the animal rendered in detail as the cat's edges blur into the composition. Upon closer look, the viewer can see evidence of the work's title: five snow white kittens suckling at their mother's teats. Here, the artist captures a maternal moment of both vulnerability and vigilance—the very essence of motherhood itself. Cats have continued to appear in Smith's more contemporary work. *Guardians*, a public art project for ArtLine Milano in 2022, comprised two oversize bronze cat sculptures, inspired by the mystical watchfulness she ascribed to the feral feline colony at the Italian city's Castello Sforzesco. Just as the mother in *Litter* protects her own, Smith's *Guardians* stand watch over their urban landscape. In both feline works, Smith celebrates the sacred relationship between bodies and their environments, whether wild or tame, keeper or kept.

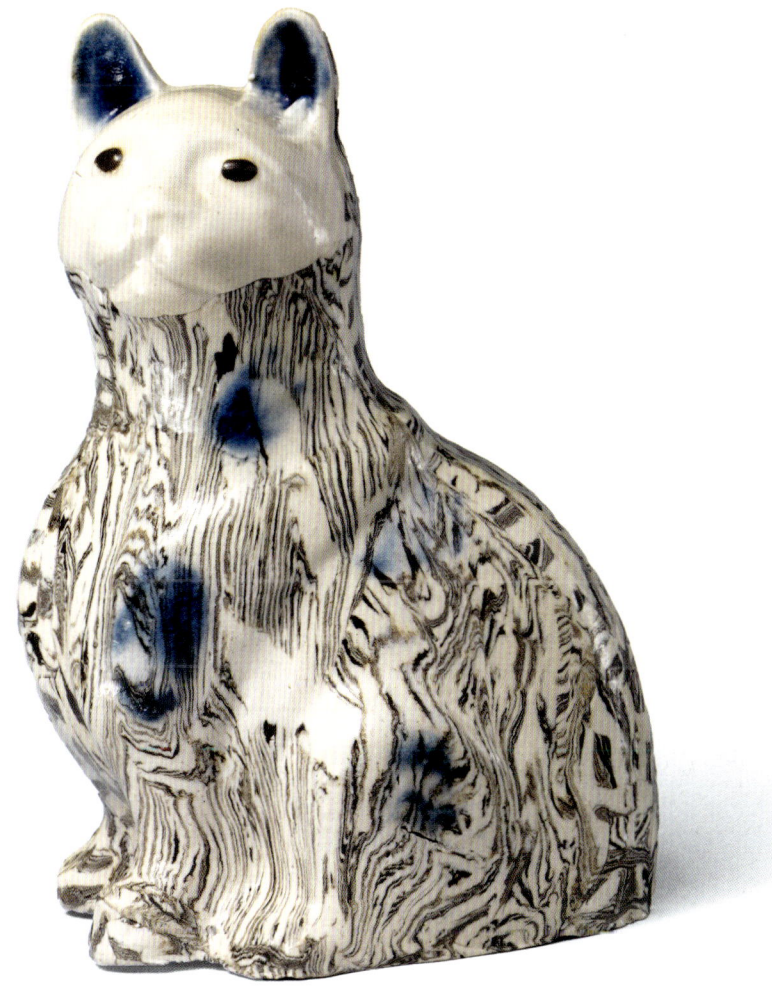

ANONYMOUS

Cat, c. 1745
Salt-glazed stoneware, H. 6⅛ in. / 15.4 cm
Metropolitan Museum of Art, New York

This ceramic cat has an unmistakable air of pride—and with good reason. Made in the mid-eighteenth century by an unknown potter in Staffordshire, England, its blue ears, blue splotches, and tabby body are a testament to the skill of contemporary artisans and the technological advances made in ceramics at that time. Since the early 1600s, Staffordshire had become the center of England's ceramic production, thanks to the ready availability of the materials needed to make pottery: clay, salt, lead for glazing, and coal for firing the kilns. Many small potteries emerged, often family businesses employing everyone, even young children, that produced a wide range of items, including decorative pieces, such as this cat. Intended for larger-scale production, the cat was press-molded with a variegated clay decoration that provides its distinctive tabby markings. It was then glazed, with common salt being added to the kiln; the resulting texture of orange peel gave the finished article the resemblance of agate, a semi-precious stone notable for its vibrant colors. Pottery cats have been popular with cultures in ancient Egypt (see p.29) and China, but this small porcelain cat tapped into a new and growing market in England for ceramic pieces that were affordable to far more people than the wealthy elite who had traditionally bought expensive porcelain. Pottery houses emerged that are still popular today, such as Spode and Wedgwood, and Staffordshire ceramics were exported around the world, particularly during the nineteenth century.

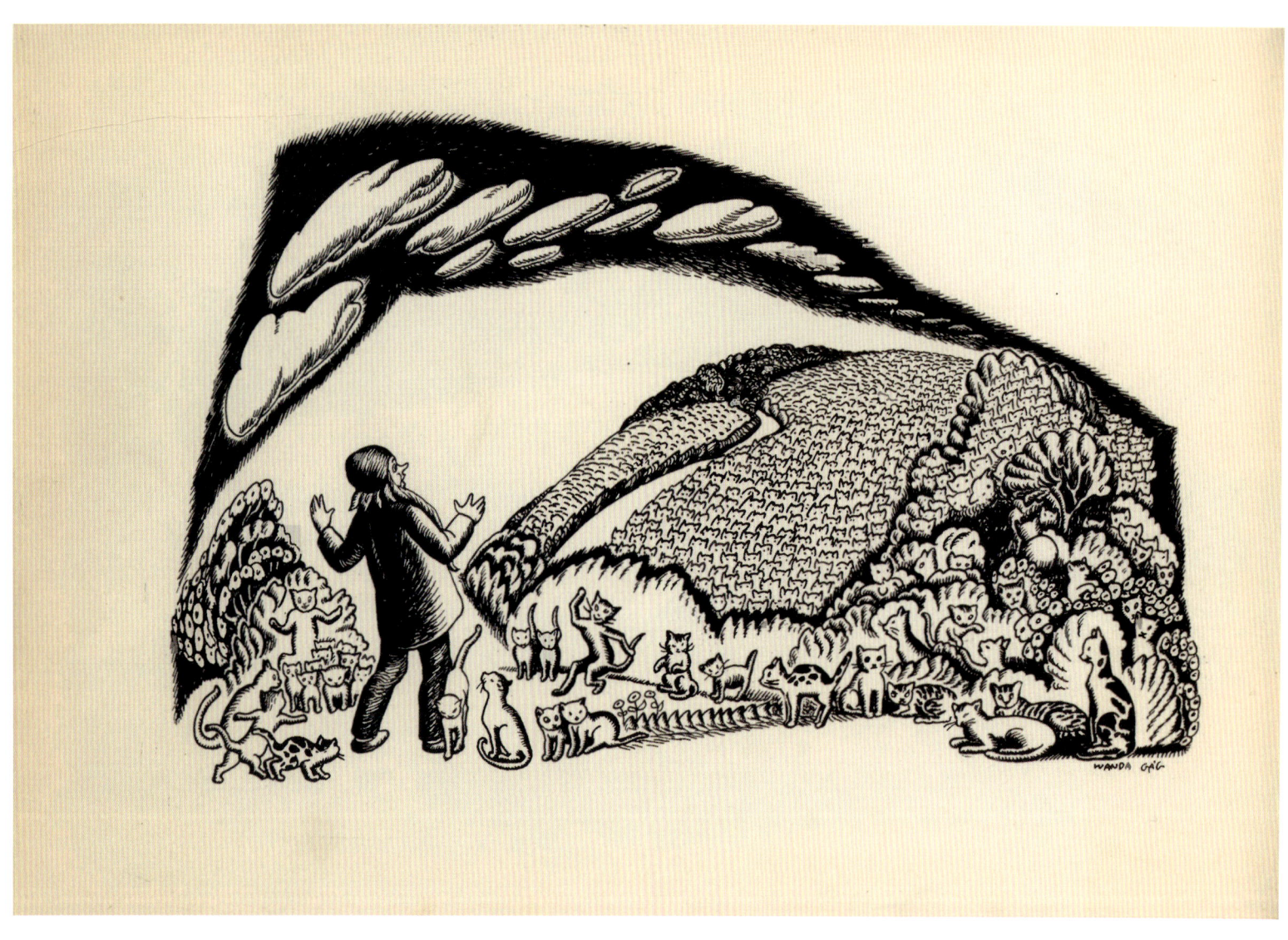

WANDA GÁG

Millions of Cats, 1928
Printed book, 6⅛ × 9¼ in. / 15.5 × 23.4 cm

There is a reason why *Millions of Cats* is the oldest American children's picture book still in print. Its lilting prose and delightful, offbeat illustrations are as fresh today as they were a century ago. Written and illustrated by Wanda Gág (1893–1946) and featuring hand-lettering by her brother Howard, the pioneering work is believed to be the first modern children's book to feature a double-page illustration and is also the first picture book to win a Newbery Honor for excellence in children's writing. It tells the story of a lonely elderly couple who decide they need a cat to keep them company. The man goes out in search of a feline companion and runs into a slight hiccup. He has not found one cat but "hundreds of cats, thousands of cats, millions and billions and trillions" of them! Unable or unwilling

to choose, the man has the entire coterie follow him home, decimating lake and stream and field as they go. When they arrive at the couple's cottage, the man's wife is gobsmacked. Naturally, they cannot take in all of the cats. Perhaps just the prettiest could stay? A terrible fight breaks out among them, until all that is left is one small, scrawny, and homely kitten, cowering in the bushes. Whether a fable about beauty being in the eye of the beholder or a commentary on the dog-eat-dog (or in this case, cat-eat-cat) nature of modern society, the book is an enduring classic beloved by generations of young readers.

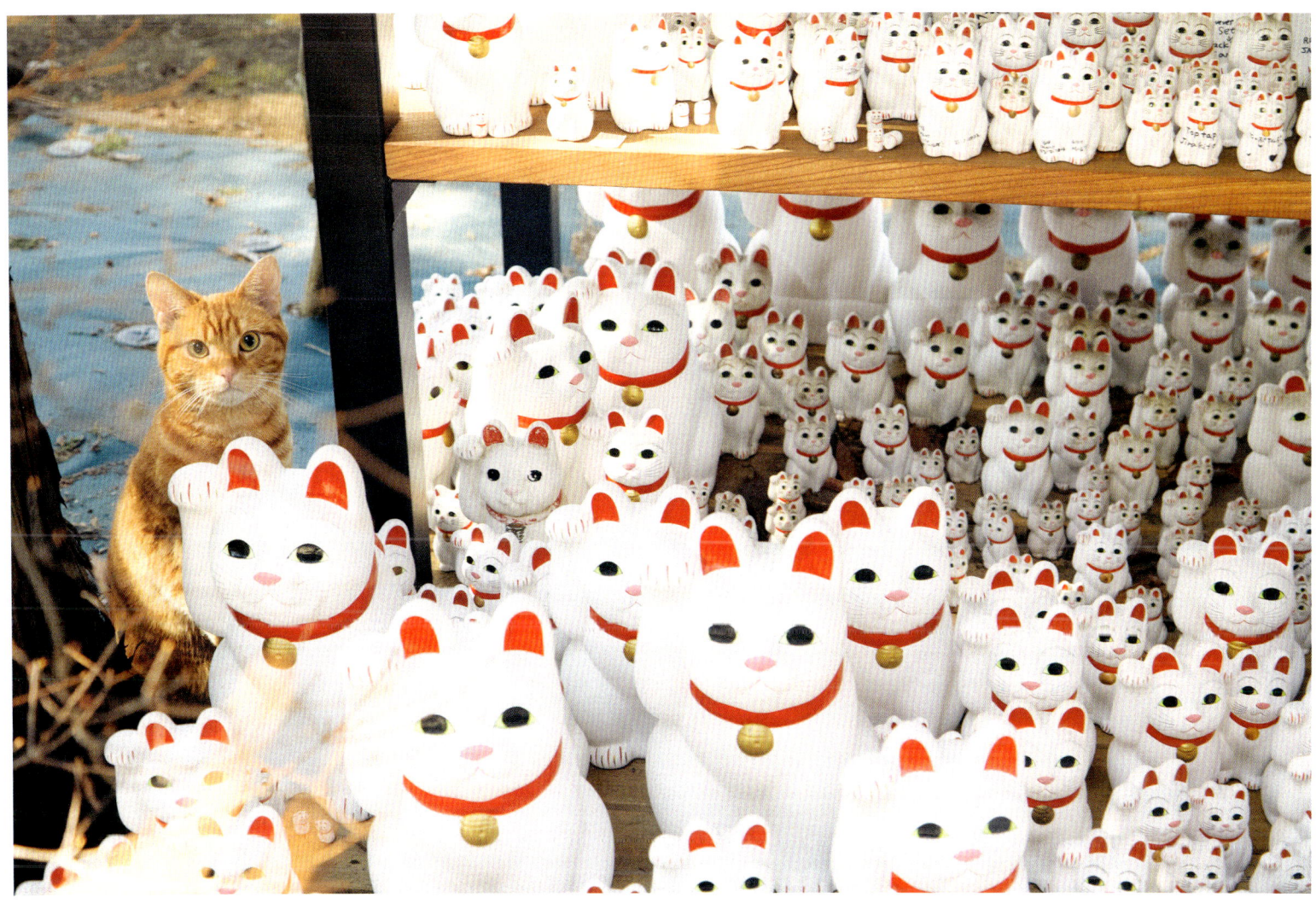

KYOKO HAMADA

Ceramic Maneki-Neko at Gotokuji Temple, 2023
Photograph, dimensions variable

An inquisitive ginger tomcat surveys the hundreds of red-and-white *maneki-neko* (beckoning cat) figurines at Tokyo's Gotokuji Temple, which is regarded as the birthplace of this iconic symbol of good fortune, here captured in abundance by Japanese American photographer Kyoko Hamada (b. 1973). The feline talismans typically depict a calico Japanese Bobtail with a raised paw—some even have moving mechanical paws—and are displayed in stores, restaurants, hotels, and other businesses throughout Japan. Many mistakenly believe that the *maneki-neko* is waving or even washing its face, but it is actually beckoning people toward it. According to one legend, the origin of the figurine dates to the seventeenth century, when a poor monk is said to have resided at the crumbling Gotokuji Temple with his pet cat. A high-ranking samurai was passing by when a large storm began to rage. While sheltering under a nearby tree, the samurai spotted the temple cat, which seemed to be motioning for him to come into the building. As he entered, the tree was suddenly destroyed by lightning. Grateful to the cat for saving his life, the samurai paid for the building's renovation, and, after his death, a small shrine was erected, which mourners decorated with cat-shaped dolls. Hamada took this photograph for a piece in *The New York Times Style Magazine* entitled "Why Do Cats Hold Such Mythic Power in Japan?" As Hamada's whimsical and informative image shows, visitors to Gotokuji continue to leave beckoning cats at the shrine, believing that their gifts will bring them protection and prosperity.

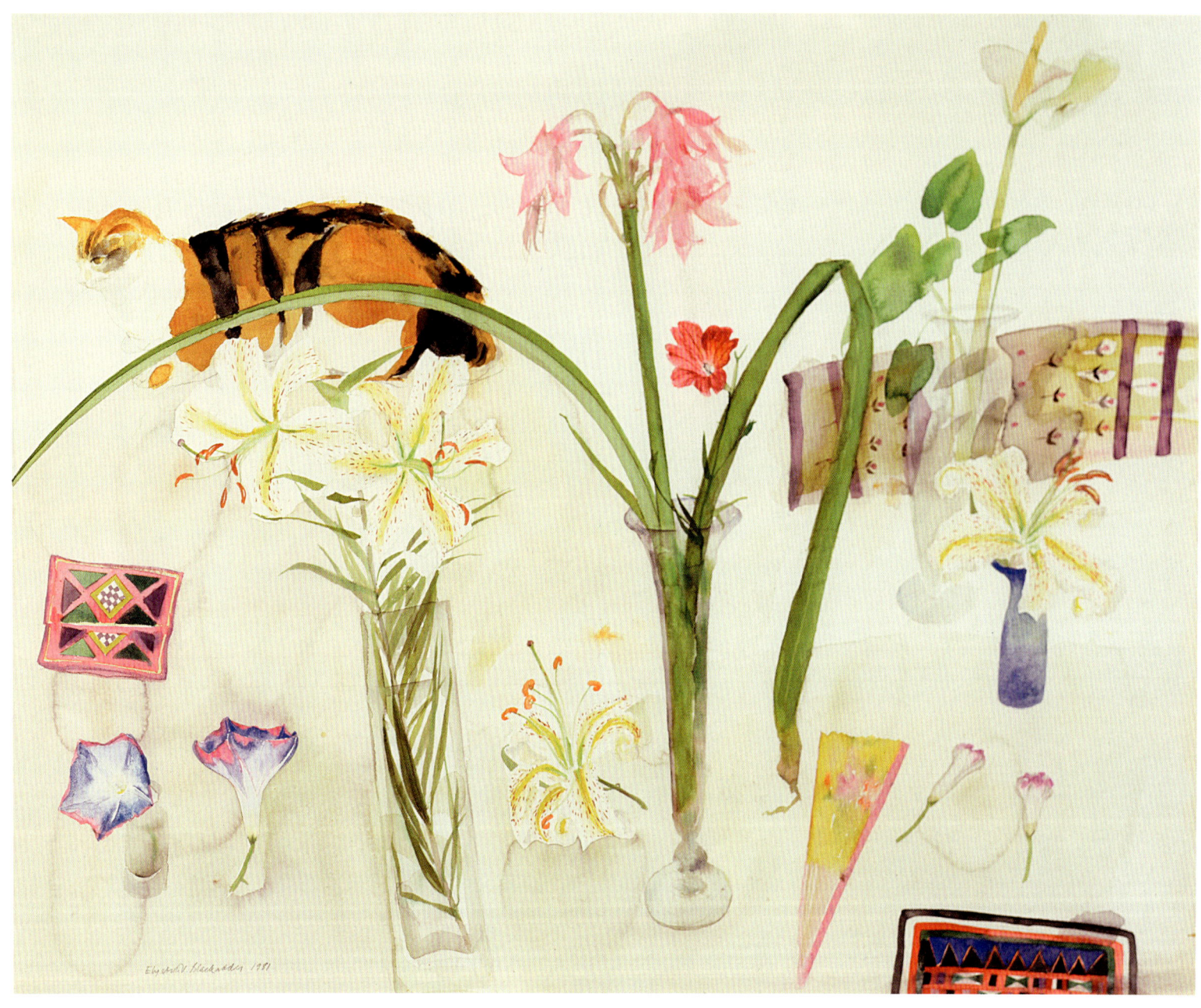

ELIZABETH BLACKADDER

Cat and Flowers, 1981
Watercolor, 30 × 37¼ in. / 76.2 × 95.8 cm
Private collection

Over a long career, Scottish artist Elizabeth Blackadder (1931–2021) repeatedly returned to painting flowers and cats almost by accident: they were, as she said, "just things in the house." The comfortable feline here is surrounded by a sea of cut flowers that includes lilies and morning glories in a variety of vases and arrangements. Appearing to float above the floral explosion, the cat is clearly at home, luxuriating in the peace and quiet. Blackadder painted her pets in many situations— asleep, with flowers, and lying on her rugs—as she did with the animals she saw on the streets of Rome, Venice, and Siena when traveling through Italy. As elusive as her cats, Blackadder rarely talked about her work, and her still lifes of plants and interiors, as well as her quiet portraits and landscapes, remained seemingly conventional at the end of the twentieth century, a period when confessional painting and the shock tactics of creatives like the Young British Artists were all the rage. However, on closer examination, her work has its own revolutionary style. The arrangement of flowers with the healthy cat is positioned against a flattened background and there is no single subject; the entire composition is the subject matter. Greatly influenced by Japanese culture and aesthetics, Blackadder believed the negative spaces between objects were as vital as the objects themselves. Her unique approach led her to become the first woman artist to belong to both the Royal Academy of Arts in England and the Royal Scottish Academy.

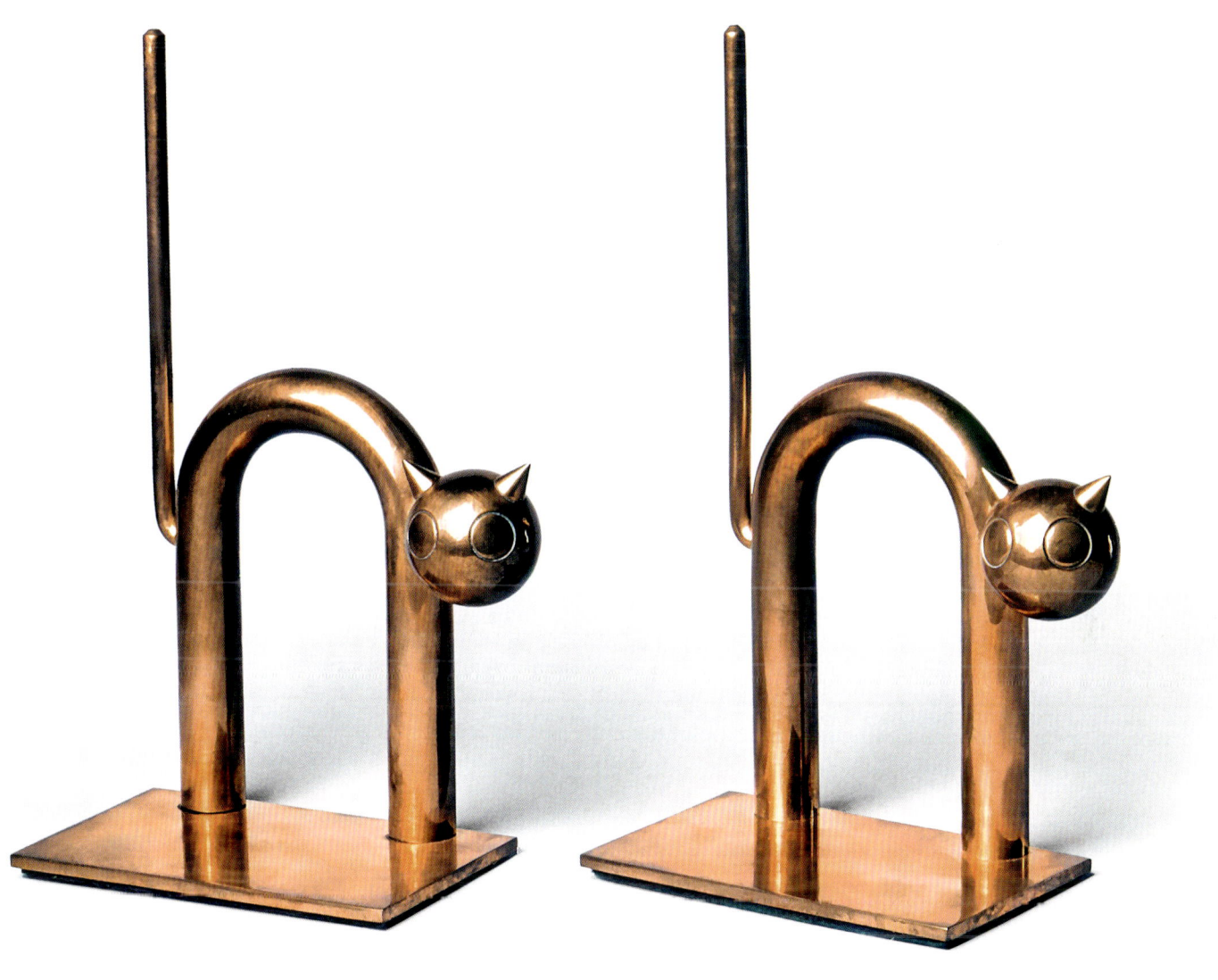

WALTER VON NESSEN

Cat Bookends, 1930–35
Copper-plated alloy, each 7⅜ × 4½ × 2½ in. /
18.7 × 11.4 × 6.4 cm
Brooklyn Museum

These two shiny scaredy-cats are more than just beautifully designed objects; they are a pair of bookends, with ramrod-straight tails and pointy ears that could keep together even the heftiest of tomes. The sleek yet evocative shapes of this Art Deco twosome prove that even in the twenty-first century the axiom of mid-century modernist design still rings true: interesting form can follow function. Created by German American designer Walter von Nessen (1889–1943) in the early 1930s, these copper-plated cats are a unique unlit offering from the craftsman who may be better known for revolutionizing lighting design. After immigrating to the United States in the early 1920s, von Nessen set up his own studio, Nessen Lighting, in 1927, at a time when the idea of illuminating spaces both practically and stylishly was still on the cutting edge. His streamline Art Deco and metallic Machine Age table, floor, and wall lamps changed the look and process of interior design, bringing modernist ideas of form into the practical realm of industrial craft. In 1927, von Nessen introduced his revolutionary swing arm lamp, which is still in production today, and fast became the preeminent lighting designer to the day's leading architects, including Eliel Saarinen. Partnering with storied manufacturers such as the Chase Brass & Copper Company, he extended his reach beyond lighting, applying his approach to an extensive range of product designs, such as these glamorous bookends, which appeal to the design aficionado, bookworm, and cat person alike.

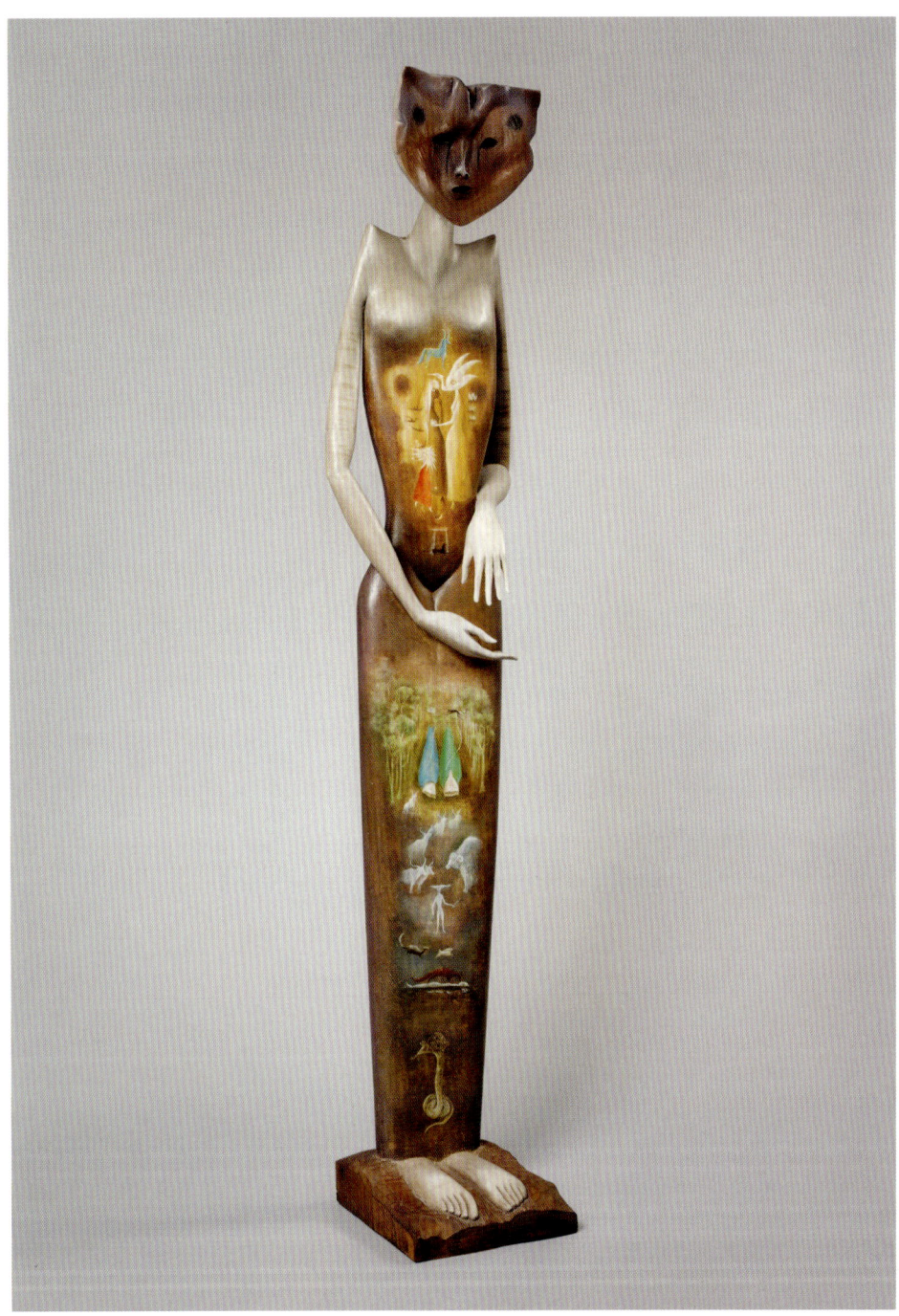

LEONORA CARRINGTON

La Grande Dame (The Cat Woman), 1951
Oil on wood, H. 79½ in. / 201.9 cm
Private collection

La Grande Dame is a towering, totemlike painted sculpture by British Surrealist Leonora Carrington (1917–2011), created almost a decade after she had emigrated to Mexico in 1942, fleeing the war in Europe. Made in collaboration with artist and woodworker José Horna, the work demonstrates Carrington's fascination with the occult, as well as her depiction of animals and fantastic beings in constant metamorphosis. As both of its titles suggest, this figure has a woman's body and a cat's head, inspired by ancient Egyptian devotional statues to the goddess Bastet (see p.29). But this woman is a strange cat whose head also resembles a butterfly or a stingray. Highly syncretic, Carrington's beings are often hybrid and undefinable, taken from mythologies as diverse as Celtic, Aztec, and Egyptian. This creature is also

present in *Samhain*, a painting from the same year, named for the Celtic festival of the dead. During Samhain, time is frozen so otherworldly spirits can wander the earth while humans explore the alternate realm. This hand-painted sculpture is adorned with several figures that signify the magical moment of reunion between worlds, representing the Celtic "white goddess," or the mistress of animals, forests, and fresh water, shown here as a white cow, bird-headed woman, and white wolf-headed female figure. For Carrington, this woman, both cat and not, encompassed all creatures, a "goddess gleaming with all the colors of the rainbow, and full of little windows with faces that looked out and sang the song of every Being living and dead."

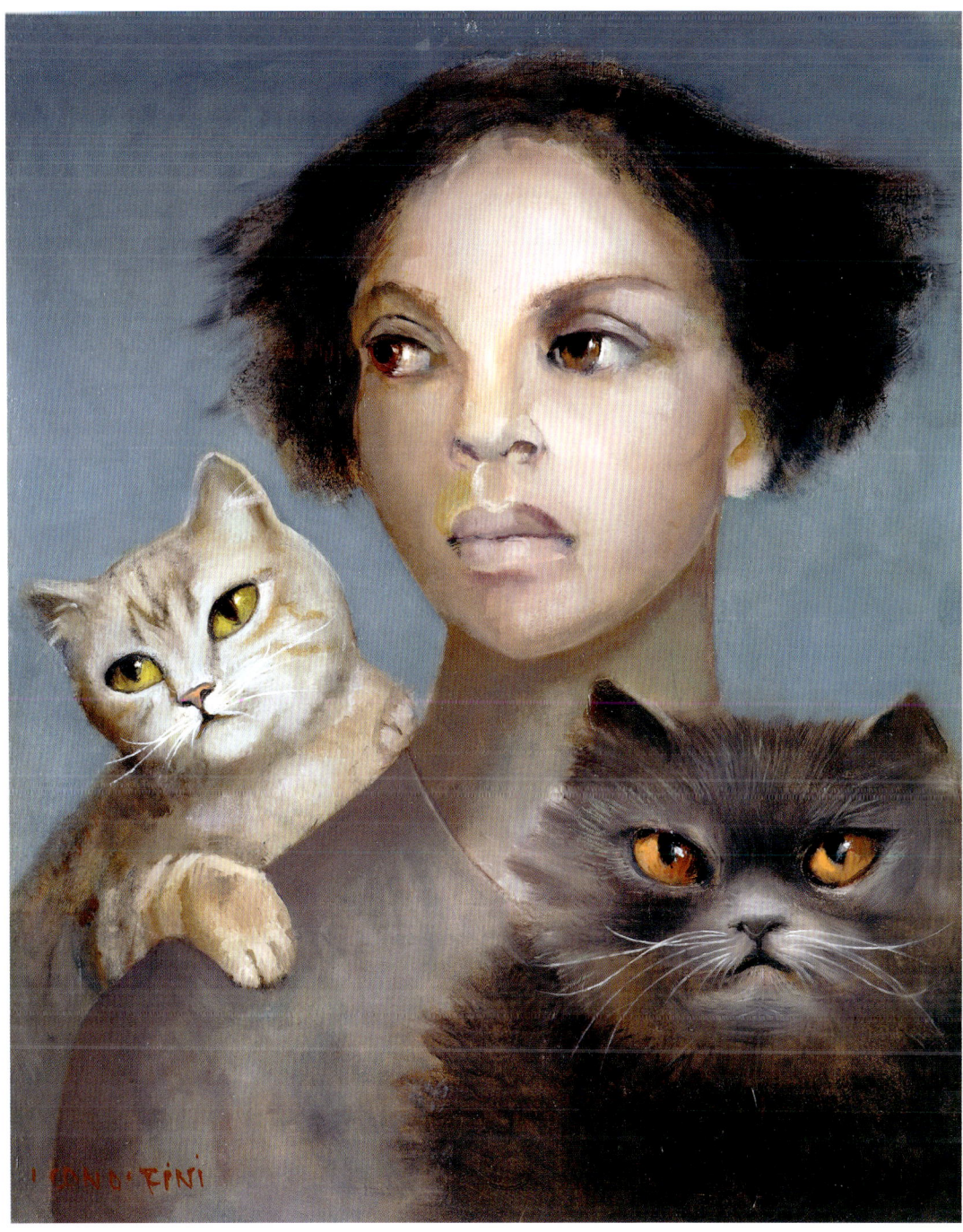

LEONOR FINI

Self-Portrait with Cats, date unknown
Oil on canvas, 16⅛ × 13 in. / 41 × 33 cm
Private collection

In this feline-filled self-portrait, Argentinian-born French artist Leonor Fini (1907–1996) expressed her passion for cats by positioning them as if they were her human children and this a family still life. A self-taught artist, illustrator, and theatrical designer, Fini was a close friend of the Surrealists, although her fiercely independent spirit and feminist principles kept her from joining the predominantly male movement. Fascinated by cats' sensuality, mystery, and the fact that they dream, Fini made the animals a recurring motif in her art, whether rendered in an impressionistic style using ink wash, humorously cartoonish line drawings, or realist depictions as here. In 1948 she even cast felines in a ballet, *Les Demoiselles de la nuit* (*The Ladies of the Evening*), and throughout her career she devoted numerous books for adults and children to her favorite animal. Fini believed cats were perfect creatures whose large eyes and small noses gave them more pleasing proportions than lions and tigers, although she did feature big cats in an arresting series of images that depict a female sphinx, a mythical creature that combines the head of a human with the body of a lion and the wings of an eagle. Here, Fini emphasizes the preciousness of these cats to her conception of self by imagining them anthropomorphically. As if they were her own children, the orange tabby rests a delicate paw on her shoulder, while its fuzzy gray sibling stares straight out from the canvas, confronting the viewer with intelligent amber eyes.

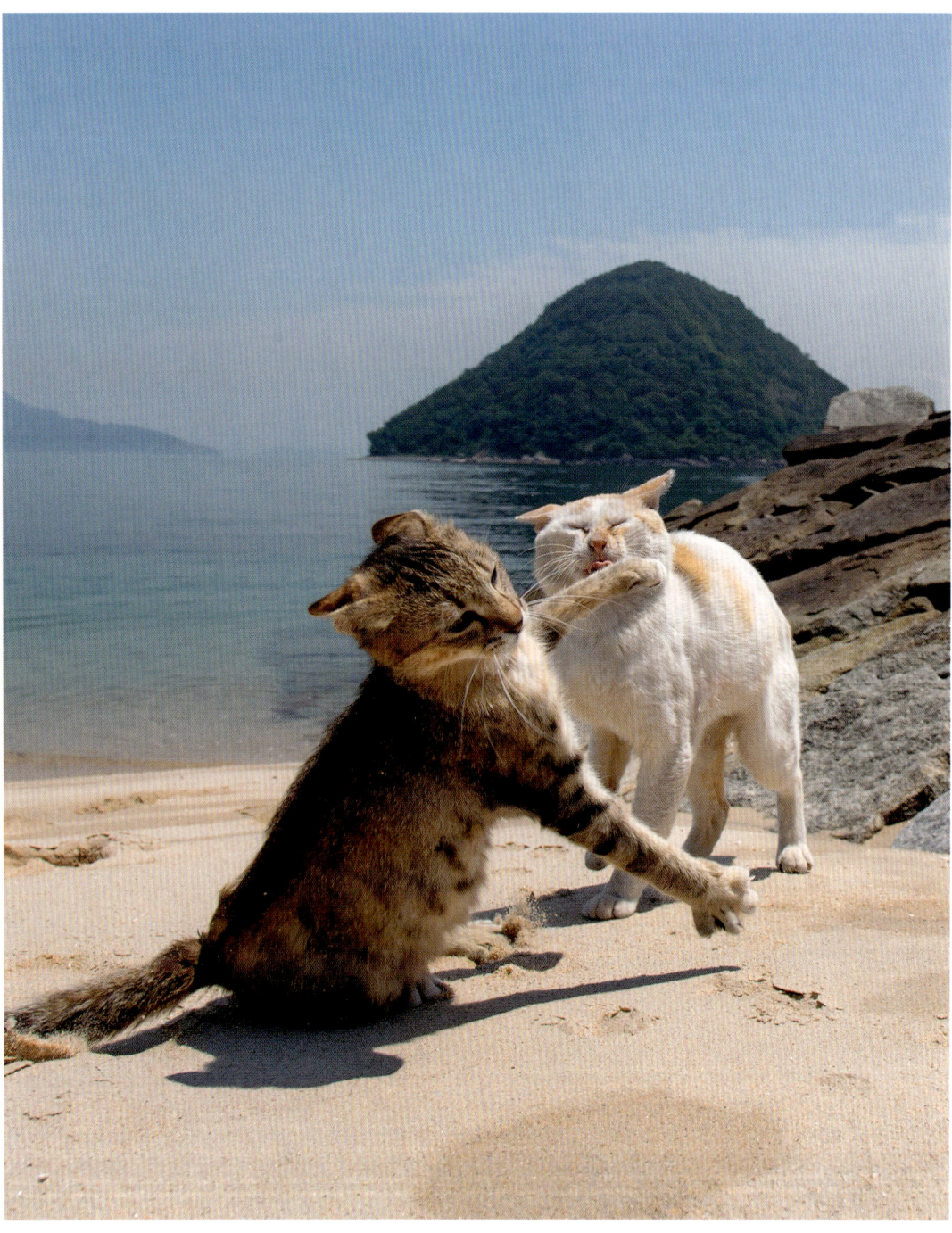

MASAYUKI OKI

Left Hook, 2017
Photograph, dimensions variable

On an idyllic beach on Sanagi island, a young female cat takes a swipe at a male during mating season. With her claws extended, the aggressor tries to stay balanced while her foe screws up his face, comically poking out his tongue. This dynamic photograph is from the book *Hisshi sugiru neko* (2017) by Japanese photographer Masayuki Oki (b. 1978), which is filled with candid portraits of Japan's street cats engaged in playful activities, mischievous moments, and humorous predicaments. A bestseller in Japan, the book's title literally translates to "Desperate Cats." The Japanese archipelago consists of more than fourteen thousand islands, including several like Sanagi that are known for their large, unchecked populations of feral cats. These *nekojima*, or "cat islands," are the result of cats having been introduced by the fishing industry in the early twentieth century to control rodents, although today their presence has turned some islands into tourist attractions, with Aoshima being the best-known. The antics of feral felines on these islands are a continual source of fascination and entertainment for Oki, who also records strays on the streets of Tokyo and other large cities. Despite being self-taught, he has developed an uncanny knack for capturing his subjects at opportune moments, revealing their individual personalities. But Oki's project is about more than securing a cute or humorous shot; he uses his lens to promote an appreciation for these resilient creatures, sharing their untold stories with the world.

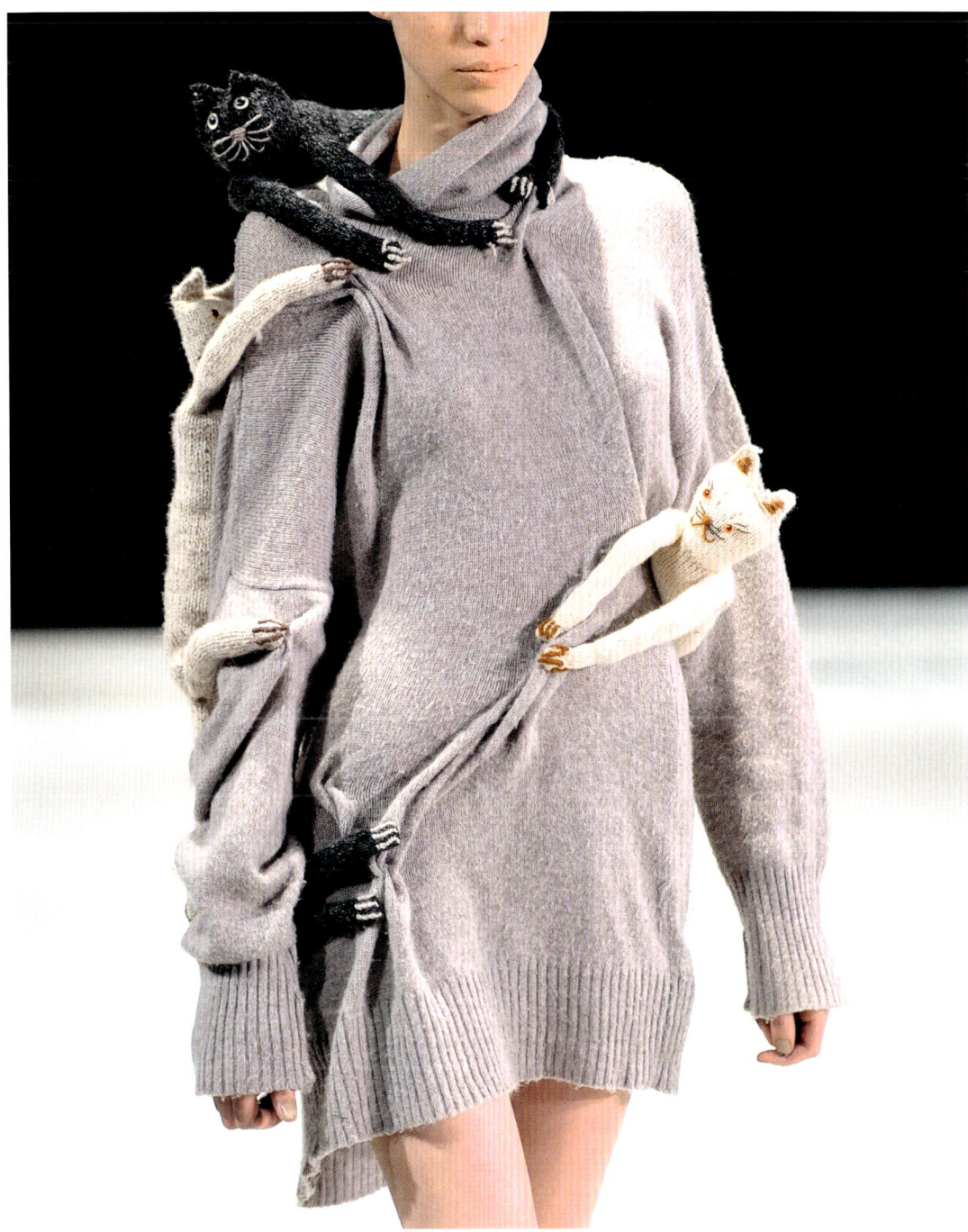

MIGUEL ADROVER

Cat Lady Sweater, from *Out of My Mind*, 2012
Knitted sweater

A model traipses down the runway, her otherwise minimal gray sweater besieged by clawing sock puppet–inspired cats. This eccentric garment formed part of the Autumn/Winter 2012 Ready-to-Wear collection of Spanish fashion designer Miguel Adrover (b. 1965). A self-taught creative, Adrover moved to London in the early 1980s, where he befriended and collaborated with fellow iconoclast and designer Alexander McQueen. He presented the first collection of his eponymous line at New York Fashion Week in 1999 to widespread acclaim. Long before sustainability became a fashion buzzword, Adrover held repurposing at the center of his practice. His first show featured a souvenir "I Love NY" T-shirt upcycled with ruffled sleeves, while his second included a dress made from a Burberry trench coat turned inside out and backward, its label and signature plaid on full display, and a coat made from a mattress discarded by British queer icon Quentin Crisp. Provocative, playful, and always experimental, Adrover's designs invariably pushed the envelope. After taking a hiatus from the fashion world, he came back with a fully repurposed collection in 2012, titled *Out of My Mind*, which was lauded by *Vogue* for its aggressive antiestablishment approach. The model seen wearing the Cat Lady Sweater also sported shoes festooned with leather gloves, each one with a middle finger raised in salute. With his collage-like fashions and radically sustainable approach, Adrover has gained new fans in the 2020s, especially of this wild piece of haute *cat*ure.

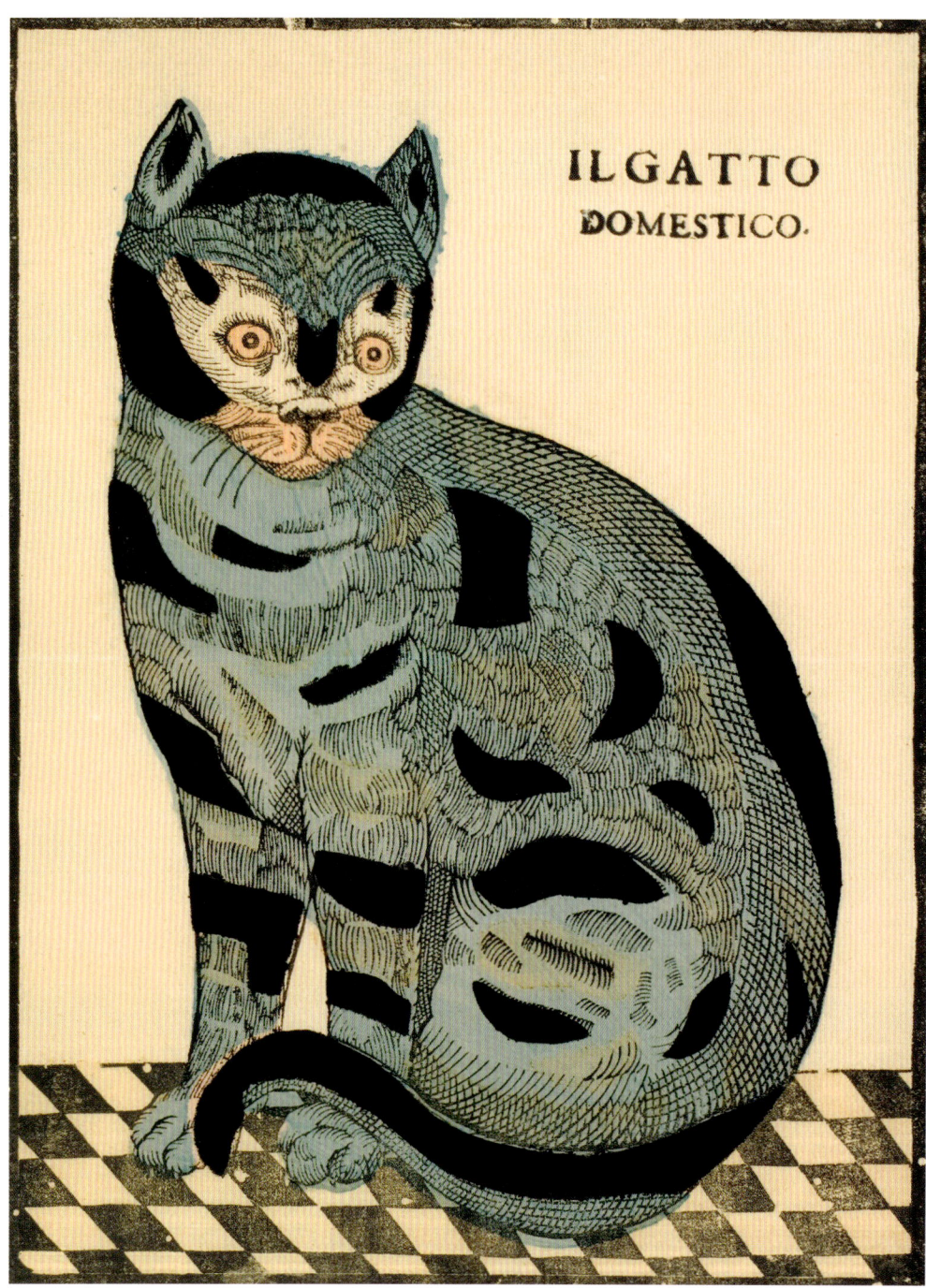

IL GATTO
DOMESTICO.

REMONDINI

Il Gatto Domestico (The House Cat), c. 1800
Stencil-colored woodcut
13⅜ × 9⅞ in. / 34.1 × 25.2 cm
Philadelphia Museum of Art

An unnaturally hued cat sits on a checkerboard floor. This is not a zombie pet, but an early nineteenth-century woodcut published by Remondini, a family of illustrators who made their name through their eponymous publishing house. Established by Giovanni Antonio Remondini in the mid-seventeenth century, the house was located in Bassano del Grappa in northern Italy, which was then under Venetian rule. Finding favor with the Venetian state, the Remondini family was able to stave off competitors at a time when printed works were seeing widespread popularity. By the next century, through the efforts of a massive corps of traveling salesmen, their publishing empire stretched across Europe and even to Asia and the American colonies, cementing their status as one of the most successful printers of

the day. At its height, the firm had eighteen movable type presses, twenty-four chalcographic (intaglio) presses, and more than a thousand workers on staff. Remondini specialized in prayer books, playing cards, illustrated atlases, and everyday prints, such as the domestic cat in this image. This feline was part of a series of prints featuring household pets, including different breeds of cats and dogs, each one posing regally on an exquisitely tiled floor. The coloration and contrasts are unusual, and the work's pastiche of graphic techniques demonstrates the deft hand of the engraver. Alas, with the fall of the Venetian empire went Remondini, but its legacy lives on in its surviving work, a visual archive of vernacular Italian iconography.

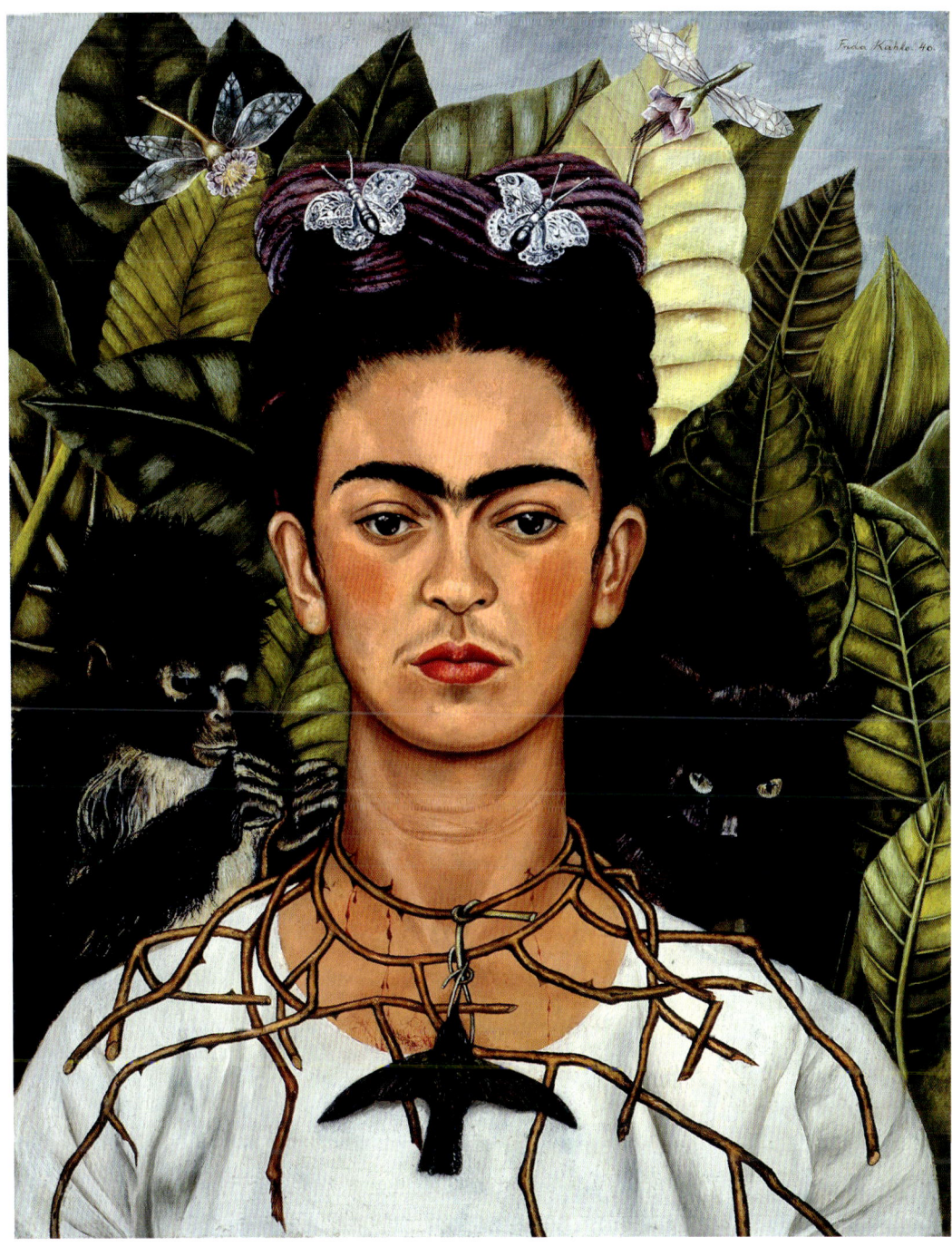

FRIDA KAHLO

Self-Portrait with Thorn Necklace and Hummingbird, 1940
Oil on canvas, 24¾ × 18⅞ in. / 62.6 × 47.9 cm
Harry Ransom Center, University of Texas at Austin

This artwork is one of fifty-five self-portraits painted by Mexican artist Frida Kahlo (1907–1954) during her lifetime. In front of verdant jungle foliage, Kahlo faces the viewer head on, weathering pain patiently. Her intricate thorn necklace, featuring a lifeless hummingbird pendant, digs into her skin, and her shoulders are flanked by two mischievous creatures, a spider monkey and a black cat. Kahlo used the self-portrait to explore her interior life, repeatedly depicting herself to reclaim her body from the patriarchal tradition of painting and showcase her identification with the indigenous culture of pre-Hispanic Mexico. She loved animals and often featured her pets, including parrots, spider monkeys, and cats, in her works. Painted after her divorce from and remarriage to fellow artist Diego Rivera, as well as the end of her affair with photographer Nickolas Muray, this small canvas overflows with symbolism. Black cats were classically associated with bad luck, but also with magic, and in Mexican folklore dead hummingbirds were good-luck charms for love. Likely a stand-in for Rivera himself, the spider monkey pulls on the thorns to inflict more pain. The necklace conjures Christ's crown of thorns, with Kahlo framing herself as a martyr, and the butterflies and surreal dragonflies above her head representing her resurrection in a new period of love. By using powerful iconography from her life, indigenous Mexican culture, and nature, Kahlo visualizes personal resilience while situating herself in a larger tradition of rebellion against patriarchal and colonial dominance.

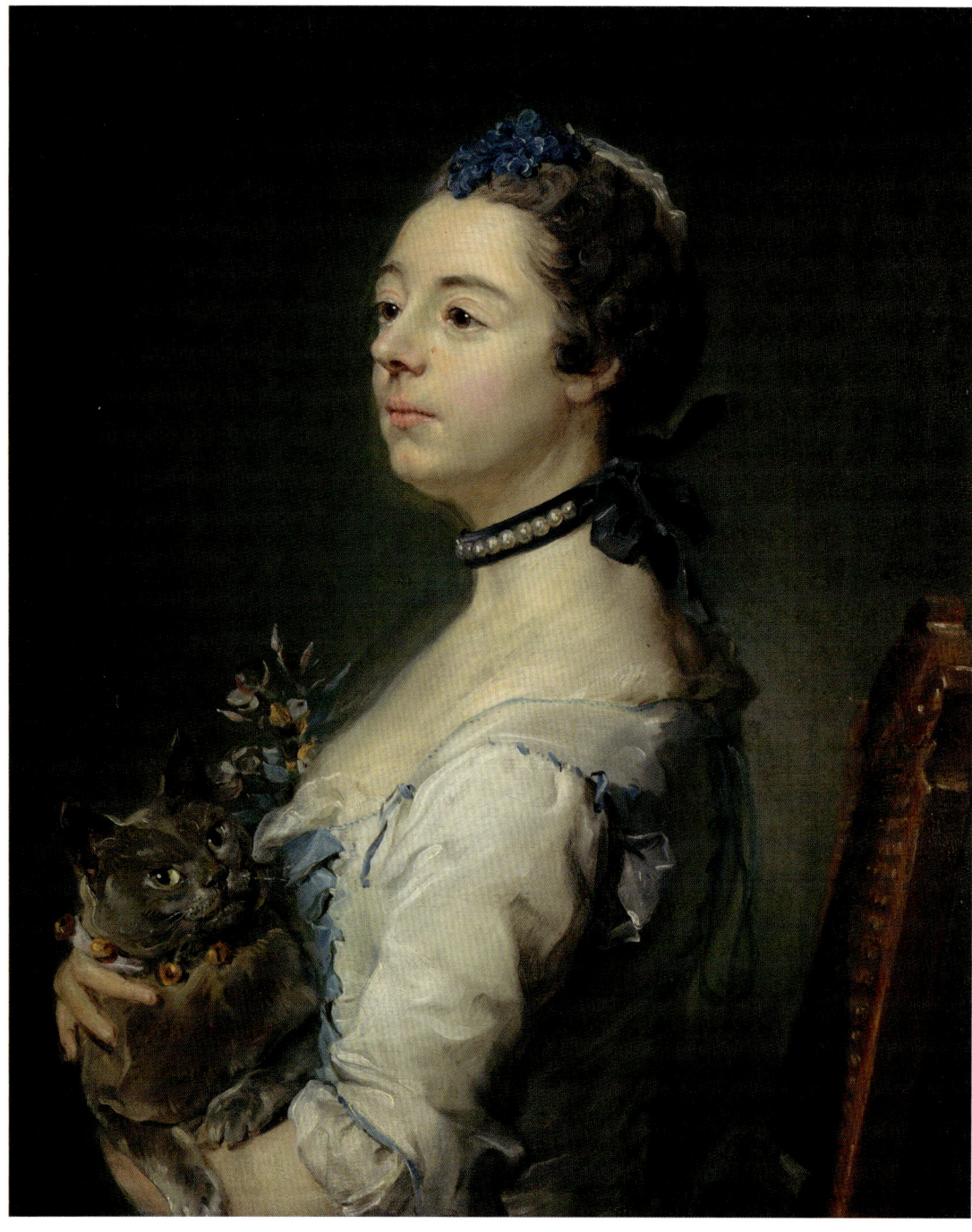

JEAN-BAPTISTE PERRONNEAU

Magdaleine Pinceloup de la Grange, née de Parseval, 1747
Oil on canvas, 25⅝ × 20⅝ in. / 65.1 × 52.4 cm
J. Paul Getty Museum, Los Angeles

Sitting bolt upright in this portrait is the elegantly attired Magdaleine Pinceloup de la Grange, the wife of Charles-François Pinceloup de la Grange, a member of the eighteenth-century French nobility. Magdaleine gazes into the distance, holding on tightly with both hands to the large gray-blue Chartreux cat in her lap, perhaps to prevent it from escaping her grasp. Painted by leading French portrait artist Jean-Baptiste Perronneau (1715–1783), the likeness was one of a pair made at the same time, the other being of Magdaleine's husband, and the commission may have been a celebration of a recent government appointment for Pinceloup. Perronneau often included cats in his feminine portraits to emphasize the sophistication of his sitters. That elegance is underlined by the neck decoration sported by both the lady and her pet: Magdaleine wears a choker studded with pearls while her cat has a matching collar with bells. The Chartreux is one of the most popular breeds of cat in France and has been owned by many distinguished figures, including the poet Charles Baudelaire, also a noted cat lover, and the writer Colette. Such was Colette's devotion to the breed that her novel *The Cat* (1933) featured a love triangle involving a man, his new wife, and his Chartreux. Spoiler alert: the man leaves his wife for the cat. As well as its distinctively colored coat, the Chartreux is celebrated for its personality, which is said to be extremely friendly, more like that of a dog than other cats.

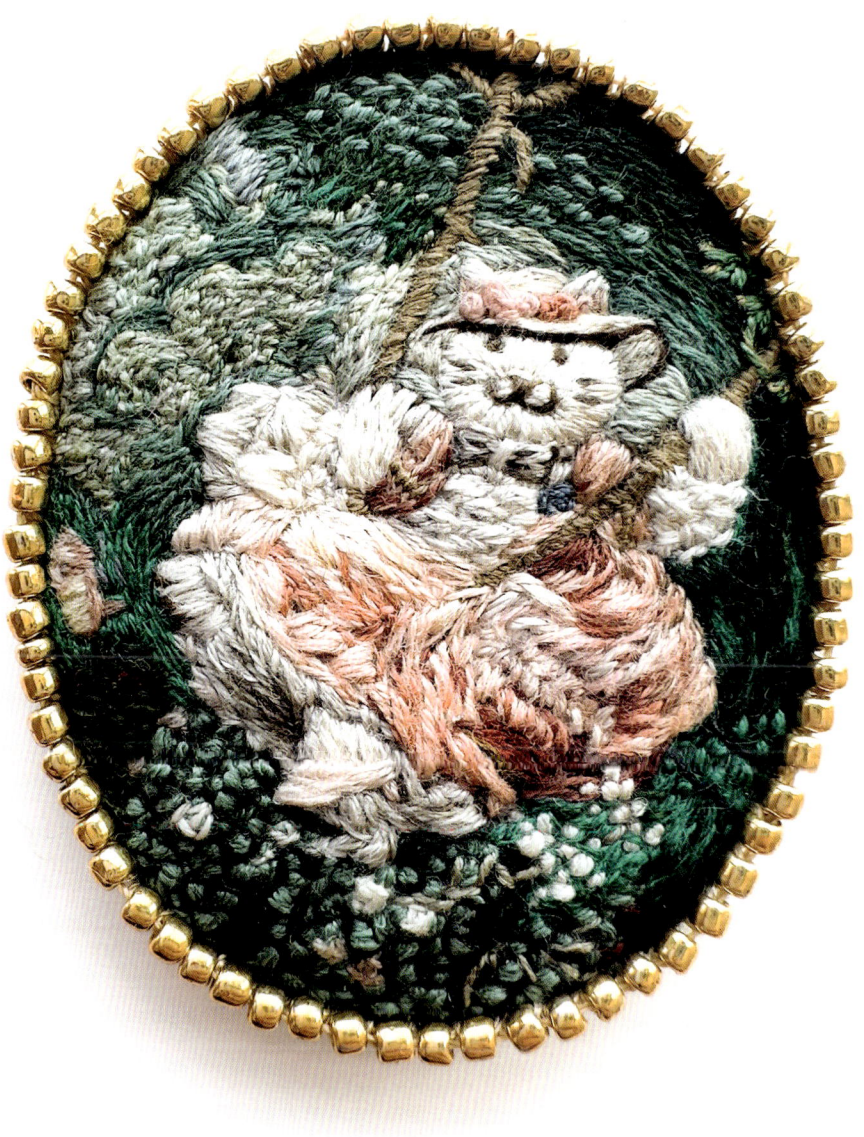

MINAMI

Cat in Jean-Honoré Fragonard's *The Swing*, 2022
Embroidered brooch, 2 × 1¾ in. / 5 × 4.3 cm

The Cat Embroidery Museum began with a question: what if the world's greatest works of art were inhabited by the world's cutest creatures? Japanese embroidery artist and cat lover Minami set out to do just that, re-creating famous works from the canon of art history with felines front and center. Launched in 2021, the Instagram page @cat_embroidery_museum boasts a wide array of artworks in miniature. Picture a silhouetted cat staring into Van Gogh's *Starry Night*. Or a circle of white Persian cats holding paws as if they were in *Dance* by Henri Matisse (see p.90). There are cats emitting Munchian screams, giving *Mona Lisa* smiles, locked in Klimtian kisses, and wearing pearl earrings; one cat even becomes the embodiment of a Hokusai wave. This work, of course, is a reimagining of Jean-Honoré

Fragonard's Rococo masterpiece, *The Swing*, originally painted in 1767. While a white cat stands in for the woman centering the painting, it radiates the same frolicking feelings of decadence as its forebear. There is abundant whimsy in each of Minami's embroidered miniatures, but importantly, there is also a skilled hand at work. The artist, who has been embroidering since the age of fifteen, showcases a wide range of techniques, from traditional Japanese styles, such as *sashiko* and *kogin*, to modern styles that include cross-stitch and freestyle. She even invented one to suit her purr-ticular needs, which she calls the "cat stitch." With more than forty thousand followers, the Cat Embroidery Museum continues to delight ailurophiles around the world.

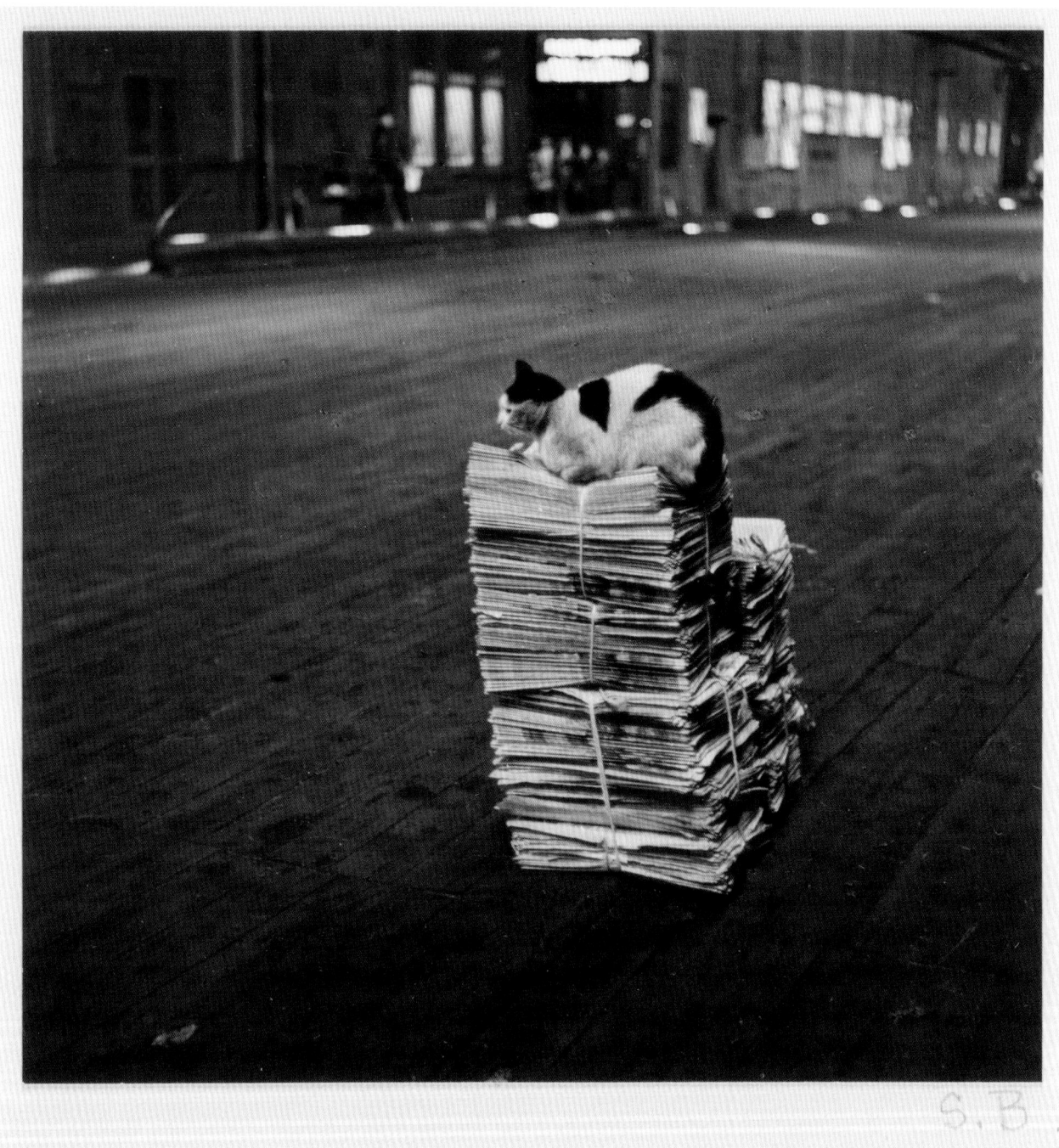

SHIRLEY BURDEN

*The Weehawken Ferry Story [Cat on a stack
of newspapers]*, 1956
Gelatin silver print, 11 × 8½ in. / 27.9 × 21.6 cm
Museum of the City of New York

A stray cat is the only living thing to be seen in this urban scene. In a prime cat move, it has perched itself atop a stack of newspapers that have been left at the deserted Weehawken Ferry Terminal and was captured in this shot by American photographer Shirley Burden (1908–1989). Burden was a descendant of the fabulously wealthy railroad and shipping magnate Cornelius Vanderbilt, the richest man in the United States when he died in 1877. As a child, Burden would ride the 42nd Street Ferry from Manhattan to Weehawken, New Jersey, to board the train, observing later, "This ferry had once brought great crowds of men and women from New York to the races in New Jersey." The ferry began crossing the Hudson River in 1700 and by the time Burden made his photographic essay about the ferry in 1956, it was in decline. It eventually disappeared in 1959 after 259 years of continuous service, during which time New York had grown from a small settlement into one of the world's greatest cities. Burden was known for photographic essays that variously looked at architecture, racial intolerance, and the Catholic Church in the United States. Here, he wanted to capture for posterity the loss of the ferry as cars, tunnels, and bridges became the preferred method of crossing the Hudson. Although the ferry route was reinstated in 1989, the year of his death, the presence of the solitary cat underlines the terminal's abandonment, lending an air of mourning to a bygone era.

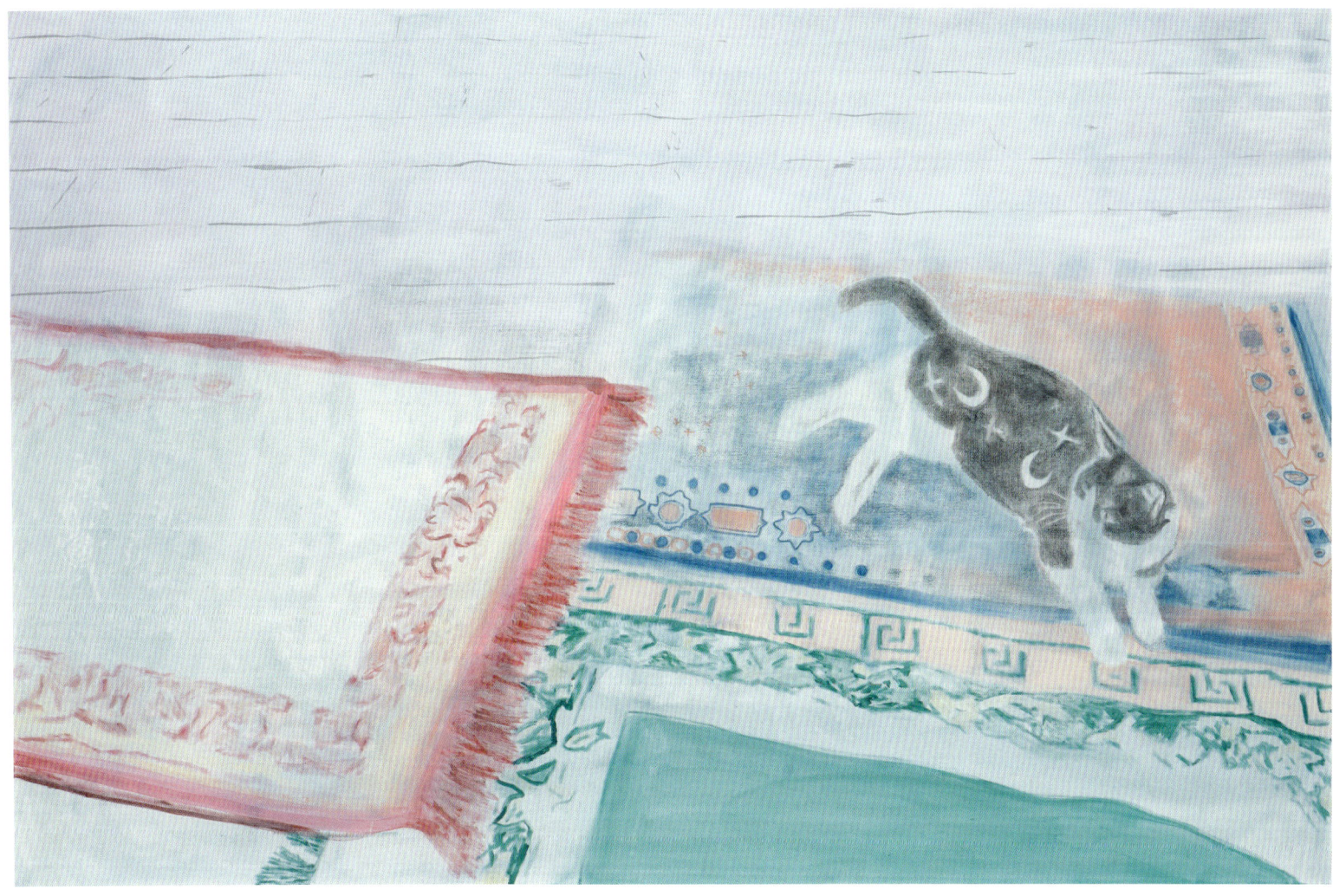

ZEINAB SALEH

The sovereignty of quiet, 2024
Acrylic, chalk, and fixative on linen
74¾ × 114⅛ in. / 190 × 290 cm
Private collection

A black-and-white cat stretches out on a rug—a classic scene. Upon closer examination, one notices the rugs are more than simple textiles, they are prayer mats, and the cat's black fur has a cosmic pattern of white crescent moons and stars. Nairobi-born, London- and Dubai-based artist Zeinab Saleh (b. 1996) paints this serene moment, entitled *The sovereignty of quiet*, with a sense of luminosity. The overlapping textiles are rendered in layers of calm colors, muted icy whites, cold blues, and soft pink edges, that appear infused with light, as do the cat's limbs. The animal's body is drawn in charcoal dust, capturing its softness and providing a contrast with the mats' pale shades. The flexible medium allowed the artist to play with the cat's fur, rubbing out parts of it to create the moons and stars. Saleh is known

for depicting the specificities of her world, especially the textiles from her home, which include bed linens as well as prayer mats, inspired by the richness of everyday spaces. Cats often feature in Saleh's work, because she is drawn to their innate unknowability and the sense of home a cat's presence can provide. The artist does not actually have a pet cat, but she often paints the feline companions of friends and family members, musing, "Every auntie in my family seems to have a cat." Making the personal universal through her calm compositions, Saleh produces a perceptual world to be enjoyed with a patient gaze, much like that of a cat.

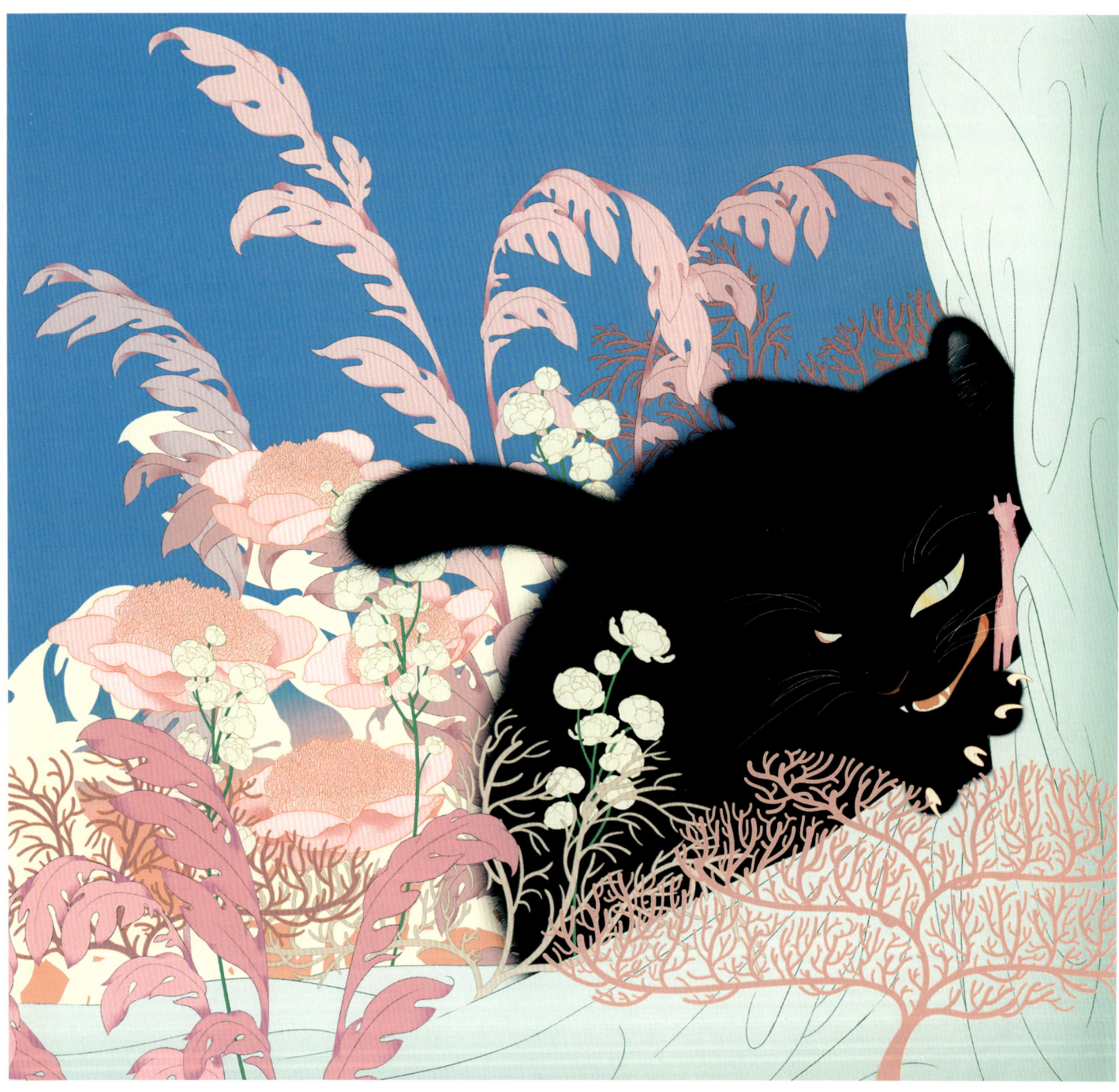

JEE-OOK CHOI

Album artwork for *Earth* by Maurice Fulton, 2020
Digital illustration, dimensions variable

A small, smiling black cat with claws curling hides amid a hallucinatory botanical landscape, clutching a piece of seafoam fabric and inexplicably accompanied by a ridiculously tiny pink giraffe. This strange scene comes from the mind of Korean digital illustrator Jee-ook Choi (b. 1987), who imbues the everyday with a subtle surrealist touch. Choi's fluid, dreamlike compositions transform familiar forms and landscapes into something else entirely, encouraging the viewer to revel in a sense of the uncanny. Her bright acid palette draws from the neon lights of Seoul, where she is based, adding a sense of dynamic movement to her altered scenes of reality. A commercial illustrator, she has more recently applied her psychedelic style to record covers, especially those produced by global dance label Gudu

Records, founded by South Korean DJ, singer, and songwriter Peggy Gou. Choi created this image of a sly, sneering black cat for Gudu Records artist Maurice Fulton's EP *Earth*. Fulton is a house music legend, known for his energetic, fusionist dance repertoire, which makes for a perfect audiovisual match between his sound and Choi's own blended aesthetic. Drawn to the possibilities created when differing images collide, Choi remembered envisioning this cat "always poised to scratch, between soft fabrics and plants" for the album cover while listening to Fulton's music. "Thinking about the sharp edges hidden within the beat," she declared, "I decided to draw [this] cat—something beautiful yet untouchable, small yet fiercely assertive."

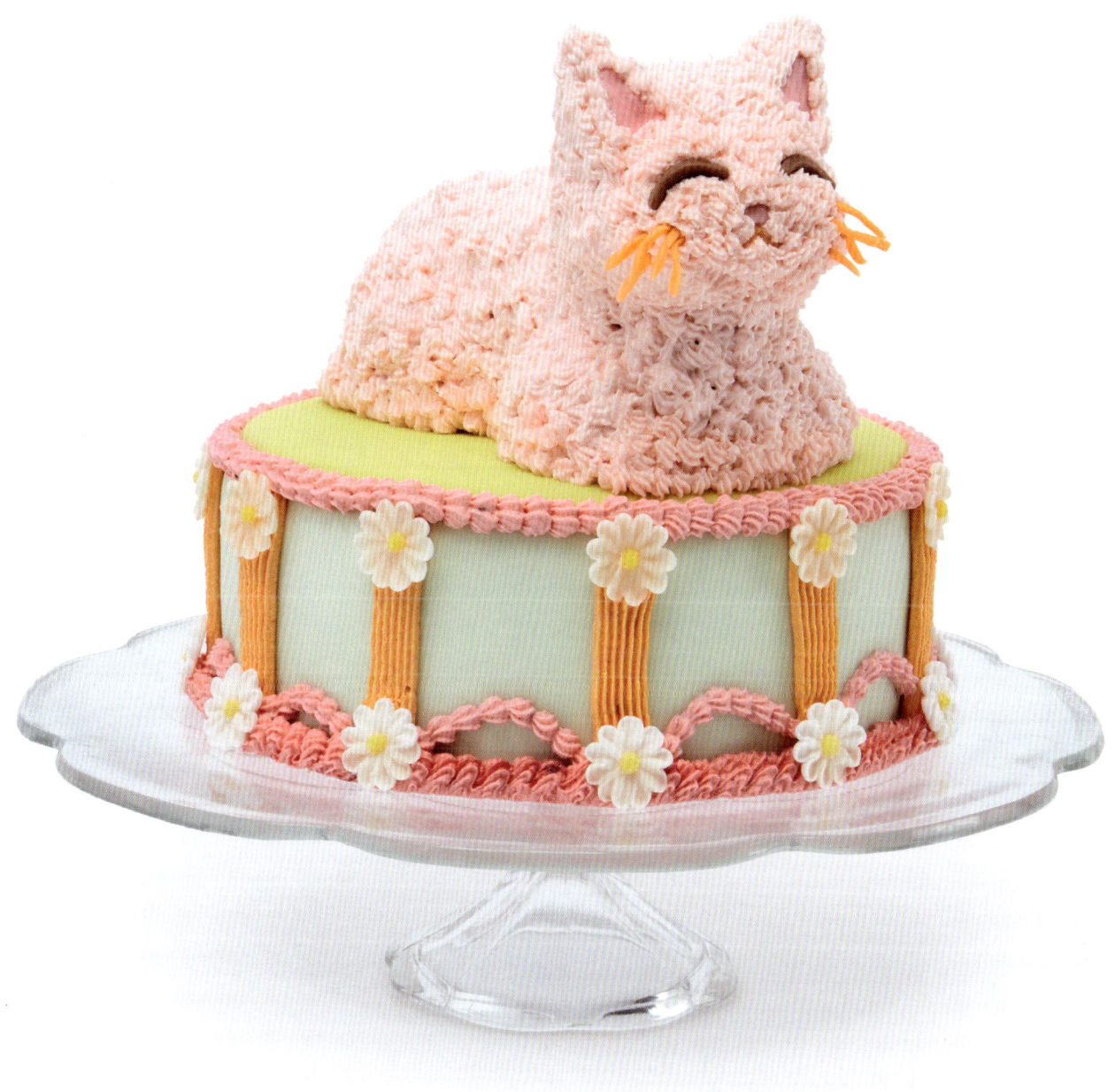

HEBE KONDITORI

Coconut Kitten Cake, 2020
Cake, dimensions variable
Photograph by Luke Stephenson

With its blissfully blinking, crescent moon eyes, pert orange whiskers, and fluffy fur piped out in pink frosting, this edible kitten is the epitome of cuteness. It sits proudly on a festive cake decorated in retro hues of green and orange, ornamented with regularly spaced delicate sugar daisies. Commissioned by the designer streetwear brand Lazy Oaf, it was made by Hebe Konditori, an online cake business started in 2017 by British artist, food stylist, and recipe developer Sarah Hardy (b. 1993), who studied sculpture at Glasgow School of Art and regularly works with well-known London bakeries and brands. Her business is named in honor of Princess Hebe, the mythological daughter of Zeus and Hera whose cup delivered nectar and ambrosia to the gods, and *konditori*, the term for a bakery specializing in sweets, cakes, and pastries used across Scandinavia. She creates stylish, glamorous, and romantic baked goods, with decorations that are rendered in a palette of soft and seductive pastel hues. Their forms are influenced by neoclassical architecture and often feature domes and trompe l'oeil colonnades made of frosting piped to resemble fluted columns. Some are adorned with sugar putti or swans, recalling eighteenth-century splendor, while others are more risqué, such as the hot pink cake in the shape of men's genitalia or the individual fancies wrapped in leopard print frosting. Although it is not Hebe Konditori's main selling point, all the cakes are vegan, ensuring that they are not only delicious but environmentally and animal friendly.

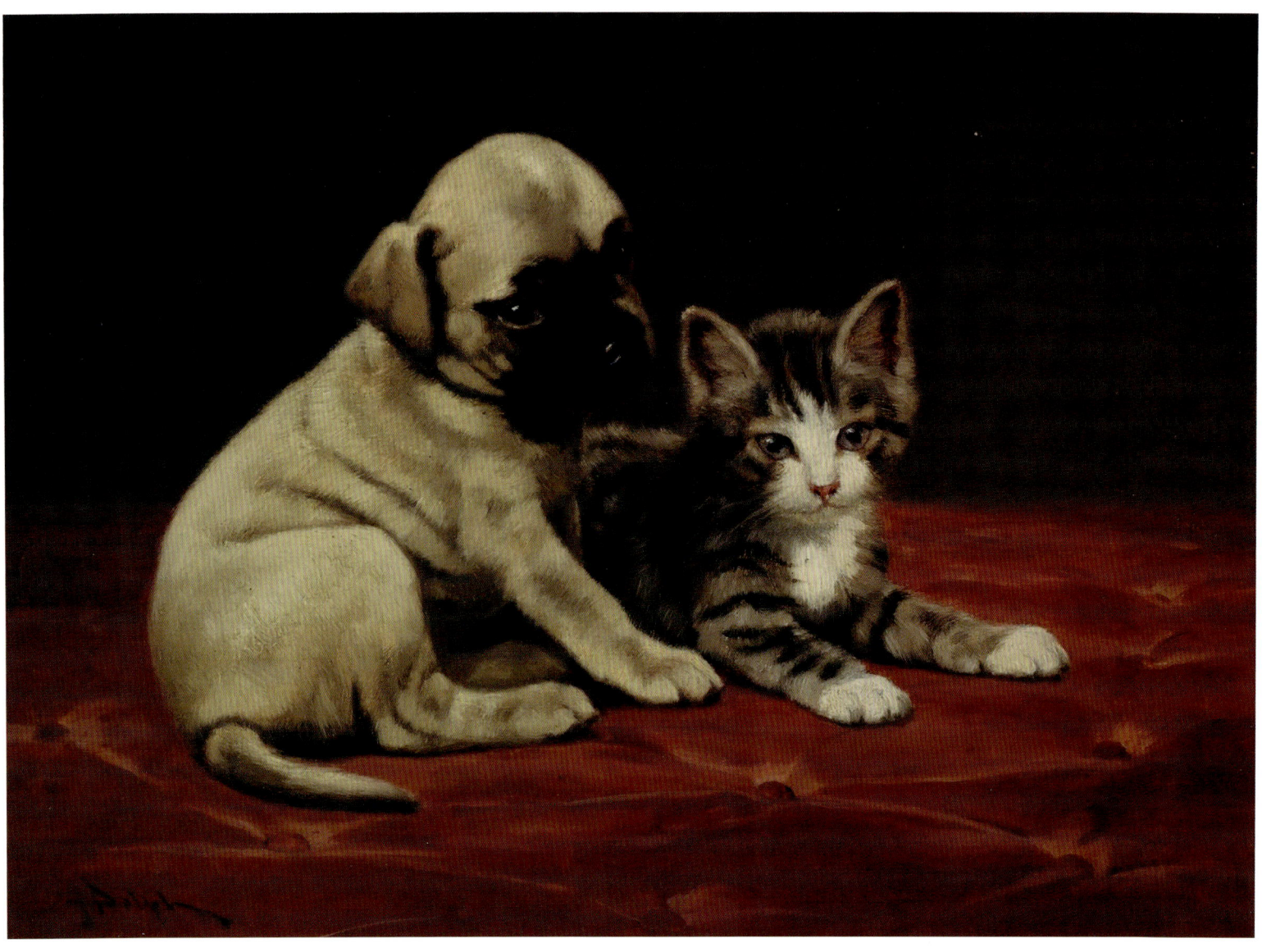

JOHN HENRY DOLPH

Good Friends (Puppy and Kitten), late 19th century
Oil on canvas, 12 × 16 in. / 30.5 × 40.6 cm
Walters Art Museum, Baltimore

Although cats and dogs are supposed to be sworn enemies, one would not know it from this sweet scene. Painted in the late nineteenth century by famed American animal artist John Henry Dolph (1835–1903), this portrait features a Pug puppy and tabby kitten thick as thieves, snuggled together familiarly on a luxurious red ottoman. After moving to New York City in the 1860s, Dolph originally made his name as a painter of Hudson River Valley landscapes, developing a reputation as "the American Landseer." Like most artists of the time, he was a member of various art academies in New York and took trips to Europe to study under masters there. From 1868 to 1873, he trained with an animal painter, known as Van Kuyck, in Antwerp and Paris. After incorporating these new skills into his works,

Dolph found great financial and critical success in 1875 with a painting of a Persian cat, leading him to turn exclusively to the creation of the dog and cat paintings for which he is now best known. Dolph painted cats in a wide variety of modes and poses, doing just about every cute thing one could imagine, from kittens roughhousing with a bowl of goldfish or standing off against some collie puppies for a saucer of milk to staring up at a vase of artfully arranged flowers. According to most pet behaviorists, feline and canine members of the family can get along with the proper socialization. This painting is further proof that puppies and kittens do not have to fight like, well, cats and dogs.

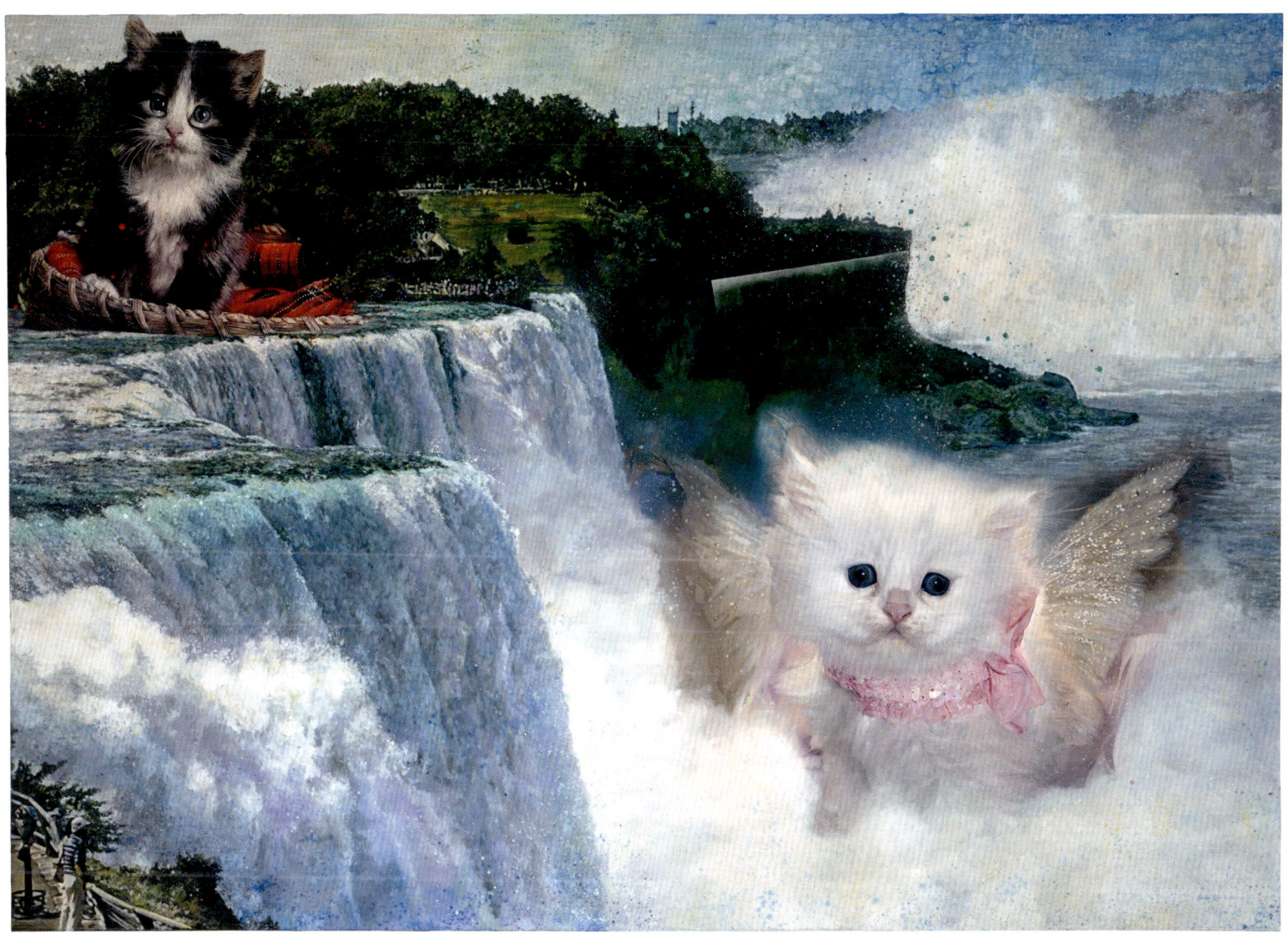

MARTIN EDER

Death (is a Candy), 2024
Oil on canvas, 90½ × 128 in. / 230 × 325 cm

With its fluffy kittens and glistening waterfalls, this painting appears like something a gentle-natured grandma might donate to goodwill. Upon further study, it takes on a darker twist: the tiny feline in the basket is actually a concerned giant, headed straight for the water's edge, obviously on its way to a similar fate as the sparkly winged angel emerging from the roar below. A perversion of kitschy cuteness, *Death (is a Candy)* is the work of German artist Martin Eder (b. 1968). Known for his oversize hyperreal canvases, Eder combines intricate painting techniques with an appropriative methodology of pastiche, deliberately collaging found imagery from sources as varied as Y2K Internet aesthetics and paint-by-number kits with motifs from the canon of art history. Although many of his works include nude figures rendered voyeuristically, cats often appear, whether hairless sphynxes amid pink-and-blue skies or kittens flying with bat wings in galactic space. The artist recycles recognizable figures from nostalgic kitsch to make paintings that are both immediately legible and unsettling. With provocation as the goal, Eder urges viewers to wrestle with basic ideas of desire and revulsion, cuteness and terror, as well as the concepts of artmaking and authorship in a digital age. As *The Art Newspaper* cheekily declared—referencing the notorious *Harry Potter* villain, whose office was adorned with portraits of cats—"for anyone who ever wondered what Dolores Umbridge's 2004 MySpace page might have looked like, Eder has the answer."

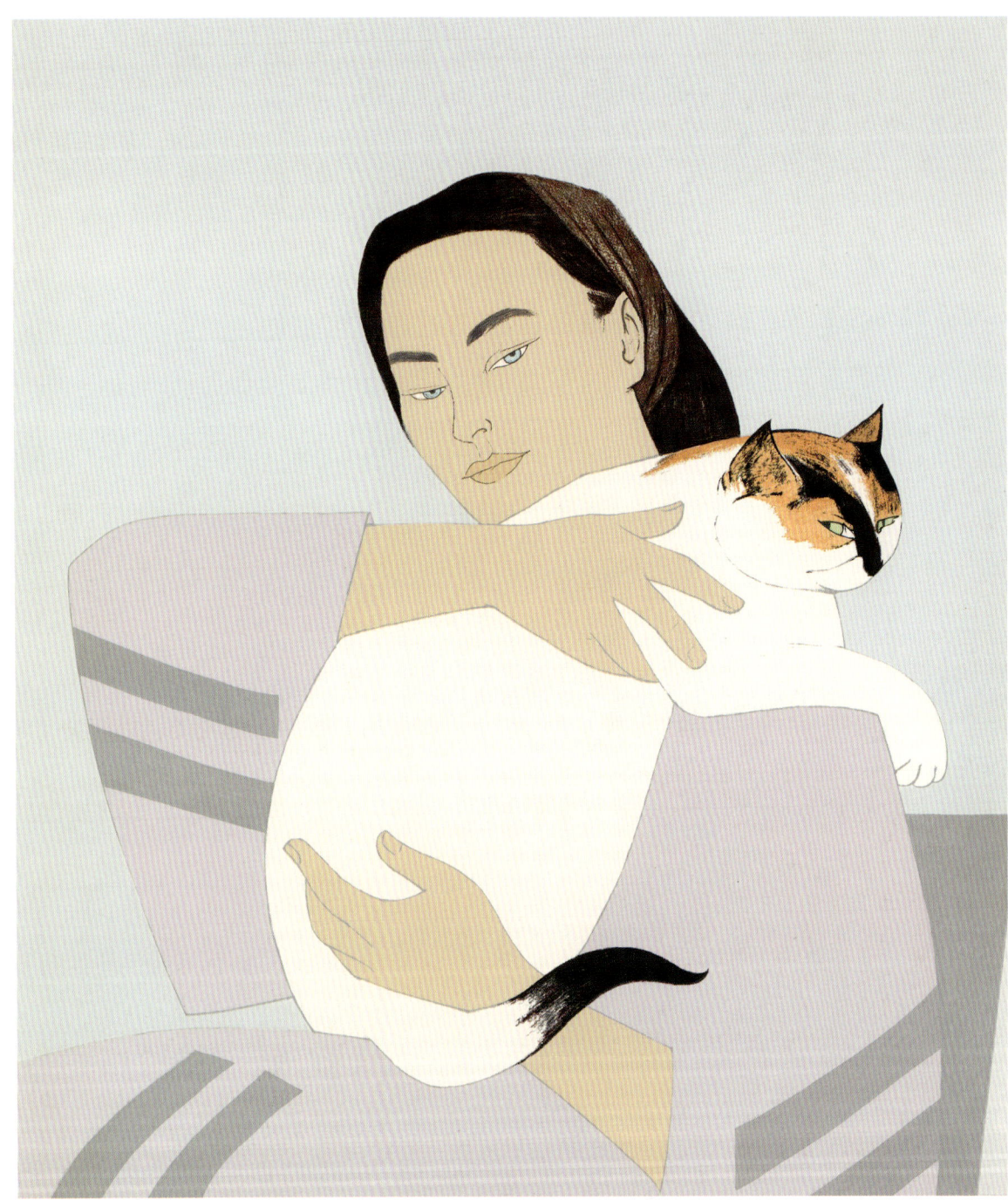

WILL BARNET

Woman & White Cat, 1971
Screenprint, 23¼ × 20 in. / 59.2 × 50.8 cm
Whitney Museum of American Art, New York

An elegant, dark-haired woman with a sultry gaze tenderly holds a minimally patterned calico cat, which turns its head toward the viewer. Charged with a latent sensuality, the domestic scene typifies the late graphic work of American painter and printmaker Will Barnet (1911–2012), whose warm portrayals of his homelife are rendered with clear, sinuous lines, flat colors, and shallow perspective. Barnet enjoyed a long career that spanned nearly eight decades, during which time he worked in a variety of styles, including social realism in the 1940s and pure abstraction in the 1950s. From the 1960s, he settled on a flattened, figurative minimalism developed from his earlier explorations. His enigmatic portraits and calm domestic scenes, which are noted for their careful balance of form and color,

convey a range of moods and feelings. As a printmaking tutor at the Art Students League in New York, he taught several generations of younger artists, including Mark Rothko, Eva Hesse, and Cy Twombly, although the student whose work was perhaps most influenced by him is Alex Katz. Barnet was a great lover of cats, and he included them in many of his later works; his pet calico, Minou, appears by his side in self-portraits, curled up, playing with his wife and daughter, or simply observing the familial goings-on. Minou was often found in Barnet's studio, and it was said that if she did not warm to you, neither would the artist.

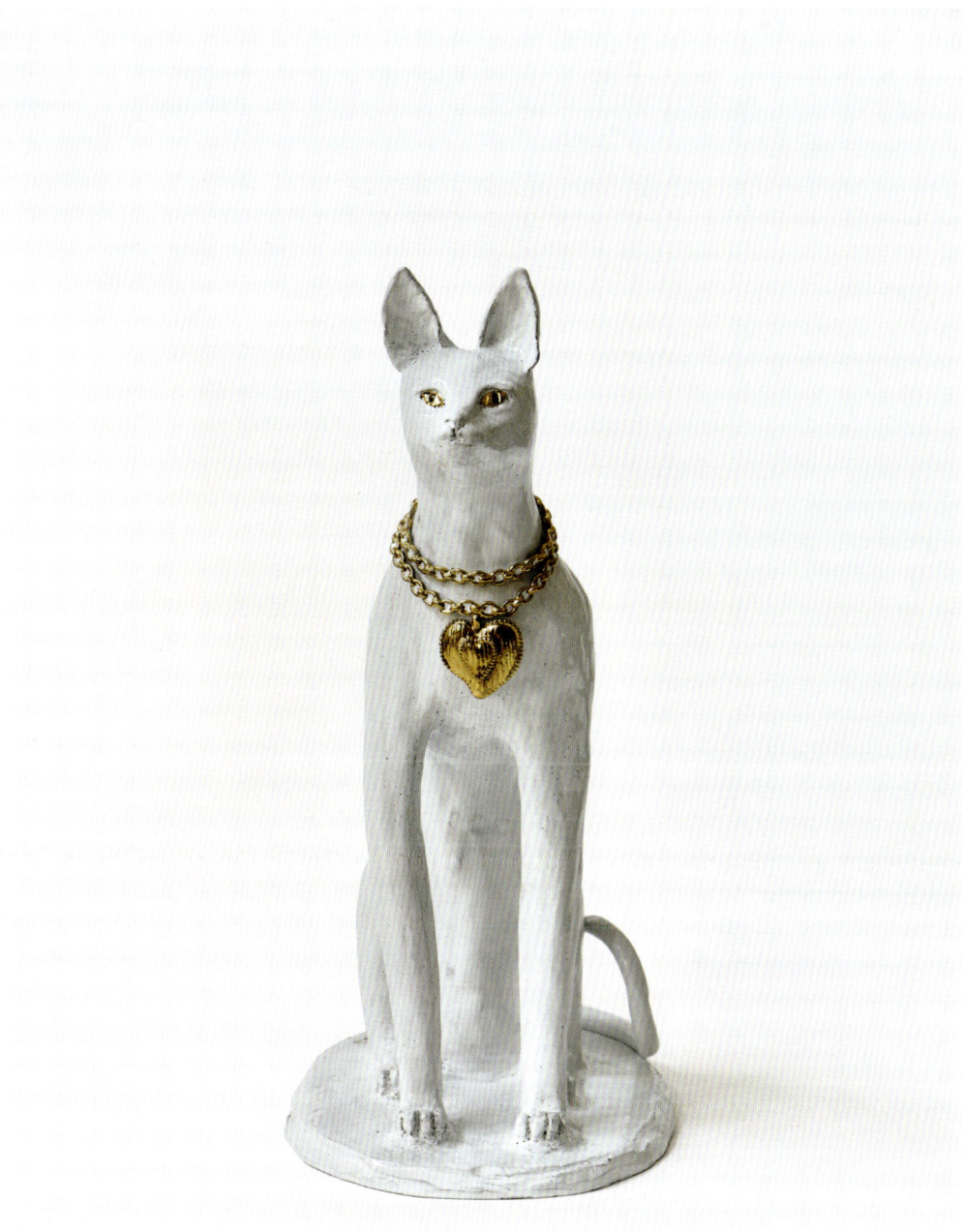

SETSUKO

Le grand chat au médaillon, 2024
Enameled ceramic
10½ × 12 × 7¾ in. / 47 × 30.5 × 19.7 cm
Private collection

Celebrated Japanese artist Setsuko (Klossowska de Rola, b. 1942) is known for her serene ceramic sculptures and paintings that capture the subtle beauty of the everyday. Her signature style, at once delicate and romantic, explores ethereal themes in nature by blending traditional motifs from Eastern and European modernist traditions with a contemporary sensibility, connecting past mythologies with present-day spiritual thinking. Just like her late husband, the French artist Balthus, Setsuko has a deep affection for cats, owning dozens over the course of her life and believing them to be symbols of independence, adventure, and courage. The noble white cat of *Le grand chat au médaillon*, made of shiny enameled ceramic, is a perfect example. Elegantly poised and gracefully alert, with disproportionately long limbs and oversize ears that appear more foxlike than feline, this cat's slinky silhouette bears a striking resemblance both to that of an ancient Egyptian feline statuette of the goddess Bastet (see p.29) and to *maneki-neko*, the lucky waving cats of Japan (see p.185). These associations naturally align the sculpture's form to ideas surrounding the sacred and the talismanic. Yet Setsuko's cat is also very much a good-luck charm for modern times. Adorned with a contemporary chunky gold necklace featuring a giant pendant heart, this cat is no shy breed, stylishly flaunting her high-ranking status as an object of desire with a look of confident sophistication.

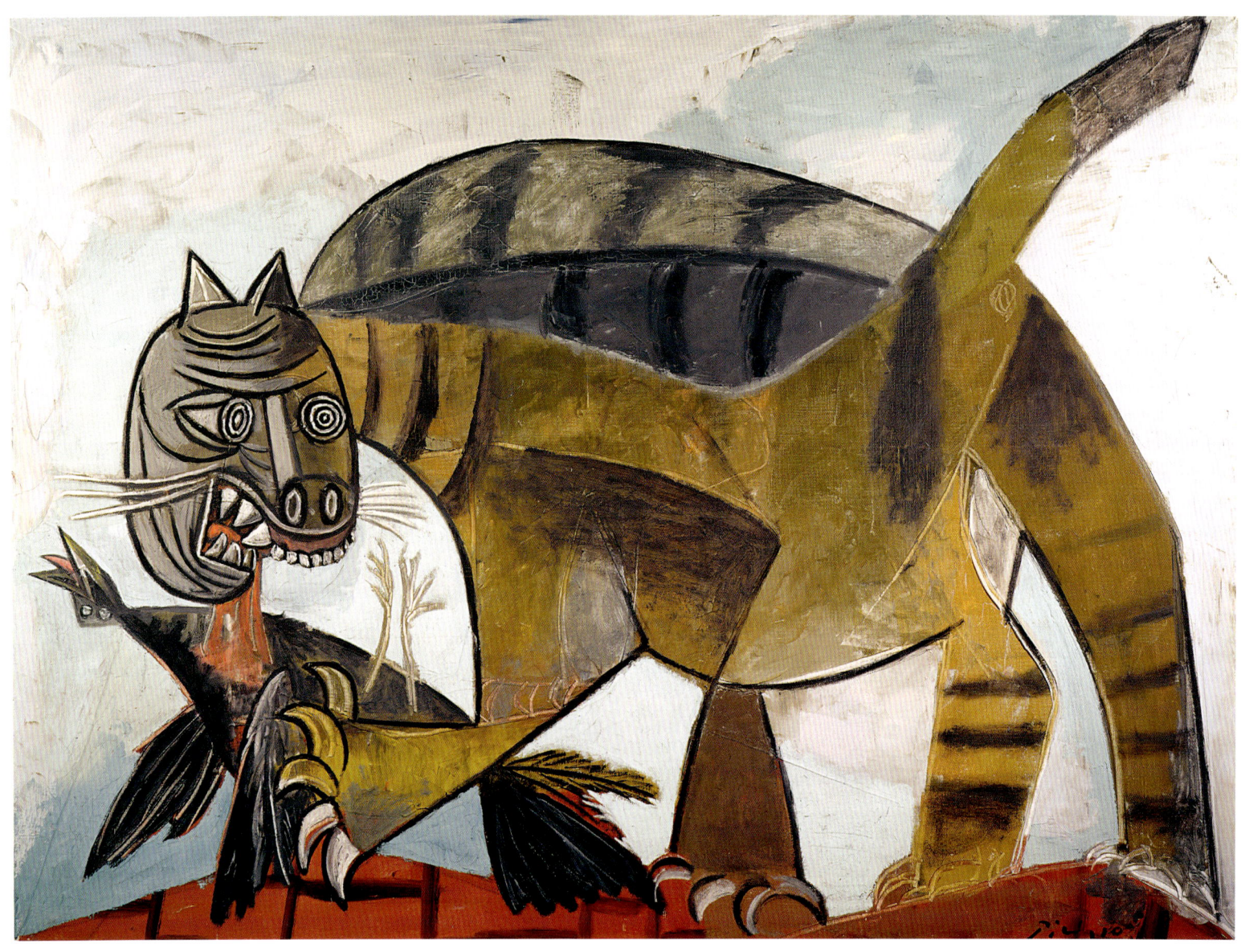

PABLO PICASSO

A Cat Devouring a Bird, 1939
Oil on canvas, 38⅛ × 50¾ in. / 97 × 129 cm
Private collection

In 1939, on the cusp of World War II, Spanish artist Pablo Picasso (1881–1973) found himself obsessively thinking about violent scenes involving cats. This painting depicts a feline hunter unleashing its predatory instinct. Holding its prey between its pincer-sharp claws, the cat has ripped open the bird's chest with its pointed teeth, tearing the bloody innards out. The hunter's spiraling eyes make the animal appear possessed and transfixed by its own savagery. Bringing this rapacious mindset into his inventive abstraction, Picasso has merged the characteristics of the wild cat with those of a domestic one. Two years earlier, the artist had painted *Guernica* (1937), a powerful protest against the devastating bombing of the Spanish town of Guernica by German Nazi forces. This massive work also depicted

battling animals, featuring an aggressive bull and an injured horse that evoked the plight of the innocent. Here, Picasso presents a less politically overt conflict between more common animals, the cat and bird, but the cruelty somehow seems more pervasive. Although this painting does not have the scale of *Guernica*, it has a similar sense of monumentality. By minimizing the background detail, the enlarged cat occupies most of the canvas and becomes even more threatening. Picasso exaggerates this menace with clashing colors and jagged Cubist forms. Indeed, this macabre scene could be read as a haunting premonition of the impending cruelties to come.

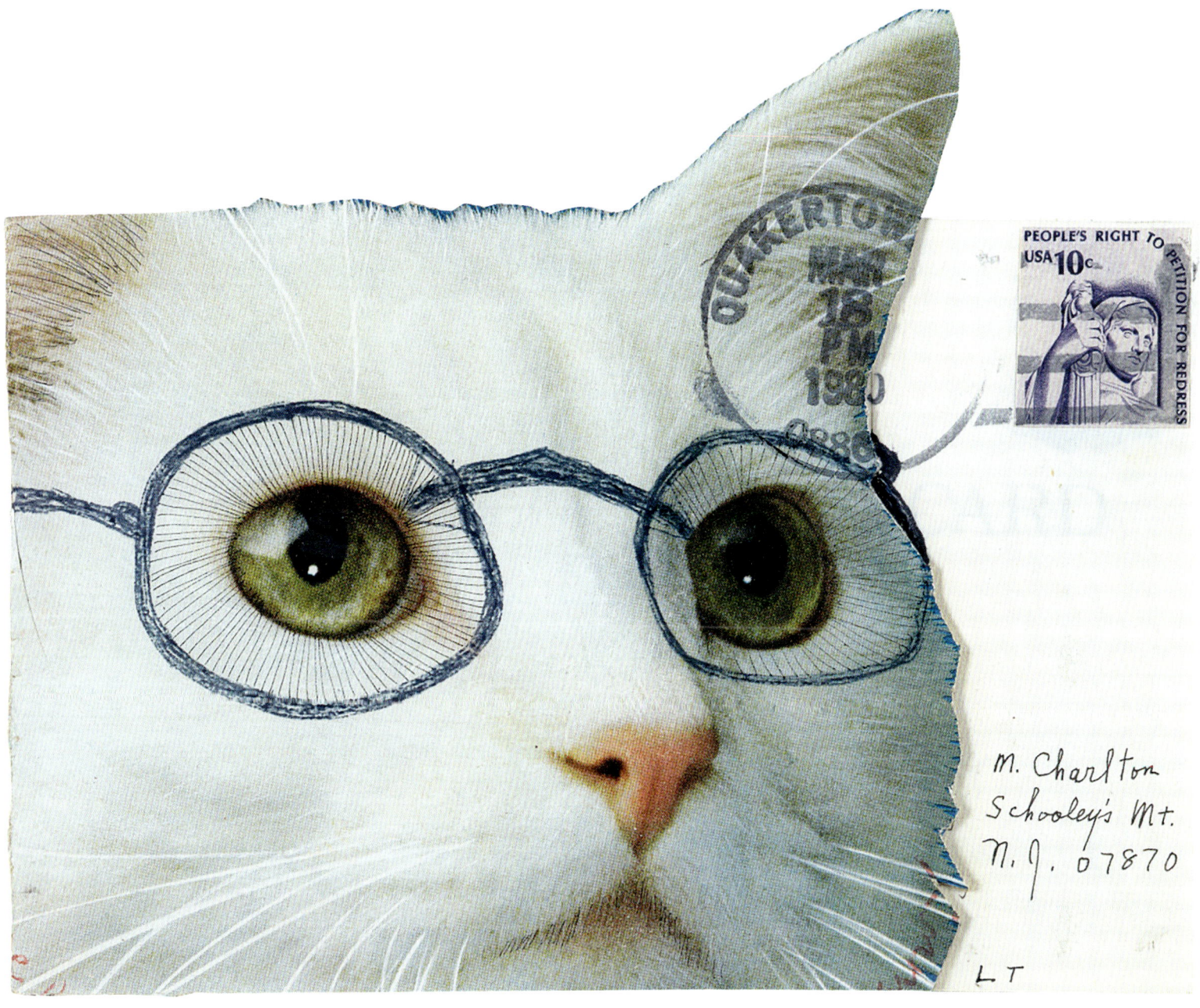

LENORE TAWNEY

Mail art to Maryette Charlton, 1980
Mixed media, 4³⁄₈ × 5½ in. / 11 × 14 cm
Archives of American Art, Smithsonian,
Washington, DC

A smartly bespectacled white cat gazes ahead on this postcard addressed to American artist and filmmaker Maryette Charlton at her New Jersey home. Made by pioneering American fiber artist Lenore Tawney (1907–2007), who began a career as an artist only in her fifties, the postcard was among hundreds of hand-decorated cards she sent to friends and fellow artists, often accompanied by cryptic and humorous messages. For this letter, Tawney cut out the fabulous cat's head from a magazine, chopping off its right ear while allowing the left to extend over the card, and drew its glasses in blue ink. On the reverse side, the feline theme continues, with an illustration of a white cat, perhaps the same one pictured on the front, sitting proudly on top of a red ottoman. Cats were an important part of

Tawney's life. After spending thirty years in Chicago—where she had studied textiles under Bauhaus luminaries László Moholy-Nagy, Marli Ehrman, Emerson Woelffer, and Alexander Archipenko—she decided to relocate to New York City in 1957, packing into her car only her refrigerator and loom, as well as her beloved cat Pansy. A breakthrough exhibition of her fiber sculptures in 1963 brought Tawney's weaving to the public's attention. She followed her woven sculptures with collages, including her envelope art, and assemblages. When she was photographed in her Manhattan studio by Nina Leen (see p.118) for *Life* magazine in 1966, the images featured Tawney with her hanging textile sculptures and, of course, Pansy the cat.

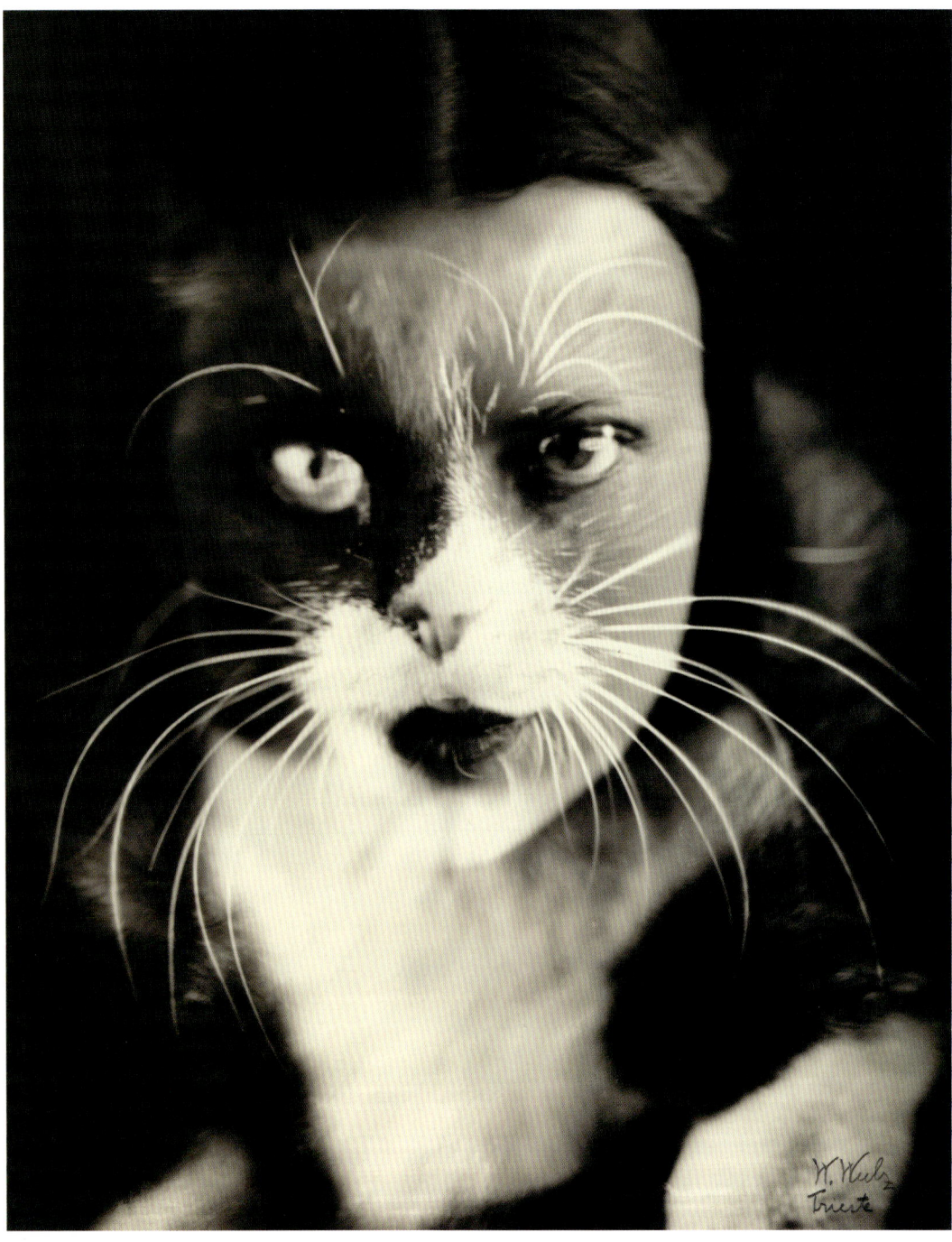

WANDA WULZ

Io + gatto (Cat and I), 1932
Gelatin silver print, 11⅝ × 9⅛ in. / 29.4 × 23.2 cm
Metropolitan Museum of Art, New York

In this fantastical self-portrait, the artist's face melds with that of a cat, as if she were metamorphosing from human to animal. Fur and whiskers sprout from her skin and, although the cat-woman's lips remain humanoid, her intently staring eyes have become feline, complete with vertical-slit pupils, recalling the mythological werecat from European folklore. The Italian photographer Wanda Wulz (1903–1984) created this striking photomontage by combining two images: one of her own face and the other of her pet cat's. Such visual trickery is easily achieved today digitally, but in Wulz's day, the process was far more involved, requiring skillful darkroom techniques to convincingly combine two different negatives. Known as combination printing, the practice was embraced by many modern artists who sought to create absurd and otherworldly images. In the 1930s, Wulz was associated with Futurism (see p.141), an Italian art movement that aimed to capture the dynamism, energy, and movement of a modern and industrialized society. However, these themes are absent in this dreamlike work, which appears more closely aligned with Surrealist strategies of image manipulation. Although Wulz's early work centered on portraits of musicians, dancers, and actors in Trieste, Italy, she became increasingly experimental as she explored Futurist-inspired photomontages and collages. Despite remaining closely associated with the Futurists until the late 1930s, her works from this period are extremely rare, with *Io + gatto* being her most famous photograph.

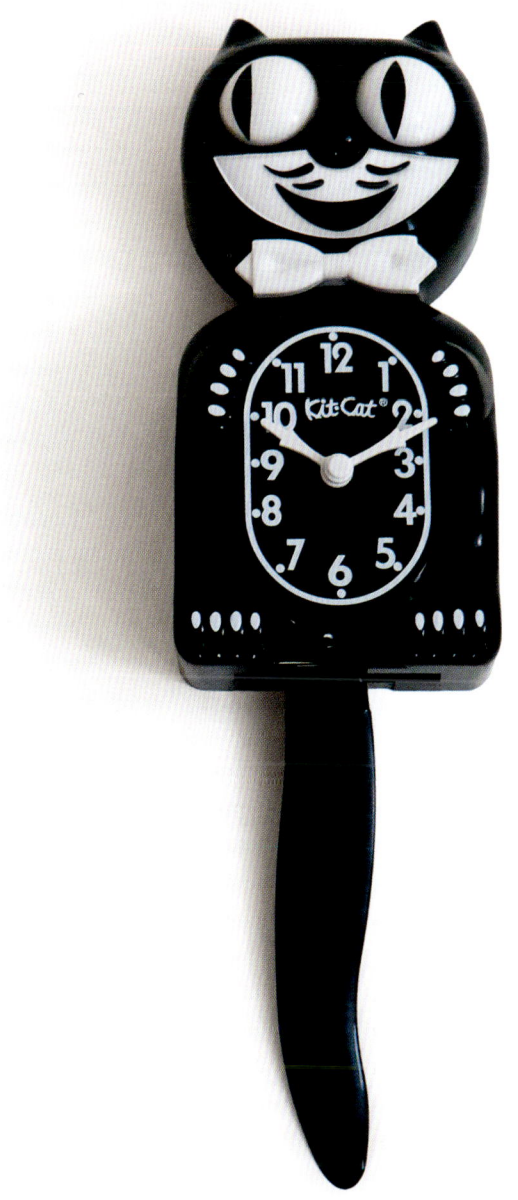

EARL ARNAULT

Kit-Cat Klock, 1932
Plastic, 15½ × 4 × 3 in. / 39.4 × 10.2 × 7.6 cm

An icon of twentieth-century industrial design, the Kit-Cat Klock was born during the heart of the Great Depression. Indeed, Portland-based designer Earl Arnault (1904–1971) would later say his intent was to create something cheerful as a salve for his customers during trying times. Bearing more than a passing resemblance to silent-era cartoon star Felix the Cat (see p.144), the Kit-Cat Klock is distinguished by its rectangular body, ear-to-ear grin, and exaggerated eyes. These wide inset eyes shift from side to side with each tick of the timepiece, and its tail similarly wags in time like a pendulum on a grandfather clock. The original version was made of metal and retailed for only $3.95. By the end of the 1930s, the clock housing had changed from metal to plastic, and Arnault had moved his

Allied Clock Company to Seattle. In the 1940s, the company manufactured equipment for Boeing as part of the war effort. After World War II, Kit-Cat Klocks became a craze on par with the Hula-Hoop, cementing their association with mid-century Americana. The American actress Lucille Ball reportedly bought them by the case and gave them out as gifts. Small innovations followed, but the overall design has stayed the same: a bow tie and top paws were added in the 1950s, and some new hues were added in the 1960s. The integrity and wit of this feline icon of mid-century modern design have kept the original clock as popular as it was nearly a century ago.

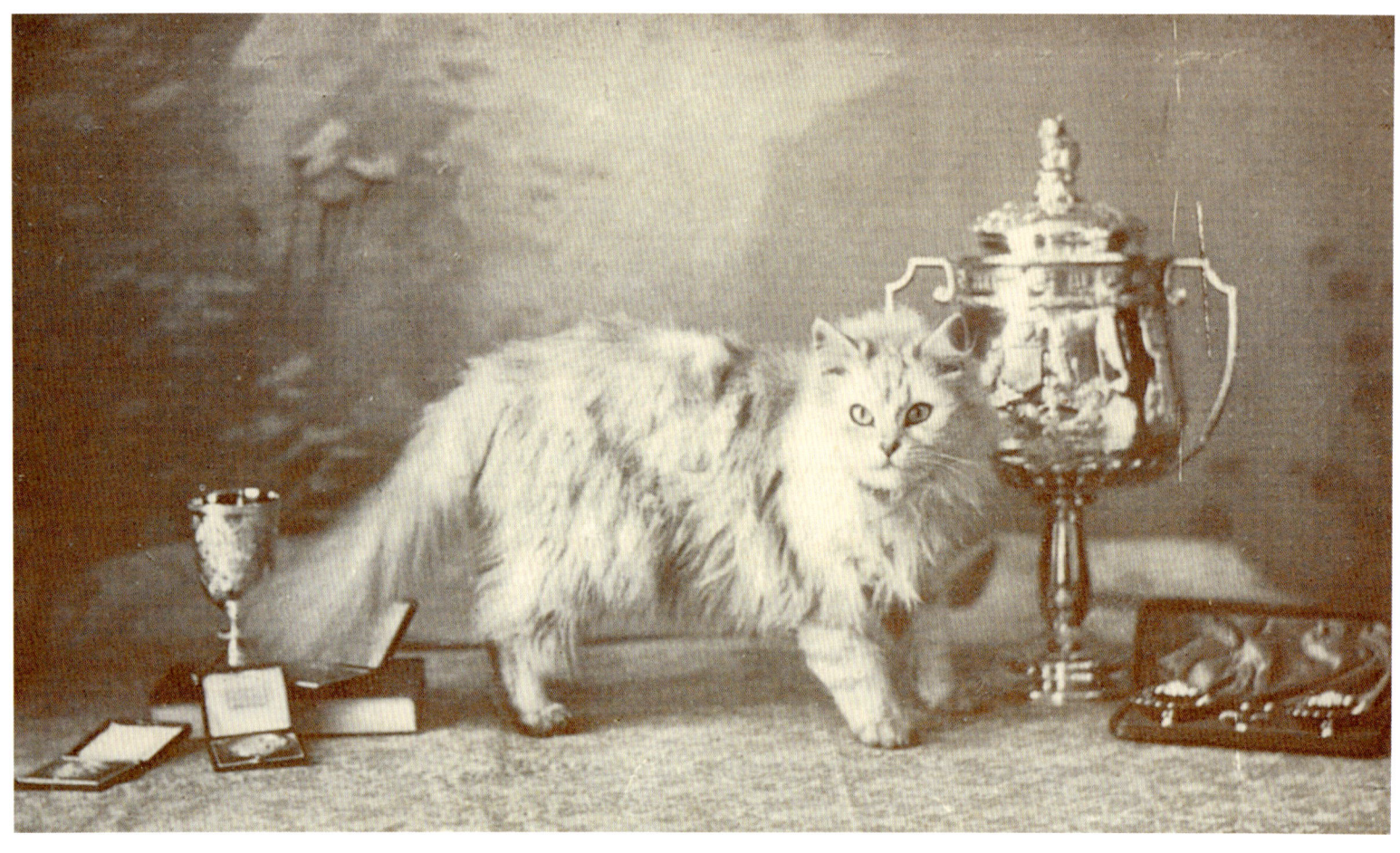

FRANCES SIMPSON

Lady Decies' Silver Champion "Fulmer Zaida,"
from *Cats and All About Them*, 1902
Photograph in printed book, H. 7½ in. / 19 cm

By the Victorian period, cats were no longer viewed just as outdoor exterminators of vermin but as pedigreed champions. With her pristine silver coat, the longhaired Chinchilla Persian Zaida certainly has the look of a winner, as the many trophies with which she is photographed attest. Zaida would collect more than 150 prizes in cat shows during her show career. The idea of a competition in which both domestic and pedigree cats could be judged against each other was first suggested by British cat breeder Harrison Weir, who became known as "The Father of the Cat Fancy." In 1871 Weir co-organized the first major Cat Fancy show at the Crystal Palace in London, which probably featured more than one hundred cats, including the first Siamese cats documented in the West and a Scottish wildcat owned by the Duke of Sutherland. The Fancy was a commercial hit, attracting more than 20,000 visitors. Weir went on to form the National Cat Club in 1887 and wrote the first book about pedigree cats, *Our Cats and All About Them*, in 1889. A decade later, Frances Simpson (c. 1857–1926) took up Weir's mantle, becoming a renowned cat fancier and judge in England. Zaida's photograph comes from Simpson's 1902 book—almost identically titled to Weir's—*Cats and All About Them*, which contained a multitude of advice on cat breeding and judging. Zaida belonged to Lady Decies, who owned two catteries and was a passionate breeder, highlighting the Victorians' obsession with all things feline.

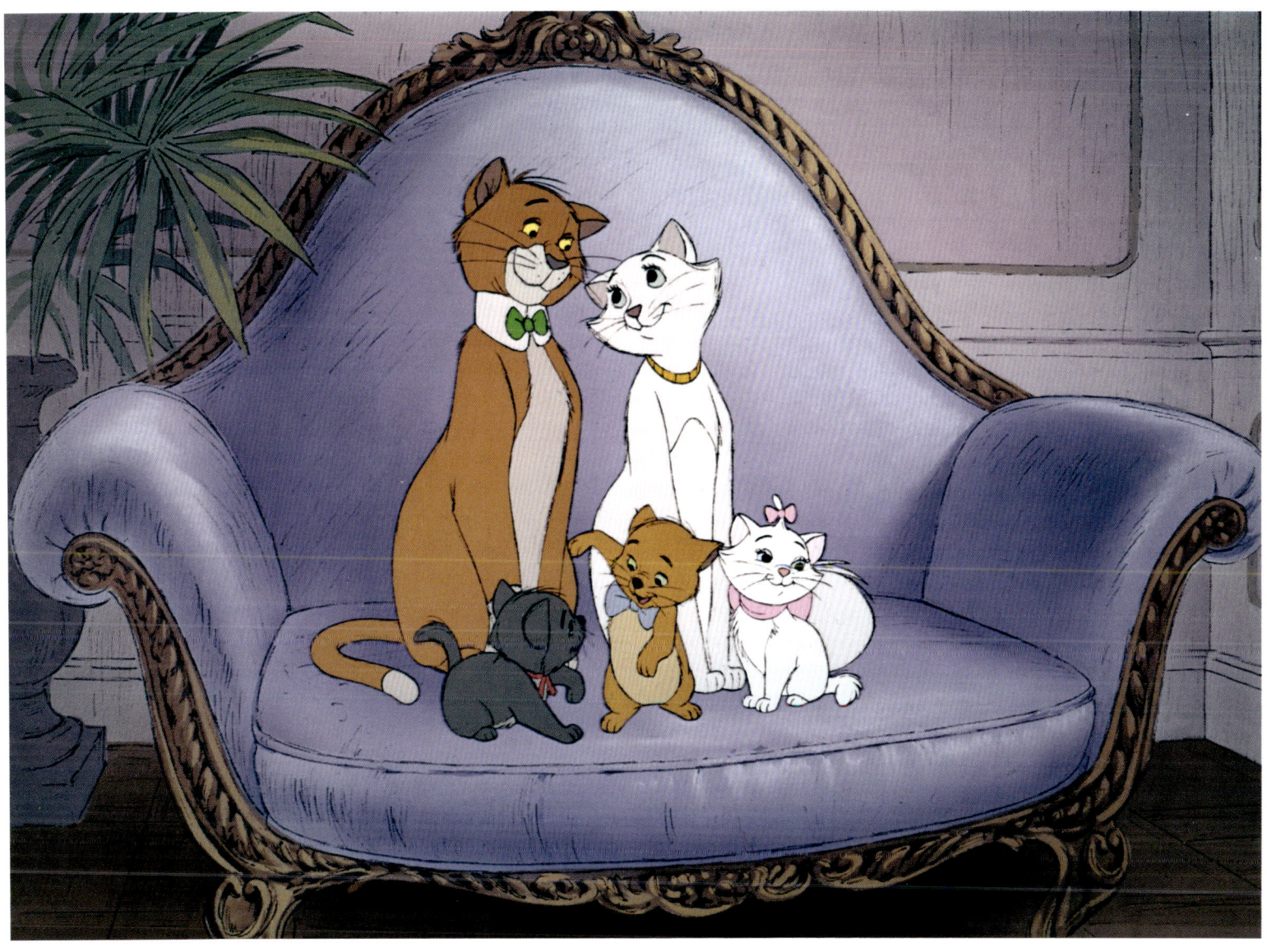

WALT DISNEY PICTURES

The Aristocats, 1970
Film still, dimensions variable

A playful romp through early twentieth-century France, *The Aristocats* is one of Walt Disney Pictures' jazziest tales, following a family of well-to-do felines in Paris. The pampered pets Duchess and her three kittens Berlioz, Marie, and Toulouse live a luxurious lifestyle as the companions of Madame, a retired opera diva. When the English butler Edgar discovers that Madame intends to leave her fortune to her beloved feline family instead of him, he kidnaps and dumps them in the French countryside. Out of their urban element, Duchess and her kittens are found by an alley cat named Thomas O'Malley, who offers to escort them back to Paris. The band of travelers meet an eccentric cast of characters on their journey home, including a goose, two stubborn hounds, and a jazz band helmed by Scat Cat. Once

reunited with her beloved pets, Madame adopts O'Malley into the family and establishes a charity that houses stray cats in her mansion, with Scat Cat and his gang being the first to move in. The commercial success of both *The Aristocats* and its animal-focused predecessor *The Jungle Book* (1967) proved to the studio that anthropomorphic films were a hit with kids and adults alike. It was also a tribute to the expertise of Disney's animators at capturing the enigmatic nature of cats. As critic Roger Ebert wrote in his review of the film, "The three little kittens are dainty, stalwart, and pugnacious by turns. It seems kind of silly to be writing about how the kittens walk, it just occurred to me, but it's in details like those that *The Aristocats* becomes delightful."

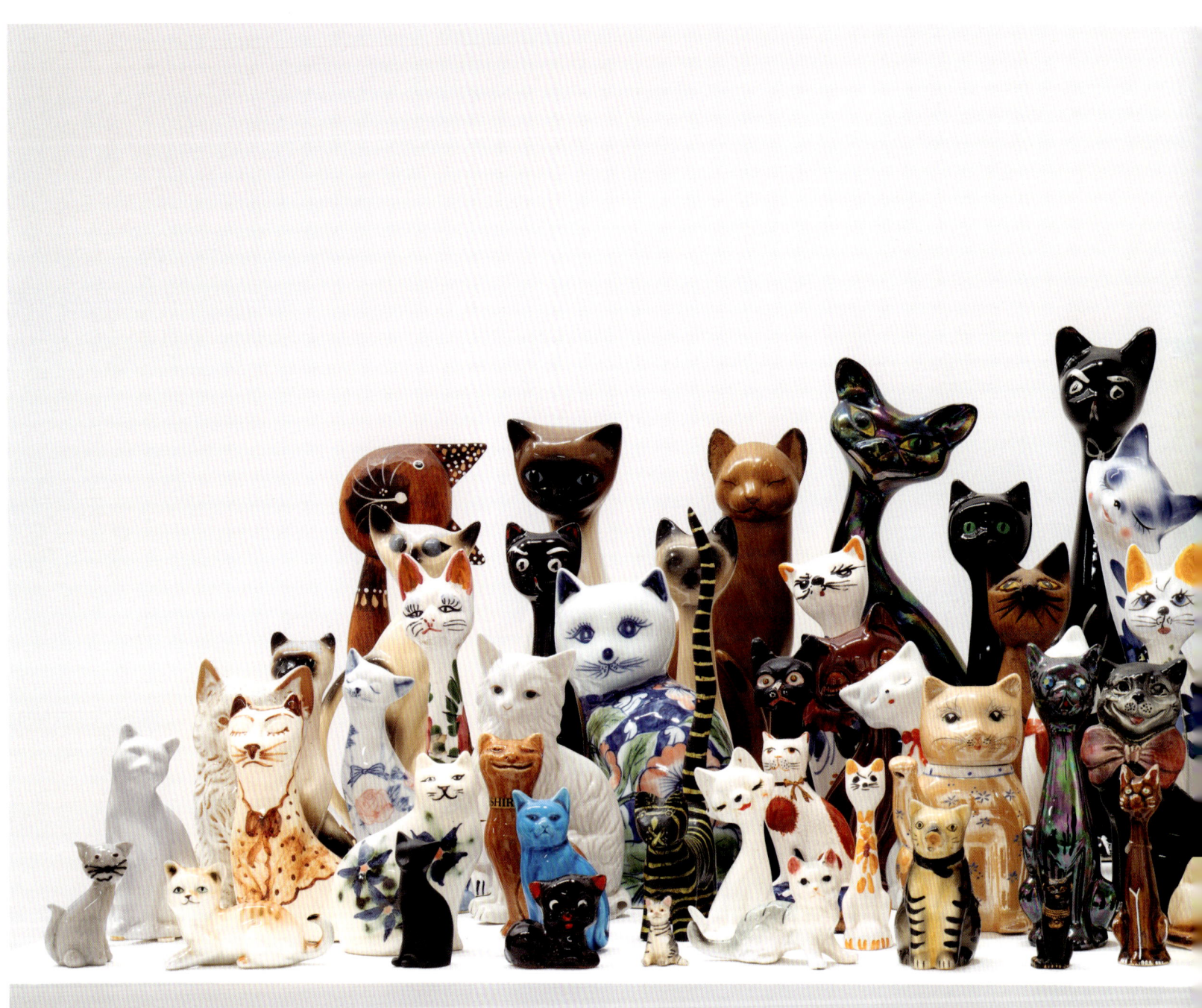

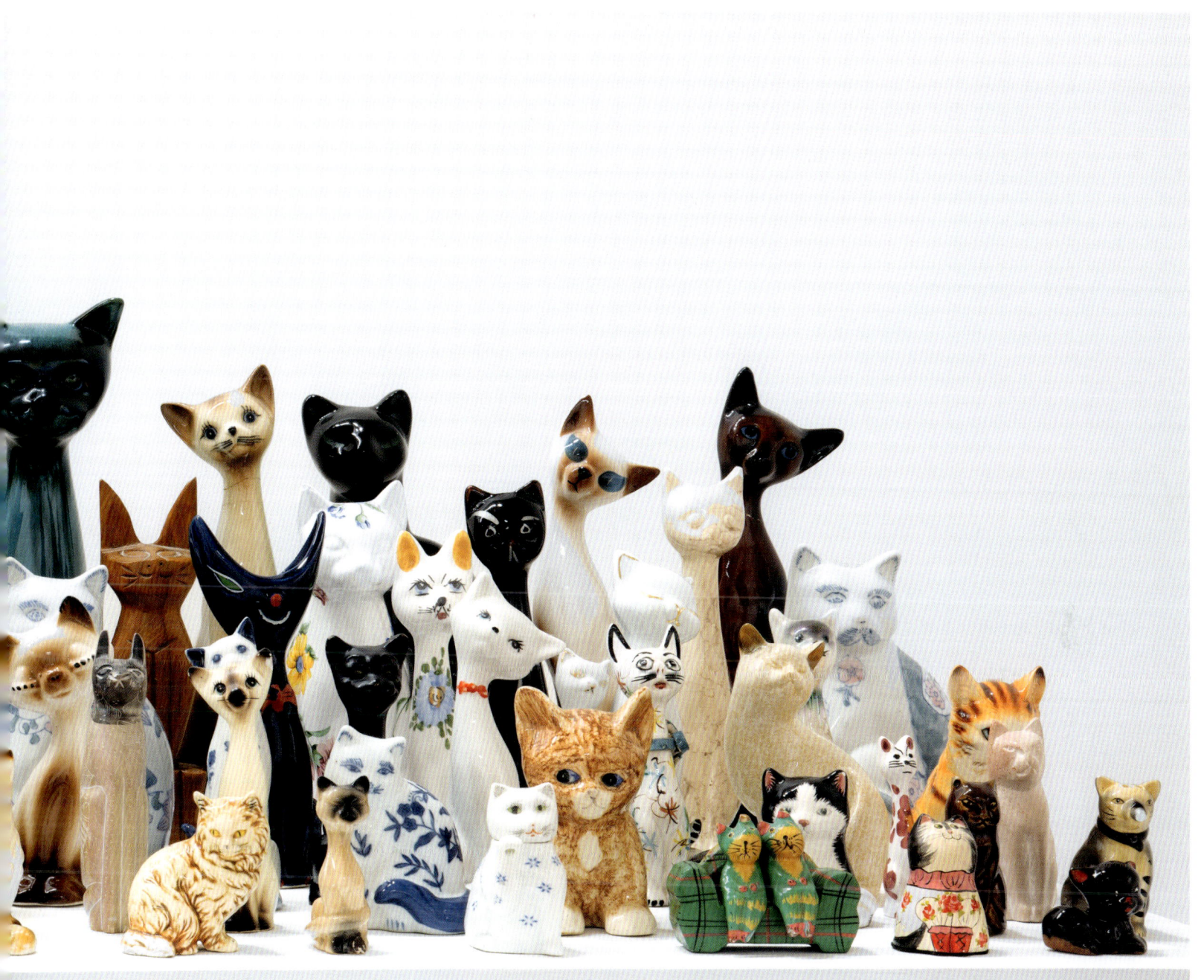

ANDY HOLDEN

Cat-tharsis, 2022
90 cat figurines and HD video with
music by The Grubby Mitts, 17 min
Private collection

When his ninety-year old grandmother died, British artist Andy Holden (b. 1982) was bequeathed eight cardboard boxes containing her extensive collection of cat figurines. Holden transformed their unboxing into an artwork. The feline forms are filmed being unwrapped from newspaper and briefly displayed on his hand. The artist narrates a deadpan monologue accompanied by lounge jazz music, which is sometimes melancholic, sometimes whimsical. He notes in his voice-over that while his grandmother's living room was filled from floor to ceiling with these cats, she never had a real one as a pet, and she only started collecting around the time of her husband's Alzheimer's diagnosis. Holden cites facts about cats: the disproportionate percentage of cat characters in cartoons and how, in 2021, there were an estimated 6.5 billion cat pictures on the Internet. He observes the ornaments' kitsch designs: big eyes, neckerchiefs, and painted floral patterns on their coats. He reveals personal insights: that he cannot recall the names of any of the seventy-three cat breeds and that he had an early erotic response to Michelle Pfeiffer's Catwoman in the film *Batman Returns* (1992). Presented alongside displays of the collection, as pictured here, *Cat-tharsis* ultimately concludes that Holden's grandmother was driven by the psychological impulse to collect more than any particular interest in this domestic animal per se, yet their easy availability in the charity shops from which she acquired them reveals a shared cultural love for cats in all shapes and forms.

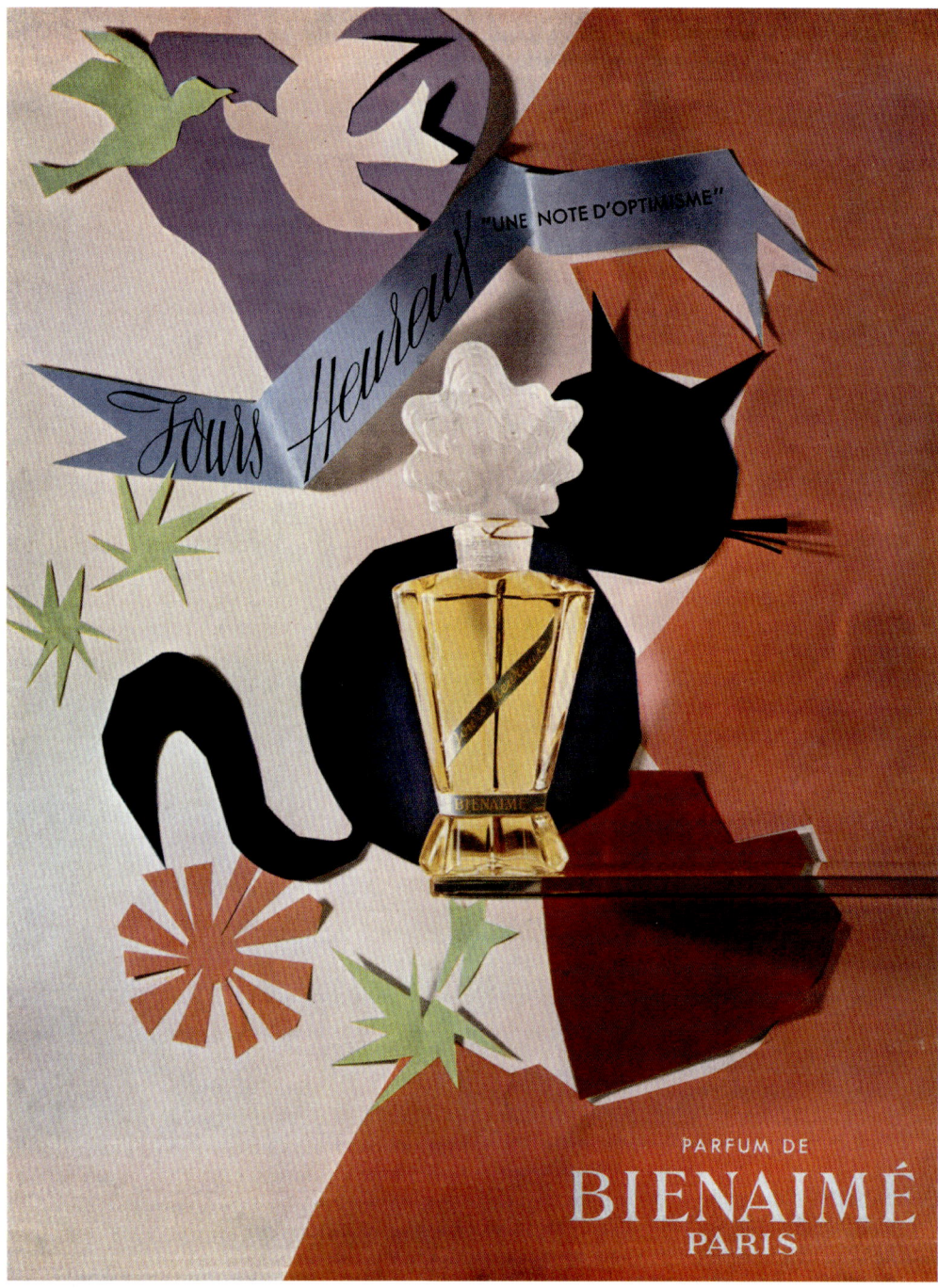

BIENAIMÉ

Advertisement for Jours Heureux, 1950
Offset lithograph
Approx. 11¾ × 8⅝ in. / 30 × 22 cm

This whimsical advertisement from 1950 promotes the fragrance Jours Heureux, a scent made by the French perfume house Bienaimé. The design showcases the scent's Art Deco bottle and its stopper shaped like a scallop against a joyful collage of roughly cutout figures that include stars, flowers, and birds. As if hiding, a large blue-black cat peers around the bottle, its whiskers and left ear slightly raised from the page to create a shadow as it watches the birds in flight, the picture of springtime. French for "happy days," Jours Heureux promises a felicitous scent, the poster's tagline translating to "a note of optimism." The perfumery's founder, Robert Bienaimé, was a pioneer in the industry: a chemist, he trained with Paul Parquet at the house of Houbigant before setting up his eponymous business in 1935 and becoming one of the first perfumers to use synthetic molecules to make his scents—some eight years before Coco Chanel famously did so with Chanel No 5. He launched Jours Heureux in 1938, with woody, floral notes designed to evoke the coming of spring, and it was in production until his death in 1960. Bienaimé's modern approach to his perfumes is captured in this advertising poster, which recalls the paper cutouts of his contemporary, artist Henri Matisse (see p.90). Modern fragrance lovers can rejoice: the Bienaimé brand was revived in 2021 with the aim of marrying its classic scents and Art Deco designs with clean ingredients and innovations in perfume production.

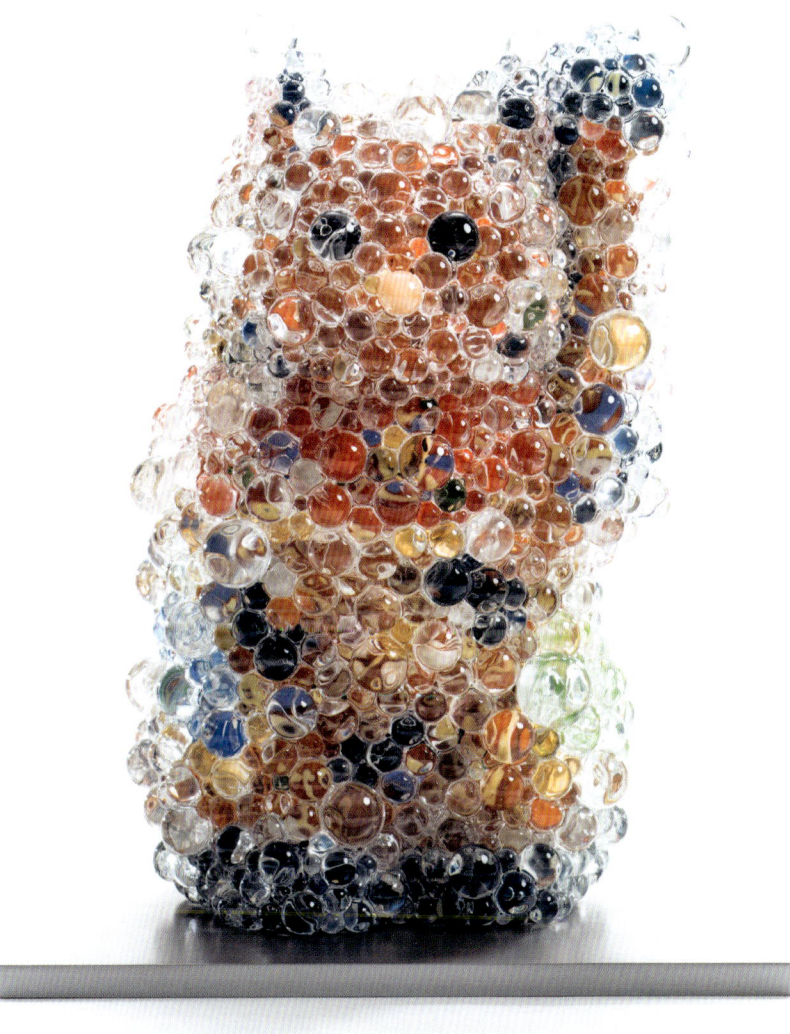

KOHEI NAWA

PixCell-Beckoning Cat, 2015
Mixed media
11¾ × 9⅝ × 9⅝ in. / 30 × 24.5 × 24.5 cm
Private collection

This is not your average lucky cat, but an unusual sculpture by Japanese artist Kohei Nawa (b. 1975) from his *PixCell* series. Nawa created these works by covering a variety of taxidermied animals and everyday objects with clear spheres of varying sizes, mimicking the way an image is presented through a computer monitor. The overall effect is discombobulating and surreal, because the underlying object can be viewed through multiple lenses and becomes magnified and warped. The term "PixCell" is Nawa's invention, a combination of "pixels" (in this case, the grouping of images that creates a larger picture, such as a digital photograph) and "cells" (the outer spheres). The project is a commentary on digital culture and the way that online data can be viewed and distorted to alter reality. This work

features a typical *maneki-neko*, the familiar Japanese waving cat figurine known by various names, including beckoning cat, lucky cat, and money cat (see p.185). Believed to be a totem of good fortune, the *maneki-neko* has its legendary origins in the seventeenth century, and the cat-shaped dolls remain good-luck charms globally, even when "PixCell"-ated. Although an icon, the *maneki-neko* is an interesting choice of subject for the artist. Nawa participated in the 2011 exhibition *Bye Bye Kitty!!!* at New York's Japan Society Gallery, where some of Japan's most cutting-edge artists rejected *kawaii* stereotypes embodied by feline figures, such as Hello Kitty, instead presenting artworks that offered a more nuanced perspective on Japanese visual culture.

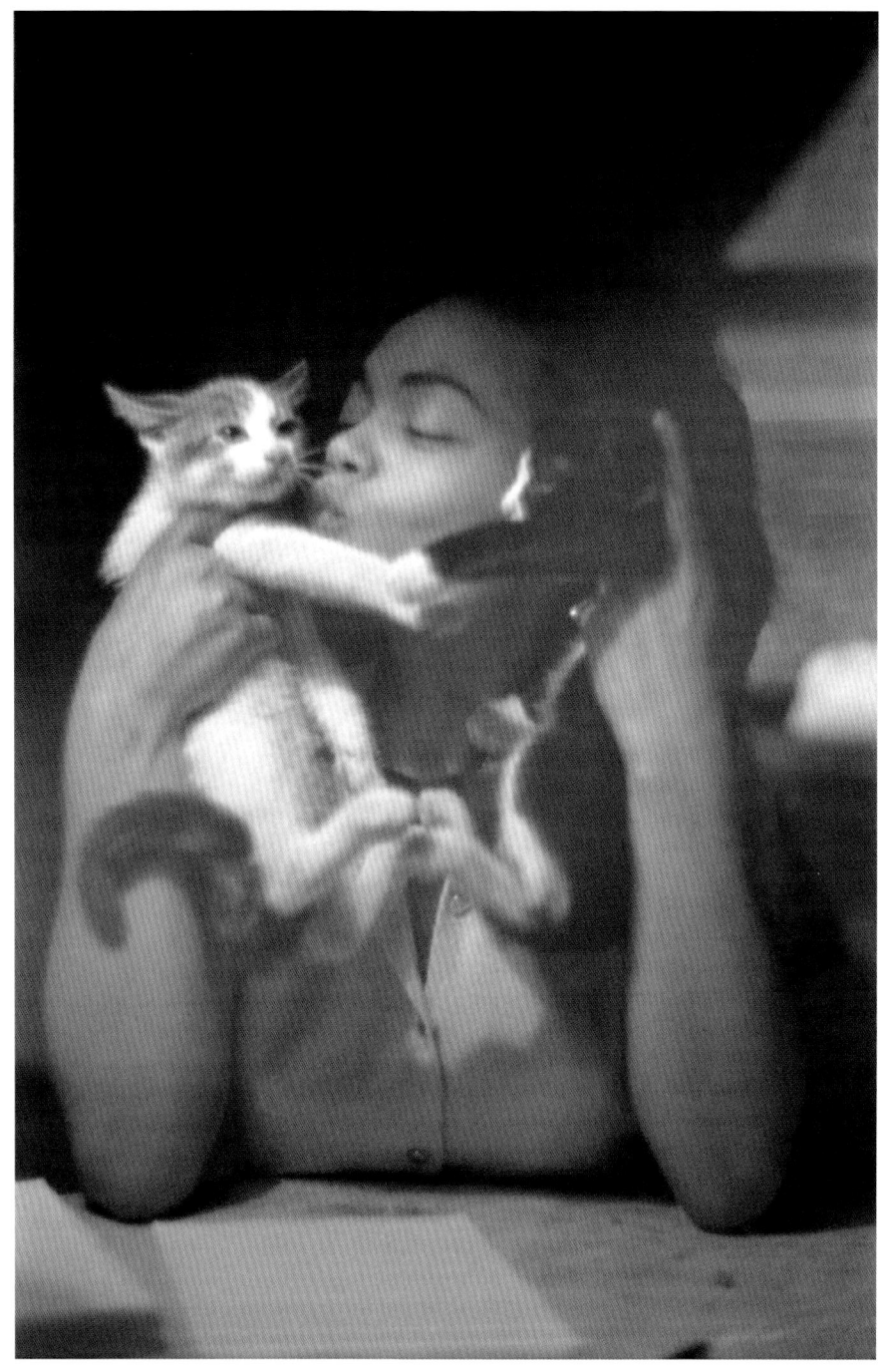

GORDON PARKS

Eartha Kitt for *Life* magazine, 1952
Photograph, dimensions variable

It is no surprise that the woman famous for playing Catwoman loved cats. *Life* magazine readers were treated to a dream pairing in the August 4, 1952, issue when American photographer Gordon Parks (1912–2006) trained his lens on singer and actress Eartha Kitt for an article entitled "Girl Who Gets Around," celebrating Kitt's transition from nightclub singer to Broadway star. Both artists were trailblazers: beginning his career as a photographer for the Farm Security Administration, Parks was the first Black American to become a *Life* magazine staff photographer in 1948 and his fashion photographs began appearing in *Vogue* in 1960. He was as adept at capturing everyday life in Harlem and the social justice revolution of the Civil Rights Movement as he was at creating fashion editorials and celebrity portraits. In this outtake that did not make it into the magazine, Kitt holds up two kittens, gently cradling them against her face and giving one a kiss. From 1967 to 1968, Kitt played the antiheroine Catwoman in the final season of the television show *Batman*, which had been adapted from the comic book, but as Parks demonstrated more than fifteen years earlier, her love of cats was not an act. She had multiple as pets throughout her life and was frequently photographed with them. Driven by a feline spirit, she even compared her ability to rise from a harsh childhood to find success on both stage and screen to a cat's smooth flexibility, wily strength, and ferocious perseverance.

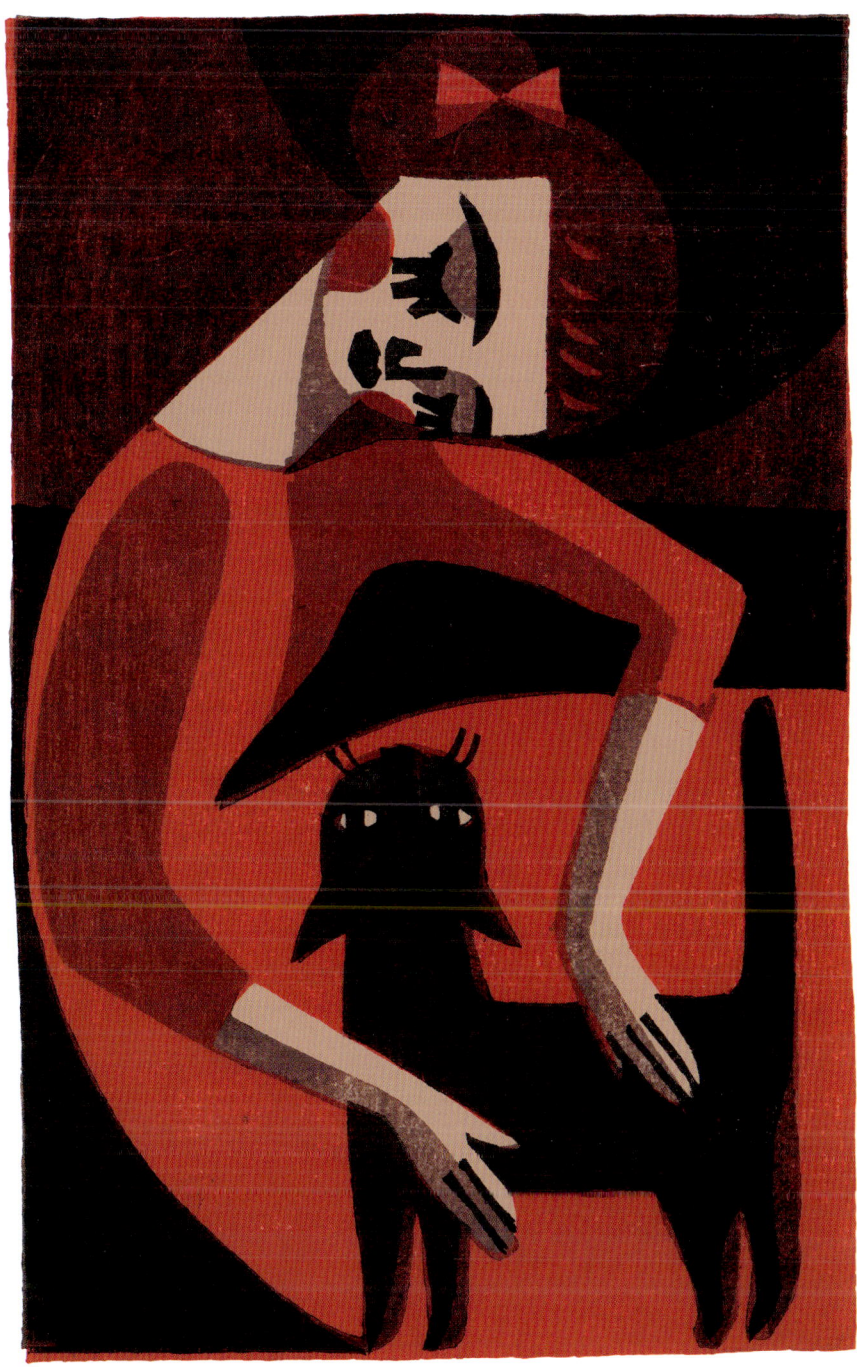

FUMI YANAGIMOTO

Dress, 2023
Woodcut, 7⅛ × 4¾ in. / 18.2 × 12 cm

There is nothing quite like the bond between a girl and her cat. The intimate and empathetic connection is captured artfully in this contemporary graphic print by Japanese artist Fumi Yanagimoto (b. 1986), a print-maker, potter, and painter based in Tokyo. In the artist's graphic style, the girl and her pot are made up of flat shapes, swooping lines, and varying tones of black and red. She folds herself around the waiting black feline, whose upright tail is a clear signal of its happiness and love, its whiskers almost the same chunky shape as her eyelashes. Cue the purrs now. The star of the print, however, is neither of the figures, but the vibrant cherry red of the girl's dress, hence the work's pithy title. A variant of the color is echoed in the blush that spreads across her cheeks and the bow that adorns her hair. Girls and their cats are a favored subject of the artist's, often depicted in simple grayscale palettes with a pop of well-placed color, but books, steaming cups of coffee, dogs, even the odd duck, also make repeated appearances. Reminiscent of both traditional nineteenth-century Japanese prints (see p.48) and the mid-century mini-malist realism of artists like Charley and Edie Harper (see p.17), her woodcuts utilize traditional printmak-ing techniques to create evocative artworks inspired by simple joys. No matter the focus, Fumi Yanagimoto always shares a sense of love, warmth, and comfort in works that reveal the tender moments between people and the animals they love.

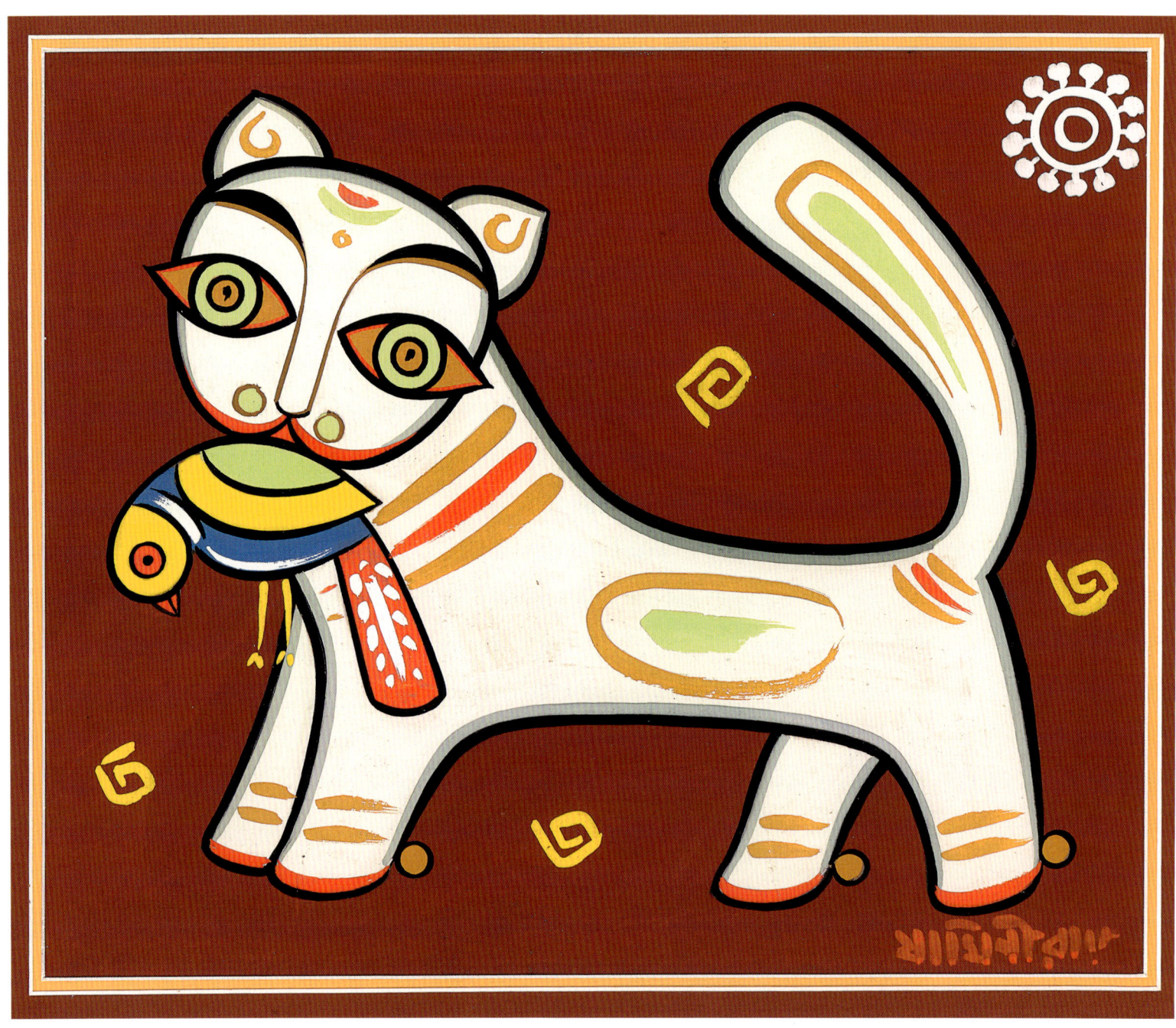

JAMINI ROY

Untitled, date unknown
Tempera on board
14 × 17⅛ in. / 35.6 × 43.5 cm
Private collection

A stylized hunter cat carries its lunch in its mouth in this striking painting by prolific Indian artist Jamini Roy (1887–1972). Notable for its simplified, flattened style, this work of tempera was influenced by the folk bazaar paintings sold for good luck in temples all over the subcontinent. Living and working in Kolkata, Roy trained in the traditional Western style of painting with Indian artist Abanindranath Tagore and began his career by making portraits. In the 1920s he abruptly switched from portrait commissions to painting in the Bengali folk style seen here, which has a distinctive geometric and brightly colorful appearance. In the hopes of promoting Bengali art, Roy wanted to make painting accessible to ordinary Indians instead of simply the wealthy patrons who could afford to commission portraits, thereby extending the reach of Indian art. Remarkably hardworking, the artist made more than twenty thousand paintings in his lifetime; he typically produced as many as ten works a day and sourced his own materials, including earth and mineral pigments and organic tempera. Best known for his epic seventeen-canvas rendition of the Hindu tale *Ramayana*, which tells the story of Rama and Sita and good versus evil, Roy also often included cats in his images, contentedly staring at the viewer as here or in classic feline action. One of his best-known paintings, *Two Cats Holding a Large Prawn* (c. 1920), features two upright black cats munching on the shellfish they have ostensibly just caught.

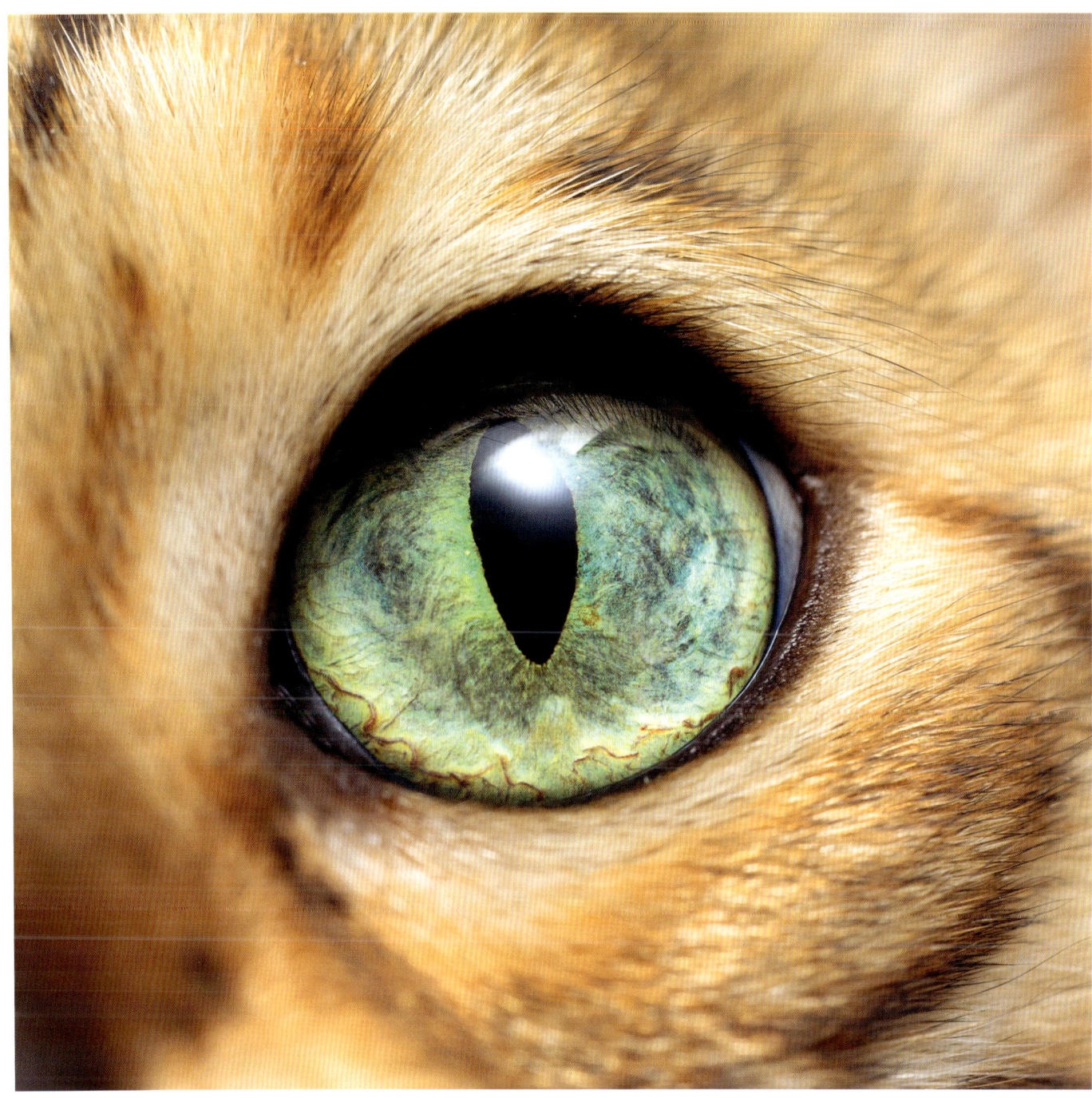

ANDREW MARTTILA

Haroun's Eye, 2023
Digital image, dimensions variable

A macro perspective of this cat's emerald iris—rimmed in yellow and brown and framed by golden-toned fur—is the centerpiece of this mesmerizing image captured by professional animal photographer Andrew Marttila (b. 1985). The feline's vertical pupil differentiates it from the circular shape of the human pupil: the elliptical form can quickly widen when more light is needed, or narrow to protect the retina from excessively bright conditions. Felines, along with other animals who are active in dim light, also have a reflective layer behind their retina, which enhances their night vision and explains why their eyes glow in the dark. While both human and cat eyes share the same types of photoreceptors in their retinas, felines are more sensitive to light and see a more limited range of color. From an evolutionary perspective, this makes sense: cats are crepuscular creatures, most active at dusk and dawn, and built to hunt stealthily at twilight. Beyond these biological functions, we can learn a great deal about a cat's feelings and state of mind from their expressive eyes. Marttila, who has been documenting felines for more than a decade—including his Bengal, Haroun, the star of this magnified photograph—has captured the vast range of their personalities and emotions in hundreds of thousands of images taken around the globe. He is a passionate advocate for animals, and along with his wife, Hannah Shaw (aka Kitten Lady and the author of this book's foreword, see p.5), helps run the Orphan Kitten Club, an impactful nonprofit that saves the lives of vulnerable kittens.

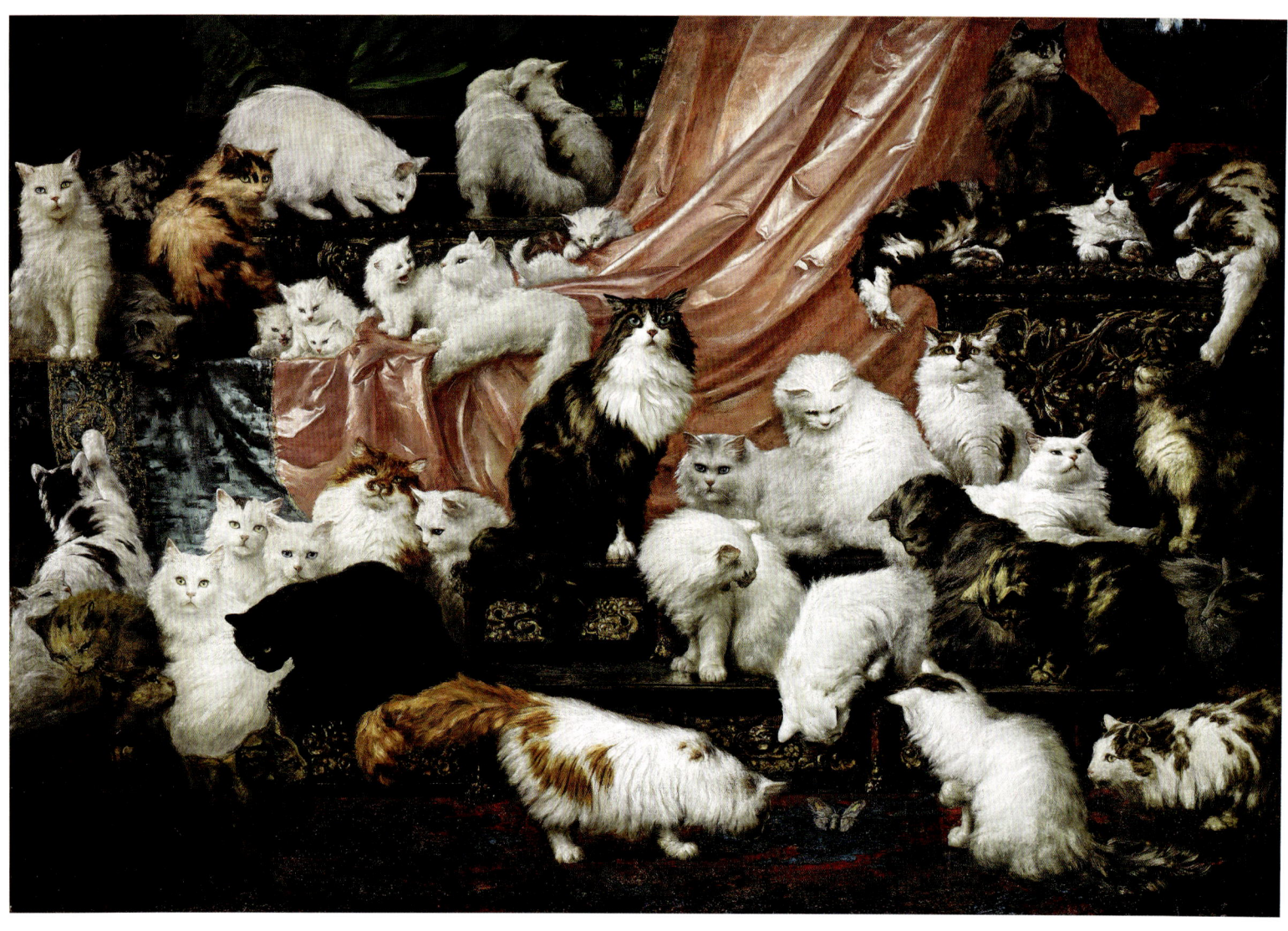

CARL KAHLER

My Wife's Lovers, 1891
Oil on canvas
70 × 101¾ in. / 177.8 × 258.4 cm
Private collection

Kate Birdsall Johnson, a Gilded Age millionaire hailing from San Francisco, was enamored with cats. She is said to have had a whopping 350 felines (but the real number was more like 50), mostly pedigreed Persian and Angora breeds, who lived at her vast summer estate in California and were taken care of by their own team of servants. On a trip to Paris, Johnson fell in love with a Persian cat named Sultan and paid a hefty sum to bring him home. She met Austrian painter Carl Kahler (1856–1906), who had just moved to San Francisco from Australia, after her return and commissioned him to commemorate forty-two of her cats in a massive painting, with Sultan at the center. Although Kahler had never painted a cat before, he spent three years studying and sketching Johnson's cats before beginning

work, learning their idiosyncrasies and personalities. His expertise is reflected in the work, which shows the fortunate felines reclining, grouped together, or even playfully chasing a moth. The mischievous title is commonly thought to have been suggested by Johnson herself, inspired by the way her late husband had always referred to her beloved pets. Dubbed by *Cat Magazine* as the "world's greatest painting of cats" in 1949, the work survived the destructive San Francisco earthquake in 1906, in which Kahler lost his life, and was eventually put up for auction in 2015. Hugely surpassing its estimate of $300,000, the painting eventually sold for $826,000.

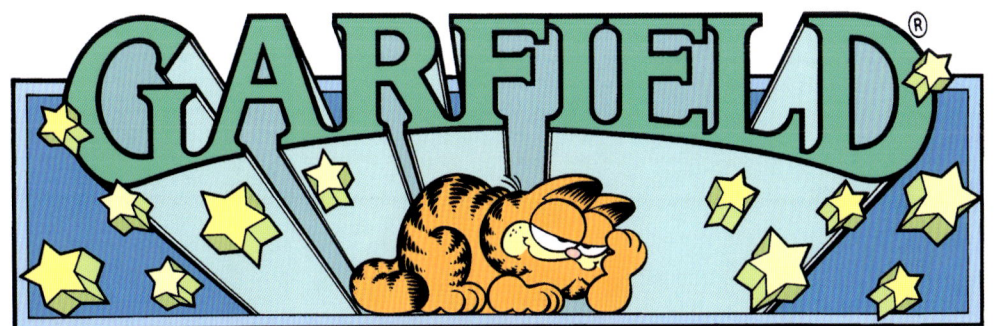

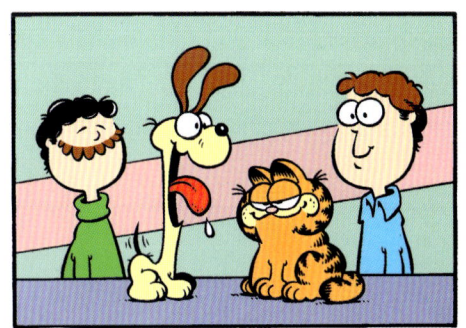

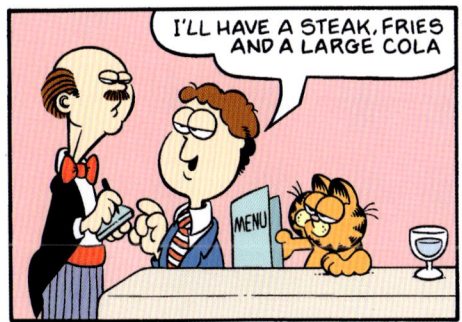

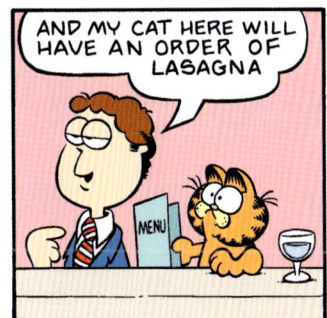

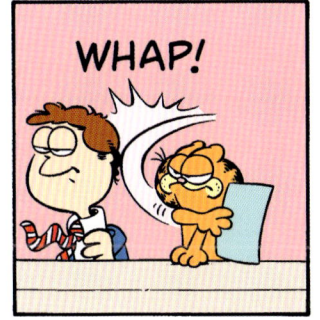

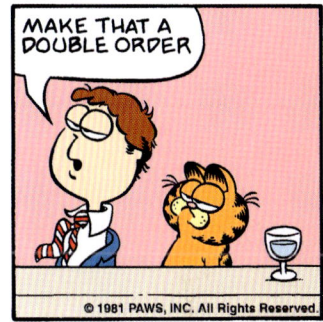

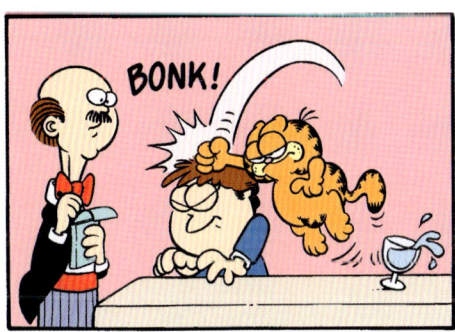

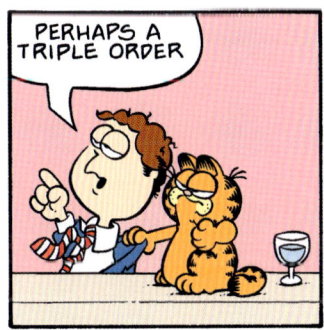

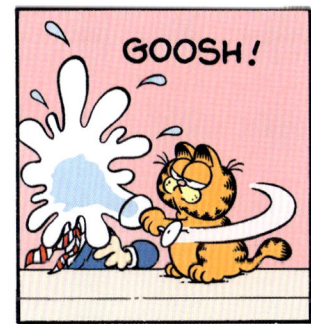

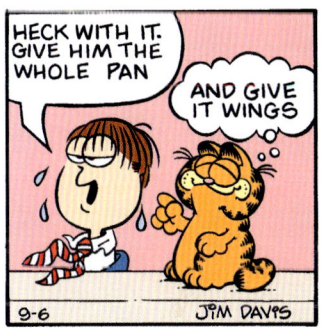

JIM DAVIS

Garfield, September 6, 1981
Comic strip

As the title character of the popular comic strip created by American cartoonist Jim Davis (b. 1945) in 1976, Garfield may be the original Grumpy Cat (see p.111). In syndication since 1978, *Garfield* has become the world's most widely circulated comic strip and now appears in nearly three thousand newspapers across the globe. The cartoon's humor derives from the contrasting personalities of its three main characters: the eponymous Garfield, an overweight, bitingly sarcastic orange tabby; Odie, a sweet but dim canine; and their nerdy, well-meaning owner, Jon Arbuckle. After realizing there were no cartoons that featured cats as the main character, dogs having long taken center stage on the funny pages, Davis decided to create a comic cat star. He felt he was up for the challenge; after all,

he had grown up on an Indiana farm alongside twenty-five barn cats. Based on the cartoonist's grouchy grandfather, Garfield has become famous for his sullen and sardonic attitude, which includes a total disdain of Monday and dieting, as well as an intense love of overeating, especially of his favorite meal, lasagna. In this strip from 1981, Davis plays up Garfield's passion for the baked pasta in a hilarious fine-dining episode. Much to the fancy waiter's surprise, but maybe not Jon's, this orange tabby is willing to go to violent lengths for a whole pan of the Italian dish.

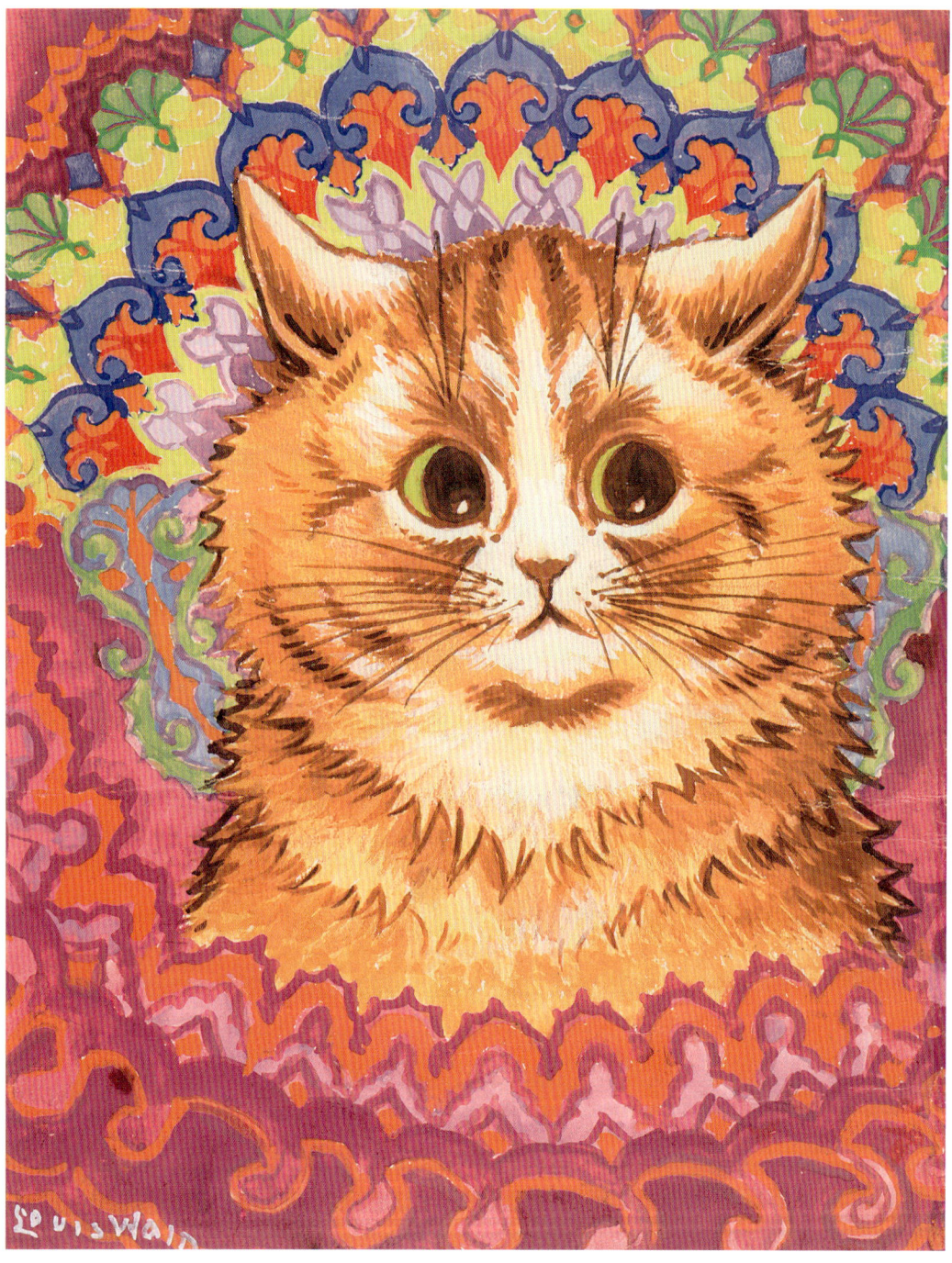

LOUIS WAIN

Kaleidoscope Cat, c. 1920s–30s
Watercolor on paper
Private collection

Known in his lifetime simply as "the man who drew cats," English artist Louis Wain (1860–1939) can claim a large share of the responsibility for changing the way people viewed cats as pets rather than pests in the United Kingdom and beyond. In Wain's anthropomorphized illustrations, cats behaved just like humans, living their best modern lives: they fell in love, drank champagne, drove cars, and played sports. As a contemporary fan, the novelist H. G. Wells remarked, "He invented a cat style, a cat society, a whole cat world." Wain's love of cats can probably be attributed to the family pet, Peter, who was a great consolation to his wife, Emily, during her fight with terminal breast cancer. Wain began drawing caricatures of Peter to amuse Emily, but when his bosses at the *Illustrated London*

News saw his work, they offered to print some of the jobbing artist's cat illustrations. *A Kitten's Christmas Party*—a collection of 11 drawings showing 150 cats doing all kinds of things—was published just before Emily's death, and Wain became an overnight sensation. A best-selling cat annual and postcards followed, but he made virtually no money from his commercial success. Later in life, Wain was admitted to mental health institutions, where he began to depict cats in increasingly colorful and abstract ways. This electrically pink watercolor is one such work, often called *Kaleidoscope Cats* for their optical appearance. Although he spent his final decades in poverty, his oeuvre is being reexamined and justly celebrated by contemporary scholars and cat lovers alike.

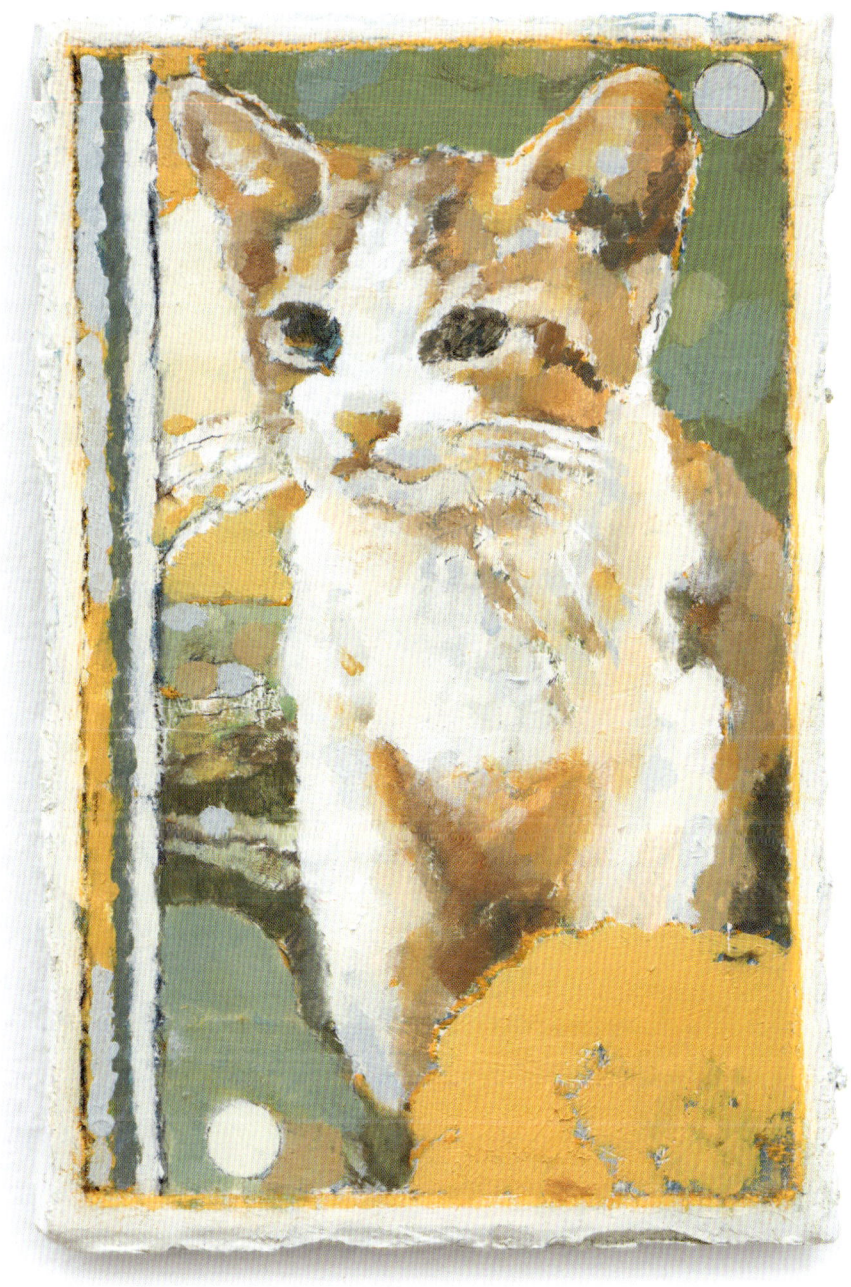

PIERRE BELLOT

Standing cat, 2025
Oil on canvas
8⅞ × 6 in. / 22.5 × 15.1 cm
Private collection

French artist Pierre Bellot (b. 1990) is a new painter of cats for a new generation. In his calm, consistent palette of greens, yellows, browns, and grays, Bellot's portraits are immediate and intimate but slightly out of focus, his cats appearing cloaked in memory instead of reality. The *Standing cat* seen here takes up most of the small composition in a familiar feline pose, its ears alert and gaze trained on something beyond the painting's edge. And yet Bellot's layered application—both of paint to create a textured surface and of shapes that surround the cat—takes the recognizable animal into a mystical realm. A graduate of the École nationale supérieure des Beaux-Arts de Paris in 2015, Bellot also paints abstract works in the same offbeat yet sensitive way. *Night* (2024) hints at a starry sky, with the circles in Bellot's customary colors appearing more planetlike than stellar, while the "landscape" *The dream at the hotel* (2023) is awash in greens, allowing the eye to flit across shapes and color fields as if in a lucid dream. In a 2025 exhibition of his work at New York's 56 Henry Gallery, the only figurative paintings included were those of cats, their small scale suggesting the portable size of religious icons and their presence meant to connect, as well as offer interludes between, the abstractions. Although worshipped for centuries, cats' proliferation in Internet memes and kitsch have seemingly lessened their divine appeal today. With quiet irony, Bellot reiterates the transcendent power of these animals in art for a contemporary age.

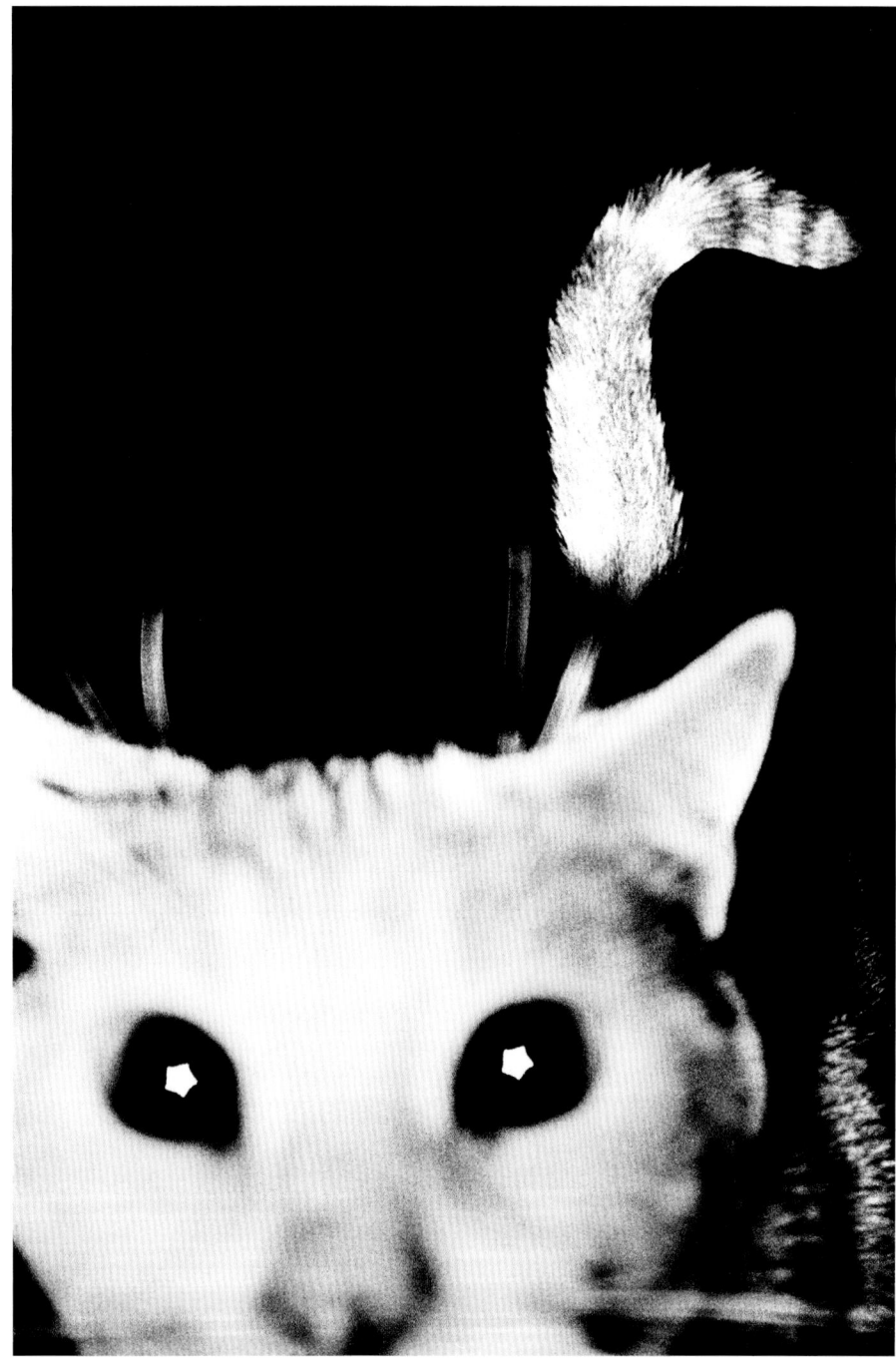

SOHRAB HURA

Francoise, the neighborhood cat. France, 2010
Photograph, 20 × 16 in. / 50.8 × 40.6 cm

It is easy to forget that cats are crepuscular, out on the prowl especially at dusk and dawn, with many active in the middle of the night, as proven by popular memes on social media showcasing the mischief they can get up to in the small hours. The unseen realities of nocturnal environments is a topic that fascinates Indian photographer Sohrab Hura (b. 1981), who likens this time of day to a kind of "theater inhabited by all kinds of different characters," at once magical and mysterious, as well as a little bit spooky. In terms of subject matter, pets figure prominently in his photography. Not only are they full of personality and charming, but, for Hura, they have a unifying presence that underlines the human need for tactility. Included in Hura's book *Life is Elsewhere* (2015), *Francoise, the neighborhood cat.*

France is certainly fearless and inquisitive, but in this close-up shot, the artist also captures a sense of the supernatural, as if she is a spectral apparition. Her markings and features are out of focus, and only the shape of her head and tail are visible through the pitch black as she approaches the photographer's lens, drawing the viewer's gaze to her piercing white pupils, which have been altered to appear as glimmering stars. The suggestion, it would seem, is that Francoise is not just blessed with night vision like her fellow felines, but endowed with additional otherworldly senses that switch on when the rest of the world sleeps.

I USED TO THINK MY SHADOW WAS
MY RIVAL

NOW I KNOW HE IS NOT MY RIVAL

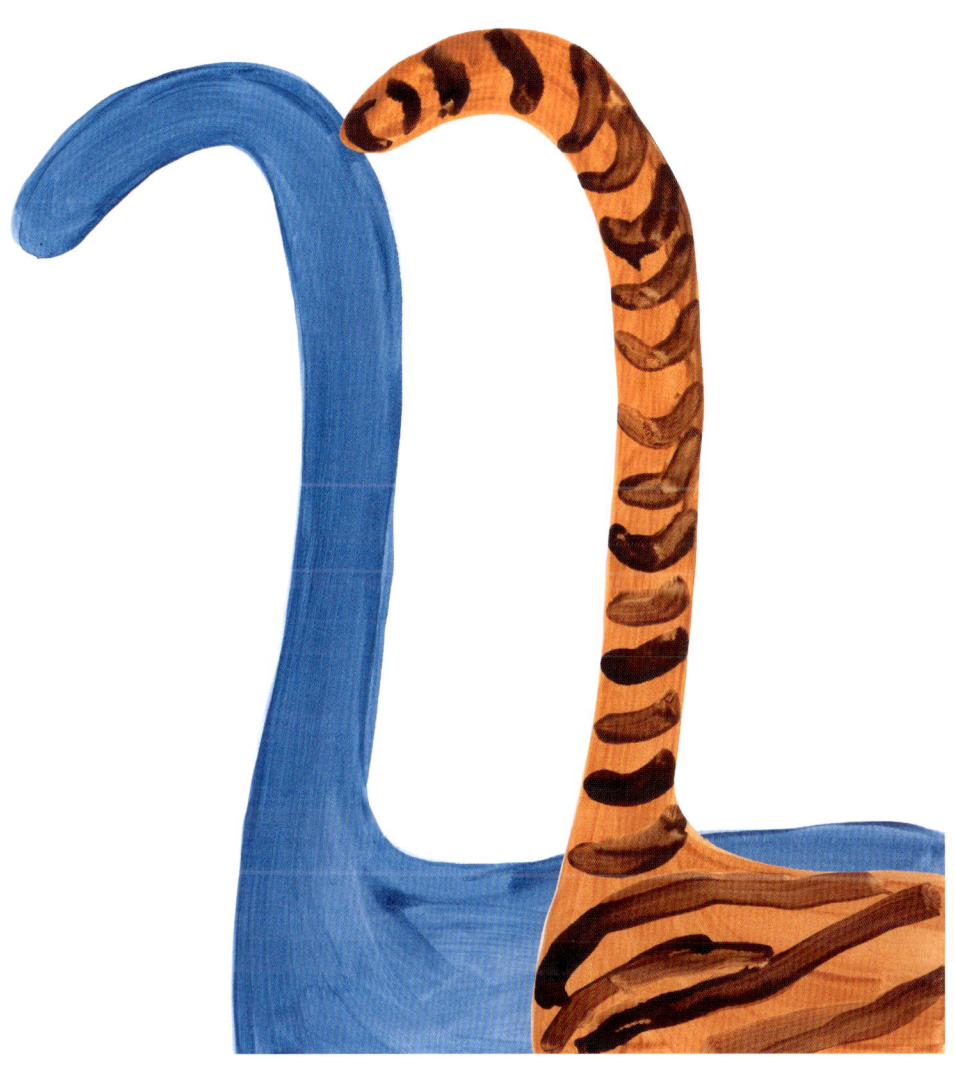

DAVID SHRIGLEY

I Used To Think My Shadow Was My Rival, 2024
Acrylic on paper, dimensions variable

Two cat tails—one a familiar tabby striped, the other an electric, unnatural blue—curl in tandem in this drawing by British artist David Shrigley (b. 1968), accompanied by a pithy message of feline camaraderie. Bringing a deadpan irreverence to paintings, drawings, sculptures, and public installations, Shrigley is drawn to the minutiae of the everyday. He often depicts household items, such as light bulbs and toothbrushes, in his trademark cartoon style, and he documents overheard snippets of conversations in his works. The deceptive childlike simplicity of his texts belies a sharp observational undercurrent, with cheerful scrawls masking a dry humor and cynical ponderings, from musings on the state of the nation to examinations of mortality and the meaning of life. Shrigley is drawn to animals, including elephants, polar bears, dogs, rabbits, and cats like these two. Familiar creatures appear as frequent motifs throughout his work to offer cute juxtapositions to stronger statements on issues, such as climate change, or to be celebrated in their own right. For Shrigley, animals are more authentic and honest than humans, but they also act as a mirror to human behavior in that they are almost like us but not quite. The artist has noted that he sees humans as the representations of culture and animals as the representations of nature—by observing us, animals reveal our own absurdities to us. Cats, in particular, are a means of conveying thought-provoking messages for Shrigley, who often accompanies their likenesses with deeper, more meaningful texts.

INDEX

ACKNOWLEDGMENTS

A project of this size requires the commitment and expertise of many people. Special thanks are due to the following for their knowledge, passion, and advice in the selection of the works for inclusion, as well as to Hannah Shaw and Leïla Jarbouai for writing the essays that open the book:

Yekaterina Barbash
Egyptologist, author, and curator of Egyptian Art at the Brooklyn Museum

Claire Catterall
Senior Curator at Somerset House, London

Anja Charbonneau
Founder of *Broccoli* and creator of collectible art books and niche magazines, including *Catnip*, a magazine for cat people

Mihoko Iida
Tokyo-based author and former *Vogue Japan* editor, bridging cultures through storytelling inspired by a lifelong love of cats—as both admirer and proud owner

Leïla Jarbouai
Art historian, writer, and Chief Curator of Graphic Arts and Paintings at the Musée d'Orsay in Paris

Jenny Pierson
Founding executive director of the Cat Museum of New York City. Her rescue cat is named Churro

Hannah Shaw aka Kitten Lady
Award-winning kitten rescuer, humane educator, *New York Times* best-selling author, and the founder of the leading nonprofit for kittens, Orphan Kitten Club

Anna Stothart
Art historian and cofounder of Davila-Villa & Stothart, specializing in institutional relations, market growth and sustainability, and studio management

BriAnne Wills
Brooklyn-based photographer and creator of *Girls and Their Cats*, a photo series debunking cat lady stereotypes through portraits of women and their feline companions

Kristiina Wilson
Clinical animal behaviorist specializing in felines and former fashion/ celebrity photographer

We are particularly grateful to Sara Bader for researching and compiling the long list of entries for inclusion. Additional thanks are due to Sarah Bell for her picture research, and to Theresa Bebbington, Vanessa Bird, Amelie Cherlin, Lynne Ciccaglione, Manon Gitton, João Mota, Deb Monti, Andrew Mott, Elizabeth O'Rourke, and Rosie Pickles for their invaluable assistance.

TEXT CREDITS

The publisher is grateful to the following writers for the individual entry texts:

Sara Bader: 19, 35, 86, 139, 158, 217; Yekaterina Barbash: 29, 132, 175; Tim Cooke: 9, 24, 27, 34, 59, 64, 84, 86, 104, 115, 128, 145, 153, 160, 166, 196, 208, 216; Anita Croy: 13, 25, 26, 30, 38, 39, 45, 55, 57, 66, 69, 71, 72, 74, 75, 76, 78, 82, 83, 96, 101, 108, 118, 120, 127, 130, 136, 138, 143, 148, 162, 163, 176, 177, 181, 183, 186, 194, 197, 205, 212, 220; Ellen Mara De Wachter: 36, 40, 102, 114, 131, 146, 150, 155, 157, 172, 189, 199; Catherine Ingram: 89, 90, 204; Leïla Jarbouai: 23, 48, 51, 68, 94, 110, 119, 147, 180, 188; Rebecca Morrill: 15, 50, 126, 211; Ilana Novick: 22, 56, 67, 112, 124, 125, 159, 170, 214; Hannah Silver: 91, 95, 178, 218, 223; Katy Sprinkel: 11, 14, 18, 28, 31, 32, 33, 37, 52, 58, 81, 92, 97, 98, 103, 105, 113, 116, 117, 122, 135, 142, 144, 151, 154, 171, 174, 182, 184, 191, 192, 195, 207, 213; David Trigg: 10, 20, 42, 44, 47, 54, 60, 61, 63, 70, 73, 106, 107, 121, 129, 152, 164, 173, 185, 190, 202, 206; Alexandra Zagalsky: 16, 41, 43, 62, 77, 80, 85, 109, 123, 133, 134, 137, 161, 165, 167, 169, 179, 198, 203, 222.

PICTURE CREDITS

We would like to thank all the artists, illustrators, photographers, collectors, libraries, institutions, and museums who have given us permission to include their images.

Slim Aarons / Stringer: 67; © Gertrude Abercrombie, Image: Smithsonian American Art Museum / Art Resource / Scala, Florence: 173; © 2025 ADAGP, Paris and DACS, London, Image: Christie's Images / Bridgeman Images: 189; © 2025 ADAGP Paris and DACS London, Courtesy Gagosian, Photo: Thomas Lannes: 203; © 2025 ADAGP, Paris and DACS, London, Image: © The Metropolitan Museum of Art / Art Resource / Scala, Florence: 80; Photo © AGIP / Bridgeman Images: 149; Album / Alamy Stock Photo: 150; Dirk Altenkirch / Courtesy of Tomi Ungerer and Ayla Suzan Yöndel: 77; Anacostia Community Museum / The Smithsonian Institution: 9; © Anne Arnold, Courtesy Alexandre Gallery, New York: 101; © 2025 ARS, NY and DACS, London, Image: Smithsonian American Art Museum / Art Resource / Scala, Florence: 31; Collection of the Art Gallery of Nova Scotia, bequest of Margaret and Ian Hill, Dartmouth, Nova Scotia, 2024: 39; ARTGEN / Alamy Stock Photo: 30, 74; The Art Institute of Chicago: 92, 163, 166; The Art Institute of Chicago / Art Resource, NY / Scala, Florence: 18, 104; © Ay-O, Image: National Museum of Asian Art, Smithsonian Institution, The Pearl and Seymour Moskowitz Collection, S2021.5.18: 161; © 2025 Estate of Will Barnet / VAGA at ARS, NY and DACS, London, Digital image Whitney Museum of American Art / Licensed by Scala: 202; Mychael Barratt: 156; © 2025 Romare Bearden Foundation / VAGA at ARS, NY and DACS, London, Image: Smithsonian American Art Museum / Art Resource / Scala, Florence: 71; Courtesy Pierre Bellot and 56 HENRY, New York: 221; © 2025 Charles Blackman / Copyright Agency. Licensed by DACS, Chau Chak Wing Museum Collection, The University of Sydney: 45; Courtesy Lydia Blakeley and Niru Ratnam, London, Photo: Lydia Blakeley: 159; Courtesy Boston Public Library: 44; Fernando Botero, Photo: Natalija Sahraj / Shutterstock: 131; Courtesy Boucheron: 25; Bridgeman Images: 36; British Library / Album / Alamy Stock Photo: 65; © The Trustees of the British Museum: 29, 175; Brooklyn Museum, 30.1478.101_PS20: 102; © Brooklyn Museum / Bridgeman Images: 187; Photo © Brooklyn Museum / Charles Edwin Wilbour Fund / Bridgeman Images: 132; Courtesy of Thom Browne: 171; © 2025 Calder Foundation, New York / DACS, London, Image: Museum of Contemporary Art Chicago / Art Resource, NY: 123; © 2025 Estate of Leonora Carrington / ARS, NY and DACS, London: 188; © Walter Chandoha / Trunk: 19; Chau Chak Wing Museum, The University of Sydney, Nicholson Collection, NM48.2, Photo: Rowan Conroy: 81; Manufactured by Chia Pet for Joseph Enterprises, Grown by Olivia Clark, Photo: Chris DeWitt: 105; © 2025 Chicago Woodman LLC Judy Chicago / DACS: 15; © Jee-ook Choi: 198; Christie's Images / Bridgeman Images: 88–9, 142, 144; Christie's Images, London / Scala, Florence: 216; B Christopher / Alamy Stock Photo: 207; Cooper-Hewitt, Smithsonian Design Museum / Art Resource, NY / Scala, Florence: 58, 169; Mike Coppola / Getty Images: 191; CPA Media Pte Ltd / Alamy Stock Photo: 106; Ralph Crane / The LIFE Picture Collection / Shutterstock: 172; © 2025 DACS: 218; © 2025 DACS, Image: Album / Fine Art Images: 140–41; © 2025 DACS, Courtesy Matthew Marks Gallery, Photo: Thomas Ruff: 136; TM © 1981 RUG LTD. CATS LOGO DESIGNED BY DEWYNTERS: 38; © 1951 Disney: 21; © 1970 Disney: 209; Dreams Inc: 179; © 2025 The Easton Foundation / VAGA at ARS, NY and DACS, London, Photo: Christopher Burke: 83; © 2025 Martin Eder, Courtesy Galerie EIGEN + ART Leipzig / Berlin / DACS, Photo: Uwe Walter: 201; Enikő Eged: 174; © Stephen Eichhorn: 135; Salah Elmur: 59; © 2025 Tracey Emin. All rights reserved, DACS: 66; M. C. Escher's "White Cat" © 2025 The M. C. Escher Company-The Netherlands. All rights reserved. www.mcescher.com: 122; Fairchild Archive / Contributor: 137; © Mary Fedden. All rights reserved 2025 / © Mary Fedden. All rights reserved 2025 / Bridgeman Images: 49; Courtesy Emir O. Filipović: 54; © Fleming-Wyfold Art Foundation / © Estate of Dame Elizabeth Blackadder. All rights reserved 2025 / Bridgeman Images: 186; © Masahisa Fukase Archives, Courtesy Atelier EXB: 40; © Nicolás García Uriburu, Image: Bridgeman Images: 134; GARFIELD © Paws, Inc. Reprinted with permission of ANDREWS MCMEEL SYNDICATION. All rights reserved: 219; The J. Paul Getty Museum, Los Angeles: 115, 194; © 2025 Succession Alberto Giacometti / DACS, Image © The Metropolitan Museum of Art / Art Resource / Scala, Florence: 51; © Edgardo Giménez, Courtesy of MC Galería: 148; © Robert Gober, Courtesy the artist, Paula Cooper Gallery, and Matthew Marks Gallery, Photo: Andrew Moore: 22; © Nan Goldin: 56; Image provided with permission of The Edward Gorey Charitable Trust: 69; Grumpy Cat Image © Grumpy Cat LTD. https://www.grumpycats.com / Used with permission: 111; The Solomon R. Guggenheim Foundation / Art Resource, NY / Scala, Florence: 50; © Philippe Halsman / Magnum Photos: 34; Kyoko Hamada: 185; Ram Han: 28; © Sally J. Han, Photo: Jason Mandella: 167; © Mikiko Hara, Courtesy IBASHO: 124; © 1980 Edie Harper: 16–7; CAVE FELEM, drawing by Christine Henry © Hermès Paris, 2025: 8; Heritage Images / Getty Images: 24; Hirshhorn Museum and Sculpture Garden: 55; Courtesy Andy Holden and Charles Moffett, New York, Photo: Thomas Barratt: 210–11; Peter Horree / Alamy Stock Photo: 82; HP Prints / Courtesy of Bienaimé: 212; © Sohrab Hura / Magnum Photos: 222; Photo © Indianapolis Museum of Art / Bridgeman Images: 86; Jazz Workshop, Inc. and Charles Mingus: 158; Photo Josse / Scala, Florence: 68; Dimitrios Kambouris / Staff: 97; © 2020 Judith Kerr, Reprinted by permission of HarperCollins Publishers Ltd: 139; Krazy Kat © 1938 King Features

Syndicate, Inc. World Rights Reserved: 63; © Jeff Koons: 91; Courtesy David Kordansky Gallery, Photo: Ed Mumford: 11; Kunsthalle Bremen, The Kunstverein in Bremen: 180; Lalique Kitten sculpture, amber crystal © Lalique SA: 117; Lawrences Auctioneers, Crewkerne: 120; Lebrecht History / Bridgeman Images: 94; Nina Leen / The LIFE Picture Collection / Shutterstock: 118; Sangsoo Lee: 73; From the Collection of Ann Lewis and Mike Sponder: 138; Library of Congress, Prints and Photographs Division: 13, 72, 133, 184; David Lichtneker / Alamy Stock Photo: 53; Courtesy Nikki Maloof and Perrotin: 37; © Kerry James Marshall, Courtesy the artist and David Zwirner, London: 125; Andrew Marttila: 217; M.Chat, Photo: Ferdinand Feys: 10; MIGUEL MEDINA / AFP via Getty Images: 75; © 2000–2026 The Metropolitan Museum of Art. All rights reserved: 26, 57, 79, 86, 96, 127, 153, 160, 183; Image © The Metropolitan Museum of Art / Art Resource / Scala, Florence: 14, 98, 206; MINAMI: 195; The Minneapolis Institute of Art: 48; Missouri History Museum: 146; Image by Bill Muganda under Kenyan Library on Instagram: 103; Digital image The Museum of Modern Art, New York / Scala, Florence: 110; Museum of the City of New York Collections: 196; Courtesy Godwin Champs Namuyimba: 170; © Yoshitomo Nara: 178; © Estate of John Northcote Nash. All rights reserved 2025 / Bridgeman Images: 130; National Gallery of Art: 99; © Kohei Nawa, Courtesy Pace Gallery, Photo: Nobutada OMOTE: 213; © The Estate of Alice Neel, Courtesy The Estate of Alice Neel and David Zwirner: 112; New York Public Library: 168, 181; Jodie Niss: 32; Masayuki Oki @okirakuoki: 190; © Gabriel Orozco, Courtesy the artist and Marian Goodman Gallery: 121; © Laura Owens, Courtesy the artist and Sadie Coles HQ, London, Photo: Douglas M. Parker Studio: 76; Michael Parkin Gallery / Bridgeman Images: 220; Gordon Parks / The LIFE Picture Collection / Shutterstock: 214; © Martin Parr / Magnum Photos: 93; Endre Penovác: 165; Philadelphia Museum of Art: 192; © 2025 Succession Picasso / DACS, London, Image: Bridgeman Images: 204; Courtesy Cait Porter and Marinaro, NY, Photo: Olympia Shannon: 100; Illustration from *The Tale of Tom Kitten* by Beatrix Potter. Copyright © Frederick Warne & Co., 1907, 2002. Frederick Warne & Co is the owner of all rights, copyrights and trademarks in the Beatrix Potter character names and illustrations: 42; © 2025 Mavis Pusey / VAGA at ARS, NY and DACS, London, Image courtesy the Petrucci Family Foundation Collection of African American Art, Photo: Phil Stein: 129; Courtesy Elizabeth Radcliffe and Margot Samel, NYC, Photo: Matthew Sherman: 52; Photo © Marco Ravenna / Bridgeman Images: 64; RMN-Grand Palais / Georges Meguerditchian / Dist. Photo SCALA, Florence: 90; Saint Louis Art Museum, Museum Purchase, Friends Endowment Fund, and funds provided by the Maymar Corporation: 154; Courtesy Zeinab Saleh and Château Shatto, Los Angeles, Photo: George Darrell: 197; Image courtesy San Antonio Museum of Art, Photo: Alayna Barrett Fox: 143; Photo Scala, Florence: 108, 147, 193; Photo Scala, Florence / Heritage Images: 47–8; HUCKLE CAT'S BUSIEST DAY EVER by Richard Scarry, Used with permission form Penguin Random House: 85; © Estate of Fritz Scholder / National Museum Of The American Indian, Smithsonian Institution (26/6393): 128; Book Cover from THE CAT IN THE HAT by Dr. Seuss, TM and copyright © by Dr. Seuss Enterprises, L.P. 1957, renewed 1985. Used by permission of Random House Children's Books, a division of Penguin Random House LLC. All rights reserved: 12; Jamel Shabazz: 43; © 2025 David Shrigley. All Rights Reserved, DACS: 223; Max Siedentopf: 113; © 1980 Sandy Skoglund: 151; © Kiki Smith, Courtesy Pace Gallery: 182; Photo Smithsonian American Art Museum / Art Resource / Scala, Florence: 27; © Linda Stark, Courtesy the artist and Ortuzar, New York, Photo: Brian Forrest: 20; Photo: Luke Stephenson: 199; Vanessa Stockard: 164; Satomi Sugiyama: 84; Swiss National Library, GS-GUGE-MIND-F-11: 60; © Tate Images: 126; Courtesy Lenore G. Tawney Foundation, Image: Archives of American Art, Smithsonian Institution: 205; Tennants Auctioneers, North Yorkshire: 33; Andrew Testa / Panos Pictures: 61; © 2025 Estate of Walasse Ting ARS, NY and DACS, London, Image: Christie's Images / Bridgeman Images: 116; Nyan Cat Image is © and ® of Christopher Orlando Torres / https://www.nyan.cat / Used with permission: 41; © Bill Traylor Family Inc., WhosBillTraylor.com, Image: Ricco/Maresca Gallery: 157; © Satoru Tsuda: 145; © 2025 Remedios Varo, DACS / VEGAP, Image: Christie's Images, London / Scala, Florence: 119; Laura Venditti: 107; © Victoria and Albert Museum, London: 62, 162; © LOUIS VUITTON MALLETIER / TOBY MCFARLAN POND: 177; Walters Art Museum: 200; © 2025 The Andy Warhol Foundation for the Visual Arts, Inc. / Licensed by DACS, London, Image: Christie's Images / Bridgeman Images: 95; Wikimedia Commons: 22, 70, 78, 114, 155, 176; Xuan Loc Xuan: 35; Fumi Yanagimoto: 215; Poster design by Gints Zilbalodis & Pēteris Tenisons, Copyright © 2024 Dream Well Studio, Sacrebleu Productions, Take Five: 152.

Phaidon Press Limited
2 Cooperage Yard
London E15 2QR

Phaidon Press Inc.
111 Broadway
New York, NY 10006

Phaidon SARL
55, rue Traversière
75012 Paris

phaidon.com

First published 2026
© 2026 Phaidon Press Limited
Foreword © 2026 Kitten Lady LLC

ISBN 978 1 83866 944 7

A CIP catalogue record for this book is
available from the British Library and the
Library of Congress.

Commissioning Editor: Olivia Clark
Production Controller: Andie Trainer
Cover Design: Julia Hasting
Layout Design: João Mota
Typesetting: Cantina

Printed in China